D1632492

Shakespeare

Volume IV

THE TRAGEDIES
and
THE POEMS

Distributed by
HERON BOOKS

*This book
was set for J. M. Dent & Sons, Ltd.,
in Caslon Old Face type.
Printed by Hazell Watson & Viney Ltd,
Aylesbury, Bucks
© J. M. Dent & Sons, Ltd.*

3538

Printed and bound in England

CONTENTS

THE TRAGEDY OF KING LEAR

DRAMATIS PERSONÆ

LEAR, *king of Britain.*
KING OF FRANCE.
DUKE OF BURGUNDY.
DUKE OF CORNWALL.
DUKE OF ALBANY.
EARL OF KENT.
EARL OF GLOUCESTER.
EDGAR, *son to Gloucester.*
EDMUND, *bastard son to Gloucester.*
CURAN, *a courtier.*
Old Man, tenant to Gloucester.

Doctor.
Fool.
OSWALD, *steward to Goneril.*
A captain employed by Edmund.
Gentleman attendant on Cordelia.
Herald.
Servants to Cornwall.

GONERIL,
REGAN, }*daughters to Lear.*
CORDELIA,

Knights of Lear's train, Captains, Messengers, Soldiers, and Attendants.

SCENE: *Britain.*

ACT I—SCENE I

King Lear's palace.

Enter Kent, Gloucester, and Edmund.

Kent. I thought the king had more affected the Duke of
Albany than Cornwall.

Glou. It did always seem so to us: but now, in the division
of the kingdom, it appears not which of the dukes he values
most; for equalities are so weighed that curiosity in neither
can make choice of either's moiety.

Kent. Is not this your son, my lord?

Glou. His breeding, sir, hath been at my charge: I have so
often blushed to acknowledge him that now I am brazed

Kent. I cannot conceive you.   [to it.

Glou. Sir, this young fellow's mother could: whereupon she
grew round wombed, and had indeed, sir, a son for her
cradle ere she had a husband for her bed. Do you smell
a fault?   [proper.

Kent. I cannot wish the fault undone, the issue of it being so

Glou. But I have, sir, a son by order of law, some year elder
than this, who yet is no dearer in my account: though this
knave came something saucily into the world before he was
sent for, yet was his mother fair; there was good sport at
his making, and the whoreson must be acknowledged. Do
you know this noble gentleman, Edmund?

Edm. No, my lord.

Glou. My lord of Kent: remember him hereafter as my
honourable friend.

Edm. My services to your lordship.

Kent. I must love you, and sue to know you better.

Edm. Sir, I shall study deserving.

Glou. He hath been out nine years, and away he shall again.
The king is coming.

1

Sennet.   Enter one bearing a coronet, King Lear, Cornwall,
*   Albany, Goneril, Regan, Cordelia, and Attendants.*

Lear. Attend the lords of France and Burgundy, Gloucester.

Glou. I shall, my liege.   [*Exeunt Gloucester and Edmund*

Lear. Meantime we shall express our darker purpose.
Give me the map there.   Know we have divided
In three our kingdom : and 'tis our fast intent
To shake all cares and business from our age,
Conferring them on younger strengths, while we
Unburthen'd crawl toward death.   Our son of Cornwall,
And you, our no less loving son of Albany,
We have this hour a constant will to publish
Our daughters' several dowers, that future strife
May be prevented now. The princes, France and Burgundy,
Great rivals in our youngest daughter's love,
Long in our court have made their amorous sojourn,
And here are to be answer'd.   Tell me, my daughters,
Since now we will divest us both of rule,
Interest of territory, cares of state,
Which of you shall we say doth love us most ?
That we our largest bounty may extend
Where nature doth with merit challenge.   Goneril,
Our eldest-born, speak first.

Gon. Sir, I love you more than words can wield the matter,
Dearer than eye-sight, space and liberty,
Beyond what can be valued, rich or rare,
No less than life, with grace, health, beauty, honour,
As much as child e'er loved or father found ;
A love that makes breath poor and speech unable;
Beyond all manner of so much I love you.

Cor. [*Aside*] What shall Cordelia do ?   Love, and be silent.

Lear. Of all these bounds, even from this line to this,
With shadowy forests and with champains rich'd,
With plenteous rivers and wide-skirted meads,
We make thee lady.   To thine and Albany's issue
Be this perpetual.   What says our second daughter,
Our dearest Regan, wife to Cornwall? Speak.

Reg. I am made of that self metal as my sister,
And prize me at her worth.   In my true heart
I find she names my very deed of love;
Only she comes too short : that I profess
Myself an enemy to all other joys
Which the most precious square of sense possesses,
And find I am alone felicitate
In your dear highness' love.

Cor. [*Aside*]   Then poor Cordelia!
  And yet not so, since I am sure my love's
  More ponderous than my tongue.
Lear. To thee and thine hereditary ever
  Remain this ample third of our fair kingdom,
  No less in space, validity and pleasure,
  Than that conferr'd on Goneril.   Now, our joy,
  Although the last, not least, to whose young love
  The vines of France and milk of Burgundy
  Strive to be interess'd, what can you say to draw
  A third more opulent than your sisters?   Speak.
Cor. Nothing, my lord.
Lear. Nothing!
Cor. Nothing.
Lear. Nothing will come of nothing: speak again.
Cor. Unhappy that I am, I cannot heave
  My heart into my mouth: I love your majesty
  According to my bond; nor more nor less.
Lear. How, how, Cordelia! mend your speech a little,
  Lest it may mar your fortunes.
Cor.   Good my lord,
  You have begot me, bred me, loved me: I
  Return those duties back as are right fit,
  Obey you, love you, and most honour you.
  Why have my sisters husbands, if they say
  They love you all?   Haply, when I shall wed,
  That lord whose hand must take my plight shall carry
  Half my love with him, half my care and duty:
  Sure, I shall never marry like my sisters,
  To love my father all.
Lear. But goes thy heart with this?
Cor.   Ay, good my lord.
Lear. So young, and so untender?
Cor. So young, my lord, and true.
Lear. Let it be so; thy truth then be thy dower:
  For, by the sacred radiance of the sun,
  The mysteries of Hecate, and the night;
  By all the operation of the orbs
  From whom we do exist and cease to be;
  Here I disclaim all my paternal care,
  Propinquity and property of blood,
  And as a stranger to my heart and me
  Hold thee from this for ever.   The barbarous Scythian,
  Or he that makes his generation messes
  To gorge his appetite, shall to my bosom

3

Be as well neighbour'd, pitied and relieved,
As thou my sometime daughter.

Kent.   Good my liege,—

Lear. Peace, Kent!
Come not between the dragon and his wrath.
I loved her most, and thought to set my rest
On her kind nursery.   Hence, and avoid my sight!
So be my grave my peace, as here I give
Her father's heart from her!   Call France.   Who stirs?
Call Burgundy.   Cornwall and Albany,
With my two daughters' dowers digest this third:
Let pride, which she calls plainness, marry her.
I do invest you jointly with my power,
Pre-eminence and all the large effects
That troop with majesty.   Ourself, by monthly course,
With reservation of an hundred knights
By you to be sustain'd, shall our abode
Make with you by due turns.   Only we still retain
The name and all the additions to a king;
The sway, revenue, execution of the rest,
Beloved sons, be yours: which to confirm,
This coronet part betwixt you.

Kent.   Royal Lear,
Whom I have ever honour'd as my king,
Loved as my father, as my master follow'd,
As my great patron thought on in my prayers,—

Lear. The bow is bent and drawn; make from the shaft.

Kent. Let it fall rather, though the fork invade
The region of my heart: be Kent unmannerly,
When Lear is mad.   What wouldst thou do, old man?
Think'st thou that duty shall have dread to speak,
When power to flattery bows?   To plainness honour's bound,
When majesty stoops to folly.   Reverse thy doom,
And in thy best consideration check
This hideous rashness: answer my life my judgement,
Thy youngest daughter does not love thee least;
Nor are those empty-hearted whose low sound
Reverbs no hollowness.

Lear.   Kent, on thy life, no more.

Kent. My life I never held but as a pawn
To wage against thy enemies, nor fear to lose it,
Thy safety being the motive.

Lear.   Out of my sight!

Kent. See better, Lear, and let me still remain
The true blank of thine eye.

4

Lear. Now, by Apollo,—
Kent.   Now, by Apollo, king,
   Thou swear'st thy gods in vain.
Lear.   O, vassal! miscreant!
                              [*Laying his hand on his sword.*

Alb. } Dear sir, forbear.
Corn. }
Kent. Do;
   Kill thy physician, and the fee bestow
   Upon the foul disease.   Revoke thy doom;
   Or, whilst I can vent clamour from my throat,
   I 'll tell thee thou dost evil.
Lear.   Hear me, recreant!
   On thy allegiance, hear me!
   Since thou hast sought to make us break our vow,
   Which we durst never yet, and with strain'd pride
   To come between our sentence and our power,
   Which nor our nature nor our place can bear,
   Our potency made good, take thy reward.
   Five days we do allot thee, for provision
   To shield thee from diseases of the world,
   And on the sixth to turn thy hated back
   Upon our kingdom: if on the tenth day following
   Thy banish'd trunk be found in our dominions,
   The moment is thy death.   Away!   By Jupiter,
   This shall not be revoked.
Kent. Fare thee well, king: sith thus thou wilt appear,
   Freedom lives hence, and banishment is here.
   [*To Cordelia*] The gods to their dear shelter take thee, maid,
   That justly think'st and hast most rightly said!
   [*To Regan and Goneril*] And your large speeches may your
      deeds approve,
   That good effects may spring from words of love.
   Thus Kent, O princes, bids you all adieu;
   He 'll shape his old course in a country new.   [*Exit.*
      Flourish.   Re-enter Gloucester, with France, Burgundy,
                     and Attendants.
Glou. Here 's France and Burgundy, my noble lord.
Lear. My lord of Burgundy,
   We first address towards you, who with this king
   Hath rivall'd for our daughter: what, in the least,
   Will you require in present dower with her,
   Or cease your quest of love?
Bur.   Most royal majesty,
   I crave no more than what your highness offer'd,

Nor will you tender less.

Lear.   Right noble Burgundy,
When she was dear to us, we did hold her so ;
But now her price is fall'n. Sir, there she stands :
If aught within that little seeming substance,
Or all of it, with our displeasure pierced,
And nothing more, may fitly like your grace,
She 's there, and she is yours.

Bur.   I know no answer.'

Lear. Will you, with those infirmities she owes,
Unfriended, new adopted to our hate,
Dower'd with our curse and stranger'd with our oath,'
Take her, or leave her ?

Bur.   Pardon me, royal sir ;
Election makes not up on such conditions.

Lear. Then leave her, sir ; for, by the power that made me,
I tell you all her wealth. [*To France*] For you, great king,
I would not from your love make such a stray,
To match you where I hate ; therefore beseech you
To avert your liking a more worthier way
Than on a wretch whom nature is ashamed
Almost to acknowledge hers.

France.   This is most strange,
That she, that even but now was your best object,
The argument of your praise, balm of your age,
Most best, most dearest, should in this trice of time
Commit a thing so monstrous, to dismantle
So many folds of favour. Sure, her offence
Must be of such unnatural degree
That monsters it, or your fore-vouch'd affection
Fall'n into taint : which to believe of her,
Must be a faith that reason without miracle
Could never plant in me.

Cor.   I yet beseech your majesty,—
If for I want that glib and oily art,
To speak and purpose not, since what I well intend,
I 'll do 't before I speak,—that you make known
It is no vicious blot, murder, or foulness,
No unchaste action, or dishonour'd step,
That hath deprived me of your grace and favour ;
But even for want of that for which I am richer,
A still-soliciting eye, and such a tongue
As I am glad I have not, though not to have it
Hath lost me in your liking.

Lear.   Better thou

Hadst not been born than not to have pleased me better.

France. Is it but this? a tardiness in nature
Which often leaves the history unspoke
That it intends to do? My lord of Burgundy,
What say you to the lady? Love's not love
When it is mingled with regards that stand
Aloof from the entire point. Will you have her?
She is herself a dowry.

Bur.　　　　　　　　Royal Lear,
Give but that portion which yourself proposed,
And here I take Cordelia by the hand,
Duchess of Burgundy.

Lear. Nothing: I have sworn; I am firm.

Bur. I am sorry then you have so lost a father
That you must lose a husband.

Cor.　　　　　　　　Peace be with Burgundy!
Since that respects of fortune are his love,
I shall not be his wife.

France. Fairest Cordelia, that art most rich being poor,
Most choice forsaken, and most loved despised,
Thee and thy virtues here I seize upon:
Be it lawful I take up what's cast away.
Gods, gods! 'tis strange that from their cold'st neglect
My love should kindle to inflamed respect.
Thy dowerless daughter, king, thrown to my chance,
Is queen of us, of ours, and our fair France:
Not all the dukes of waterish Burgundy
Can buy this unprized precious maid of me.
Bid them farewell, Cordelia, though unkind:
Thou losest here, a better where to find.

Lear. Thou hast her, France: let her be thine, for we
Have no such daughter, nor shall ever see
That face of hers again. Therefore be gone
Without our grace, our love, our benison.
Come, noble Burgundy.

[*Flourish. Exeunt all but France, Goneril, Regan, and Cordelia.*

France. Bid farewell to your sisters.

Cor. The jewels of our father, with wash'd eyes
Cordelia leaves you: I know you what you are;
And, like a sister, am most loath to call
Your faults as they are named. Use well our father:
To your professed bosoms I commit him:
But yet, alas, stood I within his grace,
I would prefer him to a better place.
So farewell to you both.

7

Reg. Prescribe not us our duties.

Gon.   Let your study
Be to content your lord, who hath received you
At fortune's alms.   You have obedience scanted,
And well are worth the want that you have wanted.

Cor. Time shall unfold what plaited cunning hides:
Who cover faults, at last shame them derides.
Well may you prosper!

France.   Come, my fair Cordelia.
                              [*Exeunt France and Cordelia.*

Gon. Sister, it is not a little I have to say of what most nearly
   appertains to us both.   I think our father will hence to-night.

Reg. That's most certain, and with you; next month with us.

Gon. You see how full of changes his age is; the observation
   we have made of it hath not been little: he always loved our
   sister most; and with what poor judgement he hath now cast
   her off appears too grossly.

Reg. 'Tis the infirmity of his age; yet he hath ever but
   slenderly known himself.

Gon. The best and soundest of his time hath been but rash;
   then must we look to receive from his age, not alone the
   imperfections of long ingrafted condition, but therewithal
   the unruly waywardness that infirm and choleric years
   bring with them.

Reg. Such unconstant starts are we like to have from him as
   this of Kent's banishment.

Gon. There is further compliment of leave-taking between
   France and him.   Pray you, let's hit together: if our father
   carry authority with such dispositions as he bears, this last
   surrender of his will but offend us.

Reg. We shall further think on't.

Gon. We must do something, and i' the heat.   [*Exeunt.*

SCENE II

The Earl of Gloucester's castle.

Enter Edmund, with a letter.

Edm. Thou, nature, art my goddess; to thy law
   My services are bound.   Wherefore should I
   Stand in the plague of custom, and permit
   The curiosity of nations to deprive me,
   For that I am some twelve or fourteen moonshines
   Lag of a brother?   Why bastard? wherefore base?
   When my dimensions are as well compact,
   My mind as generous and my shape as true,
   As honest madam's issue?   Why brand they us

8

With base? with baseness? bastardy? base, base?
Who in the lusty stealth of nature take
More composition and fierce quality
Than doth, within a dull, stale, tired bed,
Go to the creating a whole tribe of fops,
Got 'tween asleep and wake? Well then,
Legitimate Edgar, I must have your land:
Our father's love is to the bastard Edmund
As to the legitimate: fine word, 'legitimate'!
Well, my legitimate, if this letter speed
And my invention thrive, Edmund the base
Shall top the legitimate. I grow; I prosper:
Now, gods, stand up for bastards!

Enter Gloucester.

Glou. Kent banish'd thus! and France in choler parted!
And the king gone to-night! subscribed his power!
Confined to exhibition! All this done
Upon the gad! Edmund, how now! what news?

Edm. So please your lordship, none. [*Putting up the letter.*

Glou. Why so earnestly seek you to put up that letter?

Edm. I know no news, my lord.

Glou. What paper were you reading?

Edm. Nothing, my lord.

Glou. No? What needed then that terrible dispatch of it into your pocket? the quality of nothing hath not such need to hide itself. Let's see: come, if it be nothing, I shall not need spectacles.

Edm. I beseech you, sir, pardon me: it is a letter from my brother, that I have not all o'er-read; and for so much as I have perused, I find it not fit for your o'er-looking.

Glou. Give me the letter, sir.

Edm. I shall offend, either to detain or give it. The contents, as in part I understand them, are to blame.

Glou Let's see, let's see.

Edm. I hope, for my brother's justification, he wrote this but as an essay or taste of my virtue.

Glou. [*Reads*] 'This policy and reverence of age makes the world bitter to the best of our times; keeps our fortunes from us till our oldness cannot relish them. I begin to find an idle and fond bondage in the oppression of aged tyranny; who sways, not as it hath power, but as it is suffered. Come to me, that of this I may speak more. If our father would sleep till I waked him, you should enjoy half his revenue for ever, and live the beloved of your brother, EDGAR.' Hum! Conspiracy!—'Sleep till I waked him, you should enjoy half

9

his revenue,—My son Edgar! Had he a hand to write this? a heart and brain to breed it in? When came this to you? who brought it?

Edm. It was not brought me, my lord; there's the cunning of it; I found it thrown in at the casement of my closet.

Glou. You know the character to be your brother's?

Edm. If the matter were good, my lord, I durst swear it were his; but, in respect of that, I would fain think it were not.

Glou. It is his.   [*contents*.

Edm. It is his hand, my lord; but I hope his heart is not in the

Glou. Hath he never heretofore sounded you in this business?

Edm. Never, my lord: but I have heard him oft maintain it to be fit, that, sons at perfect age, and fathers declining, the father should be as ward to the son, and the son manage his revenue.

Glou. O villain, villain! His very opinion in the letter! Abhorred villain! Unnatural, detested, brutish villain! worse than brutish! Go, sirrah, seek him; ay, apprehend him: abominable villain! Where is he?

Edm. I do not well know, my lord. If it shall please you to suspend your indignation against my brother till you can derive from him better testimony of his intent, you should run a certain course; where, if you violently proceed against him, mistaking his purpose, it would make a great gap in your own honour and shake in pieces the heart of his obedience. I dare pawn down my life for him that he hath wrote this to feel my affection to your honour and to no further pretence of danger.

Glou. Think you so?

Edm. If your honour judge it meet, I will place you where you shall hear us confer of this, and by an auricular assurance have your satisfaction, and that without any further delay than this very evening.

Glou. He cannot be such a monster—

Edm. Nor is not, sure.

Glou. To his father, that so tenderly and entirely loves him. Heaven and earth! Edmund, seek him out; wind me into him, I pray you: frame the business after your own wisdom. I would unstate myself, to be in a due resolution.

Edm. I will seek him, sir, presently, convey the business as I shall find means, and acquaint you withal.

Glou. These late eclipses in the sun and moon portend no good to us: though the wisdom of nature can reason it thus and thus, yet nature finds itself scourged by the sequent effects: love cools, friendship falls off, brothers divide: in cities, mutinies; in coun*ries, discord; in palaces, treason; and the bond cracked 'twixt son and father. This villain of mine comes under the prediction; there's son against father: the king falls from bias of nature; there's father against child. We have seen the best of our time: machinations, hollowness, treachery and all ruinous disorders follow us disquietly to our graves. Find out this villain, Edmund; it shall lose thee nothing; do it carefully. And the noble and true-hearted Kent banished! his offence, honesty! 'Tis strange.   [*Exit.*

Edm. This is the excellent foppery of the world, that when we are sick in fortune—often the surfeit of our own behaviour—we make guilty of our disasters the sun, the moon and the stars: as if we were villains by necessity, fools by heavenly compulsion; knaves, thieves and treachers, by spherical predominance; drunkards, liars and adulterers, by an enforced obedience of planetary influence; and all that we are evil in, by a divine thrusting on: an admirable evasion of whoremaster man, to lay his goatish disposition to the charge of a star! My father compounded with my mother under the dragon's tail, and my nativity was under Ursa major; so that it follows I am rough and lecherous. Tut, I should have been that I am, had the maidenliest star in the firmament twinkled on my bastardizing. Edgar—

Enter Edgar.

And pat he comes like the catastrophe of the old comedy: my cue is villainous melancholy, with a sigh like Tom o' Bedlam. O, these eclipses do portend these divisions! fa, sol, la, mi.

Edg. How now, brother Edmund! what serious contemplation are you in?

Edm. I am thinking, brother, of a prediction I read this other day, what should follow these eclipses.

Edg. Do you busy yourself about that?

Edm. I promise you, the effects he writ of succeed unhappily; as of unnaturalness between the child and the parent; death, dearth, dissolutions of ancient amities; divisions in state, menaces and maledictions against king and nobles; needless diffidences, banishment of friends, dissipation of cohorts, nuptial breaches, and I know not what.

Edg. How long have you been a sectary astronomical?

Edm. Come, come; when saw you my father last?

Edg. Why, the night gone by.

Edm. Spake you with him?

Edg. Ay, two hours together.

Edm. Parted you in good terms? Found you no displeasure in him by word or countenance?

Edg. None at all.

Edm. Bethink yourself wherein you may have offended him:
and at my entreaty forbear his presence till some little time
hath qualified the heat of his displeasure, which at this instant
so rageth in him that with the mischief of your person it
would scarcely allay.

Edg. Some villain hath done me wrong.

Edm. That's my fear. I pray you, have a continent forbearance till the speed of his rage goes slower, and, as I say,
retire with me to my lodging, from whence I will fitly bring
you to hear my lord speak: pray ye, go; there's my key: if
you do stir abroad, go armed.

Edg. Armed, brother!

Edm. Brother, I advise you to the best: go armed: I am no
honest man if there be any good meaning towards you: I
have told you what I have seen and heard; but faintly,
nothing like the image and horror of it: pray you, away.

Edg. Shall I hear from you anon?

Edm. I do serve you in this business.   [*Exit Edgar.*

A credulous father, and a brother noble,
Whose nature is so far from doing harms
That he suspects none; on whose foolish honesty
My practices ride easy. I see the business.
Let me, if not by birth, have lands by wit:
All with me's meet that I can fashion fit.   [*Exit.*

SCENE III

The Duke of Albany's palace.

Enter Goneril and Oswald, her steward.

Gon. Did my father strike my gentleman for chiding of his fool?

Osw. Yes, madam.

Gon. By day and night he wrongs me; every hour
He flashes into one gross crime or other,
That sets us all at odds: I'll not endure it:
His knights grow riotous, and himself upbraids us
On every trifle. When he returns from hunting,
I will not speak with him; say I am sick:
If you come slack of former services,
You shall do well; the fault of it I'll answer.

Osw. He's coming, madam; I hear him.   [*Horns within.*

Gon. Put on what weary negligence you please,
You and your fellows; I'ld have it come to question:
If he distaste it, let him to our sister,
Whose mind and mine, I know, in that are one,
Not to be over-ruled. Idle old man,

That still would manage those authorities
That he hath given away! Now, by my life,
Old fools are babes again, and must be used
With checks as flatteries, when they are seen abused.
Remember what I tell you.

Osw.   Very well, madam.

Gon. And let his knights have colder looks among you;
What grows of it, no matter; advise your fellows so:
I would breed from hence occasions, and I shall,
That I may speak: I'll write straight to my sister,
To hold my very course. Prepare for dinner.   [*Exeunt.*

Scene IV

A hall in the same.
Enter Kent, disguised.

Kent. If but as well I other accents borrow,
That can my speech defuse, my good intent
May carry through itself to that full issue
For which I razed my likeness. Now, banish'd Kent,
If thou canst serve where thou dost stand condemn'd,
So may it come, thy master whom thou lovest
Shall find thee full of labours.

   Horns within. Enter Lear, Knights, and Attendants.

Lear. Let me not stay a jot for dinner; go get it ready. [*Exit
    an Attendant.*] How now! what art thou?

Kent. A man, sir.

Lear. What dost thou profess? What wouldst thou with us?

Kent. I do profess to be no less than I seem; to serve him
    truly that will put me in trust; to love him that is honest;
    to converse with him that is wise and says little; to fear
    judgement; to fight when I cannot choose, and to eat no

Lear. What art thou?   [fish.

Kent. A very honest-hearted fellow, and as poor as the king.

Lear. If thou be as poor for a subject as he is for a king, thou
    art poor enough. What wouldst thou?

Kent. Service.

Lear. Who wouldst thou serve?

Kent. You.

Lear. Dost thou know me, fellow?

Kent. No, sir; but you have that in your countenance which I
    would fain call master.

Lear. What's that?

Kent. Authority.

Lear. What services canst thou do?

Kent. I can keep honest counsel, ride, run, mar a curious tale in telling it, and deliver a plain message bluntly: that which ordinary men are fit for, I am qualified in, and the best of me is diligence.

Lear. How old art thou.

Kent. Not so young, sir, to love a woman for singing, nor so old to dote on her for any thing: I have years on my back forty eight.

Lear. Follow me; thou shalt serve me: if I like thee no worse after dinner, I will not part from thee yet. Dinner, ho, dinner! Where 's my knave? my fool? Go you, and call my fool hither.   [*Exit an Attendant.*

Enter Oswald.

You, you, sirrah, where 's my daughter?

Osw. So please you,—   [*Exit.*

Lear. What says the fellow there? Call the clot-poll back. [*Exit a Knight.*] Where 's my fool, ho? I think the world 's asleep.

Re-enter Knight.

How now! where 's that mongrel?

Knight. He says, my lord, your daughter is not well.

Lear. Why came not the slave back to me when I called him?

Knight. Sir, he answered me in the roundest manner, he would not.

Lear. He would not!

Knight. My lord, I know not what the matter is; but, to my judgement, your highness is not entertained with that cere- monious affection as you were wont; there 's a great abate- ment of kindness appears as well in the general dependants as in the duke himself also and your daughter.

Lear. Ha! sayest thou so?

Knight. I beseech you, pardon me, my lord, if I be mistaken; for my duty cannot be silent when I think your highness wronged.

Lear. Thou but rememberest me of mine own conception: I have perceived a most faint neglect of late; which I have rather blamed as mine own jealous curiosity than as a very pretence and purpose of unkindness: I will look further into 't. But where 's my fool? I have not seen him these two days.

Knight. Since my young lady's going into France, sir, the fool hath much pined away.

Lear. No more of that; I have noted it well. Go you, and tell my daughter I would speak with her. [*Exit an Atten- dant.*] Go you, call hither my fool.   [*Exit an Attendant.*

14

Re-enter Oswald.

O, you sir, you, come you hither, sir : who am I, sir ?

Osw. My lady's father.

Lear. My lady's father ! my lord's knave : you whoreson dog ! you slave ! you cur !

Osw. I am none of these, my lord ; I beseech your pardon.

Lear. Do you bandy looks with me, you rascal ? [*Striking him.*

Osw. I'll not be struck, my lord.

Kent. Nor tripped neither, you base foot-ball player.

[*Tripping up his heels.*

Lear. I thank thee, fellow ; thou servest me, and I'll love thee.

Kent. Come, sir, arise, away ! I'll teach you differences : away, away ! If you will measure your lubber's length again, tarry : but away ! go to ; have you wisdom ? so.

[*Pushes Oswald out.*

Lear. Now, my friendly knave, I thank thee : there's earnest of thy service.   [*Giving Kent money.*

Enter Fool.

Fool. Let me hire him too : here's my coxcomb.

[*Offering Kent his cap.*

Lear. How now, my pretty knave ! how dost thou ?

Fool. Sirrah, you were best take my coxcomb.

Kent. Why, fool ?

Fool. Why, for taking one's part that's out of favour : nay, as thou canst not smile as the wind sits, thou'lt catch cold shortly : there, take my coxcomb : why, this fellow hath banished two on's daughters, and done the third a blessing against his will ; if thou follow him, thou must needs wear my coxcomb. How now, nuncle ! Would I had two coxcombs and two daughters !

Lear. Why, my boy ?

Fool. If I gave them all my living, I'ld keep my coxcombs myself. There's mine ; beg another of thy daughters.

Lear. Take heed, sirrah ; the whip.

Fool. Truth's a dog must to kennel ; he must be whipped out, when Lady the brach may stand by the fire and stink.

Lear. A pestilent gall to me !

Fool. Sirrah, I'll teach thee a speech.

Lear. Do.

Fool. Mark it, nuncle :

> Have more than thou showest,
> Speak less than thou knowest,
> Lend less than thou owest,
> Ride more than thou goest,
> Learn more than thou trowest,

Set less than thou throwest;
Leave thy drink and thy whore,
And keep in-a-door,
And thou shalt have more
Than two tens to a score.

Kent. This is nothing, fool.

Fool. Then 'tis like the breath of an unfee'd lawyer, you gave me nothing for 't. Can you make no use of nothing, nuncle?

Lear. Why, no, boy; nothing can be made out of nothing.

Fool. [*To Kent*] Prithee, tell him, so much the rent of his land comes to: he will not believe a fool.

Lear. A bitter fool!

Fool. Dost thou know the difference, my boy, between a bitter fool and a sweet fool?

Lear. No, lad; teach me.

Fool.

That lord that counsell'd thee
  To give away thy land,
Come place him here by me;
  Do thou for him stand:
The sweet and bitter fool
  Will presently appear;
The one in motley here,
  The other found out there.

Lear. Dost thou call me fool, boy?

Fool. All thy other titles thou hast given away; that thou wast born with.

Kent. This is not altogether fool, my lord.

Fool. No, faith, lords and great men will not let me; if I had a monopoly out, they would have part on 't: and ladies too, they will not let me have all the fool to myself; they 'll be snatching. Give me an egg, nuncle, and I 'll give thee two crowns.

Lear. What two crowns shall they be?

Fool. Why, after I have cut the egg in the middle and eat up the meat, the two crowns of the egg. When thou clovest thy crown i' the middle and gavest away both parts, thou borest thine ass on thy back o'er the dirt: thou hadst little wit in thy bald crown when thou gavest thy golden one away. If I speak like myself in this, let him be whipped that first finds it so.

[*Singing*] Fools had ne'er less wit in a year;
  For wise men are grown foppish,
And know not how their wits to wear,
  Their manners are so apish.

Lear. When were you wont to be so full of songs, sirrah?

Fool. I have used it, nuncle, ever since thou madest thy daughters thy mother: for when thou gavest them the rod and puttest down thine own breeches,

> [*Singing*] Then they for sudden joy did weep,
>   And I for sorrow sung,
>   That such a king should play bo-peep,
>   And go the fools among.

Prithee, nuncle, keep a schoolmaster that can teach thy fool to lie: I would fain learn to lie.

Lear. An you lie, sirrah, we 'll have you whipped.

Fool. I marvel what kin thou and thy daughters are: they 'll have me whipped for speaking true, thou 'lt have me whipped for lying, and sometimes I am whipped for holding my peace. I had rather be any kind o' thing than a fool: and yet I would not be thee, nuncle; thou hast pared thy wit o' both sides and left nothing i' the middle. Here comes one o' the parings.

Enter Goneril.

Lear. How now, daughter! what makes that frontlet on? Methinks you are too much of late i' the frown.

Fool. Thou wast a pretty fellow when thou hadst no need to care for her frowning; now thou art an O without a figure: I am better than thou art now; I am a fool, thou art nothing. [*To Gon.*] Yes, forsooth, I will hold my tongue; so your face bids me, though you say nothing.

>   Mum, mum:
>   He that keeps nor crust nor crumb,
>   Weary of all, shall want some.

[*Pointing to Lear*] That 's a shealed peascod.

Gon. Not only, sir, this your all-licensed fool,
But other of your insolent retinue
Do hourly carp and quarrel, breaking forth
In rank and not to be endured riots.   Sir,
I had thought, by making this well known unto you,
To have found a safe redress; but now grow fearful,
By what yourself too late have spoke and done,
That you protect this course and put it on
By your allowance; which if you should, the fault
Would not 'scape censure, nor the redresses sleep,
Which, in the tender of a wholesome weal,
Might in their working do you that offence
Which else were shame, that then necessity
Will call discreet proceeding.

Fool. For, you know, nuncle,
   The hedge-sparrow fed the cuckoo so long,
   That it had its head bit off by its young.
 So out went the candle, and we were left darkling.
Lear. Are you our daughter?
Gon. Come, sir,
 I would you would make use of that good wisdom
 Whereof I know you are fraught, and put away
 These dispositions that of late transform you
 From what you rightly are.
Fool. May not an ass know when the cart draws the horse?
 Whoop, Jug! I love thee.
Lear. Doth any here know me? This is not Lear:
 Doth Lear walk thus? speak thus? Where are his eyes?
 Either his notion weakens, his discernings
 Are lethargied—Ha! waking? 'tis not so.
 Who is it that can tell me who I am?
Fool. Lear's shadow.
Lear. I would learn that; for, by the marks of sovereignty,
 knowledge and reason, I should be false persuaded I had
 daughters.
Fool. Which they will make an obedient father.
Lear. Your name, fair gentlewoman?
Gon. This admiration, sir, is much o' the savour
 Of other your new pranks. I do beseech you
 To understand my purposes aright:
 As you are old and reverend, you should be wise.
 Here do you keep a hundred knights and squires;
 Men so disorder'd, so debosh'd and bold,
 That this our court, infected with their manners,
 Shows like a riotous inn: epicurism and lust
 Make it more like a tavern or a brothel
 Than a graced palace. The shame itself doth speak
 For instant remedy: be then desired
 By her that else will take the thing she begs
 A little to disquantity your train,
 And the remainder that shall still depend,
 To be such men as may besort your age,
 Which know themselves and you.
Lear.   Darkness and devils!
 Saddle my horses; call my train together.
 Degenerate bastard! I 'll not trouble thee·
 Yet have I left a daughter.
Gon. You strike my people, and your disorder'd rabble
 Make servants of their betters.

18

Enter Albany.

Lear. Woe, that too late repents,—[*To Alb.*] O, sir, are you
  Is it your will? Speak, sir. Prepare my horses.   [come?
  Ingratitude, thou marble-hearted fiend,
  More hideous when thou show'st thee in a child
  Than the sea-monster!
Alb.   Pray, sir, be patient.
Lear. [*To Gon.*] Detested kite! thou liest.
  My train are men of choice and rarest parts,
  That all particulars of duty know,
  And in the most exact regard support
  The worships of their name. O most small fault,
  How ugly didst thou in Cordelia show!
  That, like an engine, wrench'd my frame of nature
  From the fix'd place, drew from my heart all love
  And added to the gall. O Lear, Lear, Lear!
  Beat at this gate, and let thy folly in   [*Striking his head.*
  And thy dear judgement out! Go, go, my people.
Alb. My lord, I am guiltless, as I am ignorant
  Of what hath moved you.
Lear.   It may be so, my lord.
  Hear, nature, hear; dear goddess, hear!
  Suspend thy purpose, if thou didst intend
  To make this creature fruitful:
  Into her womb convey sterility:
  Dry up in her the organs of increase,
  And from her derogate body never spring
  A babe to honour her! If she must teem,
  Create her child of spleen, that it may live
  And be a thwart disnatured torment to her.
  Let it stamp wrinkles in her brow of youth;
  With cadent tears fret channels in her cheeks;
  Turn all her mother's pains and benefits
  To laughter and contempt; that she may feel
  How sharper than a serpent's tooth it is
  To have a thankless child! Away, away!   [*Exit.*
Alb. Now, gods that we adore, whereof comes this?
Gon. Never afflict yourself to know the cause,
  But let his disposition have that scope
  That dotage gives it.
                Re-enter Lear.
Lear. What, fifty of my followers at a clap!
  Within a fortnight!
Alb.   What's the matter, sir?
Lear. I'll tell thee. [*To Gon.*] Life and death! I am ashamed

19

That thou hast power to shake my manhood thus;
That these hot tears, which break from me perforce,
Should make thee worth them.   Blasts and fogs upon thee!
The untented woundings of a father's curse
Pierce every sense about thee! Old fond eyes,
Beweep this cause again, I'll pluck ye out
And cast you with the waters that you lose
To temper clay.   Yea. is it come to this?
Let it be so: yet have I left a daughter,
Who, I am sure, is kind and comfortable:
When she shall hear this of thee, with her nails
She'll flay thy wolvish visage.   Thou shalt find
That I'll resume the shape which thou dost think
I have cast off for ever: thou shalt, I warrant thee.
                                [Exeunt Lear, Kent, and Attendants

Gon. Do you mark that, my lord?
Alb. I cannot be so partial, Goneril,
  To the great love I bear you,—
Gon. Pray you, content.   What, Oswald, ho!   [master.
  [To the Fool] You, sir, more knave than fool, after your
Fool. Nuncle Lear, nuncle Lear, tarry; take the fool with thee.

              A fox, when one has caught her,
                 And such a daughter,
                 Should sure to the slaughter,
                 If my cap would buy a halter:
                 So the fool follows after.   *[Exit.*

Gon. This man hath had good counsel: a hundred knights!
  'Tis politic and safe to let him keep
  At point a hundred knights: yes, that on every dream,
  Each buzz, each fancy, each complaint, dislike,
  He may enguard his dotage with their powers
  And hold our lives in mercy.   Oswald, I say!
Alb. Well, you may fear too far.
Gon.   Safer than trust too far:
  Let me still take away the harms I fear,
  Not fear still to be taken: I know his heart.
  What he hath utter'd I have writ my sister:
  If she sustain him and his hundred knights,
  When I have show'd the unfitness,—
                        Re-enter Oswald.

                                 How now, Oswald!
  What, have you writ that letter to my sister?
Osw. Yes, madam.
Gon. Take you some company, and away to horse:
  Inform her full of my particular fear,

                              20

And thereto add such reasons of your own
As may compact it more.   Get you gone;
And hasten your return.   [*Exit Oswald.*] No, no, my lord,
This milky gentleness and course of yours
Though I condemn not, yet, under pardon,
You are much more attask'd for want of wisdom
Than praised for harmful mildness.

Alb. How far your eyes may pierce I cannot tell:
Striving to better, oft we mar what's well.

Gon. Nay, then—

Alb. Well, well; the event.   [*Exeunt.*

SCENE V

Court before the same.

Enter Lear, Kent, and Fool.

Lear. Go you before to Gloucester with these letters. Acquaint
my daughter no further with any thing you know than comes
from her demand out of the letter.   If your diligence be not
speedy, I shall be there afore you.

Kent. I will not sleep, my lord, till I have delivered your letter.
                                                    [*Exit.*

Fool. If a man's brains were in's heels, were't not in danger of
kibes?

Lear. Ay, boy.

Fool. Then, I prithee, be merry; thy wit shall ne'er go slip-
Lear. Ha, ha, ha !   [shod.

Fool. Shalt see thy other daughter will use thee kindly; for
though she's as like this as a crab's like an apple, yet I can
tell what I can tell.

Lear. Why, what canst thou tell, my boy?

Fool. She will taste as like this as a crab does to a crab. Thou
canst tell why one's nose stands i' the middle on 'is face?

Lear. No.

Fool. Why, to keep one's eyes of either side's nose, that what
a man cannot smell out he may spy into.

Lear. I did her wrong—

Fool. Canst tell how an oyster makes his shell?

Lear. No.

Fool. Nor I neither; but I can tell why a snail has a house.

Lear. Why?

Fool. Why to put's head in; not to give it away to his daughters, and leave his horns without a case.

Lear. I will forget my nature.—So kind a father!—Be my
horses ready?

21

Fool. Thy asses are gone about 'em. The reason why the seven stars are no more than seven is a pretty reason.

Lear. Because they are not eight?

Fool. Yes, indeed : thou wouldst make a good fool.

Lear. To take 't again perforce ! Monster ingratitude !

Fool. If thou wert my fool, nuncle, I 'ld have thee beaten for being old before thy time.

Lear. How 's that?   [wise.

Fool. Thou shouldst not have been old till thou hadst been

Lear. O, let me not be mad, not mad, sweet heaven !
Keep me in temper : I would not be mad !

Enter Gentleman.

How now ! are the horses ready?

Gent. Ready, my lord.

Lear. Come, boy.

Fool. She that 's a maid now and laughs at my departure
Shall not be a maid long, unless things be cut shorter.

[*Exeunt.*

ACT II—Scene I

The Earl of Gloucester's castle.

Enter Edmund and Curan, meeting.

Edm. Save thee, Curan.

Cur. And you, sir. I have been with your father, and given him notice that the Duke of Cornwall and Regan his duchess will be here with him this night.

Edm. How comes that?

Cur. Nay, I know not. You have heard of the news abroad, I mean the whispered ones, for they are yet but ear-kissing arguments?

Edm. Not I : pray you, what are they?

Cur. Have you heard of no likely wars toward, 'twixt the Dukes of Cornwall and Albany?

Edm. Not a word.

Cur. You may do then in time. Fare you well, sir.   [*Exit.*

Edm. The duke be here to-night? The better ! best !
This weaves itself perforce into my business.
My father hath set guard to take my brother ;
And I have one thing, of a queasy question,
Which I must act : briefness and fortune, work !
Brother, a word ; descend : brother, I say !

Enter Edgar.

My father watches : O sir, fly this place ;
Intelligence is given where you are hid ;

22

You have now the good advantage of the night :
Have you not spoken 'gainst the Duke of Cornwall ?
He's coming hither, now, i' the night, i' the haste,
And Regan with him : have you nothing said
Upon his party 'gainst the Duke of Albany ?
Advise yourself.

Edg.   I am sure on 't, not a word.

Edm. I hear my father coming : pardon me :
In cunning I must draw my sword upon you :
Draw : seem to defend yourself : now quit you well.
Yield : come before my father.   Light, ho, here !
Fly, brother.   Torches, torches !   So farewell.

                                     [Exit Edgar.

Some blood drawn on me would beget opinion

                                    [Wounds his arm.

Of my more fierce endeavour : I have seen drunkards
Do more than this in sport.   Father, father !
Stop, stop !   No help ?

           Enter Gloucester, and Servants with torches.

Glou. Now, Edmund, where's the villain ?

Edm. Here stood he in the dark, his sharp sword out,
Mumbling of wicked charms, conjuring the moon
To stand 's auspicious mistress.

Glou.   But where is he ?

Edm. Look, sir, I bleed.

Glou.   Where is the villain, Edmund ?

Edm. Fled this way, sir.   When by no means he could—

Glou. Pursue him, ho !—Go after.   *[Exeunt some Servants.]*
'By no means ' what ?

Edm. Persuade me to the murder of your lordship ;
But that I told him the revenging gods
'Gainst parricides did all their thunders bend,
Spoke with how manifold and strong a bond
The child was bound to the father ; sir, in fine,
Seeing how loathly opposite I stood
To his unnatural purpose, in fell motion
With his prepared sword he charges home
My unprovided body, lanced mine arm :
But when he saw my best alarum'd spirits
Bold in the quarrel's right, roused to the encounter,
Or whether gasted by the noise I made,
Full suddenly he fled.

Glou.   Let him fly far :
Not in this land shall he remain uncaught :
And found—dispatch.   The noble duke my master,

My worthy arch and patron, comes to-night :
By his authority I will proclaim it,
That he which finds him shall deserve our thanks,
Bringing the murderous caitiff to the stake ;
He that conceals him, death.
Edm. When I dissuaded him from his intent
And found him pight to do it, with curst speech
I threaten'd to discover him : he replied,
' Thou unpossessing bastard ! dost thou think,
If I would stand against thee, could the reposure
Of any trust, virtue, or worth, in thee
Make thy words faith'd ? No : what I should deny—
As this I would ; ay, though thou didst produce
My very character—I 'ld turn it all
To thy suggestion, plot, and damned practice :
And thou must make a dullard of the world,
If they not thought the profits of my death
Were very pregnant and potential spurs
To make thee seek it.'
Glou.   Strong and fasten'd villain !
Would he deny his letter ? I never got him. [*Tucket within.*
Hark, the duke's trumpets ! I know not why he comes.
All ports I 'll bar ; the villain shall not 'scape ;
The duke must grant me that : besides, his picture
I will send far and near, that all the kingdom
May have due note of him ; and of my land,
Loyal and natural boy, I 'll work the means
To make thee capable.
              Enter Cornwall, Regan, and Attendants.
Corn. How now, my noble friend ! since I came hither,
Which I can call but now, I have heard strange news.
Reg. If it be true, all vengeance comes too short
Which can pursue the offender. How dost, my lord ?
Glou. O, madam, my old heart is crack'd, is crack'd !
Reg. What, did my father's godson seek your life ?
He whom my father named ? your Edgar ?
Glou. O, lady, lady, shame would have it hid !
Reg. Was he not companion with the riotous knights
That tend upon my father ?
Glou. I know not, madam : 'tis too bad, too bad.
Edm. Yes, madam, he was of that consort.
Reg. No marvel then, though he were ill affected :
'Tis they have put him on the old man's death,
To have the waste and spoil of his revenues.
I have this present evening from my sister

Been well inform'd of them, and with such cautions
That if they come to sojourn at my house,
I 'll not be there.

Corn.   Nor I, assure thee, Regan.
Edmund, I hear that you have shown your father
A child-like office.

Edm.   'Twas my duty, sir.

Glou. He did bewray his practice, and received
This hurt you see, striving to apprehend him.

Corn. Is he pursued?

Glou.   Ay, my good lord.

Corn. If he be taken, he shall never more
Be fear'd of doing harm : make your own purpose,
How in my strength you please.   For you, Edmund,
Whose virtue and obedience doth this instant
So much commend itself, you shall be ours:
Natures of such deep trust we shall much need:
You we first seize on.

Edm.   I shall serve you, sir,
Truly, however else.

Glou.   For him I thank your grace.

Corn. You know not why we came to visit you,—

Reg. Thus out of season, threading dark-eyed night:
Occasions, noble Gloucester, of some poise,
Wherein we must have use of your advice :
Our father he hath writ, so hath our sister,
Of differences, which I least thought it fit
To answer from our home ; the several messengers
From hence attend dispatch.   Our good old friend,
Lay comforts to your bosom, and bestow
Your needful counsel to our business,
Which craves the instant use.

Glou.   I serve you, madam:
Your graces are right welcome.   [*Flourish. Exeunt.*

Scene II

Before Gloucester's castle.

Enter Kent and Oswald, severally.

Osw. Good dawning to thee, friend : art of this house?

Kent. Ay.

Osw. Where may we set our horses?

Kent. I' the mire.

Osw. Prithee, if thou lovest me, tell me

Kent. I love thee not.

Osw. Why then I care not for thee.

Kent. If I had thee in Lipsbury pinfold, I would make thee care for me.

Osw. Why dost thou use me thus? I know thee not.

Kent. Fellow, I know thee.

Osw. What dost thou know me for?

Kent. A knave; a rascal; an eater of broken meats; a base, proud, shallow, beggarly, three-suited, hundred-pound, filthy, worsted-stocking knave; a lily-livered, action-taking knave; a whoreson, glass-gazing, superserviceable, finical rogue; one-trunk-inheriting slave; one that wouldst be a bawd in way of good service, and art nothing but the composition of a knave, beggar, coward, pandar, and the son and heir of a mongrel bitch: one whom I will beat into clamorous whining, if thou deniest the least syllable of thy addition.

Osw. Why, what a monstrous fellow art thou, thus to rail on one that is neither known of thee nor knows thee!

Kent. What a brazen-faced varlet art thou, to deny thou knowest me! Is it two days ago since I tripped up thy heels and beat thee before the king? Draw, you rogue: for, though it be night, yet the moon shines; I'll make a sop o' the moonshine of you: draw, you whoreson cullionly barber-monger, draw.   [*Drawing his sword.*

Osw. Away! I have nothing to do with thee.

Kent. Draw, you rascal: you come with letters against the king, and take vanity the puppet's part against the royalty of her father: draw, you rogue, or I'll so carbonado your shanks: draw, you rascal; come your ways.

Osw. Help, ho! murder! help!

Kent. Strike, you slave; stand, rogue; stand, you neat slave, strike.   [*Beating him.*

Osw. Help, ho! murder! murder!

Enter Edmund, with his rapier drawn, Cornwall, Regan, Gloucester, and Servants.

Edm. How now! What's the matter?   [*Parting them.*

Kent. With you, goodman boy, an you please: come, I'll flesh you; come on young master.

Glou. Weapons! arms! What's the matter here?

Corn. Keep peace, upon your lives;
   He dies that strikes again. What is the matter?

Reg. The messengers from our sister and the king.

Corn. What is your difference? speak.

Osw. I am scarce in breath, my lord.

Kent. No marvel, you have so bestirred your valour. You cowardly rascal, nature disclaims in thee: a tailor made thee.

Corn. Thou art a strange fellow: a tailor make a man?

Kent. Ay, a tailor, sir : a stone-cutter or a painter could not
   have made him so ill, though he had been but two hours at
Corn. Speak yet, how grew your quarrel?   [the trade.
Osw. This ancient ruffian, sir, whose life I have spared at suit
   of his gray beard,—
Kent. Thou whoreson zed ! thou unnecessary letter ! My lord,
   if you will give me leave, I will tread this unbolted villain
   into mortar, and daub the walls of a jakes with him. Spare
   my gray beard, you wagtail ?
Corn. Peace, sirrah !
   You beastly knave, know you no reverence ?
Kent. Yes, sir ; but anger hath a privilege.
Corn. Why art thou angry ?
Kent. That such a slave as this should wear a sword,
   Who wears no honesty. Such smiling rogues as these,
   Like rats, oft bite the holy cords a-twain
   Which are too intrinse to unloose ; smooth every passion
   That in the natures of their lords rebel ;
   Bring oil to fire, snow to their colder moods ;
   Renege, affirm, and turn their halcyon beaks
   With every gale and vary of their masters,
   Knowing nought, like dogs, but following.
   A plague upon your epileptic visage !
   Smile you my speeches, as I were a fool ?
   Goose, if I had you upon Sarum plain,
   I 'ld drive ye cackling home to Camelot.
Corn. What, art thou mad, old fellow ?
Glou. How fell you out ? say that.
Kent. No contraries hold more antipathy
   Than I and such a knave.
Corn. Why dost thou call him knave ? What is his fault ?
Kent. His countenance likes me not.
Corn. No more perchance does mine, nor his, nor hers.
Kent. Sir, 'tis my occupation to be plain :
   I have seen better faces in my time
   Than stands no any shoulder that I see
   Before me at this instant.
Corn.   This is some fellow,
   Who, having been praised for bluntness, doth affect
   A saucy roughness, and constrains the garb
   Quite from his nature : he cannot flatter, he,—
   An honest mind and plain,—he must speak truth !
   An they will take it, so ; if not, he 's plain.
   These kind of knaves I know, which in this plainness
   Harbour more craft and more corrupter ends

Than twenty silly ducking observants
That stretch their duties nicely.
Kent. Sir, in good faith, in sincere verity,
Under the allowance of your great aspect,
Whose influence, like the wreath of radiant fire
On flickering Phœbus' front,—
Corn.   What mean'st by this?
Kent. To go out of my dialect, which you discommend so
much. I know, sir, I am no flatterer : he that beguiled
you in a plain accent was a plain knave ; which, for my part,
I will not be, though I should win your displeasure to
entreat me to 't.
Corn. What was the offence you gave him?
Osw. I never gave him any :
It pleased the king his master very late
To strike at me, upon his misconstruction ;
When he, conjunct, and flattering his displeasure,
Tripp'd me behind ; being down, insulted, rail'd,
And put upon him such a deal of man,
That worthied him, got praises of the king
For him attempting who was self-subdued,
And in the fleshment of this dread exploit
Drew on me here again.
Kent.   None of these rogues and cowards
But Ajax is their fool.
Corn.   Fetch forth the stocks !
You stubborn ancient knave, you reverend braggart,
We'll teach you—
Kent.   Sir, I am too old to learn :
Call not your stocks for me : I serve the king,
On whose employment I was sent to you :
You shall do small respect, show too bold malice
Against the grace and person of my master,
Stocking his messenger.
Corn. Fetch forth the stocks ! As I have life and honour,
There shall he sit till noon.
Reg. Till noon ! till night, my lord, and all night too.
Kent. Why, madam, if I were your father's dog,
You should not use me so.
Reg.   Sir, being his knave, I will.
Corn. This is a fellow of the self-same colour
Our sister speaks of. Come, bring away the stocks !
                                   [*Stocks brought out.*
Glou. Let me beseech your grace not to do so :
His fault is much, and the good king his master

28

Will check him for 't : your purposed low correction
Is such as basest and contemned'st wretches
For pilferings and most common trespasses
Are punish'd with : the king must take it ill,
That he, so slightly valued in his messenger,
Should have him thus restrain'd.

Corn.   I 'll answer that.

Reg. My sister may receive it much more worse,
To have her gentleman abused, assaulted,
For following her affairs.   Put in his legs.

                              [*Kent is put in the stocks.*

Come, my good lord, away.

                              [*Exeunt all but Gloucester and Kent.*

Glou. I am sorry for thee, friend ; 'tis the duke's pleasure,
Whose disposition, all the world well knows,
Will not be rubb'd nor stopp'd : I 'll entreat for thee.

Kent. Pray, do not, sir : I have watch'd and travell'd hard ;
Some time I shall sleep out, the rest I 'll whistle.
A good man's fortune may grow out at heels :
Give you good morrow !

Glou. The duke 's to blame in this ! 'twill be ill taken.   [*Exit.*

Kent. Good king, that must approve the common saw,
Thou out of heaven's benediction comest
To the warm sun !
Approach, thou beacon to this under globe,
That by thy comfortable beams I may
Peruse this letter !   Nothing almost sees miracles
But misery : I know 'tis from Cordelia,
Who hath most fortunately been inform'd
Of my obscured course ; and shall find time
From this enormous state, seeking to give
Losses their remedies.   All weary and o'er-watch'd,
Take vantage, heavy eyes, not to behold
This shameful lodging.
Fortune, good night : smile once more ; turn thy wheel !

                              [*Sleeps.*

SCENE III

A wood.

Enter Edgar.

Edg. I heard myself proclaim'd ;
And by the happy hollow of a tree
Escaped the hunt.   No port is free ; no place,
That guard and most unusual vigilance
Does not attend my taking.   Whiles I may 'scape

I will preserve myself: and am bethought
To take the basest and most poorest shape
That ever penury in contempt of man
Brought near to beast: my face I'll grime with filth,
Blanket my loins, elf all my hair in knots,
And with presented nakedness out-face
The winds and persecutions of the sky.
The country gives me proof and precedent
Of Bedlam beggars, who with roaring voices
Strike in their numb'd and mortified bare arms
Pins, wooden pricks, nails, sprigs of rosemary;
And with this horrible object, from low farms,
Poor pelting villages, sheep-cotes and mills,
Sometime with lunatic bans, sometime with prayers,
Enforce their charity. Poor Turlygod! poor Tom!
That's something yet: Edgar I nothing am.   [*Exit*.

SCENE IV

Before Gloucester's castle. Kent in the stocks.

Enter Lear, Fool, and Gentleman.

Lear. 'Tis strange that they should so depart from home,
And not send back my messenger.

Gent.   As I learn'd,
The night before there was no purpose in them
Of this remove.

Kent.   Hail to thee, noble master!

Lear. Ha!
Makest thou this shame thy pastime?

Kent.   No, my lord.

Fool. Ha, ha! he wears cruel garters. Horses are tied by the
heads, dogs and bears by the neck, monkeys by the loins,
and men by the legs: when a man's over-lusty at legs, then
he wears wooden nether-stocks.

Lear. What's he that hath so much thy place mistook
To set thee here?

Kent.   It is both he and she;
Your son and daughter.

Lear. No.

Kent. Yes.

Lear. No, I say.

Kent. I say, yea.

Lear. No, no, they would not.

Kent. Yes, they have.

Lear. By Jupiter, I swear, no.

Kent. By Juno, I swear, ay.

Lear.   They durst not do 't;
   They could not, would not do 't; 'tis worse than murder,
   To do upon respect such violent outrage:
   Resolve me with all modest haste which way
   Thou mightst deserve, or they impose, this usage,
   Coming from us.
Kent.   My lord, when at their home
   I did commend your highness' letters to them,
   Ere I was risen from the place that show'd
   My duty kneeling, came there a reeking post,
   Stew'd in his haste, half breathless, panting forth
   From Goneril his mistress salutations;
   Deliver'd letters, spite of intermission,
   Which presently they read: on whose contents
   They summon'd up their meiny, straight took horse;
   Commanded me to follow and attend
   The leisure of their answer; gave me cold looks:
   And meeting here the other messenger,
   Whose welcome, I perceived, had poison'd mine—
   Being the very fellow that of late
   Display'd so saucily against your highness—
   Having more man than wit about me, drew:
   He raised the house with loud and coward cries.
   Your son and daughter found this trespass worth
   The shame which here it suffers.
Fool. Winter's not gone yet, if the wild geese fly that way
             Fathers that wear rags
                Do make their children blind;
             But fathers that bear bags
                Shall see their children kind.
             Fortune, that arrant whore,
             Ne'er turns the key to the poor.
   But, for all this, thou shalt have as many dolours for thy
   daughters as thou canst tell in a year.
Lear. O, how this mother swells up toward my heart!
   Hysterica passio, down, thou climbing sorrow,
   Thy element's below! Where is this daughter?
Kent. With the earl, sir, here within.
Lear. Follow me not; stay here.   [*Exit.*
Gent. Made you no more offence but what you speak of?
Kent. None.
   How chance the king comes with so small a train?
Fool. An thou hadst been set i' the stocks for that question,
   thou hadst well deserved it.
Kent. Why, fool?

Fool. We 'll set thee to school to an ant, to teach thee there 's
no labouring i' the winter.   All that follow their noses are
led by their eyes but blind men ; and there 's not a nose
among twenty but can smell him that 's stinking.   Let go
thy hold when a great wheel runs down a hill, lest it break
thy neck with following it ; but the great one that goes up
the hill, let him draw thee after.   When a wise man gives
thee better counsel, give me mine again : I would have none
but knaves follow it, since a fool gives it.

> That sir which serves and seeks for gain,
>   And follows but for form,
> Will pack when it begins to rain,
>   And leave thee in the storm.
> But I will tarry ; the fool will stay,
>   And let the wise man fly :
> The knave turns fool that runs away ;
>   The fool no knave, perdy.

Kent. Where learned you this, fool ?

Fool. Not i' the stocks, fool.

Re-enter Lear, with Gloucest .

Lear. Deny to speak with me ?   They are sick ? they are weary ?
They have travell'd all the night ?   Mere fetches ;
The images of revolt and flying off.
Fetch me a better answer.

Glou.   My dear lord,
You know the fiery quality of the duke ;
How unremoveable and fix'd he is
In his own course.

Lear. Vengeance ! plague ! death ! confusion !
Fiery ? what quality ? Why, Gloucester, Gloucester,
I 'ld speak with the Duke of Cornwall and his wife.

Glou. Well, my good lord, I have inform'd them so.

Lear. Inform'd them ! Dost thou understand me, man ?

Glou. Ay, my good lord.

Lear. The king would speak with Cornwall ; the dear father
Would with his daughter speak, commands her service :
Are they inform'd of this ?   My breath and blood !
'Fiery '? ' the fiery duke '? Tell the hot duke that—
No, but not yet : may be he is not well :
Infirmity doth still neglect all office
Whereto our health is bound ; we are not ourselves
When nature being oppress'd commands the mind
To suffer with the body : I 'll forbear ;
And am fall'n out with my more headier will,
To take the indisposed and sickly fit

For the sound man. [*Looking on Kent*] Death on my state!
Should he sit here? This act persuades me   [wherefore
That this remotion of the duke and her
Is practice only. Give me my servant forth.
Go tell the duke and 's wife I 'ld speak with them,
Now, presently: bid them come forth and hear me,
Or at their chamber-door I 'll beat the drum
Till it cry sleep to death.

Glou. I would have all well betwixt you.   [*Exit.*

Lear. O me, my heart, my rising heart! But down!

Fool. Cry to it, nuncle, as the cockney did to the eels when she
    put 'em i' the paste alive; she knapped 'em o' the coxcombs
    with a stick, and cried ' Down, wantons, down!' 'Twas her
    brother that, in pure kindness to his horse, buttered his hay.

Re-enter Gloucester, with Cornwall, Regan, and Servants.

Lear. Good morrow to you both.

Corn.   Hail to your grace! [*Kent is set at liberty.*

Reg. I am glad to see your highness.

Lear. Regan, I think you are; I know what reason
I have to think so: If thou shouldst not be glad,
I would divorce me from thy mother's tomb,
Sepulchring an adultress. [*To Kent*] O, are you free?
Some other time for that. Beloved Regan,
Thy sister 's naught: O Regan, she hath tied
Sharp-tooth'd unkindness, like a vulture, here:

[*Points to his heart.*

I can scarce speak to thee; thou 'lt not believe
With how depraved a quality—O Regan!

Reg. I pray you, sir, take patience: I have hope
You less know how to value her desert
Than she to scant her duty.

Lear.   Say, how is that?

Reg. I cannot think my sister in the least
Would fail her obligation: if, sir, perchance
She have restrain'd the riots of your followers,
'Tis on such ground and to such wholesome end
As clears her from all blame.

Lear. My curses on her!

Reg.   O, sir, you are old;
Nature in you stands on the very verge
Of her confine: you should be ruled and led
By some discretion that discerns your state
Better than you yourself. Therefore I pray you
That to our sister you do make return;
Say you have wrong'd her, sir.

33

Lear.   Ask her forgiveness?
  Do you but mark how this becomes the house:
  [*Kneeling*] 'Dear daughter, I confess that I am old;
  Age is unnecessary : on my knees I beg
  That you 'll vouchsafe me raiment, bed and food.'
Reg. Good sir, no more; these are unsightly tricks:
  Return you to my sister.
Lear. [*Rising*]   Never, Regan:
  She hath abated me of half my train;
  Look'd black upon me; struck me with her tongue,
  Most serpent-like, upon the very heart:
  All the stored vengeances of heaven fall
  On her ingrateful top! Strike her young bones,
  You taking airs, with lameness.
Corn.   Fie, sir, fie!
Lear. You nimble lightnings, dart your blinding flames
  Into her scornful eyes. Infect her beauty,
  You fen-suck'd fogs, drawn by the powerful sun
  To fall and blast her pride.
Reg. O the blest gods! so will you wish on me,
  When the rash mood is on.
Lear. No, Regan, thou shalt never have my curse:
  Thy tender-hefted nature shall not give
  Thee o'er to harshness: her eyes are fierce, but thine
  Do comfort and not burn. 'Tis not in thee
  To grudge my pleasures, to cut off my train,
  To bandy hasty words, to scant my sizes,
  And in conclusion to oppose the bolt
  Against my coming in : thou better know'st
  The offices of nature, bond of childhood,
  Effects of courtesy, dues of gratitude;
  Thy half o' the kingdom hast thou not forgot,
  Wherein I thee endow'd.
Reg.   Good sir, to the purpose.
Lear. Who put my man i' the stocks?   [*Tucket within*
Corn.   What trumpet's that?
Reg. I know't; my sister's: this approves her letter,
  That she would soon be here.

            Enter Oswald.

               Is your lady come?
Lear. This is a slave whose easy-borrow'd pride
  Dwells in the fickle grace of her he follows.
  Out, varlet, from my sight!
Corn.   What means your grace?
Lear. Who stock'd my servant? Regan, I have good hope

34

Thou didst not know on 't.   Who comes here?

Enter Goneril.
                                                    O heavens,
If you do love old men, if your sweet sway
Allow obedience, if yourselves are old,
Make it your cause; send down, and take my part!
[*To Gon.*] Art not ashamed to look upon this beard?
O Regan, wilt thou take her by the hand?
Gon. Why not by the hand, sir?   How have I offended?
All 's not offence that indiscretion finds
And dotage terms so.
Lear.   O sides, you are too tough;
Will you yet hold?   How came my man i' the stocks?
Corn. I set him there, sir: but his own disorders
Deserved much less advancement.
Lear.   You! did you?
Reg. I pray you, father, being weak, seem so.
If, till the expiration of your month,
You will return and sojourn with my sister,
Dismissing half your train, come then to me:
I am now from home and out of that provision
Which shall be needful for your entertainment.
Lear. Return to her, and fifty men dismiss'd?
No, rather I abjure all roofs, and choose
To wage against the enmity o' the air,
To be a comrade with the wolf and owl,—
Necessity's sharp pinch!   Return with her?
Why, the hot-blooded France, that dowerless took
Our youngest born, I could as well be brought
To knee his throne, and, squire-like, pension beg
To keep base life afoot.   Return with her?
Persuade me rather to be slave and sumpter
To this detested groom.   [*Pointing at Oswald.*
Gon.   At your choice, sir.
Lear. I prithee, daughter, do not make me mad:
I will not trouble thee, my child; farewell:
We 'll no more meet, no more see one another:
But yet thou art my flesh, my blood, my daughter;
Or rather a disease that 's in my flesh,
Which I must needs call mine: thou art a boil,
A plague-sore, an embossed carbuncle,
In my corrupted blood.   But I 'll not chide thee;
Let shame come when it will, I do not call it:
I do not bid the thunder-bearer shoot,
Nor tell tales of thee to high-judging Jove:

35

Mend when thou canst ; be better at thy leisure :
I can be patient ; I can stay with Regan,
I and my hundred knights.

Reg.   Not altogether so :
I look'd not for you yet, nor am provided
For your fit welcome.   Give ear, sir, to my sister ;
For those that mingle reason with your passion
Must be content to think you old, and so—
But she knows what she does.

Lear.   Is this well spoken ?

Reg. I dare avouch it, sir : what, fifty followers ?
Is it not well ?   What should you need of more ?
Yea, or so many, sith that both charge and danger
Speak 'gainst so great a number ?   How in one house
Should many people under two commands
Hold amity ?   'Tis hard, almost impossible.

Gon. Why might not you, my lord, receive attendance
From those that she calls servants or from mine ?

Reg. Why not, my lord ?   If then they chanced to slack you,
We could control them.   If you will come to me,
For now I spy a danger, I entreat you,
To bring but five and twenty : to no more
Will I give place or notice.

Lear. I gave you all—

Reg.   And in good time you gave it.

Lear. Made you my guardians, my depositaries,
But kept a reservation to be follow'd
With such a number.   What, must I come to you
With five and twenty, Regan ? said you so ?

Reg. And speak 't again, my lord ; no more with me.

Lear. Those wicked creatures yet do look well-favour'd,
When others are more wicked ; not being the worst
Stands in some rank of praise.   [*To Gon.*] I 'll go with thee :
Thy fifty yet doth double five and twenty,
And thou art twice her love.

Gon.   Hear me, my lord :
What need you five and twenty, ten, or five,
To follow in a house where twice so many
Have a command to tend you ?

Reg.   What need one ?

Lear. O, reason not the need : our basest beggars
Are in the poorest thing superfluous :
Allow not nature more than nature needs,
Man's life 's as cheap as beast's : thou art a lady ;
If only to go warm were gorgeous,

Why, nature needs not what thou gorgeous wear'st,
Which scarcely keeps thee warm.   But for true need,—
You heavens, give me that patience, patience I need !
You see me here, you gods, a poor old man,
As full of grief as age ; wretched in both :
If it be you that stirs these daughters' hearts
Against their father, fool me not so much
To bear it tamely ; touch me with noble anger,
And let not woman's weapons, water-drops,
Stain my man's cheeks !   No, you unnatural hags,
I will have such revenges on you both
That all the world shall—I will do such things,—
What they are, yet I know not, but they shall be
The terrors of the earth.   You think I'll weep ;
No, I'll not weep :
I have full cause of weeping ; but this heart
Shall break into a hundred thousand flaws,
Or ere I'll weep.   O fool, I shall go mad !
                    [*Exeunt Lear, Gloucester, Kent, and Fool.*

Corn. Let us withdraw ; 'twill be a storm. [*Storm and tempest.*
Reg. This house is little : the old man and his people
    Cannot be well bestow'd.
Gon. 'Tis his own blame ; hath put himself from rest,
    And must needs taste his folly.
Reg. For his particular, I'll receive him gladly,
    But not one follower.
Gon.   So am I purposed.
    Where is my lord of Gloucester ?
Corn. Follow'd the old man forth : he is return'd.

Re-enter Gloucester.

Glou. The king is in high rage.
Corn.   Whither is he going ?
Glou. He calls to horse ; but will I know not whither.
Corn. 'Tis best to give him way ; he leads himself.
Gon. My lord, entreat him by no means to stay.
Glou. Alack, the night comes on, and the bleak winds
    Do sorely ruffle ; for many miles about
    There's scarce a bush.
Reg.   O, sir, to wilful men
    The injuries that they themselves procure
    Must be their schoolmasters.   Shut up your doors !
    He is attended with a desperate train ;
    And what they may incense him to, being apt
    To have his ear abused, wisdom bids fear.

Corn. Shut up your doors, my lord; 'tis a wild night:
My Regan counsels well: come out o' the storm.   [*Exeunt.*

ACT III—Scene I

A heath.

Storm still.   Enter Kent and a Gentleman, meeting.

Kent. Who's there, besides foul weather?
Gent. One minded like the weather, most unquietly.
Kent. I know you.   Where's the king?
Gent. Contending with the fretful elements;
Bids the wind blow the earth into the sea,
Or swell the curled waters 'bove the main,
That things might change or cease; tears his white hair,
Which the impetuous blasts, with eyeless rage,
Catch in their fury, and make nothing of;
Strives in his little world of man to out-scorn
The to-and-fro-conflicting wind and rain.
This night, wherein the cub-drawn bear would couch,
The lion and the belly-pinched wolf
Keep their fur dry, unbonneted he runs,
And bids what will take all.
Kent.   But who is with him?
Gent. None but the fool; who labours to out-jest
His heart-struck injuries.
Kent.   Sir, I do know you;
And dare, upon the warrant of my note,
Commend a dear thing to you.   There is division,
Although as yet the face of it be cover'd
With mutual cunning, 'twixt Albany and Cornwall;
Who have—as who have not, that their great stars
Throned and set high?—servants, who seem no less,
Which are to France the spies and speculations
Intelligent of our state: what hath been seen,
Either in snuffs and packings of the dukes,
Or the hard rein which both of them have borne
Against the old kind king, or something deeper
Whereof perchance these are but furnishings,—
But true it is, from France there comes a power
Into this scatter'd kingdom; who already,
Wise in our negligence, have secret feet
In some of our best ports, and are at point
To show their open banner.   Now to you:
If on my credit you dare build so far
To make your speed to Dover, you shall find

Some that will thank you, making just report
Of how unnatural and bemadding sorrow
The king hath cause to plain.
I am a gentleman of blood and breeding,
And from some knowledge and assurance offer
This office to you.

Gent. I will talk further with you.

Kent.   No, do not.
For confirmation that I am much more
Than my out-wall, open this purse and take
What it contains. If you shall see Cordelia,—
As fear not but you shall,—show her this ring,
And she will tell you who your fellow is
That yet you do not know. Fie on this storm!
I will go seek the king.

Gent.   Give me your hand:
Have you no more to say?

Kent. Few words, but, to effect, more than all yet;
That when we have found the king,—in which your pain
That way, I'll this,—he that first lights on him
Holla the other.   [*Exeunt severally.*

SCENE II

Another part of the heath. Storm still
Enter Lear and Fool.

Lear. Blow, winds, and crack your cheeks! rage! blow!
You cataracts and hurricanoes, spout
Till you have drench'd our steeples, drown'd the cocks!
You sulphurous and thought-executing fires,
Vaunt-couriers to oak-cleaving thunderbolts,
Singe my white head! And thou, all-shaking thunder,
Smite flat the thick rotundity o' the world!
Crack nature's moulds, all germins spill at once
That make ingrateful man!

Fool. O nuncle, court holy-water in a dry house is better than
this rain-water out o' door. Good nuncle, in, and ask thy
daughters' blessing: here's a night pities neither wise man
nor fool.

Lear. Rumble thy bellyful! Spit, fire! spout, rain.
Nor rain, wind, thunder, fire, are my daughters:
I tax not you, you elements, with unkindness;
I never gave you kingdom, call'd you children,
You owe me no subscription: then let fall
Your horrible pleasure; here I stand, your slave,
A poor, infirm, weak and despised old man:

But yet I call you servile ministers,
That have with two pernicious daughters join'd
Your high-engender'd battles 'gainst a head
So old and white as this.   O ! O ! 'tis foul !
Fool.   He that has a house to put's head in has a good head-
     The cod-piece that will house [piece.
      Before the head has any,
     The head and he shall louse
      So beggars marry many.
     The man that makes his toe
      What he his heart should make
     Shall of a corn cry woe,
      And turn his sleep to wake.

For there was never yet fair woman but she made mouths in
Lear.   No, I will be the pattern of all patience ; [a glass.
I will say nothing.

Enter Kent.

Kent.   Who's there ?
Fool.   Marry, here's grace and a cod-piece ; that's a wise man
Kent.   Alas, sir, are you here ? things that love night [and a fool.
Love not such nights as these ; the wrathful skies
Gallow the very wanderers of the dark,
And make them keep their caves : since I was man,
Such sheets of fire, such bursts of horrid thunder,
Such groans of roaring wind and rain, I never
Remember to have heard : man's nature cannot carry
The affliction nor the fear.
Lear.   Let the great gods,
That keep this dreadful pother o'er our heads,
Find out their enemies now.   Tremble, thou wretch,
That hast within thee undivulged crimes,
Unwhipp'd of justice : hide thee, thou bloody hand ;
Thou perjured, and thou simular man of virtue
That art incestuous : caitiff, to pieces shake,
That under covert and convenient seeming
Hast practised on man's life : close pent-up guilts,
Rive your concealing continents and cry
These dreadful summoners grace.   I am a man
More sinn'd against than sinning.
Kent.   Alack, bare-headed !
Gracious my lord, hard by here is a hovel ;
Some friendship will it lend you 'gainst the tempest :
Repose you there ; while I to this hard house—
More harder than the stones whereof 'tis raised ;
Which even but now, demanding after you,

Denied me to come in—return, and force
Their scanted courtesy.

Lear.   My wits begin to turn.
Come on, my boy : how dost, my boy? art cold?
I am cold myself.   Where is this straw, my fellow?
The art of our necessities is strange,
That can make vile things precious.   Come, your hovel.
Poor fool and knave, I have one part in my heart
That 's sorry yet for thee.

Fool. [*Singing*]
  He that has and a little tiny wit,—
  With hey, ho, the wind and the rain,—
  Must make content with his fortunes fit,
  For the rain it raineth every day.

Lear. True, my good boy.   Come, bring us to this hovel.
         [*Exeunt Lear and Kent.*

Fool. This is a brave night to cool a courtezan.
I 'll speak a prophecy ere I go :
  When priests are more in word than matter ;
  When brewers mar their malt with water ;
  When nobles are their tailors' tutors ;
  No heretics burn'd, but wenches' suitors ;
  When every case in law is right ;
  No squire in debt, nor no poor knight ;
  When slanders do not live in tongues,
  Nor cutpurses come not to throngs ;
  When usurers tell their gold i' the field,
  And bawds and whores do churches build
  Then shall the realm of Albion
  Come to great confusion :
  Then comes the time, who lives to see 't,
  That going shall be used with feet.
This prophecy Merlin shall make ; for I live before his time.
         [*Exit.*

Scene III

Gloucester's castle.

Enter Gloucester and Edmund.

Glou. Alack, alack, Edmund, I like not this unnatural dealing.
When I desired their leave that I might pity him, they took
from me the use of mine own house ; charged me, on pain
of their perpetual displeasure, neither to speak of him,
entreat for him, nor any way sustain him.

Edm. Most savage and unnatural !

Glou. Go to ; say you nothing.   There 's a division betwixt

the dukes, and a worse matter than that: I have received a
letter this night; 'tis dangerous to be spoken; I have locked
the letter in my closet: these injuries the king now bears
will be revenged home; there is part of a power already
footed; we must incline to the king. I will seek him
and privily relieve him: go you, and maintain talk with the
duke, that my charity be not of him perceived: if he ask for
me, I am ill and gone to bed. Though I die for it, as no
less is threatened me, the king my old master must be
relieved. There is some strange thing toward, Edmund;
pray you, be careful.   [*Exit.*

Edm. This courtesy, forbid thee, shall the duke
Instantly know, and of that letter too:
This seems a fair deserving, and must draw me
That which my father loses; no less than all:
The younger rises when the old doth fall.

SCENE IV

The heath.   Before a hovel
Enter Lear, Kent, and Fool.

Kent. Here is the place, my lord: good my lord, enter:
The tyranny of the open night's too rough
For nature to endure.   [*Storm still.*

Lear.   Let me alone.

Kent. Good my lord, enter here.

Lear.   Wilt break my heart?

Kent. I had rather break mine own.   Good my lord, enter.

Lear. Thou think'st 'tis much that this contentious storm
Invades us to the skin: so 'tis to thee;
But where the greater malady is fix'd
The lesser is scarce felt.   Thou 'ldst shun a bear,
But if thy flight lay toward the raging sea
Thou 'ldst meet the bear i' the mouth.   When the mind's free
The body's delicate: the tempest in my mind
Doth from my senses take all feeling else
Save what beats there.   Filial ingratitude!
Is it not as this mouth should tear this hand
For lifting food to 't?   But I will punish home.
No, I will weep no more.   In such a night
To shut me out!   Pour on; I will endure.
In such a night as this!   O Regan, Goneril!
Your old kind father, whose frank heart gave you all,—
O that way madness lies; let me shun that;
No more of that.

Kent.   Good my lord, enter here.

Lear. Prithee, go in thyself; seek thine own ease:
  This tempest will not give me leave to ponder
  On things would hurt me more.   But I 'll go in.
  [*To the Fool*] In, boy; go first.   You houseless poverty,—
  Nay, get thee in.   I 'll pray, and then I 'll sleep. [*Fool goes in.*
  Poor naked wretches, wheresoe'er you are,
  That bide the pelting of this pitiless storm,
  How shall your houseless heads and unfed sides,
  Your loop'd and window'd raggedness, defend you
  From seasons such as these?   O, I have ta'en
  Too little care of this!   Take physic, pomp;
  Expose thyself to feel what wretches feel,
  That thou mayst shake the superflux to them
  And show the heavens more just.

Edg. [*Within*] Fathom and half, fathom and half!
  Poor Tom!   [*The Fool runs out from the hovel.*

Fool. Come not in here, nuncle, here 's a spirit.
  Help me, help me!

Kent. Give me thy hand.   Who 's there!

Fool. A spirit, a spirit: he says his name 's poor Tom.

Kent. What art thou that dost grumble there i' the straw
  Come forth.

                   Enter Edgar disguised as a madman.

Edg. Away! the foul fiend follows me!
  'Through the sharp hawthorn blows the cold wind.'
  Hum! go to thy cold bed and warm thee.

Lear. Hast thou given all to thy two daughters?
  And art thou come to this?

Edg. Who gives any thing to poor Tom? whom the foul fiend
  hath led through fire and through flame, through ford and
  whirlpool, o'er bog and quagmire; that hath laid knives under
  his pillow and halters in his pew; set ratsbane by his porridge;
  made him proud of heart, to ride on a bay trotting-horse over
  four-inched bridges, to course his own shadow for a traitor.
  Bless thy five wits!   Tom 's a-cold.   O, do de, do de, do de.
  Bless thee from whirlwinds, starblasting, and taking!   Do
  poor Tom some charity, whom the foul fiend vexes.   There
  could I have him now, and there, and there again, and there.
                                              [*Storm still.*

Lear. What, have his daughters brought him to this pass?
  Couldst thou save nothing?   Didst thou give them all?

Fool. Nay, he reserved a blanket, else we had been all shamed

Lear. Now, all the plagues that in the pendulous air
  Hang fated o'er men's faults light on thy daughters!

Kent. He hath no daughters, sir.

                                43

Lear. Death, traitor! nothing could have subdued nature
To such a lowness but his unkind daughters.
Is it the fashion that discarded fathers
Should have thus little mercy on their flesh?
Judicious punishment! 'twas this flesh begot
Those pelican daughters.

Edg.   Pillicock sat on Pillicock-hill:
Halloo, halloo, loo, loo!

Fool. This cold night will turn us all to fools and madmen.

Edg. Take heed o' the foul fiend: obey thy parents; keep thy
word justly; swear not; commit not with man's sworn spouse;
set not thy sweet heart on proud array. Tom's a-cold.

Lear. What hast thou been?

Edg. A serving-man, proud in heart and mind; that curled my
hair; wore gloves in my cap; served the lust of my mistress'
heart and did the act of darkness with her; swore as many
oaths as I spake words and broke them in the sweet face of
heaven: one that slept in the contriving of lust and waked to do
it: wine loved I deeply, dice dearly, and in woman out-para-
moured the Turk: false of heart, light of ear, bloody of hand;
hog in sloth, fox in stealth, wolf in greediness, dog in madness,
lion in prey. Let not the creaking of shoes nor the rustling
of silks betray thy poor heart to woman: keep thy foot out of
brothels, thy hand out of plackets, thy pen from lenders' books,
and defy the foul fiend.
'Still through the hawthorn blows the cold wind.'
Says suum, mun, ha, no, nonny.
Dolphin my boy, my boy, sessa! let him trot by. [*Storm still.*

Lear. Why, thou wert better in thy grave than to answer with
thy uncovered body this extremity of the skies. Is man no
more than this? Consider him well. Thou owest the worm
no silk, the beast no hide, the sheep no wool, the cat no
perfume. Ha! here's three on's are sophisticated. Thou
art the thing itself: unaccommodated man is no more but such
a poor, bare, forked animal as thou art. Off, off, you lendings!
come, unbutton here. .   [*Tearing off his clothes.*

Fool. Prithee, nuncle, be contented; 'tis a naughty night to swim
in. Now a little fire in a wild field were like an old lecher's
heart, a small spark, all the rest on's body cold. Look, here
comes a walking fire.

Enter Gloucester, with a torch.

Edg. This is the foul fiend Flibbertigibbet: he begins at curfew
and walks till the first cock; he gives the web and the pin,
squints the eye and makes the hare-lip; mildews the white
wheat and hurts the poor creature of earth.

44

Saint Withold footed thrice the 'old;
He met the night-mare and her nine-fold;
Bid her alight,
And her troth plight,
And aroint thee, witch, aroint thee!

Kent. How fares your grace?

Lear. What 's he?

Kent. Who 's there? What is 't you seek?

Glou. What are you there? Your names?

Edg. Poor Tom, that eats the swimming frog, the toad, the tadpole, the wall-newt and the water; that in the fury of his heart, when the foul fiend rages, eats cow-dung for sallets; swallows the old rat and the ditch-dog; drinks the green mantle of the standing pool; who is whipped from tithing to tithing, and stock-punished, and imprisoned; who hath had three suits to his back, six shirts to his body, horse to ride and weapon to wear;

But mice and rats and such small deer
Have been Tom's food for seven long year.

Beware my follower. Peace, Smulkin; peace, thou fiend!

Glou. What, hath your grace no better company?

Edg. The prince of darkness is a gentleman; Modo he 's call'd, and Mahu.

Glou. Our flesh and blood is grown so vile, my lord,
That it doth hate what gets it.

Edg. Poor Tom's a-cold.

Glou. Go in with me: my duty cannot suffer
To obey in all your daughters' hard commands:
Though their injunction be to bar my doors
And let this tyrannous night take hold upon you,
Yet have I ventured to come seek you out
And bring you where both fire and food is ready.

Lear. First let me talk with this philosopher.
What is the cause of thunder?

Kent. Good my lord, take his offer; go into the house.

Lear. I 'll talk a word with this same learned Theban.
What is your study?

Edg. How to prevent the fiend and to kill vermin.

Lear. Let me ask you one word in private.

Kent. Importune him once more to go, my lord;
His wits begin to unsettle.

Glou.   Canst thou blame him? [*Storm still.*
His daughters seek his death; ah, that good Kent!
He said it would be thus, poor banish'd man!
Thou say'st the king grows mad; I 'll tell thee, friend,

I am almost mad myself: I had a son,
Now outlaw'd from my blood ; he sought my life,
But lately, very late : I loved him, friend,
No father his son dearer : truth to tell thee,
The grief hath crazed my wits.   What a night 's this !
I do beseech your grace,—

Lear.   O, cry you mercy, sir.
Noble philosopher, your company.

Edg. Tom 's a-cold.

Glou. In, fellow, there, into the hovel ; keep thee warm.

Lear. Come, let 's in all.

Kent.   This way, my lord.

Lear.   With him ;
I will keep still with my philosopher.

Kent. Good my lord, soothe him ; let him take the fellow.

Glou. Take him you on.

Kent. Sirrah, come on ; go along with us.

Lear. Come, good Athenian.

Glou. No words, no words : hush.

Edg.   Child Rowland to the dark tower came ;
        His word was still ' Fie, foh, and fum,
          I smell the blood of a British man.'   [*Exeunt.*

Scene V

Gloucester's castle.

Enter Cornwall and Edmund.

Corn. I will have my revenge ere I depart his house.

Edm. How, my lord, I may be censured, that nature thus gives
way to loyalty, something fears me to think of.

Corn. I now perceive, it was not altogether your brother's evil
disposition made him seek his death, but a provoking merit,
set a-work by a reproveable badness in himself.

Edm. How malicious is my fortune, that I must repent to be
just ! This is the letter he spoke of, which approves him an
intelligent party to the advantages of France. O heavens !
that this treason were not, or not I the detector !

Corn. Go with me to the duchess.

Edm. If the matter of this paper be certain, you have mighty
business in hand.

Corn. True or false, it hath made thee earl of Gloucester.
Seek out where thy father is, that he may be ready for our
apprehension.

Edm. [Aside] If I find him comforting the king, it will stuff
his suspicion more fully.—I will persever in my course of

loyalty, though the conflict be sore between that and my blood.

Corn. I will lay trust upon thee, and thou shalt find a dearer
father in my love.   [*Exeunt.*

Scene VI

A chamber in a farmhouse adjoining the castle.

Enter Gloucester, Lear, Kent, Fool, and Edgar.

Glou. Here is better than the open air; take it thankfully. I
will piece out the comfort with what addition I can: I will
not be long from you.

Kent. All the power of his wits have given way to his impatience: the gods reward your kindness! [*Exit Gloucester.*

Edg. Frateretto calls me, and tells me Nero is an angler in the
lake of darkness. Pray, innocent, and beware the foul fiend.

Fool. Prithee, nuncle, tell me whether a madman be a gentleman or a yeoman.

Lear. A king, a king!

Fool. No, he 's a yeoman that has a gentleman to his son, for
he 's a mad yeoman that sees his son a gentleman before him.

Lear. To have a thousand with red burning spits
Come hissing in upon 'em,—

Edg. The foul fiend bites my back.

Fool. He 's mad that trusts in the tameness of a wolf, a horse's
health, a boy's love, or a whore's oath.

Lear. It shall be done; I will arraign them straight.
[*To Edgar*] Come, sit thou here, most learned justicer;
[*To the Fool*] Thou, sapient sir, sit here. Now, you she
foxes!

Edg. Look, where he stands and glares! Wantest thou eyes
at trial, madam?
                Come o'er the bourn, Bessy, to me.

Fool.   Her boat hath a leak,
                And she must not speak
          Why she dares not come over to thee.

Edg. The foul fiend haunts poor Tom in the voice of a
nightingale. Hopdance cries in Tom's belly for two white
herring. Croak not, black angel; I have no food for thee.

Kent. How do you, sir? Stand you not so amazed:
Will you lie down and rest upon the cushions?

Lear. I 'll see their trial first. Bring in the evidence.
[*To Edgar*] Thou robed man of justice, take thy place;
[*To the Fool*] And thou, his yoke-fellow of equity,
Bench by his side. [*To Kent*] You are o' the commission;
Sit you too.

Edg. Let us deal justly.

47

Sleepest or wakest thou, jolly shepherd:
 Thy sheep be in the corn;
And for one blast of thy minikin mouth,
 Thy sheep shall take no harm.

Pur! the cat is gray.

Lear. Arraign her first; 'tis Goneril. I here take my oath before this honourable assembly, she kicked the poor king her father.

Fool. Come hither, mistress. Is your name Goneril?

Lear. She cannot deny it.

Fool. Cry you mercy, I took you for a joint-stool.

Lear. And here's another, whose warp'd looks proclaim
What store her heart is made on. Stop her there!
Arms, arms, sword, fire! Corruption in the place!
False justicer, why hast thou let her 'scape?

Edg. Bless thy five wits!

Kent. O pity! Sir, where is the patience now,
That you so oft have boasted to retain!

Edg. [*Aside*] My tears begin to take his part so much,
They'll mar my counterfeiting.

Lear. The little dogs and all,
Tray, Blanch, and Sweet-heart, see, they bark at me.

Edg. Tom will throw his head at them. Avaunt, you curs!
   Be thy mouth or black or white,
   Tooth that poisons if it bite;
   Mastiff, greyhound, mongrel grim,
   Hound or spaniel, brach or lym,
   Or bobtail tike or trundle-tail,
   Tom will make them weep and wail:
   For, with throwing thus my head,
   Dogs leap the hatch, and all are fled.

Do de, de, de. Sessa! Come, march to wakes and fairs and market-towns. Poor Tom, thy horn is dry.

Lear. Then let them anatomize Regan; see what breeds about her heart. Is there any cause in nature that makes these hard hearts? [*To Edgar*] You sir, I entertain for one of my hundred; only I do not like the fashion of your garments. You will say they are Persian attire; but let them be changed.

Kent. Now, good my lord, lie here and rest awhile.

Lear. Make no noise, make no noise; draw the curtains: so, so, so. We'll go to supper i' the morning. So, so, so.

Fool. And I'll go to bed at noon.

Re-enter Gloucester.

Glou. Come hither, friend: where is the king my master?

Kent. Here, sir; but trouble him not: his wits are gone.

48

Glou. Good friend, I prithee, take him in thy arms;
  I have o'erheard a plot of death upon him :
  There is a litter ready; lay him in 't,
  And drive toward Dover, friend, where thou shalt meet
  Both welcome and protection. Take up thy master :
  If thou shouldst dally half an hour, his life,
  With thine and all that offer to defend him,
  Stand in assured loss. Take up, take up,
  And follow me, that will to some provision
  Give thee quick conduct.
Kent.   Oppressed nature sleeps.
  This rest might yet have balm'd thy broken sinews,
  Which, if convenience will not allow,
  Stand in hard cure. [*To the Fool*] Come, help to bear thy
  Thou must not stay behind.   [master;
Glou.   Come, come away.
                              [*Exeunt all but Edgar.*
Edg. When we our betters see bearing our woes,
  We scarcely think our miseries our foes.
  Who alone suffers suffers most i' the mind,
  Leaving free things and happy shows behind :
  But then the mind much sufferance doth o'erskip,
  When grief hath mates, and bearing fellowship.
  How light and portable my pain seems now,
  When that which makes me bend makes the king bow,
  He childed as I father'd ! Tom, away !
  Mark the high noises, and thyself bewray
  When false opinion, whose wrong thought defiles thee,
  In thy just proof repeals and reconciles thee.
  What will hap more to-night, safe 'scape the king !
  Lurk, lurk.   [*Exit.*

SCENE VII

Gloucester's castle.

Enter Cornwall, Regan, Goneril, Edmund, and Servants.

Corn. Post speedily to my lord your husband; show him this
  letter : the army of France is landed. Seek out the traitor
  Gloucester.   [*Exeunt some of the Servants.*
Reg. Hang him instantly.
Gon. Pluck out his eyes.
Corn. Leave him to my displeasure. Edmund, keep you our
  sister company : the revenges we are bound to take upon
  your traitorous father are not fit for your beholding. Advise
  the duke, where you are going, to a most festinate preparation : we are bound to the like. Our posts shall be swift

and intelligent betwixt us.   Farewell, dear sister: farewell,
my lord of Gloucester.

Enter Oswald.

How now! where's the king?

Osw. My lord of Gloucester hath convey'd him hence:
Some five or six and thirty of his knights,
Hot questrists after him, met him at gate;
Who, with some other of the lord's dependants,
Are gone with him toward Dover; where they boast
To have well-armed friends.

Corn.   Get horses for your mistress.

Gon. Farewell, sweet lord, and sister.

Corn. Edmund, farewell.

                    [*Exeunt Goneril, Edmund, and Oswald.*
                    Go seek the traitor Gloucester.

Pinion him like a thief, bring him before us.

                                   [*Exeunt other Servants.*

Though well we may not pass upon his life
Without the form of justice, yet our power
Shall do a courtesy to our wrath, which men
May blame but not control.   Who's there? the traitor?

        Enter Gloucester, brought in by two or three.

Reg. Ingrateful fox! 'tis he.

Corn. Bind fast his corky arms.

Glou. What mean your graces?   Good my friends, consider
You are my guests: do me no foul play, friends.

Corn. Bind him, I say.   [*Servants bind him.*

Reg.   Hard, hard.   O filthy traitor!

Glou. Unmerciful lady as you are, I'm none.

Corn. To this chair bind him.   Villain, thou shalt find—

                                   [*Regan plucks his beard.*

Glou. By the kind gods, 'tis most ignobly done
To pluck me by the beard.

Reg. So white, and such a traitor!

Glou.   Naughty lady,
These hairs which thou dost ravish from my chin
Will quicken and accuse thee: I am your host:
With robbers' hands my hospitable favours
You should not ruffle thus.   What will you do?

Corn. Come, sir, what letters had you late from France?

Reg. Be simple answerer, for we know the truth.

Corn. And what confederacy have you with the traitors
Late footed in the kingdom?

Reg. To whose hands have you sent the lunatic king?
Speak.

Glou. I have a letter guessingly set down,
   Which came from one that 's of a neutral heart.
   And not from one opposed.
Corn.   Cunning.
Reg.   And false.
Corn. Where hast thou sent the king?
Glou.   To Dover.
Reg. Wherefore to Dover?   Wast thou not charged at peril—
Corn. Wherefore to Dover?   Let him first answer that.
Glou. I am tied to the stake, and I must stand the course.
Reg. Wherefore to Dover, sir?
Glou. Because I would not see thy cruel nails
   Pluck out his poor old eyes, nor thy fierce sister
   In his anointed flesh stick boarish fangs.
   The sea, with such a storm as his bare head
   In hell-black night endured, would have buoy'd up,
   And quench'd the stelled fires :
   Yet, poor old heart, he holp the heavens to rain.
   If wolves had at thy gate howl'd that stern time,
   Thou shouldst have said, 'Good porter, turn the key,'
   All cruels else subscribed : but I shall see
   The winged vengeance overtake such children.
Corn. See 't shalt thou never.   Fellows, hold the chair.
   Upon these eyes of thine I 'll set my foot.
Glou. He that will think to live till he be old,
   Give me some help!   O cruel!   O you gods!
Reg. One side will mock another; the other too.
Corn. If you see vengeance—
First Serv.   Hold your hand, my lord:
   I have served you ever since I was a child;
   But better service have I never done you
   Than now to bid you hold.
Reg.   How now, you dog!
First Serv. If you did wear a beard upon your chin,
   I 'ld shake it on this quarrel.   What do you mean?
Corn. My villain!   [*They draw and fight.*
First Serv. Nay, then, come on, and take the chance of anger.
Reg. Give me thy sword.   A peasant stand up thus!
                           [*Takes a sword and runs at him behind.*
First Serv. O, I am slain!   My lord, you have one eye left
   To see some mischief on him.   O!   [*Dies.*
Corn. Lest it see more, prevent it.   Out, vile jelly!
   Where is thy lustre now?
Glou. All dark and comfortless.   Where 's my son Edmund?
   Edmund, enkindle all the sparks of nature,

    To quit this horrid act.

Reg.   Out, treacherous villain !
    Thou call'st on him that hates thee : it was he
    That made the overture of thy treasons to us :
    Who is too good to pity thee.

Glou. O my follies !   Then Edgar was abused.
    Kind gods, forgive me that, and prosper him !

Reg. Go thrust him out at gates, and let him smell
    His way to Dover.   [*Exit one with Gloucester.*]   How is 't,
    my lord ? how look you ?

Corn. I have received a hurt : follow me, lady.
    Turn out that eyeless villain : throw this slave
    Upon the dunghill.   Regan, I bleed apace :
    Untimely comes this hurt : give me your arm.
                         [*Exit Cornwall, led by Regan.*

Sec. Serv. I 'll never care what wickedness I do,
    If this man come to good.

Third Serv.   If she live long,
    And in the end meet the old course of death,
    Women will all turn monsters.

Sec. Serv. Let 's follow the old earl, and get the Bedlam
    To lead him where he would : his roguish madness
    Allows itself to any thing.

Third Serv. Go thou : I 'll fetch some flax and whites of eggs
    To apply to his bleeding face.   Now, heaven help him !
                         [*Exeunt severally.*

ACT IV—Scene I

The heath.

Enter Edgar.

Edg. Yet better thus, and known to be contemn'd,
    Than still contemn'd and flatter'd.   To be worst,
    The lowest and most dejected thing of fortune,
    Stands still in esperance, lives not in fear :
    The lamentable change is from the best ;
    The worst returns to laughter.   Welcome then,
    Thou unsubstantial air that I embrace !
    The wretch that thou hast blown unto the worst
    Owes nothing to thy blasts.   But who comes here ?

Enter Gloucester, led by an Old Man.

My father, poorly led ?   World, world, O world !
But that thy strange mutations make us hate thee,
Life would not yield to age.

Old Man. O, my good lord, I have been your tenant, and your
    father's tenant, these fourscore years.

Glou. Away, get thee away; good friend, be gone:
    Thy comforts can do me no good at all;
    Thee they may hurt.

Old Man. Alack, sir, you cannot see your way.

Glou. I have no way and therefore want no eyes;
    I stumbled when I saw: full oft 'tis seen,
    Our means secure us, and our mere defects
    Prove our commodities. Ah, dear son Edgar,
    The food of thy abused father's wrath!
    Might I but live to see thee in my touch,
    I 'ld say I had eyes again!

Old Man.   How now! Who's there?

Edg. [*Aside*] O gods! Who is 't can say 'I am at the worst'?
    I am worse than e'er I was.

Old Man.   'Tis poor mad Tom.

Edg. [*Aside*] And worse I may be yet: the worst is not
    So long as we can say 'This is the worst.'

Old Man. Fellow, where goest?

Glou.   Is it a beggar-man?

Old Man. Madman and beggar too.

Glou. He has some reason, else he could not beg.
    I' the last night's storm I such a fellow saw,
    Which made me think a man a worm: my son
    Came then into my mind, and yet my mind
    Was then scarce friends with him: I have heard more since.
    As flies to wanton boys, are we to the gods;
    They kill us for their sport.

Edg. [*Aside*]   How should this be?
    Bad is the trade that must play fool to sorrow,
    Angering itself and others. Bless thee, master!

Glou. Is that the naked fellow?

Old Man.   Ay, my lord.

Glou. Then, prithee, get thee gone: if for my sake
    Thou wilt o'ertake us hence a mile or twain
    I' the way toward Dover, do it for ancient love;
    And bring some covering for this naked soul,
    Who I 'll entreat to leave me.

Old Man.   Alack, sir, he is mad.

Glou. 'Tis the times' plague, when madmen lead the blind.
    Do as I bid thee, or rather do thy pleasure;
    Above the rest, be gone.

Old Man. I 'll bring him the best 'parel that I have,
    Come on 't what will.   [*Exit.*

Glou. Sirrah, naked fellow,—

Edg. Poor Tom 's a-cold. [*Aside*] I cannot daub it further.

Glou. Come hither, fellow.

Edg. [*Aside*] And yet I must.—Bless thy sweet eyes, they bleed.

Glou. Know'st thou the way to Dover?

Edg. Both stile and gate, horse-way and foot-path. Poor Tom
hath been scared out of his good wits. Bless thee, good
man's son, from the foul fiend ! Five fiends have been in
poor Tom at once; of lust, as Obidicut ; Hobbididence,
prince of dumbness ; Mahu, of stealing ; Modo, of murder ;
Flibbertigibbet, of mopping and mowing ; who since possesses
chambermaids and waiting-women. So, bless thee, master !

Glou. Here, take this purse, thou whom the heavens' plagues
Have humble to all strokes : that I am wretched
Makes thee the happier. Heavens, deal so still !
Let the superfluous and lust-dieted man,
That slaves your ordinance, that will not see
Because he doth not feel, feel your power quickly ;
So distribution should undo excess
And each man have enough. Dost thou know Dover?

Edg. Ay, master.

Glou. There is a cliff whose high and bending head
Looks fearfully in the confined deep :
Bring me but to the very brim of it,
And I 'll repair the misery thou dost bear
With something rich about me : from that place
I shall no leading need.

Edg.   Give me thy arm :
Poor Tom shall lead thee.   [*Exeunt.*

Scene II

Before the Duke of Albany's palace.

Enter Goneril and Edmund.

Gon. Welcome, my lord : I marvel our mild husband
Not met us on the way.

Enter Oswald.

                              Now, where 's your master?

sw. Madam, within ; but never man so changed.
I told him of the army that was landed ;
He smiled at it : I told him you were coming ;
His answer was, 'The worse :' of Gloucester's treachery
And of the loyal service of his son
When I inform'd him, then he call'd me sot
And told me I had turn'd the wrong side out :
What most he should dislike seems pleasant to him

What like, offensive.

Gon. [*To Edm.*]   Then shall you go no further.
It is the cowish terror of his spirit,
That dares not undertake : he 'll not feel wrongs,
Which tie him to an answer.   Our wishes on the way
May prove effects.   Back, Edmund, to my brother ;
Hasten his musters and conduct his powers :
I must change arms at home and give the distaff
Into my husband's hands.   This trusty servant
Shall pass between us : ere long you are like to hear,
If you dare venture in your own behalf,
A mistress's command.   Wear this ; spare speech ;
                              [*Giving a favour.*

Decline your head : this kiss, if it durst speak,
Would stretch thy spirits up into the air :
Conceive, and fare thee well.

Edm. Yours in the ranks of death.

Gon.   My most dear Gloucester !
                              [*Exit Edmund.*

O, the difference of man and man !
To thee a woman's services are due :
My fool usurps my body.

Osw.   Madam, here comes my lord.
                                        [*Exit.*

                    Enter Albany.

Gon. I have been worth the whistle.

Alb.   O Goneril !
You are not worth the dust which the rude wind
Blows in your face.   I fear your disposition :
That nature which contemns it origin
Cannot be border'd certain in itself ;
She that herself will sliver and disbranch
From her material sap, perforce must wither
And come to deadly use.

Gon. No more ; the text is foolish.

Alb. Wisdom and goodness to the vile seem vile :
Filths savour but themselves.   What have you done ?
Tigers, not daughters, what have you perform'd ?
A father, and a gracious aged man,
Whose reverence even the head-lugg'd bear would lick,
Most barbarous, most degenerate ! have you madded.
Could my good brother suffer you to do it ?
A man, a prince, by him so benefited !
If that the heavens do not their visible spirits
Send quickly down to tame these vile offences,

It will come,
Humanity must perforce prey on itself,
Like monsters of the deep.

Gon.   Milk-liver'd man!
That bear'st a cheek for blows, a head for wrongs;
Who hast not in thy brows an eye discerning
Thine honour from thy suffering; that not know'st
Fools do those villains pity who are punish'd
Ere they have done their mischief.   Where's thy drum?
France spreads his banners in our noiseless land,
With plumed helm thy state begins to threat,
Whiles thou, a moral fool, sit'st still and criest
'Alack, why does he so?'

Alb.   See thyself, devil!
Proper deformity seems not in the fiend
So horrid as in woman.

Gon.   O vain fool!

Alb. Thou changed and self-cover'd thing, for shame,
Be-monster not thy feature.   Were't my fitness
To let these hands obey my blood,
They are apt enough to dislocate and tear
Thy flesh and bones: howe'er thou art a fiend,
A woman's shape doth shield thee.

Gon. Marry, your manhood! mew!

Enter a Messenger.

Alb. What news?

Mess. O, my good lord, the Duke of Cornwall's dead,
Slain by his servant, going to put out
The other eye of Gloucester.

Alb.   Gloucester's eyes!

Mess. A servant that is bred, thrill'd with remorse,
Opposed against the act, bending his sword
To his great master; who thereat enraged
Flew on him and amongst them fell'd him dead,
But not without that harmful stroke which since
Hath pluck'd him after.

Alb.   This shows you are above,
You justicers, that these our nether crimes
So speedily can venge.   But, O poor Gloucester!
Lost he his other eye?

Mess.   Both, both, my lord.
This letter, madam, craves a speedy answer;
'Tis from your sister.

Gon. [*Aside*]   One way I like this well;
But being widow, and my Gloucester with her,

May all the building in my fancy pluck
Upon my hateful life: another way,
The news is not so tart.—I 'll read, and answer.   [*Exit.*
Alb. Where was his son when they did take his eyes?
Mess. Come with my lady hither.
Alb.   He is not here.
Mess. No, my good lord; I met him back again.
Alb. Knows he the wickedness?
Mess. Ay, my good lord; 'twas he inform'd against him,
And quit the house on purpose, that their punishment
Might have the freer course.
Alb.   Gloucester, I live
To thank thee for the love though show'dst the king,
And to revenge thine eyes.   Come hither, friend:
Tell me what more thou know'st.   [*Exeunt.*

SCENE III

The French camp near Dover.
Enter Kent and a Gentleman.

Kent. Why the King of France is so suddenly gone back know
you the reason?
Gent. Something he left imperfect in the state which since his
coming forth is thought of, which imports to the kingdom so
much fear and danger that his personal return was most
required and necessary.
Kent. Who hath he left behind him general?
Gent. The Marshal of France, Monsieur La Far.   [of grief?
Kent. Did your letters pierce the queen to any demonstration
Gent. Ay, sir; she took them, read them in my presence,
And now and then an ample tear trill'd down
Her delicate cheek: it seem'd she was a queen
Over her passion, who most rebel-like
Sought to be king o'er her.
Kent.   O, then it moved her.
Gent. Not to a rage: patience and sorrow strove
Who should express her goodliest.   You have seen
Sunshine and rain at once: her smiles and tears
Were like a better way: those happy smilets
That play'd on her ripe lip seem'd not to know
What guests were in her eyes; which parted thence
As pearls from diamonds dropp'd.   In brief,
Sorrow would be a rarity most beloved,
If all could so become it.
Kent.   Made she no verbal question?
Gent. Faith, once or twice she heaved the name of 'father'

Pantingly forth, as if it press'd her heart;
Cried 'Sisters! sisters!   Shame of ladies! sisters!
Kent! father! sisters!   What, i' the storm! i' the night?
Let pity not be believed!'   There she shook
The holy water from her heavenly eyes,
And clamour moisten'd: then away she started
To deal with grief alone.

Kent.   It is the stars,
The stars above us, govern our conditions;
Else one self mate and mate could not beget
Such different issues.   You spoke not with her since?

Gent. No.

Kent. Was this before the king return'd?

Gent.   No, since.

Kent. Well, sir, the poor distress'd Lear 's i' the town:
Who sometime in his better tune remembers
What we are come about, and by no means
Will yield to see his daughter.

Gent.   Why, good sir?

Kent. A sovereign shame so elbows him: his own unkindness
That stripp'd her from his benediction, turn'd her
To foreign casualties, gave her dear rights
To his dog-hearted daughters: these things sting
His mind so venomously that burning shame
Detains him from Cordelia.

Gent.   Alack, poor gentleman!

Kent. Of Albany's and Cornwall's powers you heard not?

Gent. 'Tis so; they are afoot.

Kent. Well, sir, I 'll bring you to our Master Lear,
And leave you to attend him: some dear cause
Will in concealment wrap me up awhile;
When I am known aright, you shall not grieve
Lending me this acquaintance.   I pray you, go
Along with me.   [*Exeunt.*

Scene IV
The same.   A tent.

Enter, with drum and colours, Cordelia, Doctor, and Soldiers.

Cor. Alack, 'tis he: why, he was met even now
As mad as the vex'd sea; singing aloud;
Crown'd with rank fumiter and furrow-weeds,
With bur-docks, hemlock, nettles, cuckoo-flowers,
Darnel, and all the idle weeds that grow
In our sustaining corn.   A century send forth;
Search every acre in the high-grown field,

And bring him to our eye. [*Exit an Officer.*] What can
In the restoring his bereaved sense ?   [man's wisdom
He that helps him take all my outward worth.
Doct. There is means, madam :
Our foster-nurse of nature is repose,
The which he lacks : that to provoke in him,
Are many simples operative, whose power
Will close the eye of anguish.
Cor.   All blest secrets,
All you unpublish'd virtues of the earth,
Spring with my tears ! be aidant and remediate
In the good man's distress ! Seek, seek for him :
Lest his ungovern'd rage dissolve the life
That wants the means to lead it.

Enter a Messenger.

Mess.   News, madam ;
The British powers are marching hitherward.
Cor. 'Tis known before ; our preparation stands
In expectation of them. O dear father,
It is thy business that I go about ;
Therefore great France
My mourning and important tears hath pitied.
No blown ambition doth our arms incite,
But love, dear love, and our aged father's right :
Soon may I hear and see him !   [*Exeunt.*

Scene V

Gloucester's castle.

Enter Regan and Oswald.

Reg. But are my brother's powers set forth ?
Osw.   Ay, madam.
Reg. Himself in person there ?
Osw.   Madam, with much ado ;
Your sister is the better soldier.
Reg. Lord Edmund spake not with your lord at home ?
Osw. No, madam.
Reg. What might import my sister's letter to him ?
Osw. I know not, lady.
Reg. Faith, he is posted hence on serious matter.
It was great ignorance, Gloucester's eyes being out,
To let him live : where he arrives he moves
All hearts against us : Edmund, I think, is gone,
In pity of his misery, to dispatch
His nighted life ; moreover, to descry
The strength o' the enemy.

Osw. I must needs after him, madam, with my letter.

Reg. Our troops set forth to-morrow: stay with us;
The ways are dangerous.

Osw.   I may not, madam:
My lady charged my duty in this business.

Reg. Why should she write to Edmund? Might not you
Transport her purposes by word? Belike,
Something—I know not what: I 'll love thee much,
Let me unseal the letter.

Osw.   Madam, I had rather—

Reg. I know your lady does not love her husband;
I am sure of that: and at her late being here
She gave strange œillades and most speaking looks
To noble Edmund. I know you are of her bosom.

Osw. I, madam?

Reg. I speak in understanding: you are; I know 't:
Therefore I do advise, you, take this note:
My lord is dead; Edmund and I have talk'd;
And more convenient is he for my hand
Than for your lady's: you may gather more.
If you do find him, pray you, give him this;
And when your mistress hears thus much from you,
I pray, desire her call her wisdom to her.
So, fare you well.
If you do chance to hear of that blind traitor,
Preferment falls on him that cuts him off.

Osw. Would I could meet him, madam! I should show
What party I do follow.

Reg.   Fare thee well.   [*Exeunt.*

Scene VI

Fields near Dover.

Enter Gloucester, and Edgar dressed like a peasant.

Glou. When shall we come to the top of that same hill?

Edg. You do climb up it now: look, how we labour.

Glou. Methinks the ground is even.

Edg.   Horrible steep.
Hark, do you hear the sea?

Glou.   No, truly.

Edg. Why then your other senses grow imperfect
By your eyes' anguish.

Glou.   So may it be indeed:
Methinks thy voice is alter'd, and thou speak'st
In better phrase and matter than thou didst.

Edg. You 're much deceived: in nothing am I changed

60

But in my garments.
Glou.   Methinks you're better spoken.
Edg. Come on, sir; here's the place: stand still. How fearful
And dizzy 'tis to cast one's eyes so low!
The crows and choughs that wing the midway air
Show scarce so gross as beetles: half way down
Hangs one that gathers samphire, dreadful trade!
Methinks he seems no bigger than his head:
The fishermen that walk upon the beach
Appear like mice; and yond tall anchoring bark
Diminish'd to her cock; her cock, a buoy
Almost too small for sight: the murmuring surge
That on the unnumber'd idle pebbles chafes
Cannot be heard so high. I'll look no more,
Lest my brain turn and the deficient sight
Topple down headlong.
Glou.   Set me where you stand.
Edg. Give me your hand: you are now within a foot
Of the extreme verge: for all beneath the moon
Would I not leap upright.
Glou.   Let go my hand.
Here, friend, 's another purse; in it a jewel
Well worth a poor man's taking: fairies and gods
Prosper it with thee! Go thou further off;
Bid me farewell, and let me hear thee going.
Edg. Now fare you well, good sir.
Glou.   With all my heart.
Edg. Why I do trifle thus with his despair
Is done to cure it.
Glou. [*Kneeling*]   O you mighty gods!
This world I do renounce, and in your sights
Shake patiently my great affliction off:
If I could bear it longer and not fall
To quarrel with your great opposeless wills,
My snuff and loathed part of nature should
Burn itself out. If Edgar live, O bless him!
Now fellow, fare thee well.   [*He falls forward.*
Edg.   Gone, sir: farewell.
And yet I know not how conceit may rob
The treasury of life, when life itself
Yields to the theft: had he been where he thought,
By this had thought been past.   Alive or dead?
Ho, you sir! friend!   Hear you, sir! speak!
Thus might he pass indeed: yet he revives.
What are you, sir?

Glou.   Away, and let me die.

Edg. Hadst thou been aught but gossamer, feathers, air,
So many fathom down precipitating,
Thou 'dst shiver'd like an egg : but thou dost breathe ;
Hast heavy substance ; bleed'st not ; speak'st ; art sound.
Ten masts at each make not the altitude
Which thou hast perpendicularly fell :
Thy life 's a miracle. Speak yet again.

Glou. But have I fall'n, or no ?

Edg. From the dread summit of this chalky bourn.
Look up a-height ; the shrill-gorged lark so far
Cannot be seen or heard : do but look up.

Glou. Alack, I have no eyes.
Is wretchedness deprived that benefit,
To end itself by death ? 'Twas yet some comfort,
When misery could beguile the tyrant's rage
And frustrate his proud will.

Edg.   Give me your arm :
Up : so. How is 't ? Feel you your legs ? You stand.

Glou. Too well, too well.

Edg.   This is above all strangeness.
Upon the crown o' the cliff, what thing was that
Which parted from you ?

Glou.   A poor unfortunate beggar.

Edg. As I stood here below, methought his eyes
Were two full moons ; he had a thousand noses,
Horns whelk'd and waved like the enridged sea :
It was some fiend ; therefore, thou happy father,
Think that the clearest gods, who make them honours
Of men's impossibilities, have preserved thee.

Glou. I do remember now : henceforth I 'll bear
Affliction till it do cry out itself
' Enough, enough,' and die. That thing you speak of,
I took it for a man ; often 'twould say
' The fiend, the fiend : ' he led me to that place.

Edg. Bear free and patient thoughts. But who comes here ?
        Enter Lear, fantastically dressed with wild flowers.
The safer sense will ne'er accommodate
His master thus.

Lear. No, they cannot touch me for coining ; I am the king

Edg. O thou side-piercing sight !   [himself.

Lear. Nature 's above art in that respect. There 's your press-
money. That fellow handles his bow like a crow-keeper ;
draw me a clothier's yard. Look, look, a mouse ! Peace,
peace ; this piece of toasted cheese will do 't. There 's my

gauntlet; I'll prove it on a giant.   Bring up the brown bills.
O, well flown, bird! i' the clout, i' the clout: hewgh!   Give
the word.

Edg. Sweet marjoram.

Lear. Pass.

Glou. I know that voice.

Lear. Ha! Goneril, with a white beard!   They flattered me
like a dog, and told me I had white hairs in my beard ere the
black ones were there.   To say 'ay' and 'no' to every thing
that I said!   'Ay' and 'no' too was no good divinity.   When
the rain came to wet me once and the wind to make me
chatter; when the thunder would not peace at my bidding;
there I found 'em, there I smelt 'em out.   Go to, they are
not men o' their words: they told me I was every thing; 'tis
a lie, I am not ague-proof.

Glou. The trick of that voice I do well remember:
Is't not the king?

Lear.   Ay, every inch a king:
When I do stare, see how the subject quakes.
I pardon that man's life.   What was thy cause?
Adultery?
Thou shalt not die: die for adultery!   No:
The wren goes to't, and the small gilded fly
Does lecher in my sight.
Let copulation thrive; for Gloucester's bastard son
Was kinder to his father than my daughters
Got 'tween the lawful sheets.
To't, luxury, pell-mell! for I lack soldiers.
Behold yond simpering dame,
Whose face between her forks presages snow,
That minces virtue and does shake the head
To hear of pleasure's name;
The fitchew, nor the soiled horse, goes to't
With a more riotous appetite.
Down from the waist they are Centaurs,
Though women all above:
But to the girdle do the gods inherit,
Beneath is all the fiends';
There's hell, there's darkness, there's the sulphurous pit,
Burning, scalding, stench, consumption; fie, fie, fie! pah,
    pah!   Give me an ounce of civet, good apothecary, to
    sweeten my imagination: there's money for thee.

Glou. O, let me kiss that hand!

Lear. Let me wipe it first; it smells of mortality.

Glou. O ruin'd piece of nature!   This great world

Shall so wear out to nought.   Dost thou know me?

Lear. I remember thine eyes well enough.   Dost thou squiny
at me?   No, do thy worst, blind Cupid; I'll not love.   Read
thou this challenge; mark but the penning on 't.

Glou. Were all the letters suns, I could not see one.

Edg. I would not take this from report: it is,
And my heart breaks at it.

Lear. Read.

Glou. What, with the case of eyes?

Lear. O, ho, are you there with me?   No eyes in your head,
nor no money in your purse?   Your eyes are in a heavy
case, your purse in a light: yet you see how this world goes.

Glou. I see it feelingly.

Lear. What, art mad?   A man may see how this world goes
with no eyes.   Look with thine ears: see how yond justice
rails upon yond simple thief.   Hark, in thine ear: change
places, and, handy-dandy, which is the justice, which is the
thief?   Thou hast seen a farmer's dog bark at a beggar?

Glou. Ay, sir.

Lear. And the creature run from the cur?   There thou mightst
behold the great image of authority: a dog's obeyed in office.
Thou rascal beadle, hold thy bloody hand!
Why dost thou lash that whore?   Strip thine own back;
Thou hotly lust'st to use her in that kind
For which thou whip'st her.   The usurer hangs the cozener.
Through tatter'd clothes small vices do appear;
Robes and furr'd gowns hide all.   Plate sin with gold,
And the strong lance of justice hurtless breaks;
Arm it in rags, a pigmy's straw does pierce it.
None does offend, none, I say, none; I'll able 'em:
Take that of me, my friend, who have the power
To seal the accuser's lips.   Get thee glass eyes,
And, like a scurvy politician, seem
To see the things thou dost not.
Now, now, now, now: pull off my boots: harder, harder: so.

Edg. O, matter and impertinency mix'd!
Reason in madness!

Lear. If thou wilt weep my fortunes, take my eyes.
I know thee well enough; thy name is Gloucester:
Thou must be patient; we came crying hither:
Thou know'st, the first time that we smell the air,
We wawl and cry.   I will preach to thee: mark.

Glou. Alack, alack the day!

Lear. When we are born, we cry that we are come
To this great stage of fools.   This's a good block.

It were a delicate stratagem, to shoe
A troop of horse with felt : I 'll put 't in proof ;
And when I have stol'n upon these sons-in-law,
Then, kill, kill, kill, kill, kill, kill !

Enter a Gentleman, with Attendants.

Gent. O, here he is : lay hand upon him. Sir,
Your most dear daughter—

Lear. No rescue? What, a prisoner? I am even
The natural fool of fortune. Use me well ;
You shall have ransom. Let me have a surgeon ;
I am cut to the brains.

Gent.   You shall have any thing.

Lear. No seconds? all myself?
Why, this would make a man a man of salt,
To use his eyes for garden water-pots,
Aye, and laying autumn's dust.

Gent. Good sir,—

Lear. I will die bravely, like a smug bridegroom. What
I will be jovial : come, come ; I am a king,
My masters, know you that.

Gent. You are a royal one, and we obey you.

Lear. Then there 's life in 't. Nay, an you get it, you shall get
it by running. Sa, sa, sa, sa.
                    [*Exit running ; Attendants follow.*

Gent. A sight most pitiful in the meanest wretch,
Past speaking of in a king ! Thou hast one daughter,
Who redeems nature from the general curse
Which twain have brought her to.

Edg. Hail, gentle sir.

Gent.   Sir, speed you : what 's your will?

Edg. Do you hear aught, sir, of a battle toward?

Gent. Most sure and vulgar : every one hears that,
Which can distinguish sound.

Edg.   But, by your favour,
How near 's the other army?

Gent. Near and on speedy foot ; the main descry
Stands on the hourly thought.

Edg.   I thank you, sir : that 's all.

Gent. Though that the queen on special cause is here,
Her army is moved on.

Edg.   I thank you, sir.   [*Exit Gent.*

Glou. You ever-gentle gods, take my breath from me ;
Let not my worser spirit tempt me again
To die before you please !

Edg.   Well pray you, father.

65

Glou. Now, good sir, what are you?

Edg. A most poor man, made tame to fortune's blows;
Who, by the art of known and feeling sorrows,
Am pregnant to good pity. Give me your hand,
I'll lead you to some biding.

Glou.   Hearty thanks;
The bounty and the benison of heaven
To boot, and boot!

                    Enter Oswald.

Osw.   A proclaim'd prize! Most happy!
That eyeless head of thine was first framed flesh,
To raise my fortunes. Thou old unhappy traitor,
Briefly thyself remember: the sword is out
That must destroy thee.

Glou.   Now let thy friendly hand
Put strength enough to 't.   [*Edgar interposes.*

Osw.   Wherefore, bold peasant,
Darest thou support a publish'd traitor? Hence!
Lest that the infection of his fortune take
Like hold on thee. Let go his arm.

Edg. Chill not let go, zir, without vurther 'casion.

Osw. Let go, slave, or thou diest!

Edg. Good gentleman, go your gait, and let poor volk pass.
An chud ha' been zwaggered out of my life, 'twould not ha'
been zo long as 'tis by a vortnight. Nay, come not near th'
old man; keep out, che vor ye, or I 'se try whether your
costard or my ballow be the harder: chill be plain with you.

Osw. Out, dunghill!   [*They fight.*

Edg. Chill pick your teeth, zir: come; no matter vor your foins.
                    [*Oswald falls.*

Osw. Slave thou hast slain me. Villain, take my purse:
If ever thou wilt thrive, bury my body;
And give the letters which thou find'st about me
To Edmund earl of Gloucester; seek him out
Upon the British party. O, untimely death!
Death!   [*Dies.*

Edg. I know thee well: a serviceable villain,
As duteous to the vices of thy mistress
As badness would desire.

Glou.   What, is he dead?

Edg. Sit you down, father; rest you.
Let 's see these pockets: the letters that he speaks of
May be my friends. He 's dead; I am only sorry
He had no other deathsman. Let us see:
Leave, gentle wax; and, manners, blame us not:

To know our enemies' minds, we 'ld rip their hearts;
Their papers, is more lawful.
[*Reads*] ' Let our reciprocal vows be remembered. You have
many opportunities to cut him off : if your will want not, time
and place will be fruitfully offered. There is nothing done,
if he return the conqueror : then am I the prisoner, and his
bed my gaol; from the loathed warmth whereof deliver me,
and supply the place for your labour.
　　　　　　　　　　' Your—wife, so I would say—
　　　　　　　　　　　　　' affectionate servant,
　　　　　　　　　　　　　　　　' Goneril.'

O undistinguish'd space of woman's will !
A plot upon her virtuous husband's life;
And the exchange my brother ! Here, in the sands,
Thee I 'll rake up, the post unsanctified
Of murderous lechers; and in the mature time
With this ungracious paper strike the sight
Of the death-practised duke : for him 'tis well
That of thy death and business I can tell.
Glou. The king is mad : how stiff is my vile sense,
That I stand up, and have ingenious feeling
Of my huge sorrows ! Better I were distract :
So should my thoughts be sever'd from my griefs,
And woes by wrong imaginations lose
The knowledge of themselves.   [*Drum afar off.*
Edg.   Give me your hand :
Far off, methinks, I hear the beaten drum :
Come, father, I 'll bestow you with a friend.   [*Exeunt.*

Scene VII

*A tent in the French camp. Lear on a bed asleep, soft music
playing ; Gentleman, and others attending.*
Enter Cordelia, Kent, and Doctor.

Cor. O thou good Kent, how shall I live and work,
To match thy goodness? My life will be too short,
And every measure fail me.
Kent. To be acknowledged, madam, is o'erpaid.
All my reports go with the modest truth,
Nor more nor clipp'd, but so.
Cor.   Be better suited :
These weeds are memories of those worser hours :
I prithee, put them off.
Kent.   Pardon me, dear madam;
Yet to be known shortens my made intent :
My boon I make it, that you know me not

Till time and I think meet.

Cor. Then be 't so, my good lord. [*To the Doctor*] How does
the King?

Doct. Madam, sleeps still.

Cor. O you kind gods,
Cure this great breach in his abused nature!
The untuned and jarring senses, O, wind up
Of this child-changed father!

Doct.   So please your majesty
That we may wake the king: he hath slept long.

Cor. Be govern'd by your knowledge, and proceed
I' the sway of your own will. Is he array'd?

Gent. Ay, madam; in the heaviness of his sleep
We put fresh garments on him.

Doct. Be by, good madam, when we do awake him;
I doubt not of his temperance.

Cor.   Very well.

Doct. Please you, draw near. Louder the music there!

Cor. O my dear father! Restoration hang
Thy medicine on my lips, and let this kiss
Repair those violent harms that my two sisters
Have in thy reverence made!

Kent.   Kind and dear princess!

Cor. Had you not been their father, these white flakes
Had challenged pity of them. Was this a face
To be opposed against the warring winds?
To stand against the deep dread-bolted thunder?
In the most terrible and nimble stroke
Of quick, cross lightning? to watch—poor perdu!—
With this thin helm? Mine enemy's dog,
Though he had bit me, should have stood that night
Against my fire; and wast thou fain, poor father,
To hovel thee with swine and rogues forlorn,
In short and musty straw? Alack, alack!
'Tis wonder that thy life and wits at once
Had not concluded all. He wakes; speak to him.

Doct. Madam, do you; 'tis fittest.

Cor. How does my royal lord? How fares your majesty?

Lear. You do me wrong to take me out o' the grave:
Thou art a soul in bliss; but I am bound
Upon a wheel of fire, that mine own tears
Do scald like molten lead.

Cor.   Sir, do you know me?

Lear. You are a spirit, I know: when did you die?

Cor. Still, still, far wide!

68

Doct. He's scarce awake : let him alone awhile.
Lear. Where have I been ?   Where am I ?   Fair daylight ?
I am mightily abused.   I should e'en die with pity,
To see another thus.   I know not what to say.
I will not swear these are my hands : let's see ;
I feel this pin prick.   Would I were assured
Of my condition !
Cor.   O, look upon me, sir,
And hold your hands in benediction o'er me.
No, sir, you must not kneel.
Lear.   Pray, do not mock me :
I am a very foolish fond old man,
Fourscore and upward, not an hour more nor less ;
And, to deal plainly,
I fear I am not in my perfect mind.
Methinks I should know you and know this man ;
Yet I am doubtful ; for I am mainly ignorant
What place this is, and all the skill I have
Remembers not these garments, nor I know not
Where I did lodge last night.   Do not laugh at me ;
For, as I am a man, I think this lady
To be my child Cordelia.
Cor.   And so I am, I am.
Lear. Be your tears wet ? yes, faith.   I pray, weep not :
If you have poison for me, I will drink it.
I know you do not love me ; for your sisters
Have, as I do remember, done me wrong :
You have some cause, they have not.
Cor.   No cause, no cause.
Lear. Am I in France ?
Kent.   In your own kingdom, sir.
Lear. Do not abuse me.
Doct. Be comforted, good madam : the great rage,
You see, is kill'd in him : and yet it is danger
To make him even o'er the time he has lost.
Desire him to go in ; trouble him no more
Till further settling.
Cor. Will't please your highness walk ?
Lear.   You must bear with me.
Pray you now, forget and forgive : I am old and foolish.
                    [*Exeunt all but Kent and Gentleman.*
Gent. Holds it true, sir, that the Duke of Cornwall was so slain ?
Kent. Most certain, sir.
Gent. Who is conductor of his people ?
Kent. As 'tis said, the bastard son of Gloucester

Gent. They say Edgar, his banished son, is with the Earl of
   Kent in Germany.
Kent. Report is changeable. 'Tis time to look about; the
   powers of the kingdom approach apace.   [*sir. Exit.*
Gent. The arbitrement is like to be bloody. Fare you well,
Kent. My point and period will be thoroughly wrought,
   Or well or ill, as this day's battle's fought.   [*Exit.*

ACT V—Scene I

The British camp near Dover.

Enter, with drum and colours, Edmund, Regan, Gentlemen, and Soldiers.

Edm. Know of the duke if his last purpose hold,
   Or whether since he is advised by aught
   To change the course : he's full of alteration
   And self-reproving : bring his constant pleasure.
                             [*To a Gentleman, who goes out.*
Reg. Our sister's man is certainly miscarried.
Edm. 'Tis to be doubted, madam.
Reg.   Now, sweet lord,
   You know the goodness I intend upon you :
   Tell me, but truly, but then speak the truth,
   Do you not love my sister?
Edm.   In honour'd love.
Reg. But have you never found my brother's way
   To the forfended place?
Edm.   That thought abuses you.
Reg. I am doubtful that you have been conjunct
   And bosom'd with her, as far as we call hers.
Edm. No, by mine honour, madam.
Reg. I never shall endure her : dear my lord,
   Be not familiar with her.
Edm.   Fear me not.—
   She and the duke her husband !
   Enter, with drum and colours, Albany, Goneril, and Soldiers.
Gon. [*Aside*] I had rather lose the battle than that sister
   Should loosen him and me.
Alb. Our very loving sister, well be-met.
   Sir, this I hear ; the king is come to his daughter,
   With others whom the rigour of our state
   Forced to cry out.   Where I could not be honest,
   I never yet was valiant: for this business,
   It toucheth us, as France invades our land,
   Not bolds the king, with others, whom, I fear,

Most just and heavy causes make oppose.
Edm. Sir, you speak nobly.
Reg.   Why is this reason'd?
Gon. Combine together 'gainst the enemy;
  For these domestic and particular broils
  Are not the question here.
Alb.   Let's then determine
  With the ancient of war on our proceedings.
Edm. I shall attend you presently at your tent.
Reg. Sister, you'll go with us?
Gon. No.
Reg. 'Tis most convenient; pray you, go with us.
Gon. [*Aside*] O, ho, I know the riddle.—I will go.
     As they are going out, enter Edgar disguised.
Edg. If e'er your grace had speech with man so poor,
  Hear me one word.
Alb.   I'll overtake you. Speak.
               [*Exeunt all but Albany and Edgar.*
Edg. Before you fight the battle, ope this letter.
  If you have victory, let the trumpet sound
  For him that brought it: wretched though I seem,
  I can produce a champion that will prove
  What is avouched there. If you miscarry,
  Your business of the world hath so an end,
  And machination ceases. Fortune love you!
Alb. Stay till I have read the letter.
Edg.   I was forbid it.
  When time shall serve, let but the herald cry,
  And I'll appear again.
Alb. Why, fare thee well: I will o'erlook thy paper.
                     [*Exit Edgar.*
         Re-enter Edmund.
Edm. The enemy's in view: draw up your powers.
  Here is the guess of their true strength and forces
  By diligent discovery; but your haste
  Is now urged on you.
Alb.   We will greet the time.   [*Exit.*
Edm. To both these sisters have I sworn my love;
  Each jealous of the other, as the stung
  Are of the adder. Which of them shall I take?
  Both? one? or neither? Neither can be enjoy'd,
  If both remain alive: to take the widow
  Exasperates, makes mad her sister Goneril;
  And hardly shall I carry out my side,
  Her husband being alive. Now then we'll use

His countenance for the battle; which being done,
Let her who would be rid of him devise
His speedy taking off.   As for the mercy
Which he intends to Lear and to Cordelia,
The battle done, and they within our power,
Shall never see his pardon; for my state
Stands on me to defend, not to debate.   [*Exit.*

SCENE II

A field between the two camps.

*Alarum within.   Enter, with drum and colours, Lear, Cordelia,
and Soldiers, over the stage; and exeunt.*

Enter Edgar and Gloucester.

Edg. Here, father, take the shadow of this tree
For your good host; pray that the right may thrive:
If ever I return to you again,
I 'll bring you comfort.
Glou.   Grace go with you, sir !
                                      [*Exit Edgar.*
      Alarum and retreat within.   Re-enter Edgar.
Edg. Away, old man; give me thy hand; away !
King Lear hath lost, he and his daughter ta'en;
Give me thy hand; come on.
Glou. No further, sir; a man may rot even here.
Edg. What, in ill thoughts again?   Men must endure
Their going hence, even as their coming hither:
Ripeness is all: come on.
Glou.   And that 's true too.   [*Exeunt.*

SCENE III

The British camp near Dover.

*Enter, in conquest, with drum and colours, Edmund ; Lear
and Cordelia, as prisoners ; Captain, Soldiers, &c.*

Edm. Some officers take them away : good guard,
Until their greater pleasures first be known
That are to censure them.
Cor.   We are not the first
Who with best meaning have incurr'd the worst.
For thee, oppressed king, am I cast down ;
Myself could else out-frown false fortune's frown.
Shall we not see these daughters and these sisters?
Lear. No, no, no, no !   Come, let 's away to prison :
We two alone will sing like birds i' the cage :

72

When thou dost ask me blessing, I 'll kneel down
And ask of thee forgiveness : so we 'll live,
And pray, and sing, and tell old tales, and laugh
At gilded butterflies, and hear poor rogues
Talk of court news ; and we 'll talk with them too,
Who loses and who wins, who 's in, who 's out;
And take upon 's the mystery of things,
As if we were God's spies : and we 'll wear out,
In a wall'd prison, packs and sects of great ones
That ebb and flow by the moon.

Edm.   Take them away

Lear. Upon such sacrifices, my Cordelia,
The gods themselves throw incense.   Have I caught thee?
He that parts us shall bring a brand from heaven,
And fire us hence like foxes.   Wipe thine eyes ;
The good-years shall devour them, flesh and fell,
Ere they shall make us weep : we 'll see 'em starve first.
Come.   [*Exeunt Lear and Cordelia, guarded.*

Edm. Come hither, captain ; hark.
Take thou this note : go follow them to prison :
One step I have advanced thee ; if thou dost
As this instructs thee, thou dost make thy way
To noble fortunes : know thou this, that men
Are as the time is : to be tender-minded
Does not become a sword : thy great employment
Will not bear question ; either say thou 'lt do 't,
Or thrive by other means.

Capt.   I 'll do 't, my lord.

Edm. About it ; and write happy when thou hast done.
Mark ; I say, instantly, and carry it so
As I have set it down.

Capt. I cannot draw a cart, nor eat dried oats ;
If it be a man's work, I 'll do 't.   [*Exit.*

*Flourish.   Enter Albany, Goneril, Regan, another Captain,
and Soldiers.*

Alb. Sir, you have shown to-day your valiant strain,
And fortune led you well : you have the captives
That were the opposites of this day's strife :
We do require them of you, so to use them
As we shall find their merits and our safety
May equally determine.

Edm.   Sir, I thought it fit
To send the old and miserable king
To some retention and appointed guard ;
Whose age has charms in it, whose title more,

73

To pluck the common bosom on his side,
And turn our impress'd lances in our eyes
Which do command them. With him I sent the queen:
My reason all the same; and they are ready
To-morrow or at further space to appear
Where you shall hold your session. At this time
We sweat and bleed: the friend hath lost his friend:
And the best quarrels, in the heat, are cursed
By those that feel their sharpness.
The question of Cordelia and her father
Requires a fitter place.

Alb.   Sir, by your patience,
I hold you but a subject of this war,
Not as a brother.

Reg.   That's as we list to grace him.
Methinks our pleasure might have been demanded,
Ere you had spoke so far. He led our powers,
Bore the commission of my place and person;
The which immediacy may well stand up
And call itself your brother.

Gon.   Not so hot:
In his own grace he doth exalt himself
More than in your addition.

Reg.   In my rights,
By me invested, he compeers the best.

Gon. That were the most, if he should husband you.

Reg. Jesters do oft prove prophets.

Gon.   Holla, holla!
That eye that told you so look'd but a-squint.

Reg. Lady, I am not well; else I should answer
From a full-flowing stomach. General,
Take thou my soldiers, prisoners, patrimony;
Dispose of them, of me; the walls are thine:
Witness the world, that I create thee here
My lord and master.

Gon.   Mean you to enjoy him?

Alb. The let-alone lies not in your good will.

Edm. Nor in thine, lord.

Alb.   Half-blooded fellow, yes.

Reg. [*To Edmund*] Let the drum strike, and prove my title

Alb. Stay yet; hear reason. Edmund, I arrest thee   [thine.
On capital treason; and in thine attaint
This gilded serpent [*pointing to Gon.*]. For your claim, fair
I bar it in the interest of my wife;   [sister,
'Tis she is sub-contracted to this lord.

And I, her husband, contradict your bans.
If you will marry, make your loves to me;
My lady is bespoke.

Gon.   An interlude!

Alb. Thou art arm'd, Gloucester: let the trumpet sound:
If none appear to prove upon thy person
Thy heinous, manifest, and many treasons,
There is my pledge [*throwing down a glove*]: I 'll prove it on
Ere I taste bread, thou art in nothing less   [thy heart,
Than I have here proclaim'd thee.

Reg.   Sick, O, sick!

Gon. [*Aside*] If not, I 'll ne'er trust medicine.

Edm. [*Throwing down a glove*] There 's my exchange: what in
   the world he is
That names me traitor, villain-like he lies:
Call by thy trumpet: he that dares approach,
On him, on you,—who not?—I will maintain
My truth and honour firmly.

Alb. A herald, ho!

Edm.   A herald, ho, a herald!

Alb. Trust to thy single virtue; for thy soldiers,
All levied in my name, have in my name
Took their discharge.

Reg.   My sickness grows upon me.

Alb. She is not well; convey her to my tent. [*Exit Regan, led.*
                              Enter a Herald.
Come hither, herald,—Let the trumpet sound,—
And read out this.

Capt. Sound, trumpet!   [*A trumpet sounds.*

Her. [*Reads*] 'If any man of quality or degree within the lists
   of the army will maintain upon Edmund, supposed Earl of
   Gloucester, that he is a manifold traitor, let him appear by
   the third sound of the trumpet: he is bold in his defence.'

Edm. Sound!   [*First trumpet.*

Her. Again!   [*Second trumpet.*

Her. Again!   [*Third trumpet.*
                              [*Trumpet answers within.*

*Enter Edgar, at the third sound, armed, with a trumpet
                    before him.*

Alb. Ask him his purposes, why he appears
Upon this call o' the trumpet.

Her.   What are you?
Your name, your quality? and why you answer
This present summons?

Edg.   Know, my name is lost;
  By treason's tooth bare-gnawn and canker-bit:
  Yet am I noble as the adversary
  I come to cope.
Alb.   Which is that adversary?
Edg. What's he that speaks for Edmund, Earl of Gloucester?
Edm. Himself: what say'st thou to him?
Edg.   Draw thy sword,
  That if my speech offend a noble heart,
  Thy arm may do thee justice: here is mine.
  Behold, it is the privilege of mine honours,
  My oath, and my profession: I protest,
  Maugre thy strength, youth, place and eminence,
  Despite thy victor sword and fire-new fortune,
  Thy valour and thy heart, thou art a traitor,
  False to thy gods, thy brother and thy father,
  Conspirant 'gainst this high illustrious prince,
  And from the extremest upward of thy head
  To the descent and dust below thy foot,
  A most toad-spotted traitor. Say thou 'No,'
  This sword, this arm and my best spirits are bent
  To prove upon thy heart, whereto I speak,
  Thou liest.
Edm. In wisdom I should ask thy name,
  But since thy outside looks so fair and warlike
  And that thy tongue some say of breeding breathes,
  What safe and nicely I might well delay
  By rule of knighthood, I disdain and spurn:
  Back do I toss these treasons to thy head;
  With the hell-hated lie o'erwhelm thy heart;
  Which for they yet glance by and scarcely bruise,
  This sword of mine shall give them instant way,
  Where they shall rest for ever. Trumpets, speak!
                    [*Alarums. They fight. Edmund falls.*
Alb. Save him, save him!
Gon.   This is practice, Gloucester:
  By the law of arms thou wast not bound to answer
  An unknown opposite; thou art not vanquish'd,
  But cozen'd and beguiled.
Alb.   Shut your mouth, dame,
  Or with this paper shall I stop it. Hold, sir;
  Thou worse than any name, read thine own evil.
  No tearing, lady; I perceive you know it.
Gon. Say, if I do, the laws are mine, not thine:
  Who can arraign me for 't?

Alb.   Most monstrous !
  Know'st thou this paper?
Gon.   Ask me not what I know.   [*Exit.*
Alb. Go after her : she 's desperate ; govern her.
Edm. What you have charged me with, that have I done ;
  And more, much more ; the time will bring it out :
  'Tis past, and so am I.   But what art thou
  That hast this fortune on me ?   If thou 'rt noble,
  I do forgive thee.
Edg.   Let 's exchange charity.
  I am no less in blood than thou art, Edmund ;
  If more, the more thou hast wrong'd me.
  My name is Edgar, and thy father's son.
  The gods are just, and of our pleasant vices
  Make instruments to plague us :
  The dark and vicious place where thee he got
  Cost him his eyes.
Edm.   Thou hast spoken right, 'tis true ;
  The wheel is come full circle ; I am here.
Alb. Methought thy very gait did prophesy
  A royal nobleness : I must embrace thee :
  Let sorrow split my heart, if ever I
  Did hate thee or thy father !
Edg.   Worthy prince, I know 't.
Alb. Where have you hid yourself ?
  How have you known the miseries of your father ?
Edg. By nursing them, my lord.   List a brief tale ;
  And when 'tis told, O, that my heart would burst !
  The bloody proclamation to escape
  That follow'd me so near,—O, our lives' sweetness :
  That we the pain of death would hourly die
  Rather than die at once !—taught me to shift
  Into a madman's rags, to assume a semblance
  That very dogs disdain'd : and in this habit
  Met I my father with his bleeding rings,
  Their precious stones new lost ; became his guide,
  Led him, begg'd for him, saved him from despair ;
  Never—O fault !—reveal'd myself unto him,
  Until some half-hour past, when I was arm'd ;
  Not sure, though hoping, of this good success,
  I ask'd his blessing, and from first to last
  Told him my pilgrimage : but his flaw'd heart,—
  Alack, too weak the conflict to support !—
  'Twixt two extremes of passion, joy and grief,
  Burst smilingly.

Edm.   This speech of yours hath moved me,
  And shall perchance do good : but speak you on;
  You look as you had something more to say.
Alb. If there be more, more woful, hold it in;
  For I am almost ready to dissolve,
  Hearing of this.
Edg.   This would have seem'd a period
  To such as love not sorrow; but another,
  To amplify too much, would make much more,
  And top extremity.
  Whilst I was big in clamour, came there in a man,
  Who, having seen me in my worst estate,
  Shunn'd my abhorr'd society; but then, finding
  Who 'twas that so endured, with his strong arms
  He fasten'd on my neck, and bellow'd out
  As he 'ld burst heaven; threw him on my father;
  Told the most piteous tale of Lear and him
  That ever ear received : which in recounting
  His grief grew puissant, and the strings of life
  Began to crack : twice then the trumpet sounded,
  And there I left him tranced.
Alb.   But who was this?
Edg. Kent, sir, the banish'd Kent; who in disguise
  Follow'd his enemy king, and did him service
  Improper for a slave.
              Enter a Gentleman, with a bloody knife.
Gent. Help, help, O, help !
Edg.   What kind of help?
Alb.   Speak, man.
Edg. What means this bloody knife?
Gent.   'Tis hot, it smokes;
  It came even from the heart of—O, she 's dead!
Alb. Who dead? speak, man.
Gent. Your lady, sir, your lady : and her sister
  By her is poisoned; she hath confess'd it.
Edm. I was contracted to them both : all three
  Now marry in an instant.
Edg.   Here comes Kent.
Alb. Produce the bodies, be they alive or dead.
                              [*Exit Gentleman.*
  This judgement of the heavens, that makes us tremble,
  Touches us not with pity.
                    Enter Kent.
                    O, is this he?
  The time will not allow the compliment
                    78

Which very manners urges.
Kent.   I am come
To bid my king and master aye good night:
Is he not here?
Alb.   Great thing of us forgot!
Speak, Edmund, where's the king? and where's Cordelia?
See'st thou this object, Kent?
                [The bodies of Goneril and Regan are brought in.
Kent. Alack, why thus?
Edm.   Yet Edmund was beloved:
The one the other poison'd for my sake,
And after slew herself.
Alb. Even so. Cover their faces.
Edm. I pant for life: some good I mean to do,
Despite of mine own nature. Quickly send,
Be brief in it, to the castle; for my writ
Is on the life of Lear and on Cordelia:
Nay, send in time.
Alb.   Run, run, O, run!
Edg. To who, my lord? Who hath the office? send
Thy token of reprieve.
Edm. Well thought on: take my sword,
Give it the captain.
Alb.   Haste thee, for thy life. *[Exit Edgar.*
Edm. He hath commission from thy wife and me
To hang Cordelia in the prison, and
To lay the blame upon her own despair,
That she fordid herself.
Alb. The gods defend her! Bear him hence awhile.
                [Edmund is borne off.
Re-enter Lear, with Cordelia dead in his arms; Edgar,
Captain, and others following.
Lear. Howl, howl, howl, howl! O, you are men of stones:
Had I your tongues and eyes, I'ld use them so
That heaven's vault should crack. She's gone for ever
I know when one is dead and when one lives;
She's dead as earth. Lend me a looking-glass;
If that her breath will mist or stain the stone,
Why, then she lives.
Kent.   Is this the promised end?
Edg. Or image of that horror?
Alb.   Fall and cease.
Lear. This feather stirs; she lives. If it be so,
It is a chance which does redeem all sorrows
That ever I have felt.

Kent. [*Kneeling*]   O my good master!
Lear. Prithee, away.
Edg.   'Tis noble Kent, your friend.
Lear. A plague upon you, murderers, traitors all!
 I might have saved her; now she 's gone for ever!
 Cordelia, Cordelia! stay a little. Ha!
 What is 't thou say'st? Her voice was ever soft,
 Gentle and low, an excellent thing in woman.
 I kill'd the slave that was a-hanging thee.
Capt. 'Tis true, my lords, he did.
Lear.   Did I not, fellow?
 I have seen the day, with my good biting falchion
 I would have made them skip: I am old now,
 And these same crosses spoil me. Who are you?
 Mine eyes are not o' the best: I 'll tell you straight.
Kent. If fortune brag of two she loved and hated,
 One of them we behold.
Lear. This is a dull sight. Are you not Kent?
Kent.   The same,
 Your servant Kent. Where is your servant Caius?
Lear. He 's a good fellow, I can tell you that;
 He 'll strike, and quickly too: he 's dead and rotten.
Kent. No, my good lord; I am the very man—
Lear. I 'll see that straight.
Kent. That from your first of difference and decay
 Have follow'd your sad steps.
Lear.   You are welcome hither.
Kent. Nor no man else: all 's cheerless, dark and deadly.
 Your eldest daughters have fordone themselves,
 And desperately are dead.
Lear.   Ay, so I think.
Alb. He knows not what he says, and vain is it
 That we present us to him.
Edg.   Very bootless.
     Enter a Captain.
Capt. Edmund is dead, my lord.
Alb.   That 's but a trifle here.
 You lords and noble friends, know our intent.
 What comfort to this great decay may come
 Shall be applied: for us, we will resign,
 During the life of this old majesty,
 To him our absolute power: [*To Edgar and Kent*] you, to
  your rights;
 With boot, and such addition as your honours
 Have more than merited. All friends shall taste

The wages of their virtue, and all foes
The cup of their deservings.   O, see, see !
Lear. And my poor fool is hang'd ! No, no, no life !
Why should a dog, a horse, a rat, have life,
And thou no breath at all ?   Thou 'lt come no more,
Never, never, never, never, never !
Pray you, undo this button : thank you, sir.
Do you see this ?   Look on her, look, her lips,
Look there, look there !   [*Dies.*
Edg.   He faints.   My lord, my lord !
Kent. Break, heart ; I prithee, break !
Edg.   Look up, my lord.
Kent. Vex not his ghost : O, let him pass ! he hates him
That would upon the rack of this tough world
Stretch him out longer.
Edg.   He is gone indeed.
Kent. The wonder is he hath endured so long :
He but usurp'd his life.
Alb. Bear them from hence.   Our present business
Is general woe.   [*To Kent and Edgar*] Friends of my soul,
    you twain
Rule in this realm and the gored state sustain.
Kent. I have a journey, sir, shortly to go ;
My master calls me, I must not say no.
Alb. The weight of this sad time we must obey,
Speak what we feel, not what we ought to say.
The oldest hath borne most : we that are young
Shall never see so much, nor live so long.
                              [*Exeunt, with a dead march.*

THE TRAGEDY OF
OTHELLO, THE MOOR OF VENICE

DRAMATIS PERSONÆ

DUKE OF VENICE.
BRABANTIO, *a senator.*
Other Senators.
GRATIANO, *brother to Brabantio.*
LODOVICO, *kinsman to Brabantio.*
OTHELLO, *a noble Moor in the service of the Venetian state.*
CASSIO, *his lieutenant.*
IAGO, *his ancient.*

RODERIGO, *a Venetian gentleman.*
MONTANO, *Othello's predecessor in the government of Cyprus.*
Clown, *servant to Othello.*

DESDEMONA, *daughter to Brabantio and wife to Othello.*
EMILIA, *wife to Iago.*
BIANCA, *mistress to Cassio.*

Sailor, Messenger, Herald, Officers, Gentlemen, Musicians, and Attendants.
SCENE : *Venice : a seaport in Cyprus.*

ACT I—SCENE I
Venice. A street.
Enter Roderigo and Iago.

Rod. Tush, never tell me ; I take it much unkindly
    That thou, Iago, who hast had my purse
    As if the strings were thine, shouldst know of this.
Iago. 'Sblood, but you will not hear me :
    If ever I did dream of such a matter,
    Abhor me.
Rod. Thou told'st me thou didst hold him in thy hate.
Iago. Despise me, if I do not.   Three great ones of the city,
    In personal suit to make me his lieutenant,
    Off-capp'd to him : and, by the faith of man,
    I know my price, I am worth no worse a place :
    But he, as loving his own pride and purposes,
    Evades them, with a bombast circumstance
    Horribly stuff'd with epithets of war ;
    And, in conclusion,
    Nonsuits my mediators ; for, 'Certes,' says he,
    'I have already chose my officer.'
    And what was he ?
    Forsooth, a great arithmetician,
    One Michael Cassio, a Florentine,
    A fellow almost damn'd in a fair wife ;
    That never set a squadron in the field,
    Nor the division of a battle knows
    More than a spinster ; unless the bookish theoric,
    Wherein the toged consuls can propose
    As masterly as he : mere prattle without practice
    Is all his soldiership.   But he, sir, had the election :
    And I, of whom his eyes had seen the proof

At Rhodes, at Cyprus, and on other grounds
Christian and heathen, must be be-lee'd and calm'd
By debitor and creditor : this counter-caster,
He, in good time, must his lieutenant be,
And I—God bless the mark !—his Moorship's ancient.
Rod. By heaven, I rather would have been his hangman.
Iago. Why, there 's no remedy ; 'tis the curse of service,
Preferment goes by letter and affection,
And not by old gradation, where each second
Stood heir to the first.   Now, sir, be judge yourself
Whether I in any just term am affined
To love the Moor.
Rod.   I would not follow him then.
Iago. O, sir, content you ;
I follow him to serve my turn upon him :
We cannot all be masters, nor all masters
Cannot be truly follow'd.   You shall mark
Many a duteous and knee-crooking knave,
That doting on his own obsequious bondage
Wears out his time, much like his master's ass,
For nought but provender, and when he 's old, cashier'd :
Whip me such honest knaves.   Others there are
Who, trimm'd in forms and visages of duty,
Keep yet their hearts attending on themselves,
And throwing but shows of service on their lords
Do well thrive by them, and when they have lined their coats
Do themselves homage : these fellows have some soul,
And such a one do I profess myself.
For, sir,
It is as sure as you are Roderigo,
Were I the Moor, I would not be Iago :
In following him, I follow but myself ;
Heaven is my judge, not I for love and duty,
But seeming so, for my peculiar end :
For when my outward action doth demonstrate
The native act and figure of my heart
In compliment extern, 'tis not long after
But I will wear my heart upon my sleeve
For daws to peck at : I am not what I am.
Rod. What a full fortune does the thick lips owe,
If he can carry 't thus !
Iago.   Call up her father,
Rouse him : make after him, poison his delight,
Proclaim him in the streets ; incense her kinsmen,
And, though he in a fertile climate dwell,

Plague him with flies : though that his joy be joy,
Yet throw such changes of vexation on 't
As it may lose some colour.

Rod. Here is her father's house ; I 'll call aloud.

Iago. Do ; with like timorous accent and dire yell
As when, by night and negligence, the fire
Is spied in populous cities.

Rod. What, ho, Brabantio ! Signior Brabantio, ho !

Iago. Awake ! what, ho, Brabantio ! thieves ! thieves ! thieves !
Look to your house, your daughter and your bags !
Thieves ! thieves !

Brabantio appears above, at a window.

Bra. What is the reason of this terrible summons ?
What is the matter there ?

Rod. Signior, is all your family within ?

Iago. Are your doors lock'd ?

Bra.   Why, wherefore ask you this ?

Iago. 'Zounds, sir, you 're robb'd ; for shame, put on your gown ;
Your heart is burst, you have lost half your soul ;
Even now, now, very now, an old black ram
Is tupping your white ewe.   Arise, arise ;
Awake the snorting citizens with the bell,
Or else the devil will make a grandsire of you ;
Arise, I say.

Bra.   What, have you lost your wits ?

Rod. Most reverend signior, do you know my voice ?

Bra. Not I : what are you ?

Rod. My name is Roderigo.

Bra.   The worser welcome :
I have charged thee not to haunt about my doors.
In honest plainness thou hast heard me say
My daughter is not for thee ; and now, in madness,
Being full of supper and distempering draughts,
Upon malicious bravery, dost thou come
To start my quiet.

Rod. Sir, sir, sir,—

Bra.   But thou must needs be sure
My spirit and my place have in them power
To make this bitter to thee.

Rod.   Patience, good sir.

Bra. What tell'st thou me of robbing ? this is Venice ;
My house is not a grange.

Rod.   Most grave Brabantio,
In simple and pure soul I come to you.

Iago. 'Zounds, sir, you are one of those that will not serve

84

God, if the devil bid you. Because we come to do you
service and you think we are ruffians, you'll have your
daughter covered with a Barbary horse; you'll have your
nephews neigh to you; you'll have coursers for cousins, and
gennets for germans.

Bra. What profane wretch art thou?

Iago. I am one, sir, that comes to tell you your daughter and
the Moor are now making the beast with two backs.

Bra. Thou art a villain.

Iago.   You are—a senator.

Bra. This thou shalt answer; I know thee, Roderigo.

Rod. Sir, I will answer any thing. But, I beseech you,
If 't be your pleasure and most wise consent,
As partly I find it is, that your fair daughter,
At this odd-even and dull watch o' the night,
Transported with no worse nor better guard
But with a knave of common hire, a gondolier,
To the gross clasps of a lascivious Moor,—
If this be known to you, and your allowance,
We then have done you bold and saucy wrongs;
But if you know not this, my manners tell me
We have your wrong rebuke. Do not believe
That, from the sense of all civility,
I thus would play and trifle with your reverence:
Your daughter, if you have not given her leave,
I say again, hath made a gross revolt,
Tying her duty, beauty, wit and fortunes,
In an extravagant and wheeling stranger
Of here and every where. Straight satisfy yourself:
If she be in her chamber or your house,
Let loose on me the justice of the state
For thus deluding you.

Bra.   Strike on the tinder, ho!
Give me a taper! call up all my people!
This accident is not unlike my dream:
Belief of it oppresses me already.
Light, I say! light!   *[Exit above.*

Iago.   Farewell; for I must leave you:
It seems not meet, nor wholesome to my place,
To be produced—as, if I stay, I shall—
Against the Moor: for I do know, the state,
However this may gall him with some check,
Cannot with safety cast him; for he's embark'd
With such loud reason to the Cyprus wars,
Which even now stand in act, that, for their souls,

Another of his fathom they have none
To lead their business: in which regard,
Though I do hate him as I do hell pains,
Yet for necessity of present life,
I must show out a flag and sign of love,
Which is indeed but sign.   That you shall surely find him,
Lead to the Sagittary the raised search;
And there will I be with him.   So farewell.   [*Exit.*

*Enter, below, Brabantio, in his night-gown, and Servants
with torches.*

Bra. It is too true an evil: gone she is;
And what's to come of my despised time
Is nought but bitterness.   Now, Roderigo,
Where didst thou see her?   O unhappy girl!
With the Moor, say'st thou?   Who would be a father!
How didst thou know 'twas she?   O, she deceives me
Past thought!   What said she to you?   Get more tapers.
Raise all my kindred.   Are they married, think you?

Rod. Truly, I think they are.

Bra. O heaven!   How got she out?   O treason of the blood!
Fathers, from hence trust not your daughters' minds
By what you see them act.   Is there not charms
By which the property of youth and maidhood
May be abused?   Have you not read, Roderigo,
Of some such thing?

Rod.   Yes, sir, I have indeed.

Bra. Call up my brother.   O, would you had had her!
Some one way, some another.   Do you know
Where we may apprehend her and the Moor?

Rod. I think I can discover him, if you please
To get good guard and go along with me.

Bra. Pray you, lead on.   At every house I'll call;
I may command at most.   Get weapons, ho!
And raise some special officers of night.
On, good Roderigo; I'll deserve your pains.   [*Exeunt.*

Scene II

Another street.

Enter Othello, Iago, and Attendants with torches.

Iago. Though in the trade of war I have slain men,
Yet do I hold it very stuff o' the conscience
To do no contrived murder: I lack iniquity
Sometimes to do me service: nine or ten times
I had thought to have yerk'd him here under under the ribs.

Oth. 'Tis better as it is.

Iago.   Nay, but he prated
  And spoke such scurvy and provoking terms
  Against your honour,
  That, with the little godliness I have,
  I did full hard forbear him.   But I pray you, sir,
  Are you fast married?   Be assured of this,
  That the magnifico is much beloved,
  And hath in his effect a voice potential
  As double as the duke's : he will divorce you,
  Or put upon you what restraint and grievance
  The law, with all his might to enforce it on,
  Will give him cable.
Oth.   Let him do his spite :
  My services, which I have done the signiory,
  Shall out-tongue his complaints.   'Tis yet to know—
  Which, when I know that boasting is an honour,
  I shall promulgate—I fetch my life and being
  From men of royal siege, and my demerits
  May speak unbonneted to as proud a fortune
  As this that I have reach'd : for know, Iago,
  But that I love the gentle Desdemona,
  I would not my unhoused free condition
  Put into circumscription and confine
  For the sea's worth.   But, look ! what lights come yond?
Iago. Those are the raised father and his friends :
  You were best go in.
Oth.   Not I; I must be found :
  My parts, my title and my perfect soul,
  Shall manifest me rightly.   Is it they?
Iago. By Janus, I think so.
          Enter Cassio, and certain Officers with torches.
Oth. The servants of the duke, and my lieutenant.
  The goodness of the night upon you, friends !
  What is the news?
Cas.   The duke does greet you, general,
  And he requires your haste-post-haste appearance,
  Even on the instant.
Oth.   What is the matter, think you?
Cas. Something from Cyprus, as I may divine :
  It is a business of some heat : the galleys
  Have sent a dozen sequent messengers
  This very night at one another's heels;
  And many of the consuls, raised and met,
  Are at the duke's already : you have been hotly call'd for;
  When, being not at your lodging to be found,

The senate hath sent about three several quests
To search you out.
Oth.   'Tis well I am found by you.
I will but spend a word here in the house,
And go with you.   [*Exit.*
Cas.   Ancient, what makes he here?
Iago. Faith, he to-night hath boarded a land carack:
If it prove lawful prize, he's made for ever.
Cas. I do not understand.
Iago.   He's married.
Cas.   To who?

                    Re-enter Othello.

Iago. Marry, to—Come, captain, will you go?
Oth.   Have with you.
Cas. Here comes another troop to seek for you.
Iago. It is Brabantio: general, be advised;
He comes to bad intent.

Enter Brabantio, Roderigo, and Officers with torches and weapons.
Oth.   Holla! stand there!
Rod. Signior, it is the Moor.
Bra.   Down with him, thief!
                              [*They draw on both sides.*
Iago. You, Roderigo! come, sir, I am for you.
Oth. Keep up your bright swords, for the dew will rust them.
Good signior, you shall more command with years
Than with your weapons.
Bra. O thou foul thief, where hast thou stow'd my daughter?
Damn'd as thou art, thou hast enchanted her;
For I'll refer me to all things of sense,
If she in chains of magic were not bound,
Whether a maid so tender, fair and happy,
So opposite to marriage that she shunn'd
The wealthy curled darlings of our nation,
Would ever have, to incur a general mock,
Run from her guardage to the sooty bosom
Of such a thing as thou, to fear, not to delight.
Judge me the world, if 'tis not gross in sense
That thou hast practised on her with foul charms,
Abused her delicate youth with drugs or minerals
That weaken motion: I'll have 't disputed on;
'Tis probable, and palpable to thinking.
I therefore apprehend and do attach thee
For an abuser of the world, a practiser
Of arts inhibited and out of warrant.
Lay hold upon him: if he do resist,
88

Subdue him at his peril.

Oth.   Hold your hands,
Both you of my inclining and the rest:
Were it my cue to fight, I should have known it
Without a prompter. Where will you that I go
To answer this your charge?

Bra.   To prison, till fit time
Of law and course of direct session
Call thee to answer.

Oth.   What if I do obey?
How may the duke be therewith satisfied,
Whose messengers are here about my side,
Upon some present business of the state
To bring me to him?

First Off.   'Tis true, most worthy signior;
The duke's in council, and your noble self,
I am sure, is sent for.

Bra.   How! the duke in council!
In this time of the night! Bring him away:
Mine's not an idle cause: the duke himself,
Or any of my brothers of the state,
Cannot but feel this wrong as 'twere their own;
For if such actions may have passage free,
Bond-slaves and pagans shall our statesmen be.   [*Exeunt.*

SCENE III

A council-chamber.

The Duke and Senators sitting at a table; Officers attending.

Duke. There is no composition in these news
That gives them credit.

First Sen.   Indeed they are disproportion'd;
My letters say a hundred and seven galleys.

Duke. And mine, a hundred and forty.

Sec. Sen.   And mine, two hundred:
But though they jump not on a just account,—
As in these cases, where the aim reports,
'Tis oft with difference,—yet do they all confirm
A Turkish fleet, and bearing up to Cyprus.

Duke. Nay, it is possible enough to judgement:
I do not so secure me in the error,
But the main article I do approve
In fearful sense.

Sailor. [*Within*] What, ho! what, ho! what, ho!

First Off. A messenger from the galleys.

Enter Sailor.

Duke.   Now, what's the business?
Sail. The Turkish preparation makes for Rhodes;
　　So was I bid report here to the state
　　By Signior Angelo.
Duke. How say you by this change?
First Sen.   This cannot be,
　　By no assay of reason: 'tis a pageant
　　To keep us in false gaze.   When we consider
　　The importancy of Cyprus to the Turk,
　　And let ourselves again but understand
　　That as it more concerns the Turk than Rhodes,
　　So may he with more facile question bear it,
　　For that it stands not in such warlike brace,
　　But altogether lacks the abilities
　　That Rhodes is dress'd in : if we make thought of this,
　　We must not think the Turk is so unskilful
　　To leave that latest which concerns him first,
　　Neglecting an attempt of ease and gain,
　　To wake and wage a danger profitless.
Duke. Nay, in all confidence, he's not for Rhodes.
First Off. Here is more news.

Enter a Messenger.

Mess. The Ottomites, reverend and gracious,
　　Steering with due course toward the isle of Rhodes
　　Have there injointed them with an after fleet.
First Sen. Ay, so I thought.   How many, as you guess?
Mess. Of thirty sail : and now they do re-stem
　　Their backward course, bearing with frank appearance
　　Their purposes toward Cyprus.   Signior Montano,
　　Your trusty and most valiant servitor,
　　With his free duty recommends you thus,
　　And prays you to believe him.
Duke. 'Tis certain then for Cyprus.
　　Marcus Luccicos, is not he in town?
First Sen. He's now in Florence.
Duke. Write from us to him ; post-post-haste dispatch.
First Sen. Here comes Brabantio and the valiant Moor.

Enter Brabantio, Othello, Iago, Roderigo, and Officers.

Duke. Valiant Othello, we must straight employ you
　　Against the general enemy Ottoman.
　　[*To Brabantio*] I did not see you ; welcome, gentle signior ;
　　We lack'd your counsel and your help to-night.
Bra. So did I yours.   Good your grace, pardon me ;
　　Neither my place nor aught I heard of business

Hath raised me from my bed, nor doth the general care
Take hold on me; for my particular grief
Is of so flood-gate and o'erbearing nature
That it engluts and swallows other sorrows,
And it is still itself.

Duke.   Why, what's the matter?

Bra. My daughter! O, my daughter!

All.   Dead?

Bra.   Ay, to me;
She is abused, stol'n from me and corrupted
By spells and medicines bought of mountebanks;
For nature so preposterously to err,
Being not deficient, blind, or lame of sense,
Sans witchcraft could not.

Duke. Whoe'er he be that in this foul proceeding
Hath thus beguiled your daughter of herself
And you of her, the bloody book of law
You shall yourself read in the bitter letter
After your own sense, yea, though our proper son
Stood in your action.

Bra.   Humbly I thank your grace.
Here is the man, this Moor; whom now, it seems,
Your special mandate for the state-affairs
Hath hither brought.

All.   We are very sorry for 't.

Duke. [*To Othello*] What in your own part can you say to this?

Bra. Nothing, but this is so.

Oth. Most potent, grave, and reverend signiors,
My very noble and approved good masters,
That I have ta'en away this old man's daughter,
It is most true; true, I have married her:
The very head and front of my offending
Hath this extent, no more. Rude am I in my speech,
And little blest with the soft phrase of peace;
For since these arms of mine had seven years' pith,
Till now some nine moons wasted, they have used
Their dearest action in the tented field;
And little of this great world can I speak,
More than pertains to feats of broil and battle;
And therefore little shall I grace my cause
In speaking for myself. Yet, by your gracious patience,
I will a round unvarnish'd tale deliver
Of my whole course of love; what drugs, what charms,
What conjuration and what mighty magic—
For such proceeding I am charged withal—

I won his daughter.

Bra.   A maiden never bold;
Of spirit so still and quiet that her motion
Blush'd at herself; and she—in spite of nature,
Of years, of country, credit, every thing—
To fall in love with what she fear'd to look on!
It is a judgement maim'd and most imperfect,
That will confess perfection so could err
Against all rules of nature; and must be driven
To find out practices of cunning hell,
Why this should be. I therefore vouch again,
That with some mixtures powerful o'er the blood,
Or with some dram conjured to this effect,
He wrought upon her.

Duke.   To vouch this, is no proof,
Without more certain and more overt test
Than these thin habits and poor likelihoods
Of modern seeming do prefer against him.

First Sen. But, Othello, speak:
Did you by indirect and forced courses
Subdue and poison this young maid's affections?
Or came it by request, and such fair question
As soul to soul affordeth?

Oth.   I do beseech you,
Send for the lady to the Sagittary,
And let her speak of me before her father:
If you do find me foul in her report,
The trust, the office I do hold of you,
Not only take away, but let your sentence
Even fall upon my life.

Duke.   Fetch Desdemona hither.

Oth. Ancient, conduct them; you best know the place.
                  [*Exeunt Iago and Attendants.*
And till she come, as truly as to heaven
I do confess the vices of my blood,
So justly to your grave ears I'll present
How I did thrive in this fair lady's love
And she in mine.

Duke. Say it, Othello.

Oth. Her father loved me, oft invited me,
Still questioned me the story of my life
From year to year, the battles, sieges, fortunes
That I have pass'd.
I ran it through, even from my boyish days
To the very moment that he bade me tell it

Wherein I spake of most disastrous chances,
Of moving accidents by flood and field,
Of hair-breadth 'scapes i' the imminent deadly breach,
Of being taken by the insolent foe,
And sold to slavery, of my redemption thence,
And portance in my travels' history:
Wherein of antres vast and deserts idle,
Rough quarries, rocks, and hills whose heads touch heaven,
It was my hint to speak,—such was the process;
And of the Cannibals that each other eat,
The Anthropophagi, and men whose heads
Do grow beneath their shoulders.   This to hear
Would Desdemona seriously incline:
But still the house-affairs would draw her thence;
Which ever as she could with haste dispatch,
She 'ld come again, and with a greedy ear
Devour up my discourse: which I observing,
Took once a pliant hour, and found good means
To draw from her a prayer of earnest heart
That I would all my pilgrimage dilate,
Whereof by parcels she had something heard,
But not intentively: I did consent,
And often did beguile her of her tears
When I did speak of some distressful stroke
That my youth suffer'd.   My story being done,
She gave me for my pains a world of sighs:
She swore, in faith, 'twas strange, 'twas passing strange;
'Twas pitiful, 'twas wondrous pitiful:
She wish'd she had not heard it, yet she wish'd
That heaven had made her such a man: she thank'd me,
And bade me, if I had a friend that loved her,
I should but teach him how to tell my story,
And that would woo her.   Upon this hint I spake:
She loved me for the dangers I had pass'd,
And I loved her that she did pity them.
This only is the witchcraft I have used.
Here comes the lady; let her witness it.

     Enter Desdemona, Iago, and Attendants.

Duke. I think this tale would win my daughter too.
Good Brabantio,
Take up this mangled matter at the best:
Men do their broken weapons rather use
Than their bare hands.

Bra.   I pray you, hear her speak:
If she confess that she was half the wooer,

Destruction on my head, if my bad blame
Light on the man ! Come hither, gentle mistress :
Do you perceive in all this noble company
Where most you owe obedience ?

Des. My noble father,
I do perceive here a divided duty :
To you I am bound for life and education ;
My life and education both do learn me
How to respect you ; you are the lord of duty,
I am hitherto your daughter : but here's my husband,
And so much duty as my mother show'd
To you, preferring you before her father,
So much I challenge that I may profess
Due to the Moor my lord.

Bra. God be with you ! I have done.
Please it your grace, on to the state-affairs :
I had rather to adopt a child than get it.
Come hither, Moor :
I here do give thee that with all my heart,
Which, but thou hast already, with all my heart
I would keep from thee. For your sake, jewel,
I am glad at soul I have no other child ;
For thy escape would teach me tyranny,
To hang clogs on them. I have done, my lord.

Duke. Let me speak like yourself, and lay a sentence
Which, as a grise or step, may help these lovers
Into your favour.
When remedies are past, the griefs are ended
By seeing the worst, which late on hopes depended.
To mourn a mischief that is past and gone
Is the next way to draw new mischief on.
What cannot be preserved when fortune takes,
Patience her injury a mockery makes.
The robb'd that smiles steals something from the thief ;
He robs himself that spends a bootless grief.

Bra. So let the Turk of Cyprus us beguile ;
We lose it not so long as we can smile.
He bears the sentence well, that nothing bears
But the free comfort which from thence he hears ;
But he bears both the sentence and the sorrow,
That, to pay grief, must of poor patience borrow.
These sentences, to sugar or to gall,
Being strong on both sides, are equivocal :
But words are words ; I never yet did hear
That the bruised heart was pierced through the ear.

I humbly beseech you, proceed to the affairs of state.

Duke. The Turk with a most mighty preparation makes for
Cyprus. Othello, the fortitude of the place is best known
to you; and though we have there a substitute of most
allowed sufficiency, yet opinion, a sovereign mistress of
effects, throws a more safer voice on you : you must therefore
be content to slubber the gloss of your new fortunes with
this more stubborn and boisterous expedition.

Oth. The tyrant custom, most grave senators,
Hath made the flinty and steel couch of war
My thrice-driven bed of down : I do agnize
A natural and prompt alacrity
I find in hardness ; and do undertake
These present wars against the Ottomites.
Most humbly therefore bending to your state,
I crave fit disposition for my wife,
Due reference of place and exhibition,
With such accommodation and besort
As levels with her breeding.

Duke.   If you please,
Be 't at her father's.

Bra.   I 'll not have it so.

Oth. Nor I.

Des.   Nor I, I would not there reside,
To put my father in impatient thoughts
By being in his eye. Most gracious duke,
To my unfolding lend your prosperous ear,
And let me find a charter in your voice
To assist my simpleness.

Duke. What would you, Desdemona ?

Des. That I did love the Moor to live with him,
My downright violence and storm of fortunes
May trumpet to the world : my heart 's subdued
Even to the very quality of my lord :
I saw Othello's visage in his mind,
And to his honours and his valiant parts
Did I my soul and fortunes consecrate.
So that, dear lords, if I be left behind,
A moth of peace, and he go to the war,
The rites for which I love him are bereft me,
And I a heavy interim shall support
By his dear absence. Let me go with him.

Oth. Let her have your voices.
Vouch with me, heaven, I therefore beg it not,
To please the palate of my appetite ;

Nor to comply with heat—the young affects
In me defunct—and proper satisfaction;
But to be free and bounteous to her mind:
And heaven defend your good souls, that you think
I will your serious and great business scant
For she is with me.　No, when light-wing'd toys
Of feather'd Cupid seel with wanton dullness
My speculative and officed instruments,
That my disports corrupt and taint my business,
Let housewives make a skillet of my helm,
And all indign and base adversities
Make head against my estimation!

Duke. Be it as you shall privately determine,
Either for her stay or going: the affair cries haste,
And speed must answer't; you must hence to-night.

Des. To-night, my lord?

Duke.　　　　　　　This night.

Oth.　　　　　　　　　With all my heart.

Duke. At nine i' the morning here we'll meet again.
Othello, leave some officer behind,
And he shall our commission bring to you;
With such things else of quality and respect
As doth import you.

Oth.　　　　　　So please your grace, my ancient;
A man he is of honesty and trust:
To his conveyance I assign my wife,
With what else needful your good grace shall think
To be sent after me.

Duke.　　　　　　Let it be so.
Good night to every one. [*To Brab.*] And, noble signior,
If virtue no delighted beauty lack,
Your son-in-law is far more fair than black.

First Sen. Adieu, brave Moor; use Desdemona well.

Bra. Look to her, Moor, if thou hast eyes to see:
She has deceived her father, and may thee.

　　　　　　　　　[*Exeunt Duke, Senators, Officers, &c.*

Oth. My life upon her faith!　Honest Iago,
My Desdemona must I leave to thee:
I prithee, let thy wife attend on her;
And bring them after in the best advantage.
Come, Desdemona; I have but an hour
Of love, of worldly matters and direction,
To spend with thee: we must obey the time.

　　　　　　　　　[*Exeunt Othello and Desdemona.*

Rod. Iago!

Iago. What say'st thou, noble heart?

Rod. What will I do, thinkest thou?

Iago. Why, go to bed and sleep.

Rod. I will incontinently drown myself.

Iago. If thou dost, I shall never love thee.
Why, thou silly gentleman!

Rod. It is silliness to live when to live is torment; and then
have we a prescription to die when death is our physician.

Iago. O villanous! I have looked upon the world for four
times seven years; and since I could distinguish betwixt a
benefit and an injury, I never found man that knew how to
love himself. Ere I would say I would drown myself for the
love of a guinea-hen, I would change my humanity with a
baboon.

Rod. What should I do? I confess it is my shame to be so
fond; but it is not in my virtue to amend it..

Iago. Virtue! a fig! 'tis in ourselves that we are thus or thus.
Our bodies are gardens; to the which our wills are gar-
deners: so that if we will plant nettles or sow lettuce, set
hyssop and weed up thyme, supply it with one gender of
herbs or distract it with many, either to have it sterile with
idleness or manured with industry, why, the power and
corrigible authority of this lies in our wills. If the balance
of our lives had not one scale of reason to poise another of
sensuality, the blood and baseness of our natures would conduct us to most preposterous conclusions: but we have
reason to cool our raging motions, our carnal stings, our
unbitted lusts; whereof I take this, that you call love, to be
a sect or scion.

Rod. It cannot be.

Iago. It is merely a lust of the blood and a permission of the
will. Come, be a man: drown thyself! drown cats and
blind puppies. I have professed me thy friend, and I
confess me knit to thy deserving with cables of perdurable
toughness: I could never better stead thee than now. Put
money in thy purse; follow thou the wars; defeat thy
favour with an usurped beard; I say, put money in thy
purse. It cannot be that Desdemona should long continue
her love to the Moor—put money in thy purse—nor he his
to her: it was a violent commencement, and thou shalt see
an answerable sequestration; put but money in thy purse.
These Moors are changeable in their wills:—fill thy purse
with money. The food that to him now is as luscious as
locusts, shall be to him shortly as bitter as coloquintida.
She must change for youth: when she is sated with his

body, she will find the error of her choice: she must have
change, she must: therefore put money in thy purse. If
thou wilt needs damn thyself, do it a more delicate way
than drowning.   Make all the money thou canst: if sancti-
mony and a frail vow betwixt an erring barbarian and a
supersubtle Venetian be not too hard for my wits and all
the tribe of hell, thou shalt enjoy her; therefore make
money.   A pox of drowning thyself! it is clean out of the
way: seek thou rather to be hanged in compassing thy joy
than to be drowned and go without her.

Rod. Wilt thou be fast to my hopes, if I depend on the issue?

Iago. Thou art sure of me: go, make money: I have told thee
often, and I re-tell thee again and again, I hate the Moor:
my cause is hearted; thine hath no less reason.   Let us be
conjunctive in our revenge against him: if thou canst cuckold him, thou dost thyself a pleasure, me a sport.   There
are many events in the womb of time, which will be delivered.   Traverse; go; provide thy money.   We will have
more of this to-morrow.   Adieu.

Rod. Where shall we meet i' the morning?

Iago. At my lodging.

Rod. I 'll be with thee betimes.

Iago. Go to; farewell.   Do you hear, Roderigo?

Rod. What say you?

Iago. No more of drowning, do you hear?

Rod. I am changed: I 'll go sell all my land.   [*Exit.*

Iago. Thus do I ever make my fool my purse;
For I mine own gain'd knowledge should profane,
If I would time expend with such a snipe
But for my sport and profit.   I hate the Moor;
And it is thought abroad that 'twixt my sheets
He has done my office: I know not if 't be true;
But I for mere suspicion in that kind
Will do as if for surety.   He holds me well:
The better shall my purpose work on him.
Cassio 's a proper man: let me see now;
To get his place, and to plume up my will
In double knavery—How, how?—Let 's see:—
After some time, to abuse Othello's ear
That he is too familiar with his wife.
He hath a person and a smooth dispose
To be suspected; framed to make women false.
The Moor is of a free and open nature,
That thinks men honest that but seem to be so;
And will as tenderly be led by the nose

As asses are.
I have 't. It is engender'd. Hell and night
Must bring this monstrous birth to the world's light. [*Exit.*

ACT II—Scene I

A sea-port in Cyprus. An open place near the quay.
Enter Montano and two Gentlemen.

Mon. What from the cape can you discern at sea?
First Gent. Nothing at all: it is a high-wrought flood;
I cannot, 'twixt the heaven and the main,
Descry a sail.
Mon. Methinks the wind hath spoke aloud at land;
A fuller blast ne'er shook our battlements:
If it hath ruffian'd so upon the sea,
What ribs of oak, when mountains melt on them,
Can hold the mortise? What shall we hear of this?
Sec. Gent. A segregation of the Turkish fleet:
For do but stand upon the foaming shore,
The chidden billow seems to pelt the clouds
The wind-shaked surge, with high and monstrous mane,
Seems to cast water on the burning bear,
And quench the guards of the ever-fixed pole:
I never did like molestation view
On the enchafed flood.
Mon.   If that the Turkish fleet
Be not enshelter'd and embay'd, they are drown'd;
It is impossible to bear it out.
                Enter a third Gentleman.
Third Gent. News, lads! our wars are done.
The desperate tempest hath so bang'd the Turks,
That their designment halts: a noble ship of Venice
Hath seen a grievous wreck and sufferance
On most part of their fleet.
Mon. How! is this true?
Third Gent.   The ship is here put in,
A Veronesa; Michael Cassio,
Lieutenant to the warlike Moor Othello,
Is come on shore: the Moor himself at sea,
And is in full commission here for Cyprus.
Mon. I am glad on 't; 'tis a worthy governor.
Third Gent. But this same Cassio, though he speak of comfort
Touching the Turkish loss, yet he looks sadly
And prays the Moor be safe; for they were parted
With foul and violent tempest.

Mon.   Pray heavens he be;
For I have served him, and the man commands
Like a full soldier.   Let's to the seaside, ho!
As well to see the vessel that's come in
As to throw out our eyes for brave Othello,
Even till we make the main and the aerial blue
An indistinct regard.

Third Gent.   Come, let's do so;
For every minute is expectancy
Of more arrivance.

Enter Cassio.

Cas. Thanks, you the valiant of this warlike isle,
That so approve the Moor!   O, let the heavens
Give him defence against the elements,
For I have lost him on a dangerous sea.

Mon. Is he well shipp'd?

Cas. His bark is stoutly timber'd, and his pilot
Of very expert and approved allowance;
Therefore my hopes, not surfeited to death,
Stand in bold cure.   [*A cry within:* 'A sail, a sail, a sail!'

Enter a fourth Gentleman.

Cas. What noise?

Fourth Gent. The town is empty; on the brow o' the sea
Stand ranks of people, and they cry 'A sail!'

Cas. My hopes do shape him for the governor. [*Guns heard.*

Sec. Gent. They do discharge their shot of courtesy:
Our friends at least.

Cas.   I pray you, sir, go forth,
And give us truth who 'tis that is arrived.

Sec. Gent. I shall.   [*Exit.*

Mon. But, good lieutenant, is your general wived?

Cas. Most fortunately: he hath achieved a maid
That paragons description and wild fame;
One that excels the quirks of blazoning pens,
And in the essential vesture of creation
Does tire the ingener.

Re-enter second Gentleman.

                    How now! who has put in?

Sec. Gent. 'Tis one Iago, ancient to the general.

Cas. He has had most favourable and happy speed:
Tempests themselves, high seas, and howling winds,
The gutter'd rocks, and congregated sands,
Traitors ensteep'd to clog the guiltless keel,
As having sense of beauty, do omit
Their moral natures, letting go safely by

The divine Desdemona.

Mon.   What is she?

Cas. She that I spake of, our great captain's captain,
Left in the conduct of the bold Iago;
Whose footing here anticipates our thoughts
A se'nnight's speed. Great Jove, Othello guard,
And swell his sail with thine own powerful breath,
That he may bless this bay with his tall ship,
Make love's quick pants in Desdemona's arms,
Give renew'd fire to our extinced spirits,
And bring all Cyprus comfort.

Enter Desdemona, Emilia, Iago, Roderigo, and Attendants.

O, behold,

The riches of the ship is come on shore!
Ye men of Cyprus, let her have your knees.
Hail to thee, lady! and the grace of heaven,
Before, behind thee, and on every hand,
Enwheel thee round!

Des.   I thank you, valiant Cassio.
What tidings can you tell me of my lord?

Cas. He is not yet arrived: nor know I aught
But that he 's well and will be shortly here.

Des. O, but I fear—How lost you company?

Cas. The great contention of the sea and skies
Parted our fellowship—But, hark! a sail.

               [*A cry within:* 'A sail, a sail!' *Guns heard.*

Sec. Gent. They give their greeting to the citadel:
This likewise is a friend.

Cas.   See for the news. [*Exit Gentleman.*
Good ancient, you are welcome. [*To Emilia*] Welcome,
Let it not gall your patience, good Iago,   [mistress:
That I extend my manners; 'tis my breeding
That gives me this bold show of courtesy.   [*Kissing her*

Iago. Sir, would she give you so much of her lips
As of her tongue she oft bestows on me,
You 'ld have enough.

Des.   Alas, she has no speech.

Iago. In faith, too much;
I find it still when I have list to sleep:
Marry, before your ladyship, I grant,
She puts her tongue a little in her heart
And chides with thinking.

Emil. You have little cause to say so.

Iago. Come on, come on; you are pictures out of doors, '
Bells in your parlours, wild-cats in your kitchens,

Saints in your injuries, devils being offended,
Players in your housewifery, and housewives in your beds.
Des. O, fie upon thee, slanderer!
Iago. Nay, it is true, or else I am a Turk:
You rise to play, and go to bed to work.
Emil. You shall not write my praise.
Iago.   No, let me not.
Des. What wouldst thou write of me, if thou shouldst praise
Iago. O gentle lady, do not put me to 't;   [me?
For I am nothing if not critical.
Des. Come on, assay—There's one gone to the harbour?
Iago. Ay, madam.
Des. I am not merry; but I do beguile
The thing I am by seeming otherwise.
Come, how wouldst thou praise me?
Iago. I am about it; but indeed my invention
Comes from my pate as birdlime does from frize;
It plucks out brains and all: but my Muse labours,
And thus she is deliver'd.
If she be fair and wise, fairness and wit,
The one's for use, the other useth it.
Des. Well praised! How if she be black and witty?
Iago. If she be black, and thereto have a wit,
She'll find a white that shall her blackness fit.
Des. Worse and worse.
Emil. How if fair and foolish?
Iago. She never yet was foolish that was fair;
For even her folly help'd her to an heir.
Des. These are old fond paradoxes to make fools laugh i' the
alehouse. What miserable praise hast thou for her that's
foul and foolish?
Iago. There's none so foul, and foolish thereunto,
But does foul pranks which fair and wise ones do.
Des. O heavy ignorance! thou praisest the worst best. But
what praise couldst thou bestow on a deserving woman
indeed, one that in the authority of her merit did justly put
on the vouch of very malice itself?
Iago. She that was ever fair and never proud,
Had tongue at will and yet was never loud,
Never lack'd gold and yet went never gay,
Fled from her wish and yet said 'Now I may;'
She that, being anger'd, her revenge being nigh,
Bade her wrong stay and her displeasure fly;
She that in wisdom never was so frail
To change the cod's head for the salmon's tail;

She that could think and ne'er disclose her mind,
See suitors following and not look behind;
She was a wight, if ever such wight were,—

Des. To do what?

Iago. To suckle fools and chronicle small beer.

Des. O most lame and impotent conclusion! Do not learn of
him, Emilia, though he be thy husband. How say you,
Cassio? is he not a most profane and liberal counsellor?

Cas. He speaks home, madam: you may relish him more in
the soldier than in the scholar.

Iago. [*Aside*] He takes her by the palm: ay, well said, whisper:
with as little a web as this will I ensnare as great a fly as
Cassio. Ay, smile upon her, do; I will gyve thee in thine
own courtship. You say true; 'tis so, indeed: if such tricks
as these strip you out of your lieutenantry, it had been better
you had not kissed your three fingers so oft, which now
again you are most apt to play the sir in. Very good; well
kissed! and excellent courtesy! 'tis so, indeed. Yet again
your fingers to your lips? would they were clyster-pipes for
your sake!—[*Trumpet within.*] The Moor! I know his
trumpet.

Cas. 'Tis truly so.

Des. Let's meet him and receive him.

Cas. Lo, where he comes!

Enter Othello and Attendants.

Oth. O my fair warrior!

Des.   My dear Othello!

Oth. It gives me wonder great as my content
To see you here before me. O my soul's joy!
If after every tempest come such calms,
May the winds blow till they have waken'd death!
And let the labouring bark climb hills of seas
Olympus-high, and duck again as low
As hell's from heaven! If it were now to die,
'Twere now to be most happy; for I fear,
My soul hath her content so absolute
That not another comfort like to this
Succeeds in unknown fate.

Des.   The heavens forbid
But that our loves and comforts should increase,
Even as our days do grow!

Oth.   Amen to that, sweet powers!
I cannot speak enough of this content;
It stops me here; it is too much of joy:
And this, and this, the greatest discords be   [*Kissing her.*

That e'er our hearts shall make!

Iago. [*Aside*]   O, you are well tuned now!
But I'll set down the pegs that make this music,
As honest as I am.

Oth.   Come, let us to the castle.
News, friends; our wars are done, the Turks are drown'd.
How does my old acquaintance of this isle?
Honey, you shall be well desired in Cyprus;
I have found great love amongst them.   O my sweet,
I prattle out of fashion, and I dote
In mine own comforts.   I prithee, good Iago,
Go to the bay, and disembark my coffers:
Bring thou the master to the citadel;
He is a good one, and his worthiness
Does challenge much respect.   Come, Desdemona,
Once more well met at Cyprus.

                         [*Exeunt all but Iago and Roderigo.*

Iago. Do thou meet me presently at the harbour.   Come
hither.   If thou be'st valiant—as, they say, base men being
in love have then a nobility in their natures more than is
native to them—list me.   The lieutenant to-night watches on
the court of guard.   First, I must tell thee this: Desdemona
is directly in love with him.

Rod. With him!   why, 'tis not possible.

Iago. Lay thy finger thus, and let thy soul be instructed.   Mark
me with what violence she first loved the Moor, but for
bragging and telling her fantastical lies: and will she love
him still for prating?   let not thy discreet heart think it.   Her
eye must be fed; and what delight shall she have to look on
the devil?   When the blood is made dull with the act of
sport, there should be, again to inflame it and to give satiety
a fresh appetite, loveliness in favour, sympathy in years,
manners and beauties; all which the Moor is defective in:
now, for want of these required conveniences, her delicate
tenderness will find itself abused, begin to heave the gorge,
disrelish and abhor the Moor; very nature will instruct her
in it and compel her to some second choice.   Now, sir, this
granted—as it is a most pregnant and unforced position—
who stands so eminently in the degree of this fortune as
Cassio does?   a knave very voluble; no further conscionable
than in putting on the mere form of civil and humane seeming, for the better compassing of his salt and most hidden loose
affection?   why, none; why, none: a slipper and subtle knave;
a finder out of occasions; that has an eye can stamp and
counterfeit advantages, though true advantage never present

itself: a devilish knave! Besides, the knave is handsome, young, and hath all those requisites in him that folly and green minds look after: a pestilent complete knave; and the woman hath found him already.   [condition.

Rod. I cannot believe that in her; she 's full of most blest

Iago. Blest fig's-end! the wine she drinks is made of grapes: if she had been blest, she would never have loved the Moor: blest pudding! Didst thou not see her paddle with the palm of his hand? didst not mark that?

Rod. Yes, that I did; but that was but courtesy.

Iago. Lechery, by this hand; an index and obscure prologue to the history of lust and foul thoughts. They met so near with their lips that their breaths embraced together. Villanous thoughts, Roderigo! when these mutualities so marshal the way, hard at hand comes the master and main exercise, the incorporate conclusion: pish! But, sir, be you ruled by me: I have brought you from Venice. Watch you to-night; for the command, I 'll lay 't upon you: Cassio knows you not: I 'll not be far from you: do you find some occasion to anger Cassio, either by speaking too loud, or tainting his discipline, or from what other course you please, which the time shall more favourably minister.

Rod. Well.

Iago. Sir, he is rash and very sudden in choler, and haply may strike at you: provoke him, that he may; for even out of that will I cause these of Cyprus to mutiny; whose qualification shall come into no true taste again but by the displanting of Cassio. So shall you have a shorter journey to your desires by the means I shall then have to prefer them, and the impediment most profitably removed, without the which there were no expectation of our prosperity.

Rod. I will do this, if I can bring it to any opportunity.

Iago. I warrant thee. Meet me by and by at the citadel: I must fetch his necessaries ashore. Farewell.

Rod. Adieu.   [*Exit.*

Iago. That Cassio loves her, I do well believe it;
That she loves him, 'tis apt and of great credit:
The Moor, howbeit that I endure him not,
Is of a constant, loving, noble nature;
And I dare think he 'll prove to Desdemona
A most dear husband. Now, I do love her too,
Not out of absolute lust, though peradventure
I stand accountant for as great a sin,
But partly led to diet my revenge,
For that I do suspect the lusty Moor

Hath leap'd into my seat : the thought whereof
Doth like a poisonous mineral gnaw my inwards ;
And nothing can or shall content my soul
Till I am even'd with him, wife for wife ;
Or failing so, yet that I put the Moor
At least into a jealousy so strong
That judgement cannot cure. Which thing to do,
If this poor trash of Venice, whom I trash
For his quick hunting, stand the putting on,
I 'll have our Michael Cassio on the hip,
Abuse him to the Moor in the rank garb ;
For I fear Cassio with my night-cap too ;
Make the Moor thank me, love me and reward me,
For making him egregiously an ass
And practising upon his peace and quiet
Even to madness. 'Tis here, but yet confused :
Knavery's plain face is never seen till used.   [*Exit.*

SCENE II

A street.

Enter a Herald with a proclamation ; People following.

Her. It is Othello's pleasure, our noble and valiant general,
that upon certain tidings now arrived, importing the mere
perdition of the Turkish fleet, every man put himself into
triumph ; some to dance, some to make bonfires, each man
to what sport and revels his addiction leads him : for, besides
these beneficial news, it is the celebration of his nuptial. So
much was his pleasure should be proclaimed. All offices
are open, and there is full liberty of feasting from this present
hour of five till the bell have told eleven. Heaven bless the
isle of Cyprus and our noble general Othello !   [*Exeunt.*

SCENE III

A hall in the castle.

Enter Othello, Desdemona, Cassio, and Attendants.

Oth. Good Michael, look you to the guard to-night :
Let 's teach ourselves that honourable stop,
Not to outsport discretion.

Cas. Iago hath direction what to do ;
But notwithstanding with my personal eye
Will I look to 't.

Oth.   Iago is most honest.
Michael, good night : to-morrow with your earliest
Let me have speech with you. Come, my dear love,
The purchase made, the fruits are to ensue ;

That profit's yet to come 'tween me and you.
Good night.   [*Exeunt Othello, Desdemona, and Attendants.*
                        Enter Iago.

Cas. Welcome, Iago; we must to the watch.

Iago. Not this hour, lieutenant; 'tis not yet ten o' the clock.
Our general cast us thus early for the love of his Desdemona;
who let us not therefore blame: he hath not yet made wanton the night with her, and she is sport for Jove.

Cas. She's a most exquisite lady.

Iago. And, I'll warrant her, full of game.

Cas. Indeed she's a most fresh and delicate creature.

Iago. What an eye she has! methinks it sounds a parley to
provocation.

Cas. An inviting eye; and yet methinks right modest.

Iago. And when she speaks, is it not an alarum to love?

Cas. She is indeed perfection.

Iago. Well, happiness to their sheets! Come, lieutenant, I
have a stoup of wine; and here without are a brace of Cyprus
gallants that would fain have a measure to the health of
black Othello.

Cas. Not to-night, good Iago: I have very poor and unhappy
brains for drinking: I could well wish courtesy would invent
some other custom of entertainment.

Iago. O, they are our friends; but one cup: I'll drink for you.

Cas. I have drunk but one cup to-night, and that was craftily
qualified too, and behold what innovation it makes here: I
am unfortunate in the infirmity, and dare not task my weakness with any more.

Iago. What, man! 'tis a night of revels: the gallants desire it.

Cas. Where are they?

Iago. Here at the door; I pray you, call them in.

Cas. I'll do 't; but it dislikes me.   [*Exit.*

Iago. If I can fasten but one cup upon him,
With that which he hath drunk to-night already,
He'll be as full of quarrel and offence
As my young mistress' dog. Now my sick fool Roderigo,
Whom love hath turn'd almost the wrong side out,
To Desdemona hath to-night caroused
Potations pottle-deep; and he's to watch:
Three lads of Cyprus, noble swelling spirits,
That hold their honours in a wary distance,
The very elements of this warlike isle,
Have I to-night fluster'd with flowing cups,
And they watch too. Now, 'mongst this flock of drunkards,
Am I to put our Cassio in some action

That may offend the isle.   But here they come:
If consequence do but approve my dream,
My boat sails freely, both with wind and stream.

Re-enter Cassio; with him Montano and Gentlemen; Servants
following with wine.

Cas. 'Fore God, they have given me a rouse already.
Mon. Good faith, a little one; not past a pint, as I am a
Iago. Some wine, ho!   [soldier.

[*Sings*]   And let me the canakin clink, clink,
                     And let me the canakin clink:
                          A soldier 's a man;
                          A life 's but a span;
                     Why then let a soldier drink.

Some wine, boys!

Cas. 'Fore God, an excellent song.
Iago. I learned it in England, where indeed they are most
potent in potting: your Dane, your German, and your swag-
bellied Hollander,—Drink, ho!—are nothing to your English.
Cas. Is your Englishman so expert in his drinking?
Iago. Why, he drinks you with facility your Dane dead drunk;
he sweats not to overthrow your Almain; he gives your
Hollander a vomit ere the next pottle can be filled.
Cas. To the health of our general!
Mon. I am for it, lieutenant, and I 'll do you justice.
Iago. O sweet England!

[*Sings*]   King Stephen was a worthy peer,
                     His breeches cost him but a crown;
                He held them sixpence all too dear,
                     With that he call'd the tailor lown.

                He was a wight of high renown,
                     And thou art but of low degree:
                'Tis pride that pulls the country down;
                     Then take thine auld cloak about thee.

Some wine, ho!

Cas. Why, this is a more exquisite song than the other.
Iago. Will you hear 't again?
Cas. No; for I hold him to be unworthy of his place that does
those things.   Well: God's above all; and there be souls
must be saved, and there be souls must not be saved.
Iago. It 's true, good lieutenant.
Cas. For mine own part—no offence to the general, nor any
man of quality—I hope to be saved.
Iago. And so do I too, lieutenant.

Cas. Ay, but, by your leave, not before me; the lieutenant is
to be saved before the ancient.   Let 's have no more of this;
let 's to our affairs.   God forgive us our sins !   Gentlemen,
let 's look to our business.   Do not think, gentlemen, I am
drunk : this is my ancient : this is my right hand, and this is
my left.   I am not drunk now; I can stand well enough,
and speak well enough.

All. Excellent well.

Cas. Why, very well then; you must not think then that I am
drunk.   [*Exit.*

Mon. To the platform, masters; come, let 's set the watch.

Iago. You see this fellow that is gone before;
He is a soldier fit to stand by Cæsar
And give direction : and do but see his vice;
'Tis to his virtue a just equinox,
The one as long as the other : 'tis pity of him.
I fear the trust Othello puts him in
On some odd time of his infirmity
Will shake this island.

Mon.   But is he often thus?

Iago. 'Tis evermore the prologue to his sleep :
He 'll watch the horologe a double set,
If drink rock not his cradle.

Mon.   It were well
The general were put in mind of it.
Perhaps he sees it not, or his good nature
Prizes the virtue that appears in Cassio
And looks not on his evils : is not this true?

Enter Roderigo.

Iago. [*Aside to him*] How now, Roderigo !
I pray you, after the lieutenant; go.   [*Exit Roderigo.*

Mon. And 'tis great pity that the noble Moor
Should hazard such a place as his own second
With one of an ingraft infirmity :
It were an honest action to say
So to the Moor.

Iago.   Not I, for this fair island :
I do love Cassio well, and would do much
To cure him of this evil :—But, hark ! what noise?
                              [*A cry within :* ' Help ! help !'

Re-enter Cassio, driving in Roderigo.

Cas. 'Zounds ! you rogue ! you rascal !

Mon. What 's the matter, lieutenant?

Cas. A knave teach me my duty !   But I 'll beat the knave into

Rod. Beat me !   [a wicker bottle.

Cas. Dost thou prate, rogue?   [*Striking Roderigo*
Mon. Nay, good lieutenant; I pray you, sir, hold your hand.
Cas. Let me go, sir, or I'll knock you o'er the mazzard.
Mon. Come, come, you're drunk.
Cas. Drunk!   [*They fight.*
Iago. [*Aside to Roderigo*] Away, I say; go out and cry a
     mutiny.   [*Exit Roderigo.*
     Nay, good lieutenant! God's will, gentlemen!
     Help, ho!—Lieutenant,—sir,—Montano,—sir;—
     Help, masters!—Here's a goodly watch indeed! [*A bell rings.*
     Who's that that rings the bell?—Diablo, ho!
     The town will rise: God's will, lieutenant, hold;
     You will be shamed for ever.
                  Re-enter Othello and Attendants.
Oth.   What is the matter here?
Mon. 'Zounds, I bleed still; I am hurt to the death.   [*Faints.*
Oth. Hold, for your lives!
Iago. Hold, ho! Lieutenant,—sir,—Montano,—gentlemen,—
     Have you forgot all sense of place and duty?
     Hold! the general speaks to you; hold, hold, for shame!
Oth. Why, how now, ho! from whence ariseth this?
     Are we turn'd Turks, and to ourselves do that
     Which heaven hath forbid the Ottomites?
     For Christian shame, put by this barbarous brawl:
     He that stirs next to carve for his own rage
     Holds his soul light; he dies upon his motion.
     Silence that dreadful bell: it frights the isle
     From her propriety. What is the matter, masters?
     Honest Iago, that look'st dead with grieving,
     Speak, who began this? on thy love, I charge thee.
Iago. I do not know: friends all but now, even now,
     In quarter, and in terms like bride and groom
     Devesting them for bed; and then, but now,
     As if some planet had unwitted men,
     Swords out, and tilting one at other's breast,
     In opposition bloody. I cannot speak
     Any beginning to this peevish odds;
     And would in action glorious I had lost
     Those legs that brought me to a part of it!
Oth. How comes it, Michael, you are thus forgot?
Cas. I pray you, pardon me; I cannot speak.
Oth. Worthy Montano, you were wont be civil;
     The gravity and stillness of your youth
     The world hath noted, and your name is great
     In mouths of wisest censure: what's the matter,

That you unlace your reputation thus,
And spend your rich opinion for the name
Of a night-brawler? give me answer to it.

Mon. Worthy Othello, I am hurt to danger:
Your officer, Iago, can inform you—
While I spare speech, which something now offends me—
Of all that I do know: nor know I aught
By me that's said or done amiss this night;
Unless self-charity be sometimes a vice,
And to defend ourselves it be a sin
When violence assails us.

Oth. Now, by heaven,
My blood begins my safer guides to rule,
And passion, having my best judgement collied,
Assays to lead the way: if I once stir,
Or do but lift this arm, the best of you
Shall sink in my rebuke. Give me to know
How this foul rout began, who set it on,
And he that is approved in this offence,
Though he had twinn'd with me, both at a birth,
Shall lose me. What! in a town of war,
Yet wild, the people's hearts brimful of fear,
To manage private and domestic quarrel,
In night, and on the court and guard of safety!
'Tis monstrous. Iago, who began't?

Mon. If partially affined, or leagued in office,
Thou dost deliver more or less than truth,
Thou art no soldier.

Iago. Touch me not so near:
I had rather have this tongue cut from my mouth
Than it should do offence to Michael Cassio;
Yet, I persuade myself, to speak the truth
Shall nothing wrong him. Thus it is, general.
Montano and myself being in speech,
There comes a fellow crying out for help,
And Cassio following him with determined sword,
To execute upon him. Sir, this gentleman
Steps in to Cassio and entreats his pause:
Myself the crying fellow did pursue,
Lest by his clamour—as it so fell out—
The town might fall in fright: he, swift of foot,
Outran my purpose; and I return'd the rather
For that I heard the clink and fall of swords,
And Cassio high in oath; which till to-night
I ne'er might say before. When I came back—

For this was brief—I found them close together,
At blow and thrust; even as again they were
When you yourself did part them.
More of this matter cannot I report:
But men are men; the best sometimes forget:
Though Cassio did some little wrong to him,
As men in rage strike those that wish them best,
Yet surely Cassio, I believe, received
From him that fled some strange indignity,
Which patience could not pass.

Oth.   I know, Iago,
Thy honesty and love doth mince this matter,
Making it light to Cassio.   Cassio, I love thee;
But never more be officer of mine.

     Re-enter Desdemona, attended.

Look, if my gentle love be not raised up!
I 'll make thee an example.

Des.   What 's the matter?
Oth. All 's well now, sweeting; come away to bed.
Sir, for your hurts, myself will be your surgeon:

       [To Montano, who is led off.

Lead him off.
Iago, look with care about the town,
And silence those whom this vile brawl distracted.
Come, Desdemona: 'tis the soldiers' life
To have their balmy slumbers waked with strife.

     [Exeunt all but Iago and Cassio.

Iago. What, are you hurt, lieutenant?
Cas. Ay, past all surgery.
Iago. Marry, heaven forbid!
Cas. Reputation, reputation, reputation! O, I have lost my
reputation! I have lost the immortal part of myself, and
what remains is bestial. My reputation, Iago, my reputation!
Iago. As I am an honest man, I thought you had received
some bodily wound; there is more sense in that than in
reputation. Reputation is an idle and most false imposition; oft got without merit and lost without deserving: you
have lost no reputation at all, unless you repute yourself
such a loser. What, man! there are ways to recover the
general again: you are but now cast in his mood, a punishment more in policy than in malice; even so as one would
beat his offenceless dog to affright an imperious lion: sue to
him again, and he 's yours.
Cas. I will rather sue to be despised than to deceive so good
a commander with so slight, so drunken, and so indiscreet

an officer. Drunk? and speak parrot? and squabble? swagger? swear? and discourse fustian with one's own shadow? O thou invisible spirit of wine, if thou hast no name to be known by, let us call thee devil!

Iago. What was he that you followed with your sword? What

Cas. I know not.   [had he done to you?

Iago. Is 't possible?

Cas. I remember a mass of things, but nothing distinctly; a quarrel, but nothing wherefore. O God, that men should put an enemy in their mouths to steal away their brains! that we should, with joy, pleasance, revel and applause, transform ourselves into beasts!

Iago. Why, but you are now well enough: how came you thus recovered?

Cas. It hath pleased the devil drunkenness to give place to the devil wrath: one unperfectness shows me another, to make me frankly despise myself.

Iago. Come, you are too severe a moraler: as the time, the place, and the condition of this country stands, I could heartily wish this had not befallen; but since it is as it is, mend it for your own good.

Cas. I will ask him for my place again; he shall tell me I am a drunkard! Had I as many mouths as Hydra, such an answer would stop them all. To be now a sensible man, by and by a fool, and presently a beast! O strange! Every inordinate cup is unblest, and the ingredient is a devil.

Iago. Come, come, good wine is a good familiar creature, if it be well used: exclaim no more against it. And, good lieutenant, I think you think I love you.

Cas. I have well approved it, sir. I drunk!

Iago. You or any man living may be drunk at some time, man. I 'll tell you what you shall do. Our general's wife is now the general. I may say so in this respect, for that he hath devoted and given up himself to the contemplation, mark and denotement of her parts and graces: confess yourself freely to her; importune her help to put you in your place again: she is of so free, so kind, so apt, so blessed a disposition, she holds it a vice in her goodness not to do more than she is requested: this broken joint between you and her husband entreat her to splinter; and, my fortunes against any lay worth naming, this crack of your love shall grow stronger than it was before.

Cas. You advise me well.

Iago. I protest, in the sincerity of love and honest kindness.

Cas. I think it freely; and betimes in the morning I will

beseech the virtuous Desdemona to undertake for me: I am
desperate of my fortunes if they check me here.

Iago. You are in the right.   Good night, lieutenant;
I must to the watch.

Cas. Good night, honest Iago.   [*Exit.*

Iago. And what's he then that says I play the villain?
When this advice is free I give and honest,
Probal to thinking, and indeed the course
To win the Moor again?   For 'tis most easy
The inclining Desdemona to subdue
In any honest suit.   She's framed as fruitful
As the free elements.   And then for her
To win the Moor, were 't to renounce his baptism,
All seals and symbols of redeemed sin,
His soul is so enfetter'd to her love,
That she may make, unmake, do what she list,
Even as her appetite shall play the god
With his weak function.   How am I then a villain
To counsel Cassio to this parallel course,
Directly to his good?   Divinity of hell!
When devils will the blackest sins put on,
They do suggest at first with heavenly shows,
As I do now: for whiles this honest fool
Plies Desdemona to repair his fortunes,
And she for him pleads strongly to the Moor,
I'll pour this pestilence into his ear,
That she repeals him for her body's lust;
And by how much she strives to do him good,
She shall undo her credit with the Moor.
So will I turn her virtue into pitch;
And out of her own goodness make the net
That shall enmesh them all.

Enter Roderigo.

How now, Roderigo!

Rod. I do follow here in the chase, not like a hound that
hunts, but one that fills up the cry.   My money is almost
spent; I have been to-night exceedingly well cudgelled; and
I think the issue will be, I shall have so much experience for
my pains; and so, with no money at all and a little more
wit, return again to Venice.

Iago. How poor are they that have not patience!
What wound did ever heal but by degrees?
Thou know'st we work by wit and not by witchcraft,
And wit depends on dilatory time.
Does 't not go well?   Cassio hath beaten thee,

And thou by that small hurt hast cashier'd Cassio:
Though other things grow fair against the sun,
Yet fruits that blossom first will first be ripe:
Content thyself awhile. By the mass, 'tis morning;
Pleasure and action make the hours seem short.
Retire thee; go where thou art billeted:
Away, I say; thou shalt know more hereafter:
Nay, get thee gone. [*Exit Rod.*] Two things are to be
My wife must move for Cassio to her mistress;   [done:
I 'll set her on;
Myself the while to draw the Moor apart,
And bring him jump when he may Cassio find
Soliciting his wife: ay, that 's the way;
Dull not device by coldness and delay.   [*Exit.*

ACT III—Scene I

Before the castle.

Enter Cassio and some Musicians.

Cas. Masters, play here; I will content your pains;
Something that 's brief; and bid 'Good-morrow, general.'
           [*Music.*

Enter Clown.

Clo. Why, masters, have your instruments been in Naples, that
they speak i' the nose thus?

First Mus. How, sir, how?

Clo. Are these, I pray you, wind-instruments?

First Mus. Ay, marry, are they, sir.

Clo. O, thereby hangs a tail.

First Mus. Whereby hangs a tale, sir?

Clo. Marry, sir, by many a wind-instrument that I know. But,
masters, here 's money for you: and the general so likes your
music, that he desires you, for love's sake, to make no more
noise with it.

First Mus. Well, sir, we will not.

Clo. If you have any music that may not be heard, to 't again:
but, as they say, to hear music the general does not
greatly care.

First Mus. We have none such, sir.

Clo. Then put up your pipes in your bag, for I 'll away: go;
vanish into air; away!   [*Exeunt Musicians.*

Cas. Dost thou hear, my honest friend?

Clo. No, I hear not your honest friend; I hear you.

Cas. Prithee, keep up thy quillets. There 's a poor piece of
gold for thee: if the gentlewoman that attends the general's

wife be stirring, tell her there's one Cassio entreats her a little favour of speech: wilt thou do this?

Clo. She is stirring, sir: if she will stir hither, I shall seem to notify unto her.

Cas. Do, good my friend.   [*Exit Clown.*

Enter Iago.

In happy time, Iago.

Iago. You have not been a-bed, then?

Cas. Why, no; the day had broke
Before we parted.   I have made bold, Iago,
To send in to your wife: my suit to her
Is, that she will to virtuous Desdemona
Procure me some access.

Iago.   I 'll send her to you presently;
And I 'll devise a mean to draw the Moor
Out of the way, that your converse and business
May be more free.

Cas. I humbly thank you for 't.   [*Exit Iago.*] I never knew
A Florentine more kind and honest.

Enter Emilia.

Emil. Good morrow, good lieutenant: I am sorry
For your displeasure; but all will sure be well.
The general and his wife are talking of it,
And she speaks for you stoutly: the Moor replies,
That he you hurt is of great fame in Cyprus
And great affinity, and that in wholesome wisdom
He might not but refuse you; but he protests he loves you,
And needs no other suitor but his likings
To take the safest occasion by the front
To bring you in again.

Cas.   Yet, I beseech you,
If you think fit, or that it may be done,
Give me advantage of some brief discourse
With Desdemona alone.

Emil.   Pray you, come in:
I will bestow you where you shall have time
To speak your bosom freely.

Cas.   I am much bound to you.

                                        [*Exeunt.*

SCENE II

A room in the castle.
Enter Othello, Iago, and Gentlemen.

Oth. These letters give, Iago, to the pilot;
And by him do my duties to the senate:
That done, I will be walking on the works;

Repair there to me.

Iago. Well, my good lord, I 'll do 't.

Oth. This fortification, gentlemen, shall we see 't?

Gent. We'll wait upon your lordship. [*Exeunt.*

SCENE III

The garden of the castle.

Enter Desdemona, Cassio, and Emilia.

Des. Be thou assured, good Cassio, I will do
 All my abilities in thy behalf.

Emil. Good madam, do: I warrant it grieves my husband
 As if the case were his.

Des. O, that 's an honest fellow. Do not doubt, Cassio,
 But I will have my lord and you again
 As friendly as you were.

Cas.   Bounteous madam,
 Whatever shall become of Michael Cassio,
 He 's never any thing but your true servant.

Des. I know 't: I thank you. You do love my lord:
 You have known him long; and be you well assured
 He shall in strangeness stand no farther off
 Than in a politic distance.

Cas.   Ay, but, lady,
 That policy may either last so long,
 Or feed upon such nice and waterish diet,
 Or breed itself so out of circumstance,
 That, I being absent and my place supplied,
 My general will forget my love and service.

Des. Do not doubt that; before Emilia here
 I give thee warrant of thy place: assure thee,
 If I do avow a friendship, I 'll perform it
 To the last article: my lord shall never rest;
 I 'll watch him tame and talk him out of patience;
 His bed shall seem a school, his board a shrift;
 I 'll intermingle every thing he does
 With Cassio's suit: therefore be merry, Cassio;
 For thy solicitor shall rather die
 Than give thy cause away.

Enter Othello and Iago, at a distance.

Emil. Madam, here comes my lord.

Cas. Madam, I 'll take my leave.

Des. Nay, stay and hear me speak.

Cas. Madam, not now: I am very ill at ease,
 Unfit for mine own purposes.

Des. Well, do your discretion. [*Exit Cassio.*

117

Iago. Ha!   I like not that.

Oth. What dost thou say?

Iago. Nothing, my lord: or if—I know not what.

Oth. Was not that Cassio parted from my wife?

Iago. Cassio, my lord! No, sure, I cannot think it,
That he would steal away so guilty-like,
Seeing you coming.

Oth.   I do believe 'twas he.

Des. How now, my lord!
I have been talking with a suitor here.
A man that languishes in your displeasure.

Oth. Who is't you mean?

Des. Why, your lieutenant, Cassio.   Good my lord,
If I have any grace or power to move you,
His present reconciliation take;
For if he be not one that truly loves you,
That errs in ignorance and not in cunning,
I have no judgement in an honest face:
I prithee, call him back.

Oth.   Went he hence now?

Des. Ay, sooth; so humbled,
That he hath left part of his grief with me,
To suffer with him.   Good love, call him back.

Oth. Not now, sweet Desdemona; some other time.

Des. But shall't be shortly?

Oth.   The sooner, sweet, for you.

Des. Shall't be to-night at supper?

Oth.   No, not to-night.

Des. To-morrow dinner then?

Oth.   I shall not dine at home;
I meet the captains at the citadel.

Des. Why then to-morrow night; or Tuesday morn:
On Tuesday noon, or night; on Wednesday morn:
I prithee, name the time; but let it not
Exceed three days: in faith, he's penitent;
And yet his trespass, in our common reason—
Save that, they say, the wars must make examples
Out of their best—is not almost a fault
To incur a private check.   When shall he come?
Tell me, Othello: I wonder in my soul,
What you would ask me, that I should deny,
Or stand so mammering on.   What! Michael Cassio,
That came a-wooing with you, and so many a time
When I have spoke of you dispraisingly
Hath ta'en your part; to have so much to do

To bring him in ! Trust me, I could do much—
Oth. Prithee, no more : let him come when he will ;
  I will deny thee nothing.
Des.   Why, this is not a boon ;
  'Tis as I should entreat you wear your gloves,
  Or feed on nourishing dishes, or keep you warm,
  Or sue to you to do a peculiar profit
  To your own person : nay, when I have a suit
  Wherein I mean to touch your love indeed,
  It shall be full of poise and difficult weight,
  And fearful to be granted.
Oth.   I will deny thee nothing :
  Whereon, I do beseech thee, grant me this,
  To leave me but a little to myself.
Des. Shall I deny you ? no : farewell, my lord.
Oth. Farewell, my Desdemona : I 'll come to thee straight.
Des. Emilia, come. Be as your fancies teach you ;
  Whate'er you be, I am obedient.
                              [*Exeunt Desdemona and Emilia.*
Oth. Excellent wretch ! Perdition catch my soul,
  But I do love thee ! and when I love thee not,
  Chaos is come again.
Iago. My noble lord,—
Oth.   What dost thou say, Iago ?
Iago. Did Michael Cassio, when you woo'd my lady,
  Know of your love ?
Oth. He did, from first to last : why dost thou ask ?
Iago. But for a satisfaction of my thought ;
  No further harm.
Oth.   Why of thy thought, Iago ?
Iago. I did not think he had been acquainted with her.
Oth. O, yes, and went between us very oft.
Iago. Indeed !
Oth. Indeed ! ay, indeed : discern'st thou aught in that ?
  Is he not honest ?
Iago. Honest, my lord !
Oth. Honest ! ay, honest.
Iago. My lord, for aught I know.
Oth. What dost thou think ?
Iago. Think, my lord !
Oth. Think, my lord ! By heaven, he echoes me,
  As if there were some monster in his thought
  Too hideous to be shown. Thou dost mean something :
  I heard thee say even now, thou likedst not that,
  When Cassio left my wife : what didst not like ?

And when I told thee he was of my counsel
In my whole course of wooing, thou criedst ' Indeed !
And didst contract and purse thy brow together,
As if thou then hadst shut up in thy brain
Some horrible conceit : if thou dost love me,
Show me thy thought.

Iago. My lord, you know I love you.

Oth.　　　　　　　　　　　　I think thou dost ;
And for I know thou 'rt full of love and honesty
And weigh'st thy words before thou givest them breath,
Therefore these stops of thine fright me the more:
For such things in a false disloyal knave
Are tricks of custom ; but in a man that 's just
They 're close delations, working from the heart,
That passion cannot rule.

Iago.　　　　　　　　　For Michael Cassio,
I dare be sworn I think that he is honest.

Oth. I think so too.

Iago.　　　　　　　Men should be what they seem ;
Or those that be not, would they might seem none !

Oth. Certain, men should be what they seem.

Iago. Why then I think Cassio 's an honest man.

Oth. Nay, yet there 's more in this :
I prithee, speak to me as to thy thinkings,
As thou dost ruminate, and give thy worst of thoughts
The worst of words.

Iago.　　　　　　　Good my lord, pardon me:
Though I am bound to every act of duty,
I am not bound to that all slaves are free to
Utter my thoughts ?　Why, say they are vile and false ;
As where 's that palace whereinto foul things
Sometimes intrude not ? who has a breast so pure
But some uncleanly apprehensions
Keep leets and law-days, and in session sit
With meditations lawful ?

Oth. Thou dost conspire against thy friend, Iago,
If thou but think'st him wrong'd and makest his ear
A stranger to thy thoughts.

Iago.　　　　　　　　I do beseech you—
Though I perchance am vicious in my guess,
As, I confess, it is my nature's plague
To spy into abuses, and oft my jealousy
Shapes faults that are not—that your wisdom yet,
From one that so imperfectly conceits,
Would take no notice, nor build yourself a trouble

Out of his scattering and unsure observance.
It were not for your quiet nor your good,
Nor for my manhood, honesty, or wisdom,
To let you know my thoughts.

Oth.   What dost thou mean?

Iago. Good name in man and woman, dear my lord,
Is the immediate jewel of their souls :
Who steals my purse steals trash ; 'tis something, nothing ;
'Twas mine, 'tis his, and has been slave to thousands ;
But he that filches from me my good name
Robs me of that which not enriches him
And makes me poor indeed.

Oth. By heaven, I 'll know thy thoughts.

Iago. You cannot, if my heart were in your hand ;
Nor shall not, whilst 'tis in my custody.

Oth. Ha !

Iago.   O, beware, my lord, of jealousy ;
It is the green-eyed monster, which doth mock
The meat it feeds on : that cuckold lives in bliss
Who, certain of his fate, loves not his wronger ;
But, O, what damned minutes tells he o'er
Who dotes, yet doubts, suspects, yet strongly loves !

Oth. O misery !

Iago. Poor and content is rich, and rich enough ;
But riches fineless is as poor as winter
To him that ever fears he shall be poor :
Good heaven, the souls of all my tribe defend
From jealousy !

Oth.   Why, why is this !
Think'st thou I 'ld make a life of jealousy,
To follow still the changes of the moon
With fresh suspicions ?   No ; to be once in doubt
Is once to be resolved : exchange me for a goat,
When I shall turn the business of my soul
To such exsufflicate and blown surmises,
Matching thy inference.   'Tis not to make me jealous
To say my wife is fair, feeds well, loves company,
Is free of speech, sings, plays and dances well ;
Where virtue is, these are more virtuous :
Nor from mine own weak merits will I draw
The smallest fear or doubt of her revolt ;
For she had eyes, and chose me.   No, Iago ;
I 'll see before I doubt ; when I doubt, prove ;
And on the proof, there is no more but this,
Away at once with love or jealousy !

Iago. I am glad of it; for now I shall have reason
　　To show the love and duty that I bear you
　　With franker spirit: therefore, as I am bound,
　　Receive it from me.　I speak not yet of proof.
　　Look to your wife: observe her well with Cassio;
　　Wear your eye thus, not jealous nor secure:
　　I would not have your free and noble nature
　　Out of self-bounty be abused; look to't:
　　I know our country disposition well;
　　In Venice they do let heaven see the pranks
　　They dare not show their husbands; their best **conscience**
　　Is not to leave't undone, but keep't unknown.
Oth. Dost thou say so?
Iago. She did deceive her father, marrying you;
　　And when she seem'd to shake and fear your looks,
　　She loved them most.
Oth.　　　　　　　　And so she did.
Iago.　　　　　　　　　　　　Why, go to then;
　　She that so young could give out such a seeming,
　　To seel her father's eyes up close as oak—
　　He thought 'twas witchcraft—but I am much to blame;
　　I humbly do beseech you of your pardon
　　For too much loving you.
Oth.　　　　　　　　I am bound to thee for ever.
Iago. I see this hath a little dash'd your spirits.
Oth. Not a jot, not a jot.
Iago.　　　　　　　I' faith, I fear it has.
　　I hope you will consider what is spoke
　　Comes from my love; but I do see you 're moved:
　　I am to pray you not to strain my speech
　　To grosser issues nor to larger reach
　　Than to suspicion.
Oth. I will not.
Iago.　　　　　Should you do so, my lord,
　　My speech should fall into such vile success
　　As my thoughts aim not at.　Cassio 's my worthy friend—
　　My lord, I see you 're moved.
Oth.　　　　　　　　No, not much moved:
　　I do not think but Desdemona 's honest.
Iago. Long live she so! and long live you to think so!
Oth. And yet, how nature erring from itself—
Iago. Ay, there 's the point: as—to be bold with you—
　　Not to affect many proposed matches
　　Of her own clime, complexion and degree,
　　Whereto we see in all things nature tends—

Foh! one may smell in such a will most rank,
Foul disproportion, thoughts unnatural.
But pardon me: I do not in position
Distinctly speak of her; though I may fear
Her will, recoiling to her better judgement,
May fall to match you with her country forms,
And happily repent.

Oth.   Farewell, farewell:
If more thou dost perceive, let me know more;
Set on thy wife to observe: leave me, Iago.

Iago. [*Going*] My lord, I take my leave.

Oth. Why did I marry? This honest creature doubtless
Sees and knows more, much more, than he unfolds.

Iago. [*Returning*] My lord, I would I might entreat your honour
To scan this thing no further; leave it to time:
Though it be fit that Cassio have his place,
For sure he fills it up with great ability,
Yet, if you please to hold him off awhile,
You shall by that perceive him and his means:
Note if your lady strain his entertainment
With any strong or vehement importunity;
Much will be seen in that. In the mean time,
Let me be thought too busy in my fears—
As worthy cause I have to fear I am—
And hold her free, I do beseech your honour.

Oth. Fear not my government.

Iago. I once more take my leave.   [*Exit.*

Oth. This fellow's of exceeding honesty,
And knows all qualities, with a learned spirit,
Of human dealings. If I do prove her haggard,
Though that her jesses were my dear heart-strings,
I 'ld whistle her off and let her down the wind
To prey at fortune. Haply, for I am black
And have not those soft parts of conversation
That chamberers have, or for I am declined
Into the vale of years,—yet that's not much—
She's gone; I am abused, and my relief
Must be to loathe her. O curse of marriage,
That we can call these delicate creatures ours,
And not their appetites! I had rather be a toad,
And live upon the vapour of a dungeon,
Than keep a corner in the thing I love
For others' uses. Yet, 'tis the plague of great ones;
Prerogatived are they less than the base;
'Tis destiny unshunnable, like death:

123

Even then this forked plague is fated to us
When we do quicken.   Desdemona comes:

Re-enter Desdemona and Emilia.

If she be false, O, then heaven mocks itself!
I 'll not believe 't.

Des.   How now, my dear Othello!
Your dinner, and the generous islanders
By you invited, do attend your presence.

Oth. I am to blame.

Des.   Why do you speak so faintly?
Are you not well?

Oth. I have a pain upon my forehead here.

Des. Faith, that 's with watching; 'twill away again:
Let me but bind it hard, within this hour
It will be well.

Oth.   Your napkin is too little;

[He puts the handkerchief from him; and she drops it.

Let it alone.   Come, I 'll go in with you.

Des. I am very sorry that you are not well.

[Exeunt Othello and Desdemona.

Emil. I am glad I have found this napkin:
This was her first remembrance from the Moor:
My wayward husband hath a hundred times
Woo'd me to steal it; but she so loves the token,
For he conjured her she should ever keep it,
That she reserves it evermore about her
To kiss and talk to.   I 'll have the work ta'en out,
And give 't Iago: what he will do with it
Heaven knows, not I;
I nothing but to please his fantasy.

Re-enter Iago.

Iago. How now! what do you do here alone?

Emil. Do not you chide; I have a thing for you.

Iago. A thing for me? it is a common thing—

Emil. Ha!

Iago. To have a foolish wife.

Emil. O, is that all?   What will you give me now
For that same handkerchief?

Iago.   What handkerchief?

Emil. What handkerchief!
Why, that the Moor first gave to Desdemona;
That which so often you did bid me steal.

Iago. Hast stol'n it from her?

Emil. No, faith! she let it drop by negligence,
And, to the advantage, I being here took 't up.

Look, here it is.

Iago.   A good wench; give it me.

Emil. What will you do with 't, that you have been so earnest
   To have me filch it?

Iago. [*Snatching it*] Why, what 's that to you?

Emil. If 't be not for some purpose of import,
   Give 't me again: poor lady, she 'll run mad
   When she shall lack it.

Iago. Be not acknown on 't; I have use for it.
   Go, leave me.   [*Exit Emilia.*
   I will in Cassio's lodging lose this napkin,
   And let him find it.   Trifles light as air
   Are to the jealous confirmations strong
   As proofs of holy writ: this may do something.
   The Moor already changes with my poison:
   Dangerous conceits are in their natures poisons:
   Which at the first are scarce found to distaste,
   But with a little act upon the blood
   Burn like the mines of sulphur.   I did say so:
   Look, where he comes!

                        Re-enter Othello.

                        Not poppy, nor mandragora,
   Nor all the drowsy syrups of the world,
   Shall ever medicine thee to that sweet sleep
   Which thou owedst yesterday.

Oth.   Ha! ha! false to me?

Iago. Why, how now, general! no more of that.

Oth. Avaunt! be gone! thou hast set me on the rack:
   I swear 'tis better to be much abused
   Than but to know 't a little.

Iago.   How now, my lord!

Oth. What sense had I of her stol'n hours of lust?
   I saw 't not, thought it not, it harm'd not me:
   I slept the next night well, was free and merry;
   I found not Cassio's kisses on her lips:
   He that is robb'd, not wanting what is stol'n,
   Let him not know 't and he 's not robbed at all.

Iago. I am sorry to hear this.

Oth. I had been happy, if the general camp,
   Pioners and all, had tasted her sweet body,
   So I had nothing known.   O, now for ever
   Farewell the tranquil mind! farewell content!
   Farewell the plumed troop and the big wars
   That make ambition virtue!   O, farewell,
   Farewell the neighing steed and the shrill trump,

The spirit-stirring drum, the ear-piercing fife,
The royal banner and all quality,
Pride, pomp and circumstance of glorious war!
And, O you mortal engines, whose rude throats
The immortal Jove's dread clamours counterfeit,
Farewell! Othello's occupation 's gone!

Iago. Is 't possible, my lord?

Oth. Villain, be sure thou prove my love a whore;
Be sure of it; give me the ocular proof;
Or, by the worth of man's eternal soul,
Thou hadst been better have been born a dog
Than answer my waked wrath!

Iago.   Is 't come to this?

Oth. Make me to see 't; or at the least so prove it,
That the probation bear no hinge nor loop·
To hang a doubt on; or woe upon thy life!

Iago. My noble lord,—

Oth. If thou dost slander her and torture me,
Never pray more; abandon all remorse;
On horror's head horrors accumulate;
Do deeds to make heaven weep, all earth amazed;
For nothing canst thou to damnation add
Greater than that.

Iago.   O grace! O heaven defend me!
Are you a man? have you a soul or sense?
God be wi' you; take mine office. O wretched fool,
That livest to make thine honesty a vice!
O monstrous world! Take note, take note, O world,
To be direct and honest is not safe.
I thank you for this profit, and from hence
I 'll love no friend sith love breeds such offence.

Oth. Nay, stay: thou shouldst be honest.

Iago. I should be wise; for honesty 's a fool,
And loses that it works for.

Oth.   By the world,
I think my wife be honest, and think she is not;
I think that thou art just, and think thou art not:
I 'll have some proof. Her name, that was as fresh
As Dian's visage, is now begrimed and black
As mine own face. If there be cords, or knives,
Poison, or fire, or suffocating streams,
I 'll not endure it. Would I were satisfied!

Iago. I see, sir, you are eaten up with passion:
I do repent me that I put it to you.
You would be satisfied?

Oth.   Would! nay, I will.

Iago. And may: but, how? how satisfied, my lord?
Would you, the supervisor, grossly gape on?
Behold her topp'd?

Oth.   Death and damnation! O!

Iago. It were a tedious difficulty, I think,
To bring them to that prospect; damn them then,
If ever mortal eyes do see them bolster
More than their own! What then? how then?
What shall I say? Where's satisfaction?
It is impossible you should see this,
Were they as prime as goats, as hot as monkeys,
As salt as wolves in pride, and fools as gross
As ignorance made drunk. But yet, I say,
If imputation and strong circumstances,
Which lead directly to the door of truth,
Will give you satisfaction, you may have 't.

Oth. Give me a living reason she's disloyal.

Iago. I do not like the office:
But sith I am enter'd in this cause so far,
Prick'd to 't by foolish honesty and love,
I will go on. I lay with Cassio lately,
And being troubled with a raging tooth,
I could not sleep.
There are a kind of men so loose of soul,
That in their sleeps will mutter their affairs:
One of this kind is Cassio:
In sleep I heard him say 'Sweet Desdemona,
Let us be wary, let us hide our loves;'
And then, sir, would he gripe and wring my hand,
Cry 'O sweet creature!' and then kiss me hard,
As if he pluck'd up kisses by the roots,
That grew upon my lips: then laid his leg
Over my thigh, and sigh'd and kiss'd, and then
Cried 'Cursed fate that gave thee to the Moor!'

Oth. O monstrous! monstrous!

Iago.   Nay, this was but his dream

Oth. But this denoted a foregone conclusion:
'Tis a shrewd doubt, though it be but a dream.

Iago. And this may help to thicken other proofs
That do demonstrate thinly.

Oth.   I'll tear her all to pieces.

Iago. Nay, but be wise: yet we see nothing done;
She may be honest yet. Tell me but this;
Have you not sometimes seen a handkerchief

  Spotted with strawberries in your wife's hand?

Oth. I gave her such a one; 'twas my first gift.

Iago. I know not that: but such a handkerchief—
  I am sure it was your wife's—did I to-day
  See Cassio wipe his beard with.

Oth.   If it be that,—

Iago. If it be that, or any that was hers,
  It speaks against her with the other proofs.

Oth. O, that the slave had forty thousand lives!
  One is too poor, too weak for my revenge.
  Now do I see 'tis true. Look here, Iago;
  All my fond love thus do I blow to heaven:
  'Tis gone.
  Arise, black vengeance, from thy hollow cell!
  Yield up, O love, thy crown and hearted throne
  To tyrannous hate! Swell, bosom, with thy fraught,
  For 'tis of aspics' tongues!

Iago.   Yet be content.

Oth. O, blood, blood, blood!

Iago. Patience, I say; your mind perhaps may change.

Oth. Never, Iago. Like to the Pontic sea,
  Whose icy current and compulsive course
  Ne'er feels retiring ebb, but keeps due on
  To the Propontic and the Hellespont;
  Even so my bloody thoughts, with violent pace,
  Shall ne'er look back, ne'er ebb to humble love,
  Till that a capable and wide revenge
  Swallow them up. Now, by yond marble heaven,
  In the due reverence of a sacred vow   *[Kneels.*
  I here engage my words.

Iago.   Do not rise yet.   *[Kneels.*
  Witness, you ever-burning lights above,
  You elements that clip us round about,
  Witness that here Iago doth give up
  The execution of his wit, hands, heart,
  To wrong'd Othello's service! Let him command,
  And to obey shall be in me remorse,
  What bloody business ever.   *[They rise.*

Oth.   I greet thy love,
  Not with vain thanks, but with acceptance bounteous,
  And will upon the instant put thee to 't:
  Within these three days let me hear thee say
  That Cassio's not alive.

Iago. My friend is dead; 'tis done at your request:
  But let her live.

Oth.   Damn her, lewd minx! O, damn her!
  Come, go with me apart; I will withdraw,
  To furnish me with some swift means of death
  For the fair devil. Now art thou my lieutenant.

Iago. I am your own for ever.   [*Exeunt.*

Scene IV

Before the castle.

Enter Desdemona, Emilia, and Clown.

Des. Do you know, sirrah, where Lieutenant Cassio lies?

Clo. I dare not say he lies any where.

Des. Why, man?

Clo. He's a soldier; and for one to say a soldier lies, is stabbing.

Des. Go to: where lodges he?

Clo. To tell you where he lodges, is to tell you where I lie.

Des. Can any thing be made of this?

Clo. I know not where he lodges; and for me to devise a
  lodging, and say he lies here or he lies there, were to lie in
  mine own throat.

Des. Can you inquire him out and be edified by report?

Clo. I will catechize the world for him; that is, make questions
  and by them answer.

Des. Seek him, bid him come hither: tell him I have moved
  my lord on his behalf and hope all will be well.

Clo. To do this is within the compass of man's wit, and therefore I will attempt the doing it.   [*Exit.*

Des. Where should I lose that handkerchief, Emilia?

Emil. I know not, madam.

Des. Believe me, I had rather have lost my purse
  Full of crusadoes: and, but my noble Moor
  Is true of mind and made of no such baseness
  As jealous creatures are, it were enough
  To put him to ill thinking.

Emil.   Is he not jealous?

Des. Who, he? I think the sun where he was born
  Drew all such humours from him.

Emil.   Look, where he comes.

Des. I will not leave him now till Cassio
  Be call'd to him.

Enter Othello.

                How is 't with you, my lord?

Oth. Well, my good lady. [*Aside*] O, hardness to dissemble!
  How do you, Desdemona?

Des.   Well, my good lord.

Oth. Give me your hand: this hand is moist, my lady.

Des. It yet has felt no age nor known no sorrow.
Oth. This argues fruitfulness and liberal heart :
  Hot, hot, and moist : this hand of yours requires
  A sequester from liberty, fasting and prayer,
  Much castigation, exercise devout ;
  For here 's a young and sweating devil here,
  That commonly rebels.   'Tis a good hand,
  A frank one.
Des.   You may, indeed, say so ;
  For 'twas that hand that gave away my heart.
Oth. A liberal hand : the hearts of old gave hands ;
  But our new heraldry is hands, not hearts.
Des. I cannot speak of this.   Come now, your promise.
Oth. What promise, chuck ?
Des. I have sent to bid Cassio come speak with you.
Oth. I have a salt and sorry rheum offends me ;
  Lend me thy handkerchief.
Des. Here, my lord.
Oth. That which I gave you.
Des. I have it not about me.
Oth. Not ?
Des. No, indeed, my lord.
Oth. That 's a fault.   That handkerchief
  Did an Egyptian to my mother give ;
  She was a charmer, and could almost read
  The thoughts of people : she told her, while she kept it
  'Twould make her amiable and subdue my father
  Entirely to her love, but if she lost it
  Or made a gift of it, my father's eye
  Should hold her loathed and his spirits should hunt
  After new fancies ; she dying gave it me,
  And bid me, when my fate would have me wife,
  To give it her.   I did so : and take heed on 't ;
  Make it a darling like your precious eye ;
  To lose 't or give 't away were such perdition
  As nothing else could match.
Des.   Is 't possible ?
Oth. 'Tis true : there 's magic in the web of it :
  A sibyl, that had number'd in the world
  The sun to course two hundred compasses,
  In her prophetic fury sew'd the work ;
  The worms were hallow'd that did breed the silk ;
  And it was dyed in mummy which the skilful
  Conserved of maidens' hearts.
Des.   Indeed ! is 't true ?

Oth. Most veritable; therefore look to 't well.

Des. Then would to God that I had never seen 't!

Oth. Ha! wherefore?

Des. Why do you speak so startingly and rash?

Oth. Is 't lost? is 't gone? speak, is it out o' the way?

Des. Heaven bless us!

Oth. Say you?

Des. It is not lost; but what an if it were?

Oth. How!

Des. I say, it is not lost.

Oth. Fetch 't, let me see it.

Des. Why, so I can, sir, but I will not now.
This is a trick to put me from my suit:
Pray you, let Cassio be received again.

Oth. Fetch me the handkerchief: my mind misgives.

Des. Come, come;
You 'll never meet a more sufficient man.

Oth. The handkerchief!

Des.   I pray, talk me of Cassio.

Oth. The handkerchief!

Des.   A man that all his time
Hath founded his good fortunes on your love,
Shared dangers with you,—

Oth. The handkerchief!

Des. In sooth, you are to blame.

Oth. Away!   [*Exit.*

Emil. Is not this man jealous?

Des. I ne'er saw this before.
Sure there 's some wonder in this handkerchief:
I am most unhappy in the loss of it.

Emil. 'Tis not a year or two shows us a man:
They are all but stomachs and we all but food;
They eat us hungerly, and when they are full
They belch us.   Look you, Cassio and my husband.

Enter Cassio and Iago.

Iago. There is no other way; 'tis she must do 't:
And, lo, the happiness! go and importune her.

Des. How now, good Cassio! what 's the news with you?

Cas. Madam, my former suit: I do beseech you
That by your virtuous means I may again
Exist, and be a member of his love
Whom I with all the office of my heart
Entirely honour: I would not be delay'd.
If my offence be of such mortal kind,
That nor my service past nor present sorrows

Nor purposed merit in futurity
Can ransom me into his love again,
But to know so must be my benefit;
So shall I clothe me in a forced content
And shut myself up in some other course
To fortune's alms.

Des.   Alas, thrice-gentle Cassio!
My advocation is not now in tune;
My lord is not my lord, nor should I know him
Were he in favour as in humour alter'd.
So help me every spirit sanctified,
As I have spoken for you all my best
And stood within the blank of his displeasure
For my free speech! You must awhile be patient:
What I can do I will; and more I will
Than for myself I dare: let that suffice you.

Iago. Is my lord angry?

Emil.   He went hence but now,
And certainly in strange unquietness.

Iago. Can he be angry? I have seen the cannon,
When it hath blown his ranks into the air,
And, like the devil, from his very arm
Puff'd his own brother; and can he be angry?
Something of moment then: I will go meet him:
There's matter in't indeed if he be angry.

Des. I prithee, do so.   [*Exit Iago.*
                    Something sure of state,
Either from Venice some unhatch'd practice
Made demonstrable here in Cyprus to him,
Hath puddled his clear spirit; and in such cases
Men's natures wrangle with inferior things,
Though great ones are their object. 'Tis even so;
For let our finger ache, and it indues
Our other healthful members even to that sense
Of pain: nay, we must think men are not gods,
Nor of them look for such observancy
As fits the bridal. Beshrew me much, Emilia,
I was, unhandsome warrior as I am,
Arraigning his unkindness with my soul;
But now I find I had suborn'd the witness,
And he's indicted falsely.

Emil. Pray heaven it be state-matters, as you think,
And no conception nor no jealous toy
Concerning you.

Des. Alas the day, I never gave him cause!

Emil. But jealous souls will not be answer'd so;
  They are not ever jealous for the cause,
  But jealous for they are jealous : 'tis a monster
  Begot upon itself, born on itself.
Des. Heaven keep that monster from Othello's mind !
Emil. Lady, amen.
Des. I will go seek him.   Cassio, walk hereabout :
  If I do find him fit, I 'll move your suit,
  And seek to effect it to my uttermost.
Cas. I humbly thank your ladyship.

> [*Exeunt Desdemona and Emilia.*
> *Enter Bianca.*

Bian. Save you, friend Cassio !
Cas.   What make you from home ?
  How is it with you, my most fair Bianca ?
  I' faith, sweet love, I was coming to your house.
Bian. And I was going to your lodging, Cassio,
  What, keep a week away ? seven days and nights ?
  Eight score eight hours ? and lovers' absent hours,
  More tedious than the dial eight score times ?
  O weary reckoning !
Cas.   Pardon me, Bianca ;
  I have this while with leaden thoughts been press'd ;
  But I shall in a more continuate time
  Strike off this score of absence.   Sweet Bianca,

> [*Giving her Desdemona's handkerchief.*

  Take me this work out.
Bian.   .O Cassio, whence came this ?
  This is some token from a newer friend :
  To the felt absence now I feel a cause :
  Is 't come to this ?   Well, well.
Cas.   Go to, woman !
  Throw your vile guesses in the devil's teeth,
  From whence you have them.   You are jealous now
  That this is from some mistress, some remembrance :
  No, by my faith, Bianca.
Bian.   Why, whose is it ?
Cas. I know not, sweet : I found it in my chamber.
  I like the work well : ere it be demanded—
  As like enough it will—I 'ld have it copied :
  Take it, and do 't ; and leave me for this time.
Bian. Leave you ! wherefore ?
Cas. I do attend here on the general ;
  And think it no addition, nor my wish,
  To have him see me woman'd.

Bian.   Why, I pray you?
Cas. Not that I love you not.
Bian.   But that you do not love me.
  I pray you, bring me on the way a little;
  And say if I shall see you soon at night.
Cas. 'Tis but a little way that I can bring you;
  For I attend here: but I'll see you soon.
Bian. 'Tis very good; I must be circumstanced.   [*Exeunt.*

ACT IV—SCENE I

Cyprus.   Before the castle.
Enter Othello and Iago.

Iago. Will you think so?
Oth.   Think so, Iago!
Iago.   What,
  To kiss in private?
Oth.   An unauthorized kiss.
Iago. Or to be naked with her friend in bed
  An hour or more, not meaning any harm?
Oth. Naked in bed, Iago, and not mean harm!
  It is hypocrisy against the devil:
  They that mean virtuously and yet do so,
  The devil their virtue tempts and they tempt heaven.
Iago. So they do nothing, 'tis a venial slip:
  But if I give my wife a handkerchief—
Oth. What then?
Iago. Why, then, 'tis hers, my lord; and being hers,
  She may, I think, bestow 't on any man.
Oth. She is protectress of her honour too:
  May she give that?
Iago. Her honour is an essence that 's not seen;
  They have it very oft that have it not:
  But for the handkerchief—
Oth. By heaven, I would most gladly have forgot it:
  Thou said'st—O, it comes o'er my memory,
  As doth the raven o'er the infected house,
  Boding to all—he had my handkerchief.
Iago. Ay, what of that?
Oth.   That 's not so good now.
Iago.   What,
  If I had said I had seen him do you wrong?
  Or heard him say—as knaves be such abroad,
  Who having, by their own importunate suit,
  Or voluntary dotage of some mistress,

Convinced or supplied them, cannot choose
But they must blab—
Oth.   Hath he said anything?
Iago. He hath, my lord; but be you well assured,
No more than he'll unswear.
Oth.   What hath he said?
Iago. Faith, that he did—I know not what he did.
Oth. What, what?
Iago. Lie—
Oth.   With her?
Iago.   With her, on her; what you will.
Oth. Lie with her! lie on her!—We say lie on her, when
they belie her.—Lie with her! 'Zounds, that's fulsome!
Handkerchief—confessions—handkerchief!—To confess, and
be hanged for his labour; first, to be hanged, and then to
confess. I tremble at it. Nature would not invest herself
in such shadowing passion without some instruction. It is
not words that shakes me thus. Pish! Noses, ears and
lips. Is't possible?—Confess?—Handkerchief?—O devil!
                                        [*Falls in a trance.*

Iago. Work on,
My medicine, work! Thus credulous fools are caught:
And many worthy and chaste dames even thus,
All guiltless, meet reproach. What, ho! my lord!
My lord, I say! Othello!

                    Enter Cassio.
                    How now, Cassio!

Cas. What's the matter?
Iago. My lord is fall'n into an epilepsy:
This is his second fit; he had one yesterday.
Cas. Rub him about the temples.
Iago.   No, forbear;
The lethargy must have his quiet course:
If not, he foams at mouth, and by and by
Breaks out to savage madness. Look, he stirs:
Do you withdraw yourself a little while,
He will recover straight: when he is gone,
I would on great occasion speak with you.   [*Exit Cassio.*
How is it, general? have you not hurt your head?
Oth. Dost thou mock me?
Iago.   I mock you! no, by heaven.
Would you would bear your fortune like a man!
Oth. A horned man's a monster and a beast.
Iago. There's many a beast then in a populous city
And many a civil monster.

Oth. Did he confess it ?
Iago.   Good sir, be a man ;
Think every bearded fellow that 's but yoked
May draw with you : there 's millions now alive
That nightly lie in those unproper beds
Which they dare swear peculiar : your case is better.
O, 'tis the spite of hell, the fiend's arch-mock,
To lip a wanton in a secure couch,
And to suppose her chaste !   No, let me know ;
And knowing what I am, I know what she shall be.
Oth. O, thou art wise ; 'tis certain.
Iago.   Stand you awhile apart ;
Confine yourself but in a patient list.
Whilst you were here o'erwhelmed with your grief—
A passion most unsuiting such a man—
Cassio came hither : I shifted him away,
And laid good 'scuse upon your ecstasy ;
Bade him anon return and here speak with me ;
The which he promised.   Do but encave yourself,
And mark the fleers, the gibes and notable scorns,
That dwell in every region of his face ;
For I will make him tell the tale anew,
Where, how, how oft, how long ago and when
He hath and is again to cope your wife :
I say, but mark his gesture.   Marry, patience ;
Or I shall say you are all in all in spleen,
And nothing of a man.
Oth.   Dost thou hear, Iago ?
I will be found most cunning in my patience ;
But—dost thou hear ?—most bloody.
Iago.   That 's not amiss
But yet keep time in all.   Will you withdraw ?
                              [*Othello retires.*

Now will I question Cassio of Bianca,
A housewife that by selling her desires
Buys herself bread and clothes : it is a creature
That dotes on Cassio ; as 'tis the strumpet's plague
To beguile many and be beguiled by one.
He, when he hears of her, cannot refrain
From the excess of laughter.   Here he comes.
                    Re-enter Cassio.
As he shall smile, Othello shall go mad ;
And his unbookish jealousy must construe
Poor Cassio's smiles, gestures and light behaviour,
Quite in the wrong.   How do you now, lieutenant ?

Cas. The worser that you give me the addition
  Whose want even kills me.
Iago. Ply Desdemona well, and you are sure on 't.
  Now, if this suit lay in Bianca's power,
  How quickly should you speed !
Cas.   Alas, poor caitiff !
Oth. Look, how he laughs already !
Iago. I never knew a woman love man so.
Cas. Alas, poor rogue ! I think, i' faith, she loves me.
Oth. Now he denies it faintly and laughs it out.
Iago. Do you hear, Cassio ?
Oth.   Now he importunes him
  To tell it o'er : go to ; well said, well said.
Iago. She gives it out that you shall marry her :
  Do you intend it ?
Cas. Ha, ha, ha !
Oth. Do you triumph, Roman ? do you triumph ?
Cas. I marry her ! what, a customer ! I prithee, bear some
  charity to my wit ; do not think it so unwholesome. Ha,
Oth. So, so, so, so : they laugh that win.   [ha, ha !
Iago. Faith, the cry goes that you shall marry her.
Cas. Prithee, say true.
Iago. I am a very villain else.
Oth. Have you scored me ? Well.
Cas. This is the monkey's own giving out : she is persuaded
  I will marry her, out of her own love and flattery, not out of
  my promise.
Oth. Iago beckons me ; now he begins the story.
Cas. She was here even now : she haunts me in every place.
  I was the other day talking on the sea-bank with certain
  Venetians ; and thither comes the bauble, and, by this hand,
  she falls me thus about my neck—
Oth. Crying 'O dear Cassio !' as it were : his gesture imports it.
Cas. So hangs and lolls and weeps upon me ; so hales and pulls
  me : ha, ha, ha !
Oth. Now he tells how she plucked him to my chamber. O,
  I see that nose of yours, but not that dog I shall throw it to.
Cas. Well, I must leave her company.
Iago. Before me ! look, where she comes.
Cas. 'Tis such another fitchew ! marry, a perfumed one.
                      Enter Bianca.
  What do you mean by this haunting of me ?
Bian. Let the devil and his dam haunt you ! What did you
  mean by that same handkerchief you gave me even now !
  I was a fine fool to take it. I must take out the work ? A

likely piece of work, that you should find it in your chamber,
and not know who left it there! This is some minx's token,
and I must take out the work? There; give it your hobby-
horse: wheresoever you had it, I'll take out no work on't.

Cas. How now, my sweet Bianca! how now! how now!

Oth. By heaven, that should be my handkerchief!

Bian. An you'll come to supper to-night, you may; an you will
not, come when you are next prepared for. [*Exit.*

Iago. After her, after her.

Cas. Faith, I must; she'll rail i' the street else.

Iago. Will you sup there?

Cas. Faith, I intend so.

Iago. Well, I may chance to see you; for I would very fain
speak with you.

Cas. Prithee, come; will you?

Iago. Go to; say no more. [*Exit Cassio.*

Oth. [*Advancing*] How shall I murder him, Iago?

Iago. Did you perceive how he laughed at his vice?

Oth. O Iago!

Iago. And did you see the handkerchief?

Oth. Was that mine?

Iago. Yours, by this hand: and to see how he prizes the foolish
woman your wife! she gave it him, and he hath given it his
whore.

Oth. I would have him nine years a-killing. A fine woman!
a fair woman! a sweet woman!

Iago. Nay, you must forget that.

Oth. Ay, let her rot, and perish, and be damned to-night; for
she shall not live: no, my heart is turned to stone; I strike
it, and it hurts my hand. O, the world hath not a sweeter
creature: she might lie by an emperor's side, and command

Iago. Nay, that's not your way. [him tasks.

Oth. Hang her! I do but say what she is: so delicate with her
needle: an admirable musician: O, she will sing the savage-
ness out of a bear: of so high and plenteous wit and
invention:—

Iago. She's the worse for all this.

Oth. O, a thousand thousand times: and then, of so gentle
a condition!

Iago. Ay, too gentle.

Oth. Nay, that's certain: but yet the pity of it, Iago! O Iago,
the pity of it, Iago!

Iago. If you are so fond over her iniquity, give her patent to
offend; for, if it touch not you, it comes near nobody.

Oth. I will chop her into messes: cuckold me!

Iago. O, 'tis foul in her.

Oth. With mine officer !

Iago. That's fouler.

Oth. Get me some poison, Iago ; this night. I 'll not expostu-
late with her, lest her body and beauty unprovide my mind
again : this night, Iago.

Iago. Do it not with poison, strangle her in her bed, even the
bed she hath contaminated.

Oth. Good, good : the justice of it pleases : very good.

Iago. And for Cassio, let me be his undertaker : you shall hear
more by midnight.

Oth. Excellent good.   [*A trumpet within.*]   What trumpet is
that same ?

Iago. Something from Venice, sure.   'Tis Lodovico
Come from the duke : and, see, your wife is with him.

      Enter Lodovico, Desdemona, and Attendants.

Lod. God save the worthy general !

Oth.   With all my heart, sir.

Lod. The duke and senators of Venice greet you.

                                [*Gives him a letter.*

Oth. I kiss the instrument of their pleasures.

                          [*Opens the letter, and reads.*

Des. And what's the news, good cousin Lodovico ?

Iago. I am very glad to see you, signior ;
Welcome to Cyprus.

Lod. I thank you.   How does Lieutenant Cassio ?

Iago. Lives, sir.

Des. Cousin, there's fall'n between him and my lord
An unkind breach : but you shall make all well.

Oth. Are you sure of that ?

Des. My lord ?

Oth. [*Reads*] 'This fail you not to do, as you will—'

Lod He did not call ; he's busy in the paper.
Is there division 'twixt my lord and Cassio ?

Des. A most unhappy one : I would do much
To atone them, for the love I bear to Cassio.

Oth. Fire and brimstone !

Des.   My lord ?

Oth.   Are you wise ?

Des. What, is he angry ?

Lod.   May be the letter moved him ;
For, as I think, they do command him home,
Deputing Cassio in his government

Des. By my troth, I am glad on 't.

Oth.   Indeed ?

Des.   My lord?

Oth. I am glad to see you mad.

Des.   Why, sweet Othello?

Oth. Devil!   [*Striking her.*

Des. I have not deserved this.

Lod. My lord, this would not be believed in Venice,
  Though I should swear I saw 't: 'tis very much:
  Make her amends; she weeps.

Oth.   O devil, devil!
  If that the earth could teem with woman's tears,
  Each drop she falls would prove a crocodile.
  Out of my sight!

Des.   I will not stay to offend you.   [*Going.*

Lod. Truly, an obedient lady:
  I do beseech your lordship, call her back

Oth. Mistress!

Des. My lord?

Oth. What would you with her, sir?

Lod.   Who, I, my lord?

Oth. Ay; you did wish that I would make her turn:
  Sir, she can turn and turn, and yet go on,
  And turn again; and she can weep, sir, weep;
  And she's obedient, as you say, obedient,
  Very obedient.   Proceed you in your tears.
  Concerning this, sir,—O well-painted passion!—
  I am commanded home.   Get you away;
  I 'll send for you anon.   Sir, I obey the mandate,
  And will return to Venice.   Hence, avaunt!
                                    [*Exit Desdemona.*
  Cassio shall have my place.   And, sir, to-night, I
  do entreat that we may sup together:
  You are welcome, sir, to Cyprus.   Goats and monkeys! [*Exit.*

Lod. Is this the noble Moor whom our full senate
  Call all in all sufficient?   Is this the nature
  Whom passion could not shake? whose solid virtue
  The shot of accident nor dart of chance
  Could neither graze nor pierce?

Iago.   He is much changed.

Lod. Are his wits safe? is he not light of brain?

Iago. He 's that he is: I may not breathe my censure
  What he might be: if what he might he is not,
  I would to heaven he were!

Lod.   What, strike his wife.

Iago. Faith, that was not so well; yet would I knew
  That stroke would prove the worst!

Lod.   Is it his use?
  Or did the letters work upon his blood,
  And new create this fault?
Iago.   Alas, alas!
  It is not honesty in me to speak
  What I have seen and known.   You shall observe him,
  And his own courses will denote him so
  That I may save my speech: do but go after,
  And mark how he continues.
Lod. I am sorry that I am deceived in him.   [*Exeunt.*

SCENE II

A room in the castle.
Enter Othello and Emilia.

Oth. You have seen nothing, then?
Emil. Nor ever heard, nor ever did suspect.
Oth. Yes, you have seen Cassio and she together.
Emil. But then I saw no harm, and then I heard
  Each syllable that breath made up between them.
Oth. What, did they never whisper?
Emil.   Never, my lord.
Oth. Nor send you out o' the way?
Emil. Never.
Oth. To fetch her fan, her gloves, her mask, nor nothing?
Emil. Never, my lord.
Oth. That's strange.
Emil. I durst, my lord, to wager she is honest,
  Lay down my soul at stake: if you think other,
  Remove your thought; it doth abuse your bosom.
  If any wretch have put this in your head,
  Let heaven requite it with the serpent's curse!
  For if she be not honest, chaste and true,
  There's no man happy; the purest of their wives
  Is foul as slander.
Oth.   Bid her come hither: go.   [*Exit Emilia.*
  She says enough: yet she's a simple bawd
  That cannot say as much.   This is a subtle whore,
  A closet lock and key of villanous secrets:
  And yet she'll kneel and pray; I have seen her do't.
    Enter Desdemona with Emilia.
Des. My lord, what is your will?
Oth.   Pray, chuck, come hither
Des. What is your pleasure?
Oth.   Let me see your eyes
  Look in my face.

Des.   What horrible fancy's this?

Oth. [*To Emilia*] Some of your function, mistress,
Leave procreants alone and shut the door;
Cough, or cry hem, if any body come:
Your mystery, your mystery: nay, dispatch.   [*Exit Emilia.*

Des. Upon my knees, what doth your speech import?
I understand a fury in your words,
But not the words.

Oth. Why, what art thou?

Des. Your wife, my lord; your true and loyal wife.

Oth. Come, swear it, damn thyself;
Lest, being like one of heaven, the devils themselves
Should fear to seize thee: therefore be double-damn'd;
Swear thou art honest.

Des.   Heaven doth truly know it.

Oth. Heaven truly knows that thou art false as hell.

Des. To whom, my lord? with whom? how am I false?

Oth. O Desdemona! Away! away! away!

Des. Alas the heavy day! Why do you weep?
Am I the motive of these tears, my lord?
If haply you my father do suspect
An instrument of this your calling back,
Lay not your blame on me: if you have lost him,
Why, I have lost him too.

Oth.   Had it pleased heaven
To try me with affliction; had they rain'd
All kinds of sores and shames on my bare head,
Steep'd me in poverty to the very lips,
Given to captivity me and my utmost hopes,
I should have found in some place of my soul
A drop of patience: but, alas, to make me
A fixed figure for the time of scorn
To point his slow unmoving finger at!
Yet could I bear that too; well, very well:
But there, where I have garner'd up my heart,
Where either I must live or bear no life,
The fountain from the which my current runs,
Or else dries up; to be discarded thence!
Or keep it as a cistern for foul toads
To knot and gender in! Turn thy complexion there,
Patience, thou young and rose-lipp'd cherubin,
Ay, there, look grim as hell!

Des. I hope my noble lord esteems me honest.

Oth. O, ay; as summer flies are in the shambles,
That quicken even with blowing.   O thou weed,

Who art so lovely fair and smell'st so sweet
That the sense aches at thee, would thou hadst ne'er been
Des. Alas, what ignorant sin have I committed? [born !
Oth. Was this fair paper, this most goodly book,
Made to write 'whore' upon? What committed !
Committed ! O thou public commoner !
I should make very forges of my cheeks,
That would to cinders burn up modesty,
Did I but speak thy deeds. What committed !
Heaven stops the nose at it, and the moon winks ;
The bawdy wind, that kisses all it meets,
Is hush'd within the hollow mine of earth,
And will not hear it. What committed !
Impudent strumpet !
Des.   By heaven, you do me wrong.
Oth. Are not you a strumpet ?
Des.   No, as I am a Christian :
If to preserve this vessel for my lord
From any other foul unlawful touch
Be not to be a strumpet, I am none.
Oth. What, not a whore ?
Des.   No, as I shall be saved.
Oth. Is 't possible ?
Des. O, heaven forgive us !
Oth.   I cry you mercy then :
I took you for that cunning whore of Venice
That married with Othello. [*Raising his voice*] You, mistress
That have the office opposite to Saint Peter,
And keep the gate of hell !

                    Re-enter Emilia.
                    You, you, ay, you !
We have done our course ; there 's money for your pains :
I pray you, turn the key, and keep our counsel. [*Exit.*
Emil. Alas, what does this gentleman conceive ?
How do you, madam ? how do you, my good lady ?
Des. Faith, half asleep.
Emil. Good madam, what 's the matter with my lord ?
Des. With who ?
Emil. Why, with my lord, madam
Des. Who is thy lord ?
Emil.   He that is yours, sweet lady.
Des. I have none : do not talk to me, Emilia ;
I cannot weep, nor answer have I none
But what should go by water. Prithee, to-night
Lay on my bed my wedding sheets : remember ;

And call thy husband hither.

Emil.   Here's a change indeed! [*Exit*

Des. 'Tis meet I should be used so, very meet.
How have I been behaved, that he might stick
The small'st opinion on my least misuse?

Re-enter Emilia, with Iago.

Iago. What is your pleasure, madam? How is't with you?

Des. I cannot tell. Those that do teach young babes
Do it with gentle means and easy tasks:
He might have chid me so; for, in good faith,
I am a child to chiding.

Iago.   What's the matter, lady?

Emil. Alas, Iago, my lord hath so bewhored her,
Thrown such despite and heavy terms upon her,
As true hearts cannot bear.

Des. Am I that name, Iago?

Iago.   What name, fair lady?

Des. Such as she says my lord did say I was.

Emil. He call'd her whore: a beggar in his drink
Could not have laid such terms upon his callet.

Iago. Why did he so?

Des. I do not know: I am sure I am none such.

Iago. Do not weep, do not weep. Alas the day!

Emil. Hath she forsook so many noble matches,
Her father and her country and her friends,
To be call'd whore? would it not make one weep?

Des. It is my wretched fortune.

Iago.   Beshrew him for't!
How comes this trick upon him?

Des.   Nay, heaven doth know.

Emil. I will be hang'd, if some eternal villain,
Some busy and insinuating rogue,
Some cogging, cozening slave, to get some office,
Have not devised this slander; I'll be hang'd else.

Iago. Fie, there is no such man; it is impossible.

Des. If any such there be, heaven pardon him!

Emil. A halter pardon him! and hell gnaw his bones?
Why should he call her whore? who keeps her company?
What place? what time? what form? what likelihood?
The Moor's abused by some most villanous knave,
Some base notorious knave, some scurvy fellow.
O heaven, that such companions thou 'ldst unfold,
And put in every honest hand a whip
To lash the rascals naked through the world
Even from the east to the west!

Iago.   Speak within door.

Emil. O, fie upon them! Some such squire he was
That turn'd your wit the seamy side without,
And made you to suspect me with the Moor.

Iago. You are a fool; go to.

Des.   O good Iago,
What shall I do to win my lord again?
Good friend, go to him; for, by this light of heaven,
I know not how I lost him. Here I kneel:
If e'er my will did trespass 'gainst his love
Either in discourse of thought or actual deed,
Or that mine eyes, mine ears, or any sense,
Delighted them in any other form,
Or that I do not yet, and ever did,
And ever will, though he do shake me off
To beggarly divorcement, love him dearly,
Comfort foreswear me! Unkindness may do much;
And his unkindness may defeat my life,
But never taint my love. I cannot say 'whore':
It doth abhor me now I speak the word;
To do the act that might the addition earn
Not the world's mass of vanity could make me.

Iago. I pray you, be content; 'tis but his humour:
The business of the state does him offence,
And he does chide with you.

Des. If 'twere no other,—

Iago.   'Tis but so, I warrant. [*Trumpets within.*
Hark, how these instruments summon to supper!
The messengers of Venice stay the meat:
Go in, and weep not; all things shall be well.
                        [*Exeunt Desdemona and Emilia.*
                Enter Roderigo.
How now, Roderigo!

Rod. I do not find that thou dealest justly with me.

Iago. What in the contrary?

Rod Every day thou daffest me with some device, Iago; and
rather, as it seems to me now, keepest from me all conveni-
ency than suppliest me with the least advantage of hope. I
will indeed no longer endure it; nor am I yet persuaded to
put up in peace what already I have foolishly suffered.

Iago. Will you hear me, Roderigo?

Rod. Faith, I have heard too much; for your words and per-
formances are no kin together.

Iago. You charge me most unjustly.

Rod. With nought but truth. I have wasted myself out of my means. The jewels you have had from me to deliver to Desdemona would half have corrupted a votarist: you have told me she hath received them and returned me expectations and comforts of sudden respect and acquaintance; but

Iago. Well; go to; very well.   [I find none.

Rod. Very well! go to! I cannot go to, man; nor 'tis not very well: by this hand, I say 'tis very scurvy, and begin to find myself fopped in it.

Iago. Very well.

Rod. I tell you 'tis not very well. I will make myself known to Desdemona: if she will return me my jewels, I will give over my suit and repent my unlawful solicitation; if not, assure yourself I will seek satisfaction of you.

Iago. You have said now.   [doing.

Rod. Ay, and said nothing but what I protest intendment of

Iago. Why, now I see there's mettle in thee; and even from this instant do build on thee a better opinion than ever before. Give me thy hand, Roderigo: thou hast taken against me a most just exception; but yet, I protest, I have dealt most directly in thy affair.

Rod. It hath not appeared.

Iago. I grant indeed it hath not appeared, and your suspicion is not without wit and judgement. But, Roderigo, if thou hast that in thee indeed, which I have greater reason to believe now than ever, I mean purpose, courage and valour, this night show it: if thou the next night following enjoy not Desdemona, take me from this world with treachery and devise engines for my life.

Rod. Well, what is it? is it within reason and compass?

Iago. Sir, there is especial commission come from Venice to depute Cassio in Othello's place.

Rod. Is that true? why then Othello and Desdemona return again to Venice.

Iago. O, no; he goes into Mauritania, and takes away with him the fair Desdemona; unless his abode be lingered here by some accident: wherein none can be so determinate as the removing of Cassio.

Rod. How do you mean, removing of him?

Iago. Why, by making him uncapable of Othello's place; knocking out his brains.

Rod. And that you would have me to do?

Iago. Ay, if you dare do yourself a profit and a right. He sups to-night with a harlotry, and thither will I go to him: he knows not yet of his honourable fortune. If you will watch his going thence, which I will fashion to fall out between twelve

and one, you may take him at your pleasure : I will be near
to second your attempt, and he shall fall between us. Come,
stand not amazed at it, but go along with me ; I will show
you such a necessity in his death that you shall think
yourself bound to put it on him. It is now high supper-
time, and the night grows to waste : about it.

Rod. I will hear further reason for this.

Iago. And you shall be satisfied.   [*Exeunt.*

SCENE III

Another room in the castle.

Enter Othello, Lodovico, Desdemona, Emilia, and Attendants.

Lod. I do beseech you, sir, trouble yourself no further.

Oth. O, pardon me ; 'twill do me good to walk.

Lod. Madam, good night ; I humbly thank your ladyship.

Des. Your honour is most welcome.

Oth.   Will you walk, sir ?
O,—Desdemona,—

Des. My lord ?

Oth. Get you to bed on the instant ; I will be returned forth
with : dismiss your attendant there : look it be done.

Des. I will, my lord. [*Exeunt Othello, Lodovico, and Attendants.*

Emil. How goes it now ? he looks gentler than he did.

Des. He says he will return incontinent :
He hath commanded me to go to bed,
And bade me to dismiss you.

Emil.   Dismiss me !

Des. It was his bidding ; therefore, good Emilia,
Give me my nightly wearing, and adieu ;
We must not now displease him.

Emil. I would you had never seen him !

Des. So would not I : my love doth so approve him,
That even his stubbornness, his checks, his frowns,—
Prithee, unpin me,—have grace and favour in them.

Emil. I have laid those sheets you bade me on the bed.

Des. All's one.   Good faith, how foolish are our minds !
If I do die before thee, prithee, shroud me
In one of those same sheets.

Emil.   Come, come, you talk.

Des. My mother had a maid call'd Barbara :
She was in love ; and he she loved proved mad
And did forsake her : she had a song of 'willow ;'
An old thing 'twas, but it express'd her fortune,
And she died singing it : that song to-night
Will not go from my mind ; I have much to do

But to go hang my head all at one side
And sing it like poor Barbara.　Prithee, dispatch.
Emil. Shall I go fetch your night-gown?
Des.　　　　　　　　　　　　No, unpin me here.
This Lodovico is a proper man.
Emil. A very handsome man.
Des. He speaks well.
Emil. I know a lady in Venice would have walked barefoot to
Palestine for a touch of his nether lip.
Des. [*Singing*] The poor soul sat sighing by a sycamore tree,
　　　　Sing all a green willow;
　　Her hand on her bosom, her head on her knee,
　　　　Sing willow, willow, willow:
　　The fresh streams ran by her, and murmur'd her moans;
　　　　Sing willow, willow, willow;
　　Her salt tears fell from her, and soften'd the stones;—
Lay by these:—
　　[*Singing*] Sing willow, willow, willow;
Prithee, hie thee; he'll come anon:—
　　[*Singing*] Sing all a green willow must be my garland.
　　　　Let nobody blame him; his scorn I approve,—
Nay, that's not next.　Hark! who is't that knocks?
Emil. It's the wind.
Des. [*Singing*] I call'd my love false love; but what said he
　　　　Sing willow, willow, willow:　　　　　　[then?
　　If I court moe women, you'll couch with moe men.
So get thee gone; good night.　Mine eyes do itch;
Doth that bode weeping?
Emil.　　　　　　　　'Tis neither here nor there.
Des. I have heard it said so.　O, these men, these men!
Dost thou in conscience think,—tell me, Emilia,—
That there be women do abuse their husbands
In such gross kind?
Emil.　　　　　There be some such, no question.
Des. Wouldst thou do such a deed for all the world?
Emil. Why, would not you?
Des.　　　　　　　　No, by this heavenly light!
Emil. Nor I neither by this heavenly light; I might do't as
well i' the dark.
Des. Wouldst thou do such a deed for all the world?
Emil. The world's a huge thing: it is a great price
For a small vice.
Des.　　　　　In troth, I think thou wouldst not.
Emil. In troth, I think I should; and undo't when I had
done.　Marry, I would not do such a thing for a joint-ring,

nor for measures of lawn, nor for gowns, petticoats, nor caps,
nor any petty exhibition; but, for the whole world,—why,
who would not make her husband a cuckold to make him a
monarch? I should venture purgatory for 't.

Des. Beshrew me, if I would do such a wrong
For the whole world.

Emil. Why, the wrong is but a wrong i' the world; and having
the world for your labour, 'tis a wrong in your own world,
and you might quickly make it right.

Des. I do not think there is any such woman.

Emil. Yes, a dozen; and as many to the vantage as would
store the world they played for.
But I do think it is their husbands' faults
If wives do fall: say that they slack their duties
And pour our treasures into foreign laps,
Or else break out in peevish jealousies,
Throwing restraint upon us, or say they strike us,
Or scant our former having in despite,
Why, we have galls, and though we have some grace,
Yet have we some revenge. Let husbands know
Their wives have sense like them: they see and smell
And have their palates both for sweet and sour,
As husbands have. What is it that they do
When they change us for others? Is it sport?
I think it is: and doth affection breed it?
I think it doth: is 't frailty that thus errs?
It is so too: and have not we affections,
Desires for sport, and frailty, as men have?
Then let them use us well: else let them know,
The ills we do, their ills instruct us so.

Des. Good night, good night: heaven me such uses send,
Not to pick bad from bad, but by bad mend! *[Exeunt.*

ACT V—Scene I

Cyprus. A street.

Enter Iago and Roderigo.

Iago. Here, stand behind this bulk; straight will he come:
Wear thy good rapier bare, and put it home:
Quick, quick; fear nothing; I 'll be at thy elbow:
It makes us, or it mars us; think on that,
And fix most firm thy resolution.

Rod. Be near at hand; I may miscarry in 't.

Iago. Here, at thy hand: be bold, and take thy stand. *[Retires.*

Rod. I have no great devotion to the deed;

And yet he hath given me satisfying reasons :
'Tis but a man gone.   Forth, my sword : he dies.
Iago. I have rubb'd this young quat almost to the sense,
And he grows angry.   Now, whether he kill Cassio,
Or Cassio him, or each do kill the other,
Every way makes my gain : live Roderigo,
He calls me to a restitution large
Of gold and jewels that I bobb'd from him,
As gifts to Desdemona :
It must not be : if Cassio do remain,
He hath a daily beauty in his life
That makes me ugly ; and besides, the Moor
May unfold me to him ; there stand I in much peril :
No, he must die.   Be 't so.   I hear him coming.

Enter Cassio.

Rod. I know his gait ; 'tis he.   Villain, thou diest !

[*Makes a pass at Cassio.*

Cas. That thrust had been mine enemy indeed,
But that my coat is better than thou know'st :
I will make proof of thine.   [*Draws, and wounds Roderigo.*
Rod.   O, I am slain !

[*Iago from behind wounds Cassio in the leg, and exit.*

Cas. I am maim'd for ever.   Help, ho ! murder ! murder !   [*Falls.*

Enter Othello.

Oth. The voice of Cassio : Iago keeps his word
Rod. O, villain that I am !
Oth.   It is even so.
Cas. O, help, ho ! light ! a surgeon !
Oth. 'Tis he.   O brave Iago, honest and just,
That hast such noble sense of thy friend's wrong !
Thou teachest me.   Minion, your dear lies dead,
And your unblest fate hies : strumpet, I come !
Forth of my heart those charms, thine eyes, are blotted :
Thy bed lust-stain'd shall with lust's blood be spotted.   [*Exit.*

Enter Lodovico and Gratiano.

Cas. What, ho ! no watch ? no passage ? murder ! murder !
Gra. 'Tis some mischance ; the cry is very direful.
Cas. O, help !
Lod. Hark !
Rod. O wretched villain !
Lod. Two or three groan : it is a heavy night :
These may be counterfeits : let 's think 't unsafe
To come into the cry without more help.
Rod. Nobody come ? then shall I bleed to death.
Lod. Hark !

Re-enter Iago, with a light.

Gra. Here's one comes in his shirt, with light and weapons.

Iago. Who's there? whose noise is this that cries on murder?

Lod. We do not know.

Iago.   Did not you hear a cry?

Cas. Here, here! for heaven's sake, help me!

Iago.   What's the matter?

Gra. This is Othello's ancient, as I take it.

Lod. The same indeed; a very valiant fellow.

Iago. What are you here that cry so grievously?

Cas. Iago? O, I am spoil'd, undone by villains!
    Give me some help.

Iago. O me, lieutenant! what villains have done this?

Cas. I think that one of them is hereabout,
    And cannot make away.

Iago.   O treacherous villains?
    What are you there? come in and give some help.
                   [*To Lodovico and Gratiano.*

Rod. O, help me here!

Cas. That's one of them.

Iago.   O murderous slave! O villain!
                       [*Stabs Roderigo.*

Rod. O damn'd Iago! O inhuman dog!

Iago. Kill men i' the dark! Where be these bloody thieves?
    How silent is this town! Ho! murder! murder!
    What may you be? are you of good or evil?

Lod. As you shall prove us, praise us.

Iago. Signior Lodovico?

Lod. He, sir.

Iago. I cry you mercy. Here's Cassio hurt by villains.

Gra. Cassio!

Iago. How is't, brother?

Cas. My leg is cut in two.

Iago.   Marry, heaven forbid!
    Light, gentlemen: I'll bind it with my shirt.

Enter Bianca.

Bian. What is the matter, ho? who is't that cried?

Iago. Who is't that cried!   [*Cassio!*

Bian. O my dear Cassio! my sweet Cassio! O Cassio, Cassio,

Iago. O notable strumpet! Cassio, may you suspect
    Who they should be that have thus mangled you?

Cas. No.

Gra. I am sorry to find you thus: I have been to seek you.

Iago. Lend me a garter. So. O, for a chair,
    To bear him easily hence!

Bian. Alas, he faints! O Cassio, Cassio, Cassio!

Iago. Gentlemen all, I do suspect this trash
   To be a party in this injury.
   Patience awhile, good Cassio.   Come, come;
   Lend me a light.   Know we this face or no?
   Alas, my friend and my dear countryman
   Roderigo? no:—yes, sure: O heaven!   Roderigo.

Gra. What, of Venice?

Iago. Even he, sir: did you know him?

Gra.   Know him! ay.

Iago. Signior Gratiano?   I cry you gentle pardon;
   These bloody accidents must excuse my manners,
   That so neglected you.

Gra.   I am glad to see you.

Iago. How do you, Cassio?   O, a chair, a chair?

Gra. Roderigo!   [the chair:

Iago. He, he, 'tis he. [*A chair brought in.*] O, that's well said;
   Some good man bear him carefully from hence;
   I'll fetch the general's surgeon.   [*To Bianca*] For you, mistress,
   Save you your labour.   He that lies slain here, Cassio,
   Was my dear friend: what malice was between you?

Cas. None in the world; nor do I know the man.

Iago. [*To Bian.*] What, look you pale?   O, bear him out o'
       the air.   [*Cassio and Roderigo are borne off.*
   Stay you, good gentlemen.   Look you pale, mistress?
   Do you perceive the gastness of her eye?
   Nay, if you stare, we shall hear more anon.
   Behold her well; I pray you, look upon her:
   Do you see, gentlemen? nay, guiltiness will speak,
   Though tongues were out of use.

                    Enter Emilia.

Emil. 'Las, what's the matter? what's the matter, husband?

Iago. Cassio hath here been set on in the dark
   By Roderigo, and fellows that are 'scaped:
   He's almost slain, and Roderigo dead.

Emil. Alas, good gentleman! alas, good Cassio!

Iago. This is the fruit of whoring.   Prithee, Emilia,
   Go know of Cassio where he supp'd to-night.
   What, do you shake at that?

Bian. He supp'd at my house; but I therefore shake not.

Iago. O, did he so?   I charge you, go with me.

Emil. Fie, fie upon thee, strumpet!

Bian. I am no strumpet; but of life as honest
   As you that thus abuse me.

Emil.   As I! foh! fie upon thee!

Iago. Kind gentlemen, let's go see poor Cassio dress'd.
Come, mistress, you must tell's another tale.
Emilia, run you to the citadel,
And tell my lord and lady what hath happ'd!
Will you go on? I pray. [*Aside*] This is the night
That either makes me or fordoes me quite. [*Exeunt.*

SCENE II

*A bedchamber in the castle: Desdemona in bed asleep;
a light burning.*

Enter Othello.

Oth. It is the cause, it is the cause, my soul:
Let me not name it to you, you chaste stars!
It is the cause. Yet I'll not shed her blood,
Nor scar that whiter skin of hers than snow
And smooth as monumental alabaster.
Yet she must die, else she'll betray more men.
Put out the light, and then put out the light:
If I quench thee, thou flaming minister,
I can again thy former light restore,
Should I repent me: but once put out thy light,
Thou cunning'st pattern of excelling nature,
I know not where is that Promethean heat
That can thy light relume. When I have pluck'd the rose,
I cannot give it vital growth again,
It must needs wither: I'll smell it on the tree. [*Kissing her.*
Ah, balmy breath, that dost almost persuade
Justice to break her sword! One more, one more:
Be thus when thou art dead, and I will kill thee,
And love thee after: once more, and this the last:
So sweet was ne'er so fatal. I must weep,
But they are cruel tears: this sorrow's heavenly;
It strikes where it doth love. She wakes.
Des. Who's there? Othello?
Oth.   Ay, Desdemona.
Des. Will you come to bed, my lord?
Oth. Have you pray'd to-night, Desdemona?
Des. Ay, my lord.
Oth. If you bethink yourself of any crime
Unreconciled as yet to heaven and grace,
Solicit for it straight.
Des. Alas, my lord, what may you mean by that?
Oth. Well, do it, and be brief; I will walk by:
I would not kill thy unprepared spirit;
No; heaven forfend! I would not kill thy soul.

Des. Talk you of killing?

Oth. Ay, I do.

Des. Then heaven have mercy on me!

Oth. Amen, with all my heart!

Des. If you say so, I hope you will not kill me.

Oth. Hum!

Des. And yet I fear you; for you are fatal then
When your eyes roll so: why I should fear I know not,
Since guiltiness I know not; but yet I feel I fear.

Oth. Think on thy sins.

Des.   They are loves I bear to you.

Oth. Ay, and for that thou diest.

Des. That death's unnatural that kills for loving.
Alas, why gnaw you so your nether lip?
Some bloody passion shakes your very frame:
These are portents; but yet I hope, I hope,
They do not point on me.

Oth.   Peace, and be still!

Des. I will so. What's the matter?

Oth. That handkerchief which I so loved and gave thee
Thou gavest to Cassio.

Des.   No, by my life and soul!
Send for the man, and ask him.

Oth.   Sweet soul, take heed,
Take heed of perjury; thou art on thy death-bed.

Des. Ay, but not yet to die.

Oth.   Yes, presently:
Therefore confess thee freely of thy sin;
For to deny each article with oath
Cannot remove nor choke the strong conception
That I do groan withal. Thou art to die.

Des. Then Lord have mercy on me!

Oth.   I say, amen.

Des. And have you mercy too! I never did
Offend you in my life; never loved Cassio
But with such general warranty of heaven
As I might love: I never gave him token.

Oth. By heaven, I saw my handkerchief in 's hand.
O perjured woman! thou dost stone my heart,
And makest me call what I intend to do
A murder, which I thought a sacrifice:
I saw the handkerchief.

Des.   He found it then;
I never gave it him: send for him hither;
Let him confess a truth.

Oth.   He hath confess'd.
Des. What, my lord?
Oth. That he hath used thee.
Des.   How? unlawfully?
Oth. Ay.
Des. He will not say so.
Oth.   No, his mouth is stopp'd;
  Honest Iago hath ta'en order for 't.
Des. O, my fear interprets! what, is he dead?
Oth. Had all his hairs been lives, my great revenge
  Had stomach for them all.
Des. Alas, he is betray'd, and I undone!
Oth. Out, strumpet! weep'st thou for him to my face?
Des. O, banish me, my lord, but kill me not!
Oth. Down, strumpet!
Des. Kill me to-morrow; let me live to-night!
Oth. Nay, if you strive,—
Des. But half an hour!
Oth.   Being done, there is no pause.
Des. But while I say one prayer!
Oth.   It is too late. [*He stifles her.*
Emil. [*Within*] My lord, my lord! what, ho! my lord, my
  lord!
Oth. What noise is this? Not dead? not yet quite dead?
  I that am cruel am yet merciful;
  I would not have thee linger in thy pain:
  So, so.
Emil. [*Within*] What, ho! my lord, my lord!
Oth.   Who's there?
Emil. [*Within*] O, good my lord, I would speak a word with
Oth. Yes: 'tis Emilia. By and by. She's dead.   [you!
  'Tis like she comes to speak of Cassio's death.
  The noise was here. Ha! no more moving?
  Still as the grave. Shall she come in? were 't good?
  I think she stirs again. No. What's best to do?
  If she come in, she 'll sure speak to my wife:
  My wife! my wife! what wife? I have no wife.
  O, insupportable! O heavy hour!
  Methinks it should be now a huge eclipse
  Of sun and moon, and that the affrighted globe
  Should yawn at alteration.
Emil. [*Within*]   I do beseech you
  That I may speak with you, O, good my lord!
Oth. I had forgot thee: O, come in, Emilia.
  Soft; by and by. Let me the curtains draw.

Where art thou?   [*Unlocks the door.*

Enter Emilia.

What's the matter with thee now?

Emil. O, my good lord, yonder's foul murders done!

Oth. What, now?

Emil. But now, my lord.

Oth. It is the very error of the moon;
   She comes more nearer earth than she was wont
   And makes men mad.

Emil. Cassio, my lord, hath kill'd a young Venetian
   Call'd Roderigo.

Oth.   Roderigo kill'd!
   And Cassio kill'd!

Emil.   No, Cassio is not kill'd.

Oth. Not Cassio kill'd! then murder's out of tune.
   And sweet revenge grows harsh.

Des. O, falsely, falsely murder'd!

Emil.   Alas, what cry is that?

Oth. That! what?

Emil. Out, and alas! that was my lady's voice.
   Help! help, ho! help! O lady, speak again!
   Sweet Desdemona! O sweet mistress, speak!

Des. A guiltless death I die.

Emil. O, who hath done this deed?

Des. Nobody; I myself.   Farewell:
   Commend me to my kind lord: O, farewell!   [*Dies.*

Oth. Why, how should she be murder'd?

Emil.   Alas, who knows?

Oth. You heard her say herself, It was not I.

Emil. She said so: I must needs report the truth.

Oth. She's like a liar gone to burning hell:
   'Twas I that kill'd her.

Emil.   O, the more angel she,
   And you the blacker devil!

Oth. She turn'd to folly, and she was a whore.

Emil. Thou dost belie her, and thou art a devil.

Oth. She was false as water.

Emil.   Thou art rash as fire, to say
   That she was false: O, she was heavenly true!

Oth. Cassio did top her; ask thy husband else.
   O, I were damn'd beneath all depth in hell,
   But that I did proceed upon just grounds
   To this extremity.   Thy husband knew it all.

Emil. My husband!

Oth. Thy husband.

Emil. That she was false to wedlock?
Oth. Ay, with Cassio.   Nay, had she been true,
  If heaven would make me such another world
  Of one entire and perfect chrysolite,
  I 'ld not have sold her for it.
Emil. My husband!
Oth.   Ay, 'twas he that told me first:
  An honest man he is, and hates the slime
  That sticks on filthy deeds.
Emil.   My husband!
Oth. What needs this iteration, woman?   I say thy husband.
Emil. O mistress, villany hath made mocks with love!
  My husband say that she was false!
Oth.   He, woman;
  I say thy husband: dost understand the word?
  My friend, thy husband, honest, honest Iago.
Emil. If he say so, may his pernicious soul
  Rot half a grain a day! he lies to the heart:
  She was too fond of her most filthy bargain.
Oth. Ha!
Emil. Do thy worst:
  This deed of thine is no more worthy heaven
  Than thou wast worthy her.
Oth.   Peace, you were best.
Emil. Thou hast not half that power to do me harm
  As I have to be hurt.   O gull!   O dolt!
  As ignorant as dirt! thou hast done a deed—
  I care not for thy sword; I 'll make thee known,
  Though I lost twenty lives.   Help! help, ho! help
  The Moor hath kill'd my mistress!   Murder! murder
          Enter Montano, Gratiano, Iago, and others.
Mon. What is the matter?   How now, general!
Emil. O, are you come, Iago? you have done well,
  That men must lay their murders on your neck.
Gra. What is the matter?
Emil. Disprove this villain, if thou be'st a man:
  He says thou told'st him that his wife was false:
  I know thou didst not, thou 'rt not such a villain.
  Speak, for my heart is full.
Iago. I told him what I thought, and told no more
  Than what he found himself was apt and true.
Emil. But did you ever tell him she was false?
Iago. I did.
Emil. You told a lie, an odious, damned lie;
  Upon my soul, a lie, a wicked lie!

She false with Cassio! Did you say with Cassio?

Iago. With Cassio, mistress. Go to, charm your tongue.

Emil. I will not charm my tongue; I am bound to speak:
My mistress here lies murder'd in her bed,—

All. O heavens forfend!

Emil. And your reports have set the murder on.

Oth. Nay, stare not, masters: it is true indeed.

Gra. 'Tis a strange truth.

Mon. O monstrous act!

Emil.   Villany, villany, villany!
I think upon 't: I think: I smell 't: O villany!
I thought so then: I 'll kill myself for grief:
O villany, villany!

Iago. What, are you mad? I charge you, get you home.

Emil. Good gentlemen, let me have leave to speak:
'Tis proper I obey him, but not now.
Perchance, Iago, I will ne'er go home.

Oth. O! O! O!   [*Falling on the bed.*

Emil.   Nay, lay thee down and roar;
For thou hast kill'd the sweetest innocent
That e'er did lift up eye.

Oth. [*Rising*]   O, she was foul!
I scarce did know you, uncle: there lies your niece,
Whose breath indeed these hands have newly stopp'd:
I know this act shows horrible and grim.

Gra. Poor Desdemona! I am glad thy father's dead:
Thy match was mortal to him, and pure grief
Shore his old thread in twain: did he live now,
This sight would make him do a desperate turn,
Yea, curse his better angel from his side,
And fall to reprobation.

Oth. 'Tis pitiful; but yet Iago knows
That she with Cassio hath the act of shame
A thousand times committed; Cassio confess'd it:
And she did gratify his amorous works
With that recognizance and pledge of love
Which I first gave her; I saw it in his hand:
It was a handkerchief, an antique token
My father gave my mother.

Emil. O heaven! O heavenly powers!

Iago. 'Zounds! hold your peace.

Emil.   'Twill out, 'twill out. I peace!
No, I will speak as liberal as the north:
Let heaven and men and devils, let them all,
All, all, cry shame against me, yet I 'll speak.

Iago. Be wise, and get you home.
Emil.   I will not.

> [*Iago offers to stab Emilia.*

Gra.   Fie!
  Your sword upon a woman!
Emil. O thou dull Moor! that handkerchief thou speak'st of
  I found by fortune and did give my husband;
  For often with a solemn earnestness,
  More than indeed belong'd to such a trifle,
  He begg'd of me to steal it.
Iago.   Villanous whore!
Emil. She gives it Cassio! no, alas, I found it,
  And I did give 't my husband.
Iago.   Filth, thou liest!
Emil. By heaven, I do not, I do not, gentlemen.
  O murderous coxcomb! what should such a fool
  Do with so good a wife?
Oth.   Are there no stones in heaven
  But what serve for the thunder? Precious villain!

> [*He runs at Iago: Iago, from behind, stabs Emilia, and exit.*

Gra. The woman falls; sure, he hath kill'd his wife.
Emil. Ay, ay: O, lay me by my mistress' side.
Gra. He's gone, but his wife's kill'd.
Mon. 'Tis a notorious villain. Take you this weapon,
  Which I have here recover'd from the Moor:
  Come, guard the door without; let him not pass,
  But kill him rather. I'll after that same villain,
  For 'tis a damned slave.

> [*Exeunt all but Othello and Emilia.*

Oth.   I am not valiant neither,
  But every puny whipster gets my sword.
  But why should honour outlive honesty?
  Let it go all.
Emil.   What did thy song bode, lady?
  Hark, canst thou hear me? I will play the swan,
  And die in music. [*Singing*] Willow, willow, willow.
  Moor, she was chaste; she loved thee, cruel Moor;
  So come my soul to bliss, as I speak true;
  So speaking as I think, I die, I die.   [*Dies.*
Oth. I have another weapon in this chamber;
  It is a sword of Spain, the ice-brook's temper.—
  O, here it is. Uncle, I must come forth.
Gra. [*Within*] If thou attempt it, it will cost thee dear:
  Thou hast no weapon, and perforce must suffer.
Oth. Look in upon me then, and speak with me,

  Or naked as I am, I will assault thee.

                   Re-enter Gratiano.

Gra. What is the matter?

Oth.   Behold, I have a weapon;

  A better never did itself sustain

  Upon a soldier's thigh: I have seen the day

  That with this little arm and this good sword

  I have made my way through more impediments

  Than twenty times your stop: but, O vain boast!

  Who can control his fate? 'tis not so now.

  Be not afraid, though you do see me weapon'd;

  Here is my journey's end, here is my butt

  And very sea-mark of my utmost sail.

  Do you go back dismay'd? 'tis a lost fear:

  Man but a rush against Othello's breast,

  And he retires.   Where should Othello go?

  Now, how dost thou look now? O ill-starr'd wench!

  Pale as thy smock! when we shall meet at compt,

  This look of thine will hurl my soul from heaven,

  And fiends will snatch at it.   Cold, cold, my girl!

  Even like thy chastity.   O cursed slave!

  Whip me, ye devils,

  From the possession of this heavenly sight!

  Blow me about in winds! roast me in sulphur!

  Wash me in steep-down gulfs of liquid fire!

  O Desdemona! Desdemona! dead!

  Oh! Oh! Oh!

Enter Lodovico, Montano, Cassio carried in a chair, and Officers
                 with Iago, prisoner.

Lod. Where is this rash and most unfortunate man?

Oth. That's he that was Othello: here I am.

Lod. Where is that viper? bring the villain forth.

Oth. I look down towards his feet; but that's a fable.

  If that thou be'st a devil, I cannot kill thee. [*Wounds Iago.*

Lod. Wrench his sword from him.

Iago.   I bleed, sir, but not kill'd.

Oth. I am not sorry neither: I 'ld have thee live;

  For, in my sense, 'tis happiness to die.

Lod. O thou Othello, that wert once so good,

  Fall'n in the practice of a damned slave,

  What shall be said to thee?

Oth.   Why, any thing:

  An honourable murderer, if you will;

  For nought did I in hate, but all in honour.

Lod. This wretch hath part confess'd his villany:

Did you and he consent in Cassio's death?

Oth. Ay.

Cas. Dear general, I never gave you cause.

Oth. I do believe it, and I ask your pardon.
Will you, I pray, demand that demi-devil
Why he hath thus ensnared my soul and body?

Iago. Demand me nothing; what you know, you know:
From this time forth I never will speak word.

Lod. What, not to pray?

Gra.   Torments will ope your lips.

Oth. Well, thou dost best.

Lod. Sir, you shall understand what hath befall'n,
Which, as I think, you know not.   Here is a letter
Found in the pocket of the slain Roderigo,
And here another: the one of them imports
The death of Cassio to be undertook
By Roderigo.

Oth. O villain!

Cas.   Most heathenish and most gross!

Lod. Now here's another discontented paper,
Found in his pocket too; and this, it seems,
Roderigo meant to have sent this damned villain;
But that, belike, Iago in the interim
Came in and satisfied him.

Oth.   O the pernicious caitiff!
How came you, Cassio, by that handkerchief
That was my wife's?

Cas.   I found it in my chamber:
And he himself confess'd but even now
That there he dropp'd it for a special purpose
Which wrought to his desire.

Oth.   O fool! fool! fool!

Cas. There is besides in Roderigo's letter,
How he upbraids Iago, that he made him
Brave me upon the watch; whereon it came
That I was cast: and even but now he spake
After long seeming dead, Iago hurt him,
Iago set him on.

Lod. You must forsake this room, and go with us:
Your power and your command is taken off,
And Cassio rules in Cyprus.   For this slave,
If there be any cunning cruelty
That can torment him much and hold him long
It shall be his.   You shall close prisoner rest,
Till that the nature of your fault be known

To the Venetian state.   Come, bring away.

Oth. Soft you ; a word or two before you go.
I have done the state some service, and they know 't.
No more of that.   I pray you, in your letters,
When you shall these unlucky deeds relate,
Speak of me as I am ; nothing extenuate,
Nor set down aught in malice : then must you speak
Of one that loved not wisely but too well ;
Of one not easily jealous, but, being wrought,
Perplex'd in the extreme ; of one whose hand,
Like the base Indian, threw a pearl away
Richer than all his tribe ; of one whose subdued eyes,
Albeit unused to the melting mood,
Drop tears as fast as the Arabian trees
Their medicinal gum.   Set you down this ;
And say besides, that in Aleppo once,
Where a malignant and a turban'd Turk
Beat a Venetian and traduced the state,
I took by the throat the circumcised dog
And smote him, thus.   [*Stabs himself.*

Lod. O bloody period !

Gra.   All that 's spoke is marr'd.

Oth. I kiss'd thee ere I kill'd thee : no way but this,
Killing myself, to die upon a kiss.

                                [*Falls on the bed, and dies.*

Cas. This did I fear, but thought he had no weapon ;
For he was great of heart.

Lod. [*To Iago*]   O Spartan dog,
More fell than anguish, hunger, or the sea !
Look on the tragic loading of this bed ;
This is thy work : the object poisons sight ;
Let it be hid.   Gratiano, keep the house,
And seize upon the fortunes of the Moor,
For they succeed on you.   To you, lord governor,
Remains the censure of this hellish villain,
The time, the place, the torture : O, enforce it !
Myself will straight aboard, and to the state
This heavy act with heavy heart relate.   [*Exeunt.*

ANTONY AND CLEOPATRA

DRAMATIS PERSONÆ

ANTONY,
OCTAVIUS CÆSAR, } triumvirs.
LEPIDUS,
SEXTUS POMPEIUS.
DOMITIUS ENOBARBUS,
VENTIDIUS,
EROS,
SCARUS,
DERCETAS,
DEMETRIUS,
PHIL ,
MÆCENAS,
AGRIPPA,
DOLABELLA,
PROCULEIUS,
THYRE S,
GALLUS,
MENAS,
MENECRATES,
} friends to
Antony.

} friends to Cæsar.

} friends to Sextus
Pompeius.

VARRIUS, friend to Sextus Pompeius.
TAURUS, lieutenant-general to Cæsar.
CANIDIUS, lieutenant-general to Antony.
SILIUS, an officer in Ventidius's army.
EUPHRONIUS, an ambassador from
Antony to Cæsar.
ALEXAS,
MARDIAN, a eunuch, } attendants on
SELEUCUS, } Cleopatra.
DIOMEDES,
A Soothsayer.
A Clown.

CLEOPATRA, queen of Egypt.
OCTAVIA, sister to Cæsar, and wife to
Antony.
CHARMIAN, } attendants on Cleopatra.
IRAS,

Officers, Soldiers, Messengers, and other Attendants.
SCENE: In several parts of the Roman Empire.

ACT I—SCENE I

Alexandria. A room in Cleopatra's palace.
Enter Demetrius and Philo.

Phi. Nay, but this dotage of our general's
O'erflows the measure: those his goodly eyes,
That o'er the files and musters of the war
Have glow'd like plated Mars, now bend, now turn,
The office and devotion of their view
Upon a tawny front: his captain's heart,
Which in the scuffles of great fights hath burst
The buckles on his breast, reneges all temper,
And is become the bellows and the fan
To cool a gipsy's lust.

Flourish. Enter Antony, Cleopatra, her Ladies, the train, with
Eunuchs fanning her.

Look, where they come:
Take but good note, and you shall see in him
The triple pillar of the world transform'd
Into a strumpet's fool: behold and see.

Cleo. If it be love indeed, tell me how much.

Ant. There's beggary in the love that can be reckon'd.

Cleo. I'll set a bourn how far to be beloved.

Ant. Then must thou needs find out new heaven, new earth

Enter an Attendant.

Att. News, my good lord, from Rome.

Ant.   Grates me: the sum.

163

Cleo. Nay, hear them, Antony:
  Fulvia perchance is angry; or, who knows
  If the scarce-bearded Cæsar have not sent
  His powerful mandate to you, 'Do this, or this
  Take in that kingdom, and enfranchise that;
  Perform 't, or else we damn thee.'
Ant.   How, my love!
Cleo. Perchance! nay, and most like:
  You must not stay here longer, your dismission
  Is come from Cæsar; therefore hear it, Antony.
  Where 's Fulvia's process? Cæsar's I would say? both?
  Call in the messengers. As I am Egypt's queen,
  Thou blushest, Antony, and that blood of thine
  Is Cæsar's homager: else so thy cheek pays shame
  When shrill-tongued Fulvia scolds. The messengers!
Ant. Let Rome in Tiber melt, and the wide arch
  Of the ranged empire fall! Here is my space.
  Kingdoms are clay: our dungy earth alike
  Feeds beast as man: the nobleness of life
  Is to do thus; when such a mutual pair   [*Embracing.*
  And such a twain can do 't, in which I bind,
  On pain of punishment, the world to weet
  We stand up peerless.
Cleo.   Excellent falschood!
  Why did he marry Fulvia, and not love her?
  I 'll seem the fool I am not; Antony
  Will be himself.
Ant.   But stirr'd by Cleopatra.
  Now, for the love of Love and her soft hours,
  Let 's not confound the time with conference harsh:
  There 's not a minute of our lives should stretch
  Without some pleasure now. What sport to-night?
Cleo. Hear the ambassadors.
Ant.   Fie, wrangling queen
  Whom every thing becomes, to chide, to laugh,
  To weep; whose every passion fully strives
  To make itself, in thee, fair and admired!
  No messenger but thine; and all alone
  To-night we 'll wander through the streets and note
  The qualities of people. Come, my queen;
  Last night you did desire it. Speak not to us.
                          [*Exeunt Ant. and Cleo. with their train.*
Dem. Is Cæsar with Antonius prized so slight?
Phi. Sir, sometimes, when he is not Antony,
  He comes too short of that great property

Which still should go with Antony.

Dem.   I am full sorry
That he approves the common liar, who
Thus speaks of him at Rome : but I will hope
Of better deeds to-morrow.   Rest you happy !   [*Exeunt.*

SCENE II

The same.   Another room.

Enter Charmian, Iras, Alexas, and a Soothsayer.

Char. Lord Alexas, sweet Alexas, most any thing Alexas,
   almost most absolute Alexas, where 's the soothsayer that
   you praised so to the queen ?   O, that I knew this husband,
   which, you say, must charge his horns with garlands !

Alex. Soothsayer !

Sooth. Your will ?

Char. Is this the man ?   Is 't you, sir, that know things ?

Sooth. In nature's infinite book of secrecy
   A little I can read.

Alex.   Show him your hand.

Enter Enobarbus.

Eno. Bring in the banquet quickly ; wine enough
   Cleopatra's health to drink.

Char. Good sir, give me good fortune.

Sooth. I make not, but foresee.

Char. Pray then, foresee me one.

Sooth. You shall be yet far fairer than you are.

Char. He means in flesh.

Iras. No, you shall paint when you are old.

Char. Wrinkles forbid !

Alex. Vex not his prescience ; be attentive.

Char. Hush !

Sooth. You shall be more beloving than beloved.

Char. I had rather heat my liver with drinking.

Alex. Nay, hear him.

Char. Good now, some excellent fortune !   Let me be married
   to three kings in a forenoon, and widow them all : let me
   have a child at fifty, to whom Herod of Jewry may do
   homage : find me to marry me with Octavius Cæsar, and
   companion me with my mistress.

Sooth. You shall outlive the lady whom you serve.

Char. O excellent ! I love long life better than figs.

Sooth. You have seen and proved a fairer former fortune
   Than that which is to approach.

Char. Then belike my children shall have no names : prithee,
   how many boys and wenches must I have ?

Sooth. If every of your wishes had a womb,
  And fertile every wish, a million.

Char. Out, fool! I forgive thee for a witch.

Alex. You think none but your sheets are privy to your wishes.

Char. Nay, come, tell Iras hers.

Alex. We'll know all our fortunes.

Eno. Mine and most of our fortunes to-night shall be—drunk

Iras. There's a palm presages chastity, if nothing else. [to bed.

Char. E'en as the o'erflowing Nilus presageth famine.

Iras. Go, you wild bedfellow, you cannot soothsay.

Char. Nay, if an oily palm be not a fruitful prognostication, I
  cannot scratch mine ear.   Prithee, tell her but a worky-day

Sooth. Your fortunes are alike.   [fortune.

Iras. But how, but how? give me particulars.

Sooth. I have said.

Iras. Am I not an inch of fortune better than she?

Char. Well, if you were but an inch of fortune better than I,
  where would you choose it?

Iras. Not in my husband's nose.

Char. Our worser thoughts heavens mend! Alexas,—come,
  his fortune, his fortune!   O, let him marry a woman that
  cannot go, sweet Isis, I beseech thee! and let her die too,
  and give him a worse! and let worse follow worse, till the
  worst of all follow him laughing to his grave, fifty-fold a
  cuckold!   Good Isis, hear me this prayer, though thou deny
  me a matter of more weight; good Isis, I beseech thee!

Iras. Amen.   Dear goddess, hear that prayer of the people!
  for, as it is a heart-breaking to see a handsome man loose-
  wived, so it is a deadly sorrow to behold a foul knave un-
  cuckolded: therefore, dear Isis, keep decorum, and fortune
  him accordingly!

Char. Amen.

Alex. Lo, now, if it lay in their hands to make me a cuckold,
  they would make themselves whores, but they'ld do't!

Eno. Hush! here comes Antony.

Char.   Not he; the queen.

                Enter Cleopatra.

Cleo. Saw you my lord?

Eno. No, lady.

Cleo. Was he not here?

Char. No, madam.

Cleo. He was disposed to mirth; but on the sudden
  A Roman thought has struck him.   Enobarbus!

Eno. Madam?

Cleo. Seek him, and bring him hither.   Where's Alexas?

Alex. Here, at your service. My lord approaches.

Cleo. We will not look upon him : go with us.   [*Exeunt.*

    Enter Antony with a Messenger and Attendants.

Mess. Fulvia thy wife first came into the field.

Ant. Against my brother Lucius ?

Mess. Ay :

    But soon that war had end, and the time's state
    Made friends of them, jointing their force 'gainst Cæsar,
    Whose better issue in the war from Italy
    Upon the first encounter drave them.

Ant.   Well, what worst ?

Mess. The nature of bad news infects the teller.

Ant. When it concerns the fool or coward.   On :

    Things that are past are done with me.   'Tis thus ;
    Who tells me true, though in his tale lie death,
    I hear him as he flatter'd.

Mess.   Labienus—

    This is stiff news—hath with his Parthian force
    Extended Asia from Euphrates,
    His conquering banner shook from Syria
    To Lydia and to Ionia,
    Whilst—

Ant. Antony, thou wouldst say,—

Mess.   O, my lord !

Ant. Speak to me home, mince not the general tongue :

    Name Cleopatra as she is call'd in Rome ;
    Rail thou in Fulvia's phrase, and taunt my faults
    With such full license as both truth and malice
    Have power to utter.   O, then we bring forth weeds
    When our quick minds lie still, and our ills told us
    Is as our earing.   Fare thee well awhile.

Mess. At your noble pleasure.   [*Exit.*

Ant. From Sicyon, ho, the news ! Speak there !

First Att. The man from Sicyon, is there such an one ?

Sec. Att. He stays upon your will.

Ant.   Let him appear.

    These strong Egyptian fetters I must break,
    Or lose myself in dotage.

        Enter another Messenger.

            What are you ?

Sec. Mess. Fulvia thy wife is dead.

Ant.   Where died she ?

Sec. Mess. In Sicyon :

    Her length of sickness, with what else more serious
    Importeth thee to know, this bears.   [*Gives a letter.*

Ant.   Forbear me. [*Exit Sec. Messenger.*
There's a great spirit gone! Thus did I desire it:
What our contempts do often hurl from us,
We wish it ours again; the present pleasure,
By revolution lowering, does become
The opposite of itself: she's good, being gone;
The hand could pluck her back that shoved her on.
I must from this enchanting queen break off:
Ten thousand harms, more than the ills I know,
My idleness doth hatch. How now! Enobarbus!

Re-enter Enobarbus.

Eno. What's your pleasure, sir?
Ant. I must with haste from hence.
Eno. Why then we kill all our women. We see how mortal an
unkindness is to them; if they suffer our departure, death's
the word.
Ant. I must be gone.
Eno. Under a compelling occasion let women die: it were pity
to cast them away for nothing; though, between them and
a great cause, they should be esteemed nothing. Cleopatra,
catching but the least noise of this, dies instantly; I have
seen her die twenty times upon far poorer moment: I do
think there is mettle in death, which commits some loving
act upon her, she hath such a celerity in dying.
Ant. She is cunning past man's thought.
Eno. Alack, sir, no; her passions are made of nothing but the
finest part of pure love: we cannot call her winds and waters
sighs and tears; they are greater storms and tempests than
almanacs can report: this cannot be cunning in her; if it be,
she makes a shower of rain as well as Jove.
Ant. Would I had never seen her!
Eno. O, sir, you had then left unseen a wonderful piece of
work; which not to have been blest withal would have
discredited your travel.
Ant. Fulvia is dead.
Eno. Sir?
Ant. Fulvia is dead.
Eno. Fulvia!
Ant. Dead.
Eno. Why, sir, give the gods a thankful sacrifice. When it
pleaseth their deities to take the wife of a man from him, it
shows to man the tailors of the earth, comforting therein,
that when old robes are worn out there are members to make
new. If there were no more women but Fulvia, then had
you indeed a cut, and the case to be lamented; this grief is

crowned with consolation; your old smock brings forth a
new petticoat: and indeed the tears live in an onion that
should water this sorrow.

Ant. The business she hath broached in the state cannot
endure my absence.

Eno. And the business you have broached here cannot be
without you; especially that of Cleopatra's, which wholly
depends on your abode.

Ant. No more light answers. Let our officers
Have notice what we purpose. I shall break
The cause of our expedience to the queen
And get her leave to part. For not alone
The death of Fulvia, with more urgent touches,
Do strongly speak to us, but the letters too
Of many our contriving friends in Rome
Petition us at home: Sextus Pompeius
Hath given the dare to Cæsar and commands
The empire of the sea: our slippery people,
Whose love is never link'd to the deserver
Till his deserts are past, begin to throw
Pompey the Great and all his dignities
Upon his son; who, high in name and power,
Higher than both in blood and life, stands up
For the main soldier: whose quality, going on,
The sides o' the world may danger. Much is breeding,
Which, like the courser's hair, hath yet but life
And not a serpent's poison. Say, our pleasure,
To such whose place is under us, requires
Our quick remove from hence.

Eno. I shall do 't.   *[Exeunt.*

Scene III

The same. Another room.

Enter Cleopatra, Charmian, Iras, and Alexas.

Cleo. Where is he?

Char.   I did not see him since.

Cleo. See where he is, who 's with him, what he does:
I did not send you: if you find him sad,
Say I am dancing; if in mirth, report
That I am sudden sick: quick, and return.   *[Exit Alexas.*

Char. Madam, methinks, if you did love him dearly,
You do not hold the method to enforce
The like from him.

Cleo.   What should I do, I do not?

Char. In each thing give him way, cross him in nothing.

Cleo. Thou teachest like a fool: the way to lose him.
Char. Tempt him not so too far; I wish, forbear:
　In time we hate that which we often fear.
　But here comes Antony.

Enter Antony.

Cleo.　　　　　　　　I am sick and sullen.
Ant. I am sorry to give breathing to my purpose,—
Cleo. Help me away, dear Charmian; I shall fall:
　It cannot be thus long, the sides of nature
　Will not sustain it.
Ant.　　　　　　Now, my dearest queen,—
Cleo. Pray you, stand farther from me.
Ant.　　　　　　　　　　What's the matter?
Cleo. I know, by that same eye, there's some good news.
　What says the married woman? You may go:
　Would she had never given you leave to come!
　Let her not say 'tis I that keep you here,
　I have no power upon you; hers you are.
Ant. The gods best know—
Cleo.　　　　　　O, never was there queen
　So mightily betray'd! yet at the first
　I saw the treasons planted.
Ant.　　　　　　Cleopatra,—
Cleo. Why should I think you can be mine and true,
　Though you in swearing shake the thronèd gods,
　Who have been false to Fulvia? Riotous madness,
　To be entangled with those mouth-made vows,
　Which break themselves in swearing!
Ant.　　　　　　　　Most sweet queen,—
Cleo. Nay, pray you, seek no colour for your going,
　But bid farewell, and go: when you sued staying,
　Then was the time for words: no going then;
　Eternity was in our lips and eyes,
　Bliss in our brows' bent, none our parts so poor
　But was a race of heaven: they are so still,
　Or thou, the greatest soldier of the world,
　Art turn'd the greatest liar.
Ant.　　　　　　How now, lady!
Cleo. I would I had thy inches; thou shouldst know
　There were a heart in Egypt.
Ant.　　　　　　Hear me, queen:
　The strong necessity of time commands
　Our services awhile: but my full heart
　Remains in use with you. Our Italy
　Shines o'er with civil swords: Sextus Pompeius

Makes his approaches to the port of Rome:
Equality of two domestic powers
Breed scrupulous faction: the hated, grown to strength,
Are newly grown to love: the condemn'd Pompey,
Rich in his father's honour, creeps apace
Into the hearts of such as have not thrived
Upon the present state, whose numbers threaten;
And quietness grown sick of rest would purge
By any desperate change. My more particular,
And that which most with you should safe my going,
Is Fulvia's death.

Cleo. Though age from folly could not give me freedom,
It does from childishness: can Fulvia die?

Ant. She's dead, my queen:
Look here, and at thy sovereign leisure read
The garboils she awaked: at the last, best;
See when and where she died.

Cleo.   O most false love!
Where be the sacred vials thou shouldst fill
With sorrowful water? Now I see, I see,
In Fulvia's death, how mine received shall be.

Ant. Quarrel no more, but be prepared to know
The purposes I bear, which are, or cease,
As you shall give the advice. By the fire
That quickens Nilus' slime, I go from hence
Thy soldier, servant, making peace or war
As thou affect'st.

Cleo.   Cut my lace, Charmian, come;
But let it be: I am quickly ill and well,
So Antony loves.

Ant.   My precious queen, forbear;
And give true evidence to his love, which stands
An honourable trial.

Cleo.   So Fulvia told me.
I prithee, turn aside and weep for her;
Then bid adieu to me, and say the tears
Belong to Egypt: good now, play one scene
Of excellent dissembling, and let it look
Like perfect honour.

Ant.   You'll heat my blood: no more.

Cleo. You can do better yet; but this is meetly.

Ant. Now, by my sword,—

Cleo.   And target. Still he mends,
But this is not the best. Look, prithee, Charmian,
How this Herculean Roman does become

The carriage of his chafe.

Ant. I 'll leave you, lady.

Cleo.   Courteous lord, one word.
Sir, you and I must part, but that 's not it :
Sir, you and I have loved, but there 's not it :
That you know well : something it is I would,—
O, my oblivion is a very Antony,
And I am all forgotten.

Ant.   But that your royalty
Holds idleness your subject, I should take you
For idleness itself.

Cleo.   'Tis sweating labour
To bear such idleness so near the heart
As Cleopatra this.   But, sir, forgive me,
Since my becomings kill me when they do not
Eye well to you.   Your honour calls you hence ;
Therefore be deaf to my unpitied folly,
And all the gods go with you !   Upon your sword
Sit laurel victory ! and smooth success
Be strew'd before your feet !

Ant.   Let us go.   Come ;
Our separation so abides and flies,
That thou residing here go'st yet with me,
And I hence fleeing here remain with thee.
Away !

                                        [*Exeunt.*

SCENE IV

Rome. Cæsar's house.

*Enter Octavius Cæsar, reading a letter, Lepidus,
and their train.*

Cæs. You may see, Lepidus, and henceforth know,
It is not Cæsar's natural vice to hate
Our great competitor : from Alexandria
This is the news : he fishes, drinks and wastes
The lamps of night in revel : is not more manlike
Than Cleopatra, nor the queen of Ptolemy
More womanly than he : hardly gave audience, or
Vouchsafed to think he had partners : you shall find there
A man who is the abstract of all faults
That all men follow.

Lep.   I must not think there are
Evils enow to darken all his goodness :
His faults in him seem as the spots of heaven
More fiery by night's blackness, hereditary
Rather than purchased, what he cannot change

172

Than what he chooses.

Cæs. You are too indulgent.   Let us grant it is not
Amiss to tumble on the bed of Ptolemy,
To give a kingdom for a mirth, to sit
And keep the turn of tippling with a slave,
To reel the streets at noon and stand the buffet
With knaves that smell of sweat : say this becomes him,—
As his composure must be rare indeed
Whom these things cannot blemish,—yet must Antony
No way excuse his soils, when we do bear
So great weight in his lightness.   If he fill'd
His vacancy with his voluptuousness,
Full surfeits and the dryness of his bones
Call on him for 't : but to confound such time
That drums him from his sport and speaks as loud
As his own state and ours, 'tis to be chid
As we rate boys, who, being mature in knowledge,
Pawn their experience to their present pleasure,
And so rebel to judgement.

Enter a Messenger.

Lep.   Here 's more news.

Mess. Thy biddings have been done ; and every hour,
Most noble Cæsar, shalt thou have report
How 'tis abroad.   Pompey is strong at sea ;
And it appears he is beloved of those
That only have fear'd Cæsar : to the ports
The discontents repair, and men's reports
Give him much wrong'd.

Cæs.   I should have known no less.
It had been taught us from the primal state,
That he which is was wish'd until he were ;
And the ebb'd man, ne'er loved till ne'er worth love,
Comes dear'd by being lack'd.   This common body,
Like to a vagabond flag upon the stream,
Goes to and back, lackeying the varying tide,
To rot itself with motion.

Mess.   Cæsar, I bring thee word,
Menecrates and Menas, famous pirates,
Make the sea serve them, which they ear and wound
With keels of every kind ; many hot inroads
They make in Italy ; the borders maritime
Lack blood to think on 't, and flush youth revolt :
No vessel can peep forth, but 'tis as soon
Taken as seen ; for Pompey's name strikes more

Than could his war resisted.

Cæs.   Antony,
Leave thy lascivious wassails.   When thou once
Wast beaten from Modena, where thou slew'st
Hirtius and Pansa, consuls, at thy heel
Did famine follow; whom thou fought'st against
Though daintily brought up, with patience more
Than savages could suffer: thou didst drink
The stale of horses and the gilded puddle
Which beasts would cough at: thy palate then did deign
The roughest berry on the rudest hedge;
Yea, like the stag, when snow the pasture sheets,
The barks of trees thou browsedst.   On the Alps
It is reported thou didst eat strange flesh,
Which some did die to look on: and all this—
It wounds thine honour that I speak it now—
Was borne so like a soldier that thy cheek
So much as lank'd not.

Lep.   'Tis pity of him.

Cæs. Let his shames quickly
Drive him to Rome: 'tis time we twain
Did show ourselves i' the field; and to that end
Assemble we immediate council: Pompey
Thrives in our idleness.

Lep.   To-morrow, Cæsar,
I shall be furnish'd to inform you rightly
Both what by sea and land I can be able
To front this present time.

Cæs.   Till which encounter,
It is my business too.   Farewell.

Lep. Farewell, my lord: what you shall know meantime
Of stirs abroad, I shall beseech you, sir,
To let me be partaker.

Cæs.   Doubt not, sir;
I knew it for my bond.   [*Exeunt.*

SCENE V

Alexandria.   Cleopatra's palace.

Enter Cleopatra, Charmian, Iras, and Mardian.

Cleo. Charmian!

Char. Madam?

Cleo. Ha, ha!
Give me to drink mandragora.

Char.   Why, madam?

Cleo. That I might sleep out this great gap of time
  My Antony is away.
Char.   You think of him too much.
Cleo. O, 'tis treason !
Char.   Madam, I trust, not so.
Cleo. Thou, eunuch Mardian !
Mar.   What's your highness' pleasure ?
Cleo. Not now to hear thee sing ; I take no pleasure
  In aught an eunuch has : 'tis well for thee,
  That, being unseminar'd, thy freer thoughts
  May not fly forth of Egypt. Hast thou affections ?
Mar. Yes, gracious madam.
Cleo. Indeed !
Mar. Not in deed, madam ; for I can do nothing
  But what indeed is honest to be done :
  Yet have I fierce affections, and think
  What Venus did with Mars.
Cleo.   O Charmian,
  Where think'st thou he is now ? Stands he, or sits he ?
  Or does he walk ? or is he on his horse ?
  O happy horse, to bear the weight of Antony !
  Do bravely, horse ! for wot'st thou whom thou movest ?
  The demi-Atlas of this earth, the arm
  And burgonet of men. He's speaking now,
  Or murmuring, ' Where's my serpent of old Nile ? '
  For so he calls me : now I feed myself
  With most delicious poison. Think on me,
  That am with Phœbus' amorous pinches black
  And wrinkled deep in time ! Broad-fronted Cæsar,
  When thou wast here above the ground, I was
  A morsel for a monarch : and great Pompey
  Would stand and make his eyes grow in my brow ;
  There would he anchor his aspect and die
  With looking on his life.

Enter Alexas.

Alex.   Sovereign of Egypt, hail !
Cleo. How much unlike art thou Mark Antony !
  Yet, coming from him, that great medicine hath
  With his tinct gilded thee.
  How goes it with my brave Mark Antony ?
Alex. Last thing he did, dear queen,
  He kiss'd—the last of many doubled kisses—
  This orient pearl. His speech sticks in my heart.
Cleo. Mine ear must pluck it thence.

Alex.   'Good friend,' quoth he,
'Say, the firm Roman to great Egypt sends
This treasure of an oyster; at whose foot,
To mend the petty present, I will piece
Her opulent throne with kingdoms; all the east,
Say thou, shall call her mistress.' So he nodded,
And soberly did mount an arm-gaunt steed,
Who neigh'd so high, that what I would have spoke
Was beastly dumb'd by him.

Cleo.   What, was he sad or merry?

Alex. Like to the time o' the year between the extremes
Of hot and cold, he was nor sad nor merry.

Cleo. O well divided disposition! Note him,
Note him, good Charmian, 'tis the man; but note him:
He was not sad, for he would shine on those
That make their looks by his; he was not merry,
Which seem'd to tell them his remembrance lay
In Egypt with his joy; but between both.
O heavenly mingle! Be'st thou sad or merry,
The violence of either thee becomes,
So does it no man else. Met'st thou my posts?

Alex. Ay, madam, twenty several messengers:
Why do you send so thick?

Cleo   Who's born that day
When I forget to send to Antony,
Shall die a beggar. Ink and paper, Charmian.
Welcome, my good Alexas. Did I, Charmian,
Ever love Cæsar so?

Char.   O that brave Cæsar!

Cleo. Be choked with such another emphasis!
Say, the brave Antony.

Char.   The valiant Cæsar!

Cleo. By Isis, I will give thee bloody teeth,
If thou with Cæsar paragon again
My man of men.

Char.   By your most gracious pardon,
I sing but after you.

Cleo.   My salad days,
When I was green in judgement: cold in blood,
To say as I said then! But come, away;
Get me ink and paper:
He shall have every day a several greeting,
Or I'll unpeople Egypt.

                                            [*Exeunt.*

ACT II—SCENE I

Messina.   Pompey's house.

Enter Pompey, Menecrates, and Menas, in warlike manner.

Pom. If the great gods be just, they shall assist
    The deeds of justest men.
Mene.   Know, worthy Pompey,
    That what they do delay, they not deny.
Pom. Whiles we are suitors to their throne, decays
    The thing we sue for.
Mene.   We, ignorant of ourselves,
    Beg often our own harms, which the wise powers
    Deny us for our good; so find we profit
    By losing of our prayers.
Pom.   I shall do well:
    The people love me, and the sea is mine;
    My powers are crescent, and my auguring hope
    Says it will come to the full.   Mark Antony
    In Egypt sits at dinner, and will make
    No wars without doors: Cæsar gets money where
    He loses hearts: Lepidus flatters both,
    Of both is flatter'd, but he neither loves,
    Nor either cares for him.
Men.   Cæsar and Lepidus
    Are in the field: a mighty strength they carry.
Pom. Where have you this? 'tis false.
Men.   From Silvius, sir.
Pom. He dreams: I know they are in Rome together,
    Looking for Antony.   But all the charms of love,
    Salt Cleopatra, soften thy waned lip!
    Let witchcraft join with beauty, lust with both!
    Tie up the libertine in a field of feasts,
    Keep his brain fuming; Epicurean cooks
    Sharpen with cloyless sauce his appetite;
    That sleep and feeding may prorogue his honour
    Even till a Lethe'd dulness!
                    Enter Varrius.
                    How now, Varrius!
Var. This is most certain that I shall deliver:
    Mark Antony is every hour in Rome
    Expected: since he went from Egypt 'tis
    A space for farther travel.
Pom.   I could have given less matter
    A better ear.   Menas, I did not think

This amorous surfeiter would have donn'd his helm
For such a petty war : his soldiership
Is twice the other twain : but let us rear
The higher our opinion, that our stirring
Can from the lap of Egypt's widow pluck
The ne'er-lust-wearied Antony.

Men.   I cannot hope
Cæsar and Antony shall well greet together :
His wife that 's dead did trespasses to Cæsar ;
His brother warr'd upon him ; although, I think,
Not moved by Antony.

Pom.   I know not, Menas,
How lesser enmities may give way to greater.
Were 't not that we stand up against them all,
'Twere pregnant they should square between themselves ;
For they have entertained cause enough
To draw their swords : but how the fear of us
May cement their divisions and bind up
The petty difference, we yet not know.
Be 't as our gods will have 't ! It only stands
Our lives upon to use our strongest hands.
Come, Menas.   [*Exeunt.*

Scene II

Rome.   The house of Lepidus.
Enter Enobarbus and Lepidus.

Lep. Good Enobarbus, 'tis a worthy deed,
And shall become you well, to entreat your captain
To soft and gentle speech.

Eno.   I shall entreat him
To answer like himself : if Cæsar move him,
Let Antony look over Cæsar's head
And speak as loud as Mars.   By Jupiter,
Were I the wearer of Antonius' beard,
I would not shave 't to-day.

Lep.   'Tis not a time
For private stomaching.

Eno.   Every time
Serves for the matter that is then born in 't.

Lep. But small to greater matters must give way.

Eno. Not if the small come first.

Lep.   Your speech is passion :
But, pray you, stir no embers up.   Here comes
The noble Antony.

Enter Antony and Ventidius.

Eno.   And yonder, Cæsar.

Enter Cæsar, Mæcenas, and Agrippa.

Ant. If we compose well here, to Parthia:
  Hark, Ventidius.

Cæs.   I do not know,
  Mæcenas; ask Agrippa.

Lep.   Noble friends,
  That which combined us was most great, and let not
  A leaner action rend us. What's amiss,
  May it be gently heard: when we debate
  Our trivial difference loud, we do commit
  Murder in healing wounds: then, noble partners,
  The rather for I earnestly beseech,
  Touch you the sourest points with sweetest terms,
  Nor curstness grow to the matter.

Ant.   'Tis spoken well.
  Were we before our armies and to fight,
  I should do thus.   *Flourish.*

Cæs. Welcome to Rome.

Ant. Thank you.

Cæs. Sit.

Ant. Sit, sir.

Cæs. Nay, then.

Ant. I learn, you take things ill which are not so,
  Or being, concern you not.

Cæs.   I must be laugh'd at,
  If, or for nothing or a little, I
  Should say myself offended, and with you
  Chiefly i' the world; more laugh'd at, that I should
  Once name you derogately, when to sound your name
  It not concern'd me.

Ant.   My being in Egypt, Cæsar,
  What was 't to you?

Cæs. No more than my residing here at Rome
  Might be to you in Egypt: yet, if you there
  Did practise on my state, your being in Egypt
  Might be my question.

Ant.   How intend you, practised?

Cæs. You may be pleased to catch at mine intent
  By what did here befal me. Your wife and brother
  Made wars upon me, and their contestation
  Was theme for you, you were the word of war.

Ant. You do mistake your business; my brother never
  Did urge me in his act: I did inquire it,

And have my learning from some true reports
That drew their swords with you.   Did he not rather
Discredit my authority with yours,
And make the wars alike against my stomach,
Having alike your cause? of this my letters
Before did satisfy you.   If you 'll patch a quarrel,
As matter whole you have not to make it with,
It must not be with this.

Cæs.   You praise yourself
By laying defects of judgement to me, but
You patch'd up your excuses.

Ant.   Not so, not so;
I know you could not lack, I am certain on 't,
Very necessity of this thought, that I,
Your partner in the cause 'gainst which he fought,
Could not with graceful eyes attend those wars
Which fronted mine own peace.   As for my wife,
I would you had her spirit in such another:
The third o' the world is yours, which with a snaffle
You may pace easy, but not such a wife.

Eno. Would we had all such wives, that the men might go to
wars with the women!

Ant. So much uncurbable, her garboils, Cæsar,
Made out of her impatience, which not wanted
Shrewdness of policy too, I grieving grant
Did you too much disquiet: for that you must
But say, I could not help it.

Cæs.   I wrote to you
When rioting in Alexandria; you
Did pocket up my letters, and with taunts
Did gibe my missive out of audience.

Ant.   Sir,
He fell upon me ere admitted: then
Three kings I had newly feasted and did want
Of what I was i' the morning: but next day
I told him of myself, which was as much
As to have ask'd him pardon.   Let this fellow
Be nothing of our strife; if we contend,
Out of our question wipe him.

Cæs.   You have broken
The article of your oath, which you shall never
Have tongue to charge me with.

Lep.   Soft, Cæsar!

Ant. No, Lepidus, let him speak:
The honour is sacred which he talks on now,

Supposing that I lack'd it.   But on, Cæsar;
The article of my oath.

Cæs. To lend me arms and aid when I required them;
The which you both denied.

Ant.   Neglected rather,
And then when poison'd hours had bound me up
From mine own knowledge.   As nearly as I may,
I 'll play the penitent to you : but mine honesty
Shall not make poor my greatness, nor my power
Work without it.   Truth is that Fulvia,
To have me out of Egypt, made wars here;
For which myself, the ignorant motive, do
So far ask pardon as befits mine honour
To stoop in such a case.

Lep.   'Tis noble spoken.

Mæc. If it might please you, to enforce no further
The griefs between ye : to forget them quite
Were to remember that the present need
Speaks to atone you.

Lep.   Worthily spoken, Mæcenas.

Eno. Or, if you borrow one another's love for the instant, you
may, when you hear no more words of Pompey, return it
again : you shall have time to wrangle in when you have
nothing else to do.

Ant. Thou art a soldier only : speak no more.

Eno. That truth should be silent I had almost forgot.

Ant. You wrong this presence ; therefore speak no more.

Eno. Go to, then ; your considerate stone.

Cæs. I do not much dislike the matter, but
The manner of his speech ; for 't cannot be
We shall remain in friendship, our conditions
So differing in their acts.   Yet, if I knew
What hoop should hold us stanch, from edge to edge
O' the world I would pursue it.

Agr.   Give me leave, Cæsar.

Cæs. Speak, Agrippa.

Agr. Thou hast a sister by the mother's side,
Admired Octavia : great Mark Antony
Is now a widower.

Cæs.   Say not so, Agrippa :
If Cleopatra heard you, your reproof
Were well deserved of rashness.

Ant. I am not married, Cæsar : let me hear
Agrippa further speak.

Agr. To hold you in perpetual amity,

To make you brothers and to knit your hearts
With an unslipping knot, take Antony
Octavia to his wife; whose beauty claims
No worse a husband than the best of men,
Whose virtue and whose general graces speak
That which none else can utter.   By this marriage
All little jealousies which now seem great,
And all great fears which now import their dangers,
Would then be nothing: truths would be tales,
Where now half tales be truths: her love to both
Would each to other and all loves to both
Draw after her.   Pardon what I have spoke,
For 'tis a studied, not a present thought,
By duty ruminated.

Ant.   Will Cæsar speak?
Cæs. Not till he hears how Antony is touch'd
With what is spoke already.
Ant.   What power is in Agrippa,
If I would say, ' Agrippa, be it so,'
To make this good?
Cæs.   The power of Cæsar, and
His power unto Octavia.
Ant.   May I never
To this good purpose, that so fairly shows,
Dream of impediment!   Let me have thy hand:
Further this act of grace; and from this hour
The heart of brothers govern in our loves
And sway out great designs!
Cæs.   There is my hand.
A sister I bequeath you, whom no brother
Did ever love so dearly: let her live
To join our kingdoms and our hearts; and never
Fly off our loves again!
Lep.   Happily, amen!
Ant. I did not think to draw my sword 'gainst Pompey
For he hath laid strange courtesies and great
Of late upon me: I must thank him only,
Lest my remembrance suffer ill report;
At heel of that, defy him.
Lep.   Time calls upon 's:
Of us must Pompey presently be sought,
Or else he seeks out us.
Ant.   Where lies he?
Cæs. About the Mount Misenum.
Ant.   What 's his strength

By land?

Cæs. Great and increasing : but by sea
  He is an absolute master.

Ant.   So is the fame.
  Would we had spoke together ! Haste we for it :
  Yet, ere we put ourselves in arms, dispatch we
  The business we have talk'd of.

Cæs.   With most gladness ;
  And do invite you to my sister's view,
  Whither straight I 'll lead you.

Ant.   Let us, Lepidus,
  Not lack your company.

Lep.   Noble Antony,
  Not sickness should detain me.

          [*Flourish. Exeunt Cæsar, Antony, and Lepidus.*

Mæc. Welcome from Egypt, sir.

Eno. Half the heart of Cæsar, worthy Mæcenas !
  My honourable friend, Agrippa !

Agr. Good Enobarbus !

Mæc. We have cause to be glad that matters are so well digested.
  You stayed well by 't in Egypt.

Eno. Ay, sir ; we did sleep day out of countenance,
  And made the night light with drinking.

Mæc. Eight wild-boars roasted whole at a breakfast, and but
  twelve persons there ; is this true ?

Eno. This was but as a fly by an eagle : we had much more
  monstrous matter of feast, which worthily deserved noting.

Mæc. She 's a most triumphant lady, if report be square to her.

Eno. When she first met Mark Antony, she pursed up his heart,
  upon the river of Cydnus.

Agr. There she appeared indeed, or my reporter devised well

Eno. I will tell you.   [for her.
  The barge she sat in, like a burnish'd throne,
  Burn'd on the water : the poop was beaten gold ;
  Purple the sails, and so perfumed that
  The winds were love-sick with them ; the oars were silver,
  Which to the tune of flutes kept stroke and made
  The water which they beat to follow faster,
  As amorous of their strokes. For her own person,
  It beggar'd all description : she did lie
  In her pavilion, cloth-of-gold of tissue,
  O'er-picturing that Venus where we see
  The fancy out-work nature : on each side her
  Stood pretty dimpled boys, like smiling Cupids,
  With divers-colour'd fans, whose wind did seem

    To glow the delicate cheeks which they did cool,
    And what they undid did.
Agr.   O, rare for Antony!
Eno. Her gentlewomen, like the Nereides,
    So many mermaids, tended her i' the eyes,
    And made their bends adornings : at the helm
    A seeming mermaid steers : the silken tackle
    Swell with the touches of those flower-soft hands,
    That yarely frame the office.   From the barge
    A strange invisible perfume hits the sense
    Of the adjacent wharfs.   The city cast
    Her people out upon her ; and Antony,
    Enthroned i' the market-place, did sit alone,
    Whistling to the air ; which, but for vacancy,
    Had gone to gaze on Cleopatra too,
    And made a gap in nature.
Agr.   Rare Egyptian!
Eno. Upon her landing, Antony sent to her,
    Invited her to supper : she replied,
    It should be better he became her guest,
    Which she entreated : our courteous Antony,
    Whom ne'er the word of 'No' woman heard speak,
    Being barber'd ten times o'er, goes to the feast,
    And, for his ordinary, pays his heart
    For what his eyes eat only.
Agr.   Royal wench !
    She made great Cæsar, lay his sword to bed :
    He plough'd her, and she cropp'd.
Eno.   I saw her once
    Hop forty paces through the public street;
    And having lost her breath, she spoke, and panted,
    That she did make defect perfection,
    And, breathless, power breathe forth.
Mæc. Now Antony must leave her utterly.
Eno. Never ; he will not :
    Age cannot wither her, nor custom stale
    Her infinite variety : other women cloy
    The appetites they feed, but she makes hungry
    Where most she satisfies : for vilest things
    Become themselves in her, that the holy priests
    Bless her when she is riggish.
Mæc. If beauty, wisdom, modesty, can settle
    The heart of Antony, Octavia is
Agr. A blessed lottery to him.
                        Let us go.

Good Enobarbus, make yourself my guest
Whilst you abide here.

Eno.   Humbly, sir, I thank you.   [*Exeunt.*

SCENE III

The same.   Cæsar's house.

Enter Antony, Cæsar, Octavia between them, and Attendants.

Ant. The world and my great office will sometimes
Divide me from your bosom.

Octa.   All which time
Before the gods my knee shall bow my prayers
To them for you.

Ant.   Good night, sir.   My Octavia,
Read not my blemishes in the world's report :
I have not kept my square ; but that to come
Shall all be done by the rule.   Good night, dear lady.
Good night, sir.

Cæs. Good night.   [*Exeunt all but Antony.*

Enter Soothsayer.

Ant. Now, sirrah, you do wish yourself in Egypt ?

Sooth. Would I had never come from thence, nor you thither !

Ant. If you can, your reason ?

Sooth.   I see it in
My notion, have it not in my tongue : but yet
Hie you to Egypt again.

Ant.   Say to me,
Whose fortunes shall rise higher, Cæsar's or mine ?

Sooth. Cæsar's.
Therefore, O Antony, stay not by his side :
Thy demon, that thy spirit which keeps thee, is
Noble, courageous, high, unmatchable,
Where Cæsar's is not ; but near him thy angel
Becomes a fear, as being o'erpower'd : therefore
Make space enough between you.

Ant.   Speak this no more.

Sooth. To none but thee ; no more but when to thee.
If thou dost play with him at any game,
Thou art sure to lose ; and, of that natural luck,
He beats thee 'gainst the odds : thy lustre thickens,
When he shines by : I say again, thy spirit
Is all afraid to govern thee near him,
But he away, 'tis noble.

Ant.   Get thee gone :
Say to Ventidius I would speak with him.   [*Exit Soothsayer.*
He shall to Parthia.   Be it art or hap,

He hath spoken true: the very dice obey him,
And in our sports my better cunning faints
Under his chance: if we draw lots, he speeds;
His cocks do win the battle still of mine
When it is all to nought, and his quails ever
Beat mine, inhoop'd, at odds.　I will to Egypt:
And though I make this marriage for my peace,
I' the east my pleasure lies.

Enter Ventidius.

　　　　　　　　　　O, come, Ventidius,
You must to Parthia: your commission 's ready;
Follow me, and receive 't.　　　　　　　　　　[*Exeunt.*

SCENE IV

The same.　A street.
Enter Lepidus, Mæcenas, and Agrippa.

Lep. Trouble yourselves no further: pray you, hasten
　Your generals after.
Agr.　　　　　　　Sir, Mark Antony
　Will e'en but kiss Octavia, and we 'll follow.
Lep. Till I shall see you in your soldier's dress,
　Which will become you both, farewell.
Mæc.　　　　　　　　　　We shall,
　As I conceive the journey, be at the Mount
　Before you, Lepidus.
Lep.　　　　　　Your way is shorter;
　My purposes do draw me much about:
　You 'll win two days upon me.
Mæc. }
Agr. }　　　　　　　Sir, good success!
Lep. Farewell.　　　　　　　　　　　　[*Exeunt.*

SCENE V

Alexandria.　Cleopatra's palace.
Enter Cleopatra, Charmian, Iras, and Alexas.

Cleo. Give me some music; music, moody food
　Of us that trade in love.
All.　　　　　　　The music, ho!

Enter Mardian the Eunuch.

Cleo. Let it alone; let 's to billiards: come, Charmian.
Char. My arm is sore: best play with Mardian.
Cleo. As well a woman with an eunuch play'd
　As with a woman.　Come, you 'll play with me, sir?
Mar. As well as I can, madam.
Cleo. And when good will is show'd, though 'to come to short,

The actor may plead pardon.   I'll none now:
Give me mine angle; we'll to the river: there,
My music playing far off, I will betray
Tawny-finn'd fishes; my bended hook shall pierce
Their slimy jaws, and as I draw them up,
I'll think them every one an Antony,
And say 'Ah, ha! you're caught.'
Char.   'Twas merry when
You wager'd on your angling; when your diver
Did hang a salt-fish on his hook, which he
With fervency drew up.
Cleo.   That time—O times!—
I laugh'd him out of patience, and that night
I laugh'd him into patience; and next morn,
Ere the ninth hour, I drunk him to his bed;
Then put my tires and mantles on him, whilst
I wore his sword Philippan.

Enter a Messenger.

                      O, from Italy!
Ram thou thy fruitful tidings in mine ears,
That long time have been barren.
Mess.   Madam, madam,—
Cleo. Antonius dead!   If thou say so, villain,
Thou kill'st thy mistress: but well and free,
If thou so yield him, there is gold, and here
My bluest veins to kiss: a hand that kings
Have lipp'd, and trembled kissing.
Mess. First, madam, he is well.
Cleo.   Why, there's more gold.
But, sirrah, mark, we use
To say the dead are well: bring it to that,
The gold I give thee will I melt and pour
Down thy ill-uttering throat.
Mess. Good madam, hear me.
Cleo.   Well, go to, I will;
But there's no goodness in thy face: if Antony
Be free and healthful,—so tart a favour
To trumpet such good tidings!   If not well,
Thou shouldst come like a Fury crown'd with snakes,
Not like a formal man.
Mess.   Will't please you hear me?
Cleo. I have a mind to strike thee ere thou speak'st:
Yet, if thou say Antony lives, is well,
Or friends with Cæsar, or not captive to him,
I'll set thee in a shower of gold, and hail

Rich pearls upon thee.

Mess.   Madam, he's well.

Cleo.   Well said.

Mess. And friends with Cæsar.

Cleo.   Thou'rt an honest man.

Mess. Cæsar and he are greater friends than ever.

Cleo. Make thee a fortune from me.

Mess.   But yet, madam,—

Cleo. I do not like 'But yet,' it does allay
   The good precedence; fie upon 'But yet'!
   'But yet' is as a gaoler to bring forth
   Some monstrous malefactor.   Prithee, friend,
   Pour out the pack of matter to mine ear,
   The good and bad together: he's friends with Cæsar,
   In state of health, thou say'st, and thou say'st, free.

Mess. Free, madam! no; I made no such report:
   He's bound unto Octavia.

Cleo.   For what good turn?

Mess. For the best turn i' the bed.

Cleo.   I am pale, Charmian.

Mess. Madam, he's married to Octavia.

Cleo. The most infectious pestilence upon thee!

                              [*Strikes him down.*

Mess. Good madam, patience.

Cleo.   What say you? Hence,

                              [*Strikes him again.*

   Horrible villain! or I'll spurn thine eyes
   Like balls before me; I'll unhair thy head:

                              [*She hales him up and down.*

   Thou shalt be whipp'd with wire, and stew'd in brine,
   Smarting in lingering pickle.

Mess.   Gracious madam,
   I that do bring the news made not the match.

Cleo. Say 'tis not so, a province I will give thee
   And make thy fortunes proud: the blow thou hadst
   Shall make thy peace for moving me to rage,
   And I will boot thee with what gift beside
   Thy modesty can beg.

Mess.   He's married, madam.

Cleo. Rogue, thou hast lived too long.   [*Draws a knife.*

Mess.   Nay, then I'll run.
   What mean you, madam? I have made no fault.   [*Exit.*

Char. Good madam, keep yourself within yourself:
   The man is innocent.

Cleo. Some innocents 'scape not the thunderbolt.

Melt Egypt into Nile ! and kindly creatures
Turn all to serpents !   Call the slave again:
Though I am mad, I will not bite him: call.
Char. He is afeard to come.
Cleo.   I will not hurt him.

                                   [*Exit Charmian.*

These hands do lack nobility, that they strike
A meaner than myself; since I myself
Have given myself the cause.

              Re-enter Charmian and Messenger.
                         Come hither, sir.

Though it be honest, it is never good
To bring bad news: give to a gracious message
An host of tongues, but let ill tidings tell
Themselves when they be felt.
Mess.   I have done my duty.
Cleo. Is he married?
I cannot hate thee worser than I do,
If thou again say ' Yes.'
Mess.   He's married, madam.
Cleo. The gods confound thee ! dost thou hold there still?
Mess. Should I lie, madam?
Cleo.   O, I would thou didst,
So half my Egypt were submerged and made
A cistern for scaled snakes !   Go get thee hence:
Hadst thou Narcissus in thy face, to me
Thou wouldst appear most ugly.   He is married?
Mess. I crave your highness' pardon.
Cleo.   He is married?
Mess. Take no offence that I would not offend you:
To punish me for what you make me do
Seems much unequal: he's married to Octavia.
Cleo. O, that his fault should make a knave of thee,
That art not what thou 'rt sure of!   Get thee hence:
The merchandise which thou hast brought from Rome
Are all too dear for me: lie they upon thy hand,
And be undone by 'em !   [*Exit Messenger.*
Char.   Good your highness, patience.
Cleo. In praising Antony, I have dispraised Cæsar.
Char. Many times, madam.
Cleo.   I am paid for 't now.
Lead me from hence;
I faint: O Iras, Charmian ! 'tis no matter.
Go to the fellow, good Alexas; bid him
Report the feature of Octavia, her years,

Her inclination; let him not leave out
The colour of her hair : bring me word quickly. [*Exit Alexas.*
Let him for ever go : let him not—Charmian,
Though he be painted one way like a Gorgon,
The other way 's a Mars. [*To Mardian*] Bid you Alexas
Bring me word how tall she is. Pity me, Charmian,
But do not speak to me. Lead me to my chamber. [*Exeunt.*

Scene VI

Near Misenum.

*Flourish. Enter Pompey and Menas from one side, with drum
and trumpet : at another, Cæsar, Antony, Lepidus, Enobarbus,
Mæcenas, with Soldiers marching.*

Pom. Your hostages I have, so have you mine;
　　And we shall talk before we fight.

Cæs.　　　　　　　　　　　　Most meet
That first we come to words ; and therefore have we
Our written purposes before us sent ;
Which, if thou hast consider'd, let us know
If 'twill tie up thy discontented sword
And carry back to Sicily much tall youth
That else must perish here.

Pom.　　　　　　　　　To you all three,
The senators alone of this great world,
Chief factors for the gods, I do not know
Wherefore my father should revengers want,
Having a son and friends ; since Julius Cæsar,
Who at Philippi the good Brutus ghosted,
There saw you labouring for him. What was 't
That moved pale Cassius to conspire, and what
Made the all-honour'd honest Roman, Brutus,
With the arm'd rest, courtiers of beautous freedom,
To drench the Capitol, but that they would
Have one man but a man ? And that is it
Hath made me rig my navy, at whose burthen
The anger'd ocean foams ; with which I meant
To scourge the ingratitude that despiteful Rome
Cast on my noble father.

Cæs.　　　　　　　　Take your time.

Ant. Thou canst not fear us, Pompey, with thy sails ;
We 'll speak with thee at sea : at land, thou know'st
How much we do o'ercount thee.

Pom.　　　　　　　　　　At land indeed
Thou dost o'ercount me of my father's house :

But since the cuckoo builds not for himself,
Remain in 't as thou mayst.

Lep.   Be pleased to tell us—
For this is from the present—how you take
The offers we have sent you.

Cæs.   There 's the point.

Ant. Which do not be entreated to, but weigh
What it is worth embraced.

Cæs.   And what may follow,
To try a larger fortune.

Pom.   You have made me offer
Of Sicily, Sardinia; and I must
Rid all the sea of pirates; then, to send
Measures of wheat to Rome! this 'greed upon
To part with unhack'd edges and bear back
Our targes undinted.

Cæs.   }
Ant.   }   That 's our offer.
Lep.   }

Pom.   Know then
I came before you here a man prepared
To take this offer: but Mark Antony
Put me to some impatience: though I lose
The praise of it by telling, you must know,
When Cæsar and your brother were at blows,
Your mother came to Sicily and did find
Her welcome friendly.

Ant.   I have heard it, Pompey,
And am well studied for a liberal thanks
Which I do owe you.

Pom.   Let me have your hand:
I did not think, sir, to have met you here.

Ant. The beds i' the east are soft; and thanks to you,
That call'd me timelier than my purpose hither;
For I have gain'd by 't.

Cæs.   Since I saw you last,
There is a change upon you.

Pom.   Well, I know not
What counts harsh fortune casts upon my face;
But in my bosom shall she never come,
To make my heart her vassal.

Lep.   Well met here.

Pom. I hope so, Lepidus. Thus we are agreed
I crave our composition may be written
And seal'd between us.

Cæs.   That's the next to do.

Pom. We'll feast each other ere we part, and let's
Draw lots who shall begin.

Ant.   That will I, Pompey.

Pom. No, Antony, take the lot:
But, first or last, your fine Egyptian cookery
Shall have the fame. I have heard that Julius Cæsar
Grew fat with feasting there.

Ant.   You have heard much.

Pom. I have fair meanings, sir.

Ant.   And fair words to them.

Pom. Then so much have I heard:
And I have heard, Apollodorus carried—

Eno. No more of that: he did so.

Pom.   What, I pray you?

Eno. A certain queen to Cæsar in a mattress.

Pom. I know thee now: how farest thou, soldier?

Eno.   Well;
And well am like to do, for I perceive
Four feasts are toward.

Pom.   Let me shake thy hand;
I never hated thee: I have seen thee fight,
When I have envied thy behaviour.

Eno.   Sir,
I never loved you much, but I ha' praised ye
When you have well deserved ten times as much
As I have said you did.

Pom.   Enjoy thy plainness,
It nothing ill becomes thee.
Aboard my galley I invite you all:
Will you lead, lords?

Cæs. ⎫
Ant. ⎬   Show us the way, sir.
Lep. ⎭

Pom.   Come.

[*Exeunt all but Menas and Enobarbus.*

Men. [*Aside*] Thy father, Pompey, would ne'er have made this
treaty.—You and I have known, sir.

Eno. At sea, I think.

Men. We have, sir.

Eno. You have done well by water.

Men. And you by land.

Eno. I will praise any man that will praise me; though it cannot be denied what I have done by land.

Men. Nor what I have done by water.

Eno. Yes, something you can deny for your own safety: you
have been a great thief by sea.

Men. And you by land.

Eno. There I deny my land service.   But give me your hand
Menas: if our eyes had authority, here they might take two
thieves kissing.

Men. All men's faces are true, whatsoe'er their hands are.

Eno. But there is never a fair woman has a true face.

Men. No slander; they steal hearts.

Eno. We came hither to fight with you.

Men. For my part, I am sorry it is turned to a drinking.
Pompey doth this day laugh away his fortune.

Eno. If he do, sure he cannot weep 't back again.

Men. You 've said, sir.   We looked not for Mark Antony here:
pray you, is he married to Cleopatra?

Eno. Cæsar's sister is called Octavia.

Men. True, sir; she was the wife of Caius Marcellus.

Eno. But she is now the wife of Marcus Antonius.

Men. Pray ye, sir?

Eno. 'Tis true.

Men. Then is Cæsar and he for ever knit together.

Eno. If I were bound to divine of this unity, I would not
prophesy so.

Men. I think the policy of that purpose made more in the
marriage than the love of the parties.

Eno. I think so too.   But you shall find, the band that seems
to tie their friendship together will be the very strangler of
their amity: Octavia is of a holy, cold and still conversation.

Men. Who would not have his wife so?

Eno. Not he that himself is not so; which is Mark Antony.
He will to his Egyptian dish again: then shall the sighs of
Octavia blow the fire up in Cæsar; and, as I said before,
that which is the strength of their amity shall prove the
immediate author of their variance.   Antony will use his
affection where it is: he married but his occasion here.

Men. And thus it may be.   Come, sir, will you aboard?   I
have a health for you.

Eno. I shall take it, sir: we have used our throats in Egypt.

Men. Come, let 's away.   [*Exeunt.*

SCENE VII

On board Pompey's galley, off Misenum.

Music plays.   Enter two or three Servants, with a banquet.

First Serv. Here they 'll be, man.   Some o' their plants are ill-
rooted already; the least wind i' the world will blow them down.

Sec. Serv. Lepidus is high-coloured.

First Serv. They have made him drink alms-drink.

Sec. Serv. As they pinch one another by the disposition, he
cries out 'No more;' reconciles them to his entreaty and
himself to the drink.

First Serv. But it raises the greater war between him and his
discretion.

Sec. Serv. Why, this it is to have a name in great men's fellowship: I had as lief have a reed that will do me no service as
a partisan I could not heave.

First Serv. To be called into a huge sphere, and not to be
seen to move in 't, are the holes where eyes should be,
which pitifully disaster the cheeks.

*A sennet sounded. Enter Cæsar, Antony, Lepidus, Pompey,
Agrippa, Mæcenas, Enobarbus, Menas, with other captains.*

Ant. [*To Cæsar*] Thus do they, sir: they take the flow o' the
By certain scales i' the pyramid; they know,   [Nile
By the height, the lowness, or the mean, if dearth
Or foison follow: the higher Nilus swells,
The more it promises: as it ebbs, the seedsman
Upon the slime and ooze scatters his grain,
And shortly comes to harvest.

Lep. You 've strange serpents there.

Ant. Ay, Lepidus.

Lep. Your serpent of Egypt is bred now of your mud by the
operation of your sun: so is your crocodile.

Ant. They are so.

Pom. Sit,—and some wine! A health to Lepidus!

Lep. I am not so well as I should be, but I 'll ne'er out.

Eno. Not till you have slept; I fear me you 'll be in till then.

Lep. Nay, certainly, I have heard the Ptolemies pyramises are
very goodly things; without contradiction, I have heard that

Men. [*Aside to Pom.*] Pompey, a word.

Pom. [*Aside to Men.*]   Say in mine ear: what is 't?

Men. [*Aside to Pom.*] Forsake thy seat, I do beseech thee
And hear me speak a word.   [captain,

Pom. [*Aside to Men.*]   Forbear me till anon.—
This wine for Lepidus?

Lep. What manner o' thing is your crocodile?

Ant. It is shaped, sir, like itself; and it is as broad as it hath
breadth: it is just so high as it is, and moves with its own
organs: it lives by that which nourisheth it; and the elements once out of it, it transmigrates.

Lep. What colour is it of?

194

Ant. Of its own colour too.

Lep. 'Tis a strange serpent.

Ant. 'Tis so.   And the tears of it are wet.

Cæs. Will this description satisfy him?   [epicure.

Ant. With the health that Pompey gives him, else he is a very

Pom. [*Aside to Men.*] Go hang, sir, hang!   Tell me of that?
Do as I bid you.—Where's this cup I call'd for?   [away!

Men. [*Aside to Pom.*] If for the sake of merit thou wilt hear me,
Rise from thy stool.

Pom. [*Aside to Men.*] I think thou'rt mad.   The matter?
                    [*Rises, and walks aside.*

Men. I have ever held my cap off to thy fortunes.

Pom. Thou hast served me with much faith.   What's else to
Be jolly, lords.   [say?

Ant.   These quick-sands, Lepidus,
Keep off them, for you sink.

Men. Wilt thou be lord of all the world?

Pom   What say'st thou?

Men. Wilt thou be lord of the whole world?   That's twice.

Pom. How should that be?

Men.   But entertain it,
And, though thou think me poor, I am the man
Will give thee all the world.

Pom   Hast thou drunk well?

Men. No, Pompey, I have kept me from the cup.
Thou art, if thou darest be, the earthly Jove:
Whate'er the ocean pales, or sky inclips,
Is thine, if thou wilt ha't.

Pom.   Show me which way.

Men. These three world-sharers, these competitors,
Are in thy vessel: let me cut the cable;
And, when we are put off, fall to their throats:
All there is thine.

Pom.   Ah, this thou shouldst have done,
And not have spoke on't!   In me 'tis villany;
In thee 't had been good service.   Thou must know,
'Tis not my profit that does lead mine honour;
Mine honour, it.   Repent that e'er thy tongue
Hath so betray'd thine act: being done unknown,
I should have found it afterwards well done,
But must condemn it now.   Desist, and drink.

Men. [*Aside*] For this
I'll never follow thy pall'd fortunes more.
Who seeks, and will not take when once 'tis offer'd,
Shall never find it more.

Pom   This health to Lepidus!
Ant. Bear him ashore. I'll pledge it for him, Pompey.
Eno. Here's to thee, Menas!
Men.   Enobarbus, welcome!
Pom. Fill till the cup be hid.
Eno. There's a strong fellow, Menas.
            [*Pointing to the Attendant who carries off Lepidus.*
Men. Why?
Eno. A' bears the third part of the world, man; see'st not?
Men. The third part then is drunk: would it were all,
    That it might go on wheels!
Eno. Drink thou; increase the reels.
Men. Come.
Pom. This is not yet an Alexandrian feast.
Ant. It ripens towards it. Strike the vessels, ho!
    Here's to Cæsar!
Cæs.   I could well forbear 't.
    It's monstrous labour, when I wash my brain
    And it grows fouler.
Ant.   Be a child o' the time.
Cæs. Possess it, I'll make answer:
    But I had rather fast from all four days
    Than drink so much in one.
Eno. [*To Antony*]   Ha, my brave emperor!
    Shall we dance now the Egyptian Bacchanals,
    And celebrate our drink?
Pom. Let's ha't, good soldier.
Ant. Come, let's all take hands,
    Till that the conquering wine hath steep'd our sense
    In soft and delicate Lethe.
Eno.   All take hands.
    Make battery to our ears with the loud music:
    The while I'll place you: then the boy shall sing;
    The holding every man shall bear as loud
    As his strong sides can volley.
            [*Music plays.   Enobarbus places them hand in hand*

THE SONG.

> Come, thou monarch of the vine,
> Plumpy Bacchus with pink eyne!
> In thy fats our cares be drown'd,
> With thy grapes our hairs be crown'd:
> Cup us, till the world go round,
> Cup us, till the world go round!

Cæs. What would you more? Pompey, good night. Good
  brother,
  Let me request you off: our graver business
  Frowns at this levity. Gentle lords, let's part;
  You see we have burnt our cheeks: strong Enobarb
  Is weaker than the wine; and mine own tongue
  Splits what it speaks: the wild disguise hath almost
  Antick'd us all. What needs more words? Good night.
  Good Antony, your hand.
Pom.   I'll try you on the shore.
Ant. And shall, sir: give's your hand.
Pom.   O Antony,
  You have my father's house,—But, what? we are friends.
  Come, down into the boat.
Eno.   Take heed you fall not.
                [*Exeunt all but Enobarbus and Menas.*
  Menas, I'll not on shore.
Men.   No, to my cabin.
  These drums! these trumpets, flutes! what!
  Let Neptune hear we bid a loud farewell
  To these great fellows: sound and be hang'd, sound out!
                  [*Sound a flourish, with drums.*
Eno. Hoo! says a'. There's my cap.
Men. Hoo! Noble captain, come.   [*Exeunt.*

ACT III—Scene I

A plain in Syria.

*Enter Ventidius as it were in triumph, with Silius, and other
  Romans, Officers, and soldiers; the dead body of Pacorus
  borne before him.*

Ven. Now, darting Parthia, art thou struck; and now
  Pleased fortune does of Marcus Crassus' death
  Make me revenger. Bear the king's son's body
  Before our army. Thy Pacorus, Orodes,
  Pays this for Marcus Crassus.
Sil.   Noble Ventidius,
  Whilst yet with Parthian blood thy sword is warm,
  The fugitive Parthians follow; spur through Media,
  Mesopotamia, and the shelters whither
  The routed fly: so thy grand captain Antony
  Shall set thee on triumphant chariots and
  Put garlands on thy head.
Ven.   O Silius, Silius,
  I have done enough: a lower place note well,

May make too great an act; for learn this, Silius,
Better to leave undone than by our deed
Acquire too high a fame when him we serve 's away.
Cæsar and Antony have ever won
More in their officer than person: Sossius,
One of my place in Syria, his lieutenant,
For quick accumulation of renown,
Which he achieved by the minute, lost his favour.
Who does i' the wars more than his captain can
Becomes his captain's captain: and ambition,
The soldier's virtue, rather makes choice of loss
Than gain which darkens him.
I could do more to do Antonius good,
But 'twould offend him, and in his offence
Should my performance perish.

Sil.   Thou hast, Ventidius, that
Without the which a soldier and his sword
Grants scarce distinction.   Thou wilt write to Antony?

Ven. I 'll humbly signify what in his name,
That magical word of war, we have effected;
How, with his banners and his well-paid ranks,
The ne'er-yet-beaten horse of Parthia
We have jaded out o' the field.

Sil.   Where is he now?

Ven. He purposeth to Athens: whither, with what haste
The weight we must convey with 's will permit,
We shall appear before him.   On, there; pass along!

                                              [*Exeunt.*

Scene II

Rome.   An ante-chamber in Cæsar's house.

Enter Agrippa at one door, and Enobarbus at another.

Agr. What, are the brothers parted?

Eno. They have dispatch'd with Pompey; he is gone;
The other three are sealing.   Octavia weeps
To part from Rome; Cæsar is sad, and Lepidus
Since Pompey's feast, as Mena says, is troubled
With the green sickness.

Agr.   'Tis a noble Lepidus.

Eno. A very fine one: O, how he loves Cæsar!

Agr. Nay, but how dearly he adores Mark Antony!

Eno. Cæsar? Why, he 's the Jupiter of men.

Agr. What 's Antony? The god of Jupiter.

Eno. Spake you of Cæsar? How! the nonpareil!

Agr. O Antony! O thou Arabian bird!

Eno. Would you praise Cæsar, say 'Cæsar': go no further.
Agr. Indeed, he plied them both with excellent praises
Eno. But he loves Cæsar best; yet he loves Antony:
  Ho! hearts, tongues, figures, scribes, bards, poets, cannot
  Think, speak, cast, write, sing, number—ho!—
  His love to Antony. But as for Cæsar,
  Kneel down, kneel down, and wonder.
Agr.   Both he loves.
Eno. They are his shards, and he their beetle. [*Trumpet within.*]
  This is to horse. Adieu, noble Agrippa.   [So;
Agr. Good fortune, worthy soldier, and farewell.

     Enter Cæsar, Antony, Lepidus, and Octavia.

Ant. No further, sir.
Cæs. You take from me a great part of myself;
  Use me well in 't. Sister, prove such a wife
  As my thoughts make thee, and as my farthest band
  Shall pass on thy approof. Most noble Antony,
  Let not the piece of virtue which is set
  Betwixt us as the cement of our love,
  To keep it builded, be the ram to batter
  The fortress of it; for better might we
  Have loved without this mean, if on both parts
  This be not cherish'd.
Ant.   Make me not offended
  In your distrust.
Cæs.   I have said.
Ant.   You shall not find,
  Though you be therein curious, the least cause
  For what you seem to fear: so, the gods keep you,
  And make the hearts of Romans serve your ends!
  We will here part.
Cæs. Farewell, my dearest sister, fare thee well:
  The elements be kind to thee, and make
  Thy spirits all of comfort! fare thee well.
Octa. My noble brother!
Ant. The April 's in her eyes: it is love's spring,
  And these the showers to bring it on. Be cheerful.
Octa. Sir, look well to my husband's house, and—
Cæs.   What,
  Octavia?
Octa. I 'll tell you in your ear.
Ant. Her tongue will not obey her heart, nor can
  Her heart inform her tongue, the swan's down-feather,
  That stands upon the swell at full of tide
  And neither way inclines.

Eno. [*Aside to Agr.*] Will Cæsar weep?
Agr. [*Aside to Eno.*]   He has a cloud in 's face.
Eno. [*Aside to Agr.*] He were the worse for that, were he a
  So is he, being a man.   [horse;
Agr. [*Aside to Eno.*] Why, Enobarbus,
  When Antony found Julius Cæsar dead,
  He cried almost to roaring; and he wept
  When at Philippi he found Brutus slain.
Eno. [*Aside to Agr.*] That year indeed he was troubled with a
  What willingly he did confound he wail'd,   [rheum;
  Believe 't, till I wept too.
Cæs.   No, sweet Octavia,
  You shall hear from me still; the time shall not
  Out-go my thinking on you.
Ant.   Come, sir, come;
  I 'll wrestle with you in my strength of love:
  Look, here I have you; thus I let you go,
  And give you to the gods.
Cæs.   Adieu; be happy!
Lep. Let all the number of the stars give light
  To thy fair way!
Cæs.   Farewell, farewell!   [*Kisses Octavia.*
Ant.   Farewell!
                                        [*Trumpets sound. Exeunt.*

Scene III

Alexandria.   Cleopatra's palace.

Enter Cleopatra, Charmain, Iras, and Alexas.

Cleo. Where is the fellow?
Alex.   Half afeard to come.
Cleo. Go to, go to.

                    Enter Messenger.
                    Come hither, sir.
Alex.   Good majesty,
  Herod of Jewry dare not look upon you
  But when you are well pleased.
Cleo.   That Herod's head
  I 'll have: but how, when Antony is gone
  Through whom I might command it?   Come thou near.
Mess. Most gracious majesty,—
Cleo.   Didst thou behold
  Octavia?
Mess. Ay, dread queen.
Cleo.   Where?
Mess.   Madam, in Rome

I look'd her in the face, and saw her led
Between her brother and Mark Antony.
Cleo. Is she as tall as me?
Mess.   She is not, madam.
Cleo. Didst hear her speak? is she shrill-tongued or low?
Mess. Madam, I heard her speak; she is low-voiced.
Cleo. That's not so good.   He cannot like her long.
Char. Like her!   O Isis! 'tis impossible.
Cleo. I think so, Charmian: dull of tongue and dwarfish.
   What majesty is in her gait?   Remember,
   If e'er thou look'dst on majesty.
Mess.   She creeps:
   Her motion and her station are as one;
   She shows a body rather than a life,
   A statue than a breather.
Cleo.   Is this certain?
Mess. Or I have no observance.
Char.   Three in Egypt
   Cannot make better note.
Cleo.   He's very knowing;
   I do perceive 't: there's nothing in her yet:
   The fellow has good judgement.
Char.   Excellent.
Cleo. Guess at her years, I prithee.
Mess.   Madam,
   She was a widow—
Cleo.   Widow!   Charmian, hark.
Mess. And I do think she's thirty.
Cleo. Bear'st thou her face in mind? is't long or round?
Mess. Round even to faultiness.
Cleo. For the most part, too, they are foolish that are so.
   Her hair, what colour?
Mess.   Brown, madam: and her forehead
   As low as she would wish it.
Cleo.   There's gold for thee.
   Thou must not take my former sharpness ill:
   I will employ thee back again; I find thee
   Most fit for business: go make thee ready;
   Our letters are prepared.   [*Exit Messenger.*
Char.   A proper man.
Cleo. Indeed, he is so: I repent me much
   That so I harried him.   Why, methinks, by him,
   This creature's no such thing.
Char.   Nothing, madam.
Cleo. The man hath seen some majesty, and should know.

Char. Hath he seen majesty ? Isis else defend,
   And serving you so long !
Cleo. I have one thing more to ask him yet, good Charmian :
   But 'tis no matter ; thou shalt bring him to me
   Where I will write. All may be well enough.
Char. I warrant you, madam.   [*Exeunt.*

SCENE IV

Athens. A room in Antony's house.
Enter Antony and Octavia.

Ant. Nay, nay, Octavia, not only that,
   That were excusable, that and thousands more
   Of semblable import, but he hath waged
   New wars 'gainst Pompey ; made his will, and read it
   To public ear :
   Spoke scantly of me : when perforce he could not
   But pay me terms of honour, cold and sickly
   He vented them ; most narrow measure lent me ;
   When the best hint was given him, he not took 't,
   Or did it from his teeth.
Octa.   O my good lord,
   Believe not all ; or, if you must believe,
   Stomach not all.   A more unhappy lady,
   If this division chance, ne'er stood between,
   Praying for both parts :
   The good gods will mock me presently,
   When I shall pray, 'O, bless my lord and husband !'
   Undo that prayer, by crying out as loud,
   'O, bless my brother !' Husband win, win brother,
   Prays, and destroys the prayer ; no midway
   'Twixt these extremes at all.
Ant.   Gentle Octavia,
   Let your best love draw to that point, which seeks
   Best to preserve it ; if I lose mine honour,
   I lose myself : better I were not yours
   Than yours so branchless.   But, as you requested,
   Yourself shall go between 's : the mean time, lady,
   I 'll raise the preparation of a war
   Shall stain your brother : make your soonest haste ;
   So your desires are yours.
Octa.   Thanks to my lord.
   The Jove of power make me most weak, most weak,
   Your reconciler ! Wars 'twixt your twain would be
   As if the world should cleave, and that slain men
   Should solder up the rift.

Ant. When it appears to you where this begins,
 Turn your displeasure that way ; for our faults
 Can never be so equal, that your love
 Can equally move with them.   Provide your going ;
 Choose your own company, and command what cost
 Your heart has mind to.   [*Exeunt.*

SCENE V

The same.   Another room.

Enter Enobarbus and Eros, meeting.

Eno. How now, friend Eros !

Eros. There 's strange news come, sir.

Eno. What, man ?

Eros. Cæsar and Lepidus have made wars upon Pompey.

Eno. This is old : what is the success ?

Eros. Cæsar, having made use of him in the wars 'gainst
 Pompey, presently denied him rivality ; would not let him
 partake in the glory of the action : and not resting here,
 accuses him of letters he had formerly wrote to Pompey ;
 upon his own appeal, seizes him : so the poor third is up,
 till death enlarge his confine.

Eno. Then, world, thou hast a pair of chaps, no more ;
 And throw between them all the food thou hast,
 They 'll grind the one the other.   Where 's Antony ?

Eros. He 's walking in the garden—thus ; and spurns
 The rush that lies before him ; cries ' Fool Lepidus ! '.
 And threats the throat of that his officer
 That murder'd Pompey.

Eno.   Our great navy 's rigg'd.

Eros. For Italy and Cæsar.   More, Domitius ;
 My lord desires you presently : my news
 I might have told hereafter.

Eno.   'Twill be naught :
 But let it be.   Bring me to Antony.

Eros. Come, sir.   [*Exeunt*

SCENE VI

Rome.   Cæsar' : house.

Enter Cæsar, Agrippa, and Mæcenas.

Cæs. Contemning Rome, he has done all this, and more,
 In Alexandria : here 's the manner of 't :
 I' the market-place, on a tribunal silver'd
 Cleopatra and himself in chairs of gold
 Were publicly enthroned : at the feet sat
 Cæsarion, whom they call my father's son,

And all the unlawful issue that their lust
Since then hath made between them.   Unto her
He gave the stablishment of Egypt; made her
Of lower Syria, Cyprus, Lydia,
Absolute queen.

Mæc.   This in the public eye?

Cæs. I' the common show-place, where they exercise.
His sons he there proclaim'd the kings of kings:
Great Media, Parthia, and Armenia,
He gave to Alexander; to Ptolemy he assign'd
Syria, Cilicia and Phœnicia: she
In the habiliments of the goddess Isis
That day appear'd, and oft before gave audience,
As 'tis reported, so.

Mæc.   Let Rome be thus
Inform'd.

Agr. Who, queasy with his insolence
Already, will their good thoughts call from him.

Cæs. The people know it, and have now received
His accusations.

Agr.   Who does he accuse?

Cæs. Cæsar: and that, having in Sicily
Sextus Pompeius spoil'd, we had not rated him
His part o' the isle: then does he say, he lent me
Some shipping unrestored: lastly, he frets
That Lepidus of the triumvirate
Should be deposed; and, being, that we detain
All his revenue.

Agr.   Sir, this should be answer'd.

Cæs. 'Tis done already, and the messenger gone.
I have told him, Lepidus was grown too cruel;
That he his high authority abused
And did deserve his change: for what I have conquer'd,
I grant him part; but then, in his Armenia
And other of his conquer'd kingdoms, I
Demand the like.

Mæc.   He'll never yield to that.

Cæs. Nor must not then be yielded to in this.

                    Enter Octavia, with her train.

Octa. Hail, Cæsar, and my lord! hail, most dear Cæsar!

Cæs. That ever I should call thee castaway!

Octa. You have not call'd me so, nor have you cause.

Cæs. Why have you stol'n upon us thus?   You come not
Like Cæsar's sister: the wife of Antony
Should have an army for an usher, and

The neighs of horse to tell of her approach
Long ere she did appear; the trees by the way
Should have borne men; and expectation fainted,
Longing for what it had not; nay, the dust
Should have ascended to the roof of heaven,
Raised by your populous troops: but you are come
A market-maid to Rome; and have prevented
The ostentation of our love, which, left unshown,
Is often left unloved: we should have met you
By sea and land, supplying every stage
With an augmented greeting.

Octa.   Good my lord,
To come thus was I not constrain'd, but did it
On my free will. My lord, Mark Antony,
Hearing that you prepared for war, acquainted
My grieved ear withal; whereon, I begg'd
His pardon for return.

Cæs.   Which soon he granted,
Being an obstruct 'tween his lust and him.

Octa. Do not say so, my lord.

Cæs.   I have eyes upon him,
And his affairs come to me on the wind.
Where is he now?

Octa.   My lord, in Athens.

Cæs. No, my most wronged sister; Cleopatra
Hath nodded him to her. He hath given his empire
Up to a whore; who now are levying
The kings o' the earth for war: he hath assembled
Bocchus, the king of Libya; Archelaus,
Of Cappadocia; Philadelphos, king
Of Paphlagonia; the Thracian king, Adallas;
King Malchus of Arabia; King of Pont;
Herod of Jewry; Mithridates, king
Of Comagene; Polemon and Amyntas,
The kings of Mede and Lycaonia,
With a more larger list of sceptres.

Octa.   Ay me, most wretched,
That have my heart parted betwixt two friends
That do afflict each other!

Cæs.   Welcome hither:
Your letters did withhold our breaking forth,
Till we perceived both how you were wrong led
And we in negligent danger. Cheer your heart:
Be you not troubled with the time, which drives
O'er your content these strong necessities;

But let determined things to destiny
Hold unbewail'd their way. Welcome to Rome;
Nothing more dear to me. You are abused
Beyond the mark of thought: and the high gods,
To do you justice, make them ministers
Of us and those that love you. Best of comfort;
And ever welcome to us.

Agr.   Welcome, lady.

Mæc. Welcome, dear madam.
Each heart in Rome does love and pity you:
Only the adulterous Antony, most large
In his abominations, turns you off;
And gives his potent regiment to a trull,
That noises it against us.

Octa.   Is it so, sir?

Cæs. Most certain. Sister, welcome: pray you,
Be ever known to patience: my dear'st sister! [*Exeunt.*

Scene VII

Near Actium. Antony's camp.

Enter Cleopatra and Enobarbus.

Cleo. I will be even with thee, doubt it not.

Eno. But why, why, why?

Cleo. Thou hast forspoke my being in these wars,
And say'st it is not fit.

Eno.   Well, is it, is it?

Cleo. If not denounced against us, why should not we
Be there in person?

Eno. [*Aside*]   Well, I could reply:
If we should serve with horse and mares together,
The horse were merely lost; the mares would bear
A soldier and his horse.

Cleo.   What is 't you say?

Eno. Your presence needs must puzzle Antony;
Take from his heart, take from his brain, from 's time,
What should not then be spared. He is already
Traduced for levity; and 'tis said in Rome
That Photinus, an eunuch and your maids
Manage this war.

Cleo.   Sink Rome, and their tongues rot
That speak against us! A charge we bear i' the war,
And, as the president of my kingdom, will
Appear there for a man. Speak not against it;
I will not stay behind.

Eno.   Nay, I have done.

Here comes the emperor.
                    Enter Antony and Canidius.
Ant.   Is it not strange, Canidius,
  That from Tarentum and Brundusium
  He could so quickly cut the Ionian sea,
  And take in Toryne?   You have heard on 't, sweet?
Cleo. Celerity is never more admired
  Than by the negligent.
Ant.   A good rebuke,
  Which might have well becomed the best of men,
  To taunt at slackness.   Canidius, we
  Will fight with him by sea.
Cleo.   By sea: what else?
Can. Why will my lord do so?
Ant.   For that he dares us to 't.
Eno. So hath my lord dared him to single fight.
Can. Ay, and to wage this battle at Pharsalia,
  Where Cæsar fought with Pompey: but these offers,
  Which serve not for his vantage, he shakes off,
  And so should you.
Eno.   Your ships are not well mann'd,
  Your mariners are muleters, reapers, people
  Ingross'd by swift impress; in Cæsar's fleet
  Are those that often have 'gainst Pompey fought:
  Their ships are yare, yours heavy: no disgrace
  Shall fall you for refusing him at sea,
  Being prepared for land.
Ant.   By sea, by sea.
Eno. Most worthy sir, you therein throw away
  The absolute soldiership you have by land,
  Distract your army, which doth most consist
  Of war-mark'd footmen, leave unexecuted
  Your own renowned knowledge, quite forgo
  The way which promises assurance, and
  Give up yourself merely to chance and hazard
  From firm security.
Ant.   I 'll fight at sea.
Cleo. I have sixty sails, Cæsar none better.
Ant. Our overplus of shipping will we burn;
  And, with the rest full-mann'd, from the head of Actium
  Beat the approaching Cæsar.   But if we fail,
  We then can do 't at land.
                    Enter a Messenger.
                    Thy business?
Mess. The news is true, my lord; he is descried;

207

Cæsar has taken Toryne.

Ant. Can he be there in person? 'tis impossible;
Strange that his power should be.   Canidius,
Our nineteen legions thou shalt hold by land,
And our twelve thousand horse.   We'll to our ships
Away, my Thetis!

Enter a Soldier.

How now, worthy soldier?

Sold. O noble emperor, do not fight by sea;
Trust not to rotten planks.   Do you misdoubt
This sword and these my wounds?   Let the Egyptians
And the Phœnicians go a-ducking: we
Have used to conquer, standing on the earth
And fighting foot to foot.

Ant.   Well, well: away!

[Exeunt Antony, Cleopatra, and Enobarbus.

Sold. By Hercules, I think I am i' the right.

Can. Soldier, thou art: but his whole action grows
Not in the power on 't: so our leader 's led,
And we are women's men.

Sold.   You keep by land
The legions and the horse whole, do you not?

Can. Marcus Octavius, Marcus Justeius,
Publicola and Cælius, are for sea:
But we keep whole by land.   This speed of Cæsar's
Carries beyond belief.

Sold.   While he was yet in Rome,
His power went out in such distractions as
Beguiled all spies.

Can.   Who's his lieutenant, hear you?

Sold. They say, one Taurus.

Can.   Well I know the man.

Enter a Messenger.

Mess. The emperor calls Canidius.

Can. With news the time's with labour, and throes forth
Each minute some.   *[Exeunt.*

SCENE VIII

A plain near Actium.

Enter Cæsar, and Taurus, with his army, marching.

Cæs. Taurus!

Taur. My lord?

Cæs. Strike not by land; keep whole: provoke not battle,
Till we have done at sea.   Do not exceed

The prescript of this scroll: our fortune lies
Upon this jump.   [*Exeunt.*

Scene IX
Another part of the plain.
Enter Antony and Enobarbus.

Ant. Set we our squadrons on yond side o' the hill,
In eye of Cæsar's battle; from which place
We may the number of the ships behold,
And so proceed accordingly.   [*Exeunt.*

Scene X
Another part of the plain.

Enter Canidius, marching with his land army one way; and
Taurus, the lieutenant of Cæsar, with his army, the other
way. After their going in, is heard the noise of a sea-fight.
Alarum. Enter Enobarbus.

Eno. Naught, naught, all naught! I can behold no longer!
The Antoniad, the Egyptian admiral,
With all their sixty, fly and turn the rudder:
To see't mine eyes are blasted.
                                    Enter Scarus.

Scar.   Gods and goddesses,
All the whole synod of them!
Eno.   What's thy passion?
Scar. The greater cantle of the world is lost
With very ignorance; we have kiss'd away
Kingdoms and provinces.
Eno.   How appears the fight?
Scar. On our side like the token'd pestilence,
Where death is sure. Yon ribaudred nag of Egypt—
Whom leprosy o'ertake!—i' the midst o' the fight,
When vantage like a pair of twins appear'd,
Both as the same, or rather ours the elder,—
The breese upon her, like a cow in June!—
Hoists sails and flies.
Eno. That I beheld:
Mine eyes did sicken at the sight, and could not
Endure a further view.
Scar.   She once being loof'd,
The noble ruin of her magic, Antony,
Claps on his sea-wing, and like a doting mallard,
Leaving the fight in height, flies after her:
I never saw an action of such shame;
Experience, manhood honour, ne'er before

Did violate so itself.

Eno.   Alack, alack !
                        Enter Canidius.

Can. Our fortune on the sea is out of breath,
  And sinks most lamentably.   Had our general
  Been what he knew himself, it had gone well:
  O, he has given example for our flight
  Most grossly by his own !

Eno. Ay, are you thereabouts ?   Why then good night,
  Indeed.

Can. Toward Peloponnesus are they fled.

Scar. 'Tis easy to 't ; and there I will attend
  What further comes.

Can.   To Cæsar will I render
  My legions and my horse : six kings already
  Show me the way of yielding.

Eno.   I 'll yet follow
  The wounded chance of Antony, though my reason
  Sits in the wind against me.   [*Exeunt.*

                        SCENE XI

                Alexandria.   Cleopatra's palace.
                Enter Antony with Attendants.

Ant. Hark ! the land bids me tread no more upon 't ;
  It is ashamed to bear me.   Friends, come hither ;
  I am so lated in the world that I
  Have lost my way for ever.   I have a ship
  Laden with gold ; take that, divide it ; fly,
  And make your peace with Cæsar.

All.   Fly ! not we.

Ant. I have fled myself, and have instructed cowards
  To run and show their shoulders.   Friends, be gone ;
  I have myself resolved upon a course
  Which has no need of you ; be gone :
  My treasure 's in the harbour, take it.   O,
  I follow'd that I blush to look upon :
  My very hairs do mutiny, for the white
  Reprove the brown for rashness, and they them
  For fear and doting.   Friends, be gone : you shall
  Have letters from me to some friends that will
  Sweep your way for you.   Pray you, look not sad,
  Nor make replies of loathness ; take the hint
  Which my despair proclaims ; let that be left
  Which leaves itself : to the sea-side straightway :
  I will possess you of that ship and treasure.

                          210

Leave me, I pray, a little: pray you now:
Nay, do so; for indeed I have lost command,
Therefore I pray you: I'll see you by and by.   [*Sits down*
          Enter Cleopatra led by Charmian and Iras; Eros following

Eros. Nay, gentle madam, to him, comfort him.

Iras. Do, most dear queen.

Char. Do! why, what else?

Cleo. Let me sit down.   O Juno!

Ant. No, no, no, no, no.

Eros. See you here, sir?

Ant. O fie, fie, fie!

Char. Madam!

Iras. Madam, O good empress!

Eros. Sir, sir!

Ant. Yes, my lord, yes; he at Philippi kept
His sword e'en like a dancer; while I struck
The lean and wrinkled Cassius; and 'twas I
That the mad Brutus ended: he alone
Dealt on lieutenantry and no practice had
In the brave squares of war: yet now—No matter.

Cleo. Ah! stand by.

Eros. The queen, my lord, the queen.

Iras. Go to him, madam, speak to him:
He is unqualitied with very shame.

Cleo. Well then, sustain me: O!

Eros. Most noble sir, arise; the queen approaches:
Her head's declined, and death will seize her, but
Your comfort makes the rescue.

Ant. I have offended reputation,
A most unnoble swerving.

Eros.   Sir, the queen.

Ant. O, whither hast thou led me, Egypt?   See,
How I convey my shame out of thine eyes
By looking back what I have left behind
Stroy'd in dishonour.

Cleo.   O my lord, my lord,
Forgive my fearful sails! I little thought
You would have follow'd.

Ant.   Egypt, thou knew'st too well
My heart was to thy rudder tied by the strings,
And thou shouldst tow me after: o'er my spirit
Thy full supremacy thou knew'st, and that
Thy beck might from the bidding of the gods
Command me.

Cleo.   O, my pardon!

211

Ant.   Now I must
  To the young man send humble treaties, dodge
  And palter in the shifts of lowness; who
  With half the bulk o' the world play'd as I pleased,
  Making and marring fortunes. You did know
  How much you were my conqueror, and that
  My sword, made weak by my affection, would
  Obey it on all cause.
Cleo.   Pardon, pardon!
Ant. Fall not a tear, I say; one of them rates
  All that is won and lost: give me a kiss;
  Even this repays me. We sent our schoolmaster;
  Is he come back? Love, I am full of lead.
  Some wine, within there, and our viands! Fortune knows
  We scorn her most when most she offers blows.   [*Exeunt.*

SCENE XII

Egypt. Cæsar's camp.

Enter Cæsar, Dolabella, Thyreus, with others.

Cæs. Let him appear that 's come from Antony.
  Know you him?
Dol.   Cæsar, 'tis his schoolmaster:
  An argument that he is pluck'd, when hither
  He sends so poor a pinion of his wing,
  Which had superfluous kings for messengers
  Not many moons gone by.

Enter Euphronius, ambassador from Antony.

Cæs.   Approach, and speak.
Euph. Such as I am, I come from Antony:
  I was of late as petty to his ends
  As is the morn-dew on the myrtle-leaf
  To his grand sea.
Cæs.   Be 't so: declare thine office.
Euph. Lord of his fortunes he salutes thee, and
  Requires to live in Egypt: which not granted,
  He lessens his requests, and to thee sues
  To let him breathe between the heavens and earth,
  A private man in Athens: this for him.
  Next, Cleopatra does confess thy greatness;
  Submits her to thy might, and of thee craves
  The circle of the Ptolemies for her heirs,
  Now hazarded to thy grace.
Cæs.   For Antony,
  I have no ears to his request. The queen
  Of audience nor desire shall fail, so she

From Egypt drive her all-disgraced friend,
Or take his life there : this if she perform,
She shall not sue unheard. So to them both.
Euph. Fortune pursue thee !
Cæs.   Bring him through the bands.
                              [*Exit Euphronius.*
[*To Thyreus*] To try thy eloquence, now 'tis time: dispatch;
From Antony win Cleopatra : promise,
And in our name, what she requires ; add more,
From thine invention, offers : women are not
In their best fortunes strong, but want will perjure
The ne'er-touch'd vestal : try thy cunning, Thyreus ;
Make thine own edict for thy pains, which we
Will answer as a law.
Thyr.   Cæsar, I go.
Cæs. Observe how Antony becomes his flaw,
And what thou think'st his very action speaks
In every power that moves.
Thyr.   Cæsar, I shall.   [*Exeunt.*

Scene XIII

Alexandria. Cleopatra's palace.

Enter Cleopatra, Enobarbus, Charmian, and Iras.

Cleo. What shall we do, Enobarbus ?
Eno.   Think, and die.
Cleo. Is Antony or we in fault for this ?
Eno. Antony only, that would make his will
Lord of his reason. What though you fled
From that great face of war, whose several ranges
Frighted each other, why should he follow ?
The itch of his affection should not then
Have nick'd his captainship ; at such a point,
When half to half the world opposed, he being
The mered question : 'twas a shame no less
Than was his loss, to course your flying flags
And leave his navy gazing.
Cleo.   Prithee, peace.

Enter Antony, with Euphronius the Ambassador

Ant. Is that his answer ?
Euph. Ay, my lord.
Ant. The queen shall then have courtesy, so she
Will yield us up.
Euph.   He says so.
Ant.   Let her know 't.
To the boy Cæsar send this grizzled head,

    And he will fill thy wishes to the brim
    With principalities.
Cleo.   That head, my lord?
Ant. To him again: tell him he wears the rose
    Of youth upon him, from which the world should note
    Something particular: his coin, ships, legions,
    May be a coward's, whose ministers would prevail
    Under the service of a child as soon
    As i' the command of Cæsar: I dare him therefore
    To lay his gay comparisons apart
    And answer me declined, sword against sword,
    Ourselves alone.   I 'll write it: follow me.
                 [*Exeunt Antony and Euphronius.*
Eno. [*Aside*] Yes, like enough, high-battled Cæsar will
    Unstate his happiness and be staged to the show
    Against a sworder!   I see men's judgements are
    A parcel of their fortunes, and things outward
    Do draw the inward quality after them,
    To suffer all alike.   That he should dream,
    Knowing all measures, the full Cæsar will
    Answer his emptiness!   Cæsar, thou hast subdued
    His judgement too.

Enter an Attendant.

Att.   A messenger from Cæsar.
Cleo. What, no more ceremony? See, my women,
    Against the blown rose may they stop their nose
    That kneel'd unto the buds. Admit him, sir. [*Exit Attend.*
Eno. [*Aside*] Mine honesty and I begin to square.
    The loyalty well held to fools does make
    Our faith mere folly: yet he that can endure
    To follow with allegiance a fall'n lord
    Does conquer him that did his master conquer,
    And earns a place i' the story.

Enter Thyreus.

Cleo.   Cæsar's will?
Thyr. Hear it apart.
Cleo.   None but friends: say boldly.
Thyr. So, haply, are they friends to Antony.
Eno. He needs as many, sir, as Cæsar has,
    Or needs not us. If Cæsar please, our master
    Will leap to be his friend: for us, you know,
    Whose he is we are, and that is Cæsar's.
Thyr.   So.
    Thus then, thou most renown'd: Cæsar entreats

Not to consider in what case thou stand'st
Further than he is Cæsar.

Cleo.   Go on : right royal.

Thyr. He knows that you embrace not Antony
As you did love, but as you fear'd him.

Cleo.   O !

Thyr. The scars upon your honour therefore he
Does pity as constrained blemishes,
Not as deserved.

Cleo.   He is a god and knows
What is most right : mine honour was not yielded,
But conquer'd merely.

Eno. [*Aside*]   To be sure of that,
I will ask Antony.   Sir, sir, thou art so leaky
That we must leave thee to thy sinking, for
Thy dearest quit thee.   [*Exit.*

Thyr.   Shall I say to Cæsar
What you require of him ? for he partly begs
To be desired to give.   It much would please him,
That of his fortunes you should make a staff
To lean upon : but it would warm his spirits,
To hear from me you had left Antony,
And put yourself under his shrowd,
The universal landlord.

Cleo.   What 's your name ?

Thyr. My name is Thyreus.

Cleo.   Most kind messenger,
Say to great Cæsar this : in deputation
I kiss his conquering hand : tell him, I am prompt
To lay my crown at 's feet, and there to kneel :
Tell him, from his all-obeying breath I hear
The doom of Egypt.

Thyr.   'Tis your noblest course.
Wisdom and fortune combating together,
If that the former dare but what it can,
No chance may shake it.   Give me grace to lay
My duty on your hand.

Cleo.   Your Cæsar's father oft,
When he hath mused of taking kingdoms in,
Bestow'd his lips on that unworthy place,
As it rain'd kisses.

Re-enter Antony and Enobarbus.

Ant.   Favours, by Jove that thunders
What art thou, fellow ?

Thyr.   One that but performs
  The bidding of the fullest man and worthiest
  To have command obey'd.
Eno. [*Aside*]   You will be whipp'd.
Ant. Approach, there! Ah, you kite! Now, gods and devils!
  Authority melts from me: of late, when I cried 'Ho!'
  Like boys unto a muss, kings would start forth,
  And cry 'Your will?' Have you no ears?
  I am Antony yet.

                Enter Attendants.
           Take hence this Jack, and whip him.
Eno. [*Aside*] 'Tis better playing with a lion's whelp
  Than with an old one dying.
Ant.   Moon and stars!
  Whip him. Were 't twenty of the greatest tributaries
  That do acknowledge Cæsar, should I find them
  So saucy with the hand of she here,—what's her name,
  Since she was Cleopatra? Whip him, fellows,
  Till, like a boy, you see him cringe his face,
  And whine aloud for mercy : take him hence
Thyr. Mark Antony,—
Ant.   Tug him away: being whipp'd,
  Bring him again: this Jack of Cæsar's shall
  Bear us an errand to him. [*Exeunt Attendants, with Thyreus.*
  You were half blasted ere I knew you: ha!
  Have I my pillow left unpress'd in Rome,
  Forborne the getting of a lawful race,
  And by a gem of women, to be abused
  By one that looks on feeders?
Cleo.   Good, my lord,—
Ant. You have been a boggler ever:
  But when we in our viciousness grow hard—
  O misery on 't!—the wise gods seel our eyes;
  In our own filth drop our clear judgements; make us
  Adore our errors; laugh at 's while we strut
  To our confusion.
Cleo.   O, is 't come to this?
Ant. I found you as a morsel cold upon
  Dead Cæsar's trencher; nay, you were a fragment
  Of Cneius Pompey's; besides what hotter hours,
  Unregister'd in vulgar fame, you have
  Luxuriously pick'd out: for I am sure,
  Though you can guess what temperance should be,
  You know not what it is.
Cleo.   Wherefore is this?

Ant. To let a fellow what will take rewards
    And say 'God quit you!' be familiar with
    My playfellow, your hand, this kingly seal
    And plighter of high hearts! O, that I were
    Upon the hill of Basan, to outroar
    The horned herd! for I have savage cause;
    And to proclaim it civilly, were like
    A halter'd neck which does the hangman thank
    For being yare about him.

Re-enter Attendants, with Thyreus.

                    Is he whipp'd?
First Att. Soundly, my lord.
Ant.   Cried he? and begg'd he pardon?
First Att. He did ask favour.
Ant. If that thy father live, let him repent
    Thou wast not made his daughter; and be thou sorry
    To follow Cæsar in his triumph, since
    Thou hast been whipp'd for following him: henceforth
    The white hand of a lady fever thee,
    Shake thou to look on 't. Get thee back to Cæsar,
    Tell him thy entertainment: look thou say
    He makes me angry with him; for he seems
    Proud and disdainful, harping on what I am,
    Not what he knew I was: he makes me angry;
    And at this time most easy 'tis to do 't,
    When my good stars that were my former guides
    Have empty left their orbs and shot their fires
    Into the abysm of hell. If he mislike
    My speech and what is done, tell him he has
    Hipparchus, my enfranched bondman, whom
    He may at pleasure whip, or hang, or torture,
    As he shall like, to quit me: urge it thou:
    Hence with thy stripes, begone!   *[Exit Thyreus.*
Cleo. Have you done yet?
Ant.   Alack, our terrene moon
    Is now eclipsed, and it portends alone
    The fall of Antony.
Cleo.   I must stay his time.
Ant. To flatter Cæsar, would you mingle eyes
    With one that ties his points?
Cleo.   Not know me yet?
Ant. Cold-hearted toward me?
Cleo.   Ah, dear, if I be so,
    From my cold heart let heaven engender hail,

And poison it in the source, and the first stone
Drop in my neck : as it determines, so
Dissolve my life ! The next Cæsarion smite!
Till by degrees the memory of my womb,
Together with my brave Egyptians all,
By the discandying of this pelleted storm
Lie graveless, till the flies and gnats of Nile
Have buried them for prey!

Ant.   I am satisfied.
Cæsar sits down in Alexandria, where
I will oppose his fate. Our force by land
Hath nobly held ; our sever'd navy too
Have knit again, and fleet, threatening most sea-like.
Where hast thou been, my heart? Dost thou hear, lady?
If from the field I shall return once more
To kiss these lips, I will appear in blood ;
I and my sword will earn our chronicle :
There's hope in 't yet.

Cleo. That's my brave lord !

Ant. I will be treble-sinew'd, hearted, breath'd,
And fight maliciously : for when mine hours
Were nice and lucky, men did ransom lives
Of me for jests : but now I 'll set my teeth,
And send to darkness all that stop me. Come,
Let 's have one other gaudy night : call to me
All my sad captains ; fill our bowls once more :
Let 's mock the midnight bell.

Cleo.   It is my birth-day :
I had thought to have held it poor, but since my lord
Is Antony again, I will be Cleopatra.

Ant. We will yet do well.

Cleo. Call all his noble captains to my lord.

Ant. Do so, we 'll speak to them ; and to-night I 'll force
The wine peep through their scars. Come on, my queen ;
There's sap in 't yet. The next time I do fight
I 'll make death love me, for I will contend
Even with his pestilent scythe. [*Exeunt all but Enobarbus.*

Eno. Now he 'll outstare the lightning. To be furious
Is to be frighted out of fear ; and in that mood
The dove will peck the estridge ; and I see still,
A diminution in our captain's brain
Restores his heart : when valour plays on reason,
It eats the sword it fights with. I will seek
Some way to leave him.   [*Exit.*

ACT IV—Scene I

Before Alexandria.   Cæsar's camp.

Enter Cæsar, Agrippa, and Mecænas, with his army:
Cæsar reading a letter.

Cæs. He calls me boy, and chides as he had power
　　To beat me out of Egypt; my messenger
　　He hath whipp'd with rods; dares me to personal combat,
　　Cæsar to Antony.   Let the old ruffian know
　　I have many other ways to die, meantime
　　Laugh at his challenge.
Mec.　　　　　　Cæsar must think,
　　When one so great begins to rage, he's hunted
　　Even to falling.   Give him no breath, but now
　　Make boot of his distraction.   Never anger
　　Made good guard for itself.
Cæs.　　　　　　Let our best heads
　　Know that to-morrow the last of many battles
　　We mean to fight.   Within our files there are,
　　Of those that served Mark Antony but late,
　　Enough to fetch him in.   See it done:
　　And feast the army; we have store to do't,
　　And they have earn'd the waste.   Poor Antony!   [*Exeunt.*

Scene II

Alexandria.   Cleopatra's palace.

Enter Antony, Cleopatra, Enobarbus, Charmian, Iras,
Alexas, with others.

Ant. He will not fight with me, Domitius?
Eno.　　　　　　　　　　　　No.
Ant. Why should he not?
Eno. He thinks, being twenty times of better fortune,
　　He is twenty men to one.
Ant.　　　　　　To-morrow, soldier,
　　By sea and land I'll fight: or I will live,
　　Or bathe my dying honour in the blood
　　Shall make it live again.   Woo't thou fight well?
Eno. I'll strike, and cry 'Take all.'
Ant.　　　　　　Well said; come on.
　　Call forth my household servants: let's to-night
　　Be bounteous at our meal.
　　　　　　Enter three or four Servitors.
　　　　　　　　Give me thy hand,
　　Thou hast been rightly honest;—so hast thou;—
　　Thou,—and thou,—and thou: you have served me well,

And kings have been your fellows.

Cleo. [*Aside to Eno.*]   What means this?

Eno. [*Aside to Cleo.*] 'Tis one of those odd tricks which sorrow
Out of the mind.   [shoots

Ant.   And thou art honest too.
I wish I could be made so many men,
And all of you clapp'd up together in
An Antony, that I might do you service
So good as you have done.

Serv.   The gods forbid!

Ant. Well, my good fellows, wait on me to-night:
Scant not my cups, and make as much of me
As when mine empire was your fellow too
And suffer'd my command.

Cleo. [*Aside to Eno.*]   What does he mean?

Eno. [*Aside to Cleo.*] To make his followers weep.

Ant.   Tend me to-night:
May be it is the period of your duty:
Haply you shall not see me more; or if,
A mangled shadow: perchance to-morrow
You'll serve another master.   I look on you
As one that takes his leave.   Mine honest friends,
I turn you not away; but, like a master
Married to your good service, stay till death:
Tend me to-night two hours, I ask no more,
And the gods yield you for't!

Eno.   What mean you, sir,
To give them this discomfort?   Look, they weep,
And I, an ass, am onion-eyed: for shame,
Transform us not to women.

Ant.   Ho, ho, ho!
Now the witch take me, if I meant it thus
Grace grow where those drops fall!   My hearty friends,
You take me in too dolorous a sense;
For I spake to you for your comfort, did desire you
To burn this night with torches: know, my hearts,
I hope well of to-morrow, and will lead you
Where rather I'll expect victorious life
Than death and honour.   Let's to supper. come,
And drown consideration.   [*Exeunt.*

SCENE III

The same.   Before the palace.

Enter two Soldiers to their guard.

First Sold. Brother, good night: to-morrow is the day.

Sec. Sold. It will determine one way : fare you well.
　Heard you of nothing strange about the streets ?
First Sold. Nothing.　What news ?
Sec. Sold. Belike 'tis but a rumour.　Good night to you.
First Sold. Well, sir, good night.
　　　　　　　　Enter two other Soldiers.
Sec. Sold. Soldiers, have careful watch.
Third Sold. And you.　Good night, good night.
　　　　　[*They place themselves in every corner of the stage.*
Fourth Sold. Here we : and if to-morrow
　Our navy thrive, I have an absolute hope
　Our landmen will stand up.
Third Sold.　　　　　　　　'Tis a brave army,
　And full of purpose.
　　　　　　　　Music of hautboys as under the stage.
Fourth Sold.　　　　　Peace ! what noise ?
First Sold.　　　　　　　　　　　List, list !
Sec. Sold. Hark !
First Sold.　　　　Music i' the air.
Third Sold.　　　　　　　　　　Under the earth.
Fourth Sold. It signs well, does it not ?
Third Sold.　　　　　　　　　　No.
First Sold.　　　　　　　　　　　Peace, I say !
　What should this mean ?
Sec. Sold. 'Tis the god Hercules, whom Antony loved,
　Now leaves him.
First Sold. Walk ; let 's see if other watchmen
　Do hear what we do.
Sec. Sold. How now, masters !
All. [*Speaking together*] How now ! How now ! Do you hear
First Sold. Ay ; is 't not strange ?　　　　　　　　[this ?
Third Sold. Do you hear, masters ? do you hear ?
First Sold. Follow the noise so far as we have quarter ;
　Let 's see how it will give off.
All. Content.　'Tis strange.　　　　　　　　[*Exeunt.*

SCENE IV

The same.　A room in the palace.

Enter Antony and Cleopatra, Charmian and others attending.
Ant. Eros ! mine armour, Eros !
Cleo.　　　　　　　　　　Sleep a little.
Ant. No, my chuck.　Eros, come ; mine armour, Eros !
　　　　　　　　Enter Eros with armour.
　Come, good fellow, put mine iron on :

If fortune be not ours to-day, it is
Because we brave her : come.

Cleo.   Nay, I 'll help too.
What 's this for?

Ant.   Ah, let be, let be ! thou art
The armourer of my heart : false, false ; this, this.

Cleo. Sooth, la, I 'll help : thus it must be.

Ant.   Well, well ;
We shall thrive now.   Seest thou, my good fellow?
Go put on thy defences.

Eros.   Briefly, sir.

Cleo. Is not this buckled well?

Ant.   Rarely, rarely :
He that unbuckles this, till we do please
To daff't for our repose, shall hear a storm.
Thou fumblest, Eros ; and my queen 's a squire
More tight at this than thou : dispatch.   O love,
That thou couldst see my wars to-day, and knew'st
The royal occupation ! thou shouldst see
A workman in 't.

          Enter an armed Soldier.

        Good morrow to thee ; welcome :
Thou look'st like him that knows a warlike charge :
To business that we love we rise betime,
And go to 't with delight.

Sold.   A thousand, sir,
Early though 't be, have on their riveted trim,
And at the port expect you.   [*Shout. Trumpets flourish.*

       Enter Captains and Soldiers.

Capt. The morn is fair.   Good morrow, general.

All. Good morrow, general.

Ant.   'Tis well blown, lads :
This morning, like the spirit of a youth
That means to be of note, begins betimes.
So, so ; come, give me that : this way ; well said.
Fare thee well, dame, whate'er becomes of me :
This is a soldier's kiss : rebukeable
And worthy shameful check it were, to stand
On more mechanic compliment ; I 'll leave thee
Now like a man of steel.   You that will fight,
Follow me close ; I 'll bring you to 't.   Adieu.

    [*Exeunt Antony, Eros, Captains, and Soldiers.*

Char. Please you, retire to your chamber.

Cleo.   Lead me.
He goes forth gallantly.   That he and Cæsar might

Determine this great war in single fight !
Then Antony—but now—Well, on.   [*Exeunt.*

SCENE V

Alexandria.   Antony's camp.

Trumpets sound.   Enter Antony and Eros ; a Soldier
meeting them.

Sold. The gods make this a happy day to Antony !

Ant. Would thou and those thy scars had once prevail'd
   To make me fight at land !

Sold.   Hadst thou done so,
   The kings that have revolted and the soldier
   That has this morning left thee would have still
   Follow'd thy heels.

Ant.   Who 's gone this morning ?

Sold.   Who !
   One ever near thee : call for Enobarbus,
   He shall not hear thee, or from Cæsar's camp
   Say ' I am none of thine.'

Ant.   What say'st thou ?

Sold.   Sir,
   He is with Cæsar.

Eros.   Sir, his chests and treasure
   He has not with him.

Ant.   Is he gone ?

Sold.   Most certain.

Ant. Go, Eros, send his treasure after ; do it ;
   Detain no jot, I charge thee : write to him—
   I will subscribe—gentle adieus and greetings ;
   Say that I wish he never find more cause
   To change a master.   O, my fortunes have
   Corrupted honest men !   Dispatch.   Enobarbus ! [*Exeunt.*

SCENE VI

Alexandria.   Cæsar's camp.

Flourish.   Enter Cæsar with Agrippa, Enobarbus, and others.

Cæs. Go forth, Agrippa, and begin the fight :
   Our will is Antony be took alive ;
   Make it so known.

Agr. Cæsar, I shall.   [*Exit.*

Cæs. The time of universal peace is near :
   Prove this a prosperous day, the three-nook'd world
   Shall bear the olive freely.

Enter a Messenger.

Mess.   Antony

223

Is come into the field.
Cæs.   Go charge Agrippa
Plant those that have revolted in the van,
That Antony may seem to spend his fury
Upon himself.   [*Exeunt all but Enobarbus.*
Eno. Alexas did revolt, and went to Jewry
On affairs of Antony; there did persuade
Great Herod to incline himself to Cæsar
And leave his master Antony : for this pains
Cæsar hath hang'd him.   Canidius and the rest
That fell away have entertainment, but
No honourable trust.   I have done ill;
Of which I do accuse myself so sorely
That I will joy no more.

Enter a Soldier of Cæsar's.
Sold.   Enobarbus, Antony
Hath after thee sent all thy treasure, with
His bounty overplus : the messenger
Came on my guard, and at thy tent is now
Unloading of his mules.
Eno.   I give it you.
Sold. Mock not, Enobarbus :
I tell you true : best you safed the bringer
Out of the host; I must attend mine office,
Or would have done 't myself.   Your emperor
Continues still a Jove.   [*Exit.*
Eno. I am alone the villain of the earth,
And feel I am so most.   O Antony,
Thou mine of bounty, how wouldst thou have paid
My better service, when my turpitude
Thou dost so crown with gold!   This blows my heart:
If swift thought break it not, a swifter mean
Shall outstrike thought : but thought will do 't, I feel.
I fight against thee!   No: I will go seek
Some ditch wherein to die; the foul'st best fits
My latter part of life.   [*Exit.*

SCENE VII

Field of battle between the camps.

Alarum.   Drums and trumpets.   Enter Agrippa and others.
Agr. Retire, we have engaged ourselves too far :
Cæsar himself has work, and our oppression
Exceeds what we expected.   [*Exeunt.*
Alarums.   Enter Antony, and Scarus wounded.
Scar. O my brave emperor, this is fought indeed!
224

Had we done so at first, we had droven them home
With clouts about their heads.

Ant.   Thou bleed'st apace.

Scar. I had a wound here that was like a T,
But now 'tis made an H.   [*Retreat afar off.*

Ant.   They do retire.

Scar. We 'll beat 'em into bench-holes: I have yet
Room for six scotches more.

                Enter Eros.

Eros. They are beaten, sir, and our advantage serves
For a fair victory.

Scar.   Let us score their backs
And snatch 'em up, as we take hares, behind:
'Tis sport to maul a runner.

Ant.   I will reward thee
Once for thy spritely comfort, and ten-fold
For thy good valour.   Come thee on.

Scar.   I'll halt after. [*Exeunt.*

SCENE VIII

Under the walls of Alexandria.

Alarum.   Enter Antony, in a march; Scarus, with others.

Ant. We have beat him to his camp: run one before,
And let the queen know of our gests.   To-morrow,
Before the sun shall see 's, we 'll spill the blood
That has to-day escaped;
For doughty-handed are you, and have fought
Not as you served the cause, but as 't had been
Each man 's like mine; you have shown all Hectors.
Enter the city, clip your wives, your friends,
Tell them your feats; whilst they with joyful tears
Wash the congealment from your wounds and kiss
The honour'd gashes whole. [*To Scarus*] Give me thy hand;

            Enter Cleopatra, attended.

To this great fairy I 'll commend thy acts,
Make her thanks bless thee.   O thou day o' the world,
Chain mine arm'd neck; leap thou, attire and all,
Through proof of harness to my heart, and there
Ride on the pants triumphing!

Cleo.   Lord of lords!
O infinite virtue, comest thou smiling from
The world's great snare uncaught?

Ant.   My nightingale,
We have beat them to their beds.   What, girl! though grey
Do something mingle with our younger brown, yet ha' we

A brain that nourishes our nerves and can
Get goal for goal of youth.　Behold this man;
Commend unto his lips thy favouring hand:
Kiss it, my warrior: he hath fought to-day
As if a god in hate of mankind had
Destroy'd in such a shape.

Cleo.　　　　　　　　I 'll give thee, friend,
An armour all of gold; it was a king's.

Ant. He has deserved it, were it carbuncled
Like holy Phœbus' car.　Give me thy hand:
Through Alexandria make a jolly march;
Bear our hack'd targets like the men that owe them:
Had our great palace the capacity
To camp this host, we all would sup together
And drink carouses to the next day's fate,
Which promises royal peril.　Trumpeters,
With brazen din blast you the city's ear;
Make mingle with our rattling tabourines;
That heaven and earth may strike their sounds together,
Applauding our approach.　　　　　　　[*Exeunt.*

Scene IX

Cæsar's camp.

Sentinels at their post.

First Sold. If we be not relieved within this hour,
We must return to the court of guard: the night
Is shiny, and they say we shall embattle
By the second hour i' the morn.

Sec. Sold.　　　　　　　This last day was
A shrewd one to 's.

Enter Enobarbus.

Eno.　　　　　O, bear me witness, night,—

Third Sold. What man is this?

Sec. Sold.　　　　　Stand close, and list him.

Eno. Be witness to me, O thou blessed moon,
When men revolted, shall upon record
Bear hateful memory, poor Enobarbus did
Before thy face repent!

First Sold.　　　　　Enobarbus!

Third Sold.　　　　　　　　Peace!
Hark further.

Eno. O sovereign mistress of true melancholy,
The poisonous damp of night disponge upon me,
That life, a very rebel to my will,
May hang no longer on me: throw my heart

226

Against the flint and hardness of my fault;
Which, being dried with grief, will break to powder,
And finish all foul thoughts.   O Antony,
Nobler than my revolt is infamous,
Forgive me in thine own particular,
But let the world rank me in register
A master-leaver and a fugitive:
O Antony! O Antony!   [*Dies.*

Sec. Sold.   Let's speak to him.
First Sold. Let's hear him, for the things he speaks
    May concern Cæsar.
Third Sold.   Let's do so.   But he sleeps.
First Sold. Swoons rather; for so bad a prayer as his
    Was never yet for sleep.
Sec. Sold.   Go we to him.
Third Sold. Awake, sir, awake; speak to us.
Sec. Sold.   Hear you, sir?
First Sold. The hand of death hath raught him.   [*Drums
    afar off.*]   Hark! the drums
Demurely wake the sleepers.   Let us bear him
To the court of guard; he is of note: our hour
Is fully out.
Third Sold. Come on, then; he may recover yet.
                                    [*Exeunt with the body.*

SCENE X

Between the two camps.

Enter Antony and Scarus, with their army.

Ant. Their preparation is to-day by sea;
    We please them not by land.
Scar.   For both, my lord.
Ant. I would they 'ld fight i' the fire or i' the air;
    We 'ld fight there to.   But this it is; our foot
    Upon the hills adjoining to the city
    Shall stay with us: order for sea is given;
    They have put forth the haven. . . . .
    Where their appointment we may best discover,
    And look on their endeavour.   [*Exeunt.*

SCENE XI

Another part of the same.
Enter Cæsar, and his army.

Cæs. But being charged, we will be still by land,
    Which, as I take 't, we shall; for his best force
227

    Is forth to man his galleys.   To the vales,
    And hold our best advantage.   [*Exeunt.*

Scene XII

Hills adjoining to Alexandria.
Enter Antony and Scarus.

Ant. Yet they are not join'd : where yond pine does stand,
    I shall discover all : I 'll bring thee word
    Straight, how 'tis like to go.   [*Exit.*
Scar.   Swallows have built
    In Cleopatra's sails their nests : the augurers
    Say they know not, they cannot tell ; look grimly
    And dare not speak their knowledge.   Antony
    Is valiant, and dejected, and by starts
    His fretted fortunes give him hope, and fear,
    Of what he has, and has not.
          [*Alarum afar off, as at a sea-fight.*
          Re-enter Antony.

Ant.   All is lost ;
    This foul Egyptian hath betrayed me :
    My fleet hath yielded to the foe ; and yonder
    They cast their caps up and carouse together
    Like friends long lost.   Triple-turn'd whore ! 'tis thou
    Has sold me to this novice, and my heart
    Makes only wars on thee.   Bid them all fly ;
    For when I am revenged upon my charm,
    I have done all.   Bid them all fly ; begone.   [*Exit Scarus.*
    O sun, thy uprise shall I see no more :
    Fortune and Antony part here, even here
    Do we shake hands.   All come to this ?   The hearts
    That spaniel'd me at heels, to whom I gave
    Their wishes, do discandy, melt their sweets
    On blossoming Cæsar ; and this pine is bark'd,
    That overtopp'd them all.   Betray'd I am.
    O this false soul of Egypt ! this grave charm,
    Whose eye beck'd forth my wars and call'd them home,
    Whose bosom was my crownet, my chief end,
    Like a right gipsy hath at fast and loose
    Beguiled me to the very heart of loss.
    What, Eros, Eros !

          Enter Cleopatra.
          Ah, thou spell !   Avaunt !
Cleo. Why is my lord enraged against his love ?
Ant. Vanish, or I shall give thee thy deserving,
    And blemish Cæsar's triumph.   Let him take thee,

And hoist thee up to the shouting plebeians:
Follow his chariot, like the greatest spot
Of all thy sex: most monster-like, be shown
For poor'st diminutives, for doits; and let
Patient Octavia plough thy visage up
With her prepared nails.   [*Exit Cleopatra.*
                          'Tis well thou 'rt gone,
If it be well to live; but better 'twere
Thou fell'st into my fury, for one death
Might have prevented many. Eros, ho!
The shirt of Nessus is upon me: teach me,
Alcides, thou mine ancestor, thy rage:
Let me lodge Lichas on the horns o' the moon,
And with those hands that grasp'd the heaviest club
Subdue my worthiest self. The witch shall die:
To the young Roman boy she hath sold me, and I fall
Under this plot: she dies for 't. Eros, ho!   [*Exit.*

Scene XIII

Alexandria. Cleopatra's palace.

Enter Cleopatra, Charmian, Iras, and Mardian.

Cleo. Help me, my women! O, he is more mad
    Than Telamon for his shield; the boar of Thessaly
    Was never so emboss'd.
Char.   To the monument!
    There lock yourself, and send him word you are dead.
    The soul and body rive not more in parting
    Than greatness going off.
Cleo.   To the monument!
    Mardian, go tell him I have slain myself;
    Say that the last I spoke was 'Antony,'
    And word it, prithee, piteously: hence, Mardian,
    And bring me how he takes my death. To the monument!
                                          [*Exeunt.*

Scene XIV

The same. Another room.

Enter Antony and Eros.

Ant. Eros, thou yet behold'st me?
Eros.   Ay, noble lord.
Ant. Sometime we see a cloud that 's dragonish,
    A vapour sometime like a bear or lion,
    A tower'd citadel, a pendent rock,
    A forked mountain, or blue promontory
    With trees upon 't, that nod unto the world

And mock our eyes with air : thou hast seen these signs ;
They are black vesper's pageants.

Eros.   Ay, my lord.

Ant. That which is now a horse, even with a thought
   The rack dislimns and makes it indistinct
   As water is in water.

Eros.   It does, my lord.

Ant. My good knave Eros, now thy captain is
   Even such a body : here I am Antony,
   Yet cannot hold this visible shape, my knave.
   I made these wars for Egypt ; and the queen—
   Whose heart I thought I had, for she had mine,
   Which, whilst it was mine, had annex'd unto 't
   A million moe, now lost,—she, Eros, has
   Pack'd cards with Cæsar, and false-play'd my glory
   Unto an enemy's triumph.
   Nay, weep not, gentle Eros ; there is left us
   Ourselves to end ourselves.

                         Enter Mardian.

                         O, thy vile lady !
   She has robb'd me of my sword.

Mar.   No, Antony ;
   My mistress loved thee, and her fortunes mingled
   With thine entirely.

Ant.   Hence, saucy eunuch ; peace !
   She hath betray'd me, and shall die the death.

Mar. Death of one person can be paid but once,
   And that she has discharged : what thou wouldst do
   Is done unto thy hand : the last she spake
   Was 'Antony ! most noble Antony !'
   Then in the midst a tearing groan did break
   The name of Antony ; it was divided
   Between her heart and lips : she render'd life,
   Thy name so buried in her.

Ant.   Dead then ?

Mar.   Dead.

Ant. Unarm, Eros ; the long day's task is done,   [safe,
   And we must sleep. [*To Mar.*] That thou depart'st hence
   Does pay thy labour richly ; go.   [*Exit Mardian.*
                         Off, pluck off :
   The seven-fold shield of Ajax cannot keep
   The battery from my heart.   O, cleave, my sides !
   Heart, once be stronger than thy continent,
   Crack thy frail case !   Apace, Eros, apace !
   No more a soldier.   Bruised pieces, go ;

You have been nobly borne.   From me awhile. [*Exit Eros.*
I will o'ertake thee, Cleopatra, and
Weep for my pardon.   So it must be, for now
All length is torture : since the torch is out,
Lie down and stray no farther : now all labour
Mars what it does ; yea, very force entangles
Itself with strength : seal then, and all is done.
Eros !—I come, my queen.   Eros !—Stay for me :
Where souls do couch on flowers, we 'll hand in hand,
And with our sprightly port make the ghosts gaze :
Dido and her Æneas shall want troops,
And all the haunt be ours.   Come, Eros, Eros !
                        Re-enter Eros.
Eros. What would my lord ?
Ant.   Since Cleopatra died
I have lived in such dishonour that the gods
Detest my baseness.   I, that with my sword
Quarter'd the world, and o'er green Neptune's back
With ships made cities, condemn myself to lack
The courage of a woman ; less noble mind
Than she which by her death our Cæsar tells
' I am conqueror of myself.'   Thou art sworn, Eros,
That, when the exigent should come—which now
Is come indeed—when I should see behind me
The inevitable prosecution of
Disgrace and horror, that, on my command,
Thou then wouldst kill me : do 't ; the time is come :
Thou strikest not me, 'tis Cæsar thou defeat'st.
Put colour in thy cheek.
Eros.   The gods withhold me !
Shall I do that which all the Parthian darts,
Though enemy, lost aim and could not ?
Ant.   Eros,
Wouldst thou be window'd in great Rome, and see
Thy master thus with pleach'd arms, bending down
His corrigible neck, his face subdued
To penetrative shame, whilst the wheel'd seat
Of fortunate Cæsar, drawn before him, branded
His baseness that ensued ?
Eros.   I would not see 't.
Ant. Come, then ; for with a wound I must be cured.
Draw that thy honest sword, which thou hast worn
Most useful for thy country.
Eros.   O, sir, pardon me !
Ant. When I did make thee free, sworest thou not then

To do this when I bade thee ?　Do it at once;
Or thy precedent services are all
But accidents unpurposed.　Draw, and come.
Eros. Turn from me then that noble countenance,
　Wherein the worship of the whole world lies.
Ant. Lo thee !　　　　　　　　　　*[Turning from him.*
Eros. My sword is drawn.
Ant. 　　　　　　　Then let it do at once
　The thing why thou hast drawn it.
Eros. 　　　　　　　　　　My dear master,
　My captain, and my emperor, let me say,
　Before I strike this bloody stroke, farewell.
Ant. 'Tis said, man ; and farewell.
Eros. Farewell, great chief.　Shall I strike now?
Ant. 　　　　　　　　　　　　Now, Eros.
Eros. Why, there then : thus I do escape the sorrow
　Of Antony's death.　　　　　　　*[Kills himself.*
Ant. 　　　　　　　Thrice-nobler than myself !
　Thou teachest me, O valiant Eros, what
　I should and thou couldst not.　My queen and Eros
　Have by their brave instruction got upon me
　A nobleness in record : but I will be
　A bridegroom in my death, and run into 't
　As to a lover's bed.　Come then ; and, Eros,
　Thy master dies thy scholar : to do thus
　　　　　　　　　　　　[Falling on his sword.
　I learn'd of thee.　How ! not dead ? not dead ?
　The guard, ho !　O, dispatch me !
　　　　　　Enter Dercetas and Guard.
First Guard. 　　　　　　　What 's the noise?
Ant. I have done my work ill, friends : O, make an end
　Of what I have begun.
Sec. Guard. 　　　　　The star is fall'n.
First Guard. And time is at his period.
All. 　　　　　　　　　　　Alas, and woe !
Ant. Let him that loves me strike me dead.
First Guard. 　　　　　　　　Not I.
Sec. Guard. Nor I.
Third Guard. Nor any one.　　　　*[Exeunt Guard.*
Der. Thy death and fortunes bid thy followers fly.
　This sword but shown to Cæsar, with this tidings,
　Shall enter me with him.
　　　　　　　　Enter Diomedes.
Dio. Where 's Antony ?
Der. 　　　　　　　There, Diomed, there.

Dio.   Lives he?
    Wilt thou not answer, man?   [*Exit Dercetas.*
Ant. Art thou there, Diomed? Draw thy sword, and give me
    Sufficing strokes for death.
Dio.   Most absolute lord,
    My mistress Cleopatra sent me to thee.
Ant. When did she send thee?
Dio.   Now, my lord.
Ant.   Where is she?
Dio. Lock'd in her monument.   She had a prophesying fear
    Of what hath come to pass: for when she saw—
    Which never shall be found—you did suspect
    She had disposed with Cæsar, and that your rage
    Would not be purged, she sent you word she was dead;
    But, fearing since how it might work, hath sent
    Me to proclaim the truth; and I am come,
    I dread, too late.
Ant. Too late, good Diomed: call my guard, I prithee.
Dio. What, ho, the emperor's guard!   The guard, what, ho!
    Come, your lord calls.
                Enter four or five of the Guard of Antony.
Ant. Bear me, good friends, where Cleopatra bides;
    'Tis the last service that I shall command you.
First Guard. Woe, woe are we, sir, you may not live to wear
    All your true followers out.
All.   Most heavy day!
Ant. Nay, good my fellows, do not please sharp fate
    To grace it with your sorrows: bid that welcome
    Which comes to punish us, and we punish it
    Seeming to bear it lightly.   Take me up:
    I have led you oft: carry me now, good friends,
    And have my thanks for all.   [*Exeunt, bearing Antony.*

                        SCENE XV

                The same.   A monument.
*Enter Cleopatra, and her maids aloft, with Charmian,
                    and Iras.*

Cleo. O Charmian, I will never go from hence.
Char. Be comforted, dear madam.
Cleo.   No, I will not:
    All strange and terrible events are welcome,
    But comforts we despise; our size of sorrow,
    Proportion'd to our cause, must be as great
    As that which makes it.
                        233

Enter, below, Diomedes.
                        How now ! is he dead ?

Dio. His death 's upon him, but not dead.
　Look out o' the other side your monument ;
　His guard have brought him thither.

　　　　Enter, below, Antony, borne by the Guard.

Cleo.   O sun,
　Burn the great sphere thou movest in ! darkling stand
　The varying shore o' the world.   O Antony,
　Antony, Antony !   Help, Charmian, help, Iras, help ;
　Help, friends below ; let 's draw him hither.

Ant.   Peace !
　Not Cæsar's valour hath o'erthrown Antony,
　But Antony's hath triumph'd on itself.

Cleo. So it should be, that none but Antony
　Should conquer Antony ; but woe 'tis so !

Ant. I am dying, Egypt, dying ; only
　I here importune death awhile, until
　Of many thousand kisses the poor last
　I lay upon thy lips.

Cleo.   I dare not, dear,
　Dear my lord, pardon, I dare not,
　Lest I be taken : not the imperious show
　Of the full-fortuned Cæsar ever shall
　Be brooch'd with me ; if knife, drugs, serpents, have
　Edge, sting, or operation, I am safe :
　Your wife Octavia, with her modest eyes
　And still conclusion, shall acquire no honour
　Demuring upon me.   But come, come, Antony,—
　Help me, my women,—we must draw thee up ;
　Assist, good friends.

Ant.   O, quick, or I am gone.

Cleo. Here 's sport indeed !   How heavy weighs my lord !
　Our strength is all gone into heaviness ;
　That makes the weight.   Had I great Juno's power,
　The strong-wing'd Mercury should fetch thee up
　And set thee by Jove's side.   Yet come a little—
　Wishers were ever fools—O, come, come, come ;

　　　　　　[*They heave Antony aloft to Cleopatra.*

　And welcome, welcome ! die where thou hast lived :
　Quicken with kissing : had my lips that power,
　Thus would I wear them out.

All.   A heavy sight !

Ant. I am dying, Egypt, dying :
　Give me some wine, and let me speak a little.

234

Cleo. No, let me speak, and let me rail so high,
  That the false housewife Fortune break her wheel,
  Provoked by my offence.

Ant. One word, sweet queen:
  Of Cæsar seek your honour, with your safety. O!

Cleo. They do not go together.

Ant. Gentle, hear me:
  None about Cæsar trust but Proculeius.

Cleo. My resolution and my hands I'll trust;
  None about Cæsar.

Ant. The miserable change now at my end
  Lament nor sorrow at, but please your thoughts
  In feeding them with those my former fortunes
  Wherein I lived, the greatest prince o' the world,
  The noblest, and do now not basely die,
  Not cowardly put off my helmet to
  My countryman, a Roman by a Roman
  Valiantly vanquish'd. Now my spirit is going;
  I can no more.

Cleo. Noblest of men, woo't die?
  Hast thou no care of me? shall I abide
  In this dull world, which in thy absence is
  No better than a sty? O, see, my women,   [*Antony dies.*
  The crown o' the earth doth melt. My lord!
  O, wither'd is the garland of the war,
  The soldier's pole is fall'n: young boys and girls
  Are level now with men; the odds is gone,
  And there is nothing left remarkable
  Beneath the visiting moon.   [*Faints.*

Char. O, quietness, lady!

Iras. She's dead too, our sovereign.

Char. Lady!

Iras. Madam!

Char. O madam, madam, madam!

Iras. Royal Egypt,
  Empress!

Char. Peace, peace, Iras!

Cleo. No more, but e'en a woman, and commanded
  By such poor passion as the maid that milks
  And does the meanest chares. It were for me
  To throw my sceptre at the injurious gods,
  To tell them that this world did equal theirs
  Till they had stol'n our jewel. All's but naught;
  Patience is sottish, and impatience does
  Become a dog that's mad: then is it sin

To rush into the secret house of death,
Ere death dare come to us? How do you, women?
What, what! good cheer! Why, how now, Charmian!
My noble girls! Ah, women, women, look,
Our lamp is spent, it 's out! Good sirs, take heart:
We 'll bury him; and then, what 's brave, what 's noble,
Let 's do it after the high Roman fashion,
And make death proud to take us. Come, away:
This case of that huge spirit now is cold:
Ah, women, women! Come; we have no friend
But resolution and the briefest end.

            [Exeunt: those above bearing off Antony's body.

ACT V—SCENE I

Alexandria. Cæsar's camp.

Enter Cæsar, Agrippa, Dolabella, Mæcenas, Gallus, Proculeius,
and others, his council of war.

Cæs. Go to him, Dolabella, bid him yield;
  Being so frustrate, tell him he mocks
  The pauses that he makes.
Dol.   Cæsar, I shall.   *[Exit.*

    Enter Dercetas, with the sword of Antony.

Cæs. Wherefore is that? and what art thou that darest
  Appear thus to us?
Der.   I am call'd Dercetas;
  Mark Antony I served, who best was worthy
  Best to be served: whilst he stood up and spoke,
  He was my master, and I wore my life
  To spend upon his haters. If thou please
  To take me to thee, as I was to him
  I 'll be to Cæsar; if thou pleasest not,
  I yield thee up my life.
Cæs.   What is 't thou say'st?
Der. I say, O Cæsar, Antony is dead.
Cæs. The breaking of so great a thing should make
  A greater crack: the round world
  Should have shook lions into civil streets,
  And citizens to their dens. The death of Antony
  Is not a single doom; in the name lay
  A moiety of the world.
Der.   He is dead, Cæsar;
  Not by a public minister of justice,
  Nor by a hired knife; but that self hand,
  Which writ his honour in the acts it did,

Hath, with the courage which the heart did lend it,
Splitted the heart.   This is his sword ;
I robb'd his wound of it ; behold it stain'd
With his most noble blood.

Cæs.   Look you sad, friends?
The gods rebuke me, but it is tidings
To wash the eyes of kings.

Agr.   And strange it is
That nature must compel us to lament
Our most persisted deeds.

Mæc.   His taints and honours
Waged equal with him.

Agr.   A rarer spirit never
Did steer humanity : but you, gods, will give us
Some faults to make us men.   Cæsar is touch'd.

Mæc. When such a spacious mirror 's set before him,
He needs must see himself.

Cæs.   O Antony !
I have follow'd thee to this.   But we do lance
Diseases in our bodies : I must perforce
Have shown to thee such a declining day,
Or look on thine ; we could not stall together
In the whole world : but yet let me lament,
With tears as sovereign as the blood of hearts,
That thou, my brother, my competitor
In top of all design, my mate in empire,
Friend and companion in the front of war,
The arm of mine own body and the heart
Where mine his thoughts did kindle, that our stars
Unreconciliable should divide
Our equalness to this.   Hear me, good friends,—
                    Enter an Egyptian.
But I will tell you at some meeter season :
The business of this man looks out of him ;
We 'll hear him what he says.   Whence are you ?

Egyp. A poor Egyptian yet.   The queen my mistress,
Confined in all she has, her monument,
Of thy intents desires instruction,
That she preparedly may frame herself
To the way she 's forced to.

Cæs.   Bid her have good heart :
She soon shall know of us, by some of ours,
How honourable and how kindly we
Determine for her ; for Cæsar cannot live
To be ungentle.

Egyp.   So the gods preserve thee!   [*Exit*

Cæs. Come hither, Proculeius.   Go and say,
  We purpose her no shame: give her what comforts
  The quality of her passion shall require,
  Lest in her greatness by some mortal stroke
  She do defeat us; for her life in Rome
  Would be eternal in our triumph: go,
  And with your speediest bring us what she says
  And how you find of her.

Pro.   Cæsar, I shall.   [*Exit.*

Cæs. Gallus, go you along.   [*Exit Gallus.*]   Where's Dolabella,
  To second Proculeius?

All.   Dolabella!

Cæs. Let him alone, for I remember now
  How he's employ'd: he shall in time be ready.
  Go with me to my tent; where you shall see
  How hardly I was drawn into this war;
  How calm and gentle I proceeded still
  In all my writings: go with me, and see
  What I can show in this.   [*Exeunt.*

SCENE II

Alexandria.   The monument.

Enter Cleopatra, Charmian, and Iras.

Cleo. My desolation does begin to make
  A better life.   'Tis paltry to be Cæsar;
  Not being Fortune, he's but Fortune's knave,
  A minister of her will: and it is great
  To do that thing that ends all other deeds;
  Which shackles accidents and bolts up change;
  Which sleeps, and never palates more the dug,
  The beggar's nurse and Cæsar's.

*Enter, to the gates of the monument, Proculeius, Gallus, and
  Soldiers.*

Pro. Cæsar sends greeting to the Queen of Egypt,
  And bids thee study on what fair demands
  Thou mean'st to have him grant thee.

Cleo.   What's thy name?

Pro. My name is Proculeius.

Cleo.   Antony
  Did tell me of you, bade me trust you, but
  I do not greatly care to be deceived,
  That have no use for trusting.   If your master
  Would have a queen his beggar, you must tell him,
  That majesty, to keep decorum, must

No less beg than a kingdom : if he please
To give me conquer'd Egypt for my son,
He gives me so much of mine own as I
Will kneel to him with thanks.

Pro.   Be of good cheer;
You 're fall'n into a princely hand; fear nothing:
Make your full reference freely to my lord,
Who is so full of grace that it flows over
On all that need. Let me report to him
Your sweet dependency, and you shall find
A conqueror that will pray in aid for kindness,
Where he for grace is kneel'd to.

Cleo.   Pray you, tell him
I am his fortune's vassal and I send him
The greatness he has got. I hourly learn
A doctrine of obedience, and would gladly
Look him i' the face.

Pro.   This I 'll report, dear lady.
Have comfort, for I know your plight is pitied
Of him that caused it.

Gal. You see how easily she may be surprised.

> [*Here Proculeius and two of the Guard ascend the monument
> by a ladder placed against a window, and, having descended,
> come behind Cleopatra. Some of the Guard unbar and
> open the gates.*

Guard her till Cæsar come.   [*Exit.*

Iras. Royal queen !

Char. O Cleopatra ! thou art taken, queen !

Cleo. Quick, quick, good hands.   [*Drawing a dagger.*

Pro.   Hold, worthy lady, hold :
                              [*Seizes and disarms her.*
Do not yourself such wrong, who are in this
Relieved, but not betray'd.

Cleo.   What, of death too,
That rids our dogs of languish ?

Pro.   Cleopatra,
Do not abuse my master's bounty by
The undoing of yourself : let the world see
His nobleness well acted, which your death
Will never let come forth.

Cleo.   Where art thou, death ?
Come hither, come ! come, come, and take a queen
Worth many babes and beggars !

Pro.   O, temperance, lady

Cleo. Sir, I will eat no meat, I 'll not drink, sir ;

If idle talk will once be necessary,
I 'll not sleep neither: this mortal house I 'll ruin,
Do Cæsar what he can.   Know, sir, that I
Will not wait pinion'd at your master's court,
Nor once be chastised with the sober eye
Of dull Octavia.   Shall they hoist me up
And show me to the shouting varletry
Of censuring Rome?   Rather a ditch in Egypt
Be gentle grave unto me! rather on Nilus' mud
Lay me stark naked, and let the water-flies
Blow me into abhorring! rather make
My country's high pyramides my gibbet,
And hang me up in chains!

Pro.   You do extend
These thoughts of horror further than you shall
Find cause in Cæsar.

                            Enter Dolabella.

Dol.   Proculeius,
What thou hast done thy master Cæsar knows,
And he hath sent for thee: for the queen,
I 'll take her to my guard.

Pro.   So, Dolabella,
It shall content me best: be gentle to her.
[*To Cleo.*] To Cæsar I will speak what you shall please,
If you 'll employ me to him.

Cleo.   Say, I would die.
                    [*Exeunt Proculeius and Soldiers.*

Dol. Most noble empress, you have heard of me?
Cleo. I cannot tell.
Dol.   Assuredly you know me.
Cleo. No matter, sir, what I have heard or known.
You laugh when boys or women tell their dreams;
Is 't not your trick?
Dol.   I understand not, madam.
Cleo. I dream'd there was an emperor Antony:
O, such another sleep, that I might see
But such another man!
Dol.   If it might please ye,—
Cleo. His face was as the heavens; and therein stuck
A sun and moon, which kept their course, and lighted
The little O, the earth.
Dol.   Most sovereign creature,—
Cleo. His legs bestrid the ocean: his rear'd arm
Crested the world: his voice was propertied
As all the tuned spheres, and that to friends;

But when he meant to quail and shake the orb,
He was as rattling thunder. For his bounty,
There was no winter in 't ; an autumn 'twas
That grew the more by reaping : his delights
Were dolphin-like ; they show'd his back above
The element they lived in : in his livery
Walk'd crowns and crownets ; realms and islands were
As plates dropp'd from his pocket.

Dol. Cleopatra,—

Cleo. Think you there was, or might be, such a man
As this I dream'd of ?

Dol. Gentle madam, no.

Cleo. You lie, up to the hearing of the gods.
But if there be, or ever were, one such,
It 's past the size of dreaming : nature wants stuff
To vie strange forms with fancy ; yet to imagine
An Antony, were nature's piece 'gainst fancy,
Condemning shadows quite.

Dol. Hear me, good madam.
Your loss is as yourself, great ; and you bear it
As answering to the weight : would I might never
O'ertake pursued success, but I do feel,
By the rebound of yours, a grief that smites
My very heart at root.

Cleo. I thank you, sir.
Know you what Cæsar means to do with me ?

Dol. I am loath to tell you what I would you knew.

Cleo. Nay, pray you, sir,—

Dol. Though he be honourable,—

Cæs. He 'll lead me then in triumph ?

Dol. Madam, he will ; I know 't.
[*Flourish and shout within :* 'Make way there : Cæsar !'
*Enter Cæsar, Gallus, Proculeius, Mæcenas, Seleucus, and
others of his Train.*

Cæs. Which is the Queen of Egypt ?

Dol. It is the emperor, madam. [*Cleopatra kneels.*

Cæs. Arise, you shall not kneel :
I pray you, rise ; rise, Egypt.

Cleo. Sir, the gods
Will have it thus ; my master and my lord
I must obey.

Cæs. Take to you no hard thoughts :
The record of what injuries you did us,
Though written in our flesh, we shall remember
As things but done by chance.

Cleo.   Sole sir o' the world,
I cannot project mine own cause so well
To make it clear: but do confess I have
Been laden with like frailties which before
Have often shamed our sex.

Cæs.   Cleopatra, know,
We will extenuate rather than enforce:
If you apply yourself to our intents,
Which towards you are most gentle, you shall find
A benefit in this change; but if you seek
To lay on me a cruelty by taking
Antony's course, you shall bereave yourself
Of my good purposes and put your children
To that destruction which I'll guard them from
If thereon you rely.   I'll take my leave.

Cleo. And may, through all the world: 'tis yours; and we,
Your scutcheons and your signs of conquest, shall
Hang in what place you please.   Here, my good lord.

Cæs. You shall advise me in all for Cleopatra.

Cleo. This is the brief of money, plate and jewels,
I am possess'd of: 'tis exactly valued,
Not petty things admitted.   Where's Seleucus?

Sel. Here, madam.

Cleo. This is my treasurer: let him speak, my lord,
Upon his peril, that I have reserved
To myself nothing.   Speak the truth, Seleucus.

Sel. Madam,
I had rather seal my lips than to my peril
Speak that which is not.

Cleo.   What have I kept back?

Sel. Enough to purchase what you have made known.

Cæs. Nay, blush not, Cleopatra; I approve
Your wisdom in the deed.

Cleo.   See, Cæsar! O, behold,
How pomp is follow'd! mine will now be yours,
And, should we shift estates, yours would be mine.
The ingratitude of this Seleucus does
Even make me wild.   O slave, of no more trust
Than love that's hired!   What, goest thou back? thou shalt
Go back, I warrant thee; but I'll catch thine eyes,
Though they had wings: slave, soulless villain, dog!
O rarely base!

Cæs.   Good queen, let us entreat you.

Cleo. O Cæsar, what a wounding shame is this,
That thou vouchsafing here to visit me,

Doing the honour of thy lordliness
To one so meek, that mine own servant should
Parcel the sum of my disgraces by
Addition of his envy ! Say, good Cæsar,
That I some lady trifles have reserved,
Immoment toys, things of such dignity
As we greet modern friends withal ; and say,
Some nobler token I have kept apart
For Livia and Octavia, to induce
Their mediation ; must I be unfolded
With one that I have bred ? The gods ! it smites me
Beneath the fall I have. [*To Seleucus*] Prithee, go hence ;
Or I shall show the cinders of my spirits
Through the ashes of my chance : wert thou a man,
Thou wouldst have mercy on me.

Cæs.   Forbear, Seleucus. [*Exit Seleucus.*

Cleo. Be it known, that we, the greatest, are mis-thought
For things that others do, and when we fall,
We answer others' merits in our name,
Are therefore to be pitied.

Cæs.   Cleopatra,
Not what you have reserved, nor what acknowledged,
Put we i' the roll of conquest : still be 't yours,
Bestow it at your pleasure, and believe
Cæsar 's no merchant, to make prize with you
Of things that merchants sold. Therefore be cheer'd ;
Make not your thoughts your prisons : no, dear queen ;
For we intend so to dispose you as
Yourself shall give us counsel. Feed, and sleep :
Our care and pity is so much upon you
That we remain your friend ; and so, adieu.

Cleo. My master, and my lord !

Cæs.   Not so. Adieu.
                    [*Flourish.   Exeunt Cæsar and his train.*

Cleo. He words me, girls, he words me, that I should not
Be noble to myself : but, hark thee, Charmian.
                              [*Whispers Charmian.*

Iras. Finish, good lady ; the bright day is done,
And we are for the dark.

Cleo.   Hie thee again :
I have spoke already, and it is provided ;
Go put it to the haste.

Char.   Madam, I will.
                    Re-enter Dolabella.

Dol. Where is the queen ?

Char.   Behold, sir.   [*Exit.*
Cleo.   Dolabella!
Dol. Madam, as thereto sworn by your command,
    Which my love makes religion to obey,
    I tell you this: Cæsar through Syria
    Intends his journey, and within three days
    You with your children will he send before:
    Make your best of this: I have perform'd
    Your pleasure and my promise.
Cleo.   Dolabella,
    I shall remain your debtor.
Dol.   I your servant.
    Adieu, good queen; I must attend on Cæsar.
Cleo. Farewell, and thanks.   [*Exit Dolabella.*
                    Now, Iras, what think'st thou?
    Thou, an Egyptian puppet, shalt be shown
    In Rome, as well as I: mechanic slaves
    With greasy aprons, rules and hammers, shall
    Uplift us to the view: in their thick breaths,
    Rank of gross diet, shall we be enclouded
    And forced to drink their vapour.
Iras.   The gods forbid!
Cleo. Nay, 'tis most certain, Iras: saucy lictors
    Will catch at us like strumpets, and scald rhymers
    Ballad us out o' tune: the quick comedians
    Extemporally will stage us and present
    Our Alexandrian revels; Antony
    Shall be brought drunken forth, and I shall see
    Some squeaking Cleopatra boy my greatness
    I' the posture of a whore.
Iras.   O the good gods!
Cleo. Nay, that's certain.
Iras. I'll never see 't; for I am sure my nails
    Are stronger than mine eyes.
Cleo.   Why, that's the way
    To fool their preparation, and to conquer
    Their most absurd intents.

                    Re-enter Charmian.

                    Now, Charmian!
    Show me, my women, like a queen: go fetch
    My best attires: I am again for Cydnus,
    To meet Mark Antony: sirrah Iras, go.
    Now, noble Charmian, we'll dispatch indeed,
    And when thou hast done this chare I'll give thee leave

To play till doomsday.   Bring our crown and all.
                              [*Exit Iras.   A noise within.*
Wherefore 's this noise?
                    Enter a Guardsman.
Guard.   Here is a rural fellow
That will not be denied your highness' presence:
He brings you figs.
Cleo. Let him come in.   [*Exit Guardsman.*
                What poor an instrument
May do a noble deed! he brings me liberty.
My resolution 's placed, and I have nothing
Of woman in me: now from head to foot
I am marble-constant; now the fleeting moon
No planet is of mine.
     Re-enter Guardsman, with Clown bringing in a basket.
Guard.   This is the man.
Cleo. Avoid, and leave him.   [*Exit Guardsman.*
Hast thou the pretty worm of Nilus there,
That kills and pains not?
Clown. Truly, I have him: but I would not be the party that
    should desire you to touch him, for his biting is immortal;
    those that do die of it do seldom or never recover.
Cleo. Rememberest thou any that have died on 't?
Clown. Very many, men and women too.   I heard of one of
    them no longer than yesterday: a very honest woman, but
    something given to lie; as a woman should not do, but in
    the way of honesty: how she died of the biting of it, what
    pain she felt: truly, she makes a very good report o' the
    worm; but he that will believe all that they say, shall never
    be saved by half that they do: but this is most fallible, the
    worm 's an odd worm.
Cleo. Get thee hence; farewell.
Clown. I wish you all joy of the worm. [*Setting down his basket.*
Cleo. Farewell.
Clown. You must think this, look you, that the worm will do
Cleo. Ay, ay; farewell.   [his kind.
Clown. Look you, the worm is not to be trusted but in the
    keeping of wise people, for indeed there is no goodness in
    the worm.
Cleo. Take thou no care; it shall be heeded.
Clown. Very good.   Give it nothing, I pray you, for it is not
    worth the feeding.
Cleo. Will it eat me?
Clown. You must not think I am so simple but I know the
    devil himself will not eat a woman: I know that a woman is

a dish for the gods, if the devil dress her not. But, truly,
these same whoreson devils do the gods great harm in their
women; for in every ten that they make, the devils mar five
Cleo. Well, get thee gone; farewell.
Clown. Yes, forsooth: I wish you joy o' the worm.   [*Exit.*

Re-enter Iras with a robe, crown, &c.

Cleo. Give me my robe, put on my crown; I have
    Immortal longings in me: now no more
    The juice of Egypt's grape shall moist this lip:
    Yare, yare, good Iras; quick. Methinks I hear
    Antony call; I see him rouse himself
    To praise my noble act; I hear him mock
    The luck of Cæsar, which the gods give men
    To excuse their after wrath. Husband, I come:
    Now to that name my courage prove my title!
    I am fire and air; my other elements
    I give to baser life. So; have you done?
    Come then and take the last warmth of my lips.
    Farewell, kind Charmian; Iras, long farewell.
                [*Kisses them.   Iras falls and dies.*
    Have I the aspic in my lips? Dost fall?
    If thou and nature can so gently part,
    The stroke of death is as a lover's pinch,
    Which hurts, and is desired. Dost thou lie still?
    If thus thou vanishest, thou tell'st the world
    It is not worth leave-taking.
Char. Dissolve, thick cloud, and rain, that I may say
    The gods themselves do weep!
Cleo.   This proves me base:
    If she first meet the curled Antony,
    He'll make demand of her, and spend that kiss
    Which is my heaven to have. Come, thou mortal wretch,
                [*To an asp, which she applies to her breast.*
    With thy sharp teeth this knot intrinsicate
    Of life at once untie: poor venomous fool,
    Be angry, and dispatch. O, couldst thou speak,
    That I might hear thee call great Cæsar ass
    Unpolicied!
Char.   O eastern star!
Cleo.   Peace, peace!
    Dost thou not see my baby at my breast,
    That sucks the nurse asleep?
Char.   O, break! O, break!
Cleo. As sweet as balm, as soft as air, as gentle,—

O Antony!—Nay, I will take thee too:
     [Applying another asp to her arm.
What should I stay—   *[Dies.*
Char. In this vile world? So, fare thee well.
 Now boast thee, death, in thy possession lies
 A lass unparallel'd. Downy windows, close;
 And golden Phœbus never be beheld
 Of eyes again so royal! Your crown's awry
 I'll mend it, and then play.

    Enter the Guard, rushing in.

First Guard. Where is the queen?
Char.   Speak softy, wake her not.
First Guard. Cæsar hath sent—
Char.   Too slow a messenger. *[Applies an asp.*
 O, come apace, dispatch: I partly feel thee.
First Guard. Approach, ho! All's not well: Cæsar's beguiled.
Sec. Guard. There's Dolabella sent from Cæsar; call him.
First Guard. What work is here! Charmian, is this well done?
Char. It is well done, and fitting for a princess
 Descended of so many royal kings.
 Ah, soldier!   *[Dies.*

    Re-enter Dolabella.

Dol. How goes it here?
Sec. Guard.   All dead.
Dol.   Cæsar, thy thoughts
 Touch their effects in this: thyself art coming
 To see perform'd the dreaded act which thou
 So sought'st to hinder.
    [Within. 'A way there, a way for Cæsar!'
    Re-enter Cæsar and his train.

Dol. O sir, you are too sure an augurer;
 That you did fear is done.
Cæs.   Bravest at the last.
 She levell'd at our purposes, and being royal
 Took her own way. The manner of their deaths?
 I do not see them bleed.
Dol.   Who was last with them?
First Guard A simple countryman, that brought her figs:
 This was his basket.
Cæs.   Poison'd then.
First Guard.   O Cæsar,
 This Charmian lived but now; she stood and spake:
 I found her trimming up the diadem
 On her dead mistress; tremblingly she stood,
 And on the sudden dropp'd.

      247

Cas.   O noble weakness!
    If they had swallow'd poison, 'twould appear
    By external swelling: but she looks like sleep,
    As she would catch another Antony
    In her strong toil of grace.
Dol.   Here, on her breast,
    There is a vent of blood, and something blown:
    The like is on her arm.
First Guard. This is an aspic's trail: and these fig-leaves
    Have slime upon them, such as the aspic leaves
    Upon the caves of Nile.
Cas.   Most probable
    That so she died; for her physician tells me
    She hath pursued conclusions infinite
    Of easy ways to die.   Take up her bed,
    And bear her women from the monument:
    She shall be buried by her Antony:
    No grave upon the earth shall clip in it
    A pair so famous.   High events as these
    Strike those that make them; and their story is
    No less in pity than his glory which
    Brought them to be lamented.   Our army shall
    In solemn show attend this funeral,
    And then to Rome.   Come, Dolabella, see
    High order in this great solemnity.

                                            [*Exeunt.*

248

PERICLES, PRINCE OF TYRE

DRAMATIS PERSONÆ

ANTIOCHUS, *king of Antioch.*
PERICLES, *prince of Tyre.*
HELICANUS,
ESCANES, } *two lords of Tyre.*
SIMONIDES, *king of Pentapolis.*
CLEON, *governor of Tarsus.*
LYSIMACHUS, *governor of Mytilene.*
CERIMON, *a lord of Ephesus.*
THALIARD, *a lord of Antioch.*
PHILEMON, *servant to Cerimon.*

LEONINE, *servant to Dionyza.*
Marshal.   A Pandar.
BOULT, *his servant.*

The daughter of Antiochus.
DIONYZA, *wife to Cleon.*
THAISA, *daughter to Simonides.*
MARINA, *daughter to Pericles and Thaisa.*
LYCHORIDA, *nurse to Marina.*
A Bawd.

Lords, Knights, Gentlemen, Sailors, Pirates, Fishermen, and Messengers.
DIANA.
GOWER, *as Chorus.*
SCENE: *Dispersedly in various countries.*

ACT I

Enter Gower.

Before the palace of Antioch.

To sing a song that old was sung,
From ashes ancient Gower is come,
Assuming man's infirmities,
To glad your ear and please your eyes.
It hath been sung at festivals,
On ember-eves and holy-ales;
And lords and ladies in their lives
Have read it for restoratives:
The purchase is to make men glorious;
Et bonum quo antiquius, eo melius.
If you, born in these latter times
When wit's more ripe, accept my rhymes,
And that to hear an old man sing
May to your wishes pleasure bring,
I life would wish, and that I might
Waste it for you like taper-light.
This Antioch then Antiochus the Great
Built up, this city, for his chiefest seat,
The fairest in all Syria:
I tell you what mine authors say:
This king unto him took a fere,
Who died and left a female heir,
So buxom, blithe and full of face
As heaven had lent her all his grace;
With whom the father liking took,
And her to incest did provoke:
Bad child, worse father! to entice his own
To evil should be done by none:

But custom what they did begin
Was with long use account no sin.
The beauty of this sinful dame
Made many princes thither frame
To seek her as a bed-fellow,
In marriage-pleasures play-fellow:
Which to prevent he made a law,
To keep her still and men in awe,
That whoso ask'd her for his wife,
His riddle told not, lost his life:
So for her many a wight did die,
As yon grim looks do testify.
What now ensues, to the judgement of your eye
I give, my cause who best can justify.   [*Exit.*

SCENE I

Antioch. A room in the palace.

Enter Antiochus, Prince Pericles and Followers.

Ant. Young prince of Tyre, you have at large received
  The danger of the task you undertake.
Per. I have, Antiochus, and, with a soul
  Embolden'd with the glory of her praise,
  Think death no hazard in this enterprise.
Ant. Bring in our daughter, clothed like a bride,
  For the embracements even of Jove himself;
  At whose conception, till Lucina reign'd,
  Nature this dowry gave, to glad her presence,
  The senate-house of planets all did sit,
  To knit in her their best perfections.

Music.   Enter Antiochus' Daughter.

Per. See where she comes, apparell'd like the spring,
  Graces her subjects, and her thoughts the king
  Of every virtue gives renown to men!
  Her face the book of praises, where is read
  Nothing but curious pleasures, as from thence
  Sorrow were ever razed, and testy wrath
  Could never be her mild companion.
  You gods that made me man and sway in love,
  That have inflamed desire in my breast
  To taste the fruit of yon celestial tree
  Or die in the adventure, be my helps,
  As I am son and servant to your will,
  To compass such a boundless happiness!
Ant. Prince Pericles,—
Per. That would be son to great Antiochus.

Ant. Before thee stands this fair Hesperides,
   With golden fruit, but dangerous to be touch'd;
   For death-like dragons here affright thee hard:
   Her face, like heaven, enticeth thee to view
   Her countless glory, which desert must gain;
   And which, without desert, because thine eye
   Presumes to reach, all thy whole heap must die.
   Yon sometimes famous princes, like thyself,
   Drawn by report, adventurous by desire,
   Tell thee, with speechless tongues and semblance pale,
   That without covering, save yon field of stars,
   Here they stand martyrs, slain in Cupid's wars;
   And with dead cheeks advise thee to desist
   For going on death's net, whom none resist.

Per. Antiochus, I thank thee, who hath taught
   My frail mortality to know itself,
   And by those fearful objects to prepare
   This body, like to them, to what I must;
   For death remember'd should be like a mirror,
   Who tells us life's but breath, to trust it error.
   I'll make my will then, and, as sick men do,
   Who know the world, see heaven, but feeling woe
   Gripe not at earthly joys as erst they did,
   So I bequeath a happy peace to you
   And all good men, as every prince should do;
   My riches to the earth from whence they came;
   But my unspotted fire of love to you.   [*To the Princess.*
   Thus ready for the way of life or death,
   I wait the sharpest blow.

Ant. Scorning advice: read the conclusion then:
   Which read and not expounded, 'tis decreed,
   As these before thee thou thyself shalt bleed.

Daugh. Of all 'say'd yet, mayst thou prove prosperous!
   Of all 'say'd yet, I wish thee happiness!

Per. Like a bold champion I assume the lists,
   Nor ask advice of any other thought
   But faithfulness and courage.

He reads the riddle.

   'I am no viper, yet I feed
      On mother's flesh which did me breed.
   I sought a husband, in which labour
   I found that kindness in a father:
   He's father, son, and husband mild;
   I mother, wife, and yet his child.

251

How they may be, and yet in two,
   As you will live, resolve it you.'
[*Aside*] Sharp physic is the last : but, O you powers
That give heaven countless eyes to view men's acts,
Why cloud they not their sights perpetually,
If this be true, which makes me pale to read it ?
Fair glass of light, I love you, and could still,
Were not this glorious casket stored with ill :
But I must tell you, now my thoughts revolt ;
For he 's no man on whom perfections wait
That, knowing sin within, will touch the gate.
You are a fair viol and your sense the strings,
Who, finger'd to make man his lawful music,
Would draw heaven down and all the gods, to hearken,
But being play'd upon before your time,
Hell only danceth at so harsh a chime.
Good sooth, I care not for you.

Ant. Prince Pericles, touch not, upon thy life,
For that 's an article within our law,
As dangerous as the rest.   Your time 's expired :
Either expound now or receive your sentence.

Per. Great king,
Few love to hear the sins they love to act ;
'Twould braid yourself too near for me to tell it.
Who has a book of all that monarchs do,
He 's more secure to keep it shut than shown :
For vice repeated is like the wandering wind,
Blows dust in others' eyes, to spread itself ;
And yet the end of all is bought thus dear,
The breath is gone, and the sore eyes see clear
To stop the air would hurt them.   The blind mole casts
Copp'd hills towards heaven, to tell the earth is throng'd
By man's oppression ; and the poor worm doth die for 't.
Kings are earth's gods ; in vice their law 's their will ;
And if Jove stray, who dares say Jove doth ill ?
It is enough you know ; and it is fit,
What being more known grows worse, to smother it.
All love the womb that their first being bred,
Then give my tongue like leave to love my head. [meaning :

Ant. [*Aside*] Heaven, that I had thy head ! He has found the
But I will gloze with him.—Young prince of Tyre,
Though by the tenour of our strict edict,
Your exposition misinterpreting,
We might proceed to cancel of your days ;
Yet hope, succeeding from so fair a tree

As your fair self, doth tune us otherwise:
Forty days longer we do respite you;
If by which time our secret be undone,
This mercy shows we 'll joy in such a son:
And until then your entertain shall be
As doth befit our honour and your worth.

[*Exeunt all but Pericles.*

Per. How courtesy would seem to cover sin,
When what is done is like an hypocrite,
The which is good in nothing but in sight!
If it be true that I interpret false,
Then were it certain you were not so bad
As with foul incest to abuse your soul;
Where now you 're both a father and a son,
By your untimely claspings with your child,
Which pleasure fits a husband, not a father;
And she an eater of her mother's flesh,
By the defiling of her parent's bed;
And both like serpents are, who though they feed
On sweetest flowers, yet they poison breed.
Antioch, farewell! for wisdom sees, those men
Blush not in actions blacker than the night,
Will shun no course to keep them from the light.
One sin, I know, another doth provoke;
Murder 's as near to lust as flame to smoke:
Poison and treason are the hands of sin,
Ay, and the targets, to put off the shame:
Then, lest my life be cropp'd to keep you clear,
By flight I 'll shun the danger which I fear.   [*Exit.*

Re-enter Antiochus.

Ant. He hath found the meaning, for the which we mean
To have his head.
He must not live to trumpet forth my infamy,
Nor tell the world Antiochus doth sin
In such a loathed manner:
And therefore instantly this prince must die;
For by his fall my honour must keep high.
Who attends us there?

Enter Thaliard.

Thal. Doth your highness call?
Ant. Thaliard,
You are of our chamber, and our mind partakes
Her private actions to your secrecy:
And for your faithfulness we will advance you.
Thaliard, behold, here 's poison, and here 's gold;

We hate the prince of Tyre, and thou must kill him:
It fits thee not to ask the reason why,
Because we bid it. Say, is it done?
Thal. My lord,
'Tis done.
Ant. Enough.

Enter a Messenger.

Let your breath cool yourself, telling your haste.
Mess. My lord, prince Pericles is fled. [*Exit.*
Ant. As thou
Wilt live, fly after: and like an arrow shot
From a well experienced archer hits the mark
His eye doth level at, so thou ne'er return
Unless thou say 'Prince Pericles is dead.'
Thal. My lord,
If I can get him within my pistol's length,
I 'll make him sure enough: so, farewell to your highness.
Ant. Thaliard, adieu! [*Exit Thal.*] Till Pericles be dead,
My heart can lend no succour to my head. [*Exit.*

SCENE II

Tyre. A room in the palace.
Enter Pericles.

Per. [*To Lords without*] Let none disturb us. Why should this change of thoughts,
The sad companion, dull-eyed melancholy,
Be my so used a guest as not an hour,
In the day's glorious walk, or peaceful night,
The tomb where grief should sleep, can breed me quiet?
Here pleasures court mine eyes, and mine eyes shun them,
And danger, which I fear'd, is at Antioch,
Whose arm seems far too short to hit me here:
Yet neither pleasure's art can joy my spirits,
Nor yet the other's distance comfort me.
Then it is thus: the passions of the mind,
That have their first conception by mis-dread,
Have after-nourishment and life by care;
And what was first but fear what might be done,
Grows elder now, and cares it be not done.
And so with me: the great Antiochus,
'Gainst whom I am too little to contend,
Since he 's so great can make his will his act,
Will think me speaking, though I swear to silence;
Nor boots it me to say I honour him,
If he suspect I may dishonour him.

And what may make him blush in being known,
He'll stop the course by which it might be known:
With hostile forces he'll o'erspread the land,
And with the ostent of war will look so huge,
Amazement shall drive courage from the state,
Our men be vanquish'd ere they do resist,
And subjects punish'd that ne'er thought offence:
Which care of them, not pity of myself,
Who am no more but as the tops of trees
Which fence the roots they grow by and defend them,
Makes both my body pine and soul to languish,
And punish that before that he would punish.

Enter Helicanus, with other Lords.

First Lord. Joy and all comfort in your sacred breast!
Sec. Lord. And keep your mind, till you return to us,
  Peaceful and comfortable!
Hel. Peace, peace, and give experience tongue.
  They do abuse the king that flatter him:
  For flattery is the bellows blows up sin;
  The thing the which is flatter'd, but a spark,
  To which that blast gives heat and stronger glowing;
  Whereas reproof, obedient and in order,
  Fits kings, as they are men, for they may err.
  When Signior Sooth here does proclaim a peace,
  He flatters you, makes war upon your life.
  Prince, pardon me, or strike me, if you please;
  I cannot be much lower than my knees.
Per. All leave us else; but let your cares o'erlook
  What shipping and what lading's in our haven,
  And then return to us. [*Exeunt Lords.*] Helicanus, thou
  Hast moved us: what seest thou in our looks?
Hel. An angry brow, dread lord.
Per. If there be such a dart in princes' frowns,
  How durst thy tongue move anger to our face?
Hel. How dare the plants look up to heaven, from whence
  They have their nourishment?
Per.   Thou know'st I have power
  To take thy life from thee.
Hel. [*Kneeling*] I have ground the axe myself;
  Do you but strike the blow.
Per. Rise, prithee, rise: sit down: thou art no flatterer:
  I thank thee for it; and heaven forbid
  That kings should let their ears hear their faults hid!
  Fit counsellor and servant for a prince,

Who by thy wisdom makest a prince thy servant,
What wouldst thou have me do?
Hel.   To bear with patience
Such griefs as you yourself do lay upon yourself.
Per. Thou speak'st like a physician, Helicanus,
That minister'st a potion unto me
That thou wouldst tremble to receive thyself.
Attend me then: I went to Antioch,
Where, as thou know'st, against the face of death,
I sought the purchase of a glorious beauty,
From whence an issue I might propagate,
Are arms to princes and bring joys to subjects.
Her face was to mine eye beyond all wonder;
The rest—hark in thine ear—as black as incest:
Which by my knowledge found, the sinful father
Seem'd not to strike, but smooth: but thou know'st this,
'Tis time to fear when tyrants seem to kiss.
Which fear so grew in me, I hither fled,
Under the covering of a careful night,
Who seem'd my good protector; and, being here,
Bethought me what was past, what might succeed.
I knew him tyrannous; and tyrants' fears
Decrease not, but grow faster than the years:
And should he doubt it, as no doubt he doth,
That I should open to the listening air
How many worthy princes' bloods were shed,
To keep his bed of blackness unlaid ope,
To lop that doubt, he'll fill this land with arms,
And make pretence of wrong that I have done him;
When all, for mine, if I may call offence,
Must feel war's blow, who spares not innocence:
Which love to all, of which thyself art one,
Who now reprovest me for it,—
Hel.   Alas, sir!
Per. Drew sleep out of mine eyes, blood from my cheeks,
Musings into my mind, with thousand doubts
How I might stop this tempest ere it came;
And finding little comfort to relieve them,
I thought it princely charity to grieve them.
Hel. Well, my lord, since you have given me leave to speak,
Freely will I speak. Antiochus you fear,
And justly too, I think, you fear the tyrant,
Who either by public war or private treason
Will take away your life.
Therefore, my lord, go travel for a while,

Till that his rage and anger be forgot,
Or till the Destinies do cut his thread of life.
Your rule direct to any; if to me,
Day serves not light more faithful than I 'll be.

Per. I do not doubt thy faith;
But should he wrong my liberties in my absence?

Hel. We 'll mingle our bloods together in the earth,
From whence we had our being and our birth.

Per. Tyre, I now look from thee then, and to Tarsus
Intend my travel, where I 'll hear from thee;
And by whose letters I 'll dispose myself.
The care I had and have of subjects' good
On thee I lay, whose wisdom's strength can bear it.
I 'll take thy word for faith, not ask thine oath:
Who shuns not to break one will sure crack both:
But in our orbs we 'll live so round and safe,
That time of both this truth shall ne'er convince,
Thou show'dst a subject's shine, I a true prince.   [*Exeunt.*

SCENE III

Tyre. An ante-chamber in the palace.
Enter Thaliard.

Thal. So, this is Tyre, and this the court. Here must I kill
King Pericles; and if I do it not, I am sure to be hanged at
home: 'tis dangerous. Well, I perceive he was a wise fellow
and had good discretion, that, being bid to ask what he
would of the king, desired he might know none of his
secrets: now I do see he had some reason for 't; for if a
king bid a man be a villain, he 's bound by the indenture of
his oath to be one. Hush! here come the lords of Tyre.

Enter Helicanus and Escanes, with other Lords.

Hel. You shall not need, my fellow peers of Tyre,
Further to question me of your king's departure:
His seal'd commission left in trust with me
Doth speak sufficiently he 's gone to travel.

Thal. [*Aside*] How! the king gone!

Hel. If further yet you will be satisfied,
Why, as it were unlicensed of your loves,
He would depart, I 'll give some light unto you.
Being at Antioch—

Thal. [*Aside*] What from Antioch?

Hel. Royal Antiochus—on what cause I know not—
Took some displeasure at him; at least he judged so:
And doubting lest that he had err'd or sinn'd,
To show his sorrow, he 'ld correct himself;

So puts himself unto the shipman's toil,
With whom each minute threatens life or death.

Thal. [*Aside*] Well, I perceive I shall not be hanged now,
although I would; but since he's gone, the king's seas must
please: he 'scaped the land, to perish at the sea. I'll present
myself. Peace to the lords of Tyre!

Hel. Lord Thaliard from Antiochus is welcome.

Thal. From him I come
With message unto princely Pericles;
But since my landing I have understood
Your lord has betook himself to unknown travels,
My message must return from whence it came.

Hel. We have no reason to desire it,
Commended to our master, not to us:
Yet, ere you shall depart, this we desire,
As friends to Antioch, we may feast in Tyre.   [*Exeunt.*

SCENE IV

Tarsus. A room in the Governor's house.

Enter Cleon the Governor of Tarsus, with Dionyza and others.

Cle. My Dionyza, shall we rest us here,
And by relating tales of others' griefs,
See if 'twill teach us to forget our own?

Dio. That were to blow at fire in hope to quench it;
For who digs hills because they do aspire
Throws down one mountain to cast up a higher.
O my distressed lord, even such our griefs are;
Here they're but felt, and seen with mischief's eyes,
But like to groves, being topp'd, they higher rise.

Cle. O Dionyza,
Who wanteth food, and will not say he wants it,
Or can conceal his hunger till he famish?
Our tongues and sorrows do sound deep
Our woes into the air; our eyes do weep,
Till tongues fetch breath that may proclaim them louder;
That, if heaven slumber while their creatures want,
They may awake their helps to comfort them.
I'll then discourse our woes, felt several years,
And wanting breath to speak help me with tears.

Dio. I'll do my best, sir.

Cle. This Tarsus, o'er which I have the government,
A city on whom plenty held full hand,
For riches strew'd herself even in the streets;
Whose towers bore heads so high they kiss'd the clouds,
And strangers ne'er beheld but wonder'd at;

Whose men and dames so jetted and adorn'd,
Like one another's glass to trim them by :
Their tables were stored full, to glad the sight,
And not so much to feed on as delight ;
All poverty was scorn'd, and pride so great,
The name of help grew odious to repeat.

Dio. O, 'tis too true.

Cle. But see what heaven can do ! By this our change,
These mouths, who but of late earth, sea and air,
Were all too little to content and please,
Although they gave their creatures in abundance,
As houses are defiled for want of use,
They are now starved for want of exercise :
Those palates who, not yet two summers younger,
Must have inventions to delight the taste,
Would now be glad of bread, and beg for it :
Those mothers who, to nousle up their babes,
Thought nought too curious, are ready now
To eat those little darlings whom they loved.
So sharp are hunger's teeth, that man and wife
Draw lots who first shall die to lengthen life :
Here stands a lord, and there a lady weeping ;
Here many sink, yet those which see them fall
Have scarce strength left to give them burial.
Is not this true ?

Dio. Our cheeks and hollow eyes do witness it.

Cle. O, let those cities that of plenty's cup
And her prosperities so largely taste,
With their superfluous riots, hear these tears !
The misery of Tarsus may be theirs.

Enter a Lord.

Lord. Where 's the lord governor ?

Cle. Here.
Speak out thy sorrows which thou bring'st in haste,
For comfort is too far for us to expect.

Lord. We have descried, upon our neighbouring shore,
A portly sail of ships make hitherward.

Cle. I thought as much.
One sorrow never comes but brings an heir,
That may succeed as his inheritor ;
And so in ours : some neighbouring nation,
Taking advantage of our misery,
Hath stuff'd these hollow vessels with their power,
To beat us down, the which are down already,

And make a conquest of unhappy me,
Whereas no glory 's got to overcome.
Lord. That 's the least fear ; for, by the semblance
Of their white flags display'd, they bring us peace,
And come to us as favourers, not as foes.
Cle. Thou speak'st like him 's untutor'd to repeat :
Who makest the fairest show means most deceit
But bring they what they will and what they can,
What need we fear ?
The ground 's the lowest, and we are half way there.
Go tell their general we attend him here,
To know for what he comes and whence he comes
And what he craves.
Lord. I go, my lord.   [*Exit.*
Cle. Welcome is peace, if he on peace consist ;
If wars, we are unable to resist.

Enter Pericles with Attendants.

Per. Lord governor, for so we hear you are,
Let not our ships and number of our men
Be like a beacon fired to amaze your eyes.
We have heard your miseries as far as Tyre,
And seen the desolation of your streets :
Nor come we to add sorrow to your tears,
But to relieve them of their heavy load ;
And these our ships, you happily may think
Are like the Trojan horse was stuff'd within
With bloody veins expecting overthrow,
Are stored with corn to make your needy bread,
And give them life whom hunger starved half dead.
All. The gods of Greece protect you !
And we 'll pray for you.
Per.   Arise, I pray you, rise :
We do not look for reverence, but for love
And harbourage for ourself, our ships and men.
Cle. The which when any shall not gratify,
Or pay you with unthankfulness in thought,
Be it our wives, our children, or ourselves,
The curse of heaven and men succeed their evils !
Till when,—the which I hope shall ne'er be seen—
Your grace is welcome to our town and us.
Per. Which welcome we 'll accept ; feast here awhile,
Until our stars that frown lend us a smile.   [*Exeunt.*

ACT II

Enter Gower.

Gow. Here have you seen a mighty king
    His child, I wis, to incest bring;
    A better prince and benign lord,
    That will prove awful both in deed and word.
    Be quiet then as men should be,
    Till he hath pass'd necessity.
    I 'll show you those in troubles reign,
    Losing a mite, a mountain gain.
    The good in conversation,
    To whom I give my benison,
    Is still at Tarsus, where each man
    Thinks all is writ he speken can;
    And, to remember what he does,
    Build his statue to make him glorious:
    But tidings to the contrary
    Are brought your eyes; what need speak I?

DUMB SHOW

*Enter, at one door, Pericles, talking with Cleon; all the train
with them. Enter, at another door, a Gentleman, with a
letter to Pericles; Pericles shows the letter to Cleon; gives the
Messenger a reward, and knights him. Exit Pericles at one
door, and Cleon at another.*

    Good Helicane, that stay'd at home,
    Not to eat honey like a drone
    From others' labours; for though he strive
    To killen bad, keep good alive;
    And to fulfil his prince' desire,
    Sends word of all that haps in Tyre:
    How Thaliard came full bent with sin
    And had intent to murder him;
    And that in Tarsus was not best
    Longer for him to make his rest.
    He, doing so, put forth to seas,
    Where when men been, there 's seldom ease;
    For now the wind begins to blow;
    Thunder above and deeps below
    Make such unquiet that the ship
    Should house him safe is wreck'd and split;
    And he, good prince, having all lost,
    By waves from coast to coast is tost:

All perishen of man, of pelf,
Ne aught escapen but himself;
Till fortune, tired with doing bad,
Threw him ashore, to give him glad:
And here he comes.   What shall be next,
Pardon old Gower,—this longs the text.   [*Exit.*

SCENE I

Pentapolis.   An open place by the sea-side.
Enter Pericles, wet.

Per. Yet cease your ire, you angry stars of heaven!
    Wind, rain, and thunder, remember, earthly man
    Is but a substance that must yield to you;
    And I, as fits my nature, do obey you:
    Alas, the sea hath cast me on the rocks,
    Wash'd me from shore to shore, and left me breath
    Nothing to think on but ensuing death:
    Let it suffice the greatness of your powers
    To have bereft a prince of all his fortunes;
    And having thrown him from your watery grave,
    Here to have death in peace is all he'll crave.

Enter three Fishermen.

First Fish. What, ho, Pilch!

Sec. Fish. Ha, come and bring away the nets!

First Fish. What, Patchbreech, I say!

Third Fish. What say you, master?

First Fish. Look how thou stirrest now! come away, or I'll
    fetch thee with a wanion.

Third Fish. Faith, master, I am thinking of the poor men that
    were cast away before us even now.

First Fish. Alas, poor souls, it grieved my heart to hear what
    pitiful cries they made to us to help them, when, well-a-day,
    we could scarce help ourselves.

Third Fish. Nay, master, said not I as much when I saw the
    porpus, how he bounced and tumbled? they say they're
    half fish, half flesh: a plague on them, they ne'er come but
    I look to be washed.   Master, I marvel how the fishes live
    in the sea.

First Fish. Why, as men do a-land; the great ones eat up the
    little ones: I can compare our rich misers to nothing so
    fitly as to a whale; a' plays and tumbles, driving the poor fry
    before him, and at last devours them all at a mouthful: such
    whales have I heard on o' the land, who never leave gaping
    till they've swallowed the whole parish, church, steeple, bells,

Per. [*Aside*] A pretty moral.   [and all.

Third Fish. But, master, if I had been the sexton, I would have
  been that day in the belfry.
Sec. Fish. Why, man?
Third Fish. Because he should have swallowed me too: and
  when I had been in his belly, I would have kept such a
  jangling of the bells, that he should never have left till he
  cast bells, steeple, church, and parish, up again.   But if the
  good King Simonides were of my mind,—
Per. [*Aside*] Simonides!
Third Fish. We would purge the land of these drones, that rob
  the bee of her honey.
Per. [*Aside*] How from the finny subject of the sea
  These fishers tell the infirmities of men;
  And from their watery empire recollect
  All that may men approve or men detect!—
  Peace be at your labour, honest fishermen.
Sec. Fish. Honest! good fellow, what's that? If it be a day
  fits you, search out of the calendar, and nobody look after it.
Per. May see the sea hath cast upon your coast.
Sec. Fish. What a drunken knave was the sea to cast thee in
Per. A man whom both the waters and the wind,   [our way!
  In that vast tennis-court, have made the ball
  For them to play upon, entreats you pity him;
  He asks of you, that never used to beg.
First Fish. No, friend, cannot you beg? Here's them in our
  country of Greece gets more with begging than we can do
  with working.
Sec. Fish. Canst thou catch any fishes then?
Per. I never practised it.
Sec. Fish. Nay, then thou wilt starve, sure; for here's nothing
  to be got now-a-days, unless thou canst fish for't.
Per. What I have been I have forgot to know!
  But what I am, want teaches me to think on:
  A man throng'd up with cold: my veins are chill,
  And have no more of life than may suffice
  To give my tongue that heat to ask your help;
  Which if you shall refuse, when I am dead,
  For that I am a man, pray see me buried.
First Fish. Die quoth-a? Now gods forbid 't!
  And I have a gown here; come, put it on; keep thee warm.
  Now, afore me, a handsome fellow! Come, thou shalt go
  home, and we'll have flesh for holidays, fish for fasting-days,
  and moreo'er puddings and flap-jacks, and thou shalt be
Per. I thank you, sir.   [welcome.
Sec. Fish. Hark you, my friend; you said you could not beg.

Per. I did but crave.

Sec. Fish. But crave! Then I'll turn craver too, and so I shall 'scape whipping.

Per. Why, are all your beggars whipped then?

Sec. Fish. O, not all, my friend, not all; for if all your beggars were whipped, I would wish no better office than to be beadle. But, master, I'll go draw up the net.

                             [Exit with Third Fisherman.

Per. [*Aside*] How well this honest mirth becomes their labour!

First Fish. Hark you, sir, do you know where ye are?

Per. Not well.

First Fish. Why, I'll tell you: this is called Pentapolis, and our king the good Simonides.

Per. The good Simonides, do you call him?

First Fish. Ay, sir; and he deserves so to be called for his peaceable reign and good government.

Per. He is a happy king, since he gains from his subjects the name of good by his government. How far is his court distant from this shore?

First Fish. Marry, sir, half a day's journey: and I'll tell you, he hath a fair daughter, and to-morrow is her birthday; and there are princes and knights come from all parts of the world to just and tourney for her love.

Per. Were my fortunes equal to my desires, I could wish to make one there.

First Fish. O, sir, things must be as they may; and what a man cannot get, he may lawfully deal for—his wife's soul.

      Re-enter Second and Third Fishermen, drawing up a net.

Sec. Fish. Help, master, help! here's a fish hangs in the net, like a poor man's right in the law; 'twill hardly come out. Ha! bots on 't, 'tis come at last, and 'tis turned to a rusty

Per. An armour, friends! I pray you, let me see it. [armour.
Thanks, fortune, yet, that after all thy crosses
Thou givest me somewhat to repair myself;
And though it was mine own, part of my heritage,
Which my dead father did bequeath to me,
With this strict charge, even as he left his life,
'Keep it, my Pericles; it hath been a shield
'Twixt me and death:'—and pointed to this brace—
'For that it saved me, keep it; in like necessity—
The which the gods protect thee from!—may defend thee.'
It kept where I kept, I so dearly loved it;
Till the rough seas, that spare not any man,
Took it in rage, though calm'd have given 't again!
I thank thee for 't: my shipwreck now's no ill,

Since I have here my father's gift in 's will.
First Fish. What mean you, sir?
Per. To beg of you, kind friends, this coat of worth
  For it was sometime target to a king;
  I know it by this mark.   He loved me dearly,
  And for his sake I wish the having of it;
  And that you 'ld guide me to your sovereign's court,
  Where with it I may appear a gentleman;
  And if that ever my low fortune 's better,
  I 'll pay your bounties; till then rest your debtor.
First Fish. Why, wilt thou tourney for the lady?
Per. I 'll show the virtue I have borne in arms.   [on 't!
First Fish. Why, do 'e take it, and the gods give thee good
Sec. Fish. Ay, but hark you, my friend; 'twas we that made
  up this garment through the rough seams of the waters:
  there are certain condolements, certain vails.   I hope, sir,
  if you thrive, you 'll remember from whence you had them.
Per. Believe 't, I will.
  By your furtherance I am clothed in steel;
  And spite of all the rapture of the sea
  This jewel holds his building on my arm:
  Unto thy value I will mount myself
  Upon a courser, whose delightful steps
  Shall make the gazer joy to see him tread.
  Only, my friend, I yet am unprovided
  Of a pair of bases.
Sec. Fish. We 'll sure provide: thou shalt have my best gown to
  make thee a pair; and I 'll bring thee to the court myself.
Per. Then honour be but a goal to my will,
  This day I 'll rise, or else add ill to ill.   [*Exeunt.*

SCENE II

*The same.   A public way or platform leading to the lists.   A
  pavilion by the side of it for the reception of the King, Princess,
  Lords, &c.*

        Enter Simonides, Thaisa, Lords, and Attendants.
Sim. Are the knights ready to begin the triumph?
First Lord. They are, my liege,
  And stay your coming to present themselves.
Sim. Return them, we are ready; and our daughter,
  In honour of whose birth these triumphs are,
  Sits here, like beauty's child, whom nature gat
  For men to see and seeing wonder at.   [*Exit a Lord.*
Thai. It pleaseth you, my royal father, to express
  My commendations great, whose merit 's less.

Sim. It's fit it should be so ; for princes are
 A model which heaven makes like to itself **:**
 As jewels lose their glory if neglected,
 So princes their renowns if not respected.
 'Tis now your honour, daughter, to entertain
 The labour of each knight in his device.
Thai. Which, to preserve mine honour, I 'll perform.
  Enter a Knight ; he passes over, and his Squire presents his
      shield to the Princess.
Sim. Who is the first that doth prefer himself ?
Thai. A knight of Sparta, my renowned father ;
 And the device he bears upon his shield
 Is a black Ethiope reaching at the sun ;
 The word, 'Lux tua vita mihi.'
Sim. He loves you well that holds his life of you.
        [*The Second Knight passes.*
 Who is the second that presents himself ?
Thai. A prince of Macedon, my royal father ;
 And the device he bears upon his shield
 Is an arm'd knight that 's conquer'd by a lady ;
 The motto thus, in Spanish, 'Piu por dulzura que por fuerza.'
        [*The Third Knight passes.*
Sim. And what 's the third ?
Thai.   The third of Antioch **;**
 And his device a wreath of chivalry ;
 The word, 'Me pompæ provexit apex.'
        [*The Fourth Knight passes.*
Sim. What is the fourth ?
Thai. A burning torch that 's turned upside down ;
 The word, 'Quod me alit, me extinguit.'
Sim. Which shows that beauty hath his power and will,
 Which can as well inflame as it can kill.
        [*The Fifth Knight passes.*
Thai. The fifth, an hand environed with clouds,
 Holding out gold that 's by the touchstone tried ;
 The motto thus, 'Sic spectanda fides.'
       [*The Sixth Knight, Pericles, passes.*
Sim. And what 's
 The sixth and last, the which the knight himself
 With such a graceful courtesy deliver'd ?
Thai. He seems to be a stranger ; but his present is
 A wither'd branch, that 's only green at top ;
 The motto, 'In hac spe vivo.'
Sim. A pretty moral ;
 From the dejected state wherein he is,

He hopes by you his fortunes yet may flourish.

First Lord. He had need mean better than his outward show
Can any way speak in his just commend;
For by his rusty outside he appears
To have practised more the whipstock than the lance.

Sec. Lord. He well may be a stranger, for he comes
To an honour'd triumph strangely furnished.

Third Lord. And on set purpose let his armour rust
Until this day, to scour it in the dust.

Sim. Opinion's but a fool, that makes us scan
The outward habit by the inward man.
But stay, the knights are coming: we will withdraw
Into the gallery.   [*Exeunt.*

[*Great shouts within, and all cry* 'The mean knight!'

SCENE III

The same.   A hall of state: a banquet prepared.

Enter Simonides, Thaisa, Lords, Knights, and Attendants.

Sim. Knights,
To say you're welcome were superfluous.
To place upon the volume of your deeds,
As in a title-page, your worth in arms,
Were more than you expect, or more than's fit,
Since every worth in show commends itself.
Prepare for mirth, for mirth becomes a feast:
You are princes and my guests.

Thai. But you, my knight and guest;
To whom this wreath of victory I give,
And crown you king of this day's happiness.

Per. 'Tis more by fortune, lady, than my merit.

Sim. Call it by what you will, the day is yours;
And here, I hope, is none that envies it.
In framing an artist, art hath thus decreed,
To make some good, but others to exceed;
And you are her labour'd scholar. Come, queen o' the feast,—
For, daughter, so you are,—here take your place:
Marshal the rest as they deserve their grace.

Knights. We are honour'd much by good Simonides.

Sim. Your presence glads our days: honour we love;
For who hates honour hates the gods above.

Marshal. Sir, yonder is your place.

Per.   Some other is more fit.

First Knight. Contend not, sir; for we are gentlemen
That neither in our hearts nor outward eyes
Envy the great nor do the low despise.

Per. You are right courteous knights.

Sim. Sit, sir, sit.

   [*Aside*] By Jove, I wonder, that is king of thoughts
These cates resist me, he not thought upon.

Thai. [*Aside*] By Juno, that is queen of marriage,
   All viands that I eat do seem unsavoury,
   Wishing him my meat.—Sure he's a gallant gentleman.

Sim. He's but a country gentleman;
   Has done no more than other knights have done;
   Has broken a staff or so; so let it pass.

Thai. [*Aside*] To me he seems like diamond to glass.

Per. [*Aside*] Yon king's to me like to my father's picture,
   Which tells me in that glory once he was;
   Had princes sit, like stars, about his throne,
   And he the sun, for them to reverence;
   None but beheld him but, like lesser lights,
   Did vail their crowns to his supremacy:
   Where now his son's like a glow-worm in the night,
   The which hath fire in darkness, none in light:
   Whereby I see that Time's the king of men;
   He's both their parent, and he is their grave,
   And gives them what he will, not what they crave.

Sim. What, are you merry, knights?

Knights. Who can be other in this royal presence?

Sim. Here, with a cup that's stored unto the brim,—
   As you do love, fill to your mistress' lips,—
   We drink this health to you.

Knights. We thank your grace.

Sim. Yet pause awhile:
   Yon knight doth sit too melancholy,
   As if the entertainment in our court
   Had not a show might countervail his worth.
   Note it not you, Thaisa?

Thai. What is it to me, my father?

Sim. O, attend, my daughter:
   Princes, in this, should live like gods above,
   Who freely give to every one that comes
   To honour them:
   And princes not doing so are like to gnats,
   Which make a sound, but kill'd are wonder'd at.
   Therefore to make his entrance more sweet,
   Here, say we drink this standing-bowl of wine to him.

Thai. Alas, my father, it befits not me
   Unto a stranger knight to be so bold:
   He may my proffer take for an offence,

Since men may take women's gifts for impudence.

Sim. How!

Do as I bid you, or you 'll move me else.

Thai. [*Aside*] Now, by the gods, he could not please me better.

Sim. And furthermore tell him, we desire to know of him,
Of whence he is, his name and parentage.

Thai. The king my father, sir, has drunk to you.

Per. I thank him.

Thai. Wishing it so much blood unto your life.

Per. I thank both him and you, and pledge him freely.

Thai. And further he desires to know of you
Of whence you are, your name and parentage.

Per. A gentleman of Tyre; my name, Pericles;
My education been in arts and arms;
Who, looking for adventures in the world,
Was by the rough seas reft of ships and men,
And after shipwreck driven upon this shore.

Thai. He thanks your grace; names himself Pericles,
A gentleman of Tyre,
Who only by misfortune of the seas
Bereft of ships and men, cast on this shore.

Sim. Now, by the gods, I pity his misfortune,
And will awake him from his melancholy.
Come, gentlemen, we sit too long on trifles,
And waste the time, which looks for other revels.
Even in your armours, as you are address'd,
Will very well become a soldier's dance.
I will not have excuse, with saying this
Loud music is too harsh for ladies' heads,
Since they love men in arms as well as beds.

[*The Knights dance.*

So, this was well ask'd, 'twas so well perform'd.
Come, sir,
Here 's a lady that wants breathing too:
And I have heard, you knights of Tyre
Are excellent in making ladies trip,
And that their measures are as excellent.

Per. In those that practise them they are, my lord.

Sim. O, that 's as much as you would be denied
Of your fair courtesy. [*The Knights and Ladies dance.*
Unclasp, unclasp:
Thanks, gentlemen, to all; all have done well,
[*To Pericles*] But you the best. Pages and lights, to conduct
These knights unto their several lodgings! - Yours, sir,
We have given order to be next our own.

Per. I am at your grace's pleasure.

Sim. Princes, it is too late to talk of love,
 And that 's the mark I know you level at :
 Therefore each one betake him to his rest ;
 To-morrow all for speeding do their best.   [*Exeunt.*

SCENE IV

Tyre. A room in the Governor's house.
Enter Helicanus and Escanes.

Hel. No, Escanes, know this of me,
 Antiochus from incest lived not free :
 For which, the most high gods not minding longer
 To withhold the vengeance that they had in store,
 Due to this heinous capital offence,
 Even in the height and pride of all his glory,
 When he was seated in a chariot
 Of an inestimable value, and his daughter with him,
 A fire from heaven came, and shrivell'd up
 Their bodies, even to loathing ; for they so stunk,
 That all those eyes adored them ere their fall
 Scorn now their hand should give them burial.

Esca. 'Twas very strange.

Hel.   And yet but justice ; for though
 The king were great, his greatness was no guard
 To bar heaven's shaft, but sin had his reward.

Esca. 'Tis very true.

Enter two or three Lords.

First Lord. See, not a man in private conference
 Or council has respect with him but he.

Sec. Lord. It shall no longer grieve without reproof.

Third Lord. And cursed be he that will not second it.

First Lord. Follow me then. Lord Helicane, a word.

Hel. With me ? and welcome : happy day, my lords.

First Lord. Know that our griefs are risen to the top,
 And now at length they overflow their banks.

Hel. Your griefs ! for what ? wrong not your prince you love.

First Lord. Wrong not yourself, then, noble Helicane ;
 But if the prince do live, let us salute him,
 Or know what ground 's made happy by his breath.
 If in the world he live, we 'll seek him out ;
 If in his grave he rest, we 'll find him there ;
 And be resolved he lives to govern us,
 Or dead, give 's cause to mourn his funeral,
 And leave us to our free election.

Sec. Lord. Whose death 's indeed the strongest in our censure :

270

And knowing this kingdom is without a head,—
Like goodly buildings left without a roof
Soon fall to ruin—your noble self,
That best know how to rule and how to reign,
We thus submit unto, our sovereign.

All. Live, noble Helicane!

Hel. For honour's cause, forbear your suffrages;
If that you love Prince Pericles, forbear.
Take I your wish, I leap into the seas,
Where's hourly trouble for a minute's ease.
A twelvemonth longer, let me entreat you
To forbear the absence of your king;
If in which time expired he not return,
I shall with aged patience bear your yoke.
But if I cannot win you to this love,
Go search like nobles, like noble subjects,
And in your search spend your adventurous worth;
Whom if you find and win unto return,
You shall like diamonds sit about his crown.

First Lord. To wisdom he's a fool that will not yield;
And since Lord Helicane enjoineth us,
We with our travels will endeavour it.

Hel. Then you love us, we you, and we'll clasp hands:
When peers thus knit, a kingdom ever stands.   [*Exeunt.*

Scene V

Pentapolis.   A room in the palace.

*Enter Simonides, reading a letter, at one door : the Knights
meet him.*

First Knight. Good morrow to the good Simonides.

Sim. Knights, from my daughter this I let you know,
That for this twelvemonth she'll not undertake
A married life.
Her reason to herself is only known,
Which from her by no means can I get.

Sec. Knight. May we not get access to her, my lord?

Sim. Faith, by no means; she hath so strictly
Tied her to her chamber, that 'tis impossible.
One twelve moons more she'll wear Diana's livery;
This by the eye of Cynthia hath she vow'd,
And on her virgin honour will not break it.

Third Knight. Loath to bid farewell, we take our leaves.
                                    [*Exeunt Knights.*

Sim. So,
They are well dispatch'd; now to my daughter's letter:

271

She tells me here, she 'll wed the stranger knight,
Or never more to view nor day nor light.
'Tis well, mistress; your choice agrees with mine;
I like that well: nay, how absolute she 's in 't,
Not minding whether I dislike or no!
Well, I do commend her choice;
And will no longer have it be delay'd.
Soft! here he comes: I must dissemble it.

Enter Pericles.

Per. All fortune to the good Simonides!
Sim. To you as much, sir! I am beholding to you
 For your sweet music this last night: I do
 Protest my ears were never better fed
 With such delightful pleasing harmony.
Per. It is your grace's pleasure to commend;
 Not my desert.
Sim.   Sir, you are music's master.
Per. The worst of all her scholars, my good lord.
Sim. Let me ask you one thing: what do you think of my
Per. A most virtuous princess.   [daughter, sir?
Sim. And she is fair too, is she not?
Per. As a fair day in summer, wondrous fair.
Sim. Sir, my daughter thinks very well of you;
 Ay, so well, that you must be her master,
 And she will be your scholar: therefore look to it.
Per. I am unworthy for her schoolmaster.
Sim. She thinks not so; peruse this writing else.
Per. [*Aside*] What 's here?
 A letter, that she loves the knight of Tyre!
 'Tis the king's subtilty to have my life.—
 O, seek not to entrap me, gracious lord,
 A stranger and distressed gentleman,
 That never aim'd so high to love your daughter,
 But bent all offices to honour her.
Sim. Thou hast bewitch'd my daughter, and thou art
 A villain.
Per. By the gods, I have not:
 Never did thought of mine levy offence;
 Nor never did my actions yet commence
 A deed might gain her love or your displeasure.
Sim. Traitor, thou liest.
Per.   Traitor!
Sim.   Ay, traitor.
Per. Even in his throat—unless it be the king—
 That calls me traitor, I return the lie.

Sim. [*Aside*] Now, by the gods, I do applaud his courage.
Per. My actions are as noble as my thoughts,
    That never relish'd of a base descent.
    I came unto your court for honour's cause,
    And not to be a rebel to her state;
    And he that otherwise accounts of me,
    This sword shall prove he's honour's enemy.
Sim. No?
    Here comes my daughter, she can witness it.
              Enter Thaisa.
Per. Then, as you are as virtuous as fair,
    Resolve your angry father, if my tongue
    Did e'er solicit, or my hand subscribe
    To any syllable that made love to you.
Thai. Why, sir, say if you had,
    Who takes offence at that would make me glad?
Sim. Yea, mistress, are you so peremptory?
    [*Aside*] I am glad on't with all my heart.—
    I'll tame you; I'll bring you in subjection.
    Will you, not having my consent,
    Bestow your love and your affections
    Upon a stranger? [*Aside*] who, for aught I know,
    May be, nor can I think the contrary,
    As great in blood as I myself.—
    Therefore hear you, mistress; either frame
    Your will to mine,—and you, sir, hear you,
    Either be ruled by me, or I'll make you—
    Man and wife:
    Nay, come, your hands and lips must seal it too:
    And being join'd, I'll thus your hopes destroy;
    And for a further grief,—God give you joy!
    What, are you both pleased?
Thai.   Yes, if you love me, sir.
Per. Even as my life my blood that fosters it.
Sim. What, are you both agreed?
Both. Yes, if't please your majesty.
Sim. It pleaseth me so well, that I will see you wed;
    And then, with what haste you can, get you to bed. [*Exeunt*

ACT III

Enter Gower.

    Gow. Now sleep y-slaked hath the rout:
        No din but snores the house about,
        Made louder by the o'er-fed breast

Of this most pompous marriage-feast.
The cat, with eyne of burning coal,
Now couches 'fore the mouse's hole;
And crickets sing at the oven's mouth,
E'er the blither for their drouth.
Hymen hath brought the bride to bed,
Where, by the loss of maidenhead,
A babe is moulded.   Be attent,
And time that is so briefly spent
With your fine fancies quaintly eche:
What 's dumb in show I 'll plain with speech.

DUMB SHOW

*Enter Pericles and Simonides at one door, with Attendants; a
Messenger meets them, kneels, and gives Pericles a letter:
Pericles shows it Simonides; the Lords kneel to the former.
Then enter Thaisa with child, with Lychorida, a nurse: the
King shows her the letter; she rejoices: she and Pericles take
leave of her father, and depart with Lychorida and their
Attendants.   Then exeunt Simonides and the rest.*

By many a dern and painful perch
Of Pericles the careful search,
By the four opposing coigns
Which the world together joins,
Is made with all due diligence
That horse and sail and high expense
Can stead the quest.   At last from Tyre,
Fame answering the most strange inquire,
To the court of King Simonides
Are letters brought, the tenour these:
Antiochus and his daughter dead;
The men of Tyrus on the head
Of Helicanus would set on
The crown of Tyre, but he will none:
The mutiny he there hastes t' oppress;
Says to 'em, if King Pericles
Come not home in twice six moons,
He, obedient to their dooms,
Will take the crown.   The sum of this,
Brought hither to Pentapolis,
Y-ravished the regions round,
And every one with claps can sound,
'Our heir-apparent is a king!
Who dream'd, who thought of such a thing?'
Brief, he must hence depart to Tyre:

His queen with child makes her desire—
Which who shall cross ?—along to go.
Omit we all their dole and woe :
Lychorida, her nurse, she takes,
And so to sea : their vessel shakes
On Neptune's billow ; half the flood
Hath their keel cut : but fortune's mood
Varies again ; the grisled north
Disgorges such a tempest forth,
That, as a duck for life that dives,
So up and down the poor ship drives :
The lady shrieks and well-a-near
Does fall in travail with her fear :
And what ensues in this fell storm
Shall for itself itself perform.
I nill relate, action may
Conveniently the rest convey ;
Which might not what by me is told.
In your imagination hold
This stage the ship, upon whose deck
The sea-tost Pericles appears to speak.   [*Exit*

SCENE I

Enter Pericles, on shipboard.

Per. Thou god of this great vast, rebuke these surges,
   Which wash both heaven and hell ; and thou, that hast
   Upon the winds command, bind them in brass,
   Having call'd them from the deep ! O, still
   Thy deafening dreadful thunders ; gently quench
   Thy nimble sulphurous flashes ! O, how, Lychorida,
   How does my queen ? Thou stormest venomously ;
   Wilt thou spit all thyself ? The seaman's whistle
   Is as a whisper in the ears of death,
   Unheard. Lychorida !—Lucina, O
   Divinest patroness and midwife gentle
   To those that cry by night, convey thy deity
   Aboard our dancing boat ; make swift the pangs
   Of my queen's travails ! Now, Lychorida !
      Enter Lychorida, with an Infant.
Lyc. Here is a thing too young for such a place,
   Who, if it had conceit, would die, as I
   Am like to do : take in your arms this piece
   Of your dead queen.
Per.   How, how, Lychorida !
Lyc. Patience, good sir ; do not assist the storm.

275

Here's all that is left living of your queen,
A little daughter : for the sake of it,
Be manly, and take comfort.

Per.   O you gods !
Why do you make us love your goodly gifts,
And snatch them straight away ? We here below
Recall not what we give, and therein may
Use honour with you.

Lyc.   Patience, good sir,
Even for this charge.

Per.   Now, mild may be thy life !
For a more blustrous birth had never babe :
Quiet and gentle thy conditions ! for
Thou art the rudeliest welcome to this world
That ever was prince's child.   Happy what follows
Thou hast as chiding a nativity
As fire, air, water, earth and heaven can make,
To herald thee from the womb : even at the first
Thy loss is more than can thy portage quit,
With all thou canst find here.   Now, the good gods
Throw their best eyes upon 't !

                        Enter two Sailors.

First Sail. What courage, sir?   God save you !

Per. Courage enough : I do not fear the flaw ;
It hath done to me the worst.   Yet, for the love
Of this poor infant, this fresh-new sea-farer,
I would it would be quiet.

First Sail. Slack the bolins there !   Thou wilt not, wilt thou ?
Blow, and split thyself.

Sec. Sail. But sea-room, an the brine and cloudy billow kiss
the moon, I care not.

First Sail. Sir, your queen must overboard : the sea works
high, the wind is loud, and will not lie till the ship be
cleared of the dead.

Per. That's your superstition.

First Sail. Pardon us, sir ; with us at sea it hath been still
observed ; and we are strong in custom.   Therefore briefly
yield her ; for she must overboard straight.

Per. As you think meet.   Most wretched queen !

Lyc. Here she lies, sir.

Per. A terrible childbed hast thou had, my dear ;
No light, no fire : the unfriendly elements
Forgot thee utterly ; nor have I time
To give thee hallow'd to thy grave, but straight
Must cast thee, scarcely coffin'd, in the ooze ;

Where, for a monument upon thy bones,
And aye-remaining lamps, the belching whale
And humming water must o'erwhelm thy corpse,
Lying with simple shells.   O Lychorida,
Bid Nestor bring me spices, ink and paper,
My casket and my jewels ; and bid Nicander
Bring me the satin coffer : lay the babe
Upon the pillow : hie thee, whiles I say
A priestly farewell to her : suddenly, woman.   [*Exit Lychorida.*

Sec. Sail. Sir, we have a chest beneath the hatches, caulked and
  bitumed ready.

Per. I thank thee.   Mariner, say what coast is this ?

Sec. Sail. We are near Tarsus.

Per. Thither, gentle mariner,
  Alter thy course for Tyre.   When canst thou reach it ?

Sec. Sail. By break of day, if the wind cease.

Per. O, make for Tarsus !
  There will I visit Cleon, for the babe
  Cannot hold out to Tyrus : there I 'll leave it
  At careful nursing.   Go thy ways, good mariner :
  I 'll bring the body presently.   [*Exeunt.*

SCENE II

Ephesus.   A room in Cerimon's house.

*Enter Cerimon, a Servant, and some Persons who have been
  shipwrecked.*

Cer. Philemon, ho !

Enter Philemon.

Phil. Doth my lord call ?

Cer. Get fire and meat for these poor men :
  'T has been a turbulent and stormy night.

Serv. I have been in many ; but such a night as this
  Till now, I ne'er endured.

Cer. Your master will be dead ere you return ;
  There 's nothing can be minister'd to nature   ['pothecary,
  That can recover him.   [*To Philemon*] Give this to the
  And tell me how it works.   [*Exeunt all but Cerimon.*

Enter two Gentlemen.

First Gent.   Good morrow

Sec. Gent. Good morrow to your lordship.

Cer.   Gentlemen,
  Why do you stir so early ?

First Gent. Sir,
  Our lodgings, standing bleak upon the sea,
  Shook as the earth did quake ;

The very principals did seem to rend
And all-to topple: pure surprise and fear
Made me to quit the house.

Sec. Gent. That is the cause we trouble you so early;
'Tis not our husbandry.

Cer. O, you say well.

First Gent. But I much marvel that your lordship, having
Rich tire about you, should at these early hours
Shake off the golden slumber of repose.
'Tis most strange,
Nature should be so conversant with pain,
Being thereto not compell'd.

Cer. I hold it ever,
Virtue and cunning were endowments greater
Than nobleness and riches: careless heirs
May the two latter darken and expend,
But immortality attends the former,
Making a man a god. 'Tis known, I ever
Have studied physic, through which secret art,
By turning o'er authorities, I have,
Together with my practice, made familiar
To me and to my aid the blest infusions
That dwell in vegetives, in metals, stones;
And I can speak of the disturbances
That nature works, and of her cures; which doth give me
A more content in course of true delight
Than to be thirsty after tottering honour,
Or tie my treasure up in silken bags,
To please the fool and death.

Sec. Gent. Your honour has through Ephesus pour'd forth
Your charity, and hundreds call themselves
Your creatures, who by you have been restored:
And not your knowledge, your personal pain, but even
Your purse, still open, hath built Lord Cerimon
Such strong renown as time shall never. . . .

Enter two or three Servants with a chest.

First Serv. So; lift there.

Cer. What's that?

First Serv. Sir,
Even now did the sea toss up upon our shore
This chest: 'tis of some wreck.

Cer. Set 't down, let's look upon 't.

Sec. Gent. 'Tis like a coffin, sir.

Cer. Whate'er it be,
'Tis wondrous heavy. Wrench it open straight:

If the sea's stomach be o'ercharged with gold,
'Tis a good constraint of fortune it belches upon us.
Sec. Gent. 'Tis so, my lord.
Cer. How close 'tis caulk'd and bitumed! Did the sea cast it up?
First Serv. I never saw so huge a billow, sir, as toss'd it upon shore.
Cer.   Wrench it open:
Soft! it smells most sweetly in my sense.
Sec. Gent. A delicate odour.
Cer. As ever hit my nostril. So, up with it.
O you most potent gods! what's here? a corse!
First Gent. Most strange!
Cer. Shrouded in cloth of state; balmed and entreasured
With full bags of spices! A passport too!
Apollo, perfect me in the characters!   [*Reads from a scroll.*
    'Here I give to understand,
        If e'er this coffin drive a-land,
        I, King Pericles, have lost
        This queen, worth all our mundane cost.
        Who finds her, give her burying;
        She was the daughter of a king:
        Besides this treasure for a fee,
        The gods requite his charity!'
If thou livest, Pericles, thou hast a heart
That even cracks for woe! This chanced to-night
Sec. Gent. Most likely, sir.
Cer.   Nay, certainly to-night;
For look how fresh she looks! They were too rough
That threw her in the sea. Make a fire within:
Fetch hither all my boxes in my closet.   [*Exit a servant.*
Death may usurp on nature many hours,
And yet the fire of life kindle again
The o'erpress'd spirits. I heard of an Egyptian
That had nine hours lien dead,
Who was by good appliance recovered.
        Re-enter a Servant, with boxes, napkins, and fire.
Well said, well said; the fire and cloths.
The rough and woful music that we have,
Cause it to sound, beseech you.
The viol once more: how thou stirr'st, thou block!
The music there! I pray you, give her air.
Gentlemen,
This queen will live: nature awakes; a warmth
Breathes out of her: she hath not been entranced
Above five hours: see how she 'gins to blow
Into life's flower again!

First Gent.   The heavens,
　Through you, increase our wonder, and set up
　Your fame for ever.
Cer.   She is alive; behold,
　Her eyelids, cases to those heavenly jewels
　Which Pericles hath lost, begin to part
　Their fringes of bright gold: the diamonds
　Of a most praised water do appear
　To make the world twice rich. Live,
　And make us weep to hear your fate, fair creature,
　Rare as you seem to be.   [*She moves.*
Thai.   O dear Diana,
　Where am I? Where's my lord? What world is this?
Sec. Gent. Is not this strange?
First Gent. Most rare.
Cer. Hush, my gentle neighbours!
　Lend me your hands; to the next chamber bear her.
　Get linen: now this matter must be look'd to,
　For her relapse is mortal. Come, come;
　And Æsculapius guide us!   [*Exeunt, carrying her away.*

SCENE III

Tarsus. A room in the Governor's house.
Enter Pericles, Cleon, Dionyza, and Lychorida with
Marina in her arms.

Per. Most honour'd Cleon, I must needs be gone;
　My twelve months are expired, and Tyrus stands
　In a litigious peace. You, and your lady,
　Take from my heart all thankfulness! The gods
　Make up the rest upon you!
Cle. Your shafts of fortune, though they hurt you mortally,
　Yet glance full wanderingly on us.
Dion.   O your sweet queen!
　That the strict fates had pleased you had brought her hither,
　To have bless'd mine eyes with her!
Per.   We cannot but obey
　The powers above us. Could I rage and roar
　As doth the sea she lies in, yet the end
　Must be as 'tis. My gentle babe Marina, whom,
　For she was born at sea, I have named so, here
　I charge your charity withal, leaving her
　The infant of your care; beseeching you
　To give her princely training, that she may be
　Manner'd as she is born.
Cle.   Fear not, my lord, but think

Your grace, that fed my country with your corn,
For which the people's prayers still fall upon you,
Must in your child be thought on.   If neglection
Should therein make me vile, the common body,
By you relieved, would force me to my duty:
But if to that my nature need a spur,
The gods revenge it upon me and mine,
To the end of generation!
Per.   I believe you;
Your honour and your goodness teach me to 't,
Without your vows.   Till she be married, madam,
By bright Diana, whom we honour, all
Unscissar'd shall this hair of mine remain,
Though I show ill in 't.   So I take my leave.
Good madam, make me blessed in your care
In bringing up my child.
Dion.   I have one myself,
Who shall not be more dear to my respect
Than yours, my lord.
Per.   Madam, my thanks and prayers.
Cle. We 'll bring your grace e'en to the edge o' the shore,
Then give you up to the mask'd Neptune and
The gentlest winds of heaven.
Per.   I will embrace
Your offer.   Come, dearest madam.   O, no tears,
Lychorida, no tears:
Look to your little mistress, on whose grace
You may depend hereafter.   Come, my lord.   [*Exeunt.*

SCENE IV

Ephesus.   A room in Cerimon's house.
Enter Cerimon and Thaisa.

Cer. Madam, this letter, and some certain jewels,
Lay with you in your coffer: which are
At your command.   Know you the character?
Thai. It is my lord's.
That I was shipp'd at sea, I well remember,
Even on my eaning time; but whether there
Delivered, by the holy gods,
I cannot rightly say.   But since King Pericles,
My wedded lord, I ne'er shall see again,
A vestal livery will I take me to,
And never more have joy.
Cer. Madam, if this you purpose as ye speak,
Diana's temple is not distant far,

Where you may abide till your date expire.
Moreover, if you please, a niece of mine
Shall there attend you.

Thai. My recompense is thanks, that's all;
    Yet my good will is great, though the gift small.   [*Exeunt.*

ACT IV
Enter Gower.

Gow. Imagine Pericles arrived at Tyre,
    Welcomed and settled to his own desire.
    His woeful queen we leave at Ephesus,
    Unto Diana there as a votaress.
    Now to Marina bend your mind,
    Whom our fast-growing scene must find
    At Tarsus, and by Cleon train'd
    In music, letters; who hath gain'd
    Of education all the grace,
    Which makes her both the heart and place
    Of general wonder. But, alack,
    That monster envy, oft the wrack
    Of earned praise, Marina's life
    Seeks to take off by treason's knife.
    And in this kind hath our Cleon
    One daughter, and a wench full grown,
    Even ripe for marriage rite; this maid
    Hight Philoten: and it is said
    For certain in our story, she
    Would ever with Marina be:
    Be't when she weaved the sleided silk
    With fingers long, small, white as milk;
    Or when she would with sharp needle wound
    The cambric, which she made more sound
    By hurting it; or when to the lute
    She sung, and made the night-bird mute,
    That still records with moan; or when
    She would with rich and constant pen
    Vail to her mistress Dian; still
    This Philoten contends in skill
    With absolute Marina: so
    With the dove of Paphos might the crow
    Vie feathers white. Marina gets
    All praises, which are paid as debts,
    And not as given. This so darks
    In Philoten all graceful marks,

That Cleon's wife, with envy rare,
A present murderer does prepare
For good Marina, that her daughter
Might stand peerless by this slaughter.
The sooner her vile thoughts to stead,
Lychorida, our nurse, is dead:
And cursed Dionyza hath
The pregnant instrument of wrath
Prest for this blow.   The unborn event
I do commend to your content:
Only I carry winged time
Post on the lame feet of my rhyme;
Which never could I so convey,
Unless your thoughts went on my way.
Dionyza does appear,
With Leonine, a murderer.   [*Exit.*

Scene I

Tarsus.   An open place near the sea-shore.
Enter Dionyza with Leonine.

Dion. Thy oath remember; thou hast sworn to do't:
  'Tis but a blow, which never shall be known.
  Thou canst not do a thing in the world so soon,
  To yield thee so much profit.   Let not conscience
  Which is but cold, inflaming love i' thy bosom,
  Inflame too nicely; nor let pity, which
  Even women have cast off, melt thee, but be
  A soldier to thy purpose.

Leon. I will do't; but yet she is a goodly creature.

Dion. The fitter then the gods should have her.   Here she comes
  weeping for her only mistress' death.   Thou art resolved?

Leon. I am resolved.

  Enter Marina, with a basket of flowers.

Mar. No, I will rob Tellus of her weed,
  To strew thy green with flowers: the yellows, blues,
  The purple violets, and marigolds,
  Shall, as a carpet, hang upon thy grave,
  While summer-days do last.   Ay me! poor maid,
  Born in a tempest, when my mother died,
  This world to me is like a lasting storm,
  Whirring me from my friends.

Dion. How now, Marina! why do you keep alone?
  How chance my daughter is not with you?
  Do not consume your blood with sorrowing:
  You have a nurse of me.   Lord, how your favour's

Changed with this unprofitable woe!
Come give me your flowers, ere the sea mar it.
Walk with Leonine; the air is quick there,
And it pierces and sharpens the stomach.
Come, Leonine, take her by the arm, walk with her.

Mar. No, I pray you;
I'll not bereave you of your servant.

Dion. Come, come;
I love the king your father and yourself
With more than foreign heart.   We every day
Expect him here: when he shall come, and find
Our paragon to all reports thus blasted,
He will repent the breadth of his great voyage;
Blame both my lord and me, that we have taken
No care to your best courses.   Go, I pray you,
Walk, and be cheerful once again; reserve
That excellent complexion, which did steal
The eyes of young and old.   Care not for me;
I can go home alone.

Mar.   Well, I will go;
But yet I have no desire to it.

Dion. Come, come, I know 'tis good for you.
Walk half an hour, Leonine, at the least:
Remember what I have said.

Leon.   I warrant you, madam.

Dion. I'll leave you, my sweet lady, for a while:
Pray, walk softly, do not heat your blood:
What! I must have care of you.

Mar.   My thanks, sweet madam. [*Exit Dionyza.*
Is this wind westerly that blows?

Leon.   South-west.

Mar. When I was born, the wind was north.

Leon.   Was't so?

Mar. My father, as nurse said, did never fear,
But cried 'Good seamen!' to the sailors, galling
His kingly hands, haling ropes;
And, clasping to the mast, endured a sea
That almost burst the deck.

Leon. When was this?

Mar. When I was born:
Never was waves nor wind more violent;
And from the ladder-tackle washes off
A canvas-climber. 'Ha!' says one, 'wilt out?
And with a dropping industry they skip
From stem to stern: the boatswain whistles, and

284

The master calls and trebles their confusion.

Leon. Come, say your prayers.

Mar. What mean you?

Leon. If you require a little space for prayer,
  I grant it: pray; but be not tedious,
  For the gods are quick of ear, and I am sworn
  To do my work with haste.

Mar.   Why will you kill me?

Leon. To satisfy my lady.

Mar. Why would she have me kill'd?
  Now, as I can remember, by my troth,
  I never did her hurt in all my life:
  I never spake bad word, nor did ill turn
  To any living creature: believe me, la,
  I never kill'd a mouse, nor hurt a fly:
  I trod upon a worm against my will,
  But I wept for it. How have I offended,
  Wherein my death might yield her any profit,
  Or my life imply her any danger?

Leon. My commission
  Is not to reason of the deed, but do 't.

Mar. You will not do 't for all the world, I hope.
  You are well favour'd, and your looks foreshow
  You have a gentle heart. I saw you lately,
  When you caught hurt in parting two that fought:
  Good sooth, it show'd well in you: do so now:
  Your lady seeks my life; come you between,
  And save poor me, the weaker.

Leon.   I am sworn,
  And will dispatch.   [*He seizes her.*

                    Enter Pirates.

First Pirate. Hold, villain!   [*Leonine runs away.*

Sec. Pirate. A prize! a prize!

Third Pirate. Half-part, mates, half-part.
  Come let 's have her aboard suddenly.

                    [*Exeunt Pirates with Marina.*
                    Re-enter Leonine.

Leon. These roguing thieves serve the great pirate Valdes;
  And they have seized Marina. Let her go:
  There 's no hope she will return. I 'll swear she 's dead,
  And thrown into the sea. But I 'll see further:
  Perhaps they will but please themselves upon her,
  Not carry her aboard. If she remain,
  Whom they have ravish'd must by me be slain.   [*Exit.*

SCENE II

Mytilene.   A room in a brothel.
Enter Pandar, Bawd, and Boult.

Pand. Boult!

Boult. Sir?

Pand. Search the market narrowly; Mytilene is full of gallants.
We lost too much money this mart by being too wenchless.

Bawd. We were never so much out of creatures. We have
but poor three, and they can do no more than they can do;
and they with continual action are even as good as rotten.

Pand. Therefore let's have fresh ones, whate'er we pay for
them. If there be not a conscience to be used in every trade,
we shall never prosper.

Bawd. Thou sayest true: 'tis not our bringing up of poor
bastards,—as, I think, I have brought up some eleven—

Boult. Ay, to eleven; and brought them down again. But
shall I search the market?

Bawd. What else, man? The stuff we have, a strong wind
will blow it to pieces, they are so pitifully sodden.

Pand. Thou sayest true; they're too unwholesome, o' conscience. The poor Transylvanian is dead, that lay with the
little baggage.

Boult. Ay, she quickly pooped him; she made him roast-meat
for worms. But I'll go search the market.   [*Exit.*

Pand. Three or four thousand chequins were as pretty a
proportion to live quietly, and so give over.

Bawd. Why to give over, I pray you? is it a shame to get
when we are old?

Pand. O, our credit comes not in like the commodity, nor the
commodity wages not with the danger: therefore, if in our
youths we could pick up some pretty estate, 'twere not amiss
to keep our door hatched. Besides, the sore terms we stand
upon with the gods will be strong with us for giving o'er.

Bawd. Come, other sorts offend as well as we.

Pand. As well as we! ay, and better too; we offend worse.
Neither is our profession any trade; it's no calling. But
here comes Boult.

Re-enter Boult, with the Pirates and Marina.

Boult. [*To Marina*] Come your ways. My masters, you say
she's a virgin?

First Pirate. O, sir, we doubt it not.

Boult. Master, I have gone through for this piece, you see: if
you like her, so; if not, I have lost my earnest.

Bawd. Boult, has she any qualities?

Boult. She has a good face, speaks well, and has excellent good
clothes : there's no farther necessity of qualities can make
her be refused.

Bawd. What's her price, Boult?

Boult. I cannot be bated one doit of a thousand pieces.

Pand. Well, follow me, my masters, you shall have your money
presently. Wife, take her in ; instruct her what she has to
do, that she may not be raw in her entertainment.

                                 [*Exeunt Pandar and Pirates.*

Bawd. Boult, take you the marks of her, the colour of her hair,
complexion, height, her age, with warrant of her virginity ;
and cry 'He that will give most shall have her first.' Such
a maidenhead were no cheap thing, if men were as they have
been. Get this done as I command you.

Boult. Performance shall follow.   [*Exit.*

Mar. Alack that Leonine was so slack, so slow !
  He should have struck, not spoke ; or that these pirates,
  Not enough barbarous, had not o'erboard thrown me
  For to seek my mother.

Bawd. Why lament you, pretty one?

Mar. That I am pretty.

Bawd. Come, the gods have done their part in you.

Mar. I accuse them not.

Bawd. You are light into my hands, where you are like to live.

Mar. The more my fault,
  To 'scape his hands where I was like to die.

Bawd. Ay, and you shall live in pleasure.

Mar. No.

Bawd. Yes, indeed shall you, and taste gentlemen of all
fashions : you shall fare well ; you shall have the difference
of all complexions. What ! do you stop your ears?

Mar. Are you a woman?

Bawd. What would you have me be, an I be not a woman?

Mar. An honest woman, or not a woman.

Bawd. Marry, whip thee, gosling : I think I shall have something to do with you. Come, you're a young foolish sapling,
and must be bowed as I would have you.

Mar. The gods defend me !

Bawd. If it please the gods to defend you by men, then men
must comfort you, men must feed you, men must stir you
up. Boult's returned.

                        Re-enter Boult.

  Now, sir, hast thou cried her through the market?

Boult. I have cried her almost to the number of her hairs : I
have drawn her picture with my voice.

Bawd. And I prithee tell me, how dost thou find the inclination of the people, especially of the younger sort?

Boult. Faith, they listened to me as they would have hearkened to their father's testament. There was a Spaniard's mouth so watered, that he went to bed to her very description.

Bawd. We shall have him here to-morrow with his best ruff on.

Boult. To-night, to-night. But, mistress, do you know the French knight that cowers i' the hams?

Bawd. Who, Monsieur Veroles?

Boult. Ay, he: he offered to cut a caper at the proclamation; but he made a groan at it, and swore he would see her to-morrow.

Bawd. Well, well; as for him, he brought his disease hither: here he does but repair it. I know he will come in our shadow, to scatter his crowns in the sun.

Boult. Well, if we had of every nation a traveller, we should lodge them with this sign.

Bawd. Pray you, come hither awhile. You have fortunes coming upon you. Mark me: you must seem to do that fearfully which you commit willingly, despise profit where you have most gain. To weep that you live as ye do makes pity in your lovers: seldom but that pity begets you a good opinion, and that opinion a mere profit.

Mar. I understand you not.

Boult. O, take her home, mistress, take her home: these blushes of hers must be quenched with some present practice.

Bawd. Thou sayest true, i' faith, so they must; for your bride goes to that with shame which is her way to go with warrant.

Boult. Faith, some do, and some do not. But, mistress, if I have bargained for the joint,—

Bawd. Thou mayst cut a morsel off the spit.

Boult. I may so.

Bawd. Who should deny it? Come, young one, I like the manner of your garments well.

Boult. Ay, by my faith, they shall not be changed yet.

Bawd. Boult, spend thou that in the town: report what a sojourner we have; you'll lose nothing by custom. When nature framed this piece, she meant thee a good turn; therefore say what a paragon she is, and thou hast the harvest out of thine own report.

Boult. I warrant you, mistress, thunder shall not so awake the beds of eels as my giving out her beauty stir up the lewdly-inclined. I'll bring home some to-night.

Bawd. Come your ways; follow me.

Mar. If fires be hot, knives sharp, or waters deep,
    Untied I still my virgin knot will keep.
    Diana, aid my purpose!
Bawd. What have we to do with Diana? Pray you, will you
    go with us?   [*Exeunt.*

Scene III

Tarsus. A room in the Governor's house.
Enter Cleon and Dionyza.

Dion. Why, are you foolish? Can it be undone?
Cle. O Dionyza, such a piece of slaughter
    The sun and moon ne'er look'd upon!
Dion.   I think
    You'll turn a child again.
Cle. Were I chief lord of all this spacious world,
    I'ld give it to undo the deed. O lady,
    Much less in blood than virtue, yet a princess
    To equal any single crown o' the earth
    I' the justice of compare! O villain Leonine!
    Whom thou hast poison'd too:
    If thou hadst drunk to him, 't had been a kindness
    Becoming well thy fact: what canst thou say
    When noble Pericles shall demand his child?
Dion. That she is dead. Nurses are not the fates,
    To foster it, nor ever to preserve.
    She died at night; I'll say so. Who can cross it?
    Unless you play the pious innocent,
    And for an honest attribute cry out
    'She died by foul play.'
Cle.   O, go to. Well, well,
    Of all the faults beneath the heavens, the gods
    Do like this worst.
Dion.   Be one of those that think
    The petty wrens of Tarsus will fly hence
    And open this to Pericles. I do shame
    To think of what a noble strain you are
    And of how coward a spirit.
Cle.   To such proceeding
    Who ever but his approbation added,
    Though not his prime consent, he did not flow
    From honourable sources.
Dion.   Be it so, then:
    Yet none does know, but you, how she came dead
    Nor none can know, Leonine being gone.
    She did distain my child, and stood between

Her and her fortunes: none would look on her,
But cast their gazes on Marina's face;
Whilst ours was blurted at, and held a malkin,
Not worth the time of day.   It pierced me thorough;
And though you call my course unnatural,
You not your child well loving, yet I find
It greets me as an enterprise of kindness
Perform'd to your sole daughter.

Cle.   Heavens forgive it!

Dion. And as for Pericles,
What should he say?   We wept after her hearse,
And yet we mourn: her monument
Is almost finish'd, and her epitaphs
In glittering golden characters express
A general praise to her, and care in us
At whose expense 'tis done.

Cle.   Thou art like the harpy,
Which, to betray, dost, with thine angel's face,
Seize with thine eagle's talons.

Dion. You are like one that superstitiously
Doth swear to the gods that winter kills the flies:
But yet I know you 'll do as I advise.   [*Exeunt.*

SCENE IV

Enter Gower, before the monument of Marina at Tarsus.

Gow. Thus time we waste, and longest leagues make short;
Sail seas in cockles, have and wish but for 't;
Making, to take our imagination,
From bourn to bourn, region to region.
By you being pardon'd, we commit no crime
To use one language in each several clime
Where our scenes seem to live.   I do beseech you
To learn of me, who stand i' the gaps to teach you
The stages of our story.   Pericles
Is now again thwarting the wayward seas,
Attended on by many a lord and knight,
To see his daughter, all his life's delight.
Old Helicanus goes along; behind
Is left to govern it, you bear in mind
Old Escanes, whom Helicanus late
Advanced in time to great and high estate.
Well-sailing ships and bounteous winds have brought
This king to Tarsus,—think his pilot thought:
So with his steerage shall your thoughts grow on,—
To fetch his daughter home, who first is gone.

Like motes and shadows see them move awhile;
Your ears unto your eyes I'll reconcile.

DUMB SHOW

*Enter Pericles at one door, with all his train; Cleon and Dionyza
    at the other. Cleon shows Pericles the tomb; whereat Pericles
    makes lamentation, puts on sackcloth, and in a mighty
    passion departs. Then exeunt Cleon, Dionyza, and the rest.*

See how belief may suffer by foul show!
This borrow'd passion stands for true old woe;
And Pericles, in sorrow all devour'd,
With sighs shot through and biggest tears o'ershower'd,
Leaves Tarsus and again embarks. He swears
Never to wash his face, nor cut his hairs:
He puts on sackcloth, and to sea. He bears
A tempest, which his mortal vessel tears,
And yet he rides it out. Now please you wit
The epitaph is for Marina writ
By wicked Dionyza.

             [Reads the inscription on Marina's monument.
'The fairest, sweet'st and best, lies here,
Who wither'd in her spring of year.
She was of Tyrus the king's daughter,
On whom foul death hath made this slaughter;
Marina was she call'd; and at her birth,
Thetis, being proud, swallow'd some part o' the earth
Therefore the earth, fearing to be o'erflow'd:
Hath Thetis' birth-child on the heavens bestow'd:
Wherefore she does, and swears she'll never stint,
Make raging battery upon shores of flint.'
No visor does become black villany
So well as soft and tender flattery.
Let Pericles believe his daughter's dead,
And bear his courses to be ordered
By Lady Fortune; while our scene must play
His daughter's woe and heavy well-a-day
In her unholy service. Patience, then,
And think you now are all in Mytilene.   *[Exit.*

SCENE V

Mytilene. A street before the brothel.
Enter, from the brothel, two Gentlemen.

First Gent. Did you ever hear the like?

Sec. Gent. No, nor never shall do in such a place as this, she
being once gone.

First Gent. But to have divinity preached there! did you ever
 dream of such a thing?

Sec. Gent. No, no.   Come, I am for no more bawdy-houses:
 shall's go hear the vestals sing?

First Gent. I'll do any thing now that is virtuous; but I am
 out of the road of rutting for ever.   [*Exeunt.*

SCENE VI

The same.   A room in the brothel.

Enter Pandar, Bawd, and Boult.

Pand. Well, I had rather than twice the worth of her she had
 ne'er come here.

Bawd. Fie, fie upon her! she's able to freeze the god Priapus,
 and undo a whole generation.   We must either get her
 ravished or be rid of her.   When she should do for clients
 her fitment and do me the kindness of our profession, she
 has me her quirks, her reasons, her master reasons, her
 prayers, her knees; that she would make a puritan of the
 devil, if he should cheapen a kiss of her.

Boult. Faith, I must ravish her, or she'll disfurnish us of all
 our cavaliers and make all our swearers priests.

Pand. Now, the pox upon her green-sickness for me!

Bawd. Faith, there's no way to be rid on't but by the way to
 the pox.   Here comes the Lord Lysimachus disguised.

Boult. We should have both lord and lown, if the peevish
 baggage would but give way to customers.

Enter Lysimachus.

Lys. How now! How a dozen of virginities?

Bawd. Now, the gods to-bless your honour!

Boult. I am glad to see your honour in good health.

Lys. You may so; 'tis the better for you that your resorters
 stand upon sound legs.   How now, wholesome iniquity have
 you that a man may deal withal, and defy the surgeon?

Bawd. We have here one, sir, if she would—but there never
 came her like in Mytilene.

Lys. If she'ld do the deed of darkness, thou wouldst say.

Bawd. Your honour knows what 'tis to say well enough.

Lys. Well, call forth, call forth.

Boult. For flesh and blood, sir, white and red, you shall see a
 rose; and she were a rose indeed, if she had but—

Lys. What, prithee?

Boult. O, sir, I can be modest.

Lys. That dignifies the renown of a bawd, no less than it gives
 a good report to a number to be chaste.   [*Exit Boult.*

Bawd. Here comes that which grows to the stalk; never plucked yet, I can assure you.

Re-enter Boult with Marina.

Is she not a fair creature?

Lys. Faith, she would serve after a long voyage at sea. Well, there's for you: leave us.

Bawd. I beseech your honour, give me leave: a word, and I'll have done presently.

Lys. I beseech you, do.

Bawd. [*To Marina*] First, I would have you note, this is an honourable man.

Mar. I desire to find him so, that I may worthily note him.

Bawd. Next, he's the governor of this country, and a man whom I am bound to.

Mar. If he govern the country, you are bound to him indeed; but how honourable he is in that, I know not.

Bawd. Pray you, without any more virginal fencing, will you use him kindly? He will line your apron with gold.

Mar. What he will do graciously, I will thankfully receive.

Lys. Ha' you done?

Bawd. My lord, she's not paced yet: you must take some pains to work her to your manage. Come, we will leave his honour and her together. Go thy ways.

[*Exeunt Bawd, Pandar, and Boult.*

Lys. Now, pretty one, how long have you been at this trade?

Mar. What trade, sir?

Lys. Why, I cannot name 't but I shall offend.

Mar. I cannot be offended with my trade. Please you to name it.

Lys. How long have you been of this profession?

Mar. E'er since I can remember.

Lys. Did you go to it so young? Were you a gamester at five or at seven?

Mar. Earlier too, sir, if now I be one.

Lys. Why, the house you dwell in proclaims you to be a creature of sale.

Mar. Do you know this house to be a place of such resort, and will come into 't? I hear say you are of honourable parts and are the governor of this place.

Lys. Why, hath your principal made known unto you who I

Mar. Who is my principal? [am?

Lys. Why, your herb-woman; she that sets seeds and roots of shame and iniquity. O, you have heard something of my power, and so stand aloof for more serious wooing. But I protest to thee, pretty one, my authority shall not see thee,

　　　or else look friendly upon thee.　Come, bring me to some
　　　private place : come, come.
Mar.　If you were born to honour, show it now ;
　　　If put upon you, make the judgement good
　　　That thought you worthy of it.
Lys.　How 's this ? how 's this ?　Some more ; be sage.
Mar.　　　　　　　　　　　　　　　　　　For me,
　　　That am a maid, though most ungentle fortune
　　　Have placed me in this sty, where, since I came,
　　　Diseases have been sold dearer than physic,
　　　O, that the gods
　　　Would set me free from this unhallow'd place,
　　　Though they did change me to the meanest bird
　　　That flies i' the purer air !
Lys.　　　　　　　　　　I did not think
　　　Thou couldst have spoke so well ; ne'er dream'd thou couldst.
　　　Had I brought hither a corrupted mind,
　　　Thy speech had alter'd it.　Hold, here 's gold for thee :
　　　Persever in that clear way thou goest,
　　　And the gods strengthen thee !
Mar.　　　　　　　　　　The good gods preserve you !
Lys.　For me, be you thoughten
　　　That I came with no ill intent ; for to me
　　　The very doors and windows savour vilely.
　　　Fare thee well.　Thou art a piece of virtue, and
　　　I doubt not but thy training hath been noble.
　　　Hold, here 's more gold for thee.
　　　A curse upon him, die he like a thief,
　　　That robs thee of thy goodness !　If thou dost
　　　Hear from me, it shall be for thy good.
　　　　　　　　　　　Re-enter Boult.
Boult.　I beseech your honour, one piece for me.
Lys.　Avaunt, thou damned door-keeper !
　　　Your house, but for this virgin that doth prop it,
　　　Would sink, and overwhelm you.　Away !　　　　　*[Exit.*
Boult.　How 's this ?　We must take another course with you.
　　　If your peevish chastity, which is not worth a breakfast in
　　　the cheapest country under the cope, shall undo a whole
　　　household, let me be gelded like a spaniel.　Come your ways.
Mar.　Whither would you have me ?
Boult.　I must have your maidenhead taken off, or the common
　　　hangman shall execute it.　Come your ways.　We 'll have
　　　no more gentlemen driven away.　Come your ways, I say.
　　　　　　　　　　　Re-enter Bawd.
Bawd.　How now !　what 's the matter ?

Boult. Worse and worse, mistress; she has here spoken holy
words to the Lord Lysimachus.

Bawd. O abominable!

Boult. She makes our profession as it were to stink afore the
face of the gods.

Bawd. Marry, hang her up for ever!

Boult. The nobleman would have dealt with her like a nobleman, and she sent him away as cold as a snowball, saying
his prayers too.

Bawd. Boult, take her away; use her at thy pleasure: crack the
glass of her virginity, and make the rest malleable.

Boult. An if she were a thornier piece of ground than she is,
she shall be ploughed.

Mar. Hark, hark, you gods!

Bawd. She conjures: away with her! Would she had never
come within my doors! Marry, hang you! She's born to
undo us. Will you not go the way of women-kind? Marry,
come up, my dish of chastity with rosemary and bays! [*Exit.*

Boult. Come, mistress; come your ways with me.

Mar. Whither wilt thou have me?

Boult. To take from you the jewel you hold so dear.

Mar. Prithee, tell me one thing first.

Boult. Come now, your one thing.

Mar. What canst thou wish thine enemy to be?

Boult. Why, I could wish him to be my master, or rather, my
[mistress.

Mar. Neither of these are so bad as thou art,
Since they do better thee in their command.
Thou hold'st a place, for which the pained'st fiend
Of hell would not in reputation change:
Thou art the damned door-keeper to every
Coistrel that comes inquiring for his Tib;
To the choleric fisting of every rogue
Thy ear is liable; thy food is such
As hath been belch'd on by infected lungs.

Boult. What would you have me do? go to the wars, would
you? where a man may serve seven years for the loss of a
leg, and have not money enough in the end to buy him a
wooden one?

Mar. Do any thing but this thou doest   Empty
Old receptacles, or common shores, of filth;
Serve by indenture to the common hangman:
Any of these ways are yet better than this;
For what thou professest, a baboon, could he speak,
Would own a name too dear. O, that the gods
Would safely deliver me from this place!

    Here, here 's gold for thee.
    If that thy master would gain by me,
    Proclaim that I can sing, weave, sew, and dance,
    With other virtues, which I 'll keep from boast;
    And I will undertake all these to teach.
    I doubt not but this populous city will
    Yield many scholars.
Boult. But can you teach all this you speak of?
Mar. Prove that I cannot, take me home again,
    And prostitute me to the basest groom
    That doth frequent your house.
Boult. Well, I will see what I can do for thee : if I can place
Mar. But amongst honest women.   [thee, I will.
Boult. Faith, my acquaintance lies little amongst them. But
    since my master and mistress have bought you, there 's no
    going but by their consent : therefore I will make them
    acquainted with your purpose, and I doubt not but I shall
    find them tractable enough. Come, I 'll do for thee what I
    can ; come your ways.   [*Exeunt.*

ACT V

Enter Gower.

Gow. Marina thus the brothel 'scapes, and chances
    Into an honest house, our story says.
    She sings like one immortal, and she dances
    As goddess-like to her admired lays;
    Deep clerks she dumbs, and with her needle composes
    Nature's own shape, of bud, bird, branch, or berry,
    That even her art sisters the natural roses ;
    Her inkle, silk, twin with the rubied cherry :
    That pupils lacks she none of noble race,
    Who pour their bounty on her, and her gain
    She gives the cursed bawd. Here we her place;
    And to her father turn our thoughts again,
    Where we left him, on the sea. We there him lost:
    Whence, driven before the winds, he is arrived
    Here where his daughter dwells ; and on this coast
    Suppose him now at anchor. The city strived
    God Neptune's annual feast to keep : from whence
    Lysimachus our Tyrian ship espies,
    His banners sable, trimm'd with rich expense;
    And to him in his barge with fervour hies.
    In your supposing once more put your sight
    Of heavy Pericles; think this his bark :

Where what is done in action, more, if might,
Shall be discover'd ; please you, sit, and hark.   [*Exit.*

SCENE I

*On board Pericles' ship, off Mytilene. A close pavilion on deck,
with a curtain before it ; Pericles within it, reclined on a
couch. A barge lying beside the Tyrian vessel.*

*Enter two sailors, one belonging to the Tyrian vessel, the other
to the barge ; to them Helicanus.*

Tyr. Sail. [*To the Sailor of Mytilene*] Where is Lord Helicanus ?
  he can resolve you.

  O, here he is.

  Sir, there is a barge put off from Mytilene,
  And in it is Lysimachus the governor,
  Who craves to come aboard.   What is your will ?

Hel. That he have his.   Call up some gentlemen.

Tyr. Sail. Ho, gentlemen ! my lord calls.

Enter two or three Gentlemen.

First Gent. Doth your lordship call ?

Hel. Gentlemen, there is some of worth would come aboard ;
  I pray, greet him fairly.

    [*The Gentlemen and the two Sailors descend, and go on
      board the barge.*

*Enter from thence, Lysimachus, and Lords ; with the Gentlemen
      and the two Sailors.*

Tyr. Sail. Sir,
  This is the man that can, in aught you would,
  Resolve you.

Lys. Hail, reverend sir ! the gods preserve you !

Hel. And you, sir, to outlive the age I am,
  And die as I would do.

Lys.   You wish me well.
  Being on shore, honouring of Neptune's triumphs,
  Seeing this goodly vessel ride before us,
  I made to it, to know of whence you are.

Hel. First, what is your place ?

Lys. I am the governor of this place you lie before.

Hel. Sir,
  Our vessel is of Tyre, in it the king ;
  A man who for this three months hath not spoken
  To any one, nor taken sustenance
  But to prorogue his grief.

Lys. Upon what ground is his distemperature ?

Hel. 'Twould be too tedious to repeat ;
  But the main grief springs from the loss

Of a beloved daughter and a wife.

Lys. May we not see him?

Hel. You may;
    But bootless is your sight; he will not speak
    To any.

Lys. Yet let me obtain my wish.

Hel. Behold him. [*Pericles discovered.*] This was a goodly
    Till the disaster that, one mortal night,   [person,
    Drove him to this.

Lys. Sir king, all hail! the gods preserve you!
    Hail, royal sir!

Hel. It is in vain; he will not speak to you.

First Lord. Sir,
    We have a maid in Mytilene, I durst wager
    Would win some words of him.

Lys.   'Tis well bethought.
    She, questionless, with her sweet harmony
    And other chosen attractions, would allure,
    And make a battery through his deafen'd parts,
    Which now are midway stopp'd:
    She is all happy as the fairest of all,
    And with her fellow maids is now upon
    The leafy shelter that abuts against
    The island's side.
        [*Whispers a Lord, who goes off in the barge of Lysimachus.*

Hel. Sure, all 's effectless; yet nothing we 'll omit
    That bears recovery's name. But, since your kindness
    We have stretch'd thus far, let us beseech you
    That for our gold we may provision have,
    Wherein we are not destitute for want,
    But weary for the staleness.

Lys.   O, sir, a courtesy
    Which if we should deny, the most just gods
    For every graff would send a caterpillar,
    And so inflict our province. Yet once more
    Let me entreat to know at large the cause
    Of your king's sorrow.

Hel.   Sit, sir, I will recount it to you.
    But, see, I am prevented.
            *Re-enter, from the barge, Lord, with Marina, and a
                            young Lady.*

Lys.   O, here is
    The lady that I sent for. Welcome, fair one!—
    Is 't not a goodly presence?

Hel.   She 's a gallant lady.

298

Lys. She 's such a one, that, were I well assured
    Came of a gentle kind and noble stock,
    I 'ld wish no better choice, and think me rarely wed.
    Fair one, all goodness that consists in bounty
    Expect even here, where is a kingly patient:
    If that thy prosperous and artificial feat
    Can draw him but to answer thee in aught,
    Thy sacred physic shall receive such pay
    As thy desires can wish.
Mar.   Sir, I will use
    My utmost skill in his recovery, provided
    That none but I and my companion maid
    Be suffer'd to come near him.
Lys.   Come, let us leave her;
    And the gods make her prosperous!   [*Marina sings.*
Lys. Mark'd he your music?
Mar.   No, nor look'd on us.
Lys. See, she will speak to him.
Mar. Hail, sir! my lord, lend ear.
Per. Hum, ha!
Mar. I am a maid,
    My lord, that ne'er before invited eyes,
    But have been gazed on like a comet: she speaks,
    My lord, that, may be, hath endured a grief
    Might equal yours, if both were justly weigh'd.
    Though wayward fortune did malign my state,
    My derivation was from ancestors
    Who stood equivalent with mighty kings:
    But time hath rooted out my parentage,
    And to the world and awkward casualties
    Bound me in servitude. [*Aside*] I will desist;
    But there is something glows upon my cheek,
    And whispers in mine ear 'Go not till he speak.'
Per. My fortunes—parentage—good parentage—
    To equal mine!—was it not thus? what say you?
Mar. I said, my lord, if you did know my parentage,
    You would not do me violence.
Per. I do think so. Pray you, turn your eyes upon me.
    You are like something that—What countrywoman?
    Here of these shores?
Mar.   No, nor of any shores:
    Yet I was mortally brought forth, and am
    No other than I appear.
Per. I am great with woe, and shall deliver weeping.
    My dearest wife was like this maid, and such a one

My daughter might have been: my queen's square brows;
Her stature to an inch; as wand-like straight,
As silver-voiced; her eyes as jewel-like
And cased as richly; in pace another Juno;
Who starves the ears she feeds, and makes them hungry,
The more she gives them speech.   Where do you live?

Mar. Where I am but a stranger: from the deck
You may discern the place.

Per.   Where were you bred?
And how achieved you these endowments, which
You make more rich to owe?

Mar. If I should tell my history, it would seem
Like lies disdain'd in the reporting.

Per.   Prithee, speak:
Falseness cannot come from thee; for thou look'st
Modest as Justice, and thou seem'st a palace
For the crown'd Truth to dwell in: I will believe thee,
And make my senses credit thy relation
To points that seem impossible; for thou look'st
Like one I loved indeed.   What were thy friends?
Didst thou not say, when I did push thee back—
Which was when I perceived thee—that thou camest
From good descending?

Mar.   So indeed I did.

Per. Report thy parentage.   I think thou said'st
Thou hadst been toss'd from wrong to injury,
And that thou thought'st thy griefs might equal mine,
If both were open'd.

Mar.   Some such thing
I said, and said no more but what my thoughts
Did warrant me was likely.

Per.   Tell thy story;
If thine consider'd prove the thousandth part
Of my endurance, thou art a man, and I
Have suffer'd like a girl: yet thou dost look
Like Patience gazing on kings' graves and smiling
Extremity out of act.   What were thy friends?
How lost thou them?   Thy name, my most kind virgin?
Recount, I do beseech thee: come, sit by me.

Mar. My name is Marina.

Per.   O, I am mock'd,
And thou by some incensed god sent hither
To make the world to laugh at me.

Mar.   Patience, good sir,
Or here I 'll cease.

Per.   Nay, I 'll be patient.
   Thou little know'st how thou dost startle me,
   To call thyself Marina.
Mar.   The name
   Was given me by one that had some power,
   My father, and a king.
Per.   How! a king's daughter?
   And call'd Marina?
Mar.   You said you would believe me;
   But, not to be a troubler of your peace,
   I will end here.
Per.   But are you flesh and blood?
   Have you a working pulse? and are no fairy?
   Motion! Well; speak on. Where were you born?
   And wherefore call'd Marina?
Mar.   Call'd Marina,
   For I was born at sea.
Per.   At sea! what mother?
Mar. My mother was the daughter of a king;
   Who died the minute I was born,
   As my good nurse Lychorida hath oft
   Deliver'd weeping.
Per.   O, stop there a little!
   [*Aside*] This is the rarest dream that e'er dull sleep
   Did mock sad fools withal: this cannot be:
   My daughter 's buried.—Well: where were you bred?
   I 'll hear you more, to the bottom of your story,
   And never interrupt you.
Mar. You scorn: believe me, 'twere best I did give o'er.
Per. I will believe you by the syllable
   Of what you shall deliver. Yet, give me leave:
   How came you in these parts? where were you bred?
Mar. The king my father did in Tarsus leave me;
   Till cruel Cleon, with his wicked wife,
   Did seek to murder me: and having woo'd
   A villain to attempt it, who having drawn to do 't,
   A crew of pirates came and rescued me;
   Brought me to Mytilene. But, good sir,
   Whither will you have me? Why do you weep? It may be,
   You think me an impostor: no, good faith;
   I am the daughter to King Pericles,
   If good King Pericles be.
Per. Ho, Helicanus!
Hel. Calls my lord?
Per. Thou art a grave and noble counsellor,

Most wise in general : tell me, if thou canst,
What this maid is, or what is like to be,
That thus hath made me weep.

Hel.   I know not; but
Here is the regent, sir, of Mytilene
Speaks nobly of her.

Lys.   She never would tell
Her parentage ; being demanded that,
She would sit still and weep.

Per. O Helicanus, strike me, honour'd sir ;
Give me a gash, put me to present pain ;
Lest this great sea of joys rushing upon me
O'erbear the shores of my mortality,
And drown me with their sweetness.   O, come hither,
Thou that beget'st him that did thee beget ;
Thou that wast born at sea, buried at Tarsus,
And found at sea again !   O Helicanus,
Down on thy knees ; thank the holy gods as loud
As thunder threatens us : this is Marina.
What was thy mother's name ? tell me but that,
For truth can never be confirm'd enough,
Though doubts did ever sleep.

Mar. First, sir, I pray, what is your title ?

Per.   I
Am Pericles of Tyre : but tell me now
My drown'd queen's name, as in the rest you said
Thou hast been godlike perfect, the heir of kingdoms,
And another like to Pericles thy father.

Mar. Is it no more to be your daughter than
To say my mother's name was Thaisa ?
Thaisa was my mother, who did end
The minute I began.

Per. Now, blessing on thee ! rise ; thou art my child.
Give me fresh garments.   Mine own, Helicanus :
She is not dead at Tarsus, as she should have been,
By savage Cleon : she shall tell thee all ;
When thou shalt kneel, and justify in knowledge
She is thy very princess.   Who is this ?

Hel. Sir, 'tis the governor of Mytilene,
Who, hearing of your melancholy state,
Did come to see you.

Per. I embrace you.
Give me my robes.   I am wild in my beholding.
O heavens bless my girl !   But, hark, what music ?
Tell Helicanus, my Marina, tell him

O'er, point by point, for yet he seems to doubt,
How sure you are my daughter.   But, what music?
Hel. My lord, I hear none.
Per. None!
The music of the spheres!   List, my Marina.
Lys. It is not good to cross him; give him way.
Per. Rarest sounds!   Do ye not hear?
Lys.   My lord, I hear.   [*Music.*
Per. Most heavenly music!
It nips me unto listening, and thick slumber
Hangs upon mine eyes : let me rest.   [*Sleeps.*
Lys. A pillow for his head :
So, leave him all.   Well, my companion friends,
If this but answer to my just belief,
I 'll well remember you.   [*Exeunt all but Pericles.*
         Diana appears to Pericles in a vision.
Dia. My temple stands in Ephesus : hie thee thither,
And do upon mine altar sacrifice.
There, when my maiden priests are met together,
Before the people all,
Reveal how thou at sea didst lose thy wife :
To mourn thy crosses, with thy daughter's, call,
And give them repetition to the life.
Or perform my bidding, or thou livest in woe;
Do it, and happy; by my silver bow!
Awake, and tell thy dream.   [*Disappears.*
Per. Celestial Dian, goddess argentine,
I will obey thee.   Helicanus!
       Re-enter Helicanus, Lysimachus, and Marina.
Hel.   Sir?
Per. My purpose was for Tarsus, there to strike
The inhospitable Cleon; but I am
For other service first : toward Ephesus
Turn our blown sails; eftsoons I 'll tell thee why.
[*To Lysimachus*] Shall we refresh us, sir, upon your shore,
And give you gold for such provision
As our intents will need?
Lys. Sir,
With all my heart; and, when you come ashore,
I have another suit.
Per.   You shall prevail,
Were it to woo my daughter; for it seems
You have been noble towards her.
Lys.   Sir, lend me your arm.
Per. Come, my Marina.   [*Exeunt.*

SCENE II

Enter Gower, before the temple of Diana at Ephesus.

Gow. Now our sands are almost run ;
　　More a little, and then dumb.
　　This, my last boon, give me,
　　For such kindness must relieve me,
　　That you aptly will suppose
　　What pageantry, what feats, what shows,
　　What minstrelsy and pretty din,
　　The regent made in Mytilene,
　　To greet the king.   So he thrived,
　　That he is promised to be wived
　　To fair Marina ; but in no wise
　　Till he had done his sacrifice,
　　As Dian bade : whereto being bound,
　　The interim, pray you, all confound.
　　In feather'd briefness sails are fill'd,
　　And wishes fall out as they're will'd.
　　At Ephesus, the temple see,
　　Our king and all his company.
　　That he can hither come so soon,
　　Is by your fancies' thankful doom.   [*Exit.*

SCENE III

*The temple of Diana at Ephesus ; Thaisa standing near the
altar, as high priestess ; a number of Virgins on each side ;
Cerimon and other Inhabitants of Ephesus attending.*

*Enter Pericles, with his train ; Lysimachus, Helicanus,
Marina, and a Lady.*

Per. Hail, Dian ! to perform thy just command,
　　I here confess myself the king of Tyre ;
　　Who, frighted from my country, did wed
　　At Pentapolis the fair Thaisa.
　　At sea in childbed died she, but brought forth
　　A maid-child call'd Marina ; who, O goddess,
　　Wears yet thy silver livery.   She at Tarsus
　　Was nursed with Cleon ; who at fourteen years
　　He sought to murder : but her better stars
　　Brought her to Mytilene ; 'gainst whose shore
　　Riding, her fortunes brought the maid aboard us,
　　Where, by her own most clear remembrance, she
　　Made known herself my daughter.

Thai.   Voice and favour !
　　You are, you are—O royal Pericles !—   [*Faints.*

Per. What means the nun? she dies! help, gentlemen!

Cer. Noble sir,
If you have told Diana's altar true,
This is your wife.

Per.   Reverend appearer, no;
I threw her overboard with these very arms.

Cer. Upon this coast, I warrant you.

Per.   'Tis most certain.

Cer. Look to the lady. O, she's but overjoy'd.
Early in blustering morn this lady was
Thrown upon this shore. I oped the coffin,
Found there rich jewels; recover'd her, and placed her
Here in Diana's temple.

Per.   May we see them?

Cer. Great sir, they shall be brought you to my house,
Whither I invite you. Look, Thaisa is
Recovered,

Thai. O, let me look!
If he be none of mine, my sanctity
Will to my sense bend no licentious ear,
But curb it, spite of seeing. O, my lord,
Are you not Pericles? Like him you spake,
Like him you are: did you not name a tempest,
A birth, and death?

Per.   The voice of dead Thaisa!

Thai. That Thaisa am I, supposed dead
And drown'd.

Per. Immortal Dian!

Thai.   Now I know you better
When we with tears parted Pentapolis,
The king my father gave you such a ring. [*Shows a ring.*

Per. This, this: no more, you gods! your present kindness
Makes my past miseries sports: you shall do well,
That on the touching of her lips I may
Melt, and no more be seen. O, come, be buried
A second time within these arms.

Mar.   My heart
Leaps to be gone into my mother's bosom. [*Kneels to Thaisa.*

Per. Look, who kneels here! Flesh of thy flesh, Thaisa;
Thy burden at the sea, and call'd Marina
For she was yielded there.

Thai.   Blest, and mine own!

Hel. Hail, madam, and my queen!

Thai.   I know you not.

Per. You have heard me say, when I did fly from Tyre,

305

I left behind an ancient substitute:
Can you remember what I call'd the man?
I have named him oft.

Thai.   'Twas Helicanus then.

Per. Still confirmation:
Embrace him, dear Thaisa; this is he.
Now do I long to hear how you were found;
How possibly preserved; and who to thank,
Besides the gods, for this great miracle.

Thai. Lord Cerimon, my lord; this man,
Through whom the gods have shown their power: that can
From first to last resolve you.

Per.   Reverend sir,
The gods can have no mortal officer
More like a god than you. Will you deliver
How this dead queen re-lives?

Cer.   I will, my lord.
Beseech you, first go with me to my house,
Where shall be shown you all was found with her;
How she came placed here in the temple;
No needful thing omitted.

Per. Pure Dian, bless thee for thy vision! I
Will offer night-oblations to thee. Thaisa,
This prince, the fair-betrothed of your daughter,
Shall marry her at Pentapolis. And now,
This ornament
Makes me look dismal will I clip to form;
And what this fourteen years no razor touch'd,
To grace thy marriage-day, I'll beautify.

Thai. Lord Cerimon hath letters of good credit, sir,
My father's dead.

Per. Heavens make a star! Yet there, my queen,
We'll celebrate their nuptials, and ourselves
Will in that kingdom spend our following days:
Our son and daughter shall in Tyrus reign.
Lord Cerimon, we do our longing stay
To hear the rest untold: sir, lead's the way.   [*Exeunt.*

Enter Gower.

Gow. In Antiochus and his daughter you have heard
Of monstrous lust the due and just reward:
In Pericles, his queen and daughter, seen,
Although assail'd with fortune fierce and keen,
Virtue preserved from fell destruction's blast,
Led on by heaven and crown'd with joy at last:
In Helicanus may you well descry

306

A figure of truth, of faith, of loyalty:
In reverend Cerimon there well appears
The worth that learned charity aye wears:
For wicked Cleon and his wife, when fame
Had spread their cursed deed and honour'd name
Of Pericles, to rage the city turn,
That him and his they in his palace burn;
The gods for murder seemed so content
To punish, although not done, but meant.
So, on your patience evermore attending,
New joy wait on you!   Here our play has ending   [Exit.

CYMBELINE

DRAMATIS PERSONÆ

CYMBELINE, *king of Britain.*
CLOTEN, *son to the Queen by a former husband.*
POSTHUMUS LEONATUS, *a gentleman, husband to Imogen.*
BELARIUS, *a banished lord, disguised under the name of Morgan.*
GUIDERIUS, } *sons to Cymbeline, disguised under the names of Polydore and Cadwal, supposed sons to Morgan.*
ARVIRAGUS, }
PHILARIO, { *friend to Posthumus,* } *Italians.*
IACHIMO, *friend to Philario,* }
CAIUS LUCIUS, *General of the Roman forces.*

PISANIO, *servant to Posthumus.*
CORNELIUS, *a physician.*

A Roman Captain.
Two British Captains.
A Frenchman, friend to Philario.
Two Lords of Cymbeline's court.
Two Gentlemen of the same.
Two Gaolers.

Queen, *wife to Cymbeline.*

IMOGEN, *daughter to Cymbeline by a former queen.*
HELEN, *a lady attending on Imogen.*

Lords, Ladies, Roman Senators, Tribunes, a Soothsayer, a Dutchman, a Spaniard, Musicians, Officers, Captains, Soldiers, Messengers, and other Attendants. Apparitions.
SCENE: *Britain: Rome.*

ACT I—SCENE I

Britain. The garden of Cymbeline's palace.
Enter two Gentlemen.

First Gent. You do not meet a man but frowns: our bloods
No more obey the heavens than our courtiers
Still seem as does the king.

Sec. Gent. But what 's the matter?

First Gent. His daughter, and the heir of 's kingdom, whom
He purposed to his wife's sole son—a widow
That late he married—hath referr'd herself
Unto a poor but worthy gentleman: she 's wedded;
Her husband banish'd; she imprison'd: all
Is outward sorrow; though I think the king
Be touch'd at very heart.

Sec. Gent. None but the king?

First Gent. He that hath lost her too: so is the queen,
That most desired the match: but not a courtier,
Although they wear their faces to the bent
Of the king's looks, hath a heart that is not
Glad at the thing they scowl at.

Sec. Gent. And why so?

First Gent. He that hath miss'd the princess is a thing
Too bad for bad report: and he that hath her,
I mean, that married her,—alack, good man!—
And therefore banish'd, is a creature such
As, to seek through the regions of the earth
For one his like, there would be something failing

    In him that should compare.   I do not think
    So fair an outward and such stuff within
    Endows a man but he.
Sec. Gent.   You speak him fair.
First Gent. I do extend him, sir, within himself,
    Crush him together rather than unfold
    His measure duly.
Sec. Gent.   What 's his name and birth?
First Gent. I cannot delve him to the root : his father
    Was call'd Sicilius, who did join his honour
    Against the Romans with Cassibelan,
    But had his titles by Tenantius, whom
    He served with glory and admired success,
    So gain'd the sur-addition Leonatus :
    And had, besides this gentleman in question,
    Two other sons, who in the wars o' the time
    Died with their swords in hand ; for which their father,
    Then old and fond of issue, took such sorrow
    That he quit being, and his gentle lady,
    Big of this gentleman, our theme, deceased
    As he was born.   The king he takes the babe
    To his protection, calls him Posthumus Leonatus,
    Breeds him and makes him of his bed-chamber :
    Puts to him all the learnings that his time
    Could make him the receiver of ; which he took,
    As we do air, fast as 'twas minister'd,
    And in 's spring became a harvest : lived in court—
    Which rare it is to do—most praised, most loved :
    A sample to the youngest, to the more mature
    A glass that feated them, and to the graver
    A child that guided dotards ; to his mistress,
    For whom he now is banish'd, her own price
    Proclaims how she esteem'd him and his virtue ;
    By her election may be truly read
    What kind of man he is.
Sec. Gent.   I honour him
    Even out of your report.   But, pray you, tell me,
    Is she sole child to the king?
First Gent.   His only child.
    He had two sons,—if this be worth your hearing,
    Mark it,—the eldest of them at three years old,
    I' the swathing clothes the other, from their nursery
    Were stolen, and to this hour no guess in knowledge
    Which way they went.
Sec. Gent.   How long is this ago?

First Gent. Some twenty years.

Sec. Gent. That a king's children should be so convey'd!
So slackly guarded! and the search so slow,
That could not trace them!

First Gent.   Howsoe'er 'tis strange,
Or that the negligence may well be laugh'd at,
Yet it is true, sir.

Sec. Gent.   I do well believe you.

First Gent. We must forbear: here comes the gentleman,
The queen and princess.   [*Exeunt.*

   Enter the Queen, Posthumus and Imogen.

Queen. No, be assured you shall not find me, daughter,
After the slander of most stepmothers,
Evil-eyed unto you: you're my prisoner, but
Your gaoler shall deliver you the keys
That lock up your restraint.   For you, Posthumus,
So soon as I can win the offended king,
I will be known your advocate: marry, yet
The fire of rage is in him, and 'twere good
You lean'd unto his sentence with what patience
Your wisdom may inform you.

Post.   Please your highness,
I will from hence to-day.

Queen.   You know the peril.
I 'll fetch a turn about the garden, pitying
The pangs of barr'd affections, though the king
Hath charged you should not speak together.   [*Exit.*

Imo.   O
Dissembling courtesy!   How fine this tyrant
Can tickle where she wounds!   My dearest husband,
I something fear my father's wrath; but nothing—
Always reserved my holy duty—what
His rage can do on me: you must be gone,
And I shall here abide the hourly shot
Of angry eyes, not comforted to live,
But that there is this jewel in the world
That I may see again.

Post.   My queen! my mistress!
O lady, weep no more, lest I give cause
To be suspected of more tenderness
Than doth become a man!   I will remain
The loyal'st husband that did e'er plight troth:
My residence in Rome at one Philario's,
Who to my father was a friend, to me
Known but by letter: thither write, my queen,

And with mine eyes I ll drink the words you send,
Though ink be made of gall.

Re-enter Queen.

Queen.   Be brief, I pray you :
If the king come, I shall incur I know not
How much of his displeasure. [*Aside*] Yet I'll move him
To walk this way : I never do him wrong
But he does buy my injuries, to be friends ;
Pays dear for my offences.   [*Exit.*

Post.   Should we be taking leave
As long a term as yet we have to live,
The loathness to depart would grow.   Adieu !

Imo. Nay, stay a little :
Were you but riding forth to air yourself,
Such parting were too petty.   Look here, love ;
This diamond was my mother's : take it, heart ;
But keep it till you woo another wife,
When Imogen is dead.

Post.   How, how ! another ?
You gentle gods, give me but this I have,
And sear up my embracements from a next   [thou here
With bonds of death ! [*Putting on the ring.*] Remain, remain
While sense can keep it on !   And, sweetest, fairest,
As I my poor self did exchange for you
To your so infinite loss, so in our trifles
I still win of you : for my sake wear this ;
It is a manacle of love ; I 'll place it
Upon this fairest prisoner.   [*Putting a bracelet on her arm.*

Imo.   O the gods !
When shall we see again ?

Enter Cymbeline and Lords.

Post.   Alack, the king !

Cym. Thou basest thing, avoid ! hence, from my sight !
If after this command thou fraught the court
With thy unworthiness, thou diest : away !
Thou 'rt poison to my blood.

Post.   The gods protect you,
And bless the good remainders of the court !
I am gone.   [*Exit.*

Imo.   There cannot be a pinch in death
More sharp than this is.

Cym.   O disloyal thing,
That shouldst repair my youth, thou heap'st
A year's age on me !

Imo.   I beseech you, sir,

Harm not yourself with your vexation:
I am senseless of your wrath; a touch more rare
Subdues all pangs, all fears.
Cym.   Past grace? obedience?
Imo. Past hope, and in despair; that way, past grace.
Cym. That mightst have had the sole son of my queen!
Imo. O blessed, that I might not! I chose an eagle,
And did avoid a puttock.
Cym. Thou took'st a beggar; wouldst have made my throne
A seat for baseness.
Imo.   No; I rather added
A lustre to it.
Cym.   O thou vile one!
Imo.   Sir,
It is your fault that I have loved Posthumus:
You bred him as my playfellow, and he is
A man worth any woman, overbuys me
Almost the sum he pays.
Cym.   What, art thou mad!
Imo. Almost, sir: heaven restore me! Would I were
A neat-herd's daughter, and my Leonatus
Our neighbour-shepherd's son!
Cym.   Thou foolish thing!
                    Re-enter Queen.
They were again together: you have done
Not after our command. Away with her,
And pen her up.
Queen.   Beseech your patience. Peace,
Dear lady daughter, peace! Sweet sovereign,
Leave us to ourselves, and make yourself some comfort
Out of your best advice.
Cym.   Nay, let her languish
A drop of blood a day; and, being aged,
Die of this folly!   [*Exeunt Cymbeline and Lords.*
Queen.   Fie! you must give way.
                    Enter Pisanio.
Here is your servant. How now, sir! What news?
Pis. My lord your son drew on my master.
Queen.   Ha!
No harm, I trust, is done?
Pis.   There might have been,
But that my master rather play'd than fought,
And had no help of anger: they were parted
By gentlemen at hand.
Queen.   I am very glad on 't.

Imo. Your son's my father's friend; he takes his part.
  To draw upon an exile!   O brave sir!
  I would they were in Afric both together;
  Myself by with a needle, that I might prick
  The goer-back.   Why came you from your master?
Pis. On his command: he would not suffer me
  To bring him to the haven: left these notes
  Of what commands I should be subject to
  When 't pleased you to employ me.
Queen.   This hath been
  Your faithful servant: I dare lay mine honour
  He will remain so.
Pis.   I humbly thank your highness.
Queen. Pray, walk awhile.
Imo.   About some half-hour hence,
  I pray you, speak with me: you shall at least
  Go see my lord aboard: for this time leave me.   [*Exeunt.*

SCENE II

The same.   A public place.
Enter Cloten and two Lords.

First Lord. Sir, I would advise you to shift a shirt; the violence
  of action hath made you reek as a sacrifice: where air comes
  out, air comes in: there's none abroad so wholesome as that
  you vent.
Clo. If my shirt were bloody, then to shift it.   Have I hurt him?
Sec. Lord. [*Aside*] No, faith; not so much as his patience.
First Lord. Hurt him! his body's a passable carcass, if he be
  not hurt: it is a throughfare for steel, if it be not hurt.
Sec. Lord. [*Aside*] His steel was in debt; it went o' the back-
  side the town.
Clo. The villain would not stand me.   [face.
Sec. Lord. [*Aside*] No, but he fled forward still, toward your
First Lord. Stand you!   You have land enough of your own;
  but he added to your having; gave you some ground.
Sec. Lord. [*Aside*] As many inches as you have oceans. Puppies!
Clo. I would they had not come between us.
Sec. Lord. [*Aside*] So would I, till you had measured how long
  a fool you were upon the ground.
Clo. And that she should love this fellow, and refuse me!
Sec. Lord. [*Aside*] If it be a sin to make a true election, she is
  damned.
First Lord. Sir, as I told you always, her beauty and her brain
  go not together: she's a good sign, but I have seen small
  reflection of her wit.

Sec. Lord. [*Aside*] She shines not upon fools, lest the reflection
    should hurt her.
Clo. Come, I 'll to my chamber.   Would there had been some
    hurt done !
Sec. Lord. [*Aside*] I wish not so ; unless it had been the fall
    of an ass, which is no great hurt.
Clo. You 'll go with us ?
First Lord. I 'll attend your lordship.
Clo. Nay, come, let 's go together.
Sec. Lord. Well, my lord.   [*Exeunt.*

SCENE III

A room in Cymbeline's palace.

Enter Imogen and Pisanio.

Imo. I would thou grew'st unto the shores o' the haven,
    And question'dst every sail : if he should write
    And I not have it, 'twere a paper lost,
    As offer'd mercy is.   What was the last
    That he spake to thee ?
Pis.   It was, his queen, his queen !
Imo. Then waved his handkerchief ?
Pis.   And kiss'd it, madam.
Imo. Senseless linen ! happier therein than I !
    And that was all ?
Pis.   No, madam ; for so long
    As he could make me with this eye or ear
    Distinguish him from others, he did keep
    The deck, with glove, or hat, or handkerchief,
    Still waving, as the fits and stirs of 's mind
    Could best express how slow his soul sail'd on,
    How swift his ship.
Imo.   Thou shouldst have made him
    As little as a crow, or less, or left
    To after-eye him.
Pis.   Madam, so I did.
Imo. I would have broke mine eye-strings, crack'd them, but
    To look upon him, till the diminution
    Of space had pointed him sharp as my needle ;
    Nay, follow'd him, till he had melted from
    The smallness of a gnat to air ; and then
    Have turn'd mine eye, and wept.   But, good Pisanio,
    When shall we hear from him ?
Pis.   Be assured, madam,
    With his next vantage.
Imo. I did not take my leave of him, but had

314

Most pretty things to say : ere I could tell him
How I would think on him at certain hours,
Such thoughts and such ; or I could make him swear
The shes of Italy should not betray
Mine interest and his honour ; or have charged him,
At the sixth hour of morn, at noon, at midnight,
To encounter me with orisons, for then
I am in heaven for him ; or ere I could
Give him that parting kiss which I had set
Betwixt two charming words, comes in my father,
And, like the tyrannous breathing of the north,
Shakes all our buds from growing.

Enter a Lady.

Lady.   The queen, madam,
Desires your highness' company.
Imo. Those things I bid you do, get them dispatch'd.
I will attend the queen.
Pis.   Madam, I shall.   [*Exeunt.*

Scene IV
Rome.   Philario's house.
*Enter Philario, Iachimo, a Frenchman, a Dutchman,
and a Spaniard.*

Iach. Believe it, sir, I have seen him in Britain : he was then of
a crescent note ; expected to prove so worthy as since he hath
been allowed the name of : but I could then have looked on
him without the help of admiration, though the catalogue of
his endowments had been tabled by his side and I to peruse
him by items.

Phi. You speak of him when he was less furnished than now he
is with that which makes him both without and within.

French. I have seen him in France : we had very many there
could behold the sun with as firm eyes as he.

Iach. This matter of marrying his king's daughter, wherein he
must be weighed ratner by her value than his own, words him,
I doubt not, a great deal from the matter.

French. And then his banishment.

Iach. Ay, and the approbation of those that weep this lamentable divorce under her colours are wonderfully to extend him ;
be it but to fortify her judgement, which else an easy battery
might lay flat, for taking a beggar without less quality.   But
how comes it he is to sojourn with you? how creeps
acquaintance?

Phi. His father and I were soldiers together ; to whom I have
been often bound for no less than my life.   Here comes the

315

Briton : let him be so entertained amongst you as suits, with
gentlemen of your knowing, to a stranger of his quality.

Enter Posthumus.

I beseech you all, be better known to this gentleman ; whom
I commend to you as a noble friend of mine : how worthy he
is I will leave to appear hereafter, rather than story him in his
own hearing.

French. Sir, we have known together in Orleans.

Post. Since when I have been debtor to you for courtesies, which
I will be ever to pay and yet pay still.

French. Sir, you o'er-rate my poor kindness : I was glad I did
atone my countryman and you ; it had been pity you should
have been put together with so mortal a purpose as then each
bore, upon importance of so slight and trivial a nature.

Post. By your pardon, sir, I was then a young traveller ; rather
shunned to go even with what I heard than in my every action
to be guided by others' experiences : but upon my mended
judgement—if I offend not to say it is mended—my quarrel
was not altogether slight.

French. Faith, yes, to be put to the arbitrement of swords, and
by such two that would, by all likelihood, have confounded
one the other, or have fallen both.

Iach. Can we with manners ask what was the difference ?

French. Safely, I think : 'twas a contention in public, which may
without contradiction suffer the report.   It is much like an
argument that fell out last night, where each of us fell in praise
of our country mistresses ; this gentleman at that time vouch-
ing—and upon warrant of bloody affirmation—his to be more
fair, virtuous, wise, chaste, constant-qualified and less attempt-
able than any the rarest of our ladies in France.

Iach. That lady is not now living, or this gentleman's opinion,
by this, worn out.

Post. She holds her virtue still and I my mind.

Iach. You must not so far prefer her 'fore ours of Italy.

Post. Being so far provoked as I was in France, I would abate
her nothing, though I profess myself her adorer, not her friend.

Iach. As fair and as good—a kind of hand-in-hand comparison
—had been something too fair and too good for any lady in
Britany.   If she went before others I have seen, as that diamond
of yours outlustres many I have beheld, I could not but believe
she excelled many : but I have not seen the most precious
diamond that is, nor you the lady.

Post. I praised her as I rated her : so do I my stone.

Iach. What do you esteem it at ?

Post. More than the world enjoys.

Iach. Either your unparagoned mistress is dead, or she's
   outprized by a trifle.

Post. You are mistaken: the one may be sold or given, if
   there were wealth enough for the purchase of merit for the
   gift: the other is not a thing for sale, and only the gift of the

Iach. Which the gods have given you?   [gods

Post. Which, by their graces, I will keep.

Iach. You may wear her in title yours: but, you know, strange
   fowl light upon neighbouring ponds. Your ring may be
   stolen too: so your brace of unprizable estimations, the one
   is but frail and the other casual; a cunning thief, or a that
   way accomplished courtier, would hazard the winning both
   of first and last.

Post. Your Italy contains none so accomplished a courtier to
   convince the honour of my mistress; if, in the holding or
   loss of that, you term her frail. I do nothing doubt you
   have store of thieves; notwithstanding, I fear not my ring.

Phi. Let us leave here, gentlemen.

Post. Sir, with all my heart. This worthy signior, I thank
   him, makes no stranger of me; we are familiar at first.

Iach. With five times so much conversation, I should get
   ground of your fair mistress, make her go back even to the
   yielding, had I admittance and opportunity to friend.

Post. No, no.

Iach. I dare thereupon pawn the moiety of my estate to your
   ring, which in my opinion o'er-values it something: but I
   make my wager rather against your confidence than her
   reputation: and, to bar your offence herein too, I durst
   attempt it against any lady in the world.

Post. You are a great deal abused in too bold a persuasion,
   and I doubt not you sustain what you're worthy of by your

Iach. What's that?   [attempt.

Post. A repulse: though your attempt, as you call it, deserve
   more; a punishment too.

Phi. Gentlemen, enough of this: it came in too suddenly; let
   it die as it was born, and, I pray you, be better acquainted.

Iach. Would I had put my estate and my neighbour's on the
   approbation of what I have spoke!

Post. What lady would you choose to a.

Iach. Yours; whom in constancy you think stands so safe. I
   will lay you ten thousand ducats to your ring, that, commend
   me to the court where your lady is, with no more advantage
   than the opportunity of a second conference, and I will
   bring from thence that honour of hers which you imagine
   so reserved.

Post. I will wage against your gold, gold to it : my ring I hold
  dear as my finger ; 'tis part of it.

Iach. You are afraid, and therein the wiser. If you buy ladies'
  flesh at a million a dram, you cannot preserve it from tainting : but I see you have some religion in you, that you fear.

Post. This is but a custom in your tongue ; you bear a graver
  purpose, I hope.

Iach. I am the master of my speeches, and would undergo
  what 's spoken, I swear.

Post. Will you ? I shall but lend my diamond till your return :
  let there be covenants drawn between 's : my mistress
  exceeds in goodness the hugeness of your unworthy thinking : I dare you to this match : here 's my ring.

Phi. I will have it no lay.

Iach. By the gods, it is one. If I bring you no sufficient
  testimony that I have enjoyed the dearest bodily part of your
  mistress, my ten thousand ducats are yours ; so is your
  diamond too : if I come off, and leave her in such honour as
  you have trust in, she your jewel, this your jewel, and my gold
  are yours ; provided I have your commendation for my more
  free entertainment.

Post. I embrace these conditions ; let us have articles betwixt
  us. Only, thus far you shall answer : if you make your
  voyage upon her, and give me directly to understand you have
  prevailed, I am no further your enemy ; she is not worth our
  debate : if she remain unseduced, you not making it appear
  otherwise, for your ill opinion and the assault you have made
  to her chastity, you shall answer me with your sword.

Iach. Your hand ; a covenant : we will have these things set
  down by lawful counsel, and straight away for Britain, lest
  the bargain should catch cold and starve : I will fetch my
  gold, and have our two wagers recorded.

Post. Agreed.   [*Exeunt Posthumus and Iachimo.*

French. Will this hold, think you ?

Phi. Signior Iachimo will not from it.   Pray let us follow 'em.
                                                              [*Exeunt.*

SCENE V

Britain.   A room in Cymbeline's palace
Enter Queen, Ladies, and Cornelius.

Queen. Whiles yet the dew 's on ground, gather those flowers ;
  Make haste : who has the note of them ?

First Lady.   I, madam.
Queen. Dispatch.   [*Exeunt Ladies.*
    Now, master doctor, have you brought those drugs ?

Cor. Pleaseth your highness, ay : here they are, madam :
                                    [*Presenting a small box.*
    But I beseech your grace, without offence,—
    My conscience bids me ask—wherefore you have
    Commanded of me these most poisonous compounds,
    Which are the movers of a languishing death,
    But, though slow, deadly.
Queen.   I wonder, doctor,
    Thou ask'st me such a question.   Have I not been
    Thy pupil long ?   Hast thou not learn'd me how
    To make perfumes ? distil ? preserve ? yea, so
    That our great king himself doth woo me oft
    For my confections ?   Having thus far proceeded,—
    Unless thou think'st me devilish—is 't not meet
    That I did amplify my judgement in
    Other conclusions ?   I will try the forces
    Of these thy compounds on such creatures as
    We count not worth the hanging, but none human,
    To try the vigour of them and apply
    Allayments to their act, and by them gather
    Their several virtues and effects.
Cor.   Your highness
    Shall from this practice but make hard your heart :
    Besides, the seeing these effects will be
    Both noisome and infectious.
Queen.   O, content thee.

Enter Pisanio.

    [*Aside*] Here comes a flattering rascal ; upon him
    Will I first work : he 's for his master,
    And enemy to my son.   How now, Pisanio !
    Doctor, your service for this time is ended ;
    Take your own way.
Cor. [*Aside*]   I do suspect you, madam ;
    But you shall do no harm.
Queen. [*To Pisanio*]   Hark thee, a word.
Cor. [*Aside*] I do not like her.   She doth think she has
    Strange lingering poisons : I do know her spirit,
    And will not trust one of her malice with
    A drug of such damn'd nature.   Those she has
    Will stupefy and dull the sense awhile ;
    Which first, perchance, she 'll prove on cats and dogs,
    Then afterward up higher : but there is
    No danger in what show of death it makes,
    More than the locking up the spirits a time,

To be more fresh, reviving.   She is fool'd
With a most false effect; and I the truer,
So to be false with her.
Queen.   No further service, doctor,
Until I send for thee.
Cor.   I humbly take my leave.   [*Exit.*
Queen. Weeps she still, say'st thou?   Dost thou think in time
She will not quench and let instructions enter
Where folly now possesses?   Do thou work:
When thou shalt bring me word she loves my son,
I'll tell thee on the instant thou art then
As great as is thy master; greater, for
His fortunes all lie speechless, and his name
Is at last gasp: return he cannot, nor
Continue where he is: to shift his being
Is to exchange one misery with another,
And every day that comes to decay
A day's work in him.   What shalt thou expect,
To be depender on a thing that leans,
Who cannot be new built, nor has no friends,
So much as but to prop him?   [*The Queen drops the box:
    Pisanio takes it up.*]   Thou takest up
Thou know'st not what; but take it for thy labour:
It is a thing I made, which hath the king
Five times redeem'd from death: I do not know
What is more cordial: nay, I prithee, take it;
It is an earnest of a further good
That I mean to thee.   Tell thy mistress how
The case stands with her; do't as from thyself.
Think what a chance thou changest on; but think
Thou hast thy mistress still, to boot, my son,
Who shall take notice of thee: I'll move the king
To any shape of thy preferment, such
As thou'lt desire; and then myself, I chiefly,
That set thee on to this desert, am bound
To load thy merit richly.   Call my women:
Think on my words.   [*Exit Pisanio.*
               A sly and constant knave;
Not to be shaked: the agent for his master;
And the remembrancer of her to hold
The hand-fast to her lord.   I have given him that
Which, if he take, shall quite unpeople her
Of liegers for her sweet; and which she after,
Except she bend her humour, shall be assured
To taste of too.

Re-enter Pisanio, with Ladies.

               So, so ; well done, well done :
The violets, cowslips, and the primroses,
Bear to my closet. Fare thee well, Pisanio ;
Think on my words.   *[Exeunt Queen and Ladies.*
Pis.   And shall do :
But when to my good lord I prove untrue,
I 'll choke myself : there 's all I 'll do for you.   *[Exit.*

SCENE VI

The same. Another room in the palace.

Enter Imogen alone.

Imo. A father cruel, and a step-dame false ;
A foolish suitor to a wedded lady,
That hath her husband banish'd ;—O, that husband !
My supreme crown of grief ! and those repeated
Vexations of it ! Had I been thief-stol'n,
As my two brothers, happy ! but most miserable
Is the desire that 's glorious : blest be those,
How mean soe'er, that hath their honest wills,
Which seasons comfort. Who may this be ? Fie !

Enter Pisanio and Iachimo.

Pis. Madam, a noble gentleman of Rome,
Comes from my lord with letters.
Iach.   Change you, madam ?
The worthy Leonatus is in safety,
And greets your highness dearly.   *[Presents a letter.*
Imo.   Thanks, good sir :
You 're kindly welcome.
Iach. *[Aside]* All of her that is out of door most rich !
If she be furnish'd with a mind so rare,
She is alone the Arabian bird, and I
Have lost the wager. Boldness be my friend !
Arm me, audacity, from head to foot !
Or, like the Parthian, I shall flying fight ;
Rather, directly fly.
Imo. *[Reads]* 'He is one of the noblest note, to whose kind-
nesses I am most infinitely tied. Reflect upon him accord-
ingly, as you value your trust—   LEONATUS.'
So far I read aloud :
But even the very middle of my heart
Is warm'd by the rest, and takes it thankfully.
You are as welcome, worthy sir, as I
Have words to bid you, and shall find it so
In all that I can do.

Iach.   Thanks, fairest lady.
  What, are men mad? Hath nature given them eyes
  To see this vaulted arch and the rich crop
  Of sea and land, which can distinguish 'twixt
  The fiery orbs above and the twinn'd stones
  Upon the number'd beach, and can we not
  Partition make with spectacles so precious
  'Twixt fair and foul?
Imo.   What makes your admiration?
Iach. It cannot be i' the eye; for apes and monkeys,
  'Twixt two such shes, would chatter this way and
  Contemn with mows the other: nor i' the judgement;
  For idiots, in this case of favour, would
  Be wisely definite: nor i' the appetite;
  Sluttery, to such neat excellence opposed,
  Should make desire vomit emptiness,
  Not so allured to feed.
Imo. What is the matter, trow?
Iach.   The cloyed will,
  That satiate yet unsatisfied desire, that tub
  Both fill'd and running, ravening first the lamb,
  Longs after for the garbage.
Imo.   What, dear sir,
  Thus raps you? Are you well?
Iach.   Thanks, madam; well.
  [*To Pisanio*] Beseech you, sir,
  Desire my man's abode where I did leave him:
  He 's strange and peevish.
Pis.   I was going, sir,   [*Exit.*
  To give him welcome.
Imo. Continues well my lord? His health, beseech you?
Iach. Well, madam.
Imo. Is he disposed to mirth? I hope he is.
Iach. Exceeding pleasant; none a stranger there
  So merry and so gamesome: he is call'd
  The Briton reveller.
Imo.   When he was here
  He did incline to sadness, and oft-times
  Not knowing why.
Iach.   I never saw him sad.
  There is a Frenchman his companion, one
  An eminent monsieur, that, it seems, much loves
  A Gallian girl at home: he furnaces
  The thick sighs from him; whiles the jolly Briton,
  Your lord, I mean, laughs from 's free lungs, cries 'O,

322

Can my sides hold, to think that man, who knows
By history, report, or his own proof,
What woman is, yea, what she cannot choose
But must be, will his free hours languish for
Assured bondage?'

Imo.   Will my lord say so?

Iach. Ay, madam; with his eyes in flood with laughter
It is a recreation to be by
And hear him mock the Frenchman.   But, heavens know,
Some men are much to blame.

Imo.   Not he, I hope.

Iach. Not he: but yet heaven's bounty towards him might
Be used more thankfully.   In himself 'tis much;
In you, which I account his beyond all talents,
Whilst I am bound to wonder, I am bound
To pity too.

Imo.   What do you pity, sir?

Iach. Two creatures heartily.

Imo.   Am I one, sir?
You look on me: what wreck discern you in me
Deserves your pity?

Iach.   Lamentable!   What,
To hide me from the radiant sun, and solace
I' the dungeon by a snuff?

Imo.   I pray you, sir,
Deliver with more openness your answers
To my demands.   Why do you pity me?

Iach. That others do,
I was about to say, enjoy your——But
It is an office of the gods to venge it,
Not mine to speak on 't.

Imo.   You do seem to know
Something of me, or what concerns me: pray you,—
Since doubting things go ill often hurts more
Than to be sure they do; for certainties
Either are past remedies, or, timely knowing,
The remedy then born,—discover to me
What both you spur and stop.

Iach.   Had I this cheek
To bathe my lips upon; this hand, whose touch,
Whose every touch, would force the feeler's soul
To the oath of loyalty; this object, which
Takes prisoner the wild motion of mine eye,
Fixing it only here; should I, damn'd then,
Slaver with lips as common as the stairs

That mount the Capitol; join gripes with hands
Made hard with hourly falsehood—falsehood, as
With labour; then by-peeping in an eye
Base and unlustrous as the smoky light
That's fed with stinking tallow; it were fit
That all the plagues of hell should at one time
Encounter such revolt.

Imo.   My lord, I fear,
Has forgot Britain.

Iach.   And himself.   Not I
Inclined to this intelligence pronounce
The beggary of his change, but 'tis your graces
That from my mutest conscience to my tongue
Charms this report out.

Imo.   Let me hear no more.

Iach. O dearest soul, your cause doth strike my heart
With pity, that doth make me sick!   A lady
So fair, and fasten'd to an empery,
Would make the great'st king double, to be partner'd
With tomboys hired with that self exhibition
Which your own coffers yield! with diseased ventures
That play with all infirmities for gold
Which rottenness can lend nature! such boil'd stuff
As well might poison poison!   Be revenged,
Or she that bore you was no queen and you
Recoil from your great stock.

Imo.   Revenged!
How should I be revenged?   If this be true,—
As I have such a heart that both mine ears
Must not in haste abuse,—if it be true,
How should I be revenged?

Iach.   Should he make me
Live like Diana's priest, betwixt cold sheets,
Whiles he is vaulting variable ramps,
In your despite, upon your purse?   Revenge it.
I dedicate myself to your sweet pleasure,
More noble than that runagate to your bed,
And will continue fast to your affection,
Still close as sure.

Imo.   What ho, Pisanio!

Iach. Let me my service tender on your lips.

Imo. Away!   I do condemn mine ears that have
So long attended thee.   If thou wert honourable,
Thou wouldst have told this tale for virtue, not
For such an end thou seek'st, as base as strange.

Thou wrong'st a gentleman who is as far
From thy report as thou from honour, and
Solicit'st here a lady that disdains
Thee and the devil alike.   What ho, Pisanio!
The king my father shall be made acquainted
Of thy assault: if he shall think it fit
A saucy stranger in his court to mart
As in a Romish stew, and to expound
His beastly mind to us, he hath a court
He little cares for, and a daughter who
He not respects at all.   What ho, Pisanio!

Iach. O happy Leonatus! I may say:
The credit that thy lady hath of thee
Deserves thy trust, and thy most perfect goodness
Her assured credit.   Blessed live you long!
A lady to the worthiest sir that ever
Country call'd his! and you his mistress, only
For the most worthiest fit! Give me your pardon.
I have spoke this to know if your affiance
Were deeply rooted, and shall make your lord
That which he is new o'er: and he is one
The truest manner'd, such a holy witch
That he enchants societies into him;
Half all men's hearts are his.

Imo.   You make amends.

Iach. He sits 'mongst men like a descended god:
He hath a kind of honour sets him off,
More than a mortal seeming.   Be not angry,
Most mighty princess, that I have adventured
To try your taking of a false report, which hath
Honour'd with confirmation your great judgement
In the election of a sir so rare,
Which you know cannot err.   The love I bear him
Made me to fan you thus, but the gods made you,
Unlike all others, chaffless.   Pray, your pardon.

Imo. All's well, sir: take my power i' the court for yours.

Iach. My humble thanks.   I had almost forgot
To entreat your grace but in a small request,
And yet of moment too, for it concerns
Your lord; myself and other noble friends
Are partners in the business.

Imo.   Pray, what is 't?

Iach. Some dozen Romans of us, and your lord—
The best feather of our wing—have mingled sums
To buy a present for the emperor;

Which I, the factor for the rest, have done
In France : 'tis plate of rare device and jewels
Of rich and exquisite form, their values great ;
And I am something curious, being strange,
To have them in safe stowage : may it please you
To take them in protection?

Imo.   Willingly ;
And pawn mine honour for their safety : since
My lord hath interest in them, I will keep them
In my bedchamber.

Iach.   They are in a trunk,
Attended by my men : I will make bold
To send them to you, only for this night ;
I must aboard to-morrow.

Imo.   O, no, no.

Iach. Yes, I beseech ; or I shall short my word
By lengthening my return.   From Gallia
I cross'd the seas on purpose and on promise
To see your grace.

Imo.   I thank you for your pains :
But not away to-morrow !

Iach.   O, I must, madam :
Therefore I shall beseech you, if you please
To greet your lord with writing, do 't to-night :
I have outstood my time, which is material
To the tender of our present.

Imo.   I will write.
Send your trunk to me ; it shall safe be kept
And truly yielded you.   You 're very welcome.   [*Exeunt.*

ACT II—SCENE I

Britain.   Before Cymbeline's palace.
Enter Cloten and two Lords.

Clo. Was there ever man had such luck ! when I kissed the
jack, upon an up-cast to be hit away ! I had a hundred
pound on 't : and then a whoreson jackanapes must take me
up for swearing ; as if I borrowed mine oaths of him, and
might not spend them at my pleasure.

First Lord. What got he by that? You have broke his pate
with your bowl.

Sec. Lord. [*Aside*] If his wit had been like him that broke it, it
would have run all out.

Clo. When a gentleman is disposed to swear, it is not for any
standers-by to curtail his oaths, ha?

Sec. Lord. No, my lord ; [*Aside*] nor crop the ears of them.

Clo. Whoreson dog ! I give him satisfaction ? Would he had
been one of my rank !

Sec. Lord. [*Aside*] To have smelt like a fool.

Clo. I am not vexed more at any thing in the earth : a pox
on 't ! I had rather not be so noble as I am ; they dare not
fight with me, because of the queen my mother : every Jack-
slave hath his bellyful of fighting, and I must go up and
down like a cock that nobody can match.

Sec. Lord. [*Aside*] You are cock and capon too ; and you crow,
cock, with your comb on.

Clo. Sayest thou ?

Sec. Lord. It is not fit your lordship should undertake every
companion that you give offence to.

Clo. No, I know that : but it is fit I should commit offence to

Sec. Lord. Ay, it is fit for your lordship only.   [my inferiors.

Clo. Why, so I say.

First Lord. Did you hear of a stranger that 's come to court

Clo. A stranger, and I not know on 't !   [to-night ?

Sec. Lord. [*Aside*] He 's a strange fellow himself, and knows it
not.   [Leonatus' friends.

First Lord. There 's an Italian come, and 'tis thought, one of

Clo. Leonatus ! a banished rascal ; and he 's another, whatsoever he be. Who told you of this stranger ?

First Lord. One of your lordship's pages.

Clo. Is it fit I went to look upon him ? is there no derogation

Sec. Lord. You cannot derogate, my lord.   [in 't ?

Clo. Not easily, I think.

Sec. Lord. [*Aside*] You are a fool granted ; therefore your
issues, being foolish, do not derogate.

Clo. Come, I 'll go see this Italian : what I have lost to-day at
bowls I 'll win to-night of him. Come, go.

Sec. Lord. I 'll attend your lordship.

[*Exeunt Cloten and First Lord.*

That such a crafty devil as is his mother
Should yield the world this ass ? a woman that
Bears all down with her brain ; and this her son
Cannot take two from twenty, for his heart,
And leave eighteen. Alas, poor princess,
Thou divine Imogen, what thou endurest,
Betwixt a father by thy step-dame govern'd,
A mother hourly coining plots, a wooer
More hateful than the foul expulsion is
Of thy dear husband, than that horrid act
Of the divorce he 'ld make ! The heavens hold firm

The walls of thy dear honour ; keep unshaked
That temple, thy fair mind ; that thou mayst stand,
To enjoy thy banish'd lord and this great land !   [*Exit.*

SCENE II

Imogen's bedchamber in Cymbeline's palace : a trunk in one corner of it.
Imogen in bed, reading ; a Lady attending.

Imo. Who's there ? my woman Helen ?

Lady.   Please you, madam.

Imo. What hour is it ?

Lady.   Almost midnight, madam.

Imo. I have read three hours then : mine eyes are weak :
Fold down the leaf where I have left : to bed :
Take not away the taper, leave it burning ;
And if thou canst awake by four o' the clock,
I prithee, call me. Sleep hath seized me wholly.   [*Exit Lady.*
To your protection I commend me, gods !
From fairies and the tempters of the night
Guard me, beseech ye ! [*Sleeps. Iachimo comes from the trunk.*

Iach. The crickets sing, and man's o'er-labour'd sense
Repairs itself by rest. Our Tarquin thus
Did softly press the rushes, ere he waken'd
The chastity he wounded. Cytherea,
How bravely thou becomest thy bed ! fresh lily !
And whiter than the sheets ! That I might touch
But kiss ; one kiss ! Rubies unparagon'd,
How dearly they do 't ! 'Tis her breathing that
Perfumes the chamber thus : the flame o' the taper
Bows toward her, and would under-peep her lids
To see the unclosed lights, now canopied
Under those windows, white and azure, laced
With blue of heaven's own tinct. But my design,
To note the chamber : I will write all down :
Such and such pictures ; there the window ; such
The adornment of her bed ; the arras, figures,
Why, such and such ; and the contents o' the story.
Ah, but some natural notes about her body
Above ten thousand meaner moveables
Would testify, to enrich mine inventory.
O sleep, thou ape of death, lie dull upon her !
And be her sense but as a monument,
Thus in a chapel lying ! Come off, come off:
                                   [*Taking off her bracelet.*
As slippery as the Gordian knot was hard !

'Tis mine; and this will witness outwardly,
As strongly as the conscience does within,
To the madding of her lord.   On her left breast
A mole cinque-spotted, like the crimson drops
I' the bottom of a cowslip: here's a voucher,
Stronger than ever law could make: this secret
Will force him think I have pick'd the lock and ta'en
The treasure of her honour.   No more.   To what end?
Why should I write this down, that's riveted,
Screw'd to my memory?   She hath been reading late
The tale of Tereus; here the leaf's turned down
Where Philomel gave up.   I have enough:
To the trunk again, and shut the spring of it.
Swift, swift, you dragons of the night, that dawning
May bare the raven's eye!   I lodge in fear;
Though this a heavenly angel, hell is here.   [*Clock strikes.*
One, two, three: time, time!
                                 [*Goes into the trunk.   The scene closes.*

Scene III

An ante-chamber adjoining Imogen's apartments.
Enter Cloten and Lords.

First Lord. Your lordship is the most patient man in loss, the
most coldest that ever turned up ace.

Clo. It would make any man cold to lose.

First Lord. But not every man patient after the noble temper
of your lordship. You are most hot and furious when you win.

Clo. Winning will put any man into courage.   If I could get this
foolish Imogen, I should have gold enough.   It's almost morn-
First Lord. Day, my lord.   [ing, is't not?

Clo. I would this music would come: I am advised to give her
music o' mornings; they say it will penetrate.

Enter Musicians.

Come on; tune: if you can penetrate her with your finger-
ing, so; we'll try with tongue too: if none will do, let her
remain; but I'll never give o'er.   First, a very excellent good-
conceited thing; after, a wonderful sweet air, with admirable
rich words to it: and then let her consider.

Song.

Hark, hark! the lark at heaven's gate sings,
    And Phœbus 'gins arise,
His steeds to water at those springs
    On chaliced flowers that lies;

>   And winking Mary-buds begin
>   To ope their golden eyes;
>   With every thing that pretty is,
>   My lady sweet, arise:
>   Arise, arise!

Clo. So, get you gone. If this penetrate, I will consider your
music the better: if it do not, it is a vice in her ears, which
horse-hairs and calves'-guts, nor the voice of unpaved eunuch
to boot, can never amend.   [*Exeunt Musicians.*

Sec. Lord. Here comes the king.

Clo. I am glad I was up so late; for that's the reason I was up
so early: he cannot choose but take this service I have done
fatherly.

Enter Cymbeline and Queen.

Good morrow to your majesty and to my gracious mother.

Cym. Attend you here the door of our stern daughter?
Will she not forth?

Clo. I have assailed her with music, but she vouchsafes no

Cym. The exile of her minion is too new;   [notice.
    She hath not yet forgot him: some more time
    Must wear the print of his remembrance out,
    And then she's yours.

Queen.   You are most bound to the king,
Who lets go by no vantages that may
Prefer you to his daughter. Frame yourself
To orderly soliciting, and be friended
With aptness of the season; make denials
Increase your services; so seem as if
You were inspired to do those duties which
You tender to her; that you in all obey her,
Save when command to your dismission tends,
And therein you are senseless.

Clo.   Senseless! not so

Enter a Messenger.

Mess. So like you, sir, ambassadors from Rome;
The one is Caius Lucius.

Cym.   A worthy fellow,
Albeit he comes on angry purpose now;
But that's no fault of his: we must receive him
According to the honour of his sender;
And towards himself, his goodness forespent on us,
We must extend our notice. Our dear son,
When you have given good morning to your mistress,
Attend the queen and us; we shall have need

To employ you towards this Roman.   Come, our queen.
                                    [*Exeunt all but Cloten.*

Clo. If she be up, I'll speak with her; if not,
  Let her lie still and dream.   By your leave, ho !   [*Knocks.*
  I know her women are about her : what
  If I do line one of their hands ?   'Tis gold
  Which buys admittance; oft it doth ; yea, and makes
  Diana's rangers false themselves, yield up
  Their deer to the stand o' the stealer; and 'tis gold
  Which makes the true man kill'd and saves the thief;
  Nay, sometime hangs both thief and true man : what
  Can it not do and undo ?   I will make
  One of her women lawyer to me, for
  I yet not understand the case myself.
  By your leave.   [*Knocks.*

                    Enter a Lady.

Lady. Who's there that knocks?
Clo.   A gentleman.
Lady.   No more?
Clo. Yes, and a gentlewoman's son.
Lady.   That's more
  Than some whose tailors are as dear as yours
  Can justly boast of.   What's your lordship's pleasure?
Clo. Your lady's person : is she ready?
Lady.   Ay,
  To keep her chamber.
Clo.   There is gold for you ;
  Sell me your good report.
Lady. How ! my good name? or to report of you
  What I shall think is good?   The princess !   [*Exit Lady.*
                    Enter Imogen.
Clo. Good morrow, fairest : sister, your sweet hand.
Imo. Good morrow, sir.   You lay out too much pains
  For purchasing but trouble : the thanks I give
  Is telling you that I am poor of thanks
  And scarce can spare them.
Clo.   Still I swear I love you.
Imo. If you but said so, 'twere as deep with me :
  If you swear still, your recompense is still
  That I regard it not.
Clo.   This is no answer.
Imo. But that you shall not say I yield being silent,
  I would not speak.   I pray you, spare me : faith,
  I shall unfold equal discourtesy
  To your best kindness : one of your great knowing

Should learn, being taught, forbearance.

Clo. To leave you in your madness, 'twere my sin:
  I will not.

Imo. Fools are not mad folks.

Clo.   Do you call me fool?

Imo. As I am mad, I do:
  If you 'll be patient, I 'll no more be mad;
  That cures us both. I am much sorry, sir,
  You put me to forget a lady's manners,
  By being so verbal: and learn now for all
  That I, which know my heart, do here pronounce,
  By the very truth of it, I care not for you,
  And am so near the lack of charity—
  To accuse myself—I hate you; which I had rather
  You felt than make 't my boast.

Clo.   You sin against
  Obedience, which you owe your father. For
  The contract you pretend with that base wretch,
  One bred of alms and foster'd with cold dishes,
  With scraps o' the court, it is no contract, none:
  And though it be allow'd in meaner parties—
  Yet who than he more mean?—to knit their souls
  On whom there is no more dependency
  But brats and beggary, in self-figured knot;
  Yet you are curb'd from that enlargement by
  The consequence o' the crown, and must not soil
  The precious note of it with a base slave,
  A hilding for a livery, a squire's cloth,
  A pantler, not so eminent.

Imo.   Profane fellow!
  Wert thou the son of Jupiter, and no more
  But what thou art besides, thou wert too base
  To be his groom: thou wert dignified enough,
  Even to the point of envy, if 'twere made
  Comparative for your virtues to be styled
  The under-hangman of his kingdom, and hated
  For being preferr'd so well.

Clo.   The south-fog rot him!

Imo. He never can meet more mischance than come
  To be but named of thee. His meanest garment,
  That ever hath but clipp'd his body, is dearer
  In my respect than all the hairs above thee,
  Were they all made such men. How now, Pisanio!

                Enter Pisanio.

Clo. 'His garment!' Now, the devil—

Imo. To Dorothy my woman hie thee presently,—
Clo. 'His garment!'
Imo.   I am sprited with a fool,
  Frighted and anger'd worse: go bid my woman
  Search for a jewel that too casually
  Hath left mine arm: it was thy master's: 'shrew me,
  If I would lose it for a revenue
  Of any king's in Europe! I do think
  I saw 't this morning: confident I am
  Last night 'twas on mine arm; I kiss'd it:
  I hope it be not gone to tell my lord
  That I kiss aught but he.
Pis.   'Twill not be lost.
Imo. I hope so: go and search.   [*Exit Pisanio.*
Clo.   You have abused me:
  'His meanest garment!'
Imo.   Ay, I said so, sir:
  If you will make 't an action, call witness to 't.
Clo. I will inform your father.
Imo.   Your mother too:
  She 's my good lady, and will conceive, I hope,
  But the worst of me. So, I leave you, sir,
  To the worst of discontent.   [*Exit.*
Clo.   I 'll be revenged:
  'His meanest garment!' Well.   [*Exit.*

Scene IV

Rome.   Philario's house.

Enter Posthumus and Philario.

Post. Fear it not, sir: I would I were so sure
  To win the king as I am bold her honour
  Will remain hers.
Phi.   What means do you make to him?
Post. Not any; but abide the change of time;
  Quake in the present winter's state, and wish
  That warmer days would come: in these fear'd hopes,
  I barely gratify your love; they failing,
  I must die much your debtor.
Phi. Your very goodness and your company
  O'erpays all I can do. By this, your king
  Hath heard of great Augustus: Caius Lucius
  Will do 's commission throughly: and I think
  He 'll grant the tribute, send the arrearages,
  Or look upon our Romans, whose remembrance
  Is yet fresh in their grief.

Post.   I do believe,
    Statist though I am none, nor like to be,
    That this will prove a war; and you shall hear
    The legions now in Gallia sooner landed
    In our not-fearing Britain than have tidings
    Of any penny tribute paid.   Our countrymen
    Are men more order'd than when Julius Cæsar
    Smiled at their lack of skill, but found their courage
    Worthy his frowning at: their discipline,
    Now mingled with their courages, will make known
    To their approvers they are people such
    That mend upon the world.
                 Enter Iachimo.

Phi.   See! Iachimo!
Post. The swiftest harts have posted you by land,
    And winds of all the corners kiss'd your sails,
    To make your vessel nimble.
Phi.   Welcome, sir.
Post. I hope the briefness of your answer made
    The speediness of your return.
Iach.   Your lady
    Is one of the fairest that I have look'd upon.
Post. And therewithal the best, or let her beauty
    Look through a casement to allure false hearts,
    And be false with them.
Iach.   Here are letters for you.
Post. Their tenour good, I trust.
Iach.   'Tis very like.
Phi. Was Caius Lucius in the Britain court
    When you were there?
Iach.   He was expected then,
    But not approach'd.
Post.   All is well yet.
    Sparkles this stone as it was wont? or is't not
    Too dull for your good wearing?
Iach.   If I had lost it,
    I should have lost the worth of it in gold.
    I'll make a journey twice as far, to enjoy
    A second night of such sweet shortness which
    Was mine in Britain; for the ring is won.
Post. The stone's too hard to come by.
Iach.   Not a whit,
    Your lady being so easy.
Post.   Make not, sir,
    Your loss your sport: I hope you know that we

Must not continue friends.

Iach. Good sir, we must,
If you keep covenant. Had I not brought
The knowledge of your mistress home, I grant
We were to question farther: but I now
Profess myself the winner of her honour,
Together with your ring, and not the wronger
Of her or you, having proceeded but
By both your wills.

Post. If you can make 't apparent
That you have tasted her in bed, my hand
And ring is yours: if not, the foul opinion
You had of her pure honour gains or loses
Your sword or mine, or masterless leaves both
To who shall find them.

Iach. Sir, my circumstances,
Being so near the truth as I will make them,
Must first induce you to believe: whose strength
I will confirm with oath; which, I doubt not,
You 'll give me leave to spare, when you shall find
You need it not.

Post. Proceed.

Iach. First, her bedchamber,—
Where, I confess, I slept not, but profess
Had that was well worth watching,—it was hang'd
With tapestry of silk and silver; the story
Proud Cleopatra, when she met her Roman,
And Cydnus swell'd above the banks, or for
The press of boats or pride: a piece of work
So bravely done, so rich, that it did strive
In workmanship and value; which I wonder'd
Could be so rarely and exactly wrought,
Since the true life on 't was—

Post. This is true;
And this you might have heard of here, by me,
Or by some other.

Iach. More particulars
Must justify my knowledge.

Post. So they must,
Or do your honour injury.

Iach. The chimney
Is south the chamber; and the chimney-piece,
Chaste Dian bathing; never saw I figures
So likely to report themselves: the cutter
Was as another nature, dumb; outwent her,

Motion and breath left out.
Post.   This is a thing
Which you might from relation likewise reap,
Being, as it is, much spoke of.
Iach.   The roof o' the chamber
With golden cherubins is fretted : her andirons—
I had forgot them—were two winking Cupids
Of silver, each on one foot standing, nicely
Depending on their brands.
Post.   This is her honour !
Let it be granted you have seen all this,—and praise
Be given to your remembrance—the description
Of what is in her chamber nothing saves
The wager you have laid.
Iach.   Then, if you can,
                                  [*Showing the bracelet.*
Be pale : I beg but leave to air this jewel ; see !
And now 'tis up again : it must be married
To that your diamond ; I 'll keep them.
Post.   Jove !
Once more let me behold it : is it that
Which I left with her ?
Iach.   Sir,—I thank her—that :
She stripp'd it from her arm ; I see her yet ;
Her pretty action did outsell her gift,
And yet enrich'd it too : she gave it me
And said she prized it once.
Post.   May be she pluck'd it off,
To send it me.
Iach.   She writes so to you, doth she ?
Post. O, no, no, no ! 'tis true.   Here, take this too ;
                                  [*Gives the ring.*
It is a basilisk unto mine eye,
Kills me to look on 't.   Let there be no honour
Where there is beauty ; truth, where semblance ; love,
Where there 's another man : the vows of women
Of no more bondage be to where they are made
Than they are to their virtues ; which is nothing.
O, above measure false !
Phi.   Have patience, sir,
And take your ring again ; 'tis not yet won :
It may be probable she lost it, or
Who knows if one of her women, being corrupted,
Hath stol'n it from her ?
Post.   Very true ;

And so, I hope, he came by 't.   Back my ring:
Render to me some corporal sign about her
More evident than this; for this was stol'n.
Iach. By Jupiter, I had it from her arm.
Post. Hark you, he swears; by Jupiter he swears.
 'Tis true:—nay, keep the ring—'tis true: I am sure
She would not lose it: her attendants are
All sworn and honourable:—they induced to steal it!
And by a stranger!—No, he hath enjoy'd her:
The cognizance of her incontinency
Is this: she hath bought the name of whore thus dearly.
There, take thy hire; and all the fiends of hell
Divide themselves between you!
Phi.   Sir, be patient:
This is not strong enough to be believed
Of one persuaded well of—
Post.   Never talk on 't;
She hath been colted by him.
Iach.   If you seek
For further satisfying, under her breast—
Worthy the pressing—lies a mole, right proud
Of that most delicate lodging: by my life,
I kiss'd it, and it gave me present hunger
To feed again, though full.   You do remember
This stain upon her?
Post.   Ay, and it doth confirm
Another stain, as big as hell can hold,
Were there no more but it.
Iach.   Will you hear more?
Post. Spare your arithmetic; never count the turns,
Once, and a million!
Iach.   I 'll be sworn—
Post.   No swearing.
If you will swear you have not done 't you lie,
And I will kill thee if thou dost deny
Thou 'st made me cuckold.
Iach.   I 'll deny nothing.
Post. O, that I had her here, to tear her limb-meal!
I will go there and do 't; i' the court; before
Her father.   I 'll do something—   *Exit.*
Phi.   Quite besides
The government of patience!   You have won:
Let 's follow him and pervert the present wrath
He hath against himself.
Iach.   With all my heart.   [*Exeunt.*

SCENE V

Another room in Philario's house.
Enter Posthumus.

Post. Is there no way for men to be, but women
  Must be half-workers? We are all bastards;
  And that most venerable man which I
  Did call my father, was I know not where
  When I was stamp'd; some coiner with his tools
  Made me a counterfeit: yet my mother seem'd
  The Dian of that time: so doth my wife
  The nonpareil of this. O, vengeance, vengeance!
  Me of my lawful pleasure she restrain'd,
  And pray'd me oft forbearance; did it with
  A pudency so rosy, the sweet view on't
  Might well have warm'd old Saturn; that I thought her
  As chaste as unsunn'd snow. O, all the devils!
  This yellow Iachimo, in an hour,—was't not?—
  Or less,—at first?—perchance he spoke not, but
  Like a full-acorn'd boar, a German one,
  Cried 'O!' and mounted; found no opposition
  But what he look'd for should oppose and she
  Should from encounter guard. Could I find out
  The woman's part in me! For there's no motion
  That tends to vice in man but I affirm
  It is the woman's part: be it lying, note it,
  The woman's; flattering, hers; deceiving, hers;
  Lust and rank thoughts, hers, hers; revenges, hers;
  Ambitions, covetings, change of prides, disdain,
  Nice longing, slanders, mutability,
  All faults that may be named, nay, that hell knows,
  Why, hers, in part or all, but rather all;
  For even to vice
  They are not constant, but are changing still
  One vice, but of a minute old, for one
  Not half so old as that. I'll write against them,
  Detest them, curse them: yet 'tis greater skill
  In a true hate, to pray they have their will:
  The very devils cannot plague them better.   [*Exit.*

ACT III—SCENE I

Britain. A hall in Cymbeline's palace.

*Enter in state, Cymbeline, Queen, Cloten, and Lords at one
    door, and at another, Caius Lucius and Attendants.*

Cym. Now say, what would Augustus Cæsar with us?
Luc. When Julius Cæsar, whose remembrance yet
Lives in men's eyes and will to ears and tongues
Be theme and hearing ever, was in this Britain
And conquer'd it, Cassibelan, thine uncle,—
Famous in Cæsar's praises, no whit less
Than in his feats deserving it—for him
And his succession granted Rome a tribute,
Yearly three thousand pounds; which by thee lately
Is left untender'd.
Queen.   And, to kill the marvel,
Shall be so ever.
Clo.   There be many Cæsars
Ere such another Julius.   Britain is
A world by itself, and we will nothing pay
For wearing our own noses.
Queen.   That opportunity,
Which then they had to take from 's, to resume
We have again.   Remember, sir, my liege,
The kings your ancestors, together with
The natural bravery of your isle, which stands
As Neptune's park, ribbed and paled in
With rocks unscaleable and roaring waters,
With sands that will not bear your enemies' boats,
But suck them up to the topmast.   A kind of conquest
Cæsar made here; but made not here his brag
Of 'Came, and saw, and overcame:' with shame—
The first that ever touch'd him—he was carried
From off our coast, twice beaten; and his shipping—
Poor ignorant baubles!—on our terrible seas,
Like egg-shells moved upon their surges, crack'd
As easily 'gainst our rocks: for joy whereof
The famed Cassibelan, who was once at point—
O giglot fortune!—to master Cæsar's sword,
Made Lud's town with rejoicing fires bright
And Britons strut with courage.
Clo. Come, there's no more tribute to be paid: our kingdom
is stronger than it was at that time; and, as I said, there is

no moe such Cæsars: other of them may have crooked
noses, but to owe such straight arms, none.

Cym. Son, let your mother end.

Clo. We have yet many among us can gripe as hard as Cassibelan: I do not say I am one; but I have a hand. Why
tribute? why should we pay tribute? If Cæsar can hide the
sun from us with a blanket, or put the moon in his pocket,
we will pay him tribute for light; else, sir, no more tribute,
pray you now.

Cym. You must know,
Till the injurious Romans did extort
This tribute from us, we were free: Cæsar's ambition,
Which swell'd so much that it did almost stretch
The sides o' the world, against all colour here
Did put the yoke upon 's; which to shake off
Becomes a warlike people, whom we reckon
Ourselves to be.

Clo. and Lords. We do.

Cym.   Say then to Cæsar,
Our ancestor was that Mulmutius which
Ordain'd our laws, whose use the sword of Cæsar
Hath too much mangled; whose repair and franchise
Shall, by the power we hold, be our good deed,
Though Rome be therefore angry. Mulmutius made our laws,
Who was the first of Britain which did put
His brows within a golden crown, and call'd
Himself a king.

Luc.   I am sorry, Cymbeline,
That I am to pronounce Augustus Cæsar—
Cæsar, that hath moe kings his servants than
Thyself domestic officers—thine enemy:
Receive it from me, then: war and confusion
In Cæsar's name pronounce I 'gainst thee: look
For fury not to be resisted. Thus defied,
I thank thee for myself.

Cym.   Thou art welcome, Caius
Thy Cæsar knighted me; my youth I spent
Much under him; of him I gather'd honour;
Which he to seek of me again, perforce,
Behoves me keep at utterance. I am perfect
That the Pannonians and Dalmatians for
Their liberties are now in arms; a precedent
Which not to read would show the Britons cold:
So Cæsar shall not find them.

Luc.   Let proof speak.

Clo. His majesty bids you welcome.   Make pastime with us a
day or two, or longer: if you seek us afterwards in other
terms, you shall find us in our salt-water girdle: if you beat
us out of it, it is yours; if you fall in the adventure, our
crows shall fare the better for you; and there's an end.
Luc. So, sir.
Cym. I know your master's pleasure, and he mine:
All the remain is 'Welcome.'   [*Exeunt.*

SCENE II

Another room in the palace.
Enter Pisanio, with a letter.

Pis. How! of adultery? Wherefore write you not
What monster's her accuser?   Leonatus!
O master! what a strange infection
Is fall'n into thy ear!   What false Italian,
As poisonous-tongued as handed, hath prevail'd
On thy too ready hearing?   Disloyal!   No:
She's punish'd for her truth, and undergoes,
More goddess-like than wife-like, such assaults
As would take in some virtue.   O my master!
Thy mind to her is now as low as were
Thy fortunes.   How! that I should murder her?
Upon the love and truth and vows which I
Have made to thy command?   I, her? her blood?
If it be so to do good service, never
Let me be counted serviceable.   How look I,
That I should seem to lack humanity
So much as this fact comes to?   [*Reading*] 'Do't: the letter
That I have sent her, by her own command
Shall give thee opportunity.'   O damn'd paper!
Black as the ink that's on thee!   Senseless bauble,
Art thou a feodary for this act, and look'st
So virgin-like without?   Lo, here she comes.
I am ignorant in what I am commanded.

Enter Imogen.

Imo. How now, Pisanio!
Pis. Madam, here is a letter from my lord.
Imo. Who? thy lord? that is my lord Leonatus!
O, learn'd indeed were that astronomer
That knew the stars as I his characters;
He'ld lay the future open.   You good gods,
Let what is here contain'd relish of love,
Of my lord's health, of his content, yet not
That we two are asunder; let that grieve him:

Some griefs are medicinable; that is one of them,
For it doth physic love: of his content,
All but in that! Good wax, thy leave. Blest be
You bees that make these locks of counsel! Lovers
And men in dangerous bonds pray not alike:
Though forfeiters you cast in prison, yet
You clasp young Cupid's tables. Good news, gods!
[*Reads*] 'Justice, and your father's wrath, should he take me
in his dominion, could not be so cruel to me, as you, O the
dearest of creatures, would even renew me with your eyes.
Take notice that I am in Cambria, at Milford-Haven: what
your own love will out of this advise you, follow. So he
wishes you all happiness, that remains loyal to his vow, and
your, increasing in love,   LEONATUS POSTHUMUS.'
O, for a horse with wings! Hear'st thou, Pisanio?
He is at Milford-Haven: read, and tell me
How far 'tis thither. If one of mean affairs
May plod it in a week, why may not I
Glide thither in a day? Then, true Pisanio,—
Who long'st, like me, to see thy lord; who long'st—
O, let me bate,—but not like me—yet long'st,
But in a fainter kind:—O, not like me;
For mine 's beyond beyond: say, and speak thick,—
Love's counsellor should fill the pores of hearing,
To the smothering of the sense—how far it is
To this same blessed Milford: and by the way
Tell me how Wales was made so happy as
To inherit such a haven: but, first of all,
How we may steal from hence: and for the gap
That we shall make in time, from our hence-going
And our return, to excuse: but first, how get hence.
Why should excuse be born or ere begot?
We'll talk of that hereafter. Prithee, speak,
How many score of miles may we well ride
'Twixt hour and hour?
Pis.   One score 'twixt sun and sun,
Madam, 's enough for you, and too much too.
Imo. Why, one that rode to 's execution, man,
Could never go so slow: I have heard of riding wagers,
Where horses have been nimbler than the sands
That run i' the clock's behalf. But this is foolery:
Go bid my woman feign a sickness, say
She'll home to her father: and provide me presently
A riding-suit, no costlier than would fit
A franklin's housewife.

Pis.   Madam, you 're best consider.
Imo. I see before me, man : nor here, nor here,
  Nor what ensues, but have a fog in them,
  That I cannot look through. Away, I prithee ;
  Do as I bid thee : there 's no more to say ;
  Accessible is none but Milford way.   [*Exeunt.*

SCENE III

Wales : a mountainous country with a cave.
Enter Belarius, Guiderius, and Arviragus.

Bel. A goodly day not to keep house with such
  Whose roof 's as low as ours ! Stoop, boys : this gate
  Instructs you how to adore the heavens, and bows you
  To a morning's holy office : the gates of monarchs
  Are arc'd so high that giants may jet through
  And keep their impious turbans on, without
  Good morrow to the sun. Hail, thou fair heaven !
  We house i' the rock, yet use thee not so hardly
  As prouder livers do.
Gui.   Hail, heaven !
Arv.   Hail, heaven !
Bel. Now for our mountain sport : up to yond hill !
  Your legs are young : I 'll tread these flat. Consider,
  When you above perceive me like a crow,
  That it is place which lessens and sets off :
  And you may then revolve what tales I have told you
  Of courts, of princes, of the tricks in war :
  This service is not service, so being done,
  But being so allow'd : to apprehend thus,
  Draws us a profit from all things we see ;
  And often, to our comfort, shall we find
  The sharded beetle in a safer hold
  Than is the full-wing'd eagle. O, this life
  Is nobler than attending for a check,
  Richer than doing nothing for a bauble,
  Prouder than rustling in unpaid-for silk :
  Such gain the cap of him that makes 'em fine,
  Yet keeps his book uncross'd : no life to ours.
Gui. Out of your proof you speak : we, poor unfledged,
  Have never wing'd from view o' the nest, nor know not
  What air 's from home. Haply this life is best
  If quiet life be best, sweeter to you
  That have a sharper known, well corresponding
  With your stiff age : but unto us it is
  A cell of ignorance, travelling a-bed,

343

          A prison for a debtor that not dares
          To stride a limit.
Arv.   What should we speak of
          When we are old as you? when we shall hear
          The rain and wind beat dark December, how
          In this our pinching cave shall we discourse
          The freezing hours away? We have seen nothing:
          We are beastly; subtle as the fox for prey,
          Like warlike as the wolf for what we eat:
          Our valour is to chase what flies; our cage
          We make a quire, as doth the prison'd bird,
          And sing our bondage freely.
Bel.   How you speak!
          Did you but know the city's usuries,
          And felt them knowingly: the art o' the court,
          As hard to leave as keep; whose top to climb
          Is certain falling, or so slippery that
          The fear 's as bad as falling: the toil o' the war,
          A pain that only seems to seek out danger
          I' the name of fame and honour, which dies i' the search,
          And hath as oft a slanderous epitaph
          As record of fair act; nay, many times,
          Doth ill deserve by doing well; what 's worse,
          Must court'sy at the censure:—O boys, this story
          The world may read in me: my body 's mark'd
          With Roman swords, and my report was once
          First with the best of note: Cymbeline loved me;
          And when a soldier was the theme, my name
          Was not far off: then was I as a tree
          Whose boughs did bend with fruit: but in one night,
          A storm, or robbery, call it what you will,
          Shook down my mellow hangings, nay, my leaves,
          And left me bare to weather.
Gui.   Uncertain favour!
Bel. My fault being nothing, as I have told you oft,
          But that two villains, whose false oaths prevail'd
          Before my perfect honour, swore to Cymbeline
          I was confederate with the Romans; so
          Follow'd my banishment; and this twenty years
          This rock and these demesnes have been my world:
          Where I have lived at honest freedom, paid
          More pious debts to heaven than in all
          The fore-end of my time. But up to the mountains!
          This is not hunters' language: he that strikes
          The venison first shall be the lord o' the feast;

To him the other two shall minister;
And we will fear no poison, which attends
In place of greater state.   I'll meet you in the valleys.
                        [Exeunt Guiderius and Arviragus.
How hard it is to hide the sparks of nature!
These boys know little they are sons to the king;
Nor Cymbeline dreams that they are alive.
They think they are mine: and though train'd up thus
I' the cave wherein they bow, their thoughts do hit [meanly
The roofs of palaces, and nature prompts them
In simple and low things to prince it much
Beyond the trick of others.   This Polydore,
The heir of Cymbeline and Britain, who
The king his father call'd Guiderius,—Jove!
When on my three-foot stool I sit and tell
The warlike feats I have done, his spirits fly out
Into my story: say 'Thus mine enemy fell,
And thus I set my foot on 's neck,' even then
The princely blood flows in his cheek, he sweats,
Strains his young nerves, and puts himself in posture
That acts my words.   The younger brother, Cadwal,
Once Arviragus, in as like a figure
Strikes life into my speech and shows much more
His own conceiving.   Hark, the game is roused!
O Cymbeline! heaven and my conscience knows
Thou didst unjustly banish me: whereon,
At three and two years old, I stole these babes,
Thinking to bar thee of succession as
Thou reft'st me of my lands.   Euriphile,
Thou wast their nurse; they took thee for their mother,
And every day do honour to her grave:
Myself, Belarius, that am Morgan call'd,
They take for natural father.   The game is up.   *[Exit.*

SCENE IV

Country near Milford-Haven.

Enter Pisanio and Imogen.

Imo. Thou told'st me, when we came from horse, the place
Was near at hand: ne'er long'd my mother so
To see me first, as I have now.   Pisanio! man!
Where is Posthumus?   What is in thy mind,
That makes thee stare thus?   Wherefore breaks that sigh
From the inward of thee?   One but painted thus
Would be interpreted a thing perplex'd
Beyond self-explication: put thyself

345

Into a haviour of less fear, ere wildness
Vanquish my staider senses.   What's the matter?
Why tender'st thou that paper to me, with
A look untender?   If't be summer news,
Smile to't before; if winterly, thou need'st
But keep that countenance still.   My husband's hand!
That drug-damn'd Italy hath out-craftied him,
And he's at some hard point.   Speak, man: thy tongue
May take of some extremity, which to read
Would be even mortal to me.
Pis.   Please you, read;
And you shall find me, wretched man, a thing
The most disdain'd of fortune.
Imo. [*Reads*] 'Thy mistress, Pisanio, hath played the strumpet
in my bed; the testimonies whereof lie bleeding in me.   I
speak not out of weak surmises; but from proof as strong as
my grief, and as certain as I expect my revenge.   That part
thou, Pisanio, must act for me, if thy faith be not tainted
with the breach of hers.   Let thine own hands take away
her life: I shall give thee opportunity at Milford Haven:
she hath my letter for the purpose: where, if thou fear to
strike, and to make me certain it is done, thou art the pandar
to her dishonour, and equally to me disloyal.'
Pis. What shall I need to draw my sword? the paper
Hath cut her throat already.   No, 'tis slander;
Whose edge is sharper than the sword; whose tongue
Outvenoms all the worms of Nile; whose breath
Rides on the posting winds, and doth belie
All corners of the world: kings, queens, and states,
Maids, matrons, nay, the secrets of the grave
This viperous slander enters.   What cheer, madam?
Imo. False to his bed!   What is it to be false?
To lie in watch there, and to think on him?
To weep 'twixt clock and clock?   if sleep charge nature,
To break it with a fearful dream of him,
And cry myself awake?   that's false to's bed, is it?
Pis. Alas, good lady!
Imo. I false!   Thy conscience witness: Iachimo,
Thou didst accuse him of incontinency;
Thou then look'dst like a villain; now, methinks,
Thy favour's good enough.   Some jay of Italy,
Whose mother was her painting, hath betray'd him:
Poor I am stale, a garment out of fashion;
And, for I am richer than to hang by the walls,
I must be ripp'd:—to pieces with me!—O,

Men's vows are women's traitors! All good seeming,
By thy revolt, O husband, shall be thought
Put on for villany; not born where 't grows,
But worn a bait for ladies.

Pis.   Good madam, hear me.

Imo. True honest men being heard, like false Æneas,
Were in his time thought false; and Sinon's weeping
Did scandal many a holy tear, took pity
From most true wretchedness: so thou Posthumus,
Wilt lay the leaven on all proper men;
Goodly and gallant shall be false and perjured
From thy great fail. Come, fellow, be thou honest:
Do thou thy master's bidding. When thou see'st him,
A little witness my obedience. Look!
I draw the sword myself: take it, and hit
The innocent mansion of my love, my heart:
Fear not; 'tis empty of all things but grief:
Thy master is not there, who was indeed
The riches of it. Do his bidding; strike.
Thou mayst be valiant in a better cause,
But now thou seem'st a coward.

Pis.   Hence, vile instrument!,
Thou shalt not damn my hand.

Imo.   Why, I must die;
And if I do not by thy hand, thou art
No servant of thy master's. Against self-slaughter
There is a prohibition so divine
That cravens my weak hand. Come, here's my heart;—
Something 's afore 't. Soft, soft! we 'll no defence;—
Obedient as the scabbard. What is here?
The scriptures of the loyal Leonatus,
All turn'd to heresy? Away, away,
Corrupters of my faith! you shall no more
Be stomachers to my heart. Thus may poor fools
Believe false teachers: though those that are betray'd
Do feel the treason sharply, yet the traitor
Stands in worse case of woe.
And thou, Posthumus, thou that didst set up
My disobedience 'gainst the king my father,
And make me put into contempt the suits
Of princely fellows, shalt hereafter find
It is no act of common passage, but
A strain of rareness: and I grieve myself
To think, when thou shalt be disedged by her
That now thou tirest on, how thy memory

Will then be pang'd by me. Prithee, dispatch:
The lamb entreats the butcher: where 's thy knife?
Thou art too slow to do thy master's bidding,
When I desire it too.

Pis.   O gracious lady,
Since I received command to do this business
I have not slept one wink.

Imo.   Do 't, and to bed then.

Pis. I 'll wake mine eye-balls blind first.

Imo.   Wherefore then
Didst undertake it? Why hast thou abused
So many miles with a pretence? this place?
Mine action, and thine own? our horses' labour?
The time inviting thee? the perturb'd court,
For my being absent? whereunto I never
Purpose return. Why hast thou gone so far,
To be unbent when thou hast ta'en thy stand,
The elected deer before thee?

Pis.   But to win time
To lose so bad employment; in the which
I have consider'd of a course. Good lady,
Hear me with patience.

Imo.   Talk thy tongue weary; speak:
I have heard I am a strumpet; and mine ear,
Therein false struck, can take no greater wound,
Nor tent to bottom that. But speak.

Pis.   Then, madam,
I thought you would not back again.

Imo.   Most like,
Bringing me here to kill me.

Pis.   Not so, neither:
But if I were as wise as honest, then
My purpose would prove well. It cannot be
But that my master is abused: some villain,
Ay, and singular in his art, hath done you both
This cursed injury.

Imo. Some Roman courtezan.

Pis.   No, on my life.
I 'll give but notice you are dead, and send him
Some bloody sign of it; for 'tis commanded
I should do so: you shall be miss'd at court,
And that will well confirm it.

Imo.   Why, good fellow,
What shall I do the while? where abide? how live?
Or in my life what comfort, when I am

Dead to my husband?
Pis.   If you'll back to the court—
Imo. No court, no father; nor no more ado
      With that harsh, noble, simple nothing,
      That Cloten, whose love-suit hath been to me
      As fearful as a siege.
Pis.   If not at court,
      Then not in Britain must you bide.
Imo.   Where then?
      Hath Britain all the sun that shines? Day, night,
      Are they not but in Britain? I' the world's volume
      Our Britain seems as of it, but not in't;
      In a great pool a swan's nest: prithee, think
      There's livers out of Britain.
Pis.   I am most glad
      You think of other place. The ambassador,
      Lucius the Roman, comes to Milford-Haven
      To-morrow: now, if you could wear a mind
      Dark as your fortune is, and but disguise
      That which, to appear itself, must not yet be
      But by self-danger, you should tread a course
      Pretty and full of view; yea, haply, near
      The residence of Posthumus; so nigh at least
      That though his actions were not visible, yet
      Report should render him hourly to your ear
      As truly as he moves.
Imo.   O, for such means,
      Though peril to my modesty, not death on't,
      I would adventure!
Pis.   Well then, here's the point:
      You must forget to be a woman; change
      Command into obedience; fear and niceness—
      The handmaids of all women, or, more truly,
      Woman its pretty self—into a waggish courage;
      Ready in jibes, quick-answer'd, saucy and
      As quarrelous as the weasel; nay, you must
      Forget that rarest treasure of your cheek,
      Exposing it—but, O, the harder heart!
      Alack, no remedy!—to the greedy touch
      Of common-kissing Titan, and forget
      Your laboursome and dainty trims, wherein
      You made great Juno angry.
Imo.   Nay, be brief:
      I see into thy end, and am almost
      A man already.

Pis.   First, make yourself but like one.
Fore-thinking this, I have already fit—
'Tis in my cloak-bag—doublet, hat, hose, all
That answer to them : would you, in their serving
And with what imitation you can borrow
From youth of such a season, 'fore noble Lucius
Present yourself, desire his service, tell him
Wherein you 're happy,—which you 'll make him know,
If that his head have ear in music,—doubtless
With joy he will embrace you ; for he 's honourable,
And, doubling that, most holy.   Your means abroad,
You have me, rich ; and I will never fail
Beginning nor supplyment.
Imo.   Thou art all the comfort
The gods will diet me with.   Prithee, away :
There 's more to be consider'd ; but we 'll even
All that good time will give us : this attempt
I am soldier to, and will abide it with
A prince's courage.   Away, I prithee.
Pis. Well, madam, we must take a short farewell,
Lest, being miss'd, I be suspected of
Your carriage from the court.   My noble mistress,
Here is a box ; I had it from the queen :
What 's in 't is precious ; if you are sick at sea,
Or stomach-qualm'd at land, a dram of this
Will drive away distemper.   To some shade,
And fit you to your manhood : may the gods
Direct you to the best ;
Imo.   Amen : I thank thee.   [*Exeunt severally.*

Scene V

A room in Cymbeline's palace.

Enter Cymbeline, Queen, Cloten, Lucius, and Lords.
Cym. Thus far ; and so farewell.
Luc.   Thanks, royal sir.
My emperor hath wrote, I must from hence ;
And am right sorry that I must report ye
My master's enemy.
Cym.   Our subjects, sir,
Will not endure his yoke ; and for ourself
To show less sovereignty than they, must needs
Appear unkinglike.
Luc.   So, sir : I desire of you
A conduct over-land to Milford-Haven.
Madam, all joy befal your grace, and you !

Cym. My lords, you are appointed for that office ;
 The due of honour in no point omit.
 So farewell, noble Lucius.
Luc.   Your hand, my lord.
Clo. Receive it friendly ; but from this time forth
 I wear it as your enemy.
Luc.   Sir, the event
 Is yet to name the winner : fare you well.
Cym. Leave not the worthy Lucius, good my lords,
 Till he have cross'd the Severn. Happiness !
                              [*Exeunt Lucius and Lords.*
Queen. He goes hence frowning : but it honours us
 That we have given him cause.
Clo.   'Tis all the better ;
 Your valiant Britons have their wishes in it.
Cym. Lucius hath wrote already to the emperor
 How it goes here. It fits us therefore ripely
 Our chariots and our horsemen be in readiness :
 The powers that he already hath in Gallia
 Will soon be drawn to head, from whence he moves
 His war for Britain.
Queen.   'Tis not sleepy business,
 But must be look'd to speedily and strongly.
Cym. Our expectation that it would be thus
 Hath made us forward. But, my gentle queen,
 Where is our daughter ? She hath not appear'd
 Before the Roman, nor to us hath tender'd
 The duty of the day : she looks us like
 A thing more made of malice than of duty :
 We have noted it. Call her before us, for
 We have been too slight in sufferance. [*Exit an Attendant.*
Queen.   Royal sir,
 Since the exile of Posthumus, most retired
 Hath her life been ; the cure whereof, my lord,
 'Tis time must do. Beseech your majesty,
 Forbear sharp speeches to her : she 's a lady
 So tender of rebukes that words are strokes,
 And strokes death to her.

                    Re-enter Attendant.
Cym.   Where is she, sir ? How
 Can her contempt be answer'd ?
Atten.   Please you, sir,
 Her chambers are all lock'd, and there 's no answer
 That will be given to the loud'st of noise we make.
Queen. My lord, when last I went to visit her,

                          351

She pray'd me to excuse her keeping close;
Whereto constrain'd by her infirmity,
She should that duty leave unpaid to you,
Which daily she was bound to proffer : this
She wish'd me to make known ; but our great court
Made me to blame in memory.
Cym.   Her doors lock'd?
Not seen of late? Grant, heavens, that which I fear
Prove false !   [*Exit.*
Queen. Son, I say, follow the king.
Clo. That man of hers, Pisanio, her old servant,
I have not seen these two days.
Queen.   Go, look after. [*Exit Cloten.*
Pisanio, thou that stand'st so for Posthumus !
He hath a drug of mine ; I pray his absence
Proceed by swallowing that ; for he believes
It is a thing most precious. But for her,
Where is she gone? Haply, despair hath seized her;
Or, wing'd with fervour of her love, she's flown
To her desired Posthumus : gone she is
To death or to dishonour ; and my end
Can make good use of either : she being down,
I have the placing of the British crown.

Re-enter Cloten.

How now, my son !
Clo.   'Tis certain she is fled.
Go in and cheer the king : he rages ; none
Dare come about him.
Queen. [*Aside*]   All the better : may
This night forestall him of the coming day !   [*Exit.*
Clo. I love and hate her : for she's fair and royal,
And that she hath all courtly parts more exquisite
Than lady, ladies, woman ; from every one
The best she hath, and she, of all compounded,
Outsells them all ; I love her therefore : but
Disdaining me and throwing favours on
The low Posthumus slanders so her judgement
That what's else rare is choked ; and in that point
I will conclude to hate her, nay, indeed,
To be revenged upon her. For when fools
Shall—

Enter Pisanio.

            Who is here? What, are you packing, sirrah?
Come hither : ah, you precious pandar ! Villain,
Where is thy lady? In a word ; or else

Thou art straightway with the fiends.

Pis. O, good my lord!

Clo. Where is thy lady? or, by Jupiter,—
I will not ask again. Close villain,
I'll have this secret from thy heart, or rip
Thy heart to find it. Is she with Posthumus?
From whose so many weights of baseness cannot
A dram of worth be drawn.

Pis. Alas, my lord,
How can she be with him? When was she miss'd?
He is in Rome.

Clo. Where is she, sir? Come nearer;
No farther halting: satisfy me home
What is become of her.

Pis. O, my all-worthy lord!

Clo. All-worthy villain!
Discover where thy mistress is at once,
At the next word: no more of 'worthy lord!'
Speak, or thy silence on the instant is
Thy condemnation and thy death.

Pis. Then, sir,
This paper is the history of my knowledge
Touching her flight. [*Presenting a letter.*

Clo. Let's see it. I will pursue her
Even to Augustus' throne.

Pis. [*Aside*] Or this, or perish.
She's far enough; and what he learns by this
May prove his travel, not her danger.

Clo. Hum!

Pis. [*Aside*] I'll write to my lord she's dead. O Imogen,
Safe mayst thou wander, safe return again!

Clo. Sirrah, is this letter true?

Pis. Sir, as I think.

Clo. It is Posthumus' hand; I know 't. Sirrah, if thou wouldst
not be a villain, but do me true service, undergo those em-
ployments wherein I should have cause to use thee with a
serious industry, that is, what villany soe'er I bid thee do, to
perform it directly and truly, I would think thee an honest
man: thou shouldst neither want my means for thy relief,
nor my voice for thy preferment.

Pis. Well, my good lord.

Clo. Wilt thou serve me? for since patiently and constantly
thou hast stuck to the bare fortune of that beggar Posthumus,
thou canst not, in the course of gratitude, but be a diligent
follower of mine. Wilt thou serve me?

Pis. Sir, I will.

Clo. Give me thy hand; here's my purse. Hast any of thy late
    master's garments in thy possession?

Pis. I have, my lord, at my lodging the same suit he wore when
    he took leave of my lady and mistress.

Clo. The first service thou dost me, fetch that suit hither: let
    it be thy first service; go.

Pis. I shall, my lord.   [*Exit.*

Clo. Meet thee at Milford-Haven!—I forgot to ask him one
    thing; I'll remember't anon:—even there, thou villain
    Posthumus, will I kill thee. I would these garments were
    come. She said upon a time—the bitterness of it I now
    belch from my heart—that she held the very garment of
    Posthumus in more respect than my noble and natural person,
    together with the adornment of my qualities. With that suit
    upon my back, will I ravish her: first kill him, and in her
    eyes; there shall she see my valour, which will then be a
    torment to her contempt. He on the ground, my speech of
    insultment ended on his dead body, and when my lust hath
    dined—which, as I say, to vex her I will execute in the
    clothes that she so praised—to the court I'll knock her back,
    foot her home again. She hath despised me rejoicingly, and
    I'll be merry in my revenge.

            Re-enter Pisanio, with the clothes.

Be those the garments?

Pis. Ay, my noble lord.

Clo. How long is't since she went to Milford-Haven?

Pis. She can scarce be there yet.

Clo. Bring this apparel to my chamber; that is the second thing
    that I have commanded thee: the third is, that thou wilt be
    a voluntary mute to my design. Be but duteous, and true pre-
    ferment shall tender itself to thee. My revenge is now at Mil-
    ford: would I had wings to follow it! Come, and be true. [*Exit.*

Pis. Thou bid'st me to my loss: for, true to thee
    Were to prove false, which I will never be,
    To him that is most true. To Milford go,
    And find not her whom thou pursuest. Flow, flow,
    You heavenly blessings, on her! This fool's speed
    Be cross'd with slowness; labour be his meed!   [*Exit.*

SCENE VI

Wales: before the cave of Belarius.

Enter Imogen, in boy's clothes.

Imo. I see a man's life is a tedious one:
    I have tired myself; and for two nights together

Have made the ground my bed.   I should be sick,
But that my resolution helps me.   Milford,
When from the mountain-top Pisanio show'd thee,
Thou wast within a ken: O Jove! I think
Foundations fly the wretched; such, I mean,
Where they should be relieved.   Two beggars told me
I could not miss my way: will poor folks lie,
That have afflictions on them, knowing 'tis
A punishment or trial?   Yes; no wonder,
When rich ones scarce tell true: to lapse in fulness
Is sorer than to lie for need; and falsehood
Is worse in kings than beggars.   My dear lord!
Thou art one o' the false ones: now I think on thee,
My hunger's gone; but even before, I was
At point to sink for food.   But what is this?
Here is a path to 't: 'tis some savage hold:
I were best not call; I dare not call: yet famine,
Ere clean it o'erthrow nature, makes it valiant.
Plenty and peace breeds cowards; hardness ever
Of hardiness is mother.   Ho! who's here?
If any thing that's civil, speak; if savage,
Take or lend.   Ho!   No answer? then I'll enter.
Best draw my sword; and if mine enemy
But fear the sword like me, he'll scarcely look on 't.
Such a foe, good heavens!   [*Exit, to the cave.*

Enter Belarius, Guiderius, and Arviragus.

Bel. You, Polydore, have proved best woodman and
Are master of the feast: Cadwal and I
Will play the cook and servant; 'tis our match:
The sweat and industry would dry and die,
But for the end it works to.   Come; our stomachs
Will make what's homely savoury: weariness
Can snore upon the flint, when resty sloth
Finds the down pillow hard.   Now, peace be here,
Poor house, that keep'st thyself!
Gui.   I am throughly weary
Arv. I am weak with toil, yet strong in appetite.
Gui. There is cold meat i' the cave; we'll browse on that,
Whilst what we have kill'd be cook'd.
Bel. [*Looking into the cave*]   Stay; come not in.
But that it eats our victuals, I should think
Here were a fairy.
Gui.   What's the matter, sir?
Bel. By Jupiter, an angel! or, if not,

355

An earthly paragon !   Behold divineness
No elder than a boy !

Re-enter Imogen.

Imo. Good masters, harm me not :
Before I enter'd here, I call'd ; and thought
To have begg'd or bought what I have took : good troth,
I have stol'n nought ; nor would not, though I had found
Gold strew'd i' the floor.   Here 's money for my meat :
I would have left it on the board so soon
As I had made my meal, and parted
With prayers for the provider.

Gui.   Money, youth?

Arv. All gold and silver rather turn to dirt !
As 'tis no better reckon'd, but of those
Who worship dirty gods.

Imo.   I see you're angry :
Know, if you kill me for my fault, I should
Have died had I not made it.

Bel.   Whither bound?

Imo. To Milford-Haven.

Bel. What 's your name?

Imo. Fidele, sir.   I have a kinsman who
Is bound for Italy ; he embark'd at Milford ;
To whom being going, almost spent with hunger,
I am fall'n in this offence.

Bel.   Prithee, fair youth,
Think us no churls, nor measure our good minds
By this rude place we live in.   Well encounter'd !
'Tis almost night : you shall have better cheer
Ere you depart : and thanks to stay and eat it.
Boys, bid him welcome.

Gui.   Were you a woman, youth,
I should woo hard but be your groom.   In honesty,
I bid for you as I 'ld buy.

Arv.   I 'll mak 't my comfort
He is a man ; I 'll love him as my brother :
And such a welcome as I 'ld give to him
After long absence, such is yours : most welcome !
Be sprightly, for you fall 'mongst friends.

Imo.   'Mongst friends,
If brothers.   [*Aside*] Would it had been so, that they
Had been my father's sons ! then had my prize
Been less, and so more equal ballasting
To thee, Posthumus.

Bel.   He wrings at some distress.

Gui. Would I could free 't!
Arv.   Or I; whate'er it be,
  What pain it cost, what danger! Gods!
Bel.   Hark, boys. [*Whispering.*
Imo. Great men,
  That had a court no bigger than this cave,
  That did attend themselves and had the virtue
  Which their own conscience seal'd them—laying by
  That nothing-gift of differing multitudes—
  Could not out-peer these twain.   Pardon me, gods!
  I 'ld change my sex to be companion with them,
  Since Leonatus' false.
Bel.   It shall be so.
  Boys, we 'll go dress our hunt.   Fair youth, come in:
  Discourse is heavy, fasting; when we have supp'd,
  We 'll mannerly demand thee of thy story,
  So far as thou wilt speak it.
Gui.   Pray, draw near.
Arv. The night to the owl and morn to the lark less welcome.
Imo. Thanks, sir.
Arv. I pray, draw near.   [*Exeunt.*

SCENE VII

Rome.   A public place.

Enter two Senators and Tribunes.

First Sen. This is the tenour of the emperor's writ:
  That since the common men are now in action
  'Gainst the Pannonians and Dalmatians,
  And that the legions now in Gallia are
  Full weak to undertake our wars against
  The fall'n-off Britons, that we do incite
  The gentry to this business.   He creates
  Lucius proconsul: and to you the tribunes,
  For this immediate levy, he commends
  His absolute commission.   Long live Cæsar!
First Tri. Is Lucius general of the forces?
Sec. Sen.   Ay.
First Tri. Remaining now in Gallia?
First Sen.   With those legions
  Which I have spoke of, whereunto your levy
  Must be supplyant: the words of your commission
  Will tie you to the numbers and the time
  Of their dispatch.
First Tri.   We will discharge our duty.   [*Exeunt.*

357

ACT IV—Scene I

Wales: near the cave of Belarius.

Enter Cloten alone.

Clo. I am near to the place where they should meet, if Pisanio
have mapped it truly. How fit his garments serve me! Why
should his mistress, who was made by him that made the
tailor, not be fit too? the rather—saving reverence of the
word—for 'tis said a woman's fitness comes by fits. Therein
I must play the workman. I dare speak it to myself—for it
is not vain-glory for a man and his glass to confer in his own
chamber—I mean, the lines of my body are as well drawn
as his; no less young, more strong, not beneath him in
fortunes, beyond him in the advantage of the time, above
him in birth, alike conversant in general services, and more
remarkable in single oppositions: yet this imperceiverant
thing loves him in my despite. What mortality is! Posthumus, thy head, which now is growing upon thy shoulders,
shall within this hour be off; thy mistress enforced; thy
garments cut to pieces before thy face: and all this done,
spurn her home to her father; who may haply be a little
angry for my so rough usage; but my mother, having power
of his testiness, shall turn all into my commendations. My
horse is tied up safe: out, sword, and to a sore purpose!
Fortune, put them into my hand! This is the very description of their meeting-place; and the fellow dares not deceive
me.   [*Exit.*

Scene II

Before the cave of Belarius.

Enter, from the cave, Belarius, Guiderius, Arviragus, and
Imogen.

Bel. [*To Imogen*] You are not well: remain here in the cave;
We 'll come to you after hunting.

Arv. [*To Imogen*]   Brother, stay here:
Are we not brothers?

Imo.   So man and man should be;
But clay and clay differs in dignity,
Whose dust is both alike. I am very sick.

Gui. Go you to hunting; I 'll abide with him.

Imo. So sick I am not, yet I am not well;
But not so citizen a wanton as
To seem to die ere sick: so please you, leave me;
Stick to your journal course: the breach of custom

Is breach of all. I am ill, but your being by me
Cannot amend me: society is no comfort
To one not sociable: I am not very sick,
Since I can reason of it. Pray you, trust me here:
I'll rob none but myself; and let me die,
Stealing so poorly.

Gui.   I love thee; I have spoke it:
How much the quantity, the weight as much,
As I do love my father.

Bel.   What! how! how!

Arv. If it be sin to say so, sir, I yoke me
In my good brother's fault: I know not why
I love this youth; and I have heard you say,
Love's reason's without reason: the bier at door
And a demand who is 't shall die, I'ld say
'My father, not this youth.'

Bel. [*Aside*]   O noble strain!
O worthiness of nature! breed of greatness!
Cowards father cowards and base things sire base:
Nature hath meal and bran, contempt and grace.
I'm not their father; yet who this should be,
Doth miracle itself, loved before me.—
'Tis the ninth hour o' the morn.

Arv.   Brother, farewell.

Imo. I wish ye sport.

Arv.   You health. So please you, sir.

Imo. [*Aside*] These are kind creatures. Gods, what lies I have
Our courtiers say all's savage but at court: [heard!
Experience, O, thou disprovest report!
The imperious seas breed monsters; for the dish
Poor tributary rivers as sweet fish.
I am sick still, heart-sick. Pisanio,
I'll now taste of thy drug.   [*Swallows some.*

Gui.   I could not stir him:
He said he was gentle, but unfortunate;
Dishonestly afflicted, but yet honest.

Arv. Thus did he answer me: yet said, hereafter
I might know more.

Bel.   To the field, to the field!
We'll leave you for this time: go in and rest.

Arv. We'll not be long away.

Bel.   Pray, be not sick,
For you must be our housewife.

Imo.   Well or ill,
I am bound to you.

Bel.   And shalt be ever.

> [*Exit Imogen, to the cave.*

This youth, howe'er distress'd, appears he hath had
Good ancestors.

Arv.   How angel-like he sings!

Gui. But his neat cookery! he cut our roots
In characters;
And sauced our broths, as Juno had been sick,
And he her dieter.

Arv.   Nobly he yokes
A smiling with a sigh, as if the sigh
Was that it was, for not being such a smile;
The smile mocking the sigh, that it would fly
From so divine a temple, to commix
With winds that sailors rail at.

Gui.   I do note
That grief and patience, rooted in him both,
Mingle their spurs together.

Arv.   Grow, patience!
And let the stinking elder, grief, untwine
His perishing root with the increasing vine!

Bel. It is great morning. Come, away!—Who's there?

Enter Cloten.

Clo. I cannot find those runagates; that villain
Hath mock'd me: I am faint.

Bel.   'Those runagates!'
Means he not us? I partly know him: 'tis
Cloten, the son o' the queen. I fear some ambush.
I saw him not these many years, and yet
I know 'tis he. We are held as outlaws: hence!

Gui. He is but one: you and my brother search
What companies are near: pray you, away;
Let me alone with him. [*Exeunt Belarius and Arviragus.*

Clo.   Soft! What are you
That fly me thus? some villain mountaineers?
I have heard of such. What slave art thou?

Gui.   A thing
More slavish did I ne'er than answering
A slave without a knock.

Clo.   Thou art a robber,
A law-breaker, a villain: yield thee, thief.

Gui. To who? to thee? What art thou? Have not I
An arm as big as thine? a heart as big?
Thy words, I grant, are bigger; for I wear not

My dagger in my mouth.   Say what thou art,
Why I should yield to thee.

Clo.   Thou villain base,
Know'st me not by my clothes?

Gui.   No, nor thy tailor, rascal,
Who is thy grandfather: he made those clothes,
Which, as it seems, make thee.

Clo.   Thou precious varlet,
My tailor made them not.

Gui.   Hence then, and thank
The man that gave them thee.   Thou art some fool;
I am loath to beat thee.

Clo.   Thou injurious thief,
Hear but my name, and tremble.

Gui.   What's thy name?

Clo. Cloten, thou villain.

Gui. Cloten, thou double villain, be thy name,
I cannot tremble at it: were it Toad, or Adder, Spider,
'Twould move me sooner.

Clo.   To thy further fear,
Nay, to thy mere confusion, thou shalt know
I am son to the queen.

Gui.   I am sorry for 't; not seeming
So worthy as thy birth.

Clo.   Art not afeard?

Gui. Those that I reverence, those I fear, the wise:
At fools I laugh, not fear them.

Clo.   Die the death:
When I have slain thee with my proper hand,
I'll follow those that even now fled hence,
And on the gates of Lud's town set your heads:
Yield, rustic mountaineer.   [*Exeunt fighting.*

            Re-enter Belarius and Arviragus.

Bel. No companies abroad?

Arv. None in the world: you did mistake him, sure.

Bel. I cannot tell: long is it since I saw him,
But time hath nothing blurr'd those lines of favour
Which then he wore; the snatches in his voice,
And burst of speaking, were as his: I am absolute
'Twas very Cloten.

Arv.   In this place we left them:
I wish my brother make good time with him,
You say he is so fell.

Bel.   Being scarce made up,
I mean, to man, he had not apprehension

361

Of roaring terrors: for defect of judgement
Is oft the cause of fear.   But see, thy brother.

Re-enter Guiderius with Cloten's head.

Gui. This Cloten was a fool, an empty purse;
There was no money in 't: not Hercules
Could have knock'd out his brains, for he had none.
Yet I not doing this, the fool had borne
My head as I do his.

Bel.   What hast thou done?

Gui. I am perfect what: cut off one Cloten's head,
Son to the queen, after his own report;
Who call'd me traitor, mountaineer; and swore,
With his own single hand he 'ld take us in,
Displace our heads where—thank the gods!—they grow,
And set them on Lud's town.

Bel.   We are all undone.

Gui. Why, worthy father, what have we to lose,
But that he swore to take, our lives?   The law
Protects not us: then why should we be tender
To let an arrogant piece of flesh threat us,
Play judge and executioner, all himself,
For we do fear the law?   What company
Discover you abroad?

Bel.   No single soul
Can we set eye on; but in all safe reason
He must have some attendants.   Though his humour
Was nothing but mutation, ay, and that
From one bad thing to worse, not frenzy, not
Absolute madness could so far have raved,
To bring him here alone: although perhaps
It may be heard at court that such as we
Cave here, hunt here, are outlaws, and in time
May make some stronger head; the which he hearing—
As it is like him—might break out, and swear
He 'ld fetch us in; yet is 't not probable
To come alone, either he so undertaking,
Or they so suffering: then on good ground we fear,
If we do fear this body hath a tail
More perilous than the head.

Arv.   Let ordinance
Come as the gods foresay it: howsoe'er,
My brother hath done well.

Bel.   I had no mind
To hunt this day: the boy Fidele's sickness
Did make my way long forth.

Gui.   With his own sword,
Which he did wave against my throat, I have ta'en
His head from him : I 'll throw 't into the creek
Behind our rock, and let it to the sea,
And tell the fishes he 's the queen's son, Cloten :
That 's all I reck.   [*Exit.*

Bel.   I fear 'twill be revenged :
Would, Polydore, thou hadst not done 't ! though valour
Becomes thee well enough.

Arv.   Would I had done 't,
So the revenge alone pursued me ! Polydore,
I love thee brotherly, but envy much
Thou hast robb'd me of this deed : I would revenges,
That possible strength might meet, would seek us through
And put us to our answer.

Bel.   Well, 'tis done :
We 'll hunt no more to-day, nor seek for danger
Where there 's no profit. I prithee, to our rock ;
You and Fidele play the cooks : I 'll stay
Till hasty Polydore return, and bring him
To dinner presently.

Arv.   Poor sick Fidele !
I 'll willingly to him : to gain his colour
I 'ld let a parish of such Clotens blood,
And praise myself for charity.   [*Exit.*

Bel.   O thou goddess,
Thou divine Nature, how thyself thou blazon'st
In these two princely boys ! They are as gentle
As zephyrs blowing below the violet,
Not wagging his sweet head ; and yet as rough,
Their royal blood enchafed, as the rudest wind
That by the top doth take the mountain pine
And make him stoop to the vale. 'Tis wonder
That an invisible instinct should frame them
To royalty unlearn'd, honour untaught,
Civility not seen from other, valour
That wildly grows in them, but yields a crop
As if it had been sow'd. Yet still it 's strange
What Cloten's being here to us portends,
Or what his death will bring us.

                    Re-enter Guiderius.

Gui.   Where 's my brother ?
I have sent Cloten's clotpoll down the stream,
In embassy to his mother : his body 's hostage
For his return.   [*Solemn music.*

                    363

Bel.   My ingenious instrument !
    Hark, Polydore, it sounds ! But what occasion
    Hath Cadwal now to give it motion ? Hark !
Gui. Is he at home ?
Bel.   He went hence even now.
Gui. What does he mean ? Since death of my dear'st mother
    It did not speak before. All solemn things
    Should answer solemn accidents. The matter ?
    Triumphs for nothing and lamenting toys
    Is jollity for apes and grief for boys.
    Is Cadwal mad ?

Re-enter Arviragus with Imogen, as dead, bearing her in his arms.

Bel.   Look, here he comes,
    And brings the dire occasion in his arms
    Of what we blame him for !
Arv.   The bird is dead
    That we have made so much on. I had rather
    Have skipp'd from sixteen years of age to sixty,
    To have turn'd my leaping-time into a crutch,
    Than have seen this.
Gui.   O sweetest, fairest lily !
    My brother wears thee not the one half so well
    As when thou grew'st thyself.
Bel.   O melancholy !
    Who ever yet could sound thy bottom ? find
    The ooze, to show what coast thy sluggish crare
    Might easiliest harbour in ? Thou blessed thing !
    Jove knows what man thou mightst have made ; but I,
    Thou diedst, a most rare boy, of melancholy.
    How found you him ?
Arv.   Stark, as you see :
    Thus smiling, as some fly had tickled slumber,
    Not as death's dart, being laugh'd at ; his right cheek
    Reposing on a cushion.
Gui.   Where ?
Arv.   O' the floor ;
    His arms thus leagued : I thought he slept, and put
    My clouted brogues from off my feet, whose rudeness
    Answer'd my steps too loud.
Gui.   Why, he but sleeps :
    If he be gone, he 'll make his grave a bed ;
    With female fairies will his tomb be haunted,
    And worms will not come to thee.
Arv.   With fairest flowers,
    Whilst summer lasts, and I live here, Fidele,

I 'll sweeten thy sad grave : thou shalt not lack
The flower that 's like thy face, pale primrose, nor
The azured harebell, like thy veins ; no, nor
The leaf of eglantine, whom not to slander,
Out-sweeten'd not thy breath : the ruddock would
With charitable bill—O bill, sore shaming
Those rich-left heirs that let their fathers lie
Without a monument !—bring thee all this ;
Yea, and furr'd moss besides, when flowers are none,
To winter-ground thy corse.

Gui.   Prithee, have done ;
And do not play in wench-like words with that
Which is so serious.   Let us bury him,
And not protract with admiration what
Is now due debt.   To the grave.

Arv.   Say, where shall 's lay him ?

Gui. By good Euriphile, our mother.

Arv.   Be 't so :
And let us, Polydore, though now our voices
Have got the mannish crack, sing him to the ground,
As once our mother ; use like note and words,
Save that 'Euriphile' must be 'Fidele.'

Gui. Cadwal,
I cannot sing : I 'll weep, and word it with thee ;
For notes of sorrow out of tune are worse
Than priests and fanes that lie.

Arv.   We 'll speak it then.

Bel. Great griefs, I see, medicine the less ; for Cloten
Is quite forgot.   He was a queen's son, boys :
And though he came our enemy, remember
He was paid for that : though mean and mighty, rotting
Together, have one dust, yet reverence,
That angel of the world, doth make distinction
Of place 'tween high and low.   Our foe was princely ;
And though you took his life as being our foe,
Yet bury him as a prince.

Gui.   Pray you, fetch him hither,
Thersites' body is as good as Ajax',
When neither are alive.

Arv.   If you 'll go fetch him,
We 'll say our song the whilst.   Brother, begin.

                                        [*Exit Belarius.*

Gui. Nay, Cadwal, we must lay his head to the east ;
My father hath a reason for 't.

Arv.   'Tis true.

Gui. Come on thenand remove him.
Arv.   So.   Begin.

SONG.

Gui.   Fear no more the heat o' the sun,
                    Nor the furious winter's rages ;
              Thou thy worldly task hast done,
                    Home art gone and ta'en thy wages :
              Golden lads and girls all must,
              As chimney-sweepers, come to dust.

Arv.   Fear no more the frown o' the great ;
                    Thou art past the tyrant's stroke ;
              Care no more to clothe and eat ;
                    To thee the reed is as the oak :
              The sceptre, learning, physic, must
              All follow this and come to dust.

Gui.   Fear no more the lightning-flash,
Arv   Nor the all-dreaded thunder-stone ;
Gui.   Fear not slander, censure rash ;
Arv.   Thou hast finish'd joy and moan :
Both.   All lovers young, all lovers must
              Consign to thee and come to dust.

Gui.   No exorciser harm thee !
Arv.   Nor no witchcraft charm thee !
Gui.   Ghost unlaid forbear thee !
Arv.   Nothing ill come near thee !
Both.   Quiet consummation have ;
              And renowned be thy grave !

Re-enter Belarius with the body of Cloten.

Gui. We have done our obsequies : come, lay him down,
Bel. Here's a few flowers, but 'bout midnight more :
    The herbs that have on them cold dew o' the night
    Are strewings fitt'st for graves.   Upon their faces.
    You were as flowers, now wither'd : even so
    These herblets shall, which we upon you strow.
    Come on, away : apart upon our knees.
    The ground that gave them first has them again :
    Their pleasures here are past, so is their pain.
                    [*Exeunt Belarius, Guiderius, and Arviragus.*
Imo. [*Awaking*] Yes, sir, to Milford-Haven ; which is the
    way ?—

I thank you.—By yond bush?—Pray, how far thither?
'Ods pittikins! can it be six mile yet?—
I have gone all night:—faith, I'll lie down and sleep.
But, soft! no bedfellow!   O gods and goddesses!
                              [Seeing the body of Cloten.
These flowers are like the pleasures of the world;
This bloody man, the care on 't.   I hope I dream;
For so I thought I was a cave-keeper,
And cook to honest creatures: but 'tis not so;
'Twas but a bolt of nothing, shot at nothing,
Which the brain makes of fumes: our very eyes
Are sometimes like our judgements, blind.   Good faith,
I tremble still with fear: but if there be
Yet left in heaven as small a drop of pity
As a wren's eye, fear'd gods, a part of it!
The dream's here still: even when I wake, it is
Without me, as within me: not imagined, felt.
A headless man.   The garments of Posthumus!
I know the shape of 's leg: this is his hand;
His foot Mercurial; his Martial thigh:
The brawns of Hercules: but his Jovial face—
Murder in heaven?—How!—'Tis gone.   Pisanio,
All curses madded Hecuba gave the Greeks,
And mine to boot, be darted on thee!   Thou,
Conspired with that irregulous devil, Cloten,
Hast here cut off my lord.   To write and read
Be henceforth treacherous!   Damn'd Pisanio
Hath with his forged letters—damn'd Pisanio—
From this most bravest vessel of the world
Struck the main-top!   O Posthumus! alas,
Where is thy head? where's that?   Ay me! where's that?
Pisanio might have kill'd thee at the heart,
And left this head on.   How should this be?   Pisanio?
'Tis he and Cloten: malice and lucre in them
Have laid this woe here.   O, 'tis pregnant, pregnant!
The drug he gave me, which he said was precious
And cordial to me, have I not found it
Murderous to the senses?   That confirms it home:
This is Pisanio's deed, and Cloten's: O!
Give colour to my pale cheek with thy blood,
That we the horrider may seem to those
Which chance to find us: O, my lord, my lord!
                              [Falls on the body.
Enter Lucius, a Captain and other Officers, and a Soothsayer.
Cap. To them the legions garrison'd in Gallia

After your will have cross'd the sea, attending
You here at Milford-Haven with your ships :
They are in readiness.

Luc.   But what from Rome ?

Cap. The senate hath stirr'd up the confiners
And gentlemen of Italy, most willing spirits
That promise noble service : and they come
Under the conduct of bold Iachimo,
Syenna's brother.

Luc.   When expect you them ?

Cap. With the next benefit o' the wind.

Luc.   This forwardness
Makes our hopes fair.   Command our present numbers
Be muster'd ; bid the captains look to 't.   Now, sir,
What have you dream'd of late of this war's purpose ?

Sooth. Last night the very gods show'd me a vision—
I fast and pray'd for their intelligence—thus :
I saw Jove's bird, the Roman eagle, wing'd
From the spongy south to this part of the west,
There vanish'd in the sunbeams : which portends—
Unless my sins abuse my divination—
Success to the Roman host.

Luc.   Dream often so,
And never false.   Soft, ho ! what trunk is here
Without his top ?   The ruin speaks that sometime
It was a worthy building.   How ! a page !
Or dead, or sleeping on him ?   But dead rather ;
For nature doth abhor to make his bed
With the defunct, or sleep upon the dead.
Let 's see the boy's face.

Cap.   He 's alive, my lord.

Luc. He 'll then instruct us of this body.   Young one,
Inform us of thy fortunes, for it seems
They crave to be demanded.   Who is this
Thou makest thy bloody pillow ?   Or who was he
That, otherwise than noble nature did,
Hath alter'd that good picture ?   What 's thy interest
In this sad wreck ?   How came it ?   Who is it ?
What art thou ?

Imo.   I am nothing : or if not,
Nothing to be were better.   This was my master,
A very valiant Briton, and a good,
That here by mountaineers lies slain.   Alas !
There is no more such masters : I may wander
From east to occident, cry out for service,

Try many, all good, serve truly, never
Find such another master.
Luc.   'Lack, good youth !
Thou movest no less with thy complaining than
Thy master in bleeding : say his name, good friend.
Imo. Richard du Champ. [*Aside*] If I do lie, and do
No harm by it, though the gods hear, I hope
They 'll pardon it.   Say you, sir?
Luc. Thy name?
Imo. Fidele, sir.
Luc. Thou dost approve thyself the very same :
Thy name well fits thy faith, thy faith thy name.
Wilt take thy chance with me ?   I will not say
Thou shalt be so well master'd, but be sure,
No less beloved.   The Roman emperor's letters
Sent by a consul to me should not sooner
Than thine own worth prefer thee : go with me.
Imo. I 'll follow, sir.   But first, an 't please the gods,
I 'll hide my master from the flies, as deep
As these poor pickaxes can dig : and when
With wild wood-leaves and weeds I ha' strew'd his grave
And on it said a century of prayers,
Such as I can, twice o'er, I 'll weep and sigh,
And leaving so his service, follow you,
So please you entertain me.
Luc.   Ay, good youth ;
And rather father thee than master thee.
My friends,
The boy hath taught us manly duties : let us
Find out the prettiest daisied plot we can,
And make him with our pikes and partisans
A grave : come, arm him.   Boy, he is preferr'd
By thee to us, and he shall be interr'd
As soldiers can.   Be cheerful ; wipe thine eyes :
Some falls are means the happier to arise.   [*Exeunt.*

Scene III

A room in Cymbeline's palace.

Enter Cymbeline, Lords, Pisanio, and Attendants.
Cym. Again ; and bring me word how 'tis with her.
                                        [*Exit an Attendant*

A fever with the absence of her son ;
A madness, of which her life 's in danger.   Heavens
How deeply you at once do touch me !   Imogen,
The great part of my comfort, gone ; my queen

Upon a desperate bed, and in a time
When fearful wars point at me ; her son gone,
So needful for this present : it strikes me, past
The hope of comfort.   But for thee, fellow,
Who needs must know of her departure and
Dost seem so ignorant, we 'll enforce it from thee
By a sharp torture.

Pis.   Sir, my life is yours,
I humbly set it at your will : but, for my mistress
I nothing know where she remains, why gone,
Nor when she purposes return.   Beseech your highness,
Hold me your loyal servant.

First Lord.   Good my liege,
The day that she was missing he was here :
I dare be bound he 's true and shall perform
All parts of his subjection loyally.   For Cloten,
There wants no diligence in seeking him,
And will, no doubt, be found.

Cym.   The time is troublesome.
[*To Pisanio*] We 'll slip you for a season ; but our jealousy
Does yet depend.

First Lord.   So please your majesty,
The Roman legions, all from Gallia drawn,
Are landed on your coast, with a supply
Of Roman gentlemen by the senate sent.

Cym. Now for the counsel of my son and queen !
I am amazed with matter.

First Lord.   Good my liege,
Your preparation can affront no less
Than what you hear of : come more, for more you 're ready :
The want is but to put those powers in motion
That long to move.

Cym.   I thank you.   Let 's withdraw ;
And meet the time as it seeks us.   We fear not
What can from Italy annoy us, but
We grieve at chances here.   Away !   [*Exeunt all but Pisanio.*

Pis. I heard no letter from my master since
I wrote him Imogen was slain : 'tis strange :
Nor hear I from my mistress, who did promise
To yield me often tidings ; neither know I
What is betid to Cloten, but remain
Perplex'd in all.   The heavens still must work.
Wherein I am false I am honest ; not true, to be true.
These present wars shall find I love my country,
Even to the note o' the king, or I 'll fall in them.

All other doubts, by time let them be clear'd:
Fortune brings in some boats that are not steer'd.   [*Exit.*

SCENE IV

Wales.   Before the cave of Belarius.
Enter Belarius, Guiderius, and Arviragus.

Gui. The noise is round about us.

Bel.   Let us from it.

Arv. What pleasure, sir, find we in life, to lock it
From action and adventure?

Gui.   Nay, what hope
Have we in hiding us?   This way, the Romans
Must or for Britons slay us or receive us
For barbarous and unnatural revolts
During their use, and slay us after.

Bel.   Sons,
We'll higher to the mountains; there secure us.
To the king's party there's no going: newness
Of Cloten's death—we being not known, not muster'd
Among the bands—may drive us to a render
Where we have lived, and so extort from 's that
Which we have done, whose answer would be death
Drawn on with torture.

Gui.   This is, sir, a doubt
In such a time nothing becoming you,
Nor satisfying us.

Arv.   It is not likely
That when they hear the Roman horses neigh,
Behold their quarter'd fires, have both their eyes
And ears so cloy'd importantly as now,
That they will waste their time upon our note,
To know from whence we are.

Bel.   O, I am known
Of many in the army: many years,
Though Cloten then but young, you see, not wore him
From my remembrance.   And besides, the king
Hath not deserved my service nor your loves;
Who find in my exile the want of breeding,
The certainty of this hard life; aye hopeless
To have the courtesy your cradle promised,
But to be still hot summer's tanlings and
The shrinking slaves of winter.

Gui.   Than be so
Better to cease to be.   Pray, sir, to the army:
I and my brother are not known; yourself

So out of thought, and thereto so o'ergrown,
Cannot be question'd.

Arv.   By this sun that shines,
I'll thither: what thing is it that I never
Did see man die! scarce ever look'd on blood,
But that of coward hares, hot goats, and venison!
Never bestrid a horse, save one that had
A rider like myself, who ne'er wore rowel
Nor iron on his heel! I am ashamed
To look upon the holy sun, to have
The benefit of his blest beams, remaining
So long a poor unknown.

Gui.   By heavens, I'll go:
If you will bless me, sir, and give me leave,
I'll take the better care, but if you will not,
The hazard therefore due fall on me by
The hands of Romans!

Arv.   So say I: amen.

Bel. No reason I, since of your lives you set
So slight a valuation, should reserve
My crack'd one to more care. Have with you, boys!
If in your country wars you chance to die,
That is my bed too, lads, and there I'll lie;   [scorn,
Lead, lead. [*Aside*] The time seems long; their blood thinks
Till it fly out and show them princes born.   [*Exeunt.*

ACT V—Scene I

Britain. The Roman camp.

Enter Posthumus, with a bloody handkerchief.

Post. Yea, bloody cloth, I'll keep thee; for I wish'd
Thou shouldst be colour'd thus. You married ones,
If each of you should take this course, how many
Must murder wives much better than themselves
For wrying but a little! O Pisanio!
Every good servant does not all commands:
No bond but to do just ones. Gods! if you
Should have ta'en vengeance on my faults, I never
Had lived to put on this: so had you saved
The noble Imogen to repent, and struck
Me, wretch more worth your vengeance. But, alack,
You snatch some hence for little faults; that's love,
To have them fall no more: you some permit
To second ills with ills, each elder worse,
And make them dread it, to the doers' thrift.

But Imogen is your own: do your best wills,
And make me blest to obey! I am brought hither
Among the Italian gentry, and to fight
Against my lady's kingdom: 'tis enough
That, Britain, I have kill'd thy mistress; peace!
I'll give no wound to thee. Therefore, good heavens,
Hear patiently my purpose: I'll disrobe me
Of these Italian weeds, and suit myself
As does a Briton peasant: so I'll fight
Against the part I come with; so I'll die
For thee, O Imogen, even for whom my life
Is, every breath, a death: and thus, unknown,
Pitied nor hated, to the face of peril
Myself I'll dedicate. Let me make men know
More valour in me than my habits show.
Gods, put the strength o' the Leonati in me!
To shame the guise o' the world, I will begin
The fashion, less without and more within.   [*Exit.*

SCENE II

Field of battle between the British and Roman camps.

Enter, from one side, Lucius, Iachimo, Imogen, and the Roman Army; from the other side, the British Army; Leonatus Posthumus following, like a poor soldier. They march over and go out. Then enter again, in skirmish, Iachimo and Posthumus: he vanquisheth and disarmeth Iachimo, and then leaves him.

Iach. The heaviness and guilt within my bosom
Takes off my manhood: I have belied a lady,
The princess of this country, and the air on't
Revengingly enfeebles me; or could this carl,
A very drudge of nature's, have subdued me
In my profession? Knighthoods and honours, borne
As I wear mine, are titles but of scorn.
If that thy gentry, Britain, go before
This lout as he exceeds our lords, the odds
Is that we scarce are men and you are gods.   [*Exit.*

The battle continues; the Britons fly; Cymbeline is taken; then enter, to his rescue, Belarius, Guiderius, and Arviragus.

Bel. Stand, stand! We have the advantage of the ground:
The lane is guarded: nothing routs us but
The villany of our fears.

Gui. }
Arv. }   Stand, stand, and fight!

Re-enter Posthumus, and seconds the Britons : they rescue Cymbe-
line and exeunt.   Then re-enter Lucius, Iachimo, and Imogen.

Luc. Away, boy, from the troops, and save thyself;
  For friends kill friends, and the disorder's such
  As war were hoodwink'd.

Iach.   'Tis their fresh supplies.

Luc. It is a day turn'd strangely : or betimes
  Let's re-inforce, or fly.   [*Exeunt.*

SCENE III

Another part of the field.

Enter Posthumus and a British Lord.

Lord. Camest thou from where they made the stand?
Post.   I did:
  Though you, it seems, come from the fliers.
Lord.   I did.
Post. No blame be to you, sir; for all was lost,
  But that the heavens fought : the king himself
  Of his wings destitute, the army broken,
  And but the backs of Britons seen, all flying
  Through a strait lane; the enemy full-hearted,
  Lolling the tongue with slaughtering, having work
  More plentiful than tools to do't, struck down
  Some mortally, some slightly touch'd, some falling
  Merely through fear; that the strait pass was damm'd
  With dead men hurt behind, and cowards living
  To die with lengthen'd shame.
Lord.   Where was this lane?
Post. Close by the battle, ditch'd, and wall'd with turf;
  Which gave advantage to an ancient soldier,
  An honest one, I warrant; who deserved
  So long a breeding as his white beard came to,
  In doing this for's country.   Athwart the lane
  He, with two striplings—lads more like to run
  The country base than to commit such slaughter;
  With faces fit for masks, or rather fairer
  Than those for preservation cased, or shame—
  Made good the passage ; cried to those that fled,
  ' Our Britain's harts die flying, not our men :
  To darkness fleet souls that fly backwards.   Stand;
  Or we are Romans, and will give you that
  Like beasts which you shun beastly, and may save
  But to look back in frown : stand, stand !'   These three,
  Three thousand confident, in act as many,—
  For three performers are the file when all

374

The rest do nothing,—with this word 'Stand, stand,'
Accommodated by the place, more charming
With their own nobleness, which could have turn'd
A distaff to a lance, gilded pale looks,
Part shame, part spirit renew'd ; that some, turn'd coward
But by example,—O, a sin in war,
Damn'd in the first beginners !—'gan to look
The way that they did, and to grin like lions
Upon the pikes o' the hunters.   Then began
A stop i' the chaser, a retire ; anon
A rout, confusion thick : forthwith they fly
Chickens, the way which they stoop'd eagles ; slaves,
The strides they victors made : and now our cowards,
Like fragments in hard voyages, became
The life o' the need : having found the back-door open
Of the unguarded hearts, heavens, how they wound !
Some slain before, some dying, some their friends
O'er-borne i' the former wave : ten chased by one
Are now each one the slaughter-man of twenty :
Those that would die or ere resist are grown
The mortal bugs o' the field.

Lord.   This was strange chance :
A narrow lane, an old man, and two boys.

Post. Nay, do not wonder at it : you are made
Rather to wonder at the things you hear
Than to work any.   Will you rhyme upon 't,
And vent it for a mockery ?   Here is one :
'Two boys, an old man twice a boy, a lane,
Preserved the Britons, was the Romans' bane.'

Lord. Nay, be not angry, sir.

Post.   'Lack, to what end ?
Who dares not stand his foe, I 'll be his friend ;
For if he 'll do as he is made to do,
I know he 'll quickly fly my friendship too.
You have put me into rhyme.

Lord.   Farewell ; you 're angry. [*Exit.*

Post. Still going ?   This is a lord !   O noble misery !
To be i' the field, and ask ' what news ? ' of me !
To-day how many would have given their honours
To have saved their carcasses ! took heel to do 't,
And yet died too ! I, in mine own woe charm'd,
Could not find death where I did hear him groan,
Nor feel him where he struck.   Being an ugly monster,
'Tis strange he hides him in fresh cups, soft beds,
Sweet words ; or hath moe ministers than we

That draw his knives i' the war.   Well, I will find him:
For being now a favourer to the Briton,
No more a Briton, I have resumed again
The part I came in: fight I will no more,
But yield me to the veriest hind that shall
Once touch my shoulder.   Great the slaughter is
Here made by the Roman; great the answer be
Britons must take.   For me, my ransom 's death:
On either side I come to spend my breath,
Which neither here I 'll keep nor bear again,
But end it by some means for Imogen.

Enter two British Captains and Soldiers.

First Cap. Great Jupiter be praised! Lucius is taken:
'Tis thought the old man and his sons were angels.
Sec. Cap. There was a fourth man, in a silly habit,
That gave the affront with them.
First Cap.   So 'tis reported:
But none of 'em can be found.   Stand! who 's there!
Post. A Roman;
Who had not now been drooping here if seconds
Had answer'd him.
Sec. Cap.   Lay hands on him; a dog!
A leg of Rome shall not return to tell
What crows have peck'd them here.   He brags his service
As if he were of note: bring him to the king.

*Enter Cymbeline, Belarius, Guiderius, Arviragus, Pisanio, and
    Roman Captives.   The Captains present Posthumus to Cym-
    beline, who delivers him over to a Gaoler: then exeunt omnes.*

SCENE IV

A British prison.

Enter Posthumus and two Gaolers.

First Gaol. You shall not now be stol'n, you have locks upon
    So graze as you shall find pasture.   [you:
Sec. Gaol.   Ay, or a stomach. [*Exeunt Gaolers.*
Post. Most welcome, bondage! for thou art a way,
    I think, to liberty: yet am I better
    Than one that 's sick o' the gout; since he had rather
    Groan so in perpetuity than be cured
    By the sure physician, death, who is the key
    To unbar these locks.   My conscience, thou art fetter'd
    More than my shanks and wrists: you good gods, give me
    The penitent instrument to pick that bolt,
    Then, free for ever!   Is 't enough I am sorry?

So children temporal fathers do appease;
Gods are more full of mercy.   Must I repent?
I cannot do it better than in gyves,
Desired more than constrain'd : to satisfy,
If of my freedom 'tis the main part, take
No stricter render of me than my all.
I know you are more clement than vile men,
Who of their broken debtors take a third,
A sixth, a tenth, letting them thrive again
On their abatement : that's not my desire:
For Imogen's dear life take mine ; and though
'Tis not so dear, yet 'tis a life; you coin'd it :
'Tween man and man they weigh not every stamp;
Though light, take pieces for the figure's sake :
You rather mine, being yours : and so, great powers,
If you will take this audit, take this life,
And cancel these cold bonds.   O Imogen!
I'll speak to thee in silence.   [Sleeps.

*Solemn music.   Enter, as in an apparition, Sicilius Leonatus,
father to Posthumus, an old man, attired like a warrior;
leading in his hand an ancient matron, his wife and mother
to Posthumus, with music before them : then, after other music,
follow the two young Leonati, brothers to Posthumus, with
wounds as they died in the war.   They circle Posthumus
round as he lies sleeping.*

Sici.   No more, thou thunder-master, show
                Thy spite on mortal flies :
            With Mars fall out, with Juno chide
                That thy adulteries
                    Rates and revenges.
            Hath my poor boy done aught but well,
                Whose face I never saw?
            I died whilst in the womb he stay'd
                Attending nature's law :
            Whose father then—as men report
                Thou orphans' father art—
            Thou shouldst have been, and shielded him,
                From this earth-vexing smart.

Moth.   Lucina lent not me her aid,
                But took me in my throes;
            That from me was Posthumus ript,
                Came crying 'mongst his foes,
                    A thing of pity!

377

Sici.　　　Great nature, like his ancestry,
　　　　　Moulded the stuff so fair,
　　　That he deserved the praise o' the world,
　　　　　As great Sicilius' heir.

First Bro.　When once he was mature for man,
　　　　　In Britain where was he
　　　That could stand up his parallel,
　　　　　Or fruitful object be
　　　In eye of Imogen, that best
　　　　　Could deem his dignity?

Moth.　　With marriage wherefore was he mock'd
　　　　　To be exiled, and thrown,
　　　From Leonati seat, and cast
　　　　　From her his dearest one,
　　　　　　Sweet Imogen?

Sici.　　Why did you suffer Iachimo,
　　　　　Slight thing of Italy,
　　　To taint his nobler heart and brain
　　　　　With needless jealousy;
　　　And to become the geck and scorn
　　　　　O' the other's villany?

Sec. Bro.　For this, from stiller seats we came,
　　　　　Our parents and us twain,
　　　That striking in our country's cause
　　　　　Fell bravely and were slain,
　　　Our fealty and Tenantius' right
　　　　　With honour to maintain.

First Bro.　Like hardiment Posthumus hath
　　　　　To Cymbeline perform'd:
　　　Then, Jupiter, thou king of gods,
　　　　　Why hast thou thus adjourn'd
　　　The graces for his merits due;
　　　　　Being all to dolours turn'd?

Sici.　　Thy crystal window ope; look out;
　　　　　No longer exercise
　　　Upon a valiant race thy harsh
　　　　　And potent injuries.

Moth.　　Since, Jupiter, our son is good,
　　　　　Take off his miseries.

Sici.   Peep through thy marble mansion; help;
                  Or we poor ghosts will cry
              To the shining synod of the rest
                  Against thy deity.

Both Bro.   Help, Jupiter; or we appeal,
                  And from thy justice fly.

*Jupiter descends in thunder and lightning, sitting upon an eagle:
he throws a thunderbolt. The Ghosts fall on their knees.*

Jup.   No more, you petty spirits of region low,
                  Offend our hearing; hush! How dare you ghosts
              Accuse the thunderer, whose bolt, you know,
                  Sky-planted, batters all rebelling coasts?
              Poor shadows of Elysium, hence, and rest
                  Upon your never-withering banks of flowers:
              Be not with mortal accidents opprest;
                  No care of yours it is; you know 'tis ours.
              Whom best I love I cross; to make my gift,
                  The more delay'd, delighted. Be content;
              Your low-laid son our godhead will uplift:
                  His comforts thrive, his trials well are spent.
              Our Jovial star reign'd at his birth, and in
                  Our temple was he married. Rise, and fade.
              He shall be lord of lady Imogen,
                  And happier much by his affliction made.
              This tablet lay upon his breast, wherein
                  Our pleasure his full fortune doth confine:
              And so away: no farther with your din
                  Express impatience, lest you stir up mine.
              Mount, eagle, to my palace crystalline.   [*Ascends.*

Sici He came in thunder; his celestial breath
      Was sulphurous to smell: the holy eagle
      Stoop'd, as to foot us: his ascension is
      More sweet than our blest fields: his royal bird
      Prunes the immortal wing and cloys his beak,
      As when his god is pleased.
All.   Thanks, Jupiter!
Sici. The marble pavement closes, he is enter'd
      His radiant roof. Away! and, to be blest,
      Let us with care perform his great behest. [*The Ghosts vanish.*
Post. [*Waking*] Sleep, thou hast been a grandsire, and begot
      A father to me; and thou hast created
      A mother and two brothers: but, O scorn!
      Gone! they went hence so soon as they were born:
      And so I am awake. Poor wretches that depend

On greatness' favour dream as I have done;
Wake, and find nothing. But, alas, I swerve:
Many dream not to find, neither deserve,
And yet are steep'd in favours; so am I,
That have this golden chance, and know not why.
What fairies haunt this ground? A book? O rare one!
Be not, as is our fangled world, a garment
Noble than that it cover: let thy effects
So follow, to be most unlike our courtiers,
As good as promise.

[*Reads*] 'When as a lion's whelp shall, to himself unknown, without seeking find, and be embraced by a piece of tender air, and when from a stately cedar shall be lopped branches, which, being dead many years, shall after revive, be jointed to the old stock and freshly grow, then shall Posthumus end his miseries, Britain be fortunate and flourish in peace and plenty.'

'Tis still a dream; or else such stuff as madmen
Tongue, and brain not: either both, or nothing:
Or senseless speaking, or a speaking such
As sense cannot untie. Be what it is,
The action of my life is like it, which
I'll keep, if but for sympathy.

Re-enter Gaolers.

First Gaol. Come, sir, are you ready for death?

Post. Over-roasted rather; ready long ago.

First Gaol. Hanging is the word, sir: if you be ready for that, you are well cooked.   [*pays the shot.*

Post. So, if I prove a good repast to the spectators, the dish

First Gaol. A heavy reckoning for you, sir. But the comfort is, you shall be called to no more payments, fear no more tavern-bills; which are often the sadness of parting, as the procuring of mirth: you come in faint for want of meat, depart reeling with too much drink; sorry that you have paid too much, and sorry that you are paid too much; purse and brain both empty, the brain the heavier for being too light, the purse too light, being drawn of heaviness: of this contradiction you shall now be quit. O, the charity of a penny cord! it sums up thousands in a trice: you have no true debitor and creditor but it; of what's past, is, and to come, the discharge: your neck, sir, is pen, book, and counters; so the acquittance follows.

Post. I am merrier to die than thou art to live.

First Gaol. Indeed, sir, he that sleeps feels not the toothache: but a man that were to sleep your sleep, and a hangman to

help him to bed, I think he would change places with his
officer; for, look you, sir, you know not which way you shall
Post. Yes, indeed do I, fellow. [*go.*
First Gaol. Your death has eyes in 's head then; I have not
seen him so pictured: you must either be directed by some
that take upon them to know, or to take upon yourself that
which I am sure you do not know, or jump the after-inquiry
on your own peril: and how you shall speed in your journey's
end, I think you 'll never return to tell one.
Post. I tell thee, fellow, there are none want eyes to direct
them the way I am going, but such as wink and will not use
them.
First Gaol. What an infinite mock is this, that a man should
have the best use of eyes to see the way of blindness! I am
sure hanging 's the way of winking.

Enter a Messenger.

Mess. Knock off his manacles; bring your prisoner to the king.
Post. Thou bringest good news, I am called to be made free.
First Gaol. I 'll be hanged then.
Post. Thou shalt be then freer than a gaoler; no bolts for the
dead. [*Exeunt all but First Gaoler.*
First Gaol. Unless a man would marry a gallows and beget
young gibbets, I never saw one so prone. Yet, on my conscience, there are verier knaves desire to live, for all he be a
Roman: and there be some of them too, that die against
their wills; so should I, if I were one. I would we were all
of one mind, and one mind good; O, there were desolation
of gaolers and gallowses! I speak against my present profit,
but my wish hath a perferment in 't. [*Exit.*

SCENE V

Cymbeline's tent.

*Enter Cymbeline, Belarius, Guiderius, Arviragus, Pisanio,
Lords, Officers, and Attendants.*

Cym. Stand by my side, you whom the gods have made
Preservers of my throne. Woe is my heart,
That the poor soldier, that so richly fought,
Whose rags shamed gilded arms, whose naked breast
Stepp'd before targes of proof, cannot be found:
He shall be happy that can find him, if
Our grace can make him so.
Bel. I never saw
Such noble fury in so poor a thing;
Such precious deeds in one that promised nought
But beggary and poor looks.

Cym.   No tidings of him?
Pis. He hath been search'd among the dead and living,
  But no trace of him.
Cym.   To my grief, I am
  The heir of his reward ;   [*To Belarius, Guiderius, and Arvi-
  ragus*] which I will add
  To you, the liver, heart, and brain of Britain,
  By whom I grant she lives. 'Tis now the time
  To ask of whence you are : report it.
Bel.   Sir,
  In Cambria are we born, and gentlemen :
  Further to boast were neither true nor modest,
  Unless I add we are honest.
Cym.   Bow your knees.
  Arise my knights o' the battle : I create you
  Companions to our person, and will fit you
  With dignities becoming your estates.
                    Enter Cornelius and Ladies.
  There's business in these faces. Why so sadly
  Greet you our victory? you look like Romans,
  And not o' the court of Britain.
Cor.   Hail, great king !
  To sour your happiness, I must report
  The queen is dead.
Cym.   Who worse than a physician
  Would this report become? But I consider,
  By medicine life may be prolong'd, yet death
  Will seize the doctor too. How ended she?
Cor. With horror, madly dying, like her life ;
  Which, being cruel to the world, concluded
  Most cruel to herself. What she confess'd
  I will report, so please you : these her women
  Can trip me if I err ; who with wet cheeks
  Were present when she finish'd.
Cym.   Prithee, say.
Cor. First, she confess'd she never loved you, only
  Affected greatness got by you, not you :
  Married your royalty, was wife to your place,
  Abhorr'd your person.
Cym.   She alone knew this ;
  And, but she spoke in dying, I would not
  Believe her lips in opening it. Proceed.
Cor. Your daughter, whom she bore in hand to love
  With such integrity, she did confess
  Was as a scorpion to her sight ; whose life,

But that her flight prevented it, she had
Ta'en off by poison.

Cym.   O most delicate fiend!
Who is't can read a woman? Is there more?

Cor. More, sir, and worse. She did confess she had
For you a mortal mineral; which, being took,
Should by the minute feed on life and lingering
By inches waste you: in which time she purposed,
By watching, weeping, tendance, kissing, to
O'ercome you with her show, and in time,
When she had fitted you with her craft, to work
Her son into the adoption of the crown:
But, failing of her end by his strange absence,
Grew shameless-desperate; open'd, in despite
Of heaven and men, her purposes; repented
The evils she hatch'd were not effected; so
Despairing died.

Cym.   Heard you all this, her women?

Ladies. We did, so please your highness.

Cym.   Mine eyes
Were not in fault, for she was beautiful,
Mine ears that heard her flattery, nor my heart
That thought her like her seeming; it had been vicious
To have mistrusted her: yet, O my daughter
That it was folly in me, thou mayst say,
And prove it in thy feeling. Heaven mend all!

*Enter Lucius, Iachimo, the Soothsayer, and other Roman
Prisoners, guarded; Posthumus behind, and Imogen.*

Thou comest not, Caius, now for tribute; that
The Britons have razed out, though with the loss
Of many a bold one; whose kinsman have made suit
That their good souls may be appeased with slaughter
Of you their captives, which ourself have granted:
So think of your estate.

Luc. Consider, sir, the chance of war: the day
Was yours by accident; had it gone with us,
We should not, when the blood was cool, have threaten'd
Our prisoners with the sword. But since the gods
Will have it thus, that nothing but our lives
May be call'd ransom, let it come: sufficeth
A Roman with a Roman's heart can suffer:
Augustus lives to think on't: and so much
For my peculiar care. This one thing only
I will entreat; my boy, a Briton born,
Let him be ransom'd: never master had

A page so kind, so duteous, diligent,
So tender over his occasions, true,
So feat, so nurse-like : let his virtue join
With my request, which I 'll make bold your highness
Cannot deny ; he hath done no Briton harm,
Though he have served a Roman : save him, sir,
And spare no blood beside.

Cym.   I have surely seen him :
His favour is familiar to me.   Boy,
Thou hast look'd thyself into my grace,
And art mine own.   I know not why, nor wherefore,
To say, live, boy : ne'er thank thy master ; live :
And ask of Cymbeline what boon thou wilt,
Fitting my bounty and thy state, I 'll give it ;
Yea, though thou do demand a prisoner,
The noblest ta'en.

Imo.   I humbly thank your highness.
Luc. I do not bid thee beg my life, good lad,
And yet I know thou wilt.

Imo.   No, no : alack,
There 's other work in hand : I see a thing
Bitter to me as death : your life, good master,
Must shuffle for itself.

Luc.   The boy disdains me,
He leaves me, scorns me : briefly die their joys
That place them on the truth of girls and boys.
Why stands he so perplex'd ?

Cym.   What wouldst thou, boy ?
I love thee more and more : think more and more
What 's best to ask.   Know'st him thou look'st on ? speak,
Wilt have him live ?   Is he thy kin ? thy friend ?

Imo. He is a Roman ; no more kin to me
Than I to your highness ; who, being born your vassal,
Am something nearer.

Cym.   Wherefore eyest him so ?
Imo. I 'll tell you, sir, in private, if you please
To give me hearing.

Cym.   Ay, with all my heart,
And lend my best attention.   What 's thy name ?
Imo. Fidele, sir.

Cym.   Thou 'rt my good youth, my page ;
I 'll be thy master : walk with me ; speak freely.

                    [*Cymbeline and Imogen converse apart.*

Bel. Is not this boy revived from death ?
Arv.   One sand another

384

Not more resembles that sweet rosy lad
Who died, and was Fidele.   What think you?
Gui. The same dead thing alive.
Bel. Peace, peace! see further; he eyes us not; forbear;
Creatures may be alike: were 't he, I am sure
He would have spoke to us.
Gui.   But we saw him dead.
Bel. Be silent; let 's see further.
Pis. [*Aside*]   It is my mistress:
Since she is living, let the time run on
To good or bad.   [*Cymbeline and Imogen come forward.*
Cym.   Come, stand thou by our side;
Make thy demand aloud.   [*To Iachimo*] Sir, step you forth;
Give answer to this boy, and do it freely;
Or, by our greatness and the grace of it,
Which is our honour, bitter torture shall
Winnow the truth from falsehood.   On, speak to him.
Imo. My boon is that this gentleman may render
Of whom he had this ring.
Post. [*Aside*]   What 's that to him?
Cym. That diamond upon your finger, say
How came it yours?
Iach. Thou 'lt torture me to leave unspoken that
Which, to be spoke, would torture thee.
Cym.   How! me?
Iach. I am glad to be constrain'd to utter that
Which torments me to conceal.   By villany
I got this ring: 'twas Leonatus' jewel;
Whom thou didst banish; and—which more may grieve thee
As it doth me,—a nobler sir ne 'er lived
'Twixt sky and ground.   Wilt thou hear more, my lord?
Cym. All that belongs to this.
Iach.   That paragon, thy daughter,
For whom my heart drops blood and my false spirits
Quail to remember—Give me leave; I faint.
Cym. My daughter? what of her?   Renew thy strength:
I had rather thou shouldst live while nature will
Than die ere I hear more: strive, man, and speak.
Iach. Upon a time—unhappy was the clock
That struck the hour!—it was in Rome,—accurst
The mansion where!—'twas at a feast,—O, would
Our viands had been poison'd, or at least
Those which I heaved to head!—the good Posthumus—
What should I say? he was too good to be
Where ill men were; and was the best of all

Amongst the rarest of good ones—sitting sadly,
Hearing us praise our loves of Italy
For beauty t..at made barren the swell'd boast
Of him that best could speak ; for feature, laming
The shrine of Venus, or straight-pight Minerva,
Postures beyond brief nature ; for condition,
A shop of all the qualities that man
Loves woman for ; besides that hook of wiving,
Fairness which strikes the eye—

Cym.   I stand on fire :
Come to the matter.

Iach.   All too soon I shall,
Unless thou wouldst grieve quickly. This Posthumus,
Most like a noble lord in love and one
That had a royal lover, took his hint,
And not dispraising whom we praised,—therein
He was as calm as virtue—he began
His mistress' picture ; which by his tongue being made,
And then a mind put in 't, either our brags
Were crack'd of kitchen-trulls, or his description
Proved us unspeaking sots.

Cym.   Nay, nay, to the purpose.

Iach. Your daughter's chastity—there it begins.
He spake of her, as Dian had hot dreams,
And she alone were cold : whereat I, wretch,
Made scruple of his praise, and wager'd with him
Pieces of gold 'gainst this which then he wore
Upon his honour'd finger, to attain
In suit the place of 's bed and win this ring
By hers and mine adultery : he, true knight,
No lesser of her honour confident
Than I did truly find her, stakes this ring ;
And would so, had it been a carbuncle
Of Phœbus' wheel ; and might so safely, had it
Been all the worth of 's car. Away to Britain
Post I in this design : well may you, sir,
Remember me at court ; where I was taught
Of your chaste daughter the wide difference
'Twixt amorous and villanous.   Being thus quench'd
Of hope, not longing, mine Italian brain
'Gan in your duller Britain operate
Most vilely ; for my vantage, excellent ;
And, to be brief, my practice so prevail'd,
That I return'd with simular proof enough
To make the noble Leonatus mad,

By wounding his belief in her renown
With tokens thus, and thus ; averring notes
Of chamber-hanging, pictures, this her bracelet,—
O cunning, how I got it !—nay some marks
Of secret on her person, that he could not
But think her bond of chastity quite crack'd
I having ta'en the forfeit.   Whereupon—
Methinks I see him now—

Post. [*Advancing*]   Ay, so thou dost,
Italian fiend !   Ay me, most credulous fool,
Egregious murderer, thief, any thing
That 's due to all the villains past, in being,
To come !   O, give me cord, or knife, or poison,
Some upright justicer !   Thou, king, send out
For torturers ingenious : it is I
That all the abhorred things o' the earth amend
By being worse than they.   I am Posthumus
That kill'd thy daughter : villain-like, I lie ;
That caused a lesser villain than myself,
A sacrilegious thief, to do 't.   The temple
Of virtue was she ; yea, and she herself.
Spit, and throw stones, cast mire upon me, set
The dogs o' the street to bay me : every villain
Be call'd Posthumus Leonatus, and
Be villany less than 'twas !   O Imogen !
My queen, my life, my wife !   O Imogen,
Imogen, Imogen !

Imo.   Peace, my lord ; hear, hear—

Post. Shall 's have a play of this ?   Thou scornful page,
There lie thy part.   [*Striking her : she falls.*

Pis.   O, gentlemen, help !
Mine and your mistress !   O, my lord Posthumus !
You ne'er kill'd Imogen till now.   Help, help !
Mine honour'd lady !

Cym.   Does the world go round ?

Post. How come these staggers on me ?

Pis.   Wake, my mistress !

Cym. If this be so, the gods do mean to strike me
To death with mortal joy.

Pis.   How fares my mistress ?

Imo. O, get thee from my sight ;
Thou gavest me poison : dangerous fellow, hence !
Breathe not where princes are.

Cym.   The tune of Imogen !

Pis. Lady,

The gods throw stones of sulphur on me, if
That box I gave you was not thought by me
A precious thing: I had it from the queen.
Cym. New matter still?
Imo.   It poison'd me.
Cor.   O gods!
I left out one thing which the queen confess'd,
Which must approve thee honest: 'If Pisanio
Have,' said she, 'given his mistress that confection
Which I gave him for cordial, she is served
As I would serve a rat.'
Cym.   What's this, Cornelius?
Cor. The queen, sir, very oft importuned me
To temper poisons for her, still pretending
The satisfaction of her knowledge only
In killing creatures vile, as cats and dogs,
Of no esteem: I, dreading that her purpose
Was of more danger, did compound for her
A certain stuff, which being ta'en would cease
The present power of life, but in short time
All offices of nature should again
Do their due functions.   Have you ta'en of it?
Imo. Most like I did, for I was dead.
Bel.   My boys,
There was our error.
Gui.   This is, sure, Fidele.
Imo. Why did you throw your wedded lady from you?
Think that you are upon a rock, and now
Throw me again.   [*Embracing him.*
Post.   Hang there like fruit, my soul,
Till the tree die!
Cym.   How now, my flesh, my child!
What, makest thou me a dullard in this act?
Wilt thou not speak to me?
Imo. [*Kneeling*]   Your blessing, sir.
Bel. [*To Gui. and Arv.*] Though you did love this youth, I
You had a motive for 't.   [blame ye not;
Cym.   My tears that fall
Prove holy water on thee!   Imogen,
Thy mother's dead.
Imo.   I am sorry for 't, my lord.
Cym. O, she was naught; and long of her it was
That we meet here so strangely: but her son
Is gone, we know not how nor where.
Pis.   My lord,

Now fear is from me, I 'll speak troth.   Lord
Upon my lady's missing, came to me
With his sword drawn ; foam'd at the mouth,
If I discover'd not which way she was gone,
It was my instant death.   By accident,
I had a feigned letter of my master's
Then in my pocket ; which directed him
To seek her on the mountains near to Milford;
Where, in a frenzy, in my master's garments,
Which he enforced from me, away he posts
With unchaste purpose, and with oath to violate
My lady's honour : what became of him
I further know not.

Gui.   Let me end the story:
I slew him there.

Cym.   Marry, the gods forfend !
I would not thy good deeds should from my lips
Pluck a hard sentence : prithee, valiant youth,
Deny 't again.

Gui.   I have spoke it, and I did it.

Cym. He was a prince.

Gui. A most incivil one : the wrongs he did me
Were nothing princelike ; for he did provoke me
With language that would make me spurn the sea,
If it could so roar to me : I cut off 's head ;
And am right glad he is not standing here
To tell this tale of mine.

Cym.   I am sorry for thee :
By thine own tongue thou art condemn'd, and must
Endure our law : thou 'rt dead.

Imo.   That headless man
I thought had been my lord.

Cym.   Bind the offender,
And take him from our presence.

Bel.   Stay, sir king :
This man is better than the man he slew,
As well descended as thyself, and hath
More of thee merited than a band of Clotens
Had ever scar for.   [*To the Guard*] Let his arms alone;
They were not born for bondage.

Cym.   Why, old soldier,
Wilt thou undo the worth thou art unpaid for,
By tasting of our wrath ?   How of descent
As good as we ?

Arv.   In that he spake too far.

Cym. And thou shalt die for 't.
Bel.   We will die all three:
But I will prove that two on 's are as good
As I have given out him.   My sons, I must
For mine own part unfold a dangerous speech,
Though haply well for you.
Arv.   Your danger 's ours.
Gui. And our good his.
Bel.   Have at it then, by leave.
Thou hadst, great king, a subject who
Was call'd Belarius.
Cym.   What of him? he is
A banish'd traitor.
Bel.   He it is that hath
Assumed this age, indeed a banish'd man;
I know not how a traitor.
Cym.   Take him hence:
The whole world shall not save him.
Bel.   Not too hot:
First pay me for the nursing of thy sons;
And let it be confiscate all, so soon
As I have received it.
Cym.   Nursing of my sons!
Bel. I am too blunt and saucy: here 's my knee:
Ere I arise I will prefer my sons;
Then spare not the old father.   Mighty sir,
These two young gentlemen, that call me father
And think they are my sons, are none of mine;
They are the issue of your loins, my liege,
And blood of your begetting.
Cym.   How! my issue!
Bel. So sure as you your father 's.   I, old Morgan,
Am that Belarius whom you sometime banish'd:
Your pleasure was my mere offence, my punishment
Itself, and all my treason: that I suffer'd
Was all the harm I did.   These gentle princes—
For such and so they are—these twenty years
Have I train'd up: those arts they have as I
Could put into them; my breeding was, sir, as
Your highness knows.   Their nurse, Euriphile,
Whom for the theft I wedded, stole these children
Upon my banishment: I moved her to 't,
Having received the punishment before
For that which I did then: beaten for loyalty
Excited me to treason: their dear loss,

The more of you 'twas felt, the more it shaped
Unto my end of stealing them.   But, gracious sir
Here are your sons again ; and I must lose
Two of the sweet'st companions in the world.
The benediction of these covering heavens
Fall on their heads like dew ! for they are worthy
To inlay heaven with stars.

Cym.   Thou weep'st, and speak'st.
The service that you three have done is more
Unlike than this thou tell'st.   I lost my children :
If these be they, I know not how to wish
A pair of worthier sons.

Bel.   Be pleased awhile.
This gentleman, whom I call Polydore,
Most worthy prince, as yours, is true Guiderius :
This gentleman, my Cadwal, Arviragus,
Your younger princely son ; he, sir, was lapp'd
In a most curious mantle, wrought by the hand
Of his queen mother, which for more probation
I can with ease produce.

Cym.   Guiderius had
Upon his neck a mole, a sanguine star ;
It is a mark of wonder.

Bel.   This is he ;
Who hath upon him still that natural stamp :
It was wise nature's end in the donation,
To be his evidence now.

Cym.   O, what am I ?
A mother to the birth of three ?   Ne'er mother
Rejoiced deliverance more.   Blest pray you be,
That, after this strange starting from your orbs,
You may reign in them now !   O Imogen,
Thou hast lost by this a kingdom.

Imo.   No, my lord ;
I have got two worlds by 't.   O my gentle brothers,
Have we thus met ?   O, never say hereafter
But I am truest speaker : you call'd me brother,
When I was but your sister ; I you brothers,
When ye were so indeed.

Cym.   Did you e'er meet ?

Arv. Ay, my good lord.

Gui.   And at first meeting loved,
Continued so, until we thought he died.

Cor. By the queen's dram she swallow'd.

Cym.   O rare instinct !

When shall I hear all through? This fierce abridgement
Hath to it circumstantial branches, which
Distinction should be rich in. Where? how lived you?
And when came you to serve our Roman captive?
How parted with your brothers? how first met them?
Why fled you from the court? and whither? These,
And your three motives to the battle, with
I know not how much more, should be demanded;
And all the other by-dependances,
From chance to chance: but nor the time nor place
Will serve our long inter'gatories. See,
Posthumus anchors upon Imogen;
And she, like harmless lightning, throws her eye
On him, her brothers, me, her master, hitting
Each object with a joy: the counterchange
Is severally in all. Let's quit this ground,
And smoke the temple with our sacrifices.
[*To Belarius*] Thou art my brother; so we'll hold thee ever.

Imo. You are my father too; and did relieve me,
   To see this gracious season.

Cym.   All o'erjoy'd,
   Save these in bonds: let them be joyful too,
   For they shall taste our comfort.

Imo.   My good master,
   I will yet do you service.

Luc.   Happy be you!

Cym. The forlorn soldier that so nobly fought,
   He would have well becomed this place and graced
   The thankings of a king.

Post.   I am, sir,
   The soldier that did company these three
   In poor beseeming; 'twas a fitment for
   The purpose I then follow'd. That I was he,
   Speak, Iachimo: I had you down, and might
   Have made you finish.

Iach.   [*Kneeling*] I am down again:
   But now my heavy conscience sinks my knee,
   As then your force did. Take that life, beseech you
   Which I so often owe: but your ring first;
   And here the bracelet of the truest princess
   That ever swore her faith.

Post.   Kneel not to me:
   The power that I have on you is to spare you;
   The malice towards you to forgive you: live,
   And deal with others better.

Cym.   Nobly doom'd!
We 'll learn our freeness of a son-in-law;
Pardon 's the word to all.
Arv.   You holp us, sir,
As you did mean indeed to be our brother;
Joy'd are we that you are.
Post. Your servant, princes. Good my lord of Rome,
Call forth your soothsayer: as I slept, methought
Great Jupiter, upon his eagle back'd,
Appear'd to me, with other spritely shows
Of mine own kindred: when I waked, I found
This label on my bosom; whose containing
Is so from sense in hardness, that I can
Make no collection of it: let him show
His skill in the construction.
Luc.   Philarmonus!
Sooth. Here, my good lord.
Luc.   Read, and declare the meaning.
Sooth. [*Reads*] 'When as a lion's whelp shall, to himself un-
known, without seeking find, and be embraced by a piece of
tender air, and when from a stately cedar shall be lopped
branches, which, being dead many years, shall after revive,
be jointed to the old stock and freshly grow, then shall
Posthumus end his miseries, Britain be fortunate and flourish
in peace and plenty.'
Thou, Leonatus, art the lion's whelp;
The fit and apt construction of thy name,
Being Leo-natus, doth import so much.
[*To Cymbeline*] The piece of tender air, thy virtuous daughter,
Which we call 'mollis aer;' and 'mollis aer'
We term it 'mulier:' which 'mulier' I divine
Is this most constant wife; who even now,
Answering the letter of the oracle,
Unknown to you, unsought, were clipp'd about
With this most tender air.
Cym.   This hath some seeming.
Sooth. The lofty cedar, royal Cymbeline,
Personates thee: and thy lopp'd branches point
Thy two sons forth; who, by Belarius stol'n,
For many years thought dead, are now revived,
To the most majestic cedar join'd, whose issue
Promises Britain peace and plenty.
Cym.   Well;
My peace we will begin. And, Caius Lucius,
Although the victor, we submit to Cæsar

393

And to the Roman empire, promising
To pay our wonted tribute, from the which
We were dissuaded by our wicked queen;
Whom heavens in justice both on her and hers
Have laid most heavy hand.

Sooth. The fingers of the powers above do tune
The harmony of this peace. The vision,
Which I made known to Lucius ere the stroke
Of this yet scarce-cold battle, at this instant
Is full accomplish'd; for the Roman eagle,
From south to west on wing soaring aloft,
Lessen'd herself and in the beams o' the sun
So vanish'd: which foreshow'd our princely eagle,
The imperial Cæsar, should again unite
His favour with the radiant Cymbeline,
Which shines here in the west.

Cym.   Laud we the gods;
And let our crooked smokes climb to their nostrils
From our blest altars. Publish we this peace
To all our subjects. Set we forward: let
A Roman and a British ensign wave
Friendly together: so through Lud's town march:
And in the temple of great Jupiter
Our peace we 'll ratify; seal it with feasts.
Set on there! Never was a war did cease,
Ere bloody hands were wash'd, with such a peace. [*Exeunt.*

VENUS AND ADONIS

Vilia miretur vulgus ; mihi flavus Apollo
Pocula Castalia plena ministret aqua

To the

RIGHT HONOURABLE HENRIE WRIOTHESLEY,

Earle of Southampton, and Baron of Titchfield.

RIGHT HONOURABLE,

I know not how I shall offend in dedicating my vnpolisht lines to your Lordship, nor how the worlde will censure me for choosing so strong a proppe to support so weake a burthen, onely if your Honour seeme but pleased, I account my selfe highly praised, and vowe to take aduantage of all idle houres, till I haue honoured you with some grauer labour. But if the first heire of my inuention proue deformed, I shall be sorry it had so noble a godfather : and neuer after eare so barren a land, for fear it yeeld me still so bad a haruest, I leaue it to your Honourable suruey, and your Honor to your hearts content which I wish may alwaies answere your owne wish, and the worlds hopefull expectation.

Your Honors in all dutie,
WILLIAM SHAKESPEARE.

EVEN as the sun with purple-colour'd face
Had ta'en his last leave of the weeping morn,
Rose-cheek'd Adonis hied him to the chase ;
Hunting he loved, but love he laugh'd to scorn :
    Sick-thoughted Venus makes amain unto him,
    And like a bold-faced suitor 'gins to woo him.

'Thrice fairer than myself,' thus she began,
'The field's chief flower, sweet above compare,
Stain to all nymphs, more lovely than a man,
More white and red than doves or roses are ;
    Nature that made thee, with herself at strife,
    Saith that the world hath ending with thy life.

'Vouchsafe, thou wonder, to alight thy steed,
And rein his proud head to the saddle-bow ;
If thou wilt deign this favour, for thy meed
A thousand honey secrets shalt thou know :
    Here come and sit, where never serpent hisses,
    And being set, I 'll smother thee with kisses ;

' And yet not cloy thy lips with loathed satiety.
But rather famish them amid their plenty,
Making them red and pale with fresh variety;
Ten kisses short as one, one long as twenty :
 A summer's day will seem an hour but short,
 Being wasted in such time-beguiling sport.'

With this she seizeth on his sweating palm,
The precedent of pith and livelihood,
And, trembling in her passion, calls it balm,
Earth's sovereign salve to do a goddess good :
 Being so enraged, desire doth lend her force
 Courageously to pluck him from his horse.

Over one arm the lusty courser's rein,
Under her other was the tender boy,
Who blush'd and pouted in a dull disdain,
With leaden appetite, unapt to toy ;
 She red and hot as coals of glowing fire,
 He red for shame, but frosty in desire.

The studded bridle on a ragged bough
Nimbly she fastens—O, how quick is love !—
The steed is stalled up, and even now
To tie the rider she begins to prove :
 Backward she push d him, as she would be thrust,
 And govern'd him in strength, though not in lust.

So soon was she along as he was down,
Each leaning on their elbows and their hips :
Now doth she stroke his cheek, now doth he frown,
And 'gins to chide, but soon she stops his lips :
 And kissing speaks, with lustful language broken,
 ' If thou wilt chide, thy lips shall never open.'

He burns with bashful shame ; she with her tears
Doth quench the maiden burning of his cheeks ;
Then with her windy sighs and golden hairs
To fan and blow them dry again she seeks :
 He saith she is immodest, blames her miss ;
 What follows more she murders with a kiss.

Even as an empty eagle, sharp by fast,
Tires with her beak on feathers, flesh and bone,
Shaking her wings, devouring all in haste,
Till either gorge be stuff'd or prey be gone ;
 Even so she kiss'd his brow, his cheek, his chin,
 And where she ends she doth anew begin.

Forced to content, but never to obey,
Panting he lies and breatheth in her face;
She feedeth on the steam as on a prey,
And calls it heavenly moisture, air of grace;
    Wishing her cheeks were gardens full of flowers,
    So they were dew'd with such distilling showers.

Look, how a bird lies tangled in a net,
So fasten'd in her arms Adonis lies;
Pure shame and awed resistance made him fret,
Which bred more beauty in his angry eyes:
    Rain added to a river that is rank
    Perforce will force it overflow the bank.

Still she entreats, and prettily entreats,
For to a pretty ear she tunes her tale;
Still is he sullen, still he lours and frets,
'Twixt crimson shame, and anger ashy-pale;
    Being red, she loves him best; and being white,
    Her best is better'd with a more delight.

Look how he can, she cannot choose but love;
And by her fair immortal hand she swears,
From his soft bosom never to remove,
Till he take truce with her contending tears,
    Which long have rain'd, making her cheeks all wet:
    And one sweet kiss shall pay this countless debt.

Upon this promise did he raise his chin,
Like a dive-dapper peering through a wave,
Who, being look'd on, ducks as quickly in;
So offers he to give what she did crave;
    But when her lips were ready for his pay,
    He winks, and turns his lips another way.

Never did passenger in summer's heat
More thirst for drink than she for this good turn.
Her help she sees, but help she cannot get;
She bathes in water, yet her fire must burn:
    'O, pity,' 'gan she cry, 'flint-hearted boy!
    'Tis but a kiss I beg; why art thou coy?

'I have been woo'd, as I entreat thee now,
Even by the stern and direful god of war,
Whose sinewy neck in battle ne'er did bow,
Who conquers where he comes in every jar;
    Yet hath he been my captive and my slave,
    And begg'd for that which thou unask'd shalt have.

'Over my altars hath he hung his lance,
His batter'd shield, his uncontrolled crest,
And for my sake hath learn'd to sport and dance,
To toy, to wanton, dally, smile and jest;
    Scorning his churlish drum and ensign red,
    Making my arms his field, his tent my bed.

'Thus he that overruled I overswayed,
Leading him prisoner in a red-rose chain:
Strong-temper'd steel his stronger strength obeyed,
Yet was he servile to my coy disdain.
    O, be not proud, nor brag not of thy might,
    For mastering her that foil'd the god of fight!

'Touch but my lips with those fair lips of thine—
Though mine be not so fair, yet are they red—
The kiss shall be thine own as well as mine:
What see'st thou in the ground? hold up thy head:
    Look in mine eyeballs, there thy beauty lies;
    Then why not lips on lips, since eyes in eyes?

'Art thou ashamed to kiss? then wink again,
And I will wink; so shall the day seem night;
Love keeps his revels where there are but twain;
Be bold to play, our sport is not in sight:
    These blue-vein'd violets whereon we lean
    Never can blab, nor know not what we mean.

'The tender spring upon thy tempting lip
Shews thee unripe; yet mayst thou well be tasted:
Make use of time, let not advantage slip;
Beauty within itself should not be wasted:
    Fair flowers that are not gather'd in their prime
    Rot and consume themselves in little time.

'Were I hard-favour'd, foul, or wrinkled-old,
Ill-nurtured, crooked, churlish, harsh in voice,
O'erworn, despised, rheumatic and cold,
Thick-sighted, barren, lean, and lacking juice,
    Then mightst thou pause, for then I were not for thee;
    But having no defects, why dost abhor me?

'Thou canst not see one wrinkle in my brow;
Mine eyes are grey and bright and quick in turning;
My beauty as the spring doth yearly grow,
My flesh is soft and plump, my marrow burning;
    My smooth moist hand, were it with thy hand felt,
    Would in thy palm dissolve, or seem to melt.

'Bid me discourse, I will enchant thine ear,
Or, like a fairy, trip upon the green,
Or, like a nymph, with long dishevell'd hair,
Dance on the sands, and yet no footing seen:
    Love is a spirit all compact of fire,
    Not gross to sink, but light, and will aspire.

'Witness this primrose bank whereon I lie;
These forceless flowers like sturdy trees support me;
Two strengthless doves will draw me through the sky,
From morn till night, even where I list to sport me:
    Is love so light, sweet boy, and may it be
    That thou shouldst think it heavy unto thee?

'Is thine own heart to thine own face affected?
Can thy right hand seize love upon thy left?
Then woo thyself, be of thyself rejected,
Steal thine own freedom, and complain on theft.
    Narcissus so himself himself forsook,
    And died to kiss his shadow in the brook.

'Torches are made to light, jewels to wear,
Dainties to taste, fresh beauty for the use,
Herbs for their smell, and sappy plants to bear;
Things growing to themselves are growth's abuse:
    Seeds spring from seeds and beauty breedeth beauty;
    Thou wast begot; to get it is thy duty.

'Upon the earth's increase why shouldst thou feed,
Unless the earth with thy increase be fed?
By law of nature thou art bound to breed,
That thine may live when thou thyself art dead;
    And so, in spite of death, thou dost survive,
    In that thy likeness still is left alive.'

By this, the love-sick queen began to sweat,
For, where they lay, the shadow had forsook them,
And Titan, tired in the mid-day heat,
With burning eye did hotly overlook them,
    Wishing Adonis had his team to guide,
    So he were like him and by Venus' side.

And now Adonis, with a lazy spright,
And with a heavy, dark, disliking eye,
His louring brows o'erwhelming his fair sight,
Like misty vapours when they blot the sky,
    Souring his cheeks, cries, 'Fie, no more of love!
    The sun doth burn my face; I must remove.'

'Ay me,' quoth Venus, 'young, and so unkind!
What bare excuses makest thou to be gone!
I 'll sigh celestial breath, whose gentle wind
Shall cool the heat of this descending sun:
    I 'll make a shadow for thee of my hairs;
    If they burn too, I 'll quench them with my tears.

'The sun that shines from heaven shines but warm,
And, lo, I lie between that sun and thee:
The heat I have from thence doth little harm,
Thine eye darts forth the fire that burneth me;
    And were I not immortal, life were done
    Between this heavenly and earthly sun.

'Art thou obdurate, flinty, hard as steel?
Nay, more than flint, for stone at rain relenteth:
Art thou a woman's son, and canst not feel
What 'tis to love? how want of love tormenteth?
    O, had thy mother borne so hard a mind,
    She had not brought forth thee, but died unkind.

'What am I, that thou shouldst contemn me this,
Or what great danger dwells upon my suit?
What were thy lips the worse for one poor kiss?
Speak, fair; but speak fair words, or else be mute:
    Give me one kiss, I 'll give it thee again,
    And one for interest, if thou wilt have twain.

'Fie, lifeless picture, cold and senseless stone,
Well painted idol, image dull and dead,
Statue contenting but the eye alone,
Thing like a man, but of no woman bred!
    Thou art no man, though of a man's complexion,
    For men will kiss even by their own direction.'

This said, impatience chokes her pleading tongue,
And swelling passion doth provoke a pause;
Red cheeks and fiery eyes blaze forth her wrong;
Being judge in love, she cannot right her cause:
    And now she weeps, and now she fain would speak,
    And now her sobs do her intendments break.

Sometimes she shakes her head, and then his hand,
Now gazeth she on him, now on the ground;
Sometimes her arms infold him like a band:
She would, he will not in her arms be bound;
    And when from thence he struggles to be gone,
    She locks her lily fingers one in one.

'Fondling,' she saith, 'since I have hemm'd thee here
Within the circuit of this ivory pale,
I'll be a park, and thou shalt be my deer;
Feed where thou wilt, on mountain or in dale:
    Graze on my lips, and if those hills be dry,
    Stray lower, where the pleasant fountains lie.

'Within this limit is relief enough,
Sweet bottom-grass and high delightful plain,
Round rising hillocks, brakes obscure and rough,
To shelter thee from tempest and from rain:
    Then be my deer, since I am such a park;
    No dog shall rouse thee, though a thousand bark.'

At this Adonis smiles as in disdain,
That in each cheek appears a pretty dimple:
Love made those hollows, if himself were slain,
He might be buried in a tomb so simple;
    Foreknowing well, if there he came to lie,
    Why, there Love lived, and there he could not die.

These lovely caves, these round enchanting pits,
Open'd their mouths to swallow Venus' liking.
Being mad before, how doth she now for wits?
Struck dead at first, what needs a second striking?
    Poor queen of love, in thine own law forlorn,
    To love a cheek that smiles at thee in scorn!

Now which way shall she turn? what shall she say?
Her words are done, her woes the more increasing;
The time is spent, her object will away
And from her twining arms doth urge releasing.
    'Pity,' she cries, 'some favour, some remorse!'
    Away he springs, and hasteth to his horse.

But, lo, from forth a copse that neighbours by,
A breeding jennet, lusty, young and proud,
Adonis' trampling courser doth espy,
And forth she rushes, snorts and neighs aloud:
    The strong-neck'd steed, being tied unto a tree,
    Breaketh his rein and to her straight goes he.

Imperiously he leaps, he neighs, he bounds,
And now his woven girths he breaks asunder;
The bearing earth with his hard hoof he wounds,
Whose hollow womb resounds like heaven's thunder;
    The iron bit he crusheth 'tween his teeth,
    Controlling what he was controlled with.

His ears up-prick'd; his braided hanging mane
Upon his compass'd crest now stand on end;
His nostrils drink the air, and forth again,
As from a furnace, vapours doth he send:
　　His eye, which scornfully glisters like fire,
　　Shows his hot courage and his high desire.

Sometime he trots, as if he told the steps,
With gentle majesty and modest pride;
Anon he rears upright, curvets and leaps,
As who should say ' Lo, thus my strength is tried;
　　And this I do to captivate the eye
　　Of the fair breeder that is standing by.'

What recketh he his rider's angry stir,
His flattering ' Holla' or his ' Stand, I say'?
What cares he now for curb or pricking spur?
For rich caparisons or trappings gay?
　　He sees his love, and nothing else he sees,
　　For nothing else with his proud sight agrees.

Look, when a painter would surpass the life,
In limning out a well proportion'd steed,
His art with nature's workmanship at strife,
As if the dead the living should exceed;
　　So did this horse excel a common one
　　In shape, in courage, colour, pace and bone.

Round-hoof'd, short-jointed, fetlocks shag and long,
Broad breast, full eye, small head and nostril wide,
High crest, short ears, straight legs and passing strong,
Thin mane, thick tail, broad buttock, tender hide:
　　Look, what a horse should have he did not lack,
　　Save a proud rider on so proud a back.

Sometime he scuds far off, and there he stares;
Anon he starts at stirring of a feather;
To bid the wind a base he now prepares,
And whether he run or fly, they know not whether;
　　For through his mane and tail the high wind sings,
　　Fanning the hairs, who wave like feather'd wings.

He looks upon his love and neighs unto her;
She answers him, as if she knew his mind:
Being proud, as females are, to see him woo her,
She puts on outward strangeness, seems unkind,
　　Spurns at his love and scorns the heat he feels,
　　Beating his kind embracements with her heels.

Then, like a melancholy malcontent,
He vails his tail, that, like a falling plume,
Cool shadow to his melting buttock lent:
He stamps, and bites the poor flies in his fume.
  His love, perceiving how he was enraged,
  Grew kinder, and his fury was assuaged.

His testy master goeth about to take him;
When, lo, the unback'd breeder, full of fear,
Jealous of catching, swiftly doth forsake him,
With her the horse, and left Adonis there:
  As they were mad, unto the wood they hie them,
  Out-stripping crows that strive to over-fly them.

All swoln with chafing, down Adonis sits,
Banning his boisterous and unruly beast:
And now the happy season once more fits,
That love-sick Love by pleading may be blest;
  For lovers say, the heart hath treble wrong
  When it is barr'd the aidance of the tongue.

An oven that is stopp'd, or river stay'd,
Burneth more hotly, swelleth with more rage:
So of concealed sorrow may be said;
Free vent of words love's fire doth assuage;
  But when the heart's attorney once is mute,
  The client breaks, as desperate in his suit.

He sees her coming, and begins to glow,
Even as a dying coal revives with wind,
And with his bonnet hides his angry brow,
Looks on the dull earth with disturbed mind,
  Taking no notice that she is so nigh,
  For all askance he holds her in his eye.

O, what a sight it was, wistly to view
How she came stealing to the wayward boy!
To note the fighting conflict of her hue,
How white and red each other did destroy!
  But now her cheek was pale, and by and by
  It flash'd forth fire, as lightning from the sky.

Now was she just before him as he sat,
And like a lowly lover down she kneels;
With one fair hand she heaveth up his hat,
Her other tender hand his fair cheek feels:
  His tenderer cheek receives her soft hand's print,
  As apt as new-fall'n snow takes any dint.

O, what a war of looks was then between them!
Her eyes petitioners to his eyes suing;
His eyes saw her eyes as they had not seen them;
Her eyes woo'd still, his eyes disdain'd the wooing:
      And all this dumb play had his acts made plain
      With tears, which chorus-like her eyes did rain.

Full gently now she takes him by the hand,
A lily prison'd in a gaol of snow,
Or ivory in an alabaster band;
So white a friend engirts so white a foe:
      This beauteous combat, wilful and unwilling,
      Show'd like two silver doves that sit a-billing.

Once more the engine of her thoughts began:
'O fairest mover on this mortal round,
Would thou wert as I am, and I a man,
My heart all whole as thine, thy heart my wound;
      For one sweet look thy help I would assure thee,
      Though nothing but my body's bane would cure thee.'

'Give me my hand,' saith he; 'why dost thou feel it!'
'Give me my heart,' saith she, 'and thou shalt have it;
O, give it me, lest thy hard heart do steel it,
And being steel'd, soft sighs can never grave it:
      Then love's deep groans I never shall regard,
      Because Adonis' heart hath made mine hard.'

'For shame,' he cries, 'let go, and let me go;
My day's delight is past, my horse is gone,
And 'tis your fault I am bereft him so:
I pray you hence, and leave me here alone;
      For all my mind, my thought, my busy care,
      Is how to get my palfrey from the mare.'

Thus she replies: 'Thy palfrey, as he should,
Welcomes the warm approach of sweet desire:
Affection is a coal that must be cool'd;
Else, suffer'd, it will set the heart on fire:
      The sea hath bounds, but deep desire hath none;
      Therefore no marvel though thy horse be gone.

'How like a jade he stood, tied to the tree,
Servilely master'd with a leathern rein!
But when he saw his love, his youth's fair fee,
He held such petty bondage in disdain;
      Throwing the base thong from his bending crest,
      Enfranchising his mouth, his back, his breast.

'Who sees his true-love in her naked bed,
Teaching the sheets a whiter hue than white,
But, when his glutton eye so full hath fed,
His other agents aim at like delight?
     Who is so faint, that dares not be so bold
     To touch the fire, the weather being cold?

'Let me excuse thy courser, gentle boy;
And learn of him, I heartily beseech thee,
To take advantage on presented joy;
Though I were dumb, yet his proceedings teach thee:
     O, learn to love; the lesson is but plain,
     And once made perfect, never lost again.'

'I know not love,' quoth he, 'nor will not know it,
Unless it be a boar, and then I chase it;
'Tis much to borrow, and I will not owe it;
My love to love is love but to disgrace it;
     For I have heard it is a life in death,
     That laughs, and weeps, and all but with a breath.

'Who wears a garment shapeless and unfinish'd?
Who plucks the bud before one leaf put forth?
If springing things be any jot diminish'd,
They wither in their prime, prove nothing worth:
     The colt that's back'd and burthen'd being young
     Loseth his pride, and never waxeth strong.

'You hurt my hand with wringing; let us part,
And leave this idle theme, this bootless chat:
Remove your siege from my unyielding heart;
To love's alarms it will not ope the gate:
     Dismiss your vows, your feigned tears, your flattery;
     For where a heart is hard they make no battery.'

'What! canst thou talk?' quoth she, 'hast thou a tongue?
O, would thou hadst not, or I had no hearing!
Thy mermaid's voice hath done me double wrong;
I had my load before, now press'd with bearing:
     Melodious discord, heavenly tune harsh-sounding,
     Ear's deep-sweet music, and heart's deep-sore wounding.

'Had I no eyes but ears, my ears would love
That inward beauty and invisible;
Or were I deaf, thy outward parts would move
Each part in me that were but sensible:
     Though neither eyes nor ears, to hear nor see,
     Yet should I be in love by touching thee.

'Say, that the sense of feeling were bereft me,
And that I could not see, nor hear, nor touch,
And nothing but the very smell were left me,
Yet would my love to thee be still as much ;
    For from the stillitory of thy face excelling
      Comes breath perfumed, that breedeth love by smelling.

'But, O, what banquet wert thou to the taste,
Being nurse and feeder of the other four !
Would they not wish the feast might ever last,
And bid Suspicion double-lock the door,
    Lest Jealousy, that sour unwelcome guest,
      Should by his stealing in disturb the feast ?'

Once more the ruby-colour'd portal open'd,
Which to his speech did honey passage yield ;
Like a red morn, that ever yet betoken'd
Wreck to the seaman, tempest to the field,
    Sorrow to shepherds, woe unto the birds,
      Gusts and foul flaws to herdmen and to herds.

This ill presage advisedly she marketh :
Even as the wind is hush'd before it raineth,
Or as the wolf doth grin before he barketh,
Or as the berry breaks before it staineth,
    Or like the deadly bullet of a gun,
      His meaning struck her ere his words begun.

And at his look she flatly falleth down,
For looks kill love, and love by looks reviveth :
A smile recures the wounding of a frown ;
But blessed bankrupt, that by love so thriveth !
    The silly boy, believing she is dead,
      Claps her pale cheek, till clapping makes it red ;

And all amazed brake off his late intent,
For sharply he did think to reprehend her,
Which cunning love did wittily prevent :
Fair fall the wit that can so well defend her !
    For on the grass she lies as she were slain,
      Till his breath breatheth life in her again.

He wrings her nose, he strikes her on the cheeks,
He bends her fingers, holds her pulses hard,
He chafes her lips ; a thousand ways he seeks
To mend the hurt that his unkindness marr'd :
    He kisses her ; and she, by her good will,
      Will never rise, so he will kiss her still.

The night of sorrow now is turn'd to day :
Her two blue windows faintly she up-heaveth,
Like the fair sun, when in his fresh array
He cheers the morn, and all the earth relieveth :
    And as the bright sun glorifies the sky,
    So is her face illumined with her eye ;

Whose beams upon his hairless face are fix'd,
As if from thence they borrowed all their shine.
Were never four such lamps together mix'd,
Had not his clouded with his brow's repine ;
    But hers, which through the crystal tears gave light,
    Shone like the moon in water seen by night.

'O, where am I ?' quoth she ; 'in earth or heaven,
Or in the ocean drench'd, or in the fire ?
What hour is this ? or morn or weary even ?
Do I delight to die, or life desire ?
    But now I lived, and life was death's annoy ;
    But now I died, and death was lively joy.

'O, thou didst kill me : kill me once again :
Thy eyes' shrewd tutor, that hard heart of thine,
Hath taught them scornful tricks, and such disdain,
That they have murder'd this poor heart of mine ;
    And these mine eyes, true leaders to their queen,
    But for thy piteous lips no more had seen.

'Long may they kiss each other, for this cure !
O, never let their crimson liveries wear !
And as they last, their verdure still endure,
To drive infection from the dangerous year !
    That the star-gazers, having writ on death,
    May say, the plague is banish'd by thy breath.

'Pure lips, sweet seals in my soft lips imprinted,
What bargains may I make, still to be sealing ?
To sell myself I can be well contented,
So thou wilt buy, and pay, and use good dealing ;
    Which purchase if thou make, for fear of slips
    Set thy seal-manual on my wax-red lips.

'A thousand kisses buys my heart from me ;
And pay them at thy leisure, one by one.
What is ten hundred touches unto thee ?
Are they not quickly told and quickly gone ?
    Say, for non-payment that the debt should double
    Is twenty hundred kisses such a trouble ?'

'Fair queen,' quoth he, 'if any love you owe me,
Measure my strangeness with my unripe years:
Before I know myself, seek not to know me;
No fisher but the ungrown fry forbears:
  The mellow plum doth fall, the green sticks fast,
  Or being early pluck'd is sour to taste.

'Look, the world's comforter, with weary gait,
His day's hot task hath ended in the west;
The owl, night's herald, shrieks, 'tis very late;
The sheep are gone to fold, birds to their nest;
  And coal-black clouds that shadow heaven's light
  Do summon us to part, and bid good night.

'Now let me say "Good night," and so say you;
If you will say so, you shall have a kiss.'
'Good night,' quoth she; and, ere he says 'Adieu,'
The honey fee of parting tender'd is:
  Her arms do lend his neck a sweet embrace;
  Incorporate then they seem; face grows to face.

Till breathless he disjoin'd, and backward drew
The heavenly moisture, that sweet coral mouth,
Whose precious taste her thirsty lips well knew,
Whereon they surfeit, yet complain on drouth:
  He with her plenty press'd, she faint with dearth,
  Their lips together glued, fall to the earth.

Now quick desire hath caught the yielding prey,
And glutton-like she feeds, yet never filleth;
Her lips are conquerors, his lips obey,
Paying what ransom the insulter willeth;
  Whose vulture thought doth pitch the price so high,
  That she will draw his lips' rich treasure dry.

And having felt the sweetness of the spoil,
With blindfold fury she begins to forage;
Her face doth reek and smoke, her blood doth boil,
And careless lust stirs up a desperate courage,
  Planting oblivion, beating reason back,
  Forgetting shame's pure blush and honour's wrack.

Hot, faint and weary, with her hard embracing,
Like a wild bird being tamed with too much handling,
Or as the fleet-foot roe that's tired with chasing,
Or like the froward infant still'd with dandling,
  He now obeys, and now no more resisteth,
  While she takes all she can, not all she listeth.

What wax so frozen but dissolves with tempering,
And yields at last to every light impression?
Things out of hope are compass'd oft with venturing,
Chiefly in love, whose leave exceeds commission:
  Affection faints not like a pale-faced coward,
  But then woos best when most his choice is froward.

When he did frown, O, had she then gave over,
Such nectar from his lips she had not suck'd.
Foul words and frowns must not repel a lover;
What though the rose have prickles, yet 'tis pluck'd:
  Were beauty under twenty locks kept fast,
  Yet love breaks through, and picks them all at last.

For pity now she can no more detain him;
The poor fool prays her that he may depart:
She is resolved no longer to restrain him;
Bids him farewell, and look well to her heart,
  The which, by Cupid's bow she doth protest,
  He carries thence incaged in his breast.

'Sweet boy,' she says, 'this night I'll waste in sorrow,
For my sick heart commands mine eyes to watch.
Tell me, love's master, shall we meet to-morrow?
Say, shall we? shall we? wilt thou make the match?
  He tells her, no; to-morrow he intends
  To hunt the boar with certain of his friends.

'The boar!' quoth she: whereat a sudden pale,
Like lawn being spread upon the blushing rose,
Usurps her cheek; she trembles at his tale,
And on his neck her yoking arms she throws:
  She sinketh down, still hanging by his neck,
  He on her belly falls, she on her back.

Now is she in the very lists of love,
Her champion mounted for the hot encounter:
All is imaginary she doth prove,
He will not manage her, although he mount her;
  That worse than Tantalus' is her annoy,
  To clip Elysium, and to lack her joy.

Even so poor birds, deceived with painted grapes,
Do surfeit by the eye and pine the maw,
Even so she languisheth in her mishaps
As those poor birds that helpless berries saw.
  The warm effects which she in him finds missing
  She seeks to kindle with continual kissing.

But all in vain ; good queen, it will not be :
She hath assay'd as much as may be proved ;
Her pleading hath deserved a greater fee ;
She 's Love, she loves, and yet she is not loved.
    ' Fie, fie,' he says, ' you crush me ; let me go ;
    You have no reason to withhold me so.'

'Thou hadst been gone,' quoth she, ' sweet boy, ere this,
But that thou told'st me thou wouldst hunt the boar.
O, be advised : thou know'st not what it is
With javelin's point a churlish swine to gore,
    Whose tushes never sheathed he whetteth still,
    Like to a mortal butcher, bent to kill.

'On his bow-back he hath a battle set
Of bristly pikes, that ever threat his foes ;
His eyes, like glow-worms, shine when he doth fret ;
His snout digs sepulchres where'er he goes ;
    Being moved, he strikes whate'er is in his way,
    And whom he strikes his crooked tushes slay.

'His brawny sides, with hairy bristles armed,
Are better proof than thy spear's point can enter ;
His short thick neck cannot be easily harmed ;
Being ireful, on the lion he will venture :
    The thorny brambles and embracing bushes,
    As fearful of him, part ; through whom he rushes.

'Alas, he nought esteems that face of thine,
To which Love's eyes pay tributary gazes ;
Nor thy soft hands, sweet lips and crystal eyne,
Whose full perfection all the world amazes ;
    But having thee at vantage—wondrous dread !—
    Would root these beauties as he roots the mead.

'O, let him keep his loathsome cabin still ;
Beauty hath nought to do with such foul fiends :
Come not within his danger by thy will ;
They that thrive well take counsel of their friends.
    When thou didst name the boar, not to dissemble,
    I fear'd thy fortune, and my joints did tremble.

'Didst thou not mark my face ? was it not white ?
Saw'st thou not signs of fear lurk in mine eye ?
Grew I not faint ? and fell I not downright ?
Within my bosom, whereon thou dost lie,
    My boding heart pants, beats, and takes no rest,
    But, like an earthquake, shakes thee on my breast.

'For where Love reigns, disturbing Jealousy
Doth call himself Affection's sentinel;
Gives false alarms, suggested mutiny,
And in a peaceful hour doth cry 'Kill, kill!'
　　Distempering gentle Love in his desire,
　　As air and water do abate the fire.

'This sour informer, this bate-breeding spy,
This canker that eats up Love's tender spring,
This carry-tale, dissentious Jealousy,
That sometime true news, sometime false doth bring,
　　Knocks at my heart, and whispers in mine ear,
　　That if I love thee, I thy death should fear:

'And more than so, presenteth to mine eye
The picture of an angry-chafing boar,
Under whose sharp fangs on his back doth lie
An image like thyself, all stain'd with gore;
　　Whose blood upon the fresh flowers being shed
　　Doth make them droop with grief and hang the head.

'What should I do, seeing thee so indeed,
That tremble at the imagination?
The thought of it doth make my faint heart bleed,
And fear doth teach it divination:
　　I prophesy thy death, my living sorrow,
　　If thou encounter with the boar to-morrow.

'But if thou needs wilt hunt, be ruled by me;
Uncouple at the timorous flying hare,
Or at the fox which lives by subtlety,
Or at the roe which no encounter dare:
　　Pursue these fearful creatures o'er the downs,
　　And on thy well-breath'd horse keep with thy hounds.

'And when thou hast on foot the purblind hare,
Mark the poor wretch, to overshoot his troubles,
How he outruns the wind, and with what care
He cranks and crosses with a thousand doubles:
　　The many musits through the which he goes
　　Are like a labyrinth to amaze his foes.

'Sometime he runs among a flock of sheep,
To make the cunning hounds mistake their smell,
And sometime where earth-delving conies keep,
To stop the loud pursuers in their yell;
　　And sometime sorteth with a herd of deer:
　　Danger deviseth shifts: wit waits on fear:

'For there his smell with others being mingled,
The hot scent-snuffing hounds are driven to doubt,
Ceasing their clamorous cry till they have singled
With much ado the cold fault cleanly out;
    Then do they spend their mouths: Echo replies,
    As if another chase were in the skies.

'By this, poor Wat, far off upon a hill,
Stands on his hinder legs with listening ear,
To hearken if his foes pursue him still:
Anon their loud alarums he doth hear;
    And now his grief may be compared well
    To one sore sick that hears the passing-bell.

'Then shalt thou see the dew-bedabbled wretch
Turn, and return, indenting with the way;
Each envious brier his weary legs doth scratch,
Each shadow makes him stop, each murmur stay:
    For misery is trodden on by many,
    And being low never relieved by any.

'Lie quietly, and hear a little more;
Nay, do not struggle, for thou shalt not rise:
To make thee hate the hunting of the boar,
Unlike myself thou hear'st me moralize,
    Applying this to that, and so to so;
    For love can comment upon every woe.

'Where did I leave?' 'No matter where,' quoth he;
'Leave me, and then the story aptly ends:
The night is spent.' 'Why, what of that?' quoth she.
'I am,' quoth he, 'expected of my friends;
    And now 'tis dark, and going I shall fall.'
    'In night,' quoth she, 'desire sees best of all.

'But if thou fall, O, then imagine this,
The earth, in love with thee, thy footing trips,
And all is but to rob thee of a kiss.
Rich preys make true men thieves; so do thy lips
    Make modest Dian cloudy and forlorn,
    Lest she should steal a kiss, and die forsworn.

'Now of this dark night I perceive the reason:
Cynthia for shame obscures her silver shine,
Till forging Nature be condemn'd of treason,
For stealing moulds from heaven that were divine;
    Wherein she framed thee, in high heaven's despite,
    To shame the sun by day and her by night.

' And therefore hath she bribed the Destinies
To cross the curious workmanship of nature,
To mingle beauty with infirmities
And pure perfection with impure defeature;
　　Making it subject to the tyranny
　　Of mad mischances and such misery;

' As burning fevers, agues pale and faint,
Life-poisoning pestilence and frenzies wood,
The marrow-eating sickness, whose attaint
Disorder breeds by heating of the blood:
　　Surfeits, imposthumes, grief and damn'd despair,
　　Swear Nature's death for framing thee so fair.

' And not the least of all these maladies
But in one minute's fight brings beauty under:
Both favour, savour, hue and qualities,
Whereat the impartial gazer late did wonder,
　　Are on the sudden wasted, thaw'd and done,
　　As mountain snow melts with the midday sun.

' Therefore, despite of fruitless chastity,
Love-lacking vestals and self-loving nuns,
That on the earth would breed a scarcity
And barren dearth of daughters and of sons,
　　Be prodigal: the lamp that burns by night
　　Dries up his oil to lend the world his light.

' What is thy body but a swallowing grave,
Seeming to bury that posterity
Which by the rights of time thou needs must have,
If thou destroy them not in dark obscurity?
　　If so, the world will hold thee in disdain,
　　Sith in thy pride so fair a hope is slain.

' So in thyself thyself art made away;
A mischief worse than civil home-bred strife,
Or theirs whose desperate hands themselves do slay,
Or butcher-sire that reaves his son of life.
　　Foul cankering rust the hidden treasure frets,
　　But gold that's put to use more gold begets.'

' Nay, then,' quoth Adon, ' you will fall again
Into your idle over-handled theme:
The kiss I gave you is bestow'd in vain,
And all in vain you strive against the stream;
　　For, by this black-faced night, desire's foul nurse,
　　Your treatise makes me like you worse and worse.

'If love have lent you twenty thousand tongues,
And every tongue more moving than your own,
Bewitching like the wanton mermaid's songs,
Yet from mine ear the tempting tune is blown;
　　　For know, my heart stands armed in mine ear,
　　　And will not let a false sound enter there;

'Lest the deceiving harmony should run
Into the quiet closure of my breast;
And then my little heart were quite undone,
In his bedchamber to be barr'd of rest.
　　　No, lady, no; my heart longs not to groan,
　　　But soundly sleeps, while now it sleeps alone.

'What have you urged that I cannot reprove?
The path is smooth that leadeth on to danger:
I hate not love, but your device in love
That lends embracements unto every stranger.
　　　You do it for increase: O strange excuse,
　　　When reason is the bawd to lust's abuse!

'Call it not love, for Love to heaven is fled
Since sweating Lust on earth usurp'd his name;
Under whose simple semblance he hath fed
Upon fresh beauty, blotting it with blame;
　　　Which the hot tyrant stains and soon bereaves,
　　　As caterpillars do the tender leaves.

'Love comforteth like sunshine after rain,
But Lust's effect is tempest after sun;
Love's gentle spring doth always fresh remain,
Lust's winter comes ere summer half be done;
　　　Love surfeits not, Lust like a glutton dies;
　　　Love is all truth, Lust full of forged lies.

'More I could tell, but more I dare not say;
The text is old, the orator too green.
Therefore, in sadness, now I will away;
My face is full of shame, my heart of teen:
　　　Mine ears, that to your wanton talk attended,
　　　Do burn themselves for having so offended.'

With this, he breaketh from the sweet embrace
Of those fair arms which bound him to her breast,
And homeward through the dark lawnd runs apace;
Leaves Love upon her back deeply distress'd.
　　　Look, how a bright star shooteth from the sky,
　　　So glides he in the night from Venus' eye:

Which after him she darts, as one on shore
Gazing upon a late embarked friend,
Till the wild waves will have him seen no more,
Whose ridges with the meeting clouds contend:
　　So did the merciless and pitchy night
　　Fold in the object that did feed her sight.

Whereat amazed, as one that unaware
Hath dropp'd a precious jewel in the flood,
Or 'stonish'd as night-wanderers often are,
Their light blown out in some mistrustful wood;
　　Even so confounded in the dark she lay,
　　Having lost the fair discovery of her way.

And now she beats her heart, whereat it groans,
That all the neighbour caves, as seeming troubled,
Make verbal repetition of her moans;
Passion on passion deeply is redoubled:
　　'Ay me!' she cries, and twenty times, 'Woe, woe!'
　　And twenty echoes twenty times cry so.

She, marking them, begins a wailing note,
And sings extemporally a woeful ditty;
How love makes young men thrall, and old men dote;
How love is wise in folly, foolish-witty:
　　Her heavy anthem still concludes in woe,
　　And still the choir of echoes answer so.

Her song was tedious, and outwore the night,
For lovers' hours are long, though seeming short:
If pleased themselves, others, they think, delight
In such-like circumstance, with such-like sport:
　　Their copious stories, oftentimes begun,
　　End without audience, and are never done.

For who hath she to spend the night withal,
But idle sounds resembling parasites;
Like shrill-tongued tapsters answering every call,
Soothing the humour of fantastic wits?
　　She says ''Tis so:' they answer all ''Tis so;'
　　And would say after her, if she said 'No.'

Lo, here the gentle lark, weary of rest,
From his moist cabinet mounts up on high,
And wakes the morning, from whose silver breast
The sun ariseth in his majesty;
　　Who doth the world so gloriously behold,
　　That cedar-tops and hills seem burnish'd gold.

Venus salutes him with this fair good-morrow:
'O thou clear god, and patron of all light,
From whom each lamp and shining star doth borrow
The beauteous influence that makes him bright,
>   There lives a son, that suck'd an earthly mother,
>   May lend thee light, as thou dost lend to other.'

This said, she hasteth to a myrtle grove,
Musing the morning is so much o'erworn,
And yet she hears no tidings of her love:
She hearkens for his hounds and for his horn:
>   Anon she hears them chant it lustily,
>   And all in haste she coasteth to the cry.

And as she runs, the bushes in the way
Some catch her by the neck, some kiss her face,
Some twine about her thigh to make her stay:
She wildly breaketh from their strict embrace,
>   Like a milch doe, whose swelling dugs do ache,
>   Hasting to feed her fawn hid in some brake.

By this she hears the hounds are at a bay;
Whereat she starts, like one that spies an adder
Wreathed up in fatal folds just in his way,
The fear whereof doth make him shake and shudder;
>   Even so the timorous yelping of the hounds
>   Appals her senses and her spirit confounds.

For now she knows it is no gentle chase,
But the blunt boar, rough bear, or lion proud,
Because the cry remaineth in one place,
Where fearfully the dogs exclaim aloud:
>   Finding their enemy to be so curst,
>   They all strain courtesy who shall cope him first.

This dismal cry rings sadly in her ear,
Through which it enters to surprise her heart;
Who, overcome by doubt and bloodless fear,
With cold-pale weakness numbs each feeling part:
>   Like soldiers, when their captain once doth yield,
>   They basely fly, and dare not stay the field.

Thus stands she in a trembling ecstasy;
Till, cheering up her senses all dismay'd,
She tells them 'tis a causeless fantasy,
And childish error, that they are afraid;
>   Bids them leave quaking, bids them fear no more:
>   And with that word she spied the hunted boar;

416

Whose frothy mouth, bepainted all with red,
Like milk and blood being mingled both together,
A second fear through all her sinews spread,
Which madly hurries her she knows not whither:
     This way she runs, and now she will no further,
     But back retires to rate the boar for murther.

A thousand spleens bear her a thousand ways;
She treads the path that she untreads again;
Her more than haste is mated with delays,
Like the proceedings of a drunken brain,
     Full of respects, yet not at all respecting:
     In hand with all things, nought at all effecting.

Here kennell'd in a brake she finds a hound,
And asks the weary caitiff for his master;
And there another licking of his wound,
'Gainst venom'd sores the only sovereign plaster;
     And here she meets another sadly scowling,
     To whom she speaks, and he replies with howling.

When he hath ceased his ill-resounding noise,
Another flap-mouth'd mourner, black and grim,
Against the welkin volleys out his voice;
Another and another answer him,
     Clapping their proud tales to the ground below,
     Shaking their scratch'd ears, bleeding as they go.

Look, how the world's poor people are amazed
At apparitions, signs, and prodigies,
Whereon with fearful eyes they long have gazed,
Infusing them with dreadful prophecies;
     So she at these sad signs draws up her breath,
     And, sighing it again, exclaims on Death.

'Hard-favour'd tyrant, ugly, meagre, lean,
Hateful divorce of love,'—thus chides she Death,—
'Grim-grinning ghost, earth's worm, what dost thou mean
To stifle beauty and to steal his breath,
     Who when he lived, his breath and beauty set
     Gloss on the rose, smell to the violet?

'If he be dead,—O no, it cannot be,
Seeing his beauty, thou shouldst strike at it;—
O yes, it may; thou hast no eyes to see,
But hatefully at random dost thou hit.
     Thy mark is feeble age; but thy false dart
     Mistakes that aim, and cleaves an infant's heart.

'Hadst thou but bid beware, then he had spoke,
And, hearing him, thy power had lost his power.
The Destinies will curse thee for this stroke;
They bid thee crop a weed, thou pluck'st a flower:
　　Love's golden arrow at him should have fled,
　　And not Death's ebon dart, to strike him dead.

'Dost thou drink tears, that thou provokest such weeping?
What may a heavy groan advantage thee?
Why hast thou cast into eternal sleeping
Those eyes that taught all other eyes to see?
　　Now Nature cares not for thy mortal vigour,
　　Since her best work is ruin'd with thy rigour.'

Here overcome, as one full of despair,
She vail'd her eyelids, who, like sluices, stopp'd
The crystal tide that from her two cheeks fair
In the sweet channel of her bosom dropp'd;
　　But through the flood-gates breaks the silver rain,
　　And with his strong course opens them again.

O, how her eyes and tears did lend and borrow!
Her eye seen in the tears, tears in her eye;
Both crystals, where they view'd each other's sorrow,
Sorrow that friendly sighs sought still to dry;
　　But like a stormy day, now wind, now rain,
　　Sighs dry her cheeks, tears make them wet again.

Variable passions throng her constant woe,
As striving who should best become her grief;
All entertain'd, each passion labours so
That every present sorrow seemeth chief,
　　But none is best: then join they all together,
　　Like many clouds consulting for foul weather.

By this, far off she hears some huntsman holloa;
A nurse's song ne'er pleased her babe so well:
The dire imagination she did follow
This sound of hope doth labour to expel;
　　For now reviving joy bids her rejoice,
　　And flatters her it is Adonis' voice.

Whereat her tears began to turn their tide,
Being prison'd in her eye like pearls in glass:
Yet sometimes falls an orient drop beside,
Which her cheek melts, as scorning it should pass
　　To wash the foul face of the sluttish ground,
　　Who is but drunken when she seemeth drown'd.

O hard-believing love, how strange it seems
Not to believe, and yet too credulous!
Thy weal and woe are both of them extremes;
Despair, and hope, makes thee ridiculous:
     The one doth flatter thee in thoughts unlikely,
     In likely thoughts the other kills thee quickly.

Now she unweaves the web that she hath wrought;
Adonis lives, and Death is not to blame;
It was not she that call'd him all to nought:
Now she adds honours to his hateful name;
     She clepes him king of graves, and grave for kings,
     Imperious supreme of all mortal things.

'No, no,' quoth she, 'sweet Death, I did but jest;
Yet pardon me, I felt a kind of fear
When as I met the boar, that bloody beast,
Which knows no pity, but is still severe;
     Then, gentle shadow,—truth I must confess,—
     I rail'd on thee, fearing my love's decease.

''Tis not my fault: the boar provoked my tongue;
Be wreak'd on him, invisible commander;
'Tis he, foul creature, that hath done thee wrong;
I did but act, he's author of thy slander:
     Grief hath two tongues; and never woman yet
     Could rule them both without ten women's wit.')

Thus hoping that Adonis is alive,
Her rash suspect she doth extenuate;
And that his beauty may the better thrive,
With Death she humbly doth insinuate;
     Tells him of trophies, statues, tombs, and stories
     His victories, his triumphs and his glories.

'O Jove,' quoth she, 'how much a fool was I
To be of such a weak and silly mind
To wail his death who lives and must not die
Till mutual overthrow of mortal kind!
     For he being dead, with him is beauty slain,
     And, beauty dead, black chaos comes again.

'Fie, fie, fond love, thou art so full of fear
As one with treasure laden, hemm'd with thieves
Trifles unwitnessed with eye or ear
Thy coward heart with false bethinking grieves.'
     Even at this word she hears a merry horn,
     Whereat she leaps that was but late forlorn.

As falcons to the lure, away she flies;
The grass stoops not, she treads on it so light;
And in her haste unfortunately spies
The foul boar's conquest on her fair delight;
    Which seen, her eyes, as murder'd with the view,
    Like stars ashamed of day, themselves withdrew;

Or, as the snail, whose tender horns being hit,
Shrinks backward in his shelly cave with pain,
And there all smother'd up in shade doth sit,
Long after fearing to creep forth again;
    So, at his bloody view, her eyes are fled
    Into the deep-dark cabins of her head;

Where they resign their office and their light
To the disposing of her troubled brain;
Who bids them still consort with ugly night,
And never wound the heart with looks again;
    Who, like a king perplexed in his throne,
    By their suggestion gives a deadly groan,

Whereat each tributary subject quakes;
As when the wind, imprison'd in the ground,
Struggling for passage, earth's foundation shakes,
Which with cold terror doth men's mind confound.
    This mutiny each part doth so surprise,
    That from their dark beds once more leap her eyes;

And being open'd threw unwilling light
Upon the wide wound that the boar had trench'd
In his soft flank; whose wonted lily white
With purple tears, that his wound wept, was drench'd:
    No flower was nigh, no grass, herb, leaf or weed,
    But stole his blood and seem'd with him to bleed.

This solemn sympathy poor Venus noteth;
Over one shoulder doth she hang her head;
Dumbly she passions, franticly she doteth;
She thinks he could not die, he is not dead:
    Her voice is stopp'd, her joints forget to bow;
    Her eyes are mad that they have wept till now.

Upon his hurt she looked so steadfastly
That her sight dazzling makes the wound seem three;
And then she reprehends her mangling eye,
That makes more gashes where no breach should be:
    His face seems twain, each several limb is doubled;
    For oft the eye mistakes, the brain being troubled.

'My tongue cannot express my grief for one,
And yet,' quoth she, ' Behold two Adons dead !
My sighs are blown away, my salt tears gone,
Mine eyes are turn'd to fire, my heart to lead :
    Heavy heart's lead, melt at mine eyes' red fire !
    So shall I die by drops of hot desire.

'Alas, poor world, what treasure hast thou lost !
What face remains alive that 's worth the viewing ?
Whose tongue is music now ? what canst thou boast
Of things long since, or any thing ensuing ?
    The flowers are sweet, their colours fresh and trim ;
    But true-sweet beauty lived and died with him.

'Bonnet nor veil henceforth no creature wear !
Nor sun nor wind will ever strive to kiss you :
Having no fair to lose, you need not fear ;
The sun doth scorn you, and the wind doth hiss you.
    But when Adonis lived, sun and sharp air
    Lurk'd like two thieves, to rob him of his fair.

'And therefore would he put his bonnet on,
Under whose brim the gaudy sun would peep ;
The wind would blow it off, and, being gone,
Play with his locks : then would Adonis weep ;
    And straight, in pity of his tender years,
    They both would strive who first should dry his tears.

'To see his face the lion walk'd along
Behind some hedge, because he would not fear him ;
To recreate himself when he hath sung,
The tiger would be tame and gently hear him ;
    If he had spoke, the wolf would leave his prey,
    And never fright the silly lamb that day.

'When he beheld his shadow in the brook,
The fishes spread on it their golden gills ;
When he was by, the birds such pleasure took,
That some would sing, some other in their bills
    Would bring him mulberries and ripe-red cherries ;
    He fed them with his sight, they him with berries.

'But this foul, grim, and urchin-snouted boar,
Whose downward eye still looketh for a grave,
Ne'er saw the beauteous livery that he wore ;
Witness the entertainment that he gave :
    If he did see his face, why then I know
    He thought to kiss him, and hath kill'd him so.

' 'Tis true, 'tis true ; thus was Adonis slain :
He ran upon the boar with his sharp spear,
Who did not whet his teeth at him again,
But by a kiss thought to persuade him there ;
    And nuzzling in his flank, the loving swine
    Sheathed unaware the tusk in his soft groin.

' Had I been tooth'd like him, I must confess,
With kissing him I should have kill'd him first ;
But he is dead, and never did he bless
My youth with his ; the more am I accurst.'
    With this, she falleth in the place she stood,
    And stains her face with his congealed blood.

She looks upon his lips, and they are pale ;
She takes him by the hand, and that is cold ;
She whispers in his ears a heavy tale,
As if they heard the woeful words she told ;
    She lifts the coffer-lids that close his eyes,
    Where, lo, two lamps, burnt out, in darkness lies ;

Two glasses, where herself herself beheld
A thousand times, and now no more reflect ;
Their virtue lost, wherein they late excell'd,
And every beauty robb'd of his effect :
    ' Wonder of time,' quoth she, ' this is my spite,
    That, thou being dead, the day should yet be light.

' Since thou art dead, lo, here I prophesy,
Sorrow on love hereafter shall attend :
It shall be waited on with jealousy,
Find sweet beginning but unsavoury end ;
    Ne'er settled equally, but high or low,
    That all love's pleasure shall not match his woe.

' It shall be fickle, false and full of fraud ;
Bud, and be blasted, in a breathing-while ;
The bottom poison, and the top o'erstraw'd
With sweets that shall the truest sight beguile :
    The strongest body shall it make most weak,
    Strike the wise dumb, and teach the fool to speak.

' It shall be sparing and too full of riot,
Teaching decrepit age to tread the measures ;
The staring ruffian shall it keep in quiet,
Pluck down the rich, enrich the poor with treasures
    It shall be raging-mad, and silly-mild,
    Make the young old, the old become a child.

'It shall suspect where is no cause of fear;
It shall not fear where it should most mistrust;
It shall be merciful and too severe,
And most deceiving when it seems most just;
    Perverse it shall be where it shows most toward,
    Put fear to valour, courage to the coward.

'It shall be cause of war and dire events,
And set dissension 'twixt the son and sire;
Subject and servile to all discontents,
As dry combustious matter is to fire:
    Sith in his prime death doth my love destroy
    That they love best their loves shall not enjoy.'

By this the boy that by her side lay kill'd
Was melted like a vapour from her sight,
And in his blood, that on the ground lay spill'd,
A purple flower sprung up, chequer'd with white,
    Resembling well his pale cheeks and the blood
    Which in round drops upon their whiteness stood.

She bows her head, the new-sprung flower to smell,
Comparing it to her Adonis' breath;
And says, within her bosom it shall dwell,
Since he himself is reft from her by death:
    She crops the stalk, and in the breach appears
    Green-dropping sap, which she compares to tears.

'Poor flower,' quoth she, 'this was thy father's guise—
Sweet issue of a more sweet-smelling sire—
For every little grief to wet his eyes:
To grow unto himself was his desire,
    And so 'tis thine; but know, it is as good
    To wither in my breast as in his blood.

'Here was thy father's bed, here in my breast;
Thou art the next of blood, and 'tis thy right:
Lo, in this hollow cradle take thy rest;
My throbbing heart shall rock thee day and night:
    There shall not be one minute in an hour
    Wherein I will not kiss my sweet love's flower.'

Thus weary of the world, away she hies,
And yokes her silver doves; by whose swift aid
Their mistress, mounted, through the empty skies
In her light chariot quickly is convey'd;
    Holding their course to Paphos, where their queen
    Means to immure herself and not be seen.

THE RAPE OF LUCRECE

To the

RIGHT HONOURABLE *HENRY WRIOTHESLEY,*
Earle of Southampton, and Baron of Titchfield.

THE loue I dedicate to your Lordship is without end : whereof this Pamphlet without beginning is but a superfluous Moity. The warrant I haue of your Honourable disposition, not the wort of my vntutord Lines makes it assured of acceptance. What I haue done is yours, what I haue to doe is yours, being part in all I haue, deuoted yours. Were my worth greater, my duety would shew greater, meane time, as it is, it is bound to your Lordship ; To whom I wish long life still lengthned with all happinesse.

Your Lordships in all duety,

WILLIAM SHAKESPEARE.

THE ARGUMENT.

LUCIUS TARQUINIUS, for his excessive pride surnamed Superbus, after he had caused his own father-in-law Servius Tullius to be cruelly murdered, and, contrary to the Roman laws and customs, not requiring or staying for the people's suffrages, had possessed himself of the kingdom, went, accompanied with his sons and other noblemen of Rome, to besiege Ardea. During which siege the principal men of the army meeting one evening at the tent of Sextus Tarquinius, the king's son, in their discourses after supper every one commended the virtues of his own wife; among whom Collatinus extolled the incomparable chastity of his wife Lucretia. In that pleasant humour they all posted to Rome; and intending, by their secret and sudden arrival, to make trial of that which every one had before avouched, only Collatinus finds his wife, though it were late in the night, spinning amongst her maids: the other ladies were all found dancing and revelling, or in several disports. Whereupon the noblemen yielded Collatinus the victory, and his wife the fame. At that time Sextus Tarquinius being inflamed with Lucrece' beauty, yet smothering his passions for the present, departed with the rest back to the camp; from whence he shortly after privily withdrew himself, and was, according to his estate, royally entertained and lodged by Lucrece at Collatium. The same night he treacherously stealeth into her chamber, violently ravished her, and early in the morning speedeth away. Lucrece, in this lamentable plight, hastily dispatcheth messengers, one to Rome for her father, another to the camp for Collatine. They came, the one accompanied with Junius Brutus, the other with Publius Valerius; and finding Lucrece attired in mourning habit, demanded the cause of her sorrow. She, first taking an oath of them for her revenge, revealed the actor and whole manner of his dealing, and withal suddenly stabbed herself. Which done, with one consent they all vowed to root out the whole hated family of the Tarquins; and bearing the dead body to Rome, Brutus acquainted the people with the doer and manner of the vile deed, with a bitter invective against the tyranny of the king: wherewith the people were so moved, that with one consent and a general acclamation the Tarquins were all exiled, and the state government changed from kings to consuls.

FROM the besieged Ardea all in post,
Borne by the trustless wings of false desire,
Lust-breathed Tarquin leaves the Roman host,
And to Collatium bears the lightless fire,
Which, in pale embers hid, lurks to aspire,
    And girdle with embracing flames the waist
    Of Collatine's fair love, Lucrece the chaste.

Haply that name of 'chaste' unhappily set
This bateless edge on his keen appetite;
When Collatine unwisely did not let
To praise the clear unmatched red and white
Which triumph'd in that sky of his delight,
    Where mortal stars, as bright as heaven's beauties,
    With pure aspects did him peculiar duties.

For he the night before, in Tarquin's tent,
Unlock'd the treasure of his happy state;
What priceless wealth the heavens had him lent
In the possession of his beauteous mate;
Reckoning his fortune at such high-proud rate,
    That kings might be espoused to more fame,
    But king nor peer to such a peerless dame.

O happiness enjoy'd but of a few!
And, if possess'd, as soon decay'd and done
As is the morning's silver-melting dew
Against the golden splendour of the sun!
An expired date, cancell'd ere well begun:
    Honour and beauty, in the owner's arms,
    Are weakly fortress'd from a world of harms.

Beauty itself doth of itself persuade
The eyes of men without an orator;
What needeth then apologies be made,
To set forth that which is so singular?
Or why is Collatine the publisher
　　　Of that rich jewel he should keep unknown
　　　From thievish ears, because it is his own?

Perchance his boast of Lucrece' sovereignty
Suggested this proud issue of a king;
For by our ears our hearts oft tainted be:
Perchance that envy of so rich a thing,
Braving compare, disdainfully did sting
　　　His high-pitch'd thoughts, that meaner men should vaunt
　　　That golden hap which their superiors want.

But some untimely thought did instigate
His all-too-timeless speed, if none of those:
His honour, his affairs, his friends, his state,
Neglected all, with swift intent he goes
To quench the coal which in his liver glows.
　　　O rash-false heat, wrapp'd in repentant cold,
　　　Thy hasty spring still blasts, and ne'er grows old!

When at Collatium this false lord arrived,
Well was he welcomed by the Roman dame,
Within whose face beauty and virtue strived
Which of them both should underprop her fame:
When virtue bragg'd, beauty would blush for shame;
　　　When beauty boasted blushes, in despite
　　　Virtue would stain that o'er with silver white.

But beauty, in that white intituled,
From Venus' doves doth challenge that fair field:
Then virtue claims from beauty beauty's red,
Which virtue gave the golden age to gild
Their silver cheeks, and call'd it then their shield;
　　　Teaching them thus to use it in the fight,
　　　When shame assail'd, the red should fence the white.

This heraldry in Lucrece' face was seen,
Argued by beauty's red and virtue's white:
Of either's colour was the other queen,
Proving from world's minority their right:
Yet their ambition makes them still to fight;
　　　The sovereignty of either being so great,
　　　That oft they interchange each other's seat.

This silent war of lilies and of roses,
Which Tarquin view'd in her fair face's field,
In their pure ranks his traitor eye encloses;
Where, lest between them both it should be kill'd,
The coward captive vanquished doth yield
    To those two armies, that would let him go
    Rather than triumph in so false a foe.

Now thinks he that her husband's shallow tongue,
The niggard prodigal that praised her so,
In that high task hath done her beauty wrong,
Which far exceeds his barren skill to show:
Therefore that praise which Collatine doth owe
    Enchanted Tarquin answers with surmise,
    In silent wonder of still-gazing eyes.

This earthly saint, adored by this devil,
Little suspecteth the false worshipper;
For unstain'd thoughts do seldom dream on evil;
Birds never limed no secret bushes fear:
So guiltless she securely gives good cheer
    And reverend welcome to her princely guest,
    Whose inward ill no outward harm express'd:

For that he colour'd with his high estate,
Hiding base sin in plaits of majesty;
That nothing in him seem'd inordinate,
Save sometime too much wonder of his eye,
Which, having all, all could not satisfy;
    But, poorly rich, so wanteth in his store,
    That, cloy'd with much, he pineth still for more.

But she, that never coped with stranger eyes,
Could pick no meaning from their parling looks,
Nor read the subtle-shining secrecies
Writ in the glassy margents of such books:
She touch'd no unknown baits, nor fear'd no hooks;
    Nor could she moralize his wanton sight,
    More than his eyes were open'd to the light.

He stories to her ears her husband's fame,
Won in the fields of fruitful Italy;
And decks with praises Collatine's high name,
Made glorious by his manly chivalry
With bruised arms and wreaths of victory:
    Her joy with heaved-up hand she doth express,
    And wordless so greets heaven for his success.

Far from the purpose of his coming hither,
He makes excuses for his being there :
No cloudy show of stormy blustering weather
Doth yet in his fair welkin once appear ;
Till sable Night, mother of dread and fear,
    Upon the world dim darkness doth display,
    And in her vaulty prison stows the day.

For then is Tarquin brought unto his bed,
Intending weariness with heavy spright ;
For after supper long he questioned
With modest Lucrece, and wore out the night :
Now leaden slumber with life's strength doth fight ;
    And every one to rest themselves betake,
    Save thieves and cares and troubled minds that wake.

As one of which doth Tarquin lie revolving
The sundry dangers of his will's obtaining ;
Yet ever to obtain his will resolving,
Though weak-built hopes persuade him to abstaining :
Despair to gain doth traffic oft for gaining,
    And when great treasure is the meed proposed,
    Though death be adjunct, there's no death supposed.

Those that much covet are with gain so fond
That what they have not, that which they possess,
They scatter and unloose it from their bond,
And so, by hoping more, they have but less ;
Or, gaining more, the profit of excess
    Is but to surfeit, and such griefs sustain,
    That they prove bankrupt in this poor-rich gain.

The aim of all is but to nurse the life
With honour, wealth and ease, in waning age ;
And in this aim there is such thwarting strife
That one for all or all for one we gage ;
As life for honour in fell battle's rage ;
    Honour for wealth ; and oft that wealth doth cost
    The death of all, and all together lost.

So that in venturing ill we leave to be
The things we are for that which we expect ;
And this ambitious foul infirmity,
In having much, torments us with defect
Of that we have : so then we do neglect
    The thing we have, and, all for want of wit,
    Make something nothing by augmenting it.

Such hazard now must doting Tarquin make,
Pawning his honour to obtain his lust;
And for himself himself he must forsake:
Then where is truth, if there be no self-trust?
When shall he think to find a stranger just,
  When he himself himself confounds, betrays
  To slanderous tongues and wretched hateful days?

Now stole upon the time the dead of night,
When heavy sleep had closed up mortal eyes:
No comfortable star did lend his light,
No noise but owls' and wolves' death-boding cries;
Now serves the season that they may surprise
  The silly lambs: pure thoughts are dead and still,
  While lust and murder wakes to stain and kill.

And now this lustful lord leap'd from his bed,
Throwing his mantle rudely o'er his arm;
Is madly toss'd between desire and dread;
Th' one sweetly flatters, th' other feareth harm;
But honest fear, bewitch'd with lust's foul charm,
  Doth too too oft betake him to retire,
  Beaten away by brain-sick rude desire.

His falchion on a flint he softly smiteth,
That from the cold stone sparks of fire do fly;
Whereat a waxen torch forthwith he lighteth,
Which must be lode-star to his lustful eye;
And to the flame thus speaks advisedly:
  'As from this cold flint I enforced this fire,
  So Lucrece must I force to my desire.'

Here pale with fear he doth premeditate
The dangers of his loathsome enterprise,
And in his inward mind he doth debate
What following sorrow may on this arise:
Then looking scornfully he doth despise
  His naked armour of still-slaughter'd lust,
  And justly thus controls his thoughts unjust:

'Fair torch, burn out thy light, and lend it not
To darken her whose light excelleth thine:
And die, unhallow'd thoughts, before you blot
With your uncleanness that which is divine:
Offer pure incense to so pure a shrine:
  Let fair humanity abhor the deed
  That spots and stains love's modest snow-white weed.

'O shame to knighthood and to shining arms!
O foul dishonour to my household's grave!
Oh impious act, including all foul harms!
A martial man to be soft fancy's slave!
True valour still a true respect should have;
　　　Then my digression is so vile, so base,
　　　That it will live engraven in my face.

'Yea, though I die, the scandal will survive
And be an eye-sore in my golden coat;
Some loathsome dash the herald will contrive,
To cipher me how fondly I did dote;
That my posterity, shamed with the note,
　　　Shall curse my bones, and hold it for no sin
　　　To wish that I their father had not bin.

'What win I, if I gain the thing I seek?
A dream, a breath, a froth of fleeting joy.
Who buys a minute's mirth to wail a week?
Or sells eternity to get a toy?
For one sweet grape who will the vine destroy?
　　　Or what fond beggar, but to touch the crown,
　　　Would with the sceptre straight be strucken down?

'If Collatinus dream of my intent,
Will he not wake, and in a desperate rage
Post hither, this vile purpose to prevent?
This siege that hath engirt his marriage,
This blur to youth, this sorrow to the sage,
　　　This dying virtue, this surviving shame,
　　　Whose crime will bear an ever-during blame.'

'O what excuse can my invention make,
When thou shalt charge me with so black a deed?
Will not my tongue be mute, my frail joints shake,
Mine eyes forgo their light, my false heart bleed?
The guilt being great, the fear doth still exceed;
　　　And extreme fear can neither fight nor fly,
　　　But coward-like with trembling terror die.

'Had Collatinus kill'd my son or sire,
Or lain in ambush to betray my life,
Or were he not my dear friend, this desire
Might have excuse to work upon his wife,
As in revenge or quittal of such strife:
　　　But as he is my kinsman, my dear friend,
　　　The shame and fault finds no excuse nor end.

430

'Shameful it is ; ay, if the fact be known :
Hateful it is ; there is no hate in loving :
I 'll beg her love ; but she is not her own :
The worst is but denial and reproving.
My will is strong, past reason's weak removing.
     Who fears a sentence or an old man's saw
     Shall by a painted cloth be kept in awe.'

Thus graceless holds he disputation
'Tween frozen conscience and hot-burning will,
And with good thoughts makes dispensation,
Urging the worser sense for vantage still ;
Which in a moment doth confound and kill
     All pure effects, and doth so far proceed
     That what is vile shows like a virtuous deed.

Quoth he, ' she took me kindly by the hand,
And gazed for tidings in my eager eyes,
Fearing some hard news from the warlike band,
Where her beloved Collatinus lies.
O, how her fear did make her colour rise !
     First red as roses that on lawn we lay,
     Then white as lawn, the roses took away.

' And how her hand, in my hand being lock'd,
Forced it to tremble with her loyal fear !
Which struck her sad, and then it faster rock'd,
Until her husband's welfare she did hear ;
Whereat she smiled with so sweet a cheer
     That had Narcissus seen her as she stood
     Self-love had never drown'd him in the flood.

' Why hunt I then for colour or excuses ?
All orators are dumb when beauty pleadeth ;
Poor wretches have remorse in poor abuses ;
Love thrives not in the heart that shadows dreadeth :
Affection is my captain, and he leadeth ;
     And when his gaudy banner is display'd,
     The coward fights, and will not be dismay'd.

' Then, childish fear avaunt ! debating die !
Respect and reason wait on wrinkled age !
My heart shall never countermand mine eye :
Sad pause and deep regard beseems the sage ;
My part is youth, and beats these from the stage :
     Desire my pilot is, beauty my prize ;
     Then who fears sinking where such treasure lies ?'

As corn o'ergrown by weeds, so heedful fear
Is almost choked by unresisted lust.
Away he steals with open listening ear,
Full of foul hope and full of fond mistrust;
Both which, as servitors to the unjust,
　　So cross him with their opposite persuasion,
　　That now he vows a league, and now invasion.

Within his thought her heavenly image sits,
And in the self-same seat sits Collatine:
That eye which looks on her confounds his wits;
That eye which him beholds, as more divine,
Unto a view so false will not incline;
　　But with a pure appeal seeks to the heart,
　　Which once corrupted takes the worser part;

And therein heartens up his servile powers,
Who, flatter'd by their leader's jocund show,
Stuff up his lust, as minutes fill up hours;
And as their captain, so their pride doth grow,
Paying more slavish tribute than they owe.
　　By reprobate desire thus madly led,
　　The Roman lord marcheth to Lucrece' bed.

The locks between her chamber and his will,
Each one by him enforced, retires his ward;
But, as they open, they all rate his ill,
Which drives the creeping thief to some regard:
The threshold grates the door to have him heard;
　　Night-wandering weasels shriek to see him there;
　　They fright him, yet he still pursues his fear.

As each unwilling portal yields him way,
Through little vents and crannies of the place
The wind wars with his torch to make him stay,
And blows the smoke of it into his face,
Extinguishing his conduct in this case;
　　But his hot heart, which fond desire doth scorch,
　　Puffs forth another wind that fires the torch:

And being lighted, by the light he spies
Lucretia's glove, wherein her needle sticks:
He takes it from the rushes where it lies,
And griping it, the needle his finger pricks;
As who should say 'This glove to wanton tricks
　　Is not inured; return again in haste;
　　Thou see'st our mistress' ornaments are chaste.'

But all these poor forbiddings could not stay him;
He in the worst sense construes their denial:
The doors, the wind, the glove, that did delay him,
He takes for accidental things of trial;
Or as those bars which stop the hourly dial,
  Who with a lingering stay his course doth let,
  Till every minute pays the hour his debt.

'So, so,' quoth he, 'these lets attend the time,
Like little frosts that sometime threat the spring,
To add a more rejoicing to the prime,
And give the sneaped birds more cause to sing.
Pain pays the income of each precious thing;
  Huge rocks, high winds, strong pirates, shelves and sands,
  The merchant fears, ere rich at home he lands.'

Now is he come unto the chamber door,
That shuts him from the heaven of his thought,
Which with a yielding latch, and with no more,
Hath barr'd him from the blessed thing he sought.
So from himself impiety hath wrought,
  That for his prey to pray he doth begin,
  As if the heavens should countenance his sin.

But in the midst of his unfruitful prayer,
Having solicited the eternal power
That his foul thoughts might compass his fair fair,
And they would stand auspicious to the hour,
Even there he starts: quoth he, 'I must deflower:
  The powers to whom I pray abhor this fact;
  How can they then assist me in the act?

'Then Love and Fortune be my gods, my guide!
My will is back'd with resolution:
Thoughts are but dreams till their effects be tried;
The blackest sin is clear'd with absolution;
Against love's fire fear's frost hath dissolution.
  The eye of heaven is out, and misty night
  Covers the shame that follows sweet delight.'

This said, his guilty hand pluck'd up the latch,
And with his knee the door he opens wide.
The dove sleeps fast that this night-owl will catch:
Thus treason works ere traitors be espied.
Who sees the lurking serpent steps aside;
  But she, sound sleeping, fearing no such thing,
  Lies at the mercy of his mortal sting.

Into the chamber wickedly he stalks
And gazeth on her yet unstained bed.
The curtains being close, about he walks,
Rolling his greedy eyeballs in his head :
By their high treason is his heart misled ;
  Which gives the watch-word to his hand full soon
  To draw the cloud that hides the silver moon.

Look, as the fair and fiery-pointed sun,
Rushing from forth a cloud, bereaves our sight ;
Even so, the curtain drawn, his eyes begun
To wink, being blinded with a greater light :
Whether it is that she reflects so bright,
  That dazzleth them, or else some shame supposed ;
  But blind they are, and keep themselves enclosed.

O, had they in that darksome prison died !
Then had they seen the period of the ill ;
Then Collatine again, by Lucrece' side,
In his clear bed might have reposed still :
But they must ope, this blessed league to kill ;
  And holy-thoughted Lucrece to their sight
  Must sell her joy, her life, her world's delight.

Her lily hand her rosy cheek lies under,
Cozening the pillow of a lawful kiss ;
Who, therefore angry, seems to part in sunder,
Swelling on either side to want his bliss ;
Between whose hills her head entombed is :
  Where, like a virtuous monument, she lies,
  To be admired of lewd unhallow'd eyes.

Without the bed her other fair hand was,
On the green coverlet ; whose perfect white
Show'd like an April daisy on the grass,
With pearly sweat, resembling dew of night.
Her eyes, like marigolds, had sheathed their light,
  And canopied in darkness sweetly lay,
  Till they might open to adorn the day.

Her hair, like golden threads, play'd with her breath ;
O modest wantons ! wanton modesty !
Showing life's triumph in the map of death,
And death's dim look in life's mortality :
Each in her sleep themselves so beautify
  As if between them twain there were no strife,
  But that life lived in death and death in life.

Her breasts, like ivory globes circled with blue,
A pair of maiden worlds unconquered,
Save of their lord no bearing yoke they knew,
And him by oath they truly honoured.
These worlds in Tarquin new ambition bred;
    Who, like a foul usurper, went about
    From this fair throne to heave the owner out.

What could he see but mightily he noted?
What did he note but strongly he desired?
What he beheld, on that he firmly doted,
And in his will his wilful eye he tired.
With more than admiration he admired
    Her azure veins, her alabaster skin,
    Her coral lips, her snow-white dimpled chin.

As the grim lion fawneth o'er his prey,
Sharp hunger by the conquest satisfied,
So o'er this sleeping soul doth Tarquin stay,
His rage of lust by gazing qualified;
Slack'd, not suppress'd; for standing by her side,
    His eye, which late this mutiny restrains,
    Unto a greater uproar tempts his veins:

And they, like straggling slaves for pillage fighting,
Obdurate vassals fell exploits effecting,
In bloody death and ravishment delighting,
Nor children's tears nor mother's groans respecting,
Swell in their pride, the onset still expecting:
    Anon his beating heart, alarum striking,
    Gives the hot charge, and bids them do their liking.

His drumming heart cheers up his burning eye,
His eye commends the leading to his hand;
His hand, as proud of such a dignity,
Smoking with pride, march'd on to make his stand
On her bare breast, the heart of all her land;
    Whose ranks of blue veins, as his hand did scale,
    Left their round turrets destitute and pale.

They, mustering to the quiet cabinet
Where their dear governess and lady lies,
Do tell her she is dreadfully beset,
And fright her with confusion of their cries:
She, much amazed, breaks ope her lock'd-up eyes,
    Who, peeping forth this tumult to behold,
    Are by his flaming torch dimm'd and controll'd.

Imagine her as one in dead of night
From forth dull sleep by dreadful fancy waking,
That thinks she hath beheld some ghastly sprite,
Whose grim aspect sets every joint a-shaking;
What terror 'tis! but she, in worser taking,
　　From sleep disturbed, heedfully doth view
　　The sight which makes supposed terror true.

Wrapp'd and confounded in a thousand fears,
Like to a new-kill'd bird she trembling lies;
She dares not look; yet, winking, there appears
Quick-shifting antics, ugly in her eyes:
Such shadows are the weak brain's forgeries;
　　Who, angry that the eyes fly from their lights,
　　In darkness daunts them with more dreadful sights.

His hand, that yet remains upon her breast,—
Rude ram, to batter such an ivory wall!—
May feel her heart, poor citizen! distress'd,
Wounding itself to death, rise up and fall,
Beating her bulk, that his hand shakes withal.
　　This moves in him more rage and lesser pity,
　　To make the breach and enter this sweet city.

First, like a trumpet, doth his tongue begin
To sound a parley to his heartless foe;
Who o'er the white sheet peers her whiter chin,
The reason of this rash alarm to know,
Which he by dumb demeanour seeks to show;
　　But she with vehement prayers urgeth still
　　Under what colour he commits this ill.

Thus he replies: 'The colour in thy face,
That even for anger makes the lily pale
And the red rose blush at her own disgrace,
Shall plead for me and tell my loving tale:
Under that colour am I come to scale
　　Thy never-conquer'd fort: the fault is thine,
　　For those thine eyes betray thee unto mine.

'Thus I forestall thee, if thou mean to chide:
Thy beauty hath ensnared thee to this night,
Where thou with patience must my will abide;
My will that marks thee for my earth's delight,
Which I to conquer sought with all my might;
　　But as reproof and reason beat it dead,
　　By thy bright beauty was it newly bred.

436

'I see what crosses my attempt will bring;
I know what thorns the growing rose defends;
I think the honey guarded with a sting;
All this beforehand counsel comprehends:
But will is deaf and hears no heedful friends;
    Only he hath an eye to gaze on beauty,
    And dotes on what he looks, 'gainst law or duty.

'I have debated, even in my soul,
What wrong, what shame, what sorrow I shall breed;
But nothing can affection's course control,
Or stop the headlong fury of his speed.
I know repentant tears ensue the deed,
    Reproach, disdain and deadly enmity;
    Yet strive I to embrace mine infamy.'

This said, he shakes aloft his Roman blade,
Which, like a falcon towering in the skies,
Coucheth the fowl below with his wings' shade,
Whose crooked beak threats if he mount he dies:
So under his insulting falchion lies
    Harmless Lucretia, marking what he tells
    With trembling fear, as fowl hear falcon's bells.

'Lucrece,' quoth he, 'this night I must enjoy thee:
If thou deny, then force must work my way,
For in thy bed I purpose to destroy thee:
That done, some worthless slave of thine I'll slay,
To kill thine honour with thy life's decay;
    And in thy dead arms do I mean to place him,
    Swearing I slew him, seeing thee embrace him.

'So thy surviving husband shall remain
The scornful mark of every open eye;
Thy kinsmen hang their heads at this disdain,
Thy issue blurr'd with nameless bastardy:
And thou, the author of their obloquy
    Shalt have thy trespass cited up in rhymes
    And sung by children in succeeding times.

'But if thou yield, I rest thy secret friend:
The fault unknown is as a thought unacted;
A little harm done to a great good end
For lawful policy remains enacted.
The poisonous simple sometime is compacted
    In a pure compound; being so applied,
    His venom in effect is purified.

'Then, for thy husband and thy children's sake,
Tender my suit : bequeath not to their lot
The shame that from them no device can take,
The blemish that will never be forgot ;
Worse than a slavish wipe or birth-hour's blot :
    For marks descried in men's nativity
    Are nature's faults, not their own infamy.'

Here with a cockatrice' dead-killing eye
He rouseth up himself, and makes a pause ;
While she, the picture of true piety,
Like a white hind under the gripe's sharp claws,
Pleads, in a wilderness where are no laws,
    To the rough beast that knows no gentle right,
    Nor aught obeys but his foul appetite.

But when a black-faced cloud the world doth threat,
In his dim mist the aspiring mountains hiding,
From earth's dark womb some gentle gust doth get,
Which blows these pitchy vapours from their biding,
Hindering their present fall by this dividing ;
    So his unhallow'd haste her words delays
    And moody Pluto winks while Orpheus plays.

Yet, foul night-waking cat, he doth but dally,
While in his hold-fast foot the weak mouse panteth :
Her sad behaviour feeds his vulture folly,
A swallowing gulf that even in plenty wanteth ;
His ear her prayers admits, but his heart granteth
    No penetrable entrance to her plaining :
    Tears harden lust, though marble wear with raining.

Her pity-pleading eyes are sadly fixed
In the remorseless wrinkles of his face ;
Her modest eloquence with sighs is mixed,
Which to her oratory adds more grace.
She puts the period often from his place,
    And midst the sentence so her accent breaks
    That twice she doth begin ere once she speaks.

She conjures him by high almighty Jove,
By knighthood, gentry, and sweet friendship's oath,
By her untimely tears, her husband's love,
By holy human law and common troth,
By heaven and earth, and all the power of both,
    That to his borrow'd bed he make retire,
    And stoop to honour, not to foul desire.

Quoth she: ' Reward not hospitality
With such black payment as thou hast pretended;
Mud not the fountain that gave drink to thee;
Mar not the thing that cannot be amended;
End thy ill aim before thy shoot be ended;
  He is no woodman that doth bend his bow
  To strike a poor unseasonable doe.

'My husband is thy friend; for his sake spare me:
Thyself art mighty; for thine own sake leave me:
Myself a weakling; do not then ensnare me:
Thou look'st not like deceit; do not deceive me.
My sighs, like whirlwinds, labour hence to heave thee:
  If ever man were moved with woman's moans,
  Be moved with my tears, my sighs, my groans:

'All which together, like a troubled ocean,
Beat at thy rocky and wreck-threatening heart,
To soften it with their continual motion;
For stones dissolved to water do convert.
O, if no harder than a stone thou art,
  Melt at my tears, and be compassionate!
  Soft pity enters at an iron gate.

'In Tarquin's likeness I did entertain thee:
Hast thou put on his shape to do him shame?
To all the host of heaven I complain me,
Thou wrong'st his honour, wound'st his princely name.
Thou art not what thou seem'st; and if the same,
  Thou seem'st not what thou art, a god, a king;
  For kings, like gods, should govern every thing.

'How will thy shame be seeded in thine age,
When thus thy vices bud before thy spring!
If in thy hope thou darest do such outrage,
What darest thou not when once thou art a king?
O, be remember'd, no outrageous thing
  From vassal actors can be wiped away;
  Then kings' misdeeds cannot be hid in clay.

'This deed will make thee only loved for fear;
But happy monarchs still are fear'd for love:
With foul offenders thou perforce must bear,
When they in thee the like offences prove:
If but for fear of this, thy will remove;
  For princes are the glass, the school, the book,
  Where subjects' eyes do learn, do read, do look.

'And wilt thou be the school where Lust shall learn?
Must he in thee read lectures of such shame?
Wilt thou be glass wherein it shall discern
Authority for sin, warrant for blame,
To privilege dishonour in thy name?
    Thou back'st reproach against long-living laud,
    And makest fair reputation but a bawd.

'Hast thou command? by him that gave it thee,
From a pure heart command thy rebel will:
Draw not thy sword to guard iniquity,
For it was lent thee all that brood to kill.
Thy princely office how canst thou fulfil,
    When, pattern'd by thy fault, foul sin may say
    He learn'd to sin and thou didst teach the way?

'Think but how vile a spectacle it were,
To view thy present trespass in another.
Men's faults do seldom to themselves appear;
Their own transgressions partially they smother:
This guilt would seem death-worthy in thy brother.
    O, how are they wrapp'd in with infamies
    That from their own misdeeds askance their eyes!

'To thee, to thee, my heaved-up hands appeal,
Not to seducing lust, thy rash relier:
I sue for exiled majesty's repeal;
Let him return, and flattering thoughts retire:
His true respect will prison false desire,
    And wipe the dim mist from thy doting eyne,
    That thou shalt see thy state and pity mine.'

'Have done,' quoth he: 'my uncontrolled tide
Turns not, but swells the higher by this let.
Small lights are soon blown out, huge fires abide,
And with the wind in greater fury fret:
The petty streams that pay a daily debt
    To their salt sovereign, with their fresh falls' haste
    Add to his flow, but alter not his taste.'

'Thou art,' quoth she, 'a sea, a sovereign king;
And, lo, there falls into thy boundless flood
Black lust, dishonour, shame, misgoverning,
Who seek to stain the ocean of thy blood.
If all these petty ills shall change thy good,
    Thy sea within a puddle's womb is hearsed,
    And not the puddle in thy sea dispersed.

'So shall these slaves be king, and thou their slave;
Thou nobly base, they basely dignified;
Thou their fair life, and they thy fouler grave:
Thou loathed in their shame, they in thy pride;
The lesser thing should not the greater hide;
    The cedar stoops not to the base shrub's foot,
    But low shrubs wither at the cedar's root.

'So let thy thoughts, low vassals to thy state'—
'No more,' quoth he; 'by heaven, I will not hear thee:
Yield to my love; if not, enforced hate,
Instead of love's coy touch, shall rudely tear thee:
That done, despitefully I mean to bear thee
    Unto the base bed of some rascal groom,
    To be thy partner in this shameful doom.'

This said, he sets his foot upon the light,
For light and lust are deadly enemies:
Shame folded up in blind concealing night,
When most unseen, then most doth tyrannize.
The wolf hath seized his prey, the poor lamb cries;
    Till with her own white fleece her voice controll'd
    Entombs her outcry in her lips' sweet fold:

For with the nightly linen that she wears
He pens her piteous clamours in her head,
Cooling his hot face in the chastest tears
That ever modest eyes with sorrow shed.
O, that prone lust should stain so pure a bed!
    The spots whereof could weeping purify,
    Her tears should drop on them perpetually.

But she hath lost a dearer thing than life,
And he hath won what he would lose again:
This forced league doth force a further strife;
This momentary joy breeds months of pain;
This hot desire converts to cold disdain:
    Pure Chastity is rifled of her store,
    And Lust, the thief, far poorer than before.

Look, as the full-fed hound or gorged hawk,
Unapt for tender smell or speedy flight,
Make slow pursuit, or altogether balk
The prey wherein by nature they delight,
So surfeit-taking Tarquin fares this night:
    His taste delicious, in digestion souring,
    Devours his will, that lived by foul devouring.

O, deeper sin than bottomless conceit
Can comprehend in still imagination!
Drunken Desire must vomit his receipt,
Ere he can see his own abomination.
While Lust is in his pride, no exclamation
　　　Can curb his heat or rein his rash desire,
　　　Till, like a jade, Self-will himself doth tire.

And then with lank and lean discolour'd cheek,
With heavy eye, knit brow, and strengthless pace,
Feeble Desire, all recreant, poor and meek,
Like to a bankrupt beggar wails his case:
The flesh being proud, Desire doth fight with Grace,
　　　For there it revels, and when that decays
　　　The guilty rebel for remission prays.

So fares it with this faultful lord of Rome,
Who this accomplishment so hotly chased;
For now against himself he sounds this doom,
That through the length of times he stands disgraced:
Besides, his soul's fair temple is defaced,
　　　To whose weak ruins muster troops of cares,
　　　To ask the spotted princess how she fares.

She says, her subjects with foul insurrection
Have batter'd down her consecrated wall,
And by their mortal fault brought in subjection
Her immortality, and made her thrall
To living death and pain perpetual:
　　　Which in her prescience she controlled still,
　　　But her foresight could not forestall their will.

Even in this thought through the dark night he stealeth,
A captive victor that hath lost in gain;
Bearing away the wound that nothing healeth,
The scar that will, despite of cure, remain;
Leaving his spoil perplex'd in greater pain.
　　　She bears the load of lust he left behind,
　　　And he the burthen of a guilty mind.

He like a thievish dog creeps sadly thence;
She like a wearied lamb lies panting there;
He scowls, and hates himself for his offence;
She, desperate, with her nails her flesh doth tear;
He faintly flies, sweating with guilty fear;
　　　She stays, exclaiming on the direful night;
　　　He runs, and chides his vanish'd, loathed delight.

He thence departs a heavy convertite;
She there remains a hopeless cast-away;
He in his speed looks for the morning light;
She prays she never may behold the day,
'For day,' quoth she, 'night's 'scapes doth open lay,
    And my true eyes have never practised how
    To cloak offences with a cunning brow.

'They think not but that every eye can see
The same disgrace which they themselves behold;
And therefore would they still in darkness be,
To have their unseen sin remain untold;
For they their guilt with weeping will unfold,
    And grave, like water that doth eat in steel,
    Upon my cheeks what helpless shame I feel.'

Here she exclaims against repose and rest,
And bids her eyes hereafter still be blind.
She wakes her heart by beating on her breast,
And bids it leap from thence, where it may find
Some purer chest to close so pure a mind.
    Frantic with grief thus breathes she forth her spite
    Against the unseen secrecy of night:

'O comfort-killing Night, image of hell!
Dim register and notary of shame!
Black stage for tragedies and murders fell!
Vast sin-concealing chaos! nurse of blame!
Blind muffled bawd! dark harbour for defame!
    Grim cave of death! whispering conspirator
    With close-tongued treason and the ravisher!

'O hateful, vaporous and foggy Night!
Since thou art guilty of my cureless crime,
Muster thy mists to meet the eastern light,
Make war against proportion'd course of time;
Or if thou wilt permit the sun to climb
    His wonted height, yet ere he go to bed,
    Knit poisonous clouds about his golden head.

'With rotten damps ravish the morning air;
Let their exhaled unwholesome breaths make sick
The life of purity, the supreme fair,
Ere he arrive his weary noon-tide prick;
And let thy misty vapours march so thick
    That in their smoky ranks his smother'd light
    May set at noon and make perpetual night.

'Were Tarquin Night, as he is but Night's child,
The silver-shining queen he would distain;
Her twinkling handmaids too, by him defiled,
Through Night's black bosom should not peep again:
So should I have co-partners in my pain;
      And fellowship in woe doth woe assuage,
      As palmers' chat makes short their pilgrimage.

'Where now I have no one to blush with me,
To cross their arms and hang their heads with mine,
To mask their brows and hide their infamy;
But I alone must sit and pine,
Seasoning the earth with showers of silver brine,
      Mingling my talk with tears, my grief with groans,
      Poor wasting monuments of lasting moans

'O Night, thou furnace of foul-reeking smoke,
Let not the jealous Day behold that face
Which underneath thy black all-hiding cloak
Immodestly lies martyr'd with disgrace!
Keep still possession of thy gloomy place,
      That all the faults which in thy reign are made
      May likewise be sepulchred in thy shade!

'Make me not object to the tell-tale Day!
The light will show, character'd in my brow,
The story of sweet chastity's decay,
The impious breach of holy wedlock vow.
Yea, the illiterate, that know not how
      To cipher what is writ in learned books,
      Will quote my loathsome trespass in my looks.

'The nurse, to still her child, will tell my story,
And fright her crying babe with Tarquin's name;
The orator, to deck his oratory,
Will couple my reproach to Tarquin's shame;
Feast-finding minstrels, tuning my defame,
      Will tie the hearers to attend each line,
      How Tarquin wronged me, I Collatine.

'Let my good name, that senseless reputation,
For Collatine's dear love be kept unspotted:
If that he made a theme for disputation,
The branches of another root are rotted,
And undeserved reproach to him allotted
      That is as clear from this attaint of mine
      As I, ere this, was pure to Collatine.

'O unseen shame ! invisible disgrace !
O unfelt sore ! crest-wounding, private scar !
Reproach is stamp'd in Collatinus' face,
And Tarquin's eye may read the mot afar,
How he in peace is wounded, not in war.
    Alas, how many bear such shameful blows,
    Which not themselves, but he that gives them knows !

'If, Collatine, thine honour lay in me,
From me by strong assault it is bereft.
My honey lost, and I, a drone-like bee,
Have no perfection of my summer left,
But robb'd and ransack'd by injurious theft :
    In thy weak hive a wandering wasp hath crept,
    And suck'd the honey which thy chaste bee kept.

'Yet am I guilty of thy honour's wrack ;
Yet for thy honour did I entertain him ;
Coming from thee, I could not put him back,
For it had been dishonour to disdain him :
Besides of weariness he did complain him,
    And talk'd of virtue : O unlook'd-for evil,
    When virtue is profaned in such a devil !

'Why should the worm intrude the maiden bud ?
Or hateful cuckoos hatch in sparrows' nests ?
Or toads infect fair founts with venom mud ?
Or tyrant folly lurk in gentle breasts ?
Or kings be breakers of their own behests ?
    But no perfection is so absolute
    That some impurity doth not pollute.

'The aged man that coffers up his gold
Is plagued with cramps and gouts and painful fits,
And scarce hath eyes his treasure to behold,
But like still-pining Tantalus he sits
And useless barns the harvest of his wits,
    Having no other pleasure of his gain
    But torment that it cannot cure his pain.

'So then he hath it when he cannot use it,
And leaves it to be master'd by his young ;
Who in their pride do presently abuse it :
Their father was too weak, and they too strong,
To hold their cursed-blessed fortune long.
    The sweets we wish for turn to loathed sours
    Even in the moment that we call them ours.

'Unruly blasts wait on the tender spring
Unwholesome weeds take root with precious flowers;
The adder hisses where the sweet birds sing;
What virtue breeds iniquity devours:
We have no good that we can say is ours,
　　　But ill-annexed Opportunity
　　　Or kills his life or else his quality.

'O Opportunity, thy guilt is great!
'Tis thou that executest the traitor's treason;
Thou set'st the wolf where he the lamb may get;
Whoever plots the sin, thou point'st the season;
'Tis thou that spurn'st at right, at law, at reason;
　　　And in thy shady cell, where none may spy him,
　　　Sits Sin, to seize the souls that wander by him.

'Thou makest the vestal violate her oath;
Thou blow'st the fire when temperance is thaw'd;
Thou smother'st honesty, thou murder'st troth;
Thou foul abettor! thou notorious bawd!
Thou plantest scandal and displacest laud:
　　　Thou ravisher, thou traitor, thou false thief,
　　　Thy honey turns to gall, thy joy to grief!

'Thy secret pleasure turns to open shame,
Thy private feasting to a public fast,
Thy smoothing titles to a ragged name,
Thy sugar'd tongue to bitter wormwood taste:
Thy violent vanities can never last.
　　　How comes it then, vile Opportunity,
　　　Being so bad, such numbers seek for thee?

'When wilt thou be the humble suppliant's friend,
And bring him where his suit may be obtained?
When wilt thou sort an hour great strifes to end?
Or free that soul which wretchedness hath chained?
Give physic to the sick, ease to the pained?
　　　The poor, lame, blind, halt, creep, cry out for thee;
　　　But they ne'er meet with Opportunity.

'The patient dies while the physician sleeps;
The orphan pines while the oppressor feeds;
Justice is feasting while the widow weeps;
Advice is sporting while infection breeds:
Thou grant'st no time for charitable deeds:
　　　Wrath, envy, treason, rape, and murder's rages,
　　　Thy heinous hours wait on them as their pages.

'When Truth and Virtue have to do with thee,
A thousand crosses keep them from thy aid:
They buy thy help, but Sin ne'er gives a fee;
He gratis comes, and thou art well appaid
As well to hear as grant what he hath said.
  My Collatine would else have come to me
  When Tarquin did, but he was stay'd by thee.

'Guilty thou art of murder and of theft,
Guilty of perjury and subornation,
Guilty of treason, forgery and shift,
Guilty of incest, that abomination;
An accessary by thine inclination
  To all sins past and all that are to come
  From the creation to the general doom.

'Mis-shapen Time, copesmate of ugly Night,
Swift subtle post, carrier of grisly care,
Eater of youth, false slave to false delight,
Base watch of woes, sin's pack-horse, virtue's snare';
Thou nursest all and murder'st all that are:
  O, hear me then, injurious, shifting Time!
  Be guilty of my death, since of my crime.

'Why hath thy servant Opportunity
Betray'd the hours thou gavest me to repose,
Cancell'd my fortunes and enchained me
To endless date of never-ending woes?
Time's office is to fine the hate of foes,
  To eat up errors by opinion bred,
  Not spend the dowry of a lawful bed.

'Time's glory is to calm contending kings,
To unmask falsehood and bring truth to light,
To stamp the seal of time in aged things,
To wake the morn and sentinel the night,
To wrong the wronger till he render right,
  To ruinate proud buildings with thy hours,
  And smear with dust their glittering golden towers;

'To fill with worm-holes stately monuments,
To feed oblivion with decay of things,
To blot old books and alter their contents,
To pluck the quills from ancient ravens' wings,
To dry the old oak's sap and cherish springs,
  To spoil antiquities of hammer'd steel
  And turn the giddy round of Fortune's wheel;

'To show the beldam daughters of her daughter,
To make the child a man, the man a child,
To slay the tiger that doth live by slaughter,
To tame the unicorn and lion wild,
To mock the subtle in themselves beguiled,
　　　To cheer the ploughman with increaseful crops,
　　　And waste huge stones with little water-drops.

'Why work'st thou mischief in thy pilgrimage,
Unless thou couldst return to make amends?
One poor retiring minute in an age
Would purchase thee a thousand thousand friends,
Lending him wit that to bad debtors lends:
　　　O, this dread night, wouldst thou one hour come back,
　　　I could prevent this storm and shun thy wrack!

'Thou ceaseless lackey to eternity,
With some mischance cross Tarquin in his flight:
Devise extremes beyond extremity,
To make him curse this cursed crimeful night:
Let ghastly shadows his lewd eyes affright,
　　　And the dire thought of his committed evil
　　　Shape every bush a hideous shapeless devil.

'Disturb his hours of rest with restless trances,
Afflict him in his bed with bedrid groans;
Let there bechance him pitiful mischances,
To make him moan; but pity not his moans.
Stone him with harden'd hearts, harder than stones;
　　　And let mild women to him lose their mildness,
　　　Wilder to him than tigers in their wildness.

'Let him have time to tear his curled hair,
Let him have time against himself to rave,
Let him have time of time's help to despair,
Let him have time to live a loathed slave,
Let him have time a beggar's orts to crave,
　　　And time to see one that by alms doth live
　　　Disdain to him disdained scraps to give.

'Let him have time to see his friends his foes,
And merry fools to mock at him resort;
Let him have time to mark how slow time goes
In time of sorrow, and how swift and short
His time of folly and his time of sport;
　　　And ever let his unrecalling crime
　　　Have time to wail the abusing of his time.

'O Time, thou tutor both to good and bad,
Teach me to curse him that thou taught'st this ill!
At his own shadow let the thief run mad,
Himself himself seek every hour to kill!
Such wretched hands such wretched blood should spill;
     For who so base would such an office have
     As slanderous deathsman to so base a slave?

'The baser is he, coming from a king,
To shame his hope with deeds degenerate:
The mightier man, the mightier is the thing
That makes him honour'd or begets him hate;
For greatest scandal waits on greatest state.
     The moon being clouded presently is miss'd,
     But little stars may hide them when they list.

'The crow may bathe his coal-black wings in mire,
And unperceived fly with the filth away;
But if the like the snow-white swan desire,
The stain upon his silver down will stay.
Poor grooms are sightless night, kings glorious day:
     Gnats are unnoted wheresoe'er they fly,
     But eagles gazed upon with every eye.

'Out, idle words, servants to shallow fools!
Unprofitable sounds, weak arbitrators!
Busy yourselves in skill-contending schools;
Debate where leisure serves with dull debaters;
To trembling clients be you mediators:
     For me, I force not argument a straw,
     Since that my case is past the help of law.

'In vain I rail at Opportunity,
At Time, at Tarquin, and uncheerful Night;
In vain I cavil with mine infamy,
In vain I spurn at my confirm'd despite:
This helpless smoke of words doth me no right.
     The remedy indeed to do me good
     Is to let forth my foul-defiled blood.

'Poor hand, why quiver'st thou at this decree?
Honour thyself to rid me of this shame;
For if I die, my honour lives in thee,
But if I live, thou livest in my defame:
Since thou couldst not defend thy loyal dame,
     And wast afeard to scratch her wicked foe,
     Kill both thyself and her for yielding so.'

This said, from her be-tumbled couch she starteth,
To find some desperate instrument of death:
But this no slaughterhouse no tool imparteth
To make more vent for passage of her breath;
Which, thronging through her lips, so vanisheth
    As smoke from Ætna that in air consumes,
    Or that which from discharged cannon fumes.

'In vain,' quoth she, 'I live, and seek in vain
Some happy mean to end a hapless life.
I feared by Tarquin's falchion to be slain,
Yet for the self-same purpose seek a knife:
But when I fear'd I was a loyal wife:
    So am I now: O no, that cannot be;
    Of that true type hath Tarquin rifled me.

'O, that is gone for which I sought to live,
And therefore now I need not fear to die.
To clear this spot by death, at least I give
A badge of fame to slander's livery
A dying life to living infamy:
    Poor helpless help, the treasure stol'n away,
    To burn the guiltless casket where it lay!

'Well, well, dear Collatine, thou shalt not know
The stained taste of violated troth;
I will not wrong thy true affection so,
To flatter thee with an infringed oath;
This bastard graff shall never come to growth:
    He shall not boast who did thy stock pollute
    That thou art doting father of his fruit.

'Nor shall he smile at thee in secret thought,
Nor laugh with his companions at thy state;
But thou shalt know thy interest was not bought
Basely with gold, but stol'n from forth thy gate.
For me, I am the mistress of my fate,
    And with my trespass never will dispense,
    Till life to death acquit my forced offence.

'I will not poison thee with my attaint,
Nor fold my fault in cleanly-coin'd excuses;
My sable ground of sin I will not paint,
To hide the truth of this false night's abuses:
My tongue shall utter all; mine eyes, like sluices,
    As from a mountain-spring that feeds a dale,
    Shall gush pure streams to purge my impure tale.'

By this, lamenting Philomel had ended
The well tuned warble of her nightly sorrow,
And solemn night with slow sad gait descended
To ugly hell; when, low, the blushing morrow
Lends light to all fair eyes that light will borrow;
　　But cloudy Lucrece shames herself to see,
　　And therefore still in night would cloister'd be.

Revealing day through every cranny spies,
And seems to point her out where she sits weeping;
To whom she sobbing speaks: 'O eye of eyes,
Why pry'st thou through my window? leave thy peeping:
Mock with thy tickling beams eyes that are sleeping:
　　Brand not my forehead with thy piercing light,
　　For day hath nought to do what's done by night.'

Thus cavils she with every thing she sees:
True grief is fond and testy as a child,
Who wayward once, his mood with nought agrees:
Old woes, not infant sorrows, bear them mild;
Continuance tames the one; the other wild,
　　Like an unpractised swimmer plunging still
　　With too much labour drowns for want of skill.

So she, deep-drenched in a sea of care,
Holds disputation with each thing she views,
And to herself all sorrow doth compare;
No object but her passion's strength renews,
And as one shifts, another straight ensues:
　　Sometime her grief is dumb and hath no words;
　　Sometime 'tis mad and too much talk affords.

The little birds that tune their morning's joy
Make her moans mad with their sweet melody:
For mirth doth search the bottom of annoy;
Sad souls are slain in merry company;
Grief best is pleased with grief's society:
　　True sorrow then is feelingly sufficed
　　When with like semblance it is sympathized.

'Tis double death to drown in ken of shore;
He ten times pines that pines beholding food;
To see the salve doth make the wound ache more;
Great grief grieves most at that would do it good;
Deep woes roll forward like a gentle flood,
　　Who, being stopp'd, the bounding banks o'erflows;
　　Grief dallied with nor law nor limit knows.

'You mocking birds,' quoth she, 'your tunes entomb
Within your hollow-swelling feather'd breasts,
And in my hearing be you mute and dumb :
My restless discord loves no stops nor rests ;
A woeful hostess brooks not merry guests :
    Relish your nimble notes to pleasing ears ;
    Distress likes dumps when time is kept with tears.

'Come, Philomel, that sing'st of ravishment,
Make thy sad grove in my dishevell'd hair :
As the dank earth weeps at thy languishment,
So I at each sad strain will strain a tear,
And with deep groans the diapason bear ;
    For burden-wise I 'll hum on Tarquin still,
    While thou on Tereus descant'st better skill.

'And whiles against a thorn thou bear'st thy part,
To keep thy sharp woes waking, wretched I,
To imitate thee well, against my heart
Will fix a sharp knife, to affright mine eye ;
Who, if it wink, shall thereon fall and die.
    These means, as frets upon an instrument,
    Shall tune our heart-strings to true languishment.

'And for, poor bird, thou sing'st not in the day,
As shaming any eye should thee behold,
Some dark deep desert, seated from the way,
That knows not parching heat nor freezing cold,
Will we find out ; and there we will unfold
    To creatures stern sad tunes, to change their kinds :
    Since men prove beasts, let beasts bear gentle minds.'

As the poor frighted deer, that stands at gaze,
Wildly determining which way to fly,
Or one encompass'd with a winding maze,
That cannot tread the way out readily ;
So with herself is she in mutiny,
    To live or die, which of the twain were better,
    When life is shamed and death reproach's debtor.

'To kill myself,' quoth she, 'alack, what were it,
But with my body my poor soul's pollution ?
They that lose half with greater patience bear it
Than they whose whole is swallow'd in confusion.
That mother tries a merciless conclusion
    Who, having two sweet babes, when death takes one
    Will slay the other and be nurse to none.

'My body or my soul, which was the dearer,
When the one pure, the other made divine?
Whose love of either to myself was nearer,
When both were kept for heaven and Collatine?
Ay me! the bark peel'd from the lofty pine,
    His leaves will wither and his sap decay;
    So must my soul, her bark being peel'd away.

'Her house is sack'd, her quiet interrupted,
Her mansion batter'd by the enemy;
Her sacred temple spotted, spoil'd, corrupted,
Grossly engirt with daring infamy:
Then let it not be call'd impiety,
    If in this blemish'd fort I make some hole
    Through which I may convey this troubled soul.

'Yet die I will not till my Collatine
Have heard the cause of my untimely death;
That he may vow, in that sad hour of mine,
Revenge on him that made me stop my breath.
My stained blood to Tarquin I'll bequeath,
    Which by him tainted shall for him be spent,
    And as his due writ in my testament.

'My honour I'll bequeath unto the knife
That wounds my body so dishonoured.
'Tis honour to deprive dishonour'd life;
The one will live, the other being dead:
So of shame's ashes shall my fame be bred;
    For in my death I murder shameful scorn:
    My shame so dead, mine honour is new-born.

'Dear lord of that dear jewel I have lost,
What legacy shall I bequeath to thee?
My resolution, love, shall be thy boast,
By whose example thou revenged mayst be.
How Tarquin must be used, read it in me:
    Myself, thy friend, will kill myself, thy foe,
    And, for my sake, serve thou false Tarquin so.

'This brief abridgement of my will I make:
My soul and body to the skies and ground;
My resolution, husband, do thou take;
Mine honour be the knife's that makes my wound;
My shame be his that did my fame confound;
    And all my fame that lives disbursed be
    To those that live and think no shame of me.

'Thou, Collatine, shalt oversee this will;
How was I overseen that thou shalt see it !
My blood shall wash the slander of mine ill ;
My life's foul deed, my life's fair end shall free it.
Faint not, faint heart, but stoutly say " So be it : "
    Yield to my hand ; my hand shall conquer thee :
    Thou dead, both die, and both shall victors be.

This plot of death when sadly she had laid,
And wiped the brinish pearl from her bright eyes,
With untuned tongue she hoarsely calls her maid,
Whose swift obedience to her mistress hies ;
For fleet-wing'd duty with thought's feathers flies.
    Poor Lucrece' cheeks unto her maid seem so
    As winter meads when sun doth melt their snow.

Her mistress she doth give demure good-morrow,
With soft slow tongue, true mark of modesty,
And sorts a sad look to her lady's sorrow,
For why her face wore sorrow's livery,
But durst not ask of her audaciously
    Why her two suns were cloud-eclipsed so,
    Nor why her fair cheeks over-wash'd with woe.

But as the earth doth weep, the sun being set,
Each flower moisten'd like a melting eye,
Even so the maid with swelling drops 'gan wet
Her circled eyne, enforced by sympathy
Of those fair suns set in her mistress' sky,
    Who in a salt-waved ocean quench their light,
    Which makes the maid weep like the dewy night.

A pretty while these pretty creatures stand.
Like ivory conduits coral cisterns filling :
One justly weeps ; the other takes in hand
No cause, but company, of her drops spilling :
Their gentle sex to weep are often willing,
    Grieving themselves to guess at others smarts,
    And then they drown their eyes or break their hearts.

For men have marble, women waxen, minds,
And therefore are they form'd as marble will ;
The weak oppress'd, the impression of strange kinds
Is form'd in them by force, by fraud, or skill :
Then call them not the authors of their ill,
    No more than wax shall be accounted evil
    Wherein is stamp'd the semblance of a devil.

Their smoothness, like a goodly champaign plain,
Lays open all the little worms that creep;
In men, as in a rough-grown grove, remain
Cave-keeping evils that obscurely sleep:
Through crystal walls each little mote will peep:
    Though men can cover crimes with bold stern looks,
    Poor women's faces are their own faults' books.

No man inveigh against the withered flower,
But chide rough winter that the flower hath kill'd:
Not that devour'd, but that which doth devour,
Is worthy blame. O, let it not be hild
Poor women's faults, that they are so fulfill'd
    With men's abuses: those proud lords to blame
    Make weak-made women tenants to their shame.

The precedent whereof in Lucrece view,
Assail'd by night with circumstances strong
Of present death, and shame that might ensue
By that her death, to do her husband wrong:
Such danger to resistance did belong,
    That dying fear through all her body spread;
    And who cannot abuse a body dead?

By this, mild patience did fair Lucrece speak
To the poor counterfeit of her complaining:
'My girl,' quoth she, ' on what occasion break
Those tears from thee, that down thy cheeks are raining?
If thou dost weep for grief of my sustaining,
    Know, gentle wench, it small avails my mood:
    If tears could help, mine own would do me good.

'But tell me, girl, when went'—and there she stay'd
Till after a deep groan—'Tarquin from hence?'
'Madam, ere I was up,' replied the maid,
'The more to blame my sluggard negligence:
Yet with the fault I thus far can dispense;
    Myself was stirring ere the break of day,
    And ere I rose was Tarquin gone away.

'But, lady, if your maid may be so bold,
She would request to know your heaviness.'
'O, peace!' quoth Lucrece: 'if it should be told,
The repetition cannot make it less,
For more it is than I can well express:
    And that deep torture may be call'd a hell
    When more is felt than one hath power to tell.

'Go, get me hither paper, ink and pen :
Yet save that labour, for I have them here.
What should I say ?　One of my husband's men
Bid thou be ready by and by to bear
A letter to my lord, my love, my dear :
　　　Bid him with speed prepare to carry it ;
　　　The cause craves haste and it will soon be writ.'

Her maid is gone, and she prepares to write,
First hovering o'er the paper with her quill :
Conceit and grief an eager combat fight ;
What wit sets down is blotted straight with will ;
This is too curious-good, this blunt and ill :
　　　Much like a press of people at the door,
　　　Throng her inventions, which shall go before.

At last she thus begins : 'Thou worthy lord
Of that unworthy wife that greeteth thee,
Health to thy person ! next vouchsafe t' afford—
If ever, love, thy Lucrece thou wilt see—
Some present speed to come and visit me.
　　　So, I commend me from our house in grief :
　　　My woes are tedious, though my words are brief.'

Here folds she up the tenor of her woe,
Her certain sorrow writ uncertainly.
By this short schedule Collatine may know
Her grief, but not her grief's true quality :
She dares not thereof make discovery,
　　　Lest he should hold it her own gross abuse,
　　　Ere she with blood had stain'd her stain'd excuse.

Besides, the life and feeling of her passion
She hoards, to spend when he is by to hear her,
When sighs and groans and tears may grace the fashion
Of her disgrace, the better so to clear her
From that suspicion which the world might bear her.
　　　To shun this blot, she would not blot the letter
　　　With words, till action might become them better.

To see sad sights moves more than hear them told ;
For then the eye interprets to the ear
The heavy motion that it doth behold,
When every part a part of woe doth bear.
'Tis but a part of sorrow that we hear :
　　　Deep sounds make lesser noise than shallow fords,
　　　And sorrow ebbs, being blown with wind of words

456

Her letter now is seal'd and on it writ
'At Ardea to my lord with more than haste.'
The post attends, and she delivers it,
Charging the sour-faced groom to hie as fast
As lagging fowls before the northern blast :
    Speed more than speed but dull and slow she deems:
    Extremity still urgeth such extremes.

The homely villain court'sies to her low,
And blushing on her, with a steadfast eye
Receives the scroll without or yea or no,
And forth with bashful innocence doth hie.
But they whose guilt within their bosoms lie
    Imagine every eye beholds their blame ;
    For Lucrece thought he blush'd to see her shame :

When, silly groom ! God wot, it was defect
Of spirit, life and bold audacity.
Such harmless creatures have a true respect
To talk in deeds, while others saucily
Promise more speed but do it leisurely :
    Even so this pattern of the worn-out age
    Pawn'd honest looks, but laid no words to gage.

His kindled duty kindled her mistrust,
That two red fires in both their faces blazed ;
She thought he blush'd, as knowing Tarquin's lust,
And blushing with him, wistly on him gazed ;
Her earnest eye did make him more amazed :
    The more she saw the blood his cheeks replenish,
    The more she thought he spied in her some blemish.

But long she thinks till he return again,
And yet the duteous vassal scarce is gone,
The weary time she cannot entertain,
For now 'tis stale to sigh, to weep and groan :
So woe hath wearied woe, moan tired moan,
    That she her plaints a little while doth stay,
    Pausing for means to mourn some newer way.

At lasts she calls to mind where hangs a piece
Of skilful painting, made for Priam's Troy ;
Before the which is drawn the power of Greece,
For Helen's rape the city to destroy,
Threatening cloud-kissing Ilion with annoy ;
    Which the conceited painter drew so proud,
    As heaven, it seem'd, to kiss the turrets bow'd.

A thousand lamentable objects there,
In scorn of nature, art gave lifeless life :
Many a dry drop seem'd a weeping tear,
Shed for the slaughter'd husband by the wife :
The red blood reeked to show the painter's strife ;
    And dying eyes gleam'd forth their ashy lights,
    Like dying coals burnt out in tedious nights.

There might you see the labouring pioneer
Begrimed with sweat and smeared all with dust ;
And from the towers of Troy there would appear
The very eyes of men through loop-holes thrust,
Gazing upon the Greeks with little lust :
    Such sweet observance in this work was had
    That one might see those far-off eyes look sad.

In great commanders grace and majesty
You might behold, triumphing in their faces,
In youth, quick bearing and dexterity ;
And here and there the painter interlaces
Pale cowards, marching on with trembling paces ;
    Which heartless peasants did so well resemble
    That one would swear he saw them quake and tremble.

In Ajax and Ulysses, O, what art
Of physiognomy might one behold !
The face of either cipher'd either's heart ;
Their face their manners most expressly told :
In Ajax' eyes blunt rage and rigour roll'd ;
    But the mild glance that sly Ulysses lent
    Show'd deep regard and smiling government.

There pleading might you see grave Nestor stand,
As 'twere encouraging the Greeks to fight,
Making such sober action with his hand
That it beguiled attention, charm'd the sight :
In speech, it seem'd, his beard all silver white
    Wagg'd up and down, and from his lips did fly
    Thin winding breath which purl'd up to the sky.

About him were a press of gaping faces,
Which seem'd to swallow up his sound advice ;
All jointly listening, but with several graces,
As if some mermaid did their ears entice,
Some high, some low, the painter was so nice ;
    The scalps of many, almost hid behind,
    To jump up higher seem'd, to mock the mind.

Here one man's hand lean'd on another's head,
His nose being shadow'd by his neighbour's ear;
Here one being throng'd bears back, all boll'n and red;
Another smother'd seems to pelt and swear;
And in their rage such signs of rage they bear
  As, but for loss of Nestor's golden words,
   It seem'd they would debate with angry swords.

For much imaginary work was there;
Conceit deceitful, so compact, so kind,
That for Achilles' image stood his spear
Griped in an armed hand; himself behind
Was left unseen, save to the eye of mind:
  A hand, a foot, a face, a leg, a head,
   Stood for the whole to be imagined.

And from the walls of strong-besieged Troy
When their brave hope, bold Hector, march'd to field,
Stood many Trojan mothers sharing joy
To see their youthful sons bright weapons wield;
And to their hope they such odd action yield
  That through their light joy seemed to appear,
   Like bright things stain'd, a kind of heavy fear.

And from the strand of Dardan, where they fought,
To Simois' reedy banks the red blood ran,
Whose waves to imitate the battle sought
With swelling ridges; and their ranks began
To break upon the galled shore, and then
  Retire again, till meeting greater ranks
   They join and shoot their foam at Simois' banks.

To this well-painted piece is Lucrece come,
To find a face where all distress is stell'd.
Many she sees where cares have carved some,
But none where all distress and dolour dwell'd,
Till she despairing Hecuba beheld,
  Staring on Priam's wounds with her old eyes,
   Which bleeding under Pyrrhus' proud foot lies.

In her the painter had anatomized
Time's ruin, beauty's wreck, and grim care's reign:
Her cheeks with chaps and wrinkles were disguised;
Of what she was no semblance did remain:
Her blue blood changed to black in every vein,
  Wanting the spring that those shrunk pipes had fed,
   Show'd life imprison'd in a body dead.

On this sad shadow Lucrece spends her eyes,
And shapes her sorrow to the beldam's woes,
Who nothing wants to answer her but cries,
And bitter words to ban her cruel foes :
The painter was no god to lend her those ;
    And therefore Lucrece swears he did her wrong,
    To give her so much grief and not a tongue.

'Poor instrument,' quoth she, 'without a sound,
I 'll tune thy woes with my lamenting tongue,
And drop sweet balm in Priam's painted wound,
And rail on Pyrrhus that hath done him wrong,
And with my tears quench Troy that burns so long,
    And with my knife scratch out the angry eyes
    Of all the Greeks that are thine enemies.

'Show me the strumpet that began this stir,
That with my nails her beauty I may tear.
Thy heat of lust, fond Paris, did incur
This load of wrath that burning Troy doth bear :
Thy eye kindled the fire that burneth here ;
    And here in Troy, for trespass of thine eye,
    The sire, the son, the dame and daughter die.

'Why should the private pleasure of some one
Become the public plague of many moe?
Let sin, alone committed, light alone
Upon his head that hath transgressed so ;
Let guiltless souls be freed from guilty woe :
    For one's offence why should so many fall,
    To plague a private sin in general?

'Lo, here weeps Hecuba, here Priam dies,
Here manly Hector faints, here Troilus swounds,
Here friend by friend in bloody channel lies,
And friend to friend gives unadvised wounds,
And one man's lust these many lives confounds :
    Had doting Priam check'd his son's desire,
    Troy had been bright with fame and not with fire.'

Here feelingly she weeps Troy's painted woes :
For sorrow, like a heavy-hanging bell
Once set on ringing, with his own weight goes ;
Then little strength rings out the doleful knell :
So Lucrece, set a-work, sad tales doth tell
    To pencill'd pensiveness and colour'd sorrow ;
    She lends them words, and she their looks doth borrow.

She throws her eyes about the painting round,
And who she finds forlorn she doth lament.
At last she sees a wretched image bound,
That piteous looks to Phrygian shepherds lent:
His face, though full of cares, yet show'd content;
    Onward to Troy with the blunt swains he goes,
    So mild that Patience seem'd to scorn his woes.

In him the painter labour'd with his skill
To hide deceit and give the harmless show
An humble gait, calm looks, eyes wailing still,
A brow unbent, that seem'd to welcome woe;
Cheeks neither red nor pale, but mingled so
    That blushing red no guilty instance gave,
    Nor ashy pale the fear that false hearts have.

But, like a constant and confirmed devil,
He entertain'd a show so seeming just,
And therein so ensconced his secret evil,
That jealousy itself could not mistrust
False-creeping craft and perjury should thrust
    Into so bright a day such black-faced storms,
    Or blot with hell-born sin such saint-like forms.

The well-skill'd workman this mild image drew
For perjured Sinon, whose enchanting story
The credulous old Priam after slew;
Whose words, like wildfire, burnt the shining glory
Of rich-built Ilion, that the skies were sorry,
    And little stars shot from their fixed places,
    When their glass fell wherein they view'd their faces.

This picture she advisedly perused,
And chid the painter for his wondrous skill,
Saying, some shape in Sinon's was abused;
So fair a form lodged not a mind so ill:
And still on him she gazed, and gazing still
    Such signs of truth in his plain face she spied
    That she concludes the picture was belied.

'It cannot be,' quoth she, 'that so much guile'—
She would have said 'can lurk in such a look;'
But Tarquin's shape came in her mind the while,
And from her tongue 'can lurk' from 'cannot' took:
'It cannot be' she in that sense forsook,
    And turn'd it thus, 'It cannot be, I find,
    But such a face should bear a wicked mind:

'For even as subtle Sinon here is painted,
So sober-sad, so weary and so mild,
As if with grief or travail he had fainted,
To me came Tarquin armed : so beguiled
With outward honesty, but yet defiled
    With inward vice : as Priam him did cherish,
    So did I Tarquin ; so my Troy did perish.

'Look, look, how listening Priam wets his eyes,
To see those borrow'd tears that Sinon sheds !
Priam, why art thou old and yet not wise ?
For every tear he falls a Trojan bleeds :
His eye drops fire, no water thence proceeds ;
    Those round clear pearls of his that move thy pity
    Are balls of quenchless fire to burn thy city.

'Such devils steal effects from lightless hell ;
For Sinon in his fire doth quake with cold,
And in that cold hot-burning fire doth dwell ;
These contraries such unity do hold,
Only to flatter fools and make them bold :
    So Priam's trust false Sinon's tears doth flatter,
    That he finds means to burn his Troy with water.'

Here, all enraged, such passion her assails,
That patience is quite beaten from her breast.
She tears the senseless Sinon with her nails,
Comparing him to that unhappy guest
Whose deed hath made herself herself detest :
    At last she smilingly with this gives o'er ;
    'Fool, fool !' quoth she, 'his wounds will not be sore.'

Thus ebbs and flows the current of her sorrow,
And time doth weary time with her complaining.
She looks for night, and then she longs for morrow,
And both she thinks too long with her remaining :
Short time seems long in sorrow's sharp sustaining :
    Though woe be heavy, yet it seldom sleeps,
    And they that watch see time how slow it creeps.

Which all this time hath overslipp'd her thought,
That she with painted images hath spent ;
Being from the feeling of her own grief brought
By deep surmise of others' detriment,
Losing her woes in shows of discontent.
    It easeth some, though none it ever cured,
    To think their dolour others have endured.

But now the mindful messenger come back
Brings home his lord and other company;
Who finds his Lucrece clad in mourning black:
And round about her tear-distained eye
Blue circles stream'd, like rainbows in the sky:
    These water-galls in her dim element
    Foretell new storms to those already spent.

Which when her sad-beholding husband saw,
Amazedly in her sad face he stares:
Her eyes, though sod in tears, look'd red and raw,
Her lively colour kill'd with deadly cares.
He hath no power to ask her how she fares:
    Both stood, like old acquaintance in a trance,
    Met far from home, wondering each other's chance.

At last he takes her by the bloodless hand,
And thus begins: 'What uncouth ill event
Hath thee befall'n, that thou dost trembling stand?
Sweet love, what spite hath thy fair colour spent?
Why art thou thus attired in discontent?
    Unmask, dear dear, this moody heaviness,
    And tell thy grief, that we may give redress.'

Three times with sighs she gives her sorrow fire,
Ere once she can discharge one word of woe:
At length address'd to answer his desire,
She modestly prepares to let them know
Her honour is ta'en prisoner by the foe;
    While Collatine and his consorted lords
    With sad attention long to hear her words.

And now this pale swan in her watery nest
Begins the sad dirge of her certain ending:
'Few words,' quoth she, 'shall fit the trespass best,
Where no excuse can give the fault amending:
In me moe woes than words are now depending;
    And my laments would be drawn out too long,
    To tell them all with one poor tired tongue.

'Then be this all the task it hath to say:
Dear husband, in the interest of thy bed
A stranger came, and on that pillow lay
Where thou wast wont to rest thy weary head;
And what wrong else may be imagined
    By foul enforcement might be done to me,
    From that, alas, thy Lucrece is not free.

'For in the dreadful dead of dark midnight,
With shining falchion in my chamber came
A creeeping creature, with a flaming light,
And softly cried "Awake, thou Roman dame,
And entertain my love; else lasting shame
      On thee and thine this night I will inflict,
      If thou my love's desire do contradict.

'"For some hard-favour'd groom of thine," quoth he,
"Unless thou yoke thy liking to my will,
I'll murder straight, and then I'll slaughter thee,
And swear I found you where you did fulfil
The loathsome act of lust, and so did kill
      The lechers in their deed: this act will be
      My fame, and thy perpetual infamy."

'With this, I did begin to start and cry;
And then against my heart he set his sword,
Swearing, unless I took all patiently,
I should not live to speak another word;
So should my shame still rest upon record,
      And never be forgot in mighty Rome
      The adulterate death of Lucrece and her groom.

'Mine enemy was strong, my poor self weak,
And far the weaker with so strong a fear:
My bloody judge forbade my tongue to speak;
No rightful plea might plead for justice there:
His scarlet lust came evidence to swear
      That my poor beauty had purloin'd his eyes;
      And when the judge is robb'd, the prisoner dies.

'O, teach me how to make mine own excuse!
Or, at the least, this refuge let me find;
Though my gross blood be stain'd with this abuse,
Immaculate and spotless is my mind;
That was not forced; that never was inclined
      To accessary yieldings, but still pure
      Doth in her poison'd closet yet endure.'

Lo, here, the hopeless merchant of this loss,
With head declined, and voice damm'd up with woe,
With sad-set eyes and wretched arms across,
From lips new-waxen pale begins to blow
The grief away that stops his answer so:
      But, wretched as he is, he strives in vain;
      What he breathes out his breath drinks up again.

As through an arch the violent roaring tide
Outruns the eye that doth behold his haste,
Yet in the eddy boundeth in his pride
Back to the strait that forced him on so fast,
In rage sent out, recall'd in rage, being past :
  Even so his sighs, his sorrows, make a saw,
  To push grief on and back the same grief draw.

Which speechless woe of his poor she attendeth
And his untimely frenzy thus awaketh :
'Dear lord, thy sorrow to my sorrow lendeth
Another power ; no flood by raining slaketh,
My woe too sensible thy passion maketh
  More feeling-painful : let it then suffice
  To drown one woe, one pair of weeping eyes.

'And for my sake, when I might charm thee so,
For she that was thy Lucrece, now attend me :
Be suddenly revenged on my foe,
Thine, mine, his own : suppose thou dost defend me
From what is past : the help that thou shalt lend me
  Comes all too late, yet let the traitor die ;
  For sparing justice feeds iniquity.

'But ere I name him, you fair lords,' quoth she,
Speaking to those that came with Collatine,
'Shall plight your honourable faiths to me,
With swift pursuit to venge this wrong of mine ;
For 'tis a meritorious fair design
  To chase injustice with revengeful arms :
  Knights, by their oaths, should right poor ladies' harms.'

At this request, with noble disposition
Each present lord began to promise aid,
As bound in knighthood to her imposition,
Longing to hear the hateful foe bewray'd.
But she, that yet her sad task hath not said,
  The protestation stops. 'O, speak,' quoth she,
  'How may this forced stain be wiped from me ?

'What is the quality of my offence,
Being constrain'd with dreadful circumstance ?
May my pure mind with the foul act dispense,
My low-declined honour to advance ?
May any terms acquit me from this chance ?
  The poison'd fountain clears itself again ;
  And why not I from this compelled stain ?'

With this, they all at once began to say,
Her body's stain her mind untainted clears;
While with a joyless smile she turns away
The face, that map which deep impression bears
Of hard misfortune, carved in it with tears.
　　'No, no,' quoth she, 'no dame hereafter living
　　By my excuse shall claim excuse's giving.'

Here with a sigh, as if her heart would break,
She throws forth Tarquin's name: 'He, he,' she says,
But more than 'he' her poor tongue could not speak;
Till after many accents and delays,
Untimely breathings, sick and short assays,
　　She utters this: 'He, he, fair lords, 'tis he,
　　That guides this hand to give this wound to me.'

Even here she sheathed in her harmless breast
A harmful knife, that thence her soul unsheathed:
That blow did bail it from the deep unrest
Of that polluted prison where it breathed:
Her contrite sighs unto the clouds bequeathed
　　Her winged sprite, and through her wounds doth fly
　　Life's lasting date from cancell'd destiny.

Stone-still, astonish'd with this deadly deed,
Stood Collatine and all his lordly crew;
Till Lucrece' father, that beholds her bleed,
Himself on her self-slaughtered body threw;
And from the purple fountain Brutus drew
　　The murderous knife, and, as it left the place,
　　Her blood, in poor revenge, held it in chase;

And bubbling from her breast, it doth divide
In two slow rivers, that the crimson blood
Circles her body in on every side,
Who, like a late-sack'd island, vastly stood
Bare and unpeopled in this fearful flood.
　　Some of her blood still pure and red remain'd,
　　And some look'd black, and that false Tarquin stain'd.

About the mourning and congealed face
Of that black blood a watery rigol goes,
Which seems to weep upon the tainted place:
And ever since, as pitying Lucrece' woes,
Corrupted blood some watery token shows;
　　And blood untainted still doth red abide,
　　Blushing at that which is so putrified.

'Daughter, dear daughter,' old Lucretius cries,
'That life was mine which thou hast here deprived.
If in the child the father's image lies,
Where shall I live now Lucrece is unlived?
Thou wast not to this end from me derived.
    If children pre-decease progenitors,
    We are their offspring, and they none of ours.

'Poor broken glass, I often did behold
In thy sweet semblance my old age new born:
But now that fair fresh mirror, dim and old,
Shows me a bare-boned death by time outworn:
O, from thy cheeks my image thou hast torn,
    And shiver'd all the beauty of my glass,
    That I no more can see what once I was.

'O time, cease thou thy course and last no longer,
If they surcease to be that should survive.
Shall rotten death make conquest of the stronger,
And leave the faltering feeble souls alive?
The old bees die, the young possess their hive:
    Then live, sweet Lucrece, live again, and see
    Thy father die, and not thy father thee!'

By this, starts Collatine as from a dream,
And bids Lucretius give his sorrow place;
And then in key-cold Lucrece' bleeding stream
He falls, and bathes the pale fear in his face,
And counterfeits to die with her a space;
    Till manly shame bids him possess his breath,
    And live to be revenged on her death.

The deep vexation of his inward soul
Hath served a dumb arrest upon his tongue;
Who, mad that sorrow should his use control
Or keep him from heart-easing words so long,
Begins to talk; but through his lips do throng
    Weak words, so thick come in his poor heart's aid
    That no man could distinguish what he said.

Yet sometime 'Tarquin' was pronounced plain,
But through his teeth, as if the name he tore.
This windy tempest, till it blow up rain,
Held back his sorrow's tide, to make it more;
At last it rains, and busy winds give o'er:
    Then son and father weep with equal strife
    Who should weep most, for daughter or for wife.

The one doth call her his, the other his,
Yet neither may possess the claim they lay.
The father says 'She 's mine.'   'O, mine she is,
Replies her husband : ' do not take away
My sorrow's interest ; let no mourner say
      He weeps for her, for she was only mine,
      And only must be wail'd by Collatine.

' O,' quoth Lucretius, ' I did give that life
Which she too early and too late hath spill'd.'
' Woe, woe,' quoth Collatine, ' she was my wife ;
I owed her, and 'tis mine that she hath kill'd.'
' My daughter ' and ' my wife ' with clamours fill'd
      The dispersed air, who, holding Lucrece' life,
      Answer'd their cries, ' my daughter ' and ' my wife.'

Brutus, who pluck'd the knife from Lucrece' side,
Seeing such emulation in their woe,
Began to clothe his wit in state and pride,
Burying in Lucrece' wound his folly's show.
He with the Romans was esteemed so
      As silly-jeering idiots are with kings,
      For sportive words and uttering foolish things :

But now he throws that shallow habit by
Wherein deep policy did him disguise,
And arm'd his long-hid wits advisedly
To check the tears in Collatinus' eyes.
' Thou wronged lord of Rome,' quoth he, ' arise :
      Let my unsounded self, supposed a fool,
      Now set thy long-experienced wit to school.

' Why, Collatine, is woe the cure for woe ?
Do wounds help wounds, or grief help grievous deeds ?
Is it revenge to give thyself a blow
For his foul act by whom thy fair wife bleeds ?
Such childish humour from weak minds proceeds :
      Thy wretched wife mistook the matter so,
      To slay herself, that should have slain her foe.

' Courageous Roman, do not steep thy heart
In such relenting dew of lamentations,
But kneel with me and help to bear thy part
To rouse our Roman gods with invocations
That they will suffer these abominations,
      Since Rome herself in them doth stand disgraced,
      By our strong arms from forth her fair streets chased.

'Now, by the Capitol that we adore,
And by this chaste blood so unjustly stained,
By heaven's fair sun that breeds the fat earth's store,
By all our country rights in Rome maintained,
And by chaste Lucrece' soul that late complained
    Her wrongs to us, and by this bloody knife,
    We will revenge the death of this true wife!

This said, he struck his hand upon his breast,
And kiss'd the fatal knife, to end his vow,
And to his protestation urged the rest,
Who, wondering at him, did his words allow:
Then jointly to the ground their knees they bow;
    And that deep vow, which Brutus made before,
    He doth again repeat, and that they swore.

When they had sworn to this advised doom,
They did conclude to bear dear Lucrece thence
To show her bleeding body thorough Rome,
And so to publish Tarquin's foul offence:
Which being done with speedy diligence,
    The Romans plausibly did give consent
    To Tarquin's everlasting banishment.

SONNETS

TO . THE . ONLIE .. BEGETTER . OF .
THESE . INSVING . SONNETS .
Mr W. H. ALL. HAPPINESSE .
AND . THAT . ETERNITIE.
PROMISED
BY .
OVR . EVER-LIVING . POET ,
WISHETH .
THE . WELL-WISHING
ADVENTVRER . IN .
SETTING .
FORTH .

T. T.

1 FROM fairest creatures we desire increase,
That thereby beauty's rose might never die,
But as the riper should by time decease,
His tender heir might bear his memory :
But thou, contracted to thine own bright eyes,
Feed'st thy light's flame with self-substantial fuel,
Making a famine where abundance lies,
Thyself thy foe, to thy sweet self too cruel.
Thou that art now the world's fresh ornament
And only herald to the gaudy spring,
Within thine own bud buriest thy content
And, tender churl, makest waste in niggarding.
    Pity the world, or else this glutton be,
    To eat the world's due, by the grave and thee.

2 When forty winters shall besiege thy brow
And dig deep trenches in thy beauty's field,
Thy youth's proud livery, so gazed on now,
Will be a tatter'd weed, of small worth held :
Then being ask'd where all thy beauty lies,
Where all the treasure of thy lusty days,
To say, within thine own deep-sunken eyes,
Were an ill-eating shame and thriftless praise.
How much more praise deserved thy beauty's use,
If thou couldst answer ' This fair child of mine
Shall sum my count and make my old excuse,'
Proving his beauty by succession thine !
    This were to be new made when thou art old,
    And see thy blood warm when thou feel'st it cold.

3 Look in thy glass, and tell the face thou viewest
  Now is the time that face should form another;
  Whose fresh repair if now thou not renewest,
  Thou dost beguile the world, unbless some mother.
  For where is she so fair whose unear'd womb
  Disdains the tillage of thy husbandry?
  Or who is he so fond will be the tomb
  Of his self-love, to stop posterity?
  Thou art thy mother's glass, and she in thee
  Calls back the lovely April of her prime:
  So thou through windows of thine age shalt see,
  Despite of wrinkles, this thy golden time.
      But if thou live, remember'd not to be,
      Die single, and thine image dies with thee.

4 Unthrifty loveliness, why dost thou spend
  Upon thyself thy beauty's legacy?
  Nature's bequest gives nothing, but doth lend,
  And being frank, she lends to those are free.
  Then, beauteous niggard, why dost thou abuse
  The bounteous largess given thee to give?
  Profitless usurer, why dost thou use
  So great a sum of sums, yet canst not live?
  For having traffic with thyself alone,
  Thou of thyself thy sweet self dost deceive.
  Then how, when nature calls thee to be gone,
  What acceptable audit canst thou leave?
      Thy unused beauty must be tomb'd with thee,
      Which, used, lives th' executor to be.

5 Those hours that with gentle work did frame
  The lovely gaze where every eye doth dwell,
  Will play the tyrants to the very same
  And that unfair which fairly doth excel:
  For never-resting time leads summer on
  To hideous winter and confounds him there;
  Sap check'd with frost and lusty leaves quite gone,
  Beauty o'ersnow'd and bareness every where:
  Then, were not summer's distillation left,
  A liquid prisoner pent in walls of glass,
  Beauty's effect with beauty were bereft,
  Nor it, nor no remembrance what it was:
      But flowers distill'd, though they with winter meet,
      Leese but their show; their substance still lives sweet

6 Then let not winter's ragged hand deface
 In thee thy summer, ere thou be distill'd:
 Make sweet some vial; treasure thou some place
 With beauty's treasure, ere it be self-kill'd.
 That use is not forbidden usury,
 Which happies those that pay the willing loan;
 That's for thyself to breed another thee,
 Or ten times happier, be it ten for one;
 Ten times thyself were happier than thou art,
 If ten of thine ten times refigured thee:
 Then what could death do, if thou shouldst depart,
 Leaving thee living in posterity?
    Be not self-will'd, for thou art much too fair
    To be death's conquest and make worms thine heir.

7 Lo, in the orient when the gracious light
 Lifts up his burning head, each under eye
 Doth homage to his new-appearing sight,
 Serving with looks his sacred majesty;
 And having climb'd the steep-up heavenly hill,
 Resembling strong youth in his middle age,
 Yet mortal looks adore his beauty still,
 Attending on his golden pilgrimage;
 But when from highmost pitch, with weary car
 Like feeble age, he reeleth from the day,
 The eyes, 'fore duteous, now converted are
 From his low tract, and look another way:
    So thou, thyself out-going in thy noon,
    Unlook'd on diest, unless thou get a son.

8 Music to hear, why hear'st thou music sadly?
 Sweets with sweets war not, joy delights in joy.
 Why lovest thou that which thou receivest not gladly,
 Or else receivest with pleasure thine annoy?
 If the true concord of well tuned sounds,
 By unions married, do offend thine ear
 They do but sweetly chide thee, who confounds
 In singleness the parts that thou shouldst bear.
 Mark how one string, sweet husband to another,
 Strikes each in each by mutual ordering;
 Resembling sire and child and happy mother,
 Who, all in one, one pleasing note do sing:
    Whose speechless song, being many, seeming one,
    Sings this to thee: 'Thou single wilt prove none.'

9 Is it for fear to wet a widow's eye
That thou consumest thyself in single life?
Ah! if thou issueless shalt hap to die,
The world will wail thee, like a makeless wife;
The world will be thy widow, and still weep
That thou no form of thee hast left behind,
When every private widow well may keep
By children's eyes her husband's shape in mind.
Look, what an unthrift in the world doth spend
Shifts but his place, for still the world enjoys it;
But beauty's waste hath in the world an end,
And kept unused, the user so destroys it.
　　No love toward others in that bosom sits
　　That on himself such murderous shame commits.

10 For shame! deny that thou bear'st love to any,
Who for thyself art so unprovident.
Grant, if thou wilt, thou art beloved of many,
But that thou none lovest is most evident;
For thou art so possess'd with murderous hate
That 'gainst thyself thou stick'st not to conspire,
Seeking that beauteous roof to ruinate
Which to repair should be thy chief desire.
O, change thy thought, that I may change my mind!
Shall hate be fairer lodged than gentle love?
Be, as thy presence is, gracious and kind,
Or to thyself at least kind-hearted prove:
　　Make thee another self, for love of me,
　　That beauty still may live in thine or thee.

11 As fast as thou shalt wane, so fast thou grow'st
In one of thine, from that which thou departest;
And that fresh blood which youngly thou bestow'st
Thou mayst call thine when thou from youth convertest.
Herein lives wisdom, beauty and increase;
Without this, folly, age and cold decay:
If all were minded so, the times should cease
And threescore year would make the world away.
Let those whom Nature hath not made for store,
Harsh, featureless and rude, barrenly perish:
Look, whom she best endow'd she gave the more;
Which bounteous gift thou shouldst in bounty cherish:
　　She carved thee for her seal, and meant thereby
　　Thou shouldst print more, not let that copy die.

473

12 When I do count the clock that tells the time,
And see the brave day sunk in hideous night;
When I behold the violet past prime,
And sable curls all silver'd o'er with white;
When lofty trees I see barren of leaves,
Which erst from heat did canopy the herd,
And summer's green all girded up in sheaves,
Borne on the bier with white and bristly beard,
Then of thy beauty do I question make,
That thou among the wastes of time must go,
Since sweets and beauties do themselves forsake
And die as fast as they see others grow;
  And nothing 'gainst Time's scythe can make defence
  Save breed, to brave him when he takes thee hence.

13 O, that you were yourself! but, love, you are
No longer yours than you yourself here live:
Against this coming end you should prepare,
And your sweet semblance to some other give.
So should that beauty which you hold in lease
Find no determination; then you were
Yourself again, after yourself's decease,
When your sweet issue your sweet form should bear.
Who lets so fair a house fall to decay,
Which husbandry in honour might uphold
Against the stormy gusts of winter's day
And barren rage of death's eternal cold?
  O, none but unthrifts: dear my love, you know
  You had a father; let your son say so.

14 Not from the stars do I my judgement pluck;
And yet methinks I have astronomy,
But not to tell of good or evil luck,
Of plagues, of dearths, or seasons' quality;
Nor can I fortune to brief minutes tell,
Pointing to each his thunder, rain and wind,
Or say with princes if it shall go well,
By oft predict that I in heaven find:
But from thine eyes my knowledge I derive,
And, constant stars, in them I read such art,
As truth and beauty shall together thrive,
If from thyself to store thou wouldst convert;
  Or else of thee this I prognosticate:
  Thy end is truth's and beauty's doom and date.

15 When I consider every thing that grows
   Holds in perfection but a little moment,
   That this huge stage presenteth nought but shows
   Whereon the stars in secret influence comment;
   When I perceive that men as plants increase,
   Cheered and check'd even by the self-same sky,
   Vaunt in their youthful sap, at height decrease,
   And wear their brave state out of memory;
   Then the conceit of this inconstant stay
   Sets you most rich in youth before my sight,
   Where wasteful Time debateth with Decay,
   To change your day of youth to sullied night;
      And all in war with Time for love of you,
      As he takes from you, I engraft you new.

16 But wherefore do not you a mightier way
   Make war upon this bloody tyrant, Time?
   And fortify yourself in your decay
   With means more blessed than my barren rhyme?
   Now stand you on the top of happy hours,
   And many maiden gardens, yet unset,
   With virtuous wish would bear your living flowers
   Much liker than your painted counterfeit:
   So should the lines of life that life repair,
   Which this, Time's pencil, or my pupil pen,
   Neither in inward worth nor outward fair,
   Can make you live yourself in eyes of men.
      To give away yourself keeps yourself still;
      And you must live, drawn by your own sweet skill.

17 Who will believe my verse in time to come,
   If it were fill'd with your most high deserts?
   Though yet, heaven knows, it is but as a tomb
   Which hides your life and shows not half your parts.
   If I could write the beauty of your eyes
   And in fresh numbers number all your graces,
   The age to come would say 'This poet lies;
   Such heavenly touches ne'er touch'd earthly faces.'
   So should my papers, yellowed with their age,
   Be scorn'd, like old men of less truth than tongue,
   And your true rights be term'd a poet's rage
   And stretched metre of an antique song:
      But were some child of yours alive that time,
      You should live twice, in it and in my rhyme.

18 Shall I compare thee to a summer's day?
    Thou art more lovely and more temperate:
    Rough winds do shake the darling buds of May,
    And summer's lease hath all too short a date:
    Sometime too hot the eye of heaven shines,
    And often is his gold complexion dimm'd;
    And every fair from fair sometime declines,
    By chance or nature's changing course untrimm'd;
    But thy eternal summer shall not fade,
    Nor lose possession of that fair thou owest;
    Nor shall Death brag thou wander'st in his shade,
    When in eternal lines to time thou grow'st:
        So long as men can breathe, or eyes can see,
        So long lives this, and this gives life to thee.

19 Devouring Time, blunt thou the lion's paws,
    And make the earth devour her own sweet brood;
    Pluck the keen teeth from the fierce tiger's jaws,
    And burn the long-lived phœnix in her blood;
    Make glad and sorry seasons as thou fleet'st,
    And do whate'er thou wilt, swift-footed Time,
    To the wide world and all her fading sweets;
    But I forbid thee one most heinous crime:
    O, carve not with thy hours my love's fair brow,
    Nor draw no lines there with thine antique pen;
    Him in thy course untainted do allow
    For beauty's pattern to succeeding men.
        Yet do thy worst, old Time: despite thy wrong,
        My love shall in my verse ever live young.

20 A woman's face with Nature's own hand painted
    Hast thou, the master-mistress of my passion;
    A woman's gentle heart, but not acquainted
    With shifting change, as is false women's fashion;
    An eye more bright than theirs, less false in rolling,
    Gilding the object whereupon it gazeth;
    A man in hue, all 'hues' in his controlling,
    Which steals men's eyes and women's souls amazeth.
    And for a woman wert thou first created;
    Till Nature, as she wrought thee, fell a-doting,
    And by addition me of thee defeated,
    By adding one thing to my purpose nothing.
        But since she prick'd thee out for women's pleasure,
        Mine be thy love, and thy love's use their treasure.

21 So is it not with me as with that Muse
   Stirr'd by a painted beauty to his verse,
   Who heaven itself for ornament doth use
   And every fair with his fair doth rehearse,
   Making a couplement of proud compare,
   With sun and moon, with earth and sea's rich gems,
   With April's first-born flowers, and all things rare
   That heaven's air in this huge rondure hems.
   O, let me, true in love, but truly write,
   And then believe me, my love is as fair
   As any mother's child, though not so bright
   As those gold candles fix'd in heaven's air :
        Let them say more that like of hearsay well ;
        I will not praise that purpose not to sell.

22 My glass shall not persuade me I am old,
   So long as youth and thou are of one date ;
   But when in thee time's furrows I behold,
   Then look I death my days should expiate.
   For all that beauty that doth cover thee
   Is but the seemly raiment of my heart,
   Which in thy breast doth live, as thine in me
   How can I then be elder than thou art?
   O, therefore, love, be of thyself so wary
   As I, not for myself, but for thee will ;
   Bearing thy heart, which I will keep so chary
   As tender nurse her babe from faring ill.
        Presume not on thy heart when mine is slain ;
        Thou gavest me thine, not to give back again.

23 As an unperfect actor on the stage,
   Who with his fear is put besides his part,
   Or some fierce thing replete with too much rage,
   Whose strength's abundance weakens his own heart ;
   So I, for fear of trust, forget to say
   The perfect ceremony of love's rite,
   And in mine own love's strength seem to decay,
   O'ercharged with burthen of mine own love's might.
   O, let my books be then the eloquence
   And dumb presagers of my speaking breast ;
   Who plead for love, and look for recompense,
   More than that tongue that more hath more express'd.
        O, learn to read what silent love hath writ :
        To hear with eyes belongs to love's fine wit.

24 Mine eye hath play'd the painter and hath stell'd
   Thy beauty's form in table of my heart;
   My body is the frame wherein 'tis held,
   And perspective it is best painter's art.
   For through the painter must you see his skill,
   To find where your true image pictured lies;
   Which in my bosom's shop is hanging still,
   That hath his windows glazed with thine eyes.
   Now see what good turns eyes for eyes have done:
   Mine eyes have drawn thy shape, and thine for me
   Are windows to my breast, where-through the sun
   Delights to peep, to gaze therein on thee;
          Yet eyes this cunning want to grace their art,
          They draw but what they see, know not the heart.

25 Let those who are in favour with their stars
   Of public honour and proud titles boast,
   Whilst I, whom fortune of such triumph bars
   Unlook'd for joy in that I honour most.
   Great princes' favourites their fair leaves spread
   But as the marigold at the sun's eye,
   And in themselves their pride lies buried,
   For at a frown they in their glory die.
   The painful warrior famoused for fight,
   After a thousand victories once foil'd
   Is from the book of honour razed quite,
   And all the rest forgot for which he toil'd:
          Then happy I, that love and am beloved
          Where I may not remove nor be removed.

26 Lord of my love, to whom in vassalage
   Thy merit hath my duty strongly knit,
   To thee I send this written ambassage,
   To witness duty, not to show my wit:
   Duty so great, which wit so poor as mine
   May make seem bare, in wanting words to show it,
   But that I hope some good conceit of thine
   In thy soul's thought, all naked, will bestow it;
   Till whatsoever star that guides my moving,
   Points on me graciously with fair aspect,
   And puts apparel on my tatter'd loving,
   To show me worthy of thy sweet respect:
          Then may I dare to boast how I do love thee:
          Till then not show my head where thou mayst prove me.

27 Weary with toil, I haste me to my bed,
   The dear repose for limbs with travel tired;
   But then begins a journey in my head,
   To work my mind, when body's work's expired:
   For then my thoughts, from far where I abide,
   Intend a zealous pilgrimage to thee,
   And keep my drooping eyelids open wide,
   Looking on darkness which the blind do see:
   Save that my soul's imaginary sight
   Presents thy shadow to my sightless view,
   Which like a jewel hung in ghastly night,
   Make black night beauteous and her old face new.
      Lo, thus, by day my limbs, by night my mind,
      For thee and for myself no quiet find.

28 How can I then return in happy plight,
   That am debarr'd the benefit of rest?
   When day's oppression is not eased by night,
   But day by night, and night by day, oppress'd?
   And each, though enemies to either's reign,
   Do in consent shake hands to torture me;
   The one by toil, the other to complain
   How far I toil, still farther off from thee.
   I tell the day, to please him thou art bright,
   And dost him grace when clouds do blot the heaven
   So flatter I the swart-complexion'd night;
   When sparkling stars twire not thou gild'st the even.
      But day doth daily draw my sorrows longer, [stronger.
      And night doth nightly make grief's strength seem

29 When, in disgrace with fortune and men's eyes,
   I all alone beweep my outcast state,
   And trouble deaf heaven with my bootless cries,
   And look upon myself, and curse my fate,
   Wishing me like to one more rich in hope,
   Featured like him, like him with friends possess'd,
   Desiring this man's art and that man's scope,
   With what I most enjoy contented least;
   Yet in these thoughts myself almost despising,
   Haply I think on thee, and then my state,
   Like to the lark at break of day arising
   From sullen earth, sings hymns at heaven's gate;
      For thy sweet love remember'd such wealth brings
      That then I scorn to change my state with kings.

30   When to the sessions of sweet silent thought
     I summon up remembrance of things past,
     I sigh the lack of many a thing I sought,
     And with old woes new wail my dear time's waste:
     Then can I drown an eye, unused to flow,
     For precious friends hid in death's dateless night,
     And weep afresh love's long since cancell'd woe,
     And moan the expense of many a vanish'd sight:
     Then can I grieve at grievances foregone,
     And heavily from woe to woe tell o'er
     The sad account of fore-bemoaned moan,
     Which I new pay as if not paid before.
         But if the while I think on thee, dear friend,
         All losses are restored and sorrows end.

31   Thy bosom is endeared with all hearts,
     Which I by lacking have supposed dead ;
     And there reigns love, and all love's loving parts,
     And all those friends which I thought buried.
     How many a holy and obsequious tear
     Hath dear religious love stol'n from mine eye,
     As interest of the dead, which now appear
     But things removed that hidden in thee lie !
     Thou art the grave where buried love doth live,
     Hung with the trophies of my lovers gone,
     Who all their parts of me to thee did give:
     That due of many now is thine alone:
         Their images I loved I view in thee,
         And thou, all they, hast all the all of me.

32   If thou survive my well-contented day
     When that churl Death my bones with dust shall cover,
     And shalt by fortune once more re-survey
     These poor rude lines of thy deceased lover,
     Compare them with the bettering of the time,
     And though they be outstripp'd by every pen,
     Reserve them for my love, not for their rhyme
     Exceeded by the height of happier men.
     O, then vouchsafe me but this loving thought:
     ' Had my friend's Muse grown with this growing age,
     A dearer birth than this his love had brought,
     To march in ranks of better equipage :
         But since he died, and poets better prove,
         Theirs for their style I 'll read, his for his love.'

33   Full many a glorious morning have I seen
     Flatter the mountain-tops with sovereign eye,
     Kissing with golden face the meadows green,
     Gilding pale streams with heavenly alchemy;
     Anon permit the basest clouds to ride
     With ugly rack on his celestial face,
     And from the forlorn world his visage hide,
     Stealing unseen to west with this disgrace:
     Even so my son one early morn did shine
     With all-triumphant splendour on my brow;
     But, out, alack! he was but one hour mine,
     The region cloud hath masked him from me now.
            Yet him for this my love no whit disdaineth;
            Suns of the world may stain when heaven's sun staineth.

34   Why didst thou promise such a beauteous day,
     And make me travel forth without my cloak,
     To let base clouds o'ertake me in my way,
     Hiding thy bravery in their rotten smoke?
     'Tis not enough that through the cloud thou break,
     To dry the rain on my storm-beaten face,
     For no man well of such a salve can speak
     That heals the wound and cures not the disgrace:
     Nor can thy shame give physic to my grief;
     Though thou repent, yet I have still the loss:
     The offender's sorrow lends but weak relief
     To him that bears the strong offence's cross.
            Ah, but those tears are pearl which thy love sheds,
            And they are rich and ransom all ill deeds.

35   No more be grieved at that which thou hast done:
     Roses have thorns, and silver fountains mud;
     Clouds and eclipses stain both moon and sun,
     And loathsome canker lives in sweetest bud.
     All men make faults, and even I in this,
     Authorizing thy trespass with compare,
     Myself corrupting, salving thy amiss,
     Excusing thy sins more than thy sins are;
     For to thy sensual fault I bring in sense—
     Thy adverse party is thy advocate—
     And 'gainst myself a lawful plea commence:
     Such civil war is in my love and hate,
            That I an accessary needs must be
            To that sweet thief which sourly robs from me.

36   Let me confess that we two must be twain,
    Although our undivided loves are one :
    So shall those blots that do with me remain,
    Without thy help, by me be borne alone.
    In our two loves there is but one respect,
    Though in our lives a separable spite,
    Which though it alter not love's sole effect,
    Yet doth it steal sweet hours from love's delight
    I may not evermore acknowledge thee,
    Lest my bewailed guilt should do thee shame,
    Nor thou with public kindness honour me,
    Unless thou take that honour from thy name :
        But do not so ; I love thee in such sort,
        As thou being mine, mine is thy good report.

37   As a decrepit father takes delight
    To see his active child do deeds of youth,
    So I, made lame by fortune's dearest spite,
    Take all my comfort of thy worth and truth ;
    For whether beauty, birth, or wealth, or wit,
    Or any of these all, or all, or more,
    Entitled in thy parts do crowned sit,
    I make my love engrafted to this store :
    So then I am not lame, poor, nor despised,
    Whilst that this shadow doth such substance give
    That I in thy abundance am sufficed
    And by a part of all thy glory live.
        Look, what is best, that best I wish in thee :
        This wish I have ; then ten times happy me !

38   How can my Muse want subject to invent
    While thou dost breathe, that pour'st into my verse
    Thine own sweet argument, too excellent
    For every vulgar paper to rehearse ?
    O, give thyself the thanks, if aught in me
    Worthy perusal stand against thy sight ;
    For who 's so dumb that cannot write to thee,
    When thou thyself dost give invention light ;
    Be thou the tenth Muse, ten times more in worth
    Than those old nine which rhymers invocate ;
    And he that calls on thee, let him bring forth
    Eternal numbers to outlive long date.
        If my slight Muse do please these curious days
        The pain be mine, but thine shall be the praise

39 O, how thy worth with manners may I sing,
    When thou art all the better part of me?
    What can mine own praise to mine own self bring?
    And what is 't but mine own when I praise thee?
    Even for this let us divided live,
    And our dear love lose name of single one,
    That by this separation I may give
    That due to thee which thou deservest alone.
    O absence, what a torment wouldst thou prove,
    Were it not thy sour leisure gave sweet leave
    To entertain the time with thoughts of love,
    Which time and thoughts so sweetly doth deceive,
        And that thou teachest how to make one twain,
        By praising him here who doth hence remain!

40 Take all my loves, my love, yea, take them all;
    What hast thou then more than thou hadst before?
    No love, my love, that thou mayst true love call;
    All mine was thine before thou hadst this more.
    Then, if for my love thou my love receivest,
    I cannot blame thee for my love thou usest;
    But yet be blamed, if thou thyself deceivest
    By wilful taste of what thyself refusest.
    I do forgive thy robbery, gentle thief,
    Although thou steal thee all my poverty;
    And yet, love knows, it is a greater grief
    To bear love's wrong than hate's known injury.
        Lascivious grace, in whom all ill well shows,
        Kill me with spites; yet we must not be foes.

41 Those pretty wrongs that liberty commits,
    When I am sometime absent from thy heart,
    Thy beauty and thy years full well befits,
    For still temptation follows where thou art.
    Gentle thou art, and therefore to be won,
    Beauteous thou art, therefore to be assailed;
    And when a woman woos, what woman's son
    Will sourly leave her till she hath prevailed?
    Ay me! but yet thou mightst my seat forbear,
    And chide thy beauty and thy straying youth,
    Who lead thee in their riot even there
    Where thou art forced to break a twofold truth,
        Hers, by thy beauty tempting her to thee,
        Thine, by thy beauty being false to me.

42 That thou hast her, it is not all my grief,
And yet it may be said I loved her dearly;
That she hath thee, is of my wailing chief,
A loss in love that touches me more nearly
Loving offenders, thus I will excuse ye:
Thou dost love her, because thou know'st I love her;
And for my sake even so doth she abuse me,
Suffering my friend for my sake to approve her.
If I lose thee, my loss is my love's gain,
And losing her, my friend hath found that loss;
Both find each other, and I lose both twain,
And both for my sake lay on me this cross:
    But here 's the joy: my friend and I are one;
    Sweet flattery! then she loves but me alone.

43 When most I wink, then do mine eyes best see,
For all the day they view things unrespected;
But when I sleep, in dreams they look on thee,
And, darkly bright, are bright in dark directed.
Then thou, whose shadow shadows doth make bright,
How would thy shadow's form form happy show
To the clear day with thy much clearer light,
When to unseeing eyes thy shade shines so!
How would, I say, mine eyes be blessed made
By looking on thee in the living day,
When in dead night thy fair imperfect shade
Through heavy sleep on sightless eyes doth stay!
    All days are nights to see till I see thee,
    And nights bright days when dreams do show thee me.

44 If the dull substance of my flesh were thought,
Injurious distance should not stop my way;
For then, despite of space, I would be brought,
From limits far remote, where thou dost stay.
No matter then although my foot did stand
Upon the farthest earth removed from thee;
For nimble thought can jump both sea and land,
As soon as think the place where he would be.
But, ah, thought kills me, that I am not thought,
To leap large lengths of miles when thou art gone,
But that, so much of earth and water wrought,
I must attend time's leisure with my moan;
    Receiving nought by elements so slow
    But heavy tears, badges of either's woe.

45 The other two, slight air and purging fire,
    Are both with thee, wherever I abide;
    The first my thought, the other my desire,
    These present-absent with swift motion slide.
    For when these quicker elements are gone
    In tender embassy of love to thee,
    My life, being made of four, with two alone
    Sinks down to death, oppress'd with melancholy;
    Until life's composition be recured
    By those swift messengers return'd from thee,
    Who even but now come back again, assured
    Of thy fair health, recounting it to me:
        This told, I joy; but then no longer glad,
        I send them back again, and straight grow sad.

46 Mine eye and heart are at a mortal war,
    How to divide the conquest of thy sight;
    Mine eye my heart thy picture's sight would bar,
    My heart mine eye the freedom of that right.
    My heart doth plead that thou in him dost lie,
    A closet never pierced with crystal eyes,
    But the defendant doth that plea deny,
    And says in him thy fair appearance lies.
    To 'cide this title is impanneled
    A quest of thoughts, all tenants to the heart;
    And by their verdict is determined
    The clear eye's moiety and the dear heart's part:
        As thus; mine eye's due is thine outward part,
        And my heart's right thine inward love of heart.

47 Betwixt mine eye and heart a league is took,
    And each doth good turns now unto the other:
    When that mine eye is famish'd for a look,
    Or heart in love with sighs himself doth smother,
    With my love's picture then my eye doth feast
    And to the painted banquet bids my heart;
    Another time mine eye is my heart's guest
    And in his thoughts of love doth share a part:
    So, either by thy picture or my love,
    Thyself away art present still with me;
    For thou not farther than my thoughts canst move,
    And I am still with them and they with thee;
        Or, if they sleep, thy picture in my sight
        Awakes my heart to heart's and eye's delight.

48 How careful was I, when I took my way,
　　Each trifle under truest bars to thrust,
　　That to my use it might unused stay
　　From hands of falsehood, in sure wards of trust!
　　But thou, to whom my jewels trifles are,
　　Most worthy comfort, now my greatest grief,
　　Thou, best of dearest and mine only care,
　　Art left the prey of every vulgar thief.
　　Thee have I not lock'd up in any chest,
　　Save where thou art not, though I feel thou art,
　　Within the gentle closure of my breast,
　　From whence at pleasure thou mayst come and part;
　　　　And even thence thou wilt be stol'n, I fear,
　　　　For truth proves thievish for a prize so dear.

49 Against that time, if ever that time come,
　　When I shall see thee frown on my defects,
　　When as thy love hath cast his utmost sum,
　　Call'd to that audit by advised respects;
　　Against that time when thou shalt strangely pass,
　　And scarcely greet me with that sun, thine eye,
　　When love, converted from the thing it was,
　　Shall reasons find of settled gravity;
　　Against that time do I ensconce me here
　　Within the knowledge of mine own desert,
　　And this my hand against myself uprear,
　　To guard the lawful reasons on thy part:
　　　　To leave poor me thou hast the strength of laws,
　　　　Since why to love I can allege no cause.

50 How heavy do I journey on the way,
　　When what I seek, my weary travel's end,
　　Doth teach that ease and that repose to say,
　　'Thus far the miles are measured from thy friend!'
　　The beast that bears me, tired with my woe,
　　Plods dully on, to bear that weight in me,
　　As if by some instinct the wretch did know
　　His rider loved not speed, being made from thee:
　　The bloody spur cannot provoke him on
　　That sometimes anger thrusts into his hide;
　　Which heavily he answers with a groan,
　　More sharp to me than spurring to his side;
　　　　For that same groan doth put this in my mind;
　　　　My grief lies onward, and my joy behind.

51 Thus can my love excuse the slow offence
     Of my dull bearer when from thee I speed:
     From where thou art why should I haste me thence?
     Till I return, of posting is no need.
     O, what excuse will my poor beast then find,
     When swift extremity can seem but slow?
     Then should I spur, though mounted on the wind,
     In winged speed no motion shall I know:
     Then can no horse with my desire keep pace;
     Therefore desire, of perfect'st love being made,
     Shall neigh—no dull flesh—in his fiery race;
     But love, for love, thus shall excuse my jade;
          Since from thee going he went wilful-slow,
          Towards thee I'll run and give him leave to go.

52 So am I as the rich, whose blessed key
     Can bring him to his sweet up-locked treasure,
     The which he will not every hour survey,
     For blunting the fine point of seldom pleasure.
     Therefore are feasts so solemn and so rare,
     Since, seldom coming, in the long year set,
     Like stones of worth they thinly placed are,
     Or captain jewels in the carcanet.
     So is the time that keeps you as my chest,
     Or as the wardrobe which the robe doth hide,
     To make some special instant special blest,
     By new unfolding his imprison'd pride.
          Blessed are you, whose worthiness gives scope,
          Being had, to triumph, being lack'd, to hope.

53 What is your substance, whereof are you made,
     That millions of strange shadows on you tend?
     Since every one hath, every one, one shade,
     And you, but one, can every shadow lend.
     Describe Adonis, and the counterfeit
     Is poorly imitated after you;
     On Helen's cheek all art of beauty set,
     And you in Grecian tires are painted new:
     Speak of the spring and foison of the year,
     The one doth shadow of your beauty show,
     The other as your bounty doth appear;
     And you in every blessed shape we know.
          In all external grace you have some part,
          But you like none, none you, for constant heart.

54 O, how much more doth beauty beauteous seem
By that sweet ornament which truth doth give!
The rose looks fair, but fairer we it deem
For that sweet odour which doth in it live.
The canker-blooms have full as deep a dye
As the perfumed tincture of the roses,
Hang on such thorns, and play as wantonly
When summer's breath their masked buds discloses:
But, for their virtue only is their show,
They live unwoo'd and unrespected fade;
Die to themselves.   Sweet roses do not so;
Of their sweet deaths are sweetest odours made:
    And so of you, beauteous and lovely youth,
      When that shall vade, by verse distills your truth.

55 Not marble, nor the gilded monuments
Of princes, shall outlive this powerful rhyme?
But you shall shine more bright in these contents
Than unswept stone, besmear'd with sluttish time.
When wasteful war shall statues overturn,
And broils root out the work of masonry,
Nor Mars his sword nor war's quick fire shall burn
The living record of your memory.
'Gainst death and all-oblivious enmity
Shall you pace forth; your praise shall still find room
Even in the eyes of all posterity
That wear this world out to the ending doom.
    So, till the judgement that yourself arise,
      You live in this, and dwell in lovers' eyes.

56 Sweet love, renew thy force; be it not said
Thy edge should blunter be than appetite,
Which but to-day by feeding is allay'd,
To-morrow sharpen'd in his former might:
So, love, be thou; although to-day thou fill
Thy hungry eyes even till they wink with fulness,
To-morrow see again, and do not kill
The spirit of love with a perpetual dulness.
Let this sad interim like the ocean be
Which parts the shore, where two contracted new
Come daily to the banks, that, when they see
Return of love, more blest may be the view;
    Or call it winter, which, being full of care,
      Makes summer's welcome thrice more wish'd, more rare.

57 Being your slave, what should I do but tend
Upon the hours and times of your desire?
I have no precious time at all to spend,
Nor services to do, till you require.
Nor dare I chide the world-without-end hour
Whilst I, my sovereign, watch the clock for you,
Nor think the bitterness of absence sour
When you have bid your servant once adieu;
Nor dare I question with my jealous thought
Where you may be, or your affairs suppose,
But, like a sad slave, stay and think of nought
Save, where you are how happy you make those.
    So true a fool is love that in your will,
    Though you do any thing, he thinks no ill.

58 What god forbid that made me first your slave,
I should in thought control your times of pleasure,
Or at your hand the account of hours to crave,
Being your vassal, bound to stay your leisure!
O, let me suffer, being at your beck,
The imprison'd absence of your liberty;
And patience, tame to sufferance, bide each check,
Without accusing you of injury.
Be where you list, your charter is so strong
That you yourself may privilege your time
To what you will; to you it doth belong
Yourself to pardon of self-doing crime.
    I am to wait, though waiting so be hell,
    Not blame your pleasure, be it ill or well.

59 If there be nothing new, but that which is
Hath been before, how are our brains beguiled,
Which, labouring for invention, bear amiss
The second burthen of a former child!
O, that record could with a backward look,
Even of five hundred courses of the sun,
Show me your image in some antique book,
Since mind at first in character was done.
That I might see what the old world could say
To this composed wonder of your frame;
Whether we are mended, or whether better they,
Or whether revolution be the same.
    O, sure I am, the wits of former days
    To subjects worse have given admiring praise.

60 Like as the waves make towards the pebbled shore,
So do our minutes hasten to their end ;
Each changing place with that which goes before,
In sequent toil all forwards do contend.
Nativity, once in the main of light,
Crawls to maturity, wherewith being crown'd,
Crooked eclipses 'gainst his glory fight,
And Time that gave doth now his gift confound.
Time doth transfix the flourish set on youth
And delves the parallels in beauty's brow,
Feeds on the rarities of nature's truth,
And nothing stands but for his scythe to mow :
    And yet to times in hope my verse shall stand,
    Praising thy worth, despite his cruel hand.

61 Is it thy will thy image should keep open
My heavy eyelids to the weary night ?
Dost thou desire my slumbers should be broken,
While shadows like to thee do mock my sight ?
Is it thy spirit that thou send'st from thee
So far from home into my deeds to pry,
To find out shames and idle hours in me,
The scope and tenour of thy jealousy ?
O, no ! thy love, though much, is not so great :
It is my love that keeps mine eye awake ;
Mine own true love that dost my rest defeat,
To play the watchman ever for thy sake :
    For thee watch I whilst thou doth wake elsewhere,
    From me far off, with others all too near.

62 Sin of self-love possesseth all mine eye
And all my soul and all my every part ;
And for this sin there is no remedy,
It is so grounded inward in my heart.
Methinks no face so gracious is as mine,
No shape so true, no truth of such account ;
And for myself mine own worth do define,
As I all other in all worths surmount.
But when my glass shows me myself indeed,
Beated and chopp'd with tann'd antiquity,
Mine own self-love quite contrary I read ;
Self so self-loving were iniquity.
    'Tis thee, myself, that for myself I praise,
    Painting my age with beauty of thy days.

63 Against my love shall be, as I am now,
  With Time's injurious hand crush'd and o'erworn;
  When hours have drain'd his blood and fill'd his brow
  With lines and wrinkles; when his youthful morn
  Hath travell'd on to age's steepy night,
  And all those beauties whereof now he's king
  Are vanishing or vanish'd out of sight,
  Stealing away the treasure of his spring;
  For such a time do I now fortify
  Against confounding age's cruel knife,
  That he shall never cut from memory
  My sweet love's beauty, though my lover's life:
      His beauty shall in these black lines be seen,
      And they shall live, and he in them still green.

64 When I have seen by Time's fell hand defaced
  The rich-proud cost of outworn buried age;
  When sometime lofty towers I see down-razed,
  And brass eternal slave to mortal rage;
  When I have seen the hungry ocean gain
  Advantage on the kingdom of the shore
  And the firm soil win of the watery main,
  Increasing store with loss and loss with store;
  When I have seen such interchange of state,
  Or state itself confounded to decay;
  Ruin hath taught me thus to ruminate,
  That Time will come and take my love away.
      This thought is as a death, which cannot choose
      But weep to have that which it fears to lose.

65 Since brass, nor stone, nor earth, nor boundless sea,
  But sad mortality o'er-sways their power,
  How with this rage shall beauty hold a plea
  Whose action is no stronger than a flower?
  O, how shall summer's honey breath hold out
  Against the wreckful siege of battering days,
  When rocks impregnable are not so stout,
  Nor gates of steel so strong, but Time decays?
  O fearful meditation! where, alack,
  Shall Time's best jewel from Time's chest lie hid?
  Or what strong hand can hold his swift foot back?
  Or who his spoil of beauty can forbid?
      O, none, unless this miracle have might,
      That in black ink my love may still shine bright.

66 Tired with all these, for restful death I cry,
    As, to behold desert a beggar born,
    And needy nothing trimm'd in jollity,
    And purest faith unhappily forsworn,
    And gilded honour shamefully misplaced,
    And maiden virtue rudely strumpeted,
    And right perfection wrongfully disgraced,
    And strength by limping sway disabled,
    And art made tongue-tied by authority,
    And folly, doctor-like, controlling skill,
    And simple truth miscall'd simplicity,
    And captive good attending captain ill:
        Tired with all these, from these would I be gone,
        Save that, to die, I leave my love alone.

67 Ah, wherefore with infection should he live
    And with his presence grace impiety,
    That sin by him advantage should achieve
    And lace itself with his society?
    Why should false painting imitate his cheek,
    And steal dead seeing of his living hue?
    Why should poor beauty indirectly seek
    Roses of shadow, since his rose is true?
    Why should he live, now Nature bankrupt is,
    Beggar'd of blood to blush through lively veins?
    For she hath no exchequer now but his,
    And, proud of many, lives upon his gains.
        O, him she stores, to show what wealth she had
        In days long since, before these last so bad.

68 Thus is his cheek the map of days outworn,
    When beauty lived and died as flowers do now,
    Before these bastard signs of fair were born,
    Or durst inhabit on a living brow;
    Before the golden tresses of the dead,
    The right of sepulchres, were shorn away,
    To live a second life on second head;
    Ere beauty's dead fleece made another gay:
    In him those holy antique hours are seen,
    Without all ornament itself and true,
    Making no summer of another's green,
    Robbing no old to dress his beauty new;
        And him as for a map doth Nature store,
        To show false Art what beauty was of yore.

69 Those parts of thee that the world's eye doth view
    Want nothing that the thought of hearts can mend;
    All tongues, the voice of souls, give thee that due,
    Uttering bare truth, even so as foes commend.
    Thy outward thus with outward praise is crown'd;
    But those same tongues, that give thee so thine own,
    In other accents do this praise confound
    By seeing farther than the eye hath shown.
    They look into the beauty of thy mind,
    And that, in guess, they measure by thy deeds;
    Then, churls, their thoughts, although their eyes were kind,
    To thy fair flower add the rank smell of weeds:
        But why thy odour matcheth not thy show,
        The soil is this, that thou dost common grow.

70 That thou art blamed shall not be thy defect,
    For slander's mark was ever yet the fair;
    The ornament of beauty is suspect,
    A crow that flies in heaven's sweetest air.
    So thou be good, slander doth but approve
    Thy worth the greater, being woo'd of time;
    For canker vice the sweetest buds doth love,
    And thou present'st a pure unstained prime.
    Thou hast pass'd by the ambush of young days,
    Either not assail'd, or victor being charged;
    Yet this thy praise cannot be so thy praise,
    To tie up envy evermore enlarged:
        If some suspect of ill mask'd not thy show,
        Then thou alone kingdoms of hearts shouldst owe.

71 No longer mourn for me when I am dead
    Than you shall hear the surly sullen bell
    Give warning to the world that I am fled
    From this vile world, with vilest worms to dwell:
    Nay, if you read this line, remember not
    The hand that writ it; for I love you so,
    That I in your sweet thoughts would be forgot,
    If thinking on me then should make you woe.
    O, if, I say, you look upon this verse
    When I perhaps compounded am with clay,
    Do not so much as my poor name rehearse,
    But let your love even with my life decay;
        Lest the wise world should look into your moan,
        And mock you with me after I am gone.

72 O, lest the world should task you to recite
   What merit lived in me, that you should love
   After my death, dear love, forget me quite,
   For you in me can nothing worthy prove;
   Unless you would devise some virtuous lie,
   To do more for me than mine own desert,
   And hang more praise upon deceased I
   Than niggard truth would willingly impart:
   O, lest your true love may seem false in this
   That you for love speak well of me untrue,
   My name be buried where my body is,
   And live no more to shame nor me nor you.
        For I am shamed by that which I bring forth,
        And so should you, to love things nothing worth.

73 That time of year thou mayst in me behold
   When yellow leaves, or none, or few, do hang
   Upon those boughs which shake against the cold,
   Bare ruin'd choirs, where late the sweet birds sang.
   In me thou see'st the twilight of such day
   As after sunset fadeth in the west;
   Which by and by black night doth take away,
   Death's second self, that seals up all in rest.
   In me thou see'st the glowing of such fire,
   That on the ashes of his youth doth lie,
   As the death-bed whereon it must expire,
   Consumed with that which it was nourish'd by.
        This thou perceivest, which makes thy love more strong,
        To love that well which thou must leave ere long.

74 But be contented: when that fell arrest
   Without all bail shall carry me away,
   My life hath in this line some interest,
   Which for memorial still with thee shall stay.
   When thou reviewest this, thou dost review
   The very part was consecrate to thee:
   The earth can have but earth, which is his due;
   My spirit is thine, the better part of me:
   So then thou hast but lost the dregs of life,
   The prey of worms, my body being dead;
   The coward conquest of a wretch's knife,
   Too base of thee to be remembered.
        The worth of that is that which it contains,
        And that is this, and this with thee remains

75 So are you to my thoughts as food to life,
Or as sweet-season'd showers are to the ground;
And for the peace of you I hold such strife
As 'twixt a miser and his wealth is found;
Now proud as an enjoyer, and anon
Doubting the filching age will steal his treasure;
Now counting best to be with you alone,
Then better'd that the world may see my pleasure:
Sometime all full with feasting on your sight,
And by and by clean starved for a look;
Possessing or pursuing no delight,
Save what is had or must from you be took.
　　　Thus do I pine and surfeit day by day,
　　　Or gluttoning on all, or all away.

76 Why is my verse so barren of new pride,
So far from variation or quick change?
Why with the time do I not glance aside
To new-found methods and to compounds strange?
Why write I still all one, ever the same,
And keep invention in a noted weed,
That every word doth almost tell my name,
Showing their birth and where they did proceed?
O, know, sweet love, I always write of you,
And you and love are still my argument;
So all my best is dressing old words new,
Spending again what is already spent:
　　　For as the sun is daily new and old,
　　　So is my love still telling what is told.

77 Thy glass will show thee how thy beauties wear,
Thy dial how thy precious minutes waste;
The vacant leaves thy mind's imprint will bear,
And of this book this learning mayst thou taste
The wrinkles which thy glass will truly show
Of mouthed graves will give thee memory;
Thou by thy dial's shady stealth mayst know
Time's thievish progress to eternity.
Look, what thy memory cannot contain
Commit to these waste blanks, and thou shalt find
Those children nursed, deliver'd from thy brain
To take a new acquaintance of thy mind.
　　　These offices, so oft as thou wilt look,
　　　Shall profit thee and much enrich thy book.

78 So oft have I invoked thee for my Muse
And found such fair assistance in my verse
As every alien pen hath got my use
And under thee their poesy disperse.
Thine eyes, that taught the dumb on high to sing
And heavy ignorance aloft to fly,
Have added feathers to the learned's wing
And given grace a double majesty.
Yet be most proud of that which I compile,
Whose influence is thine and born of thee:
In others' works thou dost but mend the style,
And arts with thy sweet graces graced be;
  But thou art all my art, and dost advance
  As high as learning my rude ignorance.

79 Whilst I alone did call upon thy aid,
My verse alone had all thy gentle grace;·
But now my gracious numbers are decay'd,
And my sick Muse doth give another place.
I grant, sweet love, thy lovely argument
Deserves the travail of a worthier pen;
Yet what of thee thy poet doth invent
He robs thee of, and pays it thee again.
He lends thee virtue, and he stole that word
For thy behaviour; beauty doth he give,
And found it in thy cheek: he can afford
No praise to thee but what in thee doth live.
  Then thank him not for that which he doth say,
  Since what he owes thee thou thyself dost pay.

80 O, how I faint when I of you do write,
Knowing a better spirit doth use your name,
And in the praise thereof spends all his might,
To make me tongue-tied, speaking of your fame!
But since your worth, wide as the ocean is,
The humble as the proudest sail doth bear,
My saucy bark, inferior far to his,
On your broad main doth wilfully appear.
Your shallowest help will hold me up afloat,
Whilst he upon your soundless deep doth ride;
Or, being wreck'd, I am a worthless boat,
He of tall building and of goodly pride:
  Then if he thrive and I be cast away,
  The worst was this; my love was my decay.

81 Or I shall live your epitaph to make,
    Or you survive when I in earth am rotten;
    From hence your memory death cannot take,
    Although in me each part will be forgotten.
    Your name from hence immortal life shall have,
    Though I, once gone, to all the world must die:
    The earth can yield me but a common grave,
    When you entombed in men's eyes shall lie.
    Your monument shall be my gentle verse,
    Which eyes not yet created shall o'er-read;
    And tongues to be your being shall rehearse,
    When all the breathers of this world are dead,
        You shall live—such virtue hath my pen—   [men.
        Where breath most breathes, even in the mouths of

82 I grant thou wert not married to my Muse,
    And therefore mayst without attaint o'erlook
    The dedicated words which writers use
    Of their fair subject, blessing every book
    Thou art as fair in knowledge as in hue,
    Finding thy worth a limit past my praise;
    And therefore art enforced to seek anew
    Some fresher stamp of the time-bettering days,
    And do so, love; yet when they have devised
    What strained touches rhetoric can lend,
    Thou truly fair wert truly sympathized
    In true plain words by thy true-telling friend;
        And their gross painting might be better used
        Where cheeks need blood; in thee it is abused.

83 I never saw that you did painting need,
    And therefore to your fair no painting set;
    I found, or thought I found, you did exceed
    The barren tender of a poet's debt:
    And therefore have I slept in your report,
    That you yourself, being extant, well might show
    How far a modern quill doth come too short,
    Speaking of worth, what worth in you doth grow.
    This silence for my sin you did impute,
    Which shall be most my glory, being dumb;
    For I impair not beauty being mute,
    When others would give life and bring a tomb
        There lives more life in one of your fair eyes
        Than both your poets can in praise devise.

497

84 Who is it that says most? which can say more
   Than this rich praise, that you alone are you?
In whose confine immured is the store
   Which should example where your equal grew.
Lean penury within that pen doth dwell
   That to his subject lends not some small glory;
But he that writes of you, if he can tell
   That you are you, so dignifies his story.
Let him but copy what in you is writ,
   Not making worse what nature made so clear,
And such a counterpart shall fame his wit,
   Making his style admired every where.
     You to your beauteous blessings add a curse,
     Being fond on praise, which makes your praises worse.

85 My tongue-tied Muse in manners holds her still,
   While comments of your praise, richly compiled,
Reserve their character with golden quill,
   And precious phrase by all the Muses filed.
I think good thoughts, whilst other write good words,
   And, like unletter'd clerk, still cry 'Amen'
To every hymn that able spirit affords,
   In polish'd form of well refined pen.
Hearing you praised, I say ''Tis so, 'tis true,'
   And to the most of praise add something more;
But that is in my thought, whose love to you,
   Though words come hindmost, holds his rank before.
     Then others for the breath of words respect,
     Me for my dumb thoughts, speaking in effect.

86 Was it the proud full sail of his great verse,
   Bound for the prize of all too precious you,
That did my ripe thoughts in my brain inhearse,
   Making their tomb the womb wherein they grew?
Was it his spirit, by spirits taught to write
   Above a mortal pitch, that struck me dead?
No, neither he, nor his compeers by night
   Giving him aid, my verse astonished.
He, nor that affable familiar ghost
   Which nightly gulls him with intelligence,
As victors, of my silence cannot boast;
   I was not sick of any fear from thence:
     But when your countenance fill'd up his line,
     Then lack'd I matter; that enfeebled mine.

87 Farewell! thou art too dear for my possessing,
And like enough thou know'st thy estimate:
The charter of thy worth gives thee releasing;
My bonds in thee are all determinate.
For how do I hold thee but by thy granting?
And for that riches where is my deserving?
The cause of this fair gift in me is wanting,
And so my patent back again is swerving.
Thyself thou gavest, thy own worth then not knowing,
Or me, to whom thou gavest it, else mistaking;
So thy great gift, upon misprision growing,
Comes home again, on better judgement making.
    Thus have I had thee, as a dream doth flatter,
    In sleep a king, but waking no such matter.

88 When thou shalt be disposed to set me light,
And place my merit in the eye of scorn,
Upon thy side against myself I'll fight,
And prove thee virtuous, though thou art forsworn.
With mine own weakness being best acquainted,
Upon thy part I can set down a story
Of faults conceal'd, wherein I am attainted;
That thou in losing me shalt win much glory:
And I by this will be a gainer too;
For bending all my loving thoughts on thee,
The injuries that to myself I do,
Doing thee vantage, double-vantage me.
    Such is my love, to thee I so belong,
    That for thy right myself will bear all wrong.

89 Say that thou didst forsake me for some fault,
And I will comment upon that offence:
Speak of my lameness, and I straight will halt,
Against thy reasons making no defence.
Thou canst not, love, disgrace me half so ill,
To set a form upon desired change,
As I'll myself disgrace; knowing thy will,
I will acquaintance strangle and look strange;
Be absent from thy walks; and in my tongue
Thy sweet beloved name no more shall dwell,
Lest I, too much profane, should do it wrong,
And haply of our old acquaintance tell.
    For thee, against myself I'll vow debate,
    For I must ne'er love him whom thou dost hate.

90 Then hate me when thou wilt; if ever, now;
    Now, while the world is bent my deeds to cross,
    Join with the spite of fortune, make me bow,
    And do not drop in for an after-loss:
    Ah, do not, when my heart hath 'scaped this sorrow,
    Come in the rearward of a conquer'd woe;
    Give not a windy night a rainy morrow,
    To linger out a purposed overthrow.
    If thou wilt leave me, do not leave me last,
    When other petty griefs have done their spite,
    But in the onset come: so shall I taste
    At first the very worst of fortune's might;
        And other strains of woe, which now seem woe,
        Compared with loss of thee will not seem so.

91 Some glory in their birth, some in their skill,
    Some in their wealth, some in their body's force;
    Some in their garments, though new-fangled ill;
    Some in their hawks and hounds, some in their horse;
    And every humour hath his adjunct pleasure,
    Wherein it finds a joy above the rest:
    But these particulars are not my measure;
    All these I better in one general best.
    Thy love is better than high birth to me,
    Richer than wealth, prouder than garments' cost,
    Of more delight than hawks or horses be;
    And having thee, of all men's pride I boast:
        Wretched in this alone, that thou mayst take)
        All this away and me most wretched make.

92 But do thy worst to steal thyself away,
    For term of life thou art assured mine;
    And life no longer than thy love will stay,
    For it depends upon that love of thine.
    Then need I not to fear the worst of wrongs,
    When in the least of them my life hath end.
    I see a better state to me belongs
    Than that which on thy humour doth depend:
    Thou canst not vex me with inconstant mind,
    Since that my life on thy revolt doth lie.
    O, what a happy title do I find,
    Happy to have thy love, happy to die!
        But what 's so blessed-fair that fears no blot?
        Thou mayst be false, and yet I know it not.

93 So shall I live, supposing thou art true,
   Like a deceived husband ; so love's face
   May still seem love to me, though alter'd new;
   Thy looks with me, thy heart in other place:
   For there can live no hatred in thine eye,
   Therefore in that I cannot know thy change.
   In many's looks the false heart's history
   Is writ in moods and frowns and wrinkles strange,
   But heaven in thy creation did decree
   That in thy face sweet love should ever dwell ;
   Whate'er thy thoughts or thy heart's workings be,
   Thy looks should nothing thence but sweetness tell.
      How like Eve's apple doth thy beauty grow,
      If thy sweet virtue answer not thy show

94 They that have power to hurt and will do none,
   That do not do the thing they most do show,
   Who, moving others, are themselves as stone,
   Unmoved, cold and to temptation slow ;
   They rightly do inherit heaven's graces
   And husband nature's riches from expense ;
   They are the lords and owners of their faces,
   Others but stewards of their excellence.
   The summer's flower is to the summer sweet,
   Though to itself it only live and die,
   But if that flower with base infection meet,
   The basest weed outbraves his dignity :
      For sweetest things turn sourest by their deeds ;
      Lilies that fester smell far worse than weeds.

95 How sweet and lovely dost thou make the shame
   Which, like a canker in the fragrant rose,
   Doth spot the beauty of thy budding name !
   O, in what sweets dost thou thy sins inclose !
   That tongue that tells the story of thy days,
   Making lascivious comments on thy sport,
   Cannot dispraise but in a kind of praise ;
   Naming thy name blesses an ill report.
   O, what a mansion have those vices got
   Which for their habitation chose out thee,
   Where beauty's veil doth cover every blot
   And all things turn to fair that eyes can see !
      Take heed, dear heart, of this large privilege ;
      The hardest knife ill used doth lose his edge.

96 Some say, thy fault is youth, some wantonness;
    Some say, thy grace is youth and gentle sport;
    Both grace and faults are loved of more and less:
    Thou makest faults graces that to thee resort.
    As on the finger of a throned queen
    The basest jewel will be well esteem'd,
    So are those errors that in thee are seen
    To truths translated and for true things deem'd.
    How many lambs might the stern wolf betray,
    If like a lamb he could his looks translate!
    How many gazers mightst thou lead away,
    If thou wouldst use the strength of all thy state!
            But do not so; I love thee in such sort,
            As thou being mine, mine is thy good report.

97 How like a winter hath my absence been
    From thee, the pleasure of the fleeting year!
    What freezings have I felt, what dark days seen!
    What old December's bareness every where!
    And yet this time removed was summer's time;
    The teeming autumn, big with rich increase,
    Bearing the wanton burthen of the prime,
    Like widowed wombs after their lords' decease:
    Yet this abundant issue seem'd to me
    But hope of orphans and unfather'd fruit;
    For summer and his pleasures wait on thee,
    And, thou away, the very birds are mute;
            Or, if they sing, 'tis with so dull a cheer
            That leaves look pale, dreading the winter's near.

98 From you have I been absent in the spring,
    When proud-pied April, dress'd in all his trim,
    Hath put a spirit of youth in every thing,
    That heavy Saturn laugh'd and leap'd with him.
    Yet nor the lay of birds, nor the sweet smell
    Of different flowers in odour and in hue,
    Could make me any summer's story tell,
    Or from their proud lap pluck them where they grew:
    Nor did I wonder at the lily's white,
    Nor praise the deep vermilion in the rose;
    They were but sweet, but figures of delight,
    Drawn after you, you pattern of all those.
            Yet seem'd it winter still, and, you away,
            As with your shadow I with these did play.

99 The forward violet thus did I chide:
    Sweet thief, whence didst thou steal thy sweet that smells,
    If not from my love's breath?   The purple pride
    Which on thy soft cheek for complexion dwells
    In my love's veins thou hast too grossly dyed.
    The lily I condemned for thy hand,
    And buds of marjoram had stol'n thy hair;
    The roses fearfully on thorns did stand,
    One blushing shame, another white despair;
    A third, nor red nor white, had stol'n of both,
    And to his robbery had annex'd thy breath;
    But, for his theft, in pride of all his growth
    A vengeful canker eat him up to death.
          More flowers I noted, yet I none could see
          But sweet or colour it had stol'n from thee.

100 Where art thou, Muse, that thou forget'st so long
    To speak of that which gives thee all thy might?
    Spend'st thou thy fury on some worthless song,
    Darkening thy power to lend base subjects light?
    Return, forgetful Muse, and straight redeem
    In gentle numbers time so idly spent;
    Sing to the ear that doth thy lays esteem
    And gives thy pen both skill and argument.
    Rise, resty Muse, my love's sweet face survey,
    If Time have any wrinkle graven there;
    If any, be a satire to decay,
    And make Time's spoils despised every where.
          Give my love fame faster than Time wastes life;
          So thou prevent'st his scythe and crooked knife.

101 O truant Muse, what shall be thy amends
    For thy neglect of truth in beauty dyed?
    Both truth and beauty on my love depends;
    So dost thou too, and therein dignified.
    Make answer, Muse: wilt thou not haply say,
    'Truth needs no colour, with his colour fix'd;
    Beauty no pencil, beauty's truth to lay;
    But best is best, if never intermix'd'?
    Because he needs no praise, wilt thou be dumb?
    Excuse not silence so, for 't lies in thee
    To make him much outlive a gilded tomb
    And to be praised of ages yet to be.
          Then do thy office, Muse; I teach thee how
          To make him seem long hence as he shows now.

102   My love is strengthen'd, though more weak in seeming;
      I love not less, though less the show appear:
      That love is merchandized whose rich esteeming
      The owner's tongue doth publish every where.
      Our love was new, and then but in the spring,
      When I was wont to greet it with my lays;
      As Philomel in summer's front doth sing,
      And stops her pipe in growth of riper days:
      Not that the summer is less pleasant now
      Than when her mournful hymns did hush the night¹
      But that wild music burthens every bough,
      And sweets grow common lose their dear delight.
          Therefore, like her, I sometime hold my tongue,
          Because I would not dull you with my song.

103   Alack, what poverty my Muse brings forth,
      That having such a scope to show her pride,
      The argument, all bare, is of more worth
      Than when it hath my added praise beside!
      O, blame me not, if I no more can write!
      Look in your glass, and there appears a face
      That over-goes my blunt invention quite,
      Dulling my lines and doing me disgrace.
      Were it not sinful then, striving to mend,
      To mar the subject that before was well?
      For to no other pass my verses tend
      Than of your graces and your gifts to tell;
          And more, much more, than in my verse can sit,
          Your own glass shows you when you look in it.

104   To me, fair friend, you never can be old,
      For as you were when first your eye I eyed,
      Such seems your beauty still.   Three winters cold
      Have from the forests shook three summers' pride,
      Three beauteous springs to yellow autumn turn'd
      In process of the seasons have I seen,
      Three April perfumes in three hot Junes burn'd,
      Since first I saw you fresh, which yet are green.
      Ah, yet doth beauty, like a dial-hand,
      Steal from his figure, and no pace perceived;
      So your sweet hue, which methinks still doth stand,
      Hath motion, and mine eye may be deceived:
          For fear of which, hear this, thou age unbred;
          Ere you were born was beauty's summer dead.

105 Let not my love be call'd idolatry,
      Nor my beloved as an idol show,
      Since all alike my songs and praises be
      To one, of one, still such, and ever so.
      Kind is my love to-day, to-morrow kind
      Still constant in a wondrous excellence;
      Therefore my verse to constancy confined,
      One thing expressing, leaves out difference.
      'Fair, kind, and true,' is all my argument,
      'Fair, kind, and true,' varying to other words;
      And in this change is my invention spent,
      Three themes in one, which wondrous scope affords.
            'Fair, kind, and true,' have often lived alone,
            Which three till now never kept seat in one.

106 When in the chronicle of wasted time
      I see descriptions of the fairest wights,
      And beauty making beautiful old rhyme
      In praise of ladies dead and lovely knights,
      Then, in the blazon of sweet beauty's best,
      Of hand, of foot, of lip, of eye, of brow,
      I see their antique pen would have express'd
      Even such a beauty as you master now.
      So all their praises are but prophecies
      Of this our time, all you prefiguring;
      And, for they look'd but with divining eyes,
      They had not skill enough your worth to sing:
            For we, which now behold these present days,
            Have eyes to wonder, but lack tongues to praise.

107 Not mine own fears, nor the prophetic soul
      Of the wide world dreaming on things to come,
      Can yet the lease of my true love control,
      Supposed as forfeit to a confined doom.
      The mortal moon hath her eclipse endured,
      And the sad augurs mock their own presage;
      Incertainties now crown themselves assured,
      And peace proclaims olives of endless age.
      Now with the drops of this most balmy time
      My love looks fresh, and Death to me subscribes,
      Since, spite of him, I'll live in this poor rhyme,
      While he insults o'er dull and speechless tribes:
            And thou in this shalt find thy monument,
            When tyrants' crests and tombs of brass are spent.

108 What's in the brain, that ink may character,
     Which hath not figured to thee my true spirit?
     What's new to speak, what new to register,
     That may express my love, or thy dear merit?
     Nothing, sweet boy; but yet, like prayers divine,
     I must each day say o'er the very same;
     Counting no old thing old, thou mine, I thine,
     Even as when first I hallowed thy fair name.
     So that eternal love in love's fresh case
     Weighs not the dust and injury of age,
     Nor gives to necessary wrinkles place,
     But makes antiquity for aye his page;
         Finding the first conceit of love there bred,
         Where time and outward form would show it dead.

109 O, never say that I was false of heart,
     Though absence seem'd my flame to qualify.
     As easy might I from myself depart
     As from my soul, which in thy breast doth lie:
     That is my home of love: if I have ranged,
     Like him that travels, I return again;
     Just to the time, not with the time exchanged,
     So that myself bring water for my stain.
     Never believe, though in my nature reign'd
     All frailties that besiege all kinds of blood,
     That it could so preposterously be stain'd,
     To leave for nothing all thy sum of good;
         For nothing this wide universe I call,
         Save thou, my rose; in it thou art my all.

110 Alas, 'tis true I have gone here and there,
     And made myself a motley to the view,
     Gored mine own thoughts, sold cheap what is most dear,
     Made old offences of affections new;
     Most true it is that I have look'd on truth
     Askance and strangely: but, by all above,
     These blenches gave my heart another youth,
     And worse essays proved thee my best of love.
     Now all is done, have what shall have no end:
     Mine appetite I never more will grind
     On newer proof, to try an older friend,
     A god in love, to whom I am confined.
         Then give me welcome, next my heaven the best,
         Even to thy pure and most most loving breast.

111 O, for my sake do you with Fortune chide,
   The guilty goddess of my harmful deeds,
   That did not better for my life provide
   Than public means which public manners breeds.
   Thence comes it that my name receives a brand,
   And almost thence my nature is subdued
   To what it works in, like the dyer's hand:
   Pity me then and wish I were renew'd;
   Whilst, like a willing patient, I will drink
   Potions of eisel 'gainst my strong infection;
   No bitterness that I will bitter think,
   Nor double penance, to correct correction.
        Pity me then, dear friend, and I assure ye
        Even that your pity is enough to cure me.

112 Your love and pity doth the impression fill
   Which vulgar scandal stamp'd upon my brow;
   For what care I who calls me well or ill,
   So you o'er-green my bad, my good allow?
   You are my all the world, and I must strive
   To know my shames and praises from your tongue;
   None else to me, nor I to none alive,
   That my steel'd sense or changes right or wrong.
   In so profound abysm I throw all care
   Of others' voices, that my adder's sense
   To critic and to flatterer stopped are.
   Mark how with my neglect I do dispense:
        You are so strongly in my purpose bred
        That all the world besides methinks are dead.

113 Since I left you mine eye is in my mind,
   And that which governs me to go about
   Doth part his function and is partly blind,
   Seems seeing, but effectually is out;
   For it no form delivers to the heart
   Of bird, of flower, or shape, which it doth latch:
   Of his quick objects hath the mind no part,
   Nor his own vision holds what it doth catch;
   For if it see the rudest or gentlest sight,
   The most sweet favour or deformed'st creature,
   The mountain or the sea, the day or night,
   The crow or dove, it shapes them to your feature:
        Incapable of more, replete with you,
        My most true mind thus maketh mine untrue.

114 Or whether doth my mind, being crown'd with you,
    Drink up the monarch's plague, this flattery?
    Or whether shall I say, mine eye saith true,
    And that your love taught it this alchemy,
    To make of monsters and things indigest
    Such cherubins as your sweet self resemble,
    Creating every bad a perfect best,
    As fast as objects to his beams assemble?
    O, 'tis the first; 'tis flattery in my seeing,
    And my great mind most kingly drinks it up:
    Mine eye well knows what with his gust is 'greeing,
    And to his palate doth prepare the cup:
        If it be poison'd, 'tis the lesser sin
        That mine eye loves it and doth first begin.

115 Those lines that I before have writ do lie,
    Even those that said I could not love you dearer:
    Yet then my judgement knew no reason why
    My most full flame should afterwards burn clearer.
    But reckoning Time, whose million'd accidents
    Creep in 'twixt vows, and change decrees of kings,
    Tan sacred beauty, blunt the sharp'st intents,
    Divert strong minds to the course of altering things;
    Alas, why, fearing of Time's tyranny,
    Might I not then say 'Now I love you best,'
    When I was certain o'er incertainty,
    Crowning the present, doubting of the rest?
        Love is a babe; then might I not say so,
        To give full growth to that which still doth grow?

116 Let me not to the marriage of true minds
    Admit impediments.   Love is not love
    Which alters when it alteration finds,
    Or bends with the remover to remove:
    O, no! it is an ever-fixed mark,
    That looks on tempests and is never shaken;
    It is the star to every wandering bark,
    Whose worth's unknown, although his height be taken.
    Love's not Time's fool, though rosy lips and cheeks
    Within his bending sickle's compass come;
    Love alters not with his brief hours and weeks,
    But bears it out even to the edge of doom.
        If this be error and upon me proved,
        I never writ, nor no man ever loved.

117 Accuse me thus: that I have scanted all
　　Wherein I should your great deserts repay.
　　Forgot upon your dearest love to call,
　　Whereto all bonds do tie me day by day;
　　That I have frequent been with unknown minds,
　　And given to time your own dear-purchased right;
　　That I have hoisted sail to all the winds
　　Which should transport me farthest from your sight.
　　Book both my wilfulness and errors down,
　　And on just proof surmise accumulate;
　　Bring me within the level of your frown,
　　But shoot not at me in your waken'd hate;
　　　　Since my appeal says I did strive to prove
　　　　The constancy and virtue of your love.

118 Like as, to make our appetites more keen,
　　With eager compounds we our palate urge;
　　As, to prevent our maladies unseen,
　　We sicken to shun sickness when we purge;
　　Even so, being full of your ne'er-cloying sweetness,
　　To bitter sauces did I frame my feeding;
　　And sick of welfare found a kind of meetness
　　To be diseased, ere that there was true needing.
　　Thus policy in love, to anticipate
　　The ills that were not, grew to faults assured,
　　And brought to medicine a healthful state,
　　Which, rank of goodness, would by ill be cured:
　　　　But thence I learn, and find the lesson true,
　　　　Drugs poison him that so fell sick of you.

119 What potions have I drunk of Siren tears,
　　Distill'd from limbecks foul as hell within,
　　Applying fears to hopes and hopes to fears,
　　Still losing when I saw myself to win!
　　What wretched errors hath my heart committed,
　　Whilst it hath thought itself so blessed never!
　　How have mine eyes out of their spheres been fitted,
　　In the distraction of this madding fever!
　　O benefit of ill! now I find true
　　That better is by evil still made better;
　　And ruin'd love, when it is built anew,
　　Grows fairer than at first, more strong, far greater.
　　　　So I return rebuked to my content,
　　　　And gain by ill thrice more than I have spent.

120 That you were once unkind befriends me now,
     And for that sorrow which I then did feel
     Needs must I under my transgression bow,
     Unless my nerves were brass or hammer'd steel.
     For if you were by my unkindness shaken,
     As I by yours, you 've pass'd a hell of time;
     And I, a tyrant, have no leisure taken
     To weigh how once I suffer'd in your crime.
     O, that our night of woe might have remember'd
     My deepest sense, how hard true sorrow hits,
     And soon to you, as you to me, then tender'd
     The humble salve which wounded bosoms fits!
         But that your trespass now becomes a fee;
         Mine ransoms yours, and yours must ransom me.

121 'Tis better to be vile than vile esteemed,
     When not to be receives reproach of being;
     And the just pleasure lost, which is so deemed
     Not by our feeling, but by others' seeing:
     For why should others' false adulterate eyes
     Give salutation to my sportive blood?
     Or on my frailties why are frailer spies,
     Which in their wills count bad what I think good?
     No, I am that I am, and they that level
     At my abuses reckon up their own:
     I may be straight, though they themselves be bevel;
     By their rank thoughts my deeds must not be shown;
         Unless this general evil they maintain,
         All men are bad and in their badness reign.

122 Thy gift, thy tables, are within my brain
     Full character'd with lasting memory,
     Which shall above; that idle rank remain,
     Beyond all date, even to eternity:
     Or, at the least, so long as brain and heart
     Have faculty by nature to subsist;
     Till each to razed oblivion yield his part
     Of thee, thy record never can be miss'd.
     That poor retention could not so much hold,
     Nor need I tallies thy dear love to score;
     Therefore to give them from me was I bold,
     To trust those tables that receive thee more:
         To keep an adjunct to remember thee
         Were to import forgetfulness in me.

123 No, Time, thou shalt not boast that I do change:
       Thy pyramids built up with newer might
       To me are nothing novel, nothing strange;
       They are but dressings of a former sight.
       Our dates are brief, and therefore we admire
       What thou dost foist upon us that is old;
       And rather make them born to our desire
       Than think that we before have heard them told.
       Thy registers and thee I both defy,
       Not wondering at the present nor the past,
       For thy records and what we see doth lie,
       Made more or less by thy continual haste.
             This I do vow, and this shall ever be,
             I will be true, despite thy scythe and thee.

124 If my dear love were but the child of state,
       It might for Fortune's bastard be unfather'd,
       As subject to Time's love or to Time's hate,
       Weeds among weeds, or flowers with flowers gather'd.
       No, it was builded far from accident;
       It suffers not in smiling pomp, nor falls
       Under the blow of thralled discontent,
       Whereto the inviting time our fashion calls:
       It fears not policy, that heretic,
       Which works on leases of short-number'd hours,
       But all alone stands hugely politic,
       That it nor grows with heat nor drowns with showers.
             To this I witness call the fools of time,
             Which die for goodness, who have lived for crime.

125 Were 't aught to me I bore the canopy,
       With my extern the outward honouring,
       Or laid great bases for eternity,
       Which prove more short than waste or ruining?
       Have I not seen dwellers on form and favour
       Lose all, and more, by paying too much rent,
       For compound sweet forgoing simple savour,
       Pitiful thrivers, in their gazing spent?
       No, let me be obsequious in thy heart,
       And take thou my oblation, poor but free,
       Which is not mix'd with seconds, knows no art
       But mutual render, only me for thee.
             Hence, thou suborn'd informer! a true soul
             When most impeach'd stands least in thy control.

511

126 O thou, my lovely boy, who in thy power
     Dost hold Time's fickle glass, his sickle, hour;
     Who hast by waning grown, and therein show'st
     Thy lovers withering as thy sweet self grow'st;
     If Nature, sovereign mistress over wrack,
     As thou goest onwards, still will pluck thee back,
     She keeps thee to this purpose, that her skill
     May time disgrace and wretched minutes kill.
     Yet fear her, O thou minion of her pleasure!
     She may detain, but not still keep, her treasure:
          Her audit, though delay'd, answer'd must be,
          And her quietus is to render thee.

127 In the old age black was not counted fair,
     Or if it were, it bore not beauty's name;
     But now is black beauty's successive heir,
     And beauty slander'd with a bastard shame:
     For since each hand hath put on nature's power,
     Fairing the foul with art's false borrow'd face,
     Sweet beauty hath no name, no holy bower,
     But is profaned, if not lives in disgrace.
     Therefore my mistress' eyes are raven black,
     Her eyes so suited, and they mourners seem
     At such who, not born fair, no beauty lack,
     Slandering creation with a false esteem:
          Yet so they mourn, becoming of their woe,
          That every tongue says beauty should look so.

128 How oft, when thou, my music, music play'st,
     Upon that blessed wood whose motion sounds
     With thy sweet fingers, when thou gently sway'st
     The wiry concord that mine ear confounds,
     Do I envy those jacks that nimble leap
     To kiss the tender inward of thy hand,
     Whilst my poor lips, which should that harvest reap,
     At the wood's boldness by thee blushing stand!
     To be so tickled, they would change their state
     And situation with those dancing chips,
     O'er whom thy fingers walk with gentle gait,
     Making dead wood more blest than living lips.
          Since saucy jacks so happy are in this,
          Give them thy fingers, me thy lips to kiss.

129 The expense of spirit in a waste of shame
Is lust in action; and till action, lust
Is perjured, murderous, bloody, full of blame,
Savage, extreme, rude, cruel, not to trust;
Enjoy'd no sooner but despised straight;
Past reason hunted; and no sooner had,
Past reason hated, as a swallowed bait,
On purpose laid to make the taker mad:
Mad in pursuit, and in possession so;
Had, having, and in quest to have, extreme;
A bliss in proof, and proved, a very woe;
Before, a joy proposed; behind, a dream.
　　All this the world well knows; yet none knows well
　　To shun the heaven that leads men to this hell.

130 My mistress' eyes are nothing like the sun;
Coral is far more red than her lips' red:
If snow be white, why then her breasts are dun;
If hairs be wires, black wires grow on her head.
I have seen roses damask'd, red and white,
But no such roses see I in her cheeks;
And in some perfumes is there more delight
Than in the breath that from my mistress reeks.
I love to hear her speak, yet well I know
That music hath a far more pleasing sound:
I grant I never saw a goddess go,
My mistress, when she walks, treads on the ground:
　　And yet, by heaven, I think my love as rare
　　As any she belied with false compare.

131 Thou art as tyrannous, so as thou art,
As those whose beauties proudly make them cruel;
For well thou know'st to my dear doting heart
Thou art the fairest and most precious jewel.
Yet, in good faith, some say that thee behold,
Thy face hath not the power to make love groan:
To say they err I dare not be so bold,
Although I swear it to myself alone.
And to be sure that is not false I swear,
A thousand groans, but thinking on thy face,
One on another's neck, do witness bear
Thy black is fairest in my judgement's place.
　　In nothing art thou black save in thy deeds,
　　And thence this slander, as I think, proceeds.

132   Thine eyes I love, and they, as pitying me,
       Knowing thy heart torments me with disdain,
       Have put on black and loving mourners be,
       Looking with pretty ruth upon my pain.
       And truly not the morning sun of heaven
       Better becomes the grey cheeks of the east,
       Nor that full star that ushers in the even
       Doth half that glory to the sober west,
       As those two mourning eyes become thy face:
       O, let it then as well beseem thy heart
       To mourn for me, since mourning doth thee grace,
       And suit thy pity like in every part.
             Then will I swear beauty herself is black,
             And all they foul that thy complexion lack.

133   Beshrew that heart that makes my heart to groan
       For that deep wound it gives my friend and me!
       Is 't not enough to torture me alone,
       But slave to slavery my sweet'st friend must be?
       Me from myself thy cruel eye hath taken,
       And my next self thou harder hast engrossed:
       Of him, myself, and thee, I am forsaken;
       A torment thrice threefold thus to be crossed.
       Prison my heart in thy steel bosom's ward,
       But then my friend's heart let my poor heart bail;
       Who'er keeps me, let my heart be his guard;
       Thou canst not then use rigour in my gaol:
             And yet thou wilt; for I, being pent in thee,
             Perforce am thine, and all that is in me.

134   So, now I have confess'd that he is thine
       And I myself am mortgaged to thy will,
       Myself I 'll forfeit, so that other mine
       Thou wilt restore, to be my comfort still:
       But thou wilt not, nor he will not be free,
       For thou art covetous and he is kind;
       He learn'd but surety-like to write for me,
       Under that bond that him as fast doth bind.
       The statute of thy beauty thou wilt take,
       Thou usurer, that put'st forth all to use,
       And sue a friend came debtor for my sake;
       So him I lose through my unkind abuse.
             Him have I lost; thou hast both him and me:
             He pays the whole, and yet am I not free.

135 Whoever hath her wish, thou hast thy 'Will,'
And 'Will' to boot, and 'Will' in overplus;
More than enough am I that vex thee still,
To thy sweet will making addition thus.
Wilt thou, whose will is large and spacious,
Not once vouchsafe to hide my will in thine?
Shall will in others seem right gracious,
And in my will no fair acceptance shine?
The sea, all water, yet receives rain still,
And in abundance addeth to his store;
So thou, being rich in 'Will,' add to thy 'Will'
One will of mine, to make thy large 'Will' more.
    Let no unkind, no fair beseechers kill;
    Think all but one, and me in that one 'Will.'

136 If thy soul check thee that I come so near,
Swear to thy blind soul that I was thy 'Will,'
And will, thy soul knows, is admitted there;
Thus far for love, my love-suit, sweet, fulfil.
'Will' will fulfil the treasure of thy love,
Ay, fill it full with wills, and my will one.
In things of great receipt with ease we prove
Among a number one is reckon'd none:
Then in the number let me pass untold,
Though in thy store's account I one must be;
For nothing hold me, so it please thee hold
That nothing me, a something sweet to thee:
    Make but my name thy love, and love that still,
    And then thou lovest me, for my name is 'Will.'

137 Thou blind fool, Love, what dost thou to mine eyes,
That they behold, and see not what they see?
They know what beauty is, see where it lies,
Yet what the best is take the worst to be.
If eyes, corrupt by over-partial looks,
Be anchor'd in the bay where all men ride,
Why of eyes' falsehood hast thou forged hooks,
Whereto the judgement of my heart is tied?
Why should my heart think that a several plot
Which my heart knows the wide world's common place?
Or mine eyes seeing this, say this is not,
To put fair truth upon so foul a face?
    In things right true my heart and eyes have erred,
    And to this false plague are they now transferred.

138 When my love swears that she is made of truth,
    I do believe her, though I know she lies,
    That she might think me some untutor'd youth,
    Unlearned in the world's false subtleties.
    Thus vainly thinking that she thinks me young,
    Although she knows my days are past the best,
    Simply I credit her false-speaking tongue :
    On both sides thus is simple truth suppress'd.
    But wherefore says she not she is unjust ?
    And wherefore say not I that I am old ?
    O, love's best habit is in seeming trust,
    And age in love loves not to have years told :
        Therefore I lie with her and she with me,
        And in our faults by lies we flatter'd be.

139 O call not me to justify the wrong
    That thy unkindness lays upon my heart ;
    Wound me not with thine eye, but with thy tongue ;
    Use power with power, and slay me not by art.
    Tell me thou lovest elsewhere ; but in my sight,
    Dear heart, forbear to glance thine eye aside :
    What need'st thou wound with cunning, when thy might
    Is more than my o'er-pressed defence can bide ?
    Let me excuse thee : ah, my love well knows
    Her pretty looks have been mine enemies ;
    And therefore from my face she turns my foes,
    That they elsewhere might dart their injuries :
        Yet do not so ; but since I am near slain,
        Kill me outright with looks, and rid my pain.

140 Be wise as thou art cruel ; do not press
    My tongue-tied patience with too much disdain ;
    Lest sorrow lends me words, and words express
    The manner of my pity-wanting pain.
    If I might teach thee wit, better it were,
    Though not to love, yet, love, to tell me so ;
    As testy sick men, when their deaths be near,
    No news but health from their physicians know ;
    For, if I should despair, I should grow mad,
    And in my madness might speak ill of thee :
    Now this ill-wresting world is grown so bad,
    Mad slanderers by mad ears believed be.
        That I may not be so, nor thou belied,
        Bear thine eyes straight, though thy proud heart go wide.

141 In faith, I do not love thee with mine eyes,
    For they in thee a thousand errors note;
    But 'tis my heart that loves what they despise,
    Who, in despite of view, is pleased to dote;
    Nor are mine ears with thy tongue's tune delighted;
    Nor tender feeling, to base touches prone,
    Nor taste, nor smell, desire to be invited
    To any sensual feast with thee alone:
    But my five wits nor my five senses can
    Dissuade one foolish heart from serving thee,
    Who leaves unsway'd the likeness of a man,
    Thy proud heart's slave and vassal wretch to be:
        Only my plague thus far I count my gain,
        That she that makes me sin awards me pain.

142 Love is my sin, and thy dear virtue hate,
    Hate of my sin, grounded on sinful loving:
    O, but with mine compare thou thine own state,
    And thou shalt find it merits not reproving;
    Or, if it do, not from those lips of thine,
    That have profaned their scarlet ornaments
    And seal'd false bonds of love as oft as mine,
    Robb'd others' beds' revenues of their rents.
    Be it lawful I love thee, as thou lovest those
    Whom thine eyes woo as mine importune thee:
    Root pity in thy heart, that, when it grows,
    Thy pity may deserve to pitied be.
        If thou dost seek to have what thou dost hide,
        By self-example mayst thou be denied!

143 Lo, as a careful housewife runs to catch
    One of her feather'd creatures broke away,
    Sets down her babe, and makes all swift dispatch
    In pursuit of the thing she would have stay;
    Whilst her neglected child holds her in chase,
    Cries to catch her whose busy care is bent
    To follow that which flies before her face,
    Not prizing her poor infant's discontent:
    So runn'st thou after that which flies from thee,
    Whilst I thy babe chase thee afar behind;
    But if thou catch thy hope, turn back to me,
    And play the mother's part, kiss me, be kind:
        So will I pray that thou mayst have thy 'Will,'
        If thou turn back and my loud crying still.

144 Two loves I have of comfort and despair,
    Which like two spirits do suggest me still :
    The better angel is a man right fair,
    The worser spirit a woman colour'd ill.
    To win me soon to hell, my female evil
    Tempteth my better angel from my side,
    And would corrupt my saint to be a devil,
    Wooing his purity with her foul pride.
    And whether that my angel be turn'd fiend
    Suspect I may, yet not directly tell ;
    But being both from me, both to each friend,
    I guess one angel in another's hell :
        Yet this shall I ne'er know, but live in doubt,
        Till my bad angel fire my good one out.

145 Those lips that Love's own hand did make
    Breathed forth the sound that said 'I hate,'
    To me that languish'd for her sake :
    But when she saw my woeful state,
    Straight in her heart did mercy come,
    Chiding that tongue that ever sweet
    Was used in giving gentle doom ;
    And taught it thus anew to greet ;
    'I hate' she alter'd with an end,
    That follow'd it as gentle day
    Doth follow night, who, like a fiend,
    From heaven to hell is flown away ;
        'I hate' from hate away she threw,
        And saved my life, saying 'not you.'

146 Poor soul, the centre of my sinful earth,
    . . . . . . these rebel powers that thee array,
    Why dost thou pine within and suffer dearth,
    Painting thy outward walls so costly gay ?
    Why so large cost, having so short a lease,
    Dost thou upon thy fading mansion spend ?
    Shall worms, inheritors of this excess,
    Eat up thy charge ? is this thy body's end ?
    Then, soul, live thou upon thy servant's loss,
    And let that pine to aggravate thy store ;
    Buy terms divine in selling hours of dross ;
    Within be fed, without be rich no more :
        So shalt thou feed on Death, that feeds on men,
        And Death once dead, there 's no more dying then.

147 My love is as a fever, longing still
     For that which longer nurseth the disease ;
     Feeding on that which doth preserve the ill,
     The uncertain sickly appetite to please.
     My reason, the physician to my love,
     Angry that his prescriptions are not kept,
     Hath left me, and I desperate now approve,
     Desire his death, which physic did except.
     Past cure I am, now reason is past care,
     And frantic-mad with evermore unrest ;
     My thoughts and my discourse as madmen's are,
     At random from the truth vainly express'd ;
          For I have sworn thee fair, and thought thee bright,
          Who art as black as hell, as dark as night.

148 O, me, what eyes hath Love put in my head,
     Which have no correspondence with true sight !
     Or, if they have, where is my judgement fled,
     That censures falsely what they see aright ?
     If that be fair whereon my false eyes dote,
     What means the world to say it is not so ?
     If it be not, then love doth well denote
     Love's eye is not so true as all men's : no,
     How can it ? O, how can Love's eye be true,
     That is so vex'd with watching and with tears ?
     No marvel then, though I mistake my view ;
     The sun itself sees not till heaven clears.
          O cunning Love ! with tears thou keep'st me blind,
          Lest eyes well-seeing thy foul faults should find.

149 Canst thou, O cruel ! say I love thee not,
     When I against myself with thee partake ?
     Do I not think on thee, when I forgot
     Am of myself, all tyrant, for thy sake ?
     Who hateth thee that I do call my friend ?
     On whom frown'st thou that I do fawn upon ?
     Nay, if thou lour'st on me, do I not spend
     Revenge upon myself with present moan ?
     What merit do I in myself respect,
     That is so proud thy service to despise,
     When all my best doth worship thy defect,
     Commanded by the motion of thine eyes ?
          But, love, hate on, for now I know thy mind ;
          Those that can see thou lovest, and I am blind.

150 O, from what power hast thou this powerful might
With insufficiency my heart to sway?
To make me give the lie to my true sight,
And swear that brightness doth not grace the day?
Whence hast thou this becoming of things ill,
That in the very refuse of thy deeds
There is such strength and warrantise of skill,
That, in my mind, thy worst all best exceeds?
Who taught thee how to make me love thee more,
The more I hear and see just cause of hate?
O, though I love what others do abhor,
With others thou shouldst not abhor my state:
    If thy unworthiness raised love in me,
    More worthy I to be beloved of thee.

151 Love is too young to know what conscience is;
Yet who knows not conscience is born of love?
Then, gentle cheater, urge not my amiss,
Lest guilty of my faults thy sweet self prove:
For, thou betraying me, I do betray
My nobler part to my gross body's treason;
My soul doth tell my body that he may
Triumph in love; flesh stays no farther reason,
But rising at thy name doth point out thee
As his triumphant prize. Proud of this pride,
He is contented thy poor drudge to be,
To stand in thy affairs, fall by thy side.
    No want of conscience hold it that I call
    Her 'love' for whose dear love I rise and fall.

152 In loving thee thou know'st I am forsworn,
But thou art twice forsworn, to me love swearing;
In act thy bed-vow broke, and new faith torn,
In vowing new hate after new love bearing.
But why of two oaths' breach do I accuse thee,
When I break twenty! I am perjured most;
For all my vows are oaths but to misuse thee,
And all my honest faith in thee is lost:
For I have sworn deep oaths of thy deep kindness,
Oaths of thy love, thy truth, thy constancy;
And, to enlighten thee, gave eyes to blindness,
Or made them swear against the thing they see;
    For I have sworn thee fair; more perjured I,
    To swear against the truth so foul a lie!

153 Cupid laid by his brand and fell asleep:
    A maid of Dian's this advantage found,
    And his love-kindling fire did quickly steep
    In a cold valley-fountain of that ground;
    Which borrow'd from this holy fire of Love
    A dateless lively heat, still to endure,
    And grew a seething bath, which yet men prove
    Against strange maladies a sovereign cure.
    But at my mistress' eye Love's brand new-fired,
    The boy for trial needs would touch my breast;
    I, sick withal, the help of bath desired,
    And thither hied, a sad distemper'd guest,
        But found no cure: the bath for my help lies
        Where Cupid got new fire, my mistress' eyes.

154 The little Love-god lying once asleep
    Laid by his side his heart-inflaming brand,
    Whilst many nymphs that vow'd chaste life to keep
    Came tripping by; but in her maiden hand
    The fairest votary took up that fire
    Which many legions of true hearts had warm'd;
    And so the general of hot desire
    Was sleeping by a virgin hand disarm'd.
    This brand she quenched in a cool well by,
    Which from Love's fire took heat perpetual,
    Growing a bath and healthful remedy
    For men diseased; but I, my mistress' thrall,
        Came there for cure, and this by that I prove,
        Love's fire heats water, water cools not love.

A LOVER'S COMPLAINT

From off a hill whose concave womb re-worded
A plaintful story from a sistering vale,
My spirits to attend this double voice accorded,
And down I laid to list the sad-tuned tale ;
Ere long espied a fickle maid full pale,
Tearing of papers, breaking rings a-twain,
Storming her world with sorrow's wind and rain.

Upon her head a platted hive of straw,
Which fortified her visage from the sun,
Whereon the thought might think sometime it saw
The carcass of a beauty spent and done :
Time had not scythed all that youth begun,
Nor youth all quit ; but, spite of heaven's fell rage,
Some beauty peep'd through lattice of sear'd age.

Oft did she heave her napkin to her eyne,
Which on it had conceited characters,
Laundering the silken figures in the brine
That season'd woe had pelleted in tears,
And often reading what contents it bears ;
As often shrieking undistinguish'd woe,
In clamours of all size, both high and low.

Sometimes her levell'd eyes their carriage ride
As they did battery to the spheres intend ;
Sometime diverted their poor balls are tied
To the orbed earth ; sometimes they do extend
Their view right on ; anon their gazes lend
To every place at once, and nowhere fix'd
The mind and sight distractedly commix'd.

Her hair, nor loose nor tied in formal plat,
Proclaim'd in her a careless hand of pride ;
For some, untuck'd, descended her sheaved hat,
Hanging her pale and pined cheek beside ;
Some in her threaden fillet still did bide,
And, true to bondage, would not break from thence,
Though slackly braided in loose negligence.

A thousand favours from a maund she drew
Of amber, crystal, and of beaded jet,
Which one by one she in a river threw,
Upon whose weeping margent she was set ;
Like usury, applying wet to wet,
Or monarch's hands that lets not bounty fall
Where want cries some, but where excess begs all.

Of folded schedules had she many a one,
Which she perused, sigh'd, tore, and gave the flood ;
Crack'd many a ring of posied gold and bone,
Bidding them find their sepulchres in mud ;
Found yet moe letters sadly penn'd in blood,
With sleided silk feat and affectedly
Enswathed, and seal'd to curious secrecy.

These often bathed she in her fluxive eyes,
And often kiss'd, and often 'gan to tear ;
Cried ' O false blood, thou register of lies,
What unapproved witness dost thou bear !
Ink would have seem'd more black and damned here !'
This said, in top of rage the lines she rents,
Big discontent so breaking their contents.

A reverend man that grazed his cattle nigh—
Sometime a blusterer, that the ruffle knew
Of court, of city, and had let go by
The swiftest hours, observed as they flew—
Towards this afflicted fancy fastly drew ;
And, privileged by age, desires to know
In brief the grounds and motives of her woe.

So slides he down upon his grained bat,
And comely-distant sits he by her side ;
When he again desires her, being sat,
Her grievance with his hearing to divide :
If that from him there may be aught applied
Which may her suffering ecstasy assuage,
'Tis promised in the charity of age.

' Father,' she says, ' though in me you behold
The injury of many a blasting hour,
Let it not tell your judgement I am old ;
Not age, but sorrow, over me hath power :
I might as yet have been a spreading flower,
Fresh to myself, if I had self-applied
Love to myself, and to no love beside.

'But, woe is me! too early I attended
A youthful suit—it was to gain my grace—
Of one by nature's outwards so commended,
That maidens' eyes stuck over all his face:
Love lack'd a dwelling and made him her place;
And when in his fair parts she did abide,
She was new lodged and newly deified.

'His browny locks did hang in crooked curls;
And every light occasion of the wind
Upon his lips their silken parcels hurls.
What's sweet to do, to do will aptly find:
Each eye that saw him did enchant the mind;
For on his visage was in little drawn
What largeness thinks in Paradise was sawn.

'Small show of man was yet upon his chin;
His phœnix down began but to appear,
Like unshorn velvet, on that termless skin,
Whose bare out-bragg'd the web it seem'd to wear.
Yet show'd his visage by that cost more dear;
And nice affections wavering stood in doubt
If best were as it was, or best without.

'His qualities were beauteous as his form,
For maiden-tongued he was, and thereof free;
Yet, if men moved him, was he such a storm
As oft 'twixt May and April is to see,
When winds breathe sweet, unruly though they be.
His rudeness so with his authorized youth
Did livery falseness in a pride of truth.

'Well could he ride, and often men would say,
"That horse his mettle from his rider takes:
Proud of subjection, noble by the sway,
What rounds, what bounds, what course, what stop he makes!"
And controversy hence a question takes,
Whether the horse by him became his deed,
Or he his manage by the well-doing steed.

'But quickly on this side the verdict went:
His real habitude gave life and grace
To appertainings and to ornament,
Accomplish'd in himself, not in his case:
All aids, themselves made fairer by their place,
Came for additions; yet their purposed trim
Pierced not his grace, but were all graced by him.

'So on the tip of his subduing tongue
All kinds of arguments and question deep,
All replication prompt and reason strong,
For his advantage still did wake and sleep :
To make the weeper laugh, the laugher weep,
He had the dialect and different skill,
Catching all passions in his craft of will;

'That he did in the general bosom reign
Of young, of old, and sexes both enchanted,
To dwell with him in thoughts, or to remain
In personal duty, following where he haunted :
Consents bewitch'd, ere he desire, have granted,
And dialogued for him what he would say,
Ask'd their own wills and made their wills obey.

'Many there were that did his picture get,
To serve their eyes, and in it put their mind ;
Like fools that in the imagination set
The goodly objects which abroad they find
Of lands and mansions, theirs in thought assign'd :
And labouring in moe pleasures to bestow them
Than the true gouty landlord which doth owe them :

'So many have, that never touch'd his hand,
Sweetly supposed them mistress of his heart.
My woeful self, that did in freedom stand,
And was my own fee-simple, not in part,
What with his art in youth and youth in art,
Threw my affections in his charmed power,
Reserved the stalk and gave him all my flower.

'Yet did I not, as some my equals did,
Demand of him, nor being desired yielded ;
Finding myself in honour so forbid,
With safest distance I mine honour shielded ;
Experience for me many bulwarks builded
Of proofs new-bleeding, which remain'd the foil
Of this false jewel, and this amorous spoil.

'But, ah, who ever shunn'd by precedent
The destined ill she must herself assay?
Or forced examples, 'gainst her own content,
To put the by-past perils in her way?
Counsel may stop awhile what will not stay ;
For when we rage, advice is often seen
By blunting us to make our wits more keen.

'Nor gives it satisfaction to our blood,
That we must curb it upon others' proof;
To be forbod the sweets that seem so good,
For fear of harms that preach in our behoof.
O appetite, from judgement stand aloof!
The one a palate hath that needs will taste,
Though Reason weep, and cry "It is thy last."

'For further I could say "This man's untrue,"
And knew the patterns of his foul beguiling;
Heard where his plants in others' orchards grew,
Saw how deceits were gilded in his smiling;
Knew vows were ever brokers to defiling;
Thought characters and words merely but art,
And bastards of his foul adulterate heart.

'And long upon these terms I held my city,
Till thus he 'gan besiege me: "Gentle maid,
Have of my suffering youth some feeling pity,
And be not of my holy vows afraid:
That 's to ye sworn to none was ever said;
For feasts of love I have been call'd unto,
Till now did ne'er invite, nor never woo.

'"All my offences that abroad you see
Are errors of the blood, none of the mind;
Love made them not: with acture they may be,
Where neither party is nor true nor kind:
They sought their shame that so their shame did find;
And so much less of shame in me remains
By how much of me their reproach contains.

'"Among the many that mine eyes have seen,
Not one whose flame my heart so much as warmed,
Or my affection put to the smallest teen,
Or any of my leisures ever charmed:
Harm have I done to them, but ne'er was harmed;
Kept hearts in liveries, but mine own was free,
And reign'd, commanding in his monarchy.

'"Look here, what tributes wounded fancies sent me
Of paled pearls and rubies red as blood;
Figuring that they their passions likewise lent me
Of grief and blushes, aptly understood
In bloodless white and the encrimson'd mood;
Effects of terror and dear modesty,
Encamp'd in hearts, but fighting outwardly.

' " And, lo, behold these talents of their hair,
With twisted metal amorously impleach'd,
I have received from many a several fair,
Their kind acceptance weepingly beseech'd,
With the annexions of fair gems enrich'd,
And deep-brain'd sonnets that did amplify
Each stone's dear nature, worth and quality.

' " The diamond, why, 'twas beautiful and hard,
Whereto his invised properties did tend;
The deep-green emerald, in whose fresh regard
Weak sights their sickly radiance do amend;
The heaven-hued sapphire and the opal blend
With objects manifold : each several stone,
With wit well blazon'd, smiled or made some moan.

' " Lo, all these trophies of affections hot,
Of pensived and subdued desires the tender,
Nature hath charged me that I hoard them not,
But yield them up where I myself must render,
That is, to you, my origin and ender;
For these, of force, must your oblations be,
Since I their altar, you enpatron me.

' " O, then, advance of yours that phraseless hand,
Whose white weighs down the airy scale of praise;
Take all these similes to your own command,
Hallow'd with sighs that burning lungs did raise;
What me your minister, for you obeys,
Works under you ; and to your audit comes
Their distract parcels in combined sums.

' " Lo, this device was sent me from a nun,
Or sister sanctified, of holiest note;
Which late her noble suit in court did shun,
Whose rarest havings made the blossoms dote;
For she was sought by spirits of richest coat,
But kept cold distance, and did thence remove,
To spend her living in eternal love.

' " But, O my sweet, what labour is 't to leave
The thing we have not, mastering what not strives,
Playing the place which did no form receive,
Playing patient sports in unconstrained gyves?
She that her fame so to herself contrives,
The scars of battle 'scapeth by the flight,
And makes her absence valiant, not her might.

'"O, pardon me, in that my boast is true:
The accident which brought me to her eye
Upon the moment did her force subdue,
And now she would the caged cloister fly:
Religious love put out Religion's eye:
Not to be tempted, would she be immured,
And now, to tempt all, liberty procured.

'"How mighty then you are, O, hear me tell!
The broken bosoms that to me belong
Have emptied all their fountains in my well,
And mine I pour your ocean all among:
I strong o'er them, and you o'er me being strong,
Must for your victory us all congest,
As compound love to physic your cold breast.

'"My parts had power to charm a sacred nun,
Who disciplined, ay, dieted in grace,
Believed her eyes when they to assail begun,
All vows and consecrations giving place:
O most potential love! vow, bond, nor space,
In thee hath neither sting, knot, nor confine,
For thou art all, and all things else are thine.

'"When thou impressest, what are precepts worth
Of stale example? When thou wilt inflame,
How boldly those impediments stand forth
Of wealth, of filial fear, law, kindred, fame!
Love's arms are peace, 'gainst rule, 'gainst sense, 'gainst shame;
And sweetens, in the suffering pangs it bears,
The aloes of all forces, shocks and fears.

'"Now all these hearts that do on mine depend,
Feeling it break, with bleeding groans they pine;
And supplicant their sighs to you extend,
To leave the battery that you make 'gainst mine,
Lending soft audience to my sweet design,
And credent soul to that strong-bonded oath
That shall prefer and undertake my troth."

'This said, his watery eyes he did dismount,
Whose sights till then were levell'd on my face;
Each cheek a river running from a fount
With brinish current downward flow'd apace:
O, how the channel to the stream gave grace!
Who glazed with crystal gate the glowing roses
That flame through water which their hue encloses.

'O father, what a hell of witchcraft lies
In the small orb of one particular tear!
But with the inundation of the eyes
What rocky heart to water will not wear?
What breast so cold that is not warmed here?
O cleft effect! cold modesty, hot wrath,
Both fire from hence and chill extincture hath.

For, lo, his passion, but an art of craft,
Even there resolved my reason into tears;
There my white stole of chastity I daff'd,
Shook off my sober guards and civil fears;
Appear to him, as he to me appears,
All melting; though our drops this difference bore,
His poison'd me, and mine did him restore.

'In him a plenitude of subtle matter,
Applied to cautels, all strange forms receives,
Of burning blushes, or of weeping water,
Or swounding paleness; and he takes and leaves,
In either's aptness, as it best deceives,
To blush at speeches rank, to weep at woes,
Or to turn white and swound at tragic shows:

'That not a heart which in his level came
Could 'scape the hail of his all-hurting aim,
Showing fair nature is both kind and tame;
And, veil'd in them, did win whom he would maim:
Against the thing he sought he would exclaim;
When he most burn'd in heart-wish'd luxury,
He preach'd pure maid and praised cold chastity.

'Thus merely with the garment of a Grace
The naked and concealed fiend he cover'd;
That the unexperient gave the tempter place,
Which, like a cherubin, above them hover'd.
Who, young and simple, would not be so lover'd?
Ay me! I fell, and yet do question make
What I should do again for such a sake.

'O, that infected moisture of his eye,
O, that false fire which in his cheek so glow'd,
O, that forced thunder from his heart did fly,
O, that sad breath his spongy lungs bestow'd,
O, all that borrow'd motion seeming owed,
Would yet again betray the fore-betray'd,
And new pervert a reconciled maid!'

THE PASSIONATE PILGRIM

1 WHEN my love swears that she is made of truth,
I do believe her, though I know she lies,
That she might think me some untutor'd youth,
Unskilful in the world's false forgeries.
Thus vainly thinking that she thinks me young,
Although I know my years be past the best,
I smiling credit her false-speaking tongue,
Outfacing faults in love with love's ill rest.
But wherefore says my love that she is young?
And wherefore say not I that I am old?
O, love's best habit is a soothing tongue,
And age, in love, loves not to have years told.
    Therefore I 'll lie with love, and love with me,
    Since that our faults in love thus smother'd be.

2 Two loves I have, of comfort and despair,
That like two spirits do suggest me still;
My better angel is a man right fair,
My worser spirit a woman colour'd ill.
To win me soon to hell, my female evil
Tempteth my better angel from my side,
And would corrupt my saint to be a devil,
Wooing his purity with her fair pride.
And whether that my angel be turn'd fiend,
Suspect I may, yet not directly tell:
For being both to me, both to each friend,
I guess one angel in another's hell:
    The truth I shall not know, but live in doubt,
    Till my bad angel fire my good one out.

3 Did not the heavenly rhetoric of thine eye,
'Gainst whom the world could not hold argument,
Persuade my heart to this false perjury?
Vows for thee broke deserve not punishment.
A woman I forswore; but I will prove,
Thou being a goddess, I forswore not thee:
My vow was earthly, thou a heavenly love;
Thy grace being gain'd cures all disgrace in me.
My vow was breath, and breath a vapour is;
Then, thou fair sun, that on this earth doth shine,

Exhale this vapour now; in thee it is:
If broken, then it is no fault of mine.
    If by me broke, what fool is not so wise
    To break an oath, to win a paradise?

4 Sweet Cytherea, sitting by a brook
With young Adonis, lovely, fresh and green,
Did court the lad with many a lovely look,
Such looks as none could look but beauty's queen.
She told him stories to delight his ear,
She show'd him favours to allure his eye;
To win his heart, she touch'd him here and there;
Touches so soft still conquer chastity.
But whether unripe years did want conceit,
Or he refused to take her figured proffer,
The tender nibbler would not touch the bait,
But smile and jest at every gentle offer:
    Then fell she on her back, fair queen, and toward:
    He rose and ran away; ah, fool too froward.

5 If love make me forsworn, how shall I swear to love?
O never faith could hold, if not to beauty vowed:
Though to myself forsworn, to thee I'll constant prove;
Those thoughts, to me like oaks, to thee like osiers bowed.
Study his bias leaves, and make his book thine eyes,
Where all those pleasures live that art can comprehend.
If knowledge be the mark, to know thee shall suffice;
Well learned is that tongue that well can thee commend:
All ignorant that soul that sees thee without wonder;
Which is to me some praise, that I thy parts admire:
Thine eye Jove's lightning seems, thy voice his dreadful
        thunder,
Which, not to anger bent, is music and sweet fire.
    Celestial as thou art, O do not love that wrong,
    To sing heaven's praise with such an earthly tongue.

6 Scarce had the sun dried up the dewy morn,
And scarce the herd gone to the hedge for shade,
When Cytherea, all in love forlorn,
A longing tarriance for Adonis made
Under an osier growing by a brook,
A brook where Adon used to cool his spleen:
Hot was the day; she hotter that did look
For his approach, that often there had been.
Anon he comes, and throws his mantle by,
And stood stark naked on the brook's green brim:

The sun look'd on the world with glorious eye,
Yet not so wistly as this queen on him.
　　He, spying her, bounced in, whereas he stood:
　　'O Jove,' quoth she, 'why was not I a flood!'

7 Fair is my love, but not so fair as fickle,
Mild as a dove, but neither true nor trusty,
Brighter than glass and yet, as glass is, brittle,
Softer than wax and yet as iron rusty:
　　A lily pale, with damask dye to grace her,
　　None fairer, nor none falser to deface her.
Her lips to mine how often hath she joined,
Between each kiss her oaths of true love swearing!
How many tales to please me hath she coined,
Dreading my love, the loss thereof still fearing!
　　Yet in the midst of all her pure protestings,
　　Her faith, her oaths, her tears, and all were jestings.

She burn'd with love, as straw with fire flameth;
She burn'd out love, as soon as straw out-burneth;
She framed the love, and yet she foil'd the framing;
She bade love last, and yet she fell a-turning.
　　Was this a lover, or a lecher whether?
　　Bad in the best. though excellent in neither.

8 If music and sweet poetry agree,
As they must needs, the sister and the brother,
Then must the love be great 'twixt thee and me,
Because thou lovest the one and I the other.
Dowland to thee is dear, whose heavenly touch
Upon the lute doth ravish human sense;
Spenser to me, whose deep conceit is such
As passing all conceit needs no defence.
Thou lovest to hear the sweet melodious sound
That Phœbus' lute, the queen of music, makes;
And I in deep delight am chiefly drown'd
When as himself to singing he betakes.
　　One god is god of both, as poets feign;
　　One knight loves both, and both in thee remain.

9 Fair was the morn when the fair queen of love,
　　.　　　　.　　　　.　　　　.
Paler for sorrow than her milk-white dove,
For Adon's sake, a youngster proud and wild;
Her stand she takes upon a steep-up hill:
Anon Adonis comes with horn and hounds;

She, silly queen, with more than love's good will,
Forbade the boy he should not pass those grounds:
'Once,' quoth she, 'did I see a fair sweet youth
Here in these brakes deep-wounded with a boar,
Deep in the thigh, a spectacle of ruth!
See in my thigh,' quoth she, 'here was the sore.'
    She showed hers: he saw more wounds than one,
    And blushing fled, and left her all alone.

10 Sweet rose, fair flower, untimely pluck'd, soon vaded,
Pluck'd in the bud and vaded in the spring!
Bright orient pearl, alack, too timely shaded!
Fair creature, kill'd too soon by death's sharp sting!
    Like a green plum that hangs upon a tree,
    And falls through wind before the fall should be.

I weep for thee and yet no cause I have;
For why thou left'st me nothing in thy will:
And yet thou left'st me more than I did crave;
For why I craved nothing of thee still:
    O yes, dear friend, I pardon crave of thee,
    Thy discontent thou didst bequeath to me.

11 Venus, with young Adonis sitting by her
Under a myrtle shade, began to woo him:
She told the youngling how god Mars did try her,
And as he fell to her, so fell she to him.
'Even thus,' quoth she, 'the warlike god embraced me,'
And then she clipp'd Adonis in her arms;
'Even thus,' quoth she, 'the warlike god unlaced me,'
As if the boy should use like loving charms;
'Even thus,' quoth she, 'he seized on my lips,'
And with her lips on his did act the seizure:
And as she fetched breath, away he skips,
And would not take her meaning nor her pleasure.
    Ah, that I had my lady at this bay,
    To kiss and clip me till I run away!

12 Crabbed age and youth cannot live together:
Youth is full of pleasance, age is full of care;
Youth like summer morn, age like winter weather;
Youth like summer brave, age like winter bare.
Youth is full of sport, age's breath is short;
    Youth is nimble, age is lame;
Youth is hot and bold, age is weak and cold;
    Youth is wild, and age is tame.

Age, I do abhor thee; youth, I do adore thee;
 O, my love, my love is young!
Age, I do defy thee: O, sweet shepherd, hie thee,
 For methinks thou stay'st too long.

13 Beauty is but a vain and doubtful good;
A shining gloss that vadeth suddenly;
A flower that dies when first it 'gins to bud;
A brittle glass that 's broken presently:
  A doubtful good, a gloss, a glass, a flower,
  Lost, vaded, broken, dead within an hour.

And as goods lost are seld or never found,
As vaded gloss no rubbing will refresh,
As flowers dead lie wither'd on the ground,
As broken glass no cement can redress,
  So beauty blemish'd once 's for ever lost,
  In spite of physic, painting, pain and cost.

14 Good night, good rest. Ah, neither be my share;
She bade good night that kept my rest away;
And daff'd me to a cabin hang'd with care,
To descant on the doubts of my decay.
  'Farewell,' quoth she, ' and come again to-morrow:'
  Fare well I could not, for I supp'd with sorrow.

Yet at my parting sweetly did she smile,
In scorn or friendship, nill I construe whether:
'T may be, she joy'd to jest at my exile,
'T may be, again to make me wander thither:
  'Wander,' a word for shadows like myself,
  As take the pain, but cannot pluck the pelf.

15 Lord, how mine eyes throw gazes to the east!
My heart doth charge the watch; the morning rise
Doth cite each moving sense from idle rest.
Not daring trust the office of mine eyes,
  While Philomela sits and sings, I sit and mark,
  And wish her lays were tuned like the lark;

For she doth welcome daylight with her ditty,
And drives away dark dreaming night;
The night so pack'd, I post unto my pretty;
Heart hath his hope and eyes their wished sight;
  Sorrow changed to solace and solace mix'd with sorrow;
  For why, she sigh'd, and bade me come to-morrow.

Were I with her, the night would post too soon;
But now are minutes added to the hours;
To spite me now, each minute seems a moon;
Yet not for me, shine sun to succour flowers!
    Pack night, peep day; good day, of night now borrow;
    Short, night, to-night, and length thyself to-morrow.

16 It was a lording's daughter, the fairest one of three,
That liked of her master as well as well might be,
Till looking on an Englishman, the fair'st that eye could see,
    Her fancy fell a-turning.
Long was the combat doubtful that love with love did fight,
To leave the master loveless, or kill the gallant knight:
To put in practice either, alas, it was a spite
    Unto the silly damsel!
But one must be refused; more mickle was the pain
That nothing could be used to turn them both to gain,
For of the two the trusty knight was wounded with disdain:
    Alas, she could not help it!
Thus art with arms contending was victor of the day,
Which by a gift of learning did bear the maid away:
Then, lullaby, the learned man hath got the lady gay;
    And now my song is ended.

17 On a day, alack the day!
    Love, whose month was ever May,
    Spied a blossom passing fair,
    Playing in the wanton air:
    Through the velvet leaves the wind
    All unseen 'gan passage find;
    That the lover, sick to death,
    Wish'd himself the heaven's breath,
    'Air,' quoth he, 'thy cheeks may blow;
    Air, would I might triumph so!
    But, alas! my hand hath sworn
    Ne'er to pluck thee from thy thorn:
    Vow, alack! for youth unmeet:
    Youth, so apt to pluck a sweet.
    Thou for whom Jove would swear
    Juno but an Ethiope were;
    And deny himself for Jove,
    Turning mortal for thy love.'

18 My flocks feed not,
    My ewes breed not,

My rams speed not ;
    All is amiss :
Love 's denying,
Faith 's defying,
Heart 's renying,
    Causer of this.
All my merry jigs are quite forgot,
All my lady's love is lost, God wot :
Where her faith was firmly fix'd in love,
There a nay is placed without remove.
One silly cross
Wrought all my loss ;
    O frowning Fortune, cursed, fickle dame !
For now I see
Inconstancy
    More in women than in men remain.

In black mourn I,
All fears scorn I,
Love hath forlorn me,
    Living in thrall :
Heart is bleeding,
All help needing,
O cruel speeding,
    Fraughted with gall.
My shepherd's pipe can sound no deal :
My wether's bell rings doleful knell ;
My curtal dog, that wont to have play'd,
Plays not at all, but seems afraid ;
My sighs so deep
Procure to weep,
    In howling wise, to see my doleful plight.
How sighs resound
Through heartless ground,
    Like a thousand vanquish'd men in bloody fight !

Clear wells spring not,
Sweet birds sing not,
Green plants bring not
    Forth their dye ;
Herds stand weeping,
Flocks all sleeping,
Nymphs back peeping
    Fearfully :
All our pleasure known to us poor swains,
All our merry meetings on the plains,

All our evening sport from us is fled,
All our love is lost, for Love is dead.
Farewell, sweet lass,
Thy like ne'er was
    For a sweet content, the cause of all my moan:
Poor Corydon
Must live alone;
    Other help for him I see that there is none.

19 When as thine eye hath chose the dame,
And stall'd the deer that thou shouldst strike,
Let reason rule things worthy blame,
As well as fancy, partial wight:
    Take counsel of some wiser head,
    Neither too young nor yet unwed.

And when thou comest thy tale to tell,
Smooth not thy tongue with filed talk,
Lest she some subtle practice smell,—
A cripple soon can find a halt;—
    But plainly say thou lovest her well,
    And set thy person forth to sell.

What though her frowning brows be bent,
Her cloudy looks will calm ere night:
And then too late she will repent
That thus dissembled her delight;
    And twice desire, ere it be day,
    That which with scorn she put away.

What though she strive to try her strength,
And ban and brawl, and say thee nay,
Her feeble force will yield at length,
When craft hath taught her thus to say;
    'Had women been so strong as men,
    In faith, you had not had it then.'

And to her will frame all thy ways;
Spare not to spend, and chiefly there
Where thy desert may merit praise,
By ringing in thy lady's ear:
    The strongest castle, tower and town,
    The golden bullet beats it down.

Serve always with assured trust,
And in thy suit be humble true;

Unless thy lady prove unjust,
Press never thou to choose anew :
    When time shall serve, be thou not slack
    To proffer, though she put thee back.

The wiles and guiles that women work,
Dissembled with an outward show,
The tricks and toys that in them lurk,
The cock that treads them shall not know.
    Have you not heard it said full oft,
    A woman's nay doth stand for nought?

Think women still to strive with men,
To sin and never for to saint :
There is no heaven, by holy then,
When time with age shall them attaint.
    Were kisses all the joys in bed,
    One woman would another wed.

But, soft! enough—too much, I fear—
Lest that my mistress hear my song :
She will not stick to round me on th' ear,
To teach my tongue to be so long :
    Yet will she blush, here be it said,
    To hear her secrets so bewray'd.

20 Live with me, and be my love,
And we will all the pleasures prove
That hills and valleys, dales and fields,
And all the craggy mountains yields.

There will we sit upon the rocks,
And see the shepherds feed their flocks,
By shallow rivers, by whose falls
Melodious birds sing madrigals.

There will I make thee a bed of roses,
With a thousand fragrant posies,
A cap of flowers, and a kirtle
Embroider'd all with leaves of myrtle.

A belt of straw and ivy buds,
With coral clasps and amber studs;
And if these pleasures may thee move,
Then live with me and be my love.

LOVE'S ANSWER

If that the world and love were young,
And truth in every shepherd's tongue,
These pretty pleasures might me move
To live with thee and be thy love.

21 As it fell upon a day
In the merry month of May,
Sitting in a pleasant shade
Which a grove of myrtles made,
Beasts did leap and birds did sing,
Trees did grow and plants did spring;
Every thing did banish moan,
Save the nightingale alone:
She, poor bird, as all forlorn,
Lean'd her breast up-till a thorn,
And there sung the dolefull'st ditty,
That to hear it was great pity:
'Fie, fie, fie,' now would she cry;
'Tereu, Tereu!' by and by;
That to hear her so complain,
Scarce I could from tears refrain;
For her griefs so lively shown
Made me think upon mine own.
Ah, thought I, thou mourn'st in vain!
None takes pity on thy pain:
Senseless trees they cannot hear thee;
Ruthless beasts they will not cheer thee:
King Pandion he is dead;
All thy friends are lapp'd in lead;
All thy fellow birds do sing,
Careless of thy sorrowing.
Even so, poor bird, like thee,
None alive will pity me.
Whilst as fickle Fortune smiled,
Thou and I were both beguiled.
   Every one that flatters thee
Is no friend in misery.
Words are easy, like the wind;
Faithful friends are hard to find:
Every man will be thy friend
Whilst thou hast wherewith to spend;
But if store of crowns be scant,
No man will supply thy want.

If that one be prodigal,
Bountiful they will him call,
And with such-like flattering,
'Pity but he were a king;'
If he be addict to vice,
Quickly him they will entice;
If to women he be bent,
They have at commandment:
But if Fortune once do frown,
Then farewell his great renown;
They that fawn'd on him before
Use his company no more.
He that is thy friend indeed,
He will help thee in thy need:
If thou sorrow, he will weep;
If thou wake, he cannot sleep;
Thus of every grief in heart
He with thee doth bear a part.
These are certain signs to know
Faithful friend from flattering foe.

THE PHŒNIX AND TURTLE

LET the bird of loudest lay,
On the sole Arabian tree,
Herald sad and trumpet be,
To whose sound chaste wings obey.

But thou shrieking harbinger,
Foul precurrer of the fiend,
Augur of the fever's end,
To this troop come thou not near!

From this session interdict
Every fowl of tyrant wing,
Save the eagle, feather'd king:
Keep the obsequy so strict.

Let the priest in surplice white,
That defunctive music can,
Be the death-divining swan,
Lest the requiem lack his right.

And thou treble-dated crow,
That thy sable gender makest
With the breath thou givest and takest,
'Mongst our mourners shalt thou go.

Here the anthem doth commence:
Love and constancy is dead;
Phœnix and the turtle fled
In a mutual flame from hence.

So they loved, as love in twain
Had the essence but in one;
Two distincts, division none:
Number there in love was slain.

Hearts remote, yet not asunder;
Distance, and no space was seen
'Twixt the turtle and his queen:
But in them it were a wonder.

So between them love did shine,
That the turtle saw his right
Flaming in the phœnix' sight;
Either was the other's mine.

Property was thus appalled,
That the self was not the same;
Single nature's double name
Neither two nor one was called.

Reason, in itself confounded,
Saw division grow together,
To themselves yet either neither,
Simple were so well compounded;

That it cried, How true a twain
Seemeth this concordant one!
Love hath reason, reason none,
If what parts can so remain.

Whereupon it made this threne
To the phœnix and the dove,
Co-supremes and stars of love,
As chorus to their tragic scene.

THRENOS

Beauty, truth, and rarity,
Grace in all simplicity,
Here enclosed in cinders lie.

Death is now the phœnix' nest;
And the turtle's loyal breast
To eternity doth rest,

Leaving no posterity:
'Twas not their infirmity,
It was married chastity.

Truth may seem, but cannot be;
Beauty brag, but 'tis not she;
Truth and beauty buried be.

To this urn let those repair
That are either true or fair;
For these dead birds sigh a prayer.

THE END